Fish & Shellfish

Fish & Shellfish

James Peterson

WILLIAM MORROW AND COMPANY, INC.

NEW YORK

Library of Congress Cataloging-in-Publication Data

Peterson, James.
        Fish and shellfish / James Peterson : photographs by James Peterson.
            p.   cm.
        Includes index.
        ISBN 0-688-12737-1
        1. Cookery (Fish)   2. Cookery (Shellfish)   I. Title.
TX747.P464 1996
641.6′92—dc20   95-38375
                                                                                                              CIP

Printed in the United States of America

First Edition

        5   6   7   8   9   10

ORIGINAL DESIGN BY JANET ODGIS

ADDITIONAL DESIGN BY JOEL AVIROM & JASON SNYDER

To my parents and brothers

Acknowledgments

It would be impossible to thank all those who have taught me over the years to appreciate and respect good food or to thank the dozens of people who have helped me, in so many ways, to write this book.

I will never forget my first seafood mentor, Claude Peyrot, owner/chef of Paris's Le Vivarois, who twenty years ago showed me to use the finest and freshest seafood only and to cook with a profound respect for all ingredients. I also wish to thank Julia Child who first introduced me to French cooking with her TV shows in the 1960s and Richard Olney who has always been an inspiration and a measure of what is genuine and good in the kitchen and at the table.

For their more immediate help I would like to thank Tony Nunziato who took me on my first trip to the Fulton fish market at 3:00 A.M. and introduced me to many of the suppliers there. I also wish to thank Richard Lord, fish expert par excellence, who accompanied me to the Fulton fish market and who was very helpful with my many questions both in person and on the telephone. And I would like to give very special thanks to Ken Gall of New York Sea Grants who meticulously went over the species identification sections of the manuscript to help me spot errors and omissions. I would also like to thank those people who have sent me numerous materials and have answered my many phone calls and have patiently answered my questions, specifically:

Ken Coons of the New England Fishery Development Association; Susan Day of the Oregon Department of Agriculture; Howard Deese of the State of Hawaii Department of Business, Economic Development and Tourism; Donna Florio of the South Carolina Wildlife and Marine Resources Department; R. Ganapathy of The Marine Products Export Development Authority; Emily Holt of the National Fisheries Institute; Jeffrey H. Kaelin of the Maine Sardine Council; Karen J. LaFlamme of the New Zealand Fishing Industry Board; Joseph McCraren of the United States Trout Farmers Association; Doland Pichon of the Louisiana Seafood Promotion and Marketing Board; Bill Sieling of the Maryland Department of Agriculture; and the many other representatives of various organizations from around the world.

To write this book I have relied on the works of literally hundreds of cookbook and seafood authors, but there are several authors who deserve special mention because of their exhaustive knowledge and the helpfulness of their writings. A.J. McClane's *Encyclopedia of Fish Cookery* has been an invaluable resource. Mr. McClane's lifetime of fishing and travel would be difficult if not impossible to match. His book has been especially helpful for characterizing exotic and foreign fish species. Alan Davidson's careful seafood categorization in *North Atlantic Seafood* has been extremely helpful for finding substi-

tutes for fish called for in European recipes. Jacques Le Divellec's *La Cuisine de la Mer* has been a helpful resource for French cooking techniques, and Mr. Le Divellec's inspiring Paris restaurant has served as the ultimate ideal when cooking seafood. There are also those cookbook authors who specialize in ethnic cuisines and who have provided me, through their writings, with starting points for many a seafood recipe. Shizuo Tsuji's *Japanese Cooking: A Simple Art* has been an invaluable resource for understanding the intricacies and subtleties of Japanese food. Julie Sahni's mouth-watering *Classic Indian Cooking* has revealed a world of flavors I would never have suspected; Sri Owen's erudite and thorough *Indonesian Food and Cookery* has kept me up late, stomach growling, with tales of exotic feasts; and Rick and Deann Bayless's *Authentic Mexican* has revealed the beauty and complexity of a little understood cuisine.

There are, of course, those who have helped me in a very direct hard-working way without whom this book wouldn't have been possible. I'd like to thank Rhona Lauvand whose lovely hands grace the how-to photographs; she was not only a "hand model" but a great friend who has supported me through the many ups and downs of being a food writer. Many thanks to my dear friend Megan Moore who styled the finished food shots and patiently stood by me as I struggled with the many photographic mysteries of my first food ``shoot.'' I'd also like to thank Elise Abrams and Robert Kraus of Elise Abrams Antiques in Great Barrington, Massachusetts, who lent us many pieces from their precious collection of antique china and glass. Special thanks to Carl Lipsky of the New Marlborough Hunt Club in New Marlborough, Massachusetts, for the use of the club as a photo studio and for the use of many of his antiques, which appear in the photographs.

There is one special person who has been by my side during this project and who has helped more than I would ever have thought possible. Geraldine Cresci not only cooked all the recipes—a nine-month process of almost daily testing—but drove me all over New York to shop for seafood and exotic ingredients. She also spent weeks compiling the list of sources given in the back of the book. Her friendship, support, and advice have been invaluable.

I wish to thank Maria Guarnaschelli who first encouraged me to write a seafood book. I also, of course, wish to thank my editor Ann Bramson who has stuck by me and supported me throughout this lengthy project. I am especially thankful to Ann for taking a chance and allowing me—a beginning photographer—to do the photography for the book. Her guidance, love, gentle criticism, and encouragement have been essential.

It's impossible to imagine the number of hours that are spent by dedicated professional people to bring a book such as this one from manuscript to finished book. I wish to thank Ann Cahn, Gail Kinn, Karen Lumley, and the many people at William Morrow for their hard work, professionalism, and obsessive attention to detail.

Special thanks to Chris Benton, my copy editor, for her rigorous reading and rereading of the one thousand five hundred-page manuscript and for her many helpful queries and suggestions. And to Jayne Lathrop, my proofreader, for her painstaking work. I would also like to thank Joel Avirom and his staff for their careful and meticulous design, made especially difficult by the size of the manuscript.

Special thanks to my super-agents Elise and Arnold Goodman who have always believed in me and been there for me and who have become much more than agents. They have become dear friends.

I would like also to thank Sarah Leuze for her support and compassion and for letting me talk.

And lastly and perhaps most importantly, I would like to thank Zelik Mintz for his love, support, and for putting up with a diet composed almost exclusively of seafood for so long. I owe him a lot of good steaks.

Contents

~ *Finfish*

~ *Shellfish*

❧ *Seafood in Other Guises*

❧ *Finfish Dictionary*

Color plates follow page 114

Introduction

My fascination with seafood began at the age of seven, on a camping trip with my mother, a trip that gave me one of my first gastronomic insights. When our trout catch came up short, we cheated and drove down the mountain to a local fish market. The farm-raised trout we bought to round out our catch, I soon realized, had almost no taste next to the wonderful little rainbows my mother pulled out of her creel.

In those days—the 1950s—it was hard to find truly fresh fish. The country, caught up by postwar technology, was entranced by frozen foods and packaged pudding. Home cooks seemed not to notice what had been lost. It's no wonder that to most Americans brought up during this era *fish* often meant frozen breaded fish sticks and *shellfish* signified doughy fried shrimp. For me only the occasional catch—such as the steelhead from Oregon's Rogue River—brought back memories of those first succulent trout.

It was years later, when I went to Paris to study cooking, that my real romance with seafood began. I was instantly drawn to the colorful fish markets, lively and vital places filled with people haggling and gossiping. But oh the seafood: dozens of varieties of sparkling fresh fish, from the familiar Dover sole to the inconceivable scorpion fish. Later, while apprenticing in Paris's restaurants, I was initiated into the many arcane splendors of

seafood cookery and launched onto an adventure that continues to this day and led me to write this book.

While I was grappling happily with the task of producing a perfect sole au beurre blanc and learning the intricacies of scallop quenelles, my compatriots across the ocean were languishing, even in the seventies, in a culinary milieu sorely lacking in fine fish cookery. When I first came to New York in 1979, I was devastated to find that even in this largest American metropolis I couldn't find my beloved sea robin or monkfish because, as fishmongers told me ad infinitum, there simply wasn't a market for these delicious species. A few such specimens went directly to fine restaurants, which were the only places where Americans could (for a price) count on experiencing the full delights of fresh seafood, unless they were lucky enough to live or vacation near a watery habitat. Long Islanders have long prized the nutty sweetness of tiny bay scallops plucked from the Sound minutes before being shelled and tossed into a hot pan. San Franciscans understand why Dungeness crabs are worth lining up for. And, of course, fishermen nationwide appreciate the glistening trout pulled from pristine mountain streams—both for their sport and for their inimitable flavor.

But it wasn't long before I noticed that a slow but steady change was taking place. Cities like Chicago, which could boast only one, perhaps two,

top-notch seafood restaurants two decades ago, now offer diners a wealth of worthy choices, in part because of the growing appreciation of ethnic cuisines, from which so many great fish preparation traditions have sprung. American attitudes toward cooking in general and fish in particular have changed dramatically since my Paris days. We now have not only sophisticated and specialized restaurants but excellent food and wine magazines and cooking schools. Armed with a new awareness of seafood's nutritional value, we are more likely than ever to opt for the grilled "catch of the day" at our local restaurants. More and more we're taking our appreciation of seafood back to our own kitchens, too. And thanks to vastly improved fish farming, we can now easily find excellent salmon and hybrid striped bass in most parts of the country. Even excellent farmed trout is available!

Access to good fish and shellfish is only one half of the equation. What do you do with it when you get it home? My experience with guests and students revealed a need for a book that teaches many of the things that until now could be learned only by working in a restaurant—a book that clearly described and illustrated the many techniques for preparing fish and shellfish. Many volumes on bookstore shelves tell us a great deal about fish and shellfish but give us little information on how to cook them. Others are simply cookbooks with little information on where the seafood comes from or on the basic techniques for scaling, filleting, and shucking. Here I have combined both approaches so avid cooks will learn to select and prepare the best fish and shellfish and avid fishermen will learn how best to cook their catch.

My own knowledge of seafood has been acquired a little bit at a time. I've spent over twenty years traveling, working in restaurants, teaching cooking classes, and bringing home weird or unknown fish to cook for sometimes dubious family and friends. I have used books about seafood, many of them in foreign languages, in my quest for more understanding, but I've realized that there's no book that really demystifies all the various techniques. So I've written this book with the intention of making cooking seafood—especially whole fish and shellfish—seem as easy as it really is. I hope you'll use it as a sort of fundamental course in your formal seafood education.

I also hope you'll pursue your own informal education as I continue to do, treating your exploration of seafood as an ongoing adventure. This means being willing to ask questions everywhere (even at the risk of appearing stupid) and most of all keeping an open mind. You never know how or where you're going to pick up some piece of essential information. I remember traveling in Portugal, which is famous for its sardines. In the many little towns along the Mediterranean there are simple restaurants with little grills next to the entrance. At lunchtime the grills are covered with sizzling and juicy fresh sardines. When presented with my first plate of these crispy little fish, I had deftly cut the fillets away from the bones with knife and fork before I realized the snickering I heard all around was aimed at me, the effete tourist. I was saved when someone kindly showed me how to pick the sardines up with my fingers and eat them like corn on the cob.

Once in a Paris restaurant well known for its seafood I ordered the *assiette de fruits de mer*—a platter of both raw and cooked shellfish served in the shell. As I was waiting for the *assiette* to arrive, the waiter placed before me eight different implements that looked like a set of medieval dental tools. The platter arrived groaning with various shellfish, some recognizable, some not. After attacking the more familiar pieces of lobster and shrimp, I was confronted with an odd, rather frightening-looking crab, various sea snails, and a raw sea urchin. I considered slipping the rest of the shellfish into my friend's purse, but finally in desperation (all the while trying to look sophisticated enough to know what everything was) I asked the waiter for a demonstration. He arrived in starched shirt and bow tie and carefully and patiently showed me how to dissect, crack, and extract the meat from the rest of the shellfish. Some of these very techniques appear in this book, many with full-color photos to illustrate.

Over the years I've learned in fact that European waiters are the world's experts on cutting up and serving cooked seafood. If your culinary (or other) adventures take you abroad, be sure to learn what you can from them. In Italy, for example, fish are usually cooked very simply, and while smaller fish are often fried, larger fish are usually grilled whole and then filleted at the table. I always watch intently as the waiter carves and serves the fish, proudly and quickly dissecting it with the dexterity of a surgeon. It would, of course, be a lot easier to fillet the fish in the kitchen and serve it already on the plate, but, as the Italians know, fish cooked whole has a much better flavor than fish that has been filleted. And of course we would all miss the show in the dining room.

Believe it or not, it's not difficult to apply these principles in your own home. Several summers ago I had two unexpected house guests from the Midwest, so I rushed out to Chinatown to buy some big whole red snappers. As I paraded the baked whole fish from kitchen to dining room, jaws dropped in horror and I heard the usual exclamations about fish eyes and heads and everyone's fear of bones. I gathered my patience and turned the dinner into a miniature lesson on carving whole fish and avoiding bones—the same instructions, with photos, that you'll find in this book—while describing how whole fish has a better flavor. Soon everyone was merrily slicing and munching. These friends still talk about their wonderful meal in Brooklyn.

The pursuit of a seafood education is often embarrassing. My first bite of raw fish was in a restaurant in Tokyo where I was staying with a Japanese family, in the days before sushi restaurants had become popular in the United States. I had braced myself for this much-feared adventure. The plan was for me and the family to go to the public baths at about 10:30 at night and then on the way back home, refreshed and squeaky clean, to make a stop for some sake and raw fish. When we arrived at the restaurant—we sat at the sushi bar—I was presented with a lovely menu, a booklet really, with the selections listed in beautifully brush-stroked calligraphy. When I started to study the menu—upside down and backward—the whole restaurant broke into hysterics. Fortunately, my friends helped translate, and soon there appeared a little wooden tray of raw fish. Except for some slices of giant squid, which had the texture of bubble gum, the fish was a revelation—so delicious that I could only think of all the fish that had been wasted by being cooked. To this day my favorite way to eat most fish and shellfish is completely raw, and I'm amazed that so many are reluctant to entertain the idea.

But then I'm often struck by people's attitudes toward food. I remember a woman in a fur coat who strolled into the kitchen of my restaurant and let out a screech when she saw me cutting up whole rabbits. Many of us forget that we eat living creatures because we buy our food at the supermarket, where chickens no longer have heads or feet, meat comes presliced and packaged under cellophane wrapping, and fish comes disembodied and headless in strips of white fillets. It's easy to understand why many of us are squeamish about fish and shellfish in their natural state. Fish have guts and scales and sharp fins, and shellfish have hard and unyielding shells. While a good fish market will clean and help you get your seafood ready for cooking, I've tried to show—with words and photography—how to start with whole, and sometimes living, creatures. While many of us may never want to bother with the messy job of scaling or struggling to open a tightly closed oyster, it is often these experiences, even if tried only once, that connect us with our food and give us a better feel for our ingredients—an experience that doesn't occur when we rely exclusively on the plastic-wrapped boneless fillet. I don't want to discourage those readers who live where the local supermarket is the only place to shop, but I would like to impart a spirit of adventure and encourage the willingness to experiment.

At my first fish class—for a group of well-dressed young women—I insisted that everyone clean her own fish. The scaling and subsequent filleting went reasonably well, but as we all sat down to eat the meal we'd prepared I looked on in horror as I realized that everyone's hair was flecked with fish scales. Fortunately all my students were good sports, and we spent the rest of the class time picking the scales off one another. All agreed that the experience was worth the mess.

Writing this book has been its own adventure. It's the result of more than one thousand five hundred manuscript pages and three years of almost daily forays to New York's fish markets. Its recipes and techniques spring from nearly continuous experimentation and recipe testing on patient friends (who have lately been clamoring for steaks). The final product is, I hope, a book that will add basic cooking techniques for both fish and shellfish, freshwater and saltwater, to your regular repertoire and give you the power of flexibility and spontaneity that will make you an accomplished seafood cook.

If this book seems to lean heavily on a few cuisines, I can only respond by admitting to certain prejudices. I offer a lot of French recipes because the French have systematized cooking more than any other culture and for centuries writers from this food-obsessed country have described the nuances of fish cookery and invented marvelous recipes. French cooks have always been compulsive categorizers and have managed to organize and label cooking techniques so that the techniques form parts of a complex puzzle that once understood fits neatly together. I also have a special fondness for Japanese cooking. The very light touch the Japanese use when cooking (or not cooking) fish and shellfish gives Japanese dishes a clean simplicity that shows off the quality of the best seafood. Japanese dishes often contain little more than a piece of lightly cooked fish or shellfish surrounded by a few spoonfuls of broth, but it's the infinite care that is taken and the obsession with freshness that make these dishes so satisfying. Finally, Southeast Asian cooking has a special fascination simply because it's delicious (and not always hot), but also because the techniques, so similar to European techniques, illustrate how the same methods can produce radically different dishes thanks to different ingredients.

I've always been bored by cookbooks that contain only recipes and give no sense of where the recipes come from or why and how they work. Therefore I've tried to include the logic behind different cooking techniques so that you can apply them to recipes and ideas of your own. In this way you might eventually free yourself from recipes and improvise dishes according to what's in season or to a simple flight of fancy. Some cooks—even very experienced ones—ask me how I know which ingredients to combine. A hundred years ago our decisions were based almost exclusively on what was in season and on what grew, swam, or flew within a fifty-mile radius, but today a well-stocked market is likely to have vegetables and seafood from all around the country and even from different parts of the world; we're working with an almost limitless number of ingredients. Part of the secret to understanding how ingredients work with each other is to confine your cooking to a particular tradition and to appreciate ethnic foods through travel, reading, or dining out. In this way you'll begin to discover a natural relationship among certain flavors and ingredients so that your cooking will make good aesthetic sense. The best meals evoke memories of distant places or times past.

Recipes in this book sometimes call for making requests of purveyors that may seem weird—such as that the seafood be alive or whole or filleted only at the last minute before your eyes. Don't be afraid to ask for these things. You may get a funny look or two, but ultimately the fishmonger or supermarket manager will respect you and appreciate your interest in his or her products. You will also run into recipes that call for exotic ingredients. While I usually suggest substitutes, some of these ingredients are essential to the special character of the dish and may be easier to find than you think. Many communities now have Asian grocers that carry not only ingredients from one or two countries but those from all over Asia. And if you're completely stumped, you can mail order from one of the sources listed at the back of this book.

You may also encounter recipes for fish or shellfish varieties that are difficult or impossible to find where you live. While it's fun to cook with a lot of different fish and shellfish, many of us, especially those living in between the coasts, may be able to find only two or three kinds of fish. Consequently, every recipe suggests substitutes, and most recipes, especially those for finfish, can be made with dozens of different species so you needn't ever feel limited to the swordfish or red snapper called for in a recipe.

You'll notice that many of the recipes in this book call for unsalted butter. I live on the East Coast where unsalted butter is as common as salted butter, but friends on the West Coast and in the Midwest tell me that unsalted butter isn't always easy to find. I use unsalted butter because that's what I'm used to and because I like its delicate flavor, but don't hestitate to use salted butter if it's all you have. You may just need to cut down on any salt called for in the recipe.

You may also notice frequent mention of olive oil, both extra-virgin olive oil and the relatively light-flavored olive oil called simply "pure" olive oil. While some recipes call for one or the other and a few even call for both, I call for the more expensive extra-virgin olive oil when its delicacy is not going to be destroyed by high heat and for "pure" olive oil for deep-frying or for sautéing over high heat. But you can certainly use one in place of the other. I would hesitate, however, to deep-fry in extra-virgin olive oil (which wouldn't be bad, only expensive) or to use "pure" olive oil in a Mediterranean dish where the flavor of olives is essential to the dish.

This book has been designed to be accessible to all kinds of cooks and readers since people approach cookbooks in many different ways. You can explore the pages according to cooking method, by type of fish or shellfish, or by style of ethnic cooking. The book is divided into four sections. The first part is organized by cooking technique, particularly those techniques commonly used for finfish. If you want to know, for example, how to steam, sauté, or smoke whole fish, fish steaks,

or fillets, you can look up the appropriate chapters in the first section. The second part includes recipes and techniques for cooking and serving lobster, crab, clams, and other shellfish. The third section goes beyond basic techniques and gives recipes for salads, soups, stews, and more elaborate seafood dishes such as mousses and soufflés. The last section, a finfish dictionary, includes tips for identifying and cooking more than two hundred species.

One way to get started reading this book is to look up a particular kind of fish or shellfish. Imagine that you see a particularly beautiful rockfish at the market, and in a moment of daring you buy it and take it home. You examine it and find it has scales and sharp fins and looks at you cynically. You panic. You can look up rockfish in the index and go straight to a recipe, you can consult the color photos on filleting it or trimming it for cooking whole, or you can look up rockfish in the finfish dictionary, where you will find the best ways to cook and serve the species. You then need only flip to the corresponding technique chapter. Another scenario might be that you encounter a delicious dish in a restaurant and ask how it was cooked. When you get home, you can look up the technique and find out how to do it. Once you've learned the technique, you'll be able to adapt it to other recipes or to improvise.

Whichever path you take, I hope you find this book to be an adventure, not just in the art of cooking seafood but in all the joys and pleasures of the table.

From Market to Table
How to Buy, Store, Prepare, and Serve Seafood

What food could better capture the magical essence of the sea than a piece of perfect raw tuna, an oyster glistening in its shell, or a freshly opened sea urchin? Only somewhat removed from this ascetic purity is a whole fish roasted in the oven, a small fish or fillet browned in butter, its skin crispy and golden, or a salmon steak sizzling on the grill. The simplest food is always the best, a principle that certainly applies to seafood. Whether you choose to fuss over your fish or not, the quality of the seafood you buy will have much more influence over the finished dish than anything you do in the kitchen. So, even when you have a taste for a certain dish or a particular fish, try to head for the fish market with an open mind.

HOW TO BUY AND STORE SEAFOOD

The most important step in any seafood dish is tracking down good fish or shellfish, but because finding good fresh seafood—especially if it's already filleted—can be tricky, your best bet is to find and cultivate a fishmonger you can rely on. Patronize the store regularly, ask questions to show you're interested and informed, and show a willingness to try new or unusual things. Hopefully the fishmonger will respect you for this and steer you toward the best seafood.

If you live in a big city with several fish stores, do some preliminary investigation to see which store handles its fish best. If there is a Japanese fish store in your area, investigate it first—the Japanese have very high standards, although the seafood is likely to be expensive.

When you walk into the fish store, give a sniff. A well-kept fish store should *not* smell like fish but should have a sealike smell. Look at the floors and the display cases. Is the floor clean? If sawdust is used, is it fresh? Everything should be spotless and arranged carefully—not heaped carelessly on piles of ice. Whole fish should be covered with clean crushed ice. Fillets and steaks should not be allowed to come directly in contact with ice but should be arranged on trays that in turn are set on the ice. In addition to the ice, the fillets should be kept in a refrigerated case—left out, they won't be chilled throughout. Are the steaks all the same size and carefully arranged? Does all the fish appear to be of high quality, or is some clearly of inferior quality?

Once you've found a decent fish store, you must figure out what fish is best. If you trust the fishmonger, ask for guidance. If it's your first time in the store, use the guidelines in the boxes. I always recommend keeping cooking plans flexible because sometimes the very best locally caught seafood shows up unexpectedly. You might also try to find out if there are certain days when the fish is freshest or when there's more variety available. If the wholesale market in your area is closed on the weekend, fish sold on Sunday, even at its freshest, will be Friday's catch. In neighborhoods with a large Catholic population, fish markets often get a larger and more varied shipment of fresh fish on Fridays.

Whenever possible, buy whole fish and have the fishmonger prepare it. The quality of whole fish is easier to judge than that of fillets or steaks, and if you're making a soup, stew, or sauced dish you'll need the head and bones for broth.

JUDGING THE QUALITY OF WHOLE FISH

sheen. A fresh fish should be shiny and sparkling. Any film or mucus on the fish should be transparent and glistening.

stiffness. Most fresh fish—there are some exceptions—should not hang limply but should stick out somewhat when held by the head.

firmness. Fresh fish should be firm, and the skin should be taut. If the fishmonger will let you, press your finger against the side of the fish—your finger shouldn't leave an imprint. Avoid fish with wrinkled skin (wolffish is an exception).

odor. Fresh fish should not have a fishy smell but should smell like the ocean or— if it's a freshwater fish—a clean pond. If the fishmonger will let you, lift up the gill cover and give a sniff.

scales. The scales on a fresh fish should adhere tightly. Loose scales indicate that the fish is not fresh or has been improperly handled.

gills. Lift the gill cover and inspect the gills. The gills of a fresh fish should be cherry-red (although sometimes they get covered with mud) and should not have any white slime.

eyes. The appearance of the eyes depends on the type of fish, but in general, look for clear protruding eyes. Some fish such as walleye never have clear eyes.

tail. The tail of a really fresh fish should not be dried out or curled up at the end.

bruising. Look for red bruises, which may mean the fish was injured when it was caught. These are especially easy to spot on the white side of flatfish.

Buying fresh shellfish has its own pitfalls. Bivalve shellfish are legally required to be labeled according to origin and date of harvest, so even if none of this information is displayed you should be able to find out by asking.

Beware of buying fish that is *too* fresh. This is a problem only in ethnic markets, where fish is sometimes sold alive directly out of tanks. The problem centers around rigor mortis, a dramatic stiffening of the fish, which occurs usually within several hours after the fish dies. If the fish is cooked before or near the beginning of rigor mortis, it will contract on contact with heat and pull itself apart. The result will be a very mushy fish. If you end up with a just-caught or just-killed fish, ice it down immediately. If you check it in a few hours, you'll notice that it has grown very stiff. Continue to store the fish packed in ice. When it begins to lose some of its stiffness—in anywhere from several hours to several days—it is ready for cooking. What's important is that the fish not pass too quickly through rigor mortis due to elevated temperatures.

FROZEN FISH

Nowadays much of the fish we eat has been frozen whether we know it or not. Some of the tastiest and "freshest" fish to be found in American cities is in a good sushi bar, and most of this fish has been frozen on fishing boats immediately after being caught. The problem with much "fresh" fish is that fishing boats no longer go out for a day or two at a time but may instead spend several weeks at sea. Fish that has spent two weeks packed in ice in the hold of a large fishing boat is going to be much less fresh than fish that is frozen on board as soon as it is caught.

Much of the quality depends on the freezing method. The best-quality frozen fish is called *clipper grade* and is flash-frozen on board ship as soon as it is caught. Japanese fishing ships use this technique for sashimi-quality fish. Lesser-quality frozen fish results from less efficient freezers that freeze the fish more slowly and cause ice crystals to form within the fish's cells. These ice crystals in turn damage the cell walls and cause the fish to lose moisture— so-called drip loss—when the fish is thawed and cooked. The result is fish that is dry and flavorless. The least desirable freezing method is freezing twice, sometimes done with fish sold as fillets. The whole fish are caught and frozen whole at sea. When the ship returns to port, the fish is thawed and processed into fillets. The fillets are then refrozen. It's of course not always easy to know what you're getting, but if you're buying a package of frozen fillets, look for the words *once-frozen*. Ask your fishmonger about this also.

Frozen fish should be thawed as slowly as possible to prevent the formation of crystals that would damage the fish's texture. It's best to thaw fish overnight in the refrigerator, but if you're in a hurry, the next-best method is to put the tightly wrapped fish in a bowl of cold water and change the water every 30 minutes until the fish is thawed. Don't thaw fish under warm water or in a microwave oven.

SEAFOOD SAFETY

The media attention given to the dangers of eating certain foods has by no means left seafood unscathed. Every

JUDGING THE QUALITY OF STEAKS AND FILLETS

sheen. The surface of steaks and fillets should have a moist sheen with no hint of a film or slime layer.

color. The coloration on white or pale steaks or fillets should be cherry-red and not brown. This coloration is especially noticeable on swordfish and shark steaks. Irregular red coloring on white fillets or steaks may indicate bruising if the fish was mishandled when caught.

translucence. Fish fillets and steaks should appear slightly translucent. Fish that looks opaque may not be fresh or may have been frozen improperly.

handling. Tuna should not be sliced into steaks but should be kept in as large a piece as possible. Tuna should be wrapped tightly in plastic wrap and should be translucent pink or red with no hint of brown.

opalescence. Some fish, especially tuna, may develop a rainbowlike opalescence on their surface when handled improperly. While some very oily fish take on this opalescence even when in perfect condition, it's best to play it safe and avoid buying fish with this appearance.

grain. Don't buy fillets or steaks with spaces in the flake. All fish should be dense with no gaping visible anywhere on the steak or fillet.

packaging. If you buy fish in those little cellophane packages popular in supermarkets—not a bad system in itself—make sure the container contains no liquid.

buying tricks. Avoid buying what look like the last pieces of a large fillet—such as a salmon tail piece—or the last slice of a tuna or swordfish loin. I usually tell the fishmonger that I want to cook a whole large piece—so I get a piece off a new fillet or loin—and then cut it myself into steaks or smaller fillets when I get it home.

---

few years there is a new wave of panic and a plethora of warnings about some new disease or exotic toxin. I am especially rankled when my favorite foods are accused of some insidious health treachery, but while some of the dangers of eating seafood are grossly exaggerated, some are certainly real and should be addressed.

First, it might help to keep in mind a few reassuring facts: Despite the dangers of eating seafood—which are in fact minimal—seafood is one of the most nutritionally complete foods we can eat. It is high in protein and low in fat. It contains a variety of minerals and the now-famous omega-3 fatty acids, which lower triglycerides and reduce the likelihood of strokes and certain cardiac problems. It is low in cholesterol—only a few shellfish have moderate levels of cholesterol—and some studies even suggest that eating fish can lower cholesterol. (In any case, crab and lobster have about the same amount of cholesterol as skinless chicken and most bivalve shellfish about half as much.) The small amount of fat that seafood does contain is mostly so-called good fat—polyunsaturated fat—which does little in the way of clogging arteries or causing health problems.

Seafood-related illness accounts for only 5 percent of all foodborne illness and of that 5 percent more than half is from shellfish. While eating any food has its risks—a friend of mine found a shard of glass in a box of cookies—certain foods are riskier than others. Eating raw shellfish is relatively high-risk and eating raw fish—from a reputable supplier—a distant second. So if you're worried, don't eat raw shellfish at all. Even I, with my live-for-the-moment attitude, don't make a steady diet of raw shellfish, although my wintertime oyster consumption must be dozens of times higher than the national average. Certainly you should heed the safety warnings in the chapter "Preparing Seafood to Serve Raw."

Seafood is also rich in vitamins and minerals; fatty fish especially are important sources of vitamins A, D, E, and B. Seafood contains all the minerals present in the ocean and is especially rich in copper, iodine, iron, cobalt, zinc, fluorine, phosphorus, magnesium, and selenium. Oysters contain more zinc than any other food.

Minimize consumption of raw mollusks, such as oysters, clams, and mussels, if you are worried about eating them safely. Raw scallops—provided you don't eat the roe or surrounding viscera—are safer because only the abductor muscle, which doesn't absorb toxins, is eaten. If you want to be especially careful, avoid the roe and liver altogether.

Buy shellfish from a reliable fishmonger. I buy fish from all over New York, from hole-in-the-wall stalls in Chinatown to chic upscale markets, but I recommend buying shellfish from only more expensive markets, where they are unlikely to cut costs by buying shellfish on the "gray" market. If you eat raw fish, be sure to buy it from a reliable source that specializes in sashimi or eat it in a reliable Japanese restaurant, where the personnel are well trained to select fish. Never eat raw any freshwater fish or any fish you've caught yourself. If you do your own fishing or harvesting, check with local authorities to make sure the water is deemed safe.

Avoid eating the same kind of fish, or fish from the same waters, day in and day out. Small and harmless quantities of contaminents may present more of a risk if consumed often. This may be especially important to pregnant women.

Deep-sea fish are in general less likely to contain certain contaminants than fish caught in bays or near the mouths of rivers.

Inspect fish closely. Most parasites are visible to the naked eye, and while they present little danger, if the fish is being cooked, they are unpleasant to look at. Strips of dark muscle or fatty tissue can be trimmed off, because in most cases toxins accumulate in these areas.

Food Poisoning Food poisoning is caused by particular kinds of pathogenic bacteria that secrete toxins that cause illness when ingested. Food poisoning is of course not limited to seafood but can result from eating almost any kind of food that has been handled or stored improperly. Fresh-smelling seafood bought from a reliable fishmonger is very unlikely to cause food poisoning unless you mistreat the seafood once you get it home. A common cause of seafood poisoning is allowing cooked seafood to come into contact with raw meat (e.g., chicken), other raw seafood, or utensils, such as cutting boards or knives, that have come into contact with raw fish. Cutting boards and knives must be washed thoroughly before they are allowed to come into contact with cooked seafood. Thoroughly clean any containers used for raw foods before

TIPS ON BUYING SHELLFISH

in the shell. Whenever possible, avoid shellfish already out of the shell. Shucked shellfish die quickly, are more susceptible to cross-contamination, and don't have as good a flavor. It is unusual to find scallops or bay scallops for sale in the shell, but when you do see them, snatch them up; you'll find none fresher.

origin. Ask the fishmonger to show you the tags on bivalve shellfish if you're curious about where they came from. (The source must be kept on record to trace possible sources of illness.) The tags will also show when they were harvested, but knowing this date will be of little help if the shellfish has been stored improperly.

shells tightly closed. Shellfish should have tightly closed shells, although this is more important for some shellfish than for others. Perfectly healthy mussels will sometimes gape slightly, but if you tap two together they should close quickly. In any case, avoid mussels that gape more than $1/4$ inch. Hard-shell clams also gape slightly but less so than mussels and like mussels should close quickly when tapped. Soft-shell clams and geoducks always gape—

they can't close because of their protruding siphons—but the siphon should pull in when you touch it. Oysters should always be tightly closed. Never buy an oyster that gapes. Oysters should be stored flat—not just heaped up in a pile—so their delicious briny liquid has no chance of draining out.

storage. Check to see how shellfish are stored. Bivalve shellfish should be well iced or kept in the refrigerator but should never be immersed in liquid or melted ice. Avoid buying bivalve shellfish from those pretty plastic tanks that continuously recycle the water—this can cause cross-contamination such that one dead shellfish will contaminate all the others.

Crustaceans such as lobsters, crabs, and shellfish should be frisky. If these shellfish are kept alive in tanks, ask how long they've been in the tank and reject any that have been there for more than a week. The flavor and texture suffer when crustaceans are kept in tanks for long periods. Avoid buying cooked crustaceans from a store that also sells them live. Some fish stores cook up the crustaceans that die in the tank.

using them to store cooked seafood. Thoroughly wash your hands after handling raw seafood and before touching cooked seafood. Sponges and towels used for wiping surfaces should also be kept clean. While problems of cross-contamination are more likely to occur in restaurants or where large amounts of different foods are handled in a small area, there are also precautions you should take at home:

Always keep seafood cold. Don't leave seafood sitting outside the refrigerator while you're getting ready to cook it. Marinate fish in the refrigerator and remember to put the leftovers back in the fridge immediately. It's safest to eat leftovers within 24 hours. Remember that, unlike parasites, bacteria are not killed by freezing.

STORING FISH AND
SHELLFISH AT HOME

Fish or shellfish should be stored properly from the minute you get it out of the store. The main thing to remember is to keep it cold. Bacteria on fish and shellfish grow twice as fast for every 10 degrees above freezing.

Always try to make the fish store your last shopping stop so you can rush right home and get the seafood in the refrigerator. If the seafood is going to be out of a refrigerator for more than 30 minutes, bring along a Styrofoam or plastic cooler with 3 or 4 frozen gel packs for storing the seafood until you get it home. Or in a pinch, ask the fishmonger for some ice.

As soon as you get home, remove whole fish from its wrapping and rinse it off with cold water—more bacteria grow in the moisture surrounding the fish than in the flesh itself. Unless you're using the fish within an hour or two, set a colander over a large bowl and fill the colander half full of ice. Arrange the fish on the ice, cover it with more ice, and store it in the refrigerator. Never store fish in a bowl with ice, or the ice may melt and leave the fish sitting in a puddle of water, damaging the fish's texture and flavor.

Fish fillets and steaks should be stored in the same way as whole fish except they should be left in their wrappers—or rewrapped in clean wax paper—so the fish doesn't come in direct contact with the ice.

In-the-shell shellfish such as mussels and clams should be kept in the refrigerator in a bowl covered with a wet towel. Shellfish should never be kept in water or in a bowl with melting ice. Oysters can also be kept in a bowl covered with a wet towel, but they should be arranged carefully so that they lie flat; otherwise their briny liquid may drain out.

HOW TO PREPARE AND SERVE SEAFOOD

Leave home determined to prepare roast monkfish with sage and whole garlic cloves for dinner and you're bound to return with a passel of succulent soft-shell crab—because that's what turned out to be freshest and most inviting at the market. Some cooks switch culinary gears to adapt to the daily catch without batting an eye; others are thrown by changes in their well-laid menu plans. There are, fortunately, several ways to decide how to prepare fish for a given meal. You can simply let what looks best at the market dictate the dish. In that case all you need to know beforehand is how many people you're serving (see box on page 6); then, when you get home, you can look up the fish or shellfish in this book to find out which cooking techniques work best. You can also start out with a general idea of how you want to prepare the seafood. If you're in the mood for grilling, check the chapter on that technique for the types of fish that cook well over coals. A third possibility: If you're wedded to the idea of a particular recipe, go ahead and plan on it, but be sure to check the substitutions box with the recipe before leaving home so you'll have some alternatives to choose from at the market.

Beyond the choice of seafood, matters like your family's or guests' preferences and the type of occasion will determine how you choose to prepare the seafood you buy. The fact that the simplest food is always best does not mean, for instance, that it will always be the easiest or the least expensive to prepare. Once you've tracked down a good piece of seafood, the prime directive to follow is not to alter the seafood's intrinsic flavor. The flavor of a perfect piece of seafood is ruined when the seafood is left in a strong marinade of herbs and garlic, when the fish is grilled over a too-smoky fire or smothered in too spicy a sauce. A simple cooking method will reveal the seafood's intrinsic merits. There is, for example, little more perfect than a simple steamed lobster. A more complicated avenue allows you to amplify and intensify the seafood's flavor. By gently cooking the lobster only long enough to get it out of its shell and then breaking up the shell and simmering it with a few carefully chosen herbs and vegetables, you can create a sauce that tastes more like lobster than lobster itself—a profoundly satisfying feat. So while the best cooks always strive for the simplest effect—a lobster with a little sauce—they may have followed a very convoluted path to arrive at a simple and pure flavor.

When you get your seafood home from the market, you can look the creature up in the Finfish Dictionary or the Shellfish section of this book to get an idea of what techniques are best and then choose one of the complexity you prefer. But myriad other variables also come into play when planning a meal. Is the seafood being served as a first or a main course? What are the other dishes? Does the meal have a national or cultural theme? What will your family or guests prefer? A few guidelines might help:

1. The type of fish available will vary widely. Most of the recipes in this book suggest possible substitutes, but if none of these is available, look at the chart on page 7 to find fish with a similar texture and intensity of flavor. Keep in mind also the shape of the fish called for in the recipe. If the recipe calls for salmon steaks and you wish to substitute another fish, use steaks or firm fillets.

2. If you're serving finfish as a main course, serve the fish in as simple a way as possible. A whole fish straight off the grill, out of the oven, or out of the fish poacher always makes a dramatic sight, and carving the fish at the table for the diners always creates a congenial atmosphere. When serving smaller fish as a main course, simply panfry, steam, or grill the fish and serve them at the table, one to a diner. When serving fillets or steaks, select those that are full-flavored or distinctive in some way unless you've managed to find them in especially impeccable condition or you're giving them an especially robust treatment such as frying or serving with a deeply flavored sauce.

3. Seafood served as a first course should contrast with the main course and yet remain in the style of the dinner. A simple roast can be preceded by something more elaborate and rich, such as a shellfish or finfish stew. A complicated or especially rich main course calls for a simple and modest first course.

4. Especially for a more formal dinner, there is something offputting about mixing foods from different countries or at least different regions of the world. Don't serve a plate of Italian seafood pasta after a bowl of Thai shrimp soup or a boeuf bourguignon after a tray of sushi.

5. Know how your guests feel about the use of fats. Many of the dishes in this book contain butter, cream, olive oil, or coconut milk but in such small amounts that one serving is equivalent to less than a small scoop of ice cream. In fact one way I justify eating rich sauces is by avoiding rich or very sweet desserts and serving fruit instead. But if even that much is too much, consider these possibilities:

- Serve poached, roasted, or braised fish.
- Use a nonstick pan for panfrying or sautéing. You'll be able to use only a teaspoon or two of oil to prevent sticking, hardly any of which will be absorbed by the seafood.
- Substitute olive oil for butter, especially when panfrying or sautéing.
- Leave the cream, butter, or coconut milk out of sauce and soup recipes to turn richer liquids into lean and satisfying broths.

WHAT WINE TO SERVE?

Once you have your menu planned, you'll have to give some thought to what to drink. Other than beer served at an outdoor barbecue or the occasional sake served at a Japanese dinner, the best accompaniment to

HOW MUCH TO SERVE?

Knowing how much seafood to serve depends on the appetite of your guests and how many other dishes are being served. The amounts given here are for the average eater. For small eaters you can halve the amounts, but for big eaters you may need to serve almost twice as much.

For a main course, count on 6 to 8 ounces of fish fillet or steak per serving and twice that much whole fish.

Count on 3 to 4 ounces of fillet or steak (or 6 to 8 ounces of whole fish) per serving as a first course.

Shellfish amounts are more complicated. I usually serve 6 raw or cooked oysters as a first course, a pound (about a dozen medium) clams for a first course, 4 ounces headless shrimp for a first course, and 6 to 8 ounces for a main course. I usually serve a pound of mussels as a first course and twice that amount for a main course. Serve small (1¼-pound) lobsters—1 per person—as a first course and a large lobster, at least 1½ pounds, as a main course.

LOBSTERS, CRABS, OTHER CRUSTACEANS

Because most toxins and microorganisms accumulate in the filtration apparatus of bivalve shellfish, in the fatty tissue of finfish, or in the roe and liver of both, lobsters, crabs, and other crustaceans make extremely safe eating provided you don't eat the tomalley or roe. Of course the tomalley is the tastiest part of the lobster and the liver—the "mustard"—one of the tastiest parts of the crab. What is one to do? My own response is to compromise. Because I'm unlikely to eat crustaceans, with the possible exception of shrimp, more than a couple of times a month, I go ahead and eat the tomalley and roe. But for those who eat these delicacies more often, it might be a good idea not to eat the tomalley and roe every time. Pregnant women should avoid the tomalley and roe at all times.

FAT CONTENT

TEXTURE	VERY LOW	LOW	MODERATE	HIGH
SOFT	American Sole Flounder Freshwater Bass Sea Trout, Weakfish Whiting	Anchovies (m) Rainbow Smelts*	Bluefish* (f) Butterfish* European Sardines* (f)	Atlantic Mackerel* (f) Eulachons* (f) Herring* (m) Shad* (m) Buffalofish*
SLIGHTLY FIRM	Atlantic Croaker Black Sea Bass Fluke Hake Ocean Perch Pike Pollack Rockfish Snapper Walleye Sunfish	Porgy Tilapia Tilefish Trout (not including Lake Trout) (m)	Spanish Mackerel* (m)	Lake Trout (m) Sablefish
MODERATELY FIRM	Cod, Scrod Grouper Haddock Halibut Mahimahi Monkfish Orange Roughy Red Drum Sea Robin Striped Bass White Hake Yellow Perch	Chum Salmon* (m) Pink Salmon* (m) Red Mullet (m) Skipjack Tuna (f) Wahoo* (m) Wolffish	Atlantic Salmon* (m) Arctic Char* (m) Pacific Barracuda (m) Chilean Sea Bass Coho Salmon* (m) King Mackerel* (m) Mullet* (m) Sockeye Salmon* (m)	King Salmon* (m) Whitefish
FIRM	Atlantic Bonito* (m) Bigeye Tuna* (m) Black Drum Blackfish Blowfish Cusk Dover Sole John Dory Kingclip Lingcod Ocean Pout Skate (m) Yellowfin Tuna* (m)	Catfish Shark (m) Swordfish (m)	Amberjack* (f) Bluefin Tuna* (m) Carp* Pompano Sturgeon	Eel Yellowtail (m)

(f) full flavor   (m) moderate flavor   delicate flavor (no initial)

* off-white, dark, or colored flesh

seafood is wine. Most of us assume that white wine is best, but there are times when red wine is better. I've always disliked those dogmatic little charts that imply that only a very particular—and usually expensive—wine can be served with a certain kind of dish. The best approach is to fumble around and experiment to find which wines you like best with certain foods and in certain situations. If this seems like too much freedom, a few guidelines can be helpful, but keep in mind that it's almost impossible to spoil a dinner by choosing the wrong wine.

With raw shellfish such as oysters or clams or raw fish I like to serve an austere white wine with a lot of acidity and a mineral or flinty flavor. The ultimate wine for this is a fine French Chablis or French Champagne (a good Coteaux Champenois—a still Champagne—is particularly wonderful) but these wines are expensive. Down the ladder somewhat but still wonderful (and still not cheap) is a Sancerre (made from sauvignon blanc grapes), which usually has a somewhat herbaceous flavor, a good amount of acidity, and, if well made, a mineral flavor and aroma. My old standby shellfish wine (one of the few I can still regularly afford) is Muscadet, from Brittany, with a clean flinty flavor and aroma and a good amount of acidity. An Italian pinot grigio from the Veneto or Friuli-Venezia Giulia can also make an interesting accompaniment to shellfish and simple fish dishes.

Any of these wines will be delicious with almost any cooked fish or shellfish dish, but as seafood dishes get more robust and their flavors more complex, rounder, more assertive wines can also be served. For an everyday or casual meal I buy California sauvignon blanc—which is more likely to have the necessary acidity than chardonnay—inexpensive Italian whites such as pinot grigio, Soave Classico, or Orvieto Classico; French whites such as Alsatian pinot blanc, sylvaner, or riesling (riesling usually runs a bit more); French chardonnay such as Mâcon-Villages or Saint-Véran; or French sauvignon blanc such as Pouilly-Fumé. For outdoor barbecues I like to serve red wine such as chilled Beaujolais or cool barbera. None of these wines is cheap, but none will break the bank either, and any will be delicious with seafood. Even if you decide on a bottle of inexpensive

---

SPECIAL EQUIPMENT FOR PREPARING AND COOKING FISH

Good tools always make the cook's work easier, so it's worth the trouble to keep on hand sharp knives (I use a long flexible knife for filleting and skinning fish), various baking dishes, heavy-bottomed nonstick or well-seasoned cast-iron pans, thick metal pots, long spatulas (there's even one aptly called a *fish slice*), specialty cutters such as a mandoline or a Japanese benriner cutter, baking sheets, and strainers. These are, of course, the same tools you'll use to cook other foods, and you'll find that most fish recipes require no special equipment at all. The following few items are exceptions that you might consider purchasing:

Grills: There are several very handy gadgets for grilling fish, including a fish-shaped wire cage for whole fish (eliminating the need for lifing the fish off the grill and possible sticking), a square grilling basket consisting of two small square grills held together with a hinge for small fish such as sardines (again eliminating the need for sliding a spatula under the fish to turn it), and a grilling grate, which is simply a fine-mesh grill used for small pieces of seafood such as scallops. Grills themselves vary widely in price.

Fish poachers: It probably isn't worth buying a fish poacher unless you regularly poach large fish. If you do invest in a poacher, buy a large one; you can always accommodate small fish in a large poacher but not the other way around.

Oval pans: Practically all pans are round, but if you cook a lot of fish, consider buying an oval pan or two. Whole fish and fillets will fit more snugly into an oval pan and, especially if you cook with butter, will be less likely to cause burning than round pans. Oval sauté pans are available in both cast iron (a French import) and nonstick surfaces.

Needlenose pliers, pincers, and tweezers: Long pointed pliers are useful for pulling out the pin bones in fish fillets. Special pincers available at gourmet cooking supply stores work especially well for very small bones, such as those found in trout fillets, as do tweezers.

Oyster/clam knives: Several kinds of knives are available for shucking oysters and clams. The standard oyster knife has a stubby triangular blade, a sturdy handle, and a guard between handle and blade to prevent injury. Clam knives usually have longer and thinner blades and handles without guards. For tough-to-open oysters an oyster knife is indispensable, but because the blade is so short it's not usually long enough to slide along the underside of the top shell to detach it. This requires switching to another, longer knife. I sometimes use clam knives to shuck oysters with more delicate shells such as Belons or other round oysters.

generic white wine, it's unlikely that it will detract from your enjoyment of a seafood meal.

For more formal dinners, wine selection gets more complicated—and more expensive. Part of the reason for serving food formally is that the ritual gets the diners to focus on the food more intently than when food is served casually. Because a formal dinner involves a succession of courses, there should be at least two or three wines (I sometimes get crazy and serve even more), which is what makes such a dinner so exciting. The trick is for the wines and foods to build up in depth and complexity of flavor as the meal progresses so that at no point do the wines or dishes seem anticlimactic. In a traditional dinner seafood is served before the main course, which is almost invariably some kind of meat. All-seafood dinners—or seafood courses interspersed with vegetable courses—are great alternatives when you're having guests who don't eat meat. But regardless of whether you're serving meat or all fish, you'll need to consider the succession of dishes.

One of my favorite predinner wines is a German riesling—a Mosel or a Rheingau—which has a delicate sweetness and low alcohol content that make it a pleasant drink independent of food. If you're serving seafood hors d'oeuvres, however, the sweetness of the German wine may clash, and you'll be better off serving a simple dry white such as an Alsatian pinot blanc. Champagne is an obvious predinner possibility, but it's a hard act to follow. White wines—even very fine wines—tend to taste flat when they follow Champagne. A marvelous and luxurious solution to this problem is of course to serve Champagne throughout dinner—or at least until it's time for a red—but as wonderful as Champagne is, drinking only one kind of wine throughout a meal can get monotonous. You can of course serve different Champagnes, starting with a lighter-style Champagne as the aperitif and then building up to fuller-bodied Champagnes—perhaps even a rosé Champagne—later in the meal. This requires a knowledge of Champagnes or a very trustworthy and knowledgeable wine merchant.

The best way to make sure the wines build to a climax is to serve a simple, inexpensive, but very well chosen wine for the first course. Any of the wines mentioned already as accompaniments to a casual dinner would be appropriate, but the wine should be the very best example of its type. If you decide to serve a finer wine—such as a French Chablis—with the first course, be warned that the wines that follow will have to be very fine indeed not to taste cheap after the Chablis.

While you can certainly serve a white wine with the main course, I prefer to serve a red, even at an all-seafood dinner. Red wine is delicious with fish, especially when the fish has been stewed in red wine, grilled, smoked, or has an assertive sauce. Lighter-style reds such as cool Beaujolais or barbera d'Alba are best, in casual circumstances, but for a more formal dinner my favorites are French red Burgundies, especially softer wines such as those from Vosne-Romanée and the Côte de Beaune. A Burgundy-style California or Oregon pinot noir can also be excellent. These wines—especially the Burgundies—can be exorbitant, so I'm always looking for interesting alternatives. There are less expensive red Burgundies from the Côte Chalonnaise (a region in southern Burgundy)—Rully, Mercurey, and Givry reds—or from the northern part of Burgundy (Marsannay is one example) as well as interesting red wines from the Loire Valley, especially Chinon. If you're serving an all-Champagne dinner, an interesting climax might be a red still wine from the Champagne region such as a Chigny. (This is pretty obscure and may be hard to track down.)

If you're serving a richer seafood as a second course before the main course, you'll probably want to stick with white wine. Serve the same wine you served with the first course or move on to a richer and fuller-bodied white such as white Burgundy. Almost all white Burgundies are made from the chardonnay grape, and there are many price and quality levels, ranging from a simple Mâcon-Villages to a Montrachet the price of liquid gold. Fortunately there are some excellent and reasonably priced white Burgundies from the Côte Chalonnaise such as Rully, Montagny, Mercurey, and Givry or the more expensive Meursault, Puligny-Montrachet, and Chassagne-Montrachet.

To make matters simpler, you may want to choose a chardonnay from California or Australia made in a similar style.

Keep in mind that the best way to choose wine for everyday meals is to experiment with wines you can afford and not worry about the "right" wine. You'd have to go very far afield indeed to end up with a wine that spoils your dinner, and in any case the matching of wine and food is entirely subjective. In the early part of this century Sauternes (a very sweet dessert wine) was popular with oysters!

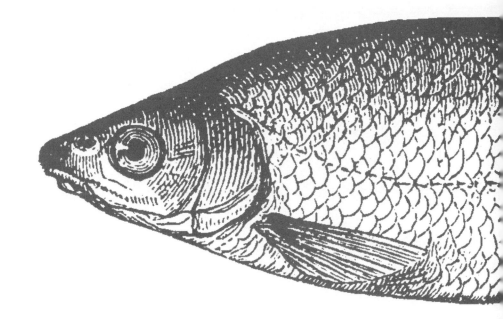

Finfish

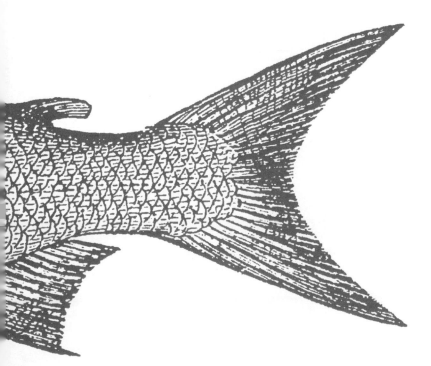

Baking

One of the best and easiest ways to cook a fish is just to slide it into a hot oven and bake it. This way the fish's flavor is unaltered, and for whole fish all the juices stay sealed in. The only tricky part of baking whole fish is filleting the cooked fish (preferably at the table) and leaving the bones behind. This isn't as hard as it sounds, but I recommend practicing on close friends or family—and maybe cutting up the fish in the kitchen—before you parade out to the dining room, fish and knife in hand. With fillets, you just scoop them out of the baking dish, right onto the plates.

BAKING WHOLE FISH

The easiest way to bake a whole fish is to put it in a lightly oiled oval casserole or sauté pan—an oiled sheet pan will also work—and bake it in a hot oven until done.

EQUIPMENT

The best-looking pan for baking a whole fish is a copper oval fish pan lined with tin or stainless steel. Unfortunately these are expensive, and you'll need a couple of different sizes to accommodate different fish. Copper pans, as beautiful as they are, also tend to stick to whole fish. I sometimes cheat and bake fish in something else, transferring the fish to a decorative copper pan for serving in the dining room. A good all-around baking dish is a large porcelain gratin dish—much less expensive than copper and almost as attractive. If you're in a real pinch, just bake the fish on a sheet pan and transfer it (carefully!) to a large plate or platter for carving. Some recipes suggest making deep cuts in the fish, the idea being that this helps the heat penetrate the fish more efficiently. I haven't found that the gashes make any difference and in fact make the fish less appealing to look at.

BAKING TIME AND TEMPERATURE

The exact oven temperature depends on the size of the fish—the smaller, the hotter—but should usually be somewhere between 400°F and 450°F. Whole fish usually bake somewhat more slowly than fillets or when cooked using other techniques, so I count around 15 minutes per inch of thickness at the thickest part—usually near the base of the head. Fillets and steaks are usually done after baking for 12 minutes per inch at the thickest part.

DETERMINING WHEN THE FISH IS DONE

To tell if the fish is done, stick a knife carefully (don't damage the fillets) into the back of the fish just alongside the dorsal fin and gently try to pull the top

---

BAKING AND ROASTING

Even though we often talk about baking and roasting as though they are the same thing, *roasting* means cooking in the open air on a spit, and *baking* means cooking in the oven. Roasting ensures that no moisture surrounds the fish while it's on the spit so that its skin turns crispy and the juices are sealed inside. Not many of us have a spit handy for roasting, however, so we simulate actual roasting in the oven, by baking.

A fish baked in a hot oven with no liquids or moist ingredients will come out almost the same as a fish that was authentically roasted. When we bake fish in the oven with liquids or moist ingredients such as vegetables—which create steam—the effect is more like braising.

---

fillet away from the backbone by lifting gently. When the fish is done, the top fillet should pull away from the bone. It's OK if the flesh is moist near the center of the spine—in fact this is good—but make sure it isn't raw. Don't bake fish until it is "flaky," or it will end up overdone and dried out.

You can also find out if the fish is done by sticking an instant-read thermometer into its back, running parallel with the dorsal fin so as not to poke a hole in its side and spoil the fish's appearance. The thermometer should read between 135°F and 140°F.

TO SCALE OR NOT TO SCALE

One of the problems with baking a whole fish is that the skin sometimes sticks to the bottom of the pan and tears when you try to serve it. One way around this is to bake the fish with its scales still on. The scales also form a kind of carapace that helps seal in the fish's juices. When it comes time to carve, the skin is easy to remove—you just have to be careful that none of the scales come loose. This is the absolute easiest way to cook a fish. Baking it in an elegant copper fish pan—sticking won't be a problem with the scales intact—makes a striking dish with no effort.

One of the disadvantages of baking a fish with the scales still attached is that no one can eat the skin. You may also want to bake a whole fish on a bed of flavorful vegetables (more about this later), and you don't dare do this with the scales still on the fish, or they may come loose into the vegetables.

If you do decide to scale the fish, follow the illustrated directions on color page 26.

SAUCES

When I serve whole baked fish at home, I usually just put a little bottle of extra-virgin olive oil and some lemon wedges on the table, but when guests show up I sometimes whip up a simple sauce. In the winter my favorite sauce is a hollandaise or béarnaise sauce, but in the summer I serve something less rich such as a salsa, basil or cilantro and mint pesto, or a light homemade mayonnaise (see "Sauces and Salsas, Condiments and Broths"). Whichever sauce you do decide to serve, serve it in a bowl or sauceboat—not on the fish—so guests can help themselves.

Whole Baked Red Snapper

Nothing quickens my appetite like the sight of a whole cooked fish, still sizzling hot, resting on an oval platter. Whole cooked fish is not only dramatic to look at but will be a lot juicier and tastier than fish fillets or steaks. You can use this technique for any firm-fleshed round fish with scales. When shopping for a whole fish, I usually figure about 12 ounces to 1 pound per person as a main course (for a fish yielding 50 percent, this makes a 6- to 8-ounce serving) or 6 to 8 ounces per person as a first course. I always try to find a fish large enough to feed everyone—a large fish looks so dramatic—but when I can't, I bake more than one.

MAKES 4 MAIN-COURSE SERVINGS

one 3- to 4-pound or two 1½- to 2-pound red snappers, gutted, gills removed, and scales left on

2 tablespoons olive oil

salt and pepper

extra-virgin olive oil and lemon wedges for serving

Preheat the oven to 400°F. Rub the fish with olive oil and place it in an oiled oval pan, gratin dish, or sheet pan. Bake for about 15 minutes per inch of thickness at the thickest part. Check for doneness by carefully sliding a paring knife into the back at the thickest part, gently lifting the top fillet, and peeking inside to make sure the fish pulls away from the bone and the flesh is opaque (but still moist) rather than translucent and raw.

Serve on hot plates in the dining room Let the guests season their own fish with salt, pepper, olive oil, and lemon.

Substitutes Whole fish such as blackfish, black sea bass, freshwater bass, drums, porgy, rockfish, sea robin, sea trout, tilapia, weakfish

BAKING WHOLE FISH WITH VEGETABLES

One attractive way to serve whole fish is to bake it on a bed of lightly cooked vegetables. The vegetables are colorful to look at when the fish is served at the table, they absorb any juices given off by the fish during baking, and they prevent the fish from sticking to the pan. They are also delicious and turn the baked fish into a whole meal.

Unlike vegetables roasted with meats, which are added raw to the roasting pan, vegetables baked with fish should be lightly precooked. Raw vegetables will not have enough time to cook in the pan with the quick-cooking fish.

When baking fish with vegetables, make sure the fish is thoroughly scaled so none of the scales ends up in the vegetables.

Baked Whole Striped Bass with Provençal Vegetables

I've always been a fan of dishes where every element in the meal is cooked and served together. In this recipe the flavors of whole fish and vegetables meld together into a complete country French meal. The vegetables absorb juices released by the fish and provide a satisfying sauce. This vegetable combination is really a ratatouille, but you can use any combination you like. Just make sure the vegetables are partially cooked before you put them in the roasting pan.

Any whole fish should of course be cooked the day it is bought. The vegetable mixture can be cooked earlier the same day.

MAKES 4 MAIN-COURSE SERVINGS

one 3-pound or two 1½-pound striped bass, gutted, gills and scales removed

1 medium onion, sliced

2 garlic cloves, chopped

½ teaspoon fresh thyme or marjoram leaves or ¼ teaspoon dried

1 red or yellow bell pepper, cut into ¼-inch cubes

3 tablespoons extra-virgin olive oil or more as needed

1 zucchini, cut into ⅓-inch cubes

3 tomatoes, peeled, seeded, and coarsely chopped

salt and pepper

Use the back of a small knife to scrape off any scales adhering to the fish. Rinse and dry the fish and refrigerate it until needed.

Cook the onion, garlic, thyme, and bell pepper in a heavy pot in olive oil over low to medium heat for about 15 minutes, until the onions are translucent and the other vegetables soft. Stir every few minutes to prevent browning.

Stir in the zucchini and cook over medium heat for about 10 minutes more. Add the tomatoes and continue stirring for about 5 minutes, until the tomatoes release their liquid. The mixture should be quite runny so it doesn't dry out and burn in the oven. Season with salt and pepper to taste.

Preheat the oven to 400°F. Spread the vegetable mixture in an even layer on the bottom of an oval roasting pan or gratin dish and place the fish on top. Season the fish with salt and pepper.

Bake for about 15 inches per inch of thickness at the thickest part. Check

for doneness by carefully sliding a paring knife into the back at the thickest part, gently lifting the top fillet, and peeking inside to make sure the fish pulls away from the bone and the flesh is opaque (but still moist) rather than translucent and raw.

Serve the fish accompanied by a large spoonful of the vegetable mixture on hot plates at the table.

Substitutes Whole fish such as blackfish, black sea bass, freshwater bass, drums, porgy, rockfish, sea robin, sea trout, Spanish mackerel, tilapia, weakfish

Baked Whole Sea Bass with Potatoes

LLABARRO AL FORN

(color page 10)

*I*t wasn't until I traveled to the Mediterranean, along the coasts of Italy, Spain, and Portugal, that I really fell in love with olives. While most of us nibble on them as snacks before dinner, olives give an exciting dissonant and slightly bitter note to cooked foods, especially seafood. In this recipe the sharp taste of the olive is juxtaposed with whole fish baked on a bed of potatoes richly flavored with garlic and olive oil. In one of my favorite books on Mediterranean cooking, *Catalan Cuisine*, Colman Andrews describes *llabarro al forn* as "one of the culture's greatest single contributions to Western civilization." Hyperbole aside, I'm predisposed to whole baked fish, especially if there's some savory little extra baked alongside or underneath. This recipe serves only 2, but if you use a 4-pound fish the rest of the

---

MEDITERRANEAN BAKING AND BRAISING

Mediterranean cooks are fond of baking whole fish or large chunks of fish, the most popular method being to rub a whole fish with a little olive oil and bake it in a very hot oven.

Mediterranean cooks also like to bake fish on a bed of aromatic ingredients, usually vegetables and herbs, to come up with a sort of braise. The flavorful drippings from the fish combine with the surrounding, often semiliquid vegetable mixture, to form a rough-hewn saucelike vegetable accompaniment. While the typical Mediterranean cook rarely thinks about technical fine distinctions, fish baked with a little olive oil is considered a roast (Fr. *rôti au four*; Ital. *arrosto*), but if liquids or moist ingredients such as wine or vegetables are baked in the same dish as the fish, the dish is a braise (Fr. *braisé*; Ital. *in umido*).

ingredients are easily doubled.

Here is Mr. Andrews's recipe with a few minor adjustments.

MAKES 2 MAIN-COURSE SERVINGS

one 2-pound sea bass, gutted and scaled

½ cup extra-virgin olive oil

2 large Idaho potatoes, peeled and cut into ⅛-inch-thick slices

2 garlic cloves, finely chopped

½ teaspoon finely chopped fresh thyme leaves or ¼ teaspoon dried

salt and pepper

3 tomatoes, peeled, seeded, and coarsely chopped

15 brine-cured (not canned) black olives, pitted and coarsely chopped

Rinse the fish in cold water. Use the back of a small knife to scrape off any scales adhering to the fish. Preheat the oven to 400°F.

Coat the bottom of an oval baking dish with olive oil and arrange an overlapping layer of potatoes on top. Sprinkle with garlic, thyme, salt, pepper, and more olive oil. Spread on another layer of potatoes and sprinkle on more garlic, thyme, olive oil, salt, and pepper. Continue in this way until you've used up all the potatoes.

Bake for 20 minutes so the potatoes get a start on the fish. Rub the fish with olive oil and season it with salt and pepper. Place the fish on top of the potatoes, arrange the chopped tomatoes and olives around the fish, and bake for about 30 minutes, about 15 minutes per inch of thickness. Check for doneness by carefully sliding a paring knife in along the backbone. The fish is done when the flesh is opaque and pulls away from the bone. Carve and serve the fish and potato mixture at the table.

Substitutes Whole fish such as blackfish, drums, red snapper, rockfish, sea trout, striped bass, weakfish

BAKING FILLETS AND STEAKS

One of the easiest ways to cook fish fillets and steaks is to stick them in the oven topped with a little butter—plain or herb—or sprinkled with olive oil. The result is almost the same as when fish are braised except there's no sauce besides the juices left in the pan. I sometimes break the rule against adding liquid and sprinkle a little wine over the steaks or fillets before baking.

Baked Scrod Fillets with Butter and Sherry

*A*ny firm-fleshed nonoily fish will work here, but be careful with flounder fillets (so-called fillets of sole), because they are so fragile that they're almost impossible to get out of the pan intact. True Dover sole from the other side of the Atlantic are delicious when cooked using this method and will *not* break or fall apart.

While this may not be an impressive dinner-party dish, it's a simple and healthful way of cooking fish when you don't feel like expending much effort. You can perk this dish up by using herb butter—tarragon is especially good—instead of plain butter or olive oil.

MAKES 4 MAIN-COURSE SERVINGS

1½ to 2 pounds scrod fillets

salt and pepper

3 tablespoons unsalted butter, herb butter (pages 329–331), or extra-virgin olive oil

3 tablespoons dry sherry or dry white wine

1 tablespoon finely chopped parsley

Preheat the oven to 400°F. Pull any pin bones out of the fish and sprinkle the fillets with salt and pepper.

Rub the bottom of a square casserole just large enough to hold the fillets in a single layer with a tablespoon of butter or olive oil. Arrange the fillets in an even layer on top.

Dot the tops of the fillets with butter or sprinkle them with olive oil. Sprinkle with the sherry and parsley. Bake for about 12 minutes per inch of thickness. Check for doneness by cutting into a fillet at the thickest part to see if it's opaque inside and pulls apart.

If you have only 1 or 2 fillets, cut them into a total of 4 servings and place on hot plates. Spoon the melted butter and juices in the bottom of the pan over the fillets. Serve immediately.

Substitutes Skinless fillets such as black sea bass, flatfish fillets such as large flounder or fluke or sole fillets, drums, grouper, haddock, hake, halibut, mullet, ocean perch, orange roughy, rockfish, tilefish, red snapper, salmon, striped bass, wolffish

Roast Monkfish with Sage and Whole Garlic Cloves

(color page 9)

*A*mericans have only recently discovered the monkfish, which until a decade ago was more likely to be thrown over the side of the boat than to be sold at a fancy fish store. The French and Italians have long appreciated the firm boneless flesh of the monkfish tail, and a southern French favorite is a dish called *gigot de lotte roti*, which is monkfish (*lotte*) roasted like a leg of lamb (*gigot*). Whole monkfish and monkfish fillets taper at one end and in fact look vaguely like small legs. In the classic recipe the monkfish is surrounded with assorted vegetables in the same way as the earlier recipe for baked whole striped bass with Provençal vegetables. This version is inspired by another Provençal dish, roast chicken with 40 cloves of garlic.

You can use this recipe with other kinds of fish, but the effect won't be quite as dramatic. I've never seen whole monkfish for sale in the United States, probably because the head is so frightful it would scare most people off. The headless monkfish is usually sold with the dark gray or black skin removed. Depending on the size of monkfish you find, you can either roast fillets or the whole headless fish trimmed of its dark skin and purple coloration. The whole fish is easy to carve at the table because it has one central bone that is easy to cut around.

The monkfish of course has to be roasted just before serving, but it can be browned an hour or two ahead, and the garlic cloves can be prepared up to a day in advance.

MAKES 4 MAIN-COURSE SERVINGS

4 heads of garlic

four 8-ounce monkfish fillets or two 1-pound whole monkfish tails

salt and pepper

½ cup all-purpose flour

6 tablespoons olive oil

1½ cups chicken broth (page 344), fish broth (page 343), or water

2 sage leaves, preferably fresh

½ cup heavy cream

2 tablespoons finely chopped parsley or chives

Separate the heads of garlic into individual cloves and peel each clove.

Simmer the cloves in just enough water to cover until they soften but are not mushy, about 20 minutes. Scoop out half of the cloves with a slotted spoon and reserve. Leave the remaining cloves in the simmering water until they turn very soft, about 10 minutes more. Drain the cloves in a fine-mesh strainer and then work them through with the back of a spoon or ladle. You should end up with about ¼ cup garlic puree. Reserve this puree in a small bowl covered with plastic wrap in the refrigerator.

Preheat the oven to 400°F. Trim the translucent membrane and any dark purple sections off the monkfish with a sharp paring or boning knife as shown on color page 25. To trim off the purple you may have to cut about ⅛ inch into the flesh.

Season the monkfish with salt and pepper and roll it in flour. Pat off the excess and brown the monkfish quickly in olive oil in a sauté pan. Place the monkfish in an oval fish pan or roasting pan, surround it with the reserved peeled garlic cloves, and bake until the monkfish bounces back to the touch, about 12 minutes per inch of thickness at the thickest part. If any liquid starts running out of the monkfish into the roasting pan—indicating the fish is starting to over-cook—immediately remove the fish from the oven.

While the monkfish is baking, bring the garlic puree, broth, sage leaves, cream, and parsley to a simmer in a small saucepan while whisking. Cook for about 5 minutes, until the mixture thickens slightly. Pour this sauce over the fish about 5 minutes before you think the fish will be done. Baste the monkfish once or twice with the sauce during the last 5 minutes of cooking.

When the monkfish is done, serve immediately at the table on hot plates. If the monkfish is already filleted, simply slice it into ⅓-inch medallions. If you've baked a whole monkfish tail, first slice along each side of the central bone to separate the fillets and then slice these into medallions. Spoon the sauce and a few garlic cloves over each serving.

SPECIAL TECHNIQUES FOR BAKING FISH

STUFFING
(*WHOLE FISH*)

One way to make a whole fish even more dramatic is to fill it with a simple stuffing.

Most traditional recipes for stuffing round fish recommend inserting the stuffing into the gutted cavity and sealing in the stuffing either by sewing up the fish with needle and thread or by gutting the fish through the gills by reaching into the fish with the hooked handle of a kitchen ladle. I don't like either of these techniques because they make carving the fish very tricky—it's hard to get the stuffing out of the cavity without serving up a lot of bones. My favorite stuffing technique—which sounds more difficult than it is—is to bone the ungutted fish through the back (see color page 27) and insert the stuffing into the cavity. In this way the cooked fish can be cut *crosswise* into attractive and boneless sections.

BONING FLATFISH FOR STUFFING

Flatfish can also be stuffed, but I rarely bother unless I come across a particularly large and fresh specimen of fluke or flounder. To stuff a flatfish, have the fishmonger scale the underside—the white side—and, if he or she is cooperative, remove the dark skin. (Otherwise, remove the dark skin yourself.) The dark skin of firm-fleshed flatfish such as Dover sole is easy to remove because once you've cut around the periphery of the fish (see color page 30) you can just peel the dark skin off. If you're using more fragile fish—most American flatfish—you'll have to coax off the dark skin by alternately pulling, peeling, and slicing between skin and flesh with a sharp knife. Once you've removed the dark skin, cut between the skinless fillets with a long flexible knife, sliding the knife under the fillets—exposing the backbone—but not cutting all the way through to the edge and detaching the fillets. Once you've exposed the backbone, cut it in two or three places with a sturdy pair of scissors and slide a knife along its underside to detach it in sections. The stuffing can now be slid under the two top fillets.

KINDS OF STUFFING

A stuffing for a whole fish can be as simple or elaborate as you like. One of my favorites is a simple mixture of cooked onions and chopped mushrooms seasoned with chopped fresh herbs and held together with a few bread crumbs, but you can also include cubes of shellfish, chopped green vegetables, fish or shellfish mousseline, or even another fish fillet. A stuffed fish is baked in the same way as a fish without stuffing, although a stuffed fish will, of course, require a few extra minutes in the oven.

❧

Stuffed Striped Bass with Spinach, Shrimp, and Mushrooms

I've selected striped bass for this dish because it is usually available ungutted—essential for boning through the back. Larger, more dramatic fish such as grouper also work well, but it is sometimes difficult to find them in ungutted whole form.

You can bone the fish and make the mushroom stuffing earlier in the same day, but the fish should be stuffed at the last minute (otherwise bacteria can grow within the stuffed cavity) and baked just before serving.

If you like, you can serve this fish with a sauce such as hollandaise (page 335), béarnaise (page 336), a light tomato puree (page 337), or flavored oil (see page 254).

MAKES 6 MAIN-COURSE SERVINGS

one 4-pound or two 2-pound striped bass or other round fish, scaled but not gutted, fins trimmed, and gills removed

1 medium onion, finely chopped

1 garlic clove, finely chopped

4 tablespoons unsalted butter

¹⁄₂ pound mushrooms, finely chopped

1 pound medium shrimp, peeled, deveined, and cut into ¹⁄₂-inch pieces

1 tablespoon chopped fresh tarragon or ¹⁄₂ teaspoon chopped fresh marjoram or thyme leaves or ¹⁄₄ teaspoon dried leaves from 1 large bunch of spinach, blanched and coarsely chopped

¹⁄₂ cup fresh bread crumbs, softened in ¹⁄₄ cup milk

salt and pepper

Bone the striped bass through the back (see color page 27), remove any stray bones, and store fish in the refrigerator.

Cook the onion and garlic in a tablespoon of the butter in a medium-size sauté pan over medium heat until the onion is translucent, about 10 minutes. Add the mushrooms, turn the heat up to high, and continue cooking until all the liquid released by the mushrooms evaporates. Remove the pan from the heat and immediately stir in the shrimp so it is cooked by the hot mushroom mixture. Transfer the mixture to a mixing bowl.

Stir the rest of the ingredients—except the remaining butter—into the mushroom mixture and let cool for at least an hour in the refrigerator.

Preheat the oven to 400°F and spread the stuffing evenly into the fish. Butter a roasting pan or oval casserole with half the remaining butter and carefully set the fish on its side in the pan. Dot the fish with the remaining butter. Bake for approximately 20 minutes (about 15 inches per inch of thickness including the stuffing). To check for doneness, carefully slide a knife between the stuffing and the top fillet to see if the fish is opaque or check the stuffing temperature with an instant-read thermometer—it should be 135°F (about 5° cooler than the fish itself).

Cut the fish crosswise into 6 sections (3 each if you've used 2 smaller fish) and serve on hot plates. Pass any sauce in a sauceboat at the table.

Substitutes Whole fish such as blackfish, large drums, grouper, large porgies, ocean perch, red snapper, rockfish, sea bass, sea trout, walleye, weakfish, tilapia

COATINGS, CRUSTS, AND RUBS

Both whole fish and fillets can be coated with mixtures of bread crumbs, chopped nuts, herbs, and condiments or rubbed lightly with spice mixtures before baking. A savory crust adds both flavor and texture to fish and fish fillets.

Indian cooks are especially expert at coating fish with delicious spice mixtures before baking or grilling. These mixtures usually include yogurt and may also include mixtures of chopped mint or cilantro, tamarind, mustard, coconut milk, and hot chilies in addition to several ground spices. Some Indian recipes suggest marinating the fish in the spice mixtures for an hour or two before cooking; others suggest coating the fish with the flavorful paste immediately before cooking.

❧

Baked Mackerel with Mustard and Bread Crumbs

When I first cooked this dish while chefing at a popular Parisian bistro, I wasn't sure whether the French would go for it. As it turned out, this simple dish became one of the most popular plates on the menu.

For reasons I don't understand, Americans usually make a face when I mention mackerel, thinking of it as somehow strong or unsavory. My own experience with mackerel (and Spanish mackerel) is that it's inexpensive, often available very fresh, and has a delicate yet full flavor. If you're still hesitant about mackerel, however,

---

MAKING YOUR OWN BREAD CRUMBS

Many cooks assume that bread crumbs should be made from stale bread. While stale bread crumbs will do in a pinch, fresh bread crumbs will provide a much more delicate coating for baked and sautéed seafood. I don't recommend bread crumbs that come in a box; they're almost always dry and usually taste like stale vegetable oil.

The easiest way to make your own bread crumbs is to buy a loaf of good-quality white bread—I usually use Pepperidge Farm—cut off the crusts, and zap it for 30 seconds in a food processor. To make even finer bread crumbs, I then work them through a drum sieve. You can also use the largest kitchen strainer you have or skip this last step altogether—it isn't essential.

---

this technique also works very well with trout.

In France we served these mackerel whole, but you can also use this technique with fillets.

MAKES 4 MAIN-COURSE SERVINGS

four 14-ounce to 1-pound mackerel or two 2-pound Spanish mackerel, gutted, gills and fins removed

1 cup Dijon mustard

2 cups fresh bread crumbs

melted unsalted butter or olive oil

Preheat the oven to 450°F. Smear the whole mackerel with a thick layer of mustard and press on a layer of bread crumbs. Place the mackerel in a buttered or oiled casserole or square baking pan in a single layer and bake for about 15 minutes per inch of thickness at the thickest part. If the bread crumbs look like they're about to burn, turn the fish over so the bread crumbs brown on both sides. If the bread crumbs have not browned, slide the fish under the broiler for a few seconds—just long enough to brown the crumbs.

Substitutes Scaled whole fish weighing 1 to 2 pounds such as porgy, sea trout, small rockfish, trout, weakfish

---

❧

Indian-Style Baked Pompano with Yogurt and Spices

I call for pompano here because of its firm flesh and its close resemblance to the pomfret, which is very popular in India. If you can't find pompano, use another firm-fleshed fish such as sea bass or thin swordfish steaks. I like to bake whole fish, but you can also fillet the fish before baking and cut the baking times accordingly.

MAKES 4 MAIN-COURSE SERVINGS

1 cup plain yogurt

1 teaspoon ground turmeric

1 teaspoon ground cumin

½ tightly packed cup fresh cilantro leaves

½ tightly packed cup fresh mint leaves

3 garlic cloves, coarsely chopped

2 Thai or serrano chilies, halved, seeded, and coarsely chopped

salt

2 tablespoons olive oil or vegetable oil

four 1-pound pompanos, cleaned and dressed, left whole or filleted

Pour the yogurt into a strainer lined with a paper coffee filter or paper towel and let drain over a bowl for 2 hours to thicken.

Stir the turmeric and cumin into the yogurt and puree it in a blender or food processor with the cilantro and mint leaves, garlic, and chilies. Season the mixture with salt to taste.

Preheat the oven to 400°F. Oil 4 rectangular sheets of aluminum foil, each about 2 inches larger on each side than the pompano.

Dip the fish or fillets in the yogurt mixture so they are well coated and arrange on the foil. Place on a baking sheet and fold each sheet of foil up along the sides of each fish so the yogurt mixture doesn't run onto the baking sheet and burn. If you're serving fillets, skip the foil and bake them in a square baking dish. You should end up using all the yogurt mixture.

Bake the whole fish or fillets for about 15 minutes per inch of thickness for whole fish and 12 minutes per inch for fillets and serve immediately on hot plates.

❧

Halibut Fillets with Curry, Herb, and Almond Crust

If you have difficulty finding halibut fillets (halibut is often marketed as steaks), this coating of almonds and herbs works with any firm-fleshed nonoily fillet or small whole fish. You can also substitute pine nuts, pecans, walnuts, hazelnuts, or macadamia nuts for the almonds—almost any nut will give the fish a delightful and crunchy outer crust. You don't really need to serve this dish with a sauce, but the curry and herb sauce goes especially well.

MAKES **4** LIGHT MAIN-COURSE OR FIRST-COURSE SERVINGS

four 6-ounce pieces of halibut fillet, without skin

2 teaspoons curry powder

salt and pepper

¼ cup fresh bread crumbs

¼ cup shelled almonds with skin

1 teaspoon fresh thyme leaves or ½ teaspoon dried

melted unsalted butter or olive oil

For the Curry Sauce (optional):

2 teaspoons good-quality curry powder

1 tablespoon unsalted butter

½ cup fish broth (page 343) or chicken broth (page 344)

½ cup heavy cream

2 tablespoons finely chopped fresh cilantro, parsley, or chives

salt and pepper

1 to 2 teaspoons fresh lemon juice

Preparing the Fish: Sprinkle the most attractive side of the halibut fillets with curry powder, salt, and pepper.

Process the bread crumbs, almonds, and thyme together in a food processor for about 1 minute. Press the fillets, attractive side down, into this mixture so the tops of the fillets are coated with an even layer. If necessary, press additional nut mixture onto the fish so that it's well coated. Refrigerate for 20 minutes to 2 hours.

Preparing the Sauce: Cook the curry powder in butter in a small saucepan over low heat until the curry starts to smell fragrant, about 2 minutes. (Be careful; curry burns quickly.)

Whisk in the broth and boil until the broth reduces by about half, about 5 minutes. Add the cream and simmer until the sauce has the consistency you like. (I like a thin almost brothlike

sauce, which I then serve *around* the fish in wide soup plates so the breading doesn't get soggy.) Stir in the cilantro, simmer gently for 1 minute more, and season with salt, pepper, and lemon juice to taste.

Baking and Serving: Preheat the oven to 450°F and carefully transfer the fillets to a buttered or oiled baking sheet. Bake the fillets for about 6 minutes (assuming they're about ½ inch thick) and transfer them to hot plates. Spoon the sauce around—not over—and serve.

Substitutes Fillets such as blackfish, grouper, John Dory, lingcod, mahimahi, rockfish, sablefish, sea trout, shark, swordfish, tilefish

BAKING FISH IN A SACK

A great trick for trapping the flavor of baked fish and at the same time making a savory sauce is to enclose the fish in a special paper or cellophane bag. Aromatic vegetables, herbs, and small amounts of liquid such as wine or fish broth can also be sealed up with the fish so that the fish actually steams or braises, locking in all the flavors from the fish and vegetables.

There are two ways to use this bag technique. One, best used for large whole fish, is to seal the fish in one of the cellophane roasting bags sold at supermarkets and then bake the fish in a 375°F oven. Because the outer surfaces of large fish, especially lean fish such as cod or pollack, tend to dry out when simply baked, the roasting bag keeps the entire fish moist. The bag also keeps in all the fish's juices, which can be spooned over the fish when it is served.

The second method, used for individual servings, is to cook the fish *en papillote*. Baking a fish *en papillote* seals in the juices and aromas from vegetables or other ingredients such as herbs or truffles, which are then released only at the moment the diners (or the waiter in a fancy restaurant) cut into their own little bags. Fish baked *en papillote* also makes its own sauce as the juices from the fish mingle with the flavors of lightly precooked vegetables and butter or extra-virgin olive oil.

Papillotes are traditionally made with a square of parchment paper sealed with egg white. If you can't find parchment paper, use aluminum foil and forget about the egg white.

❧

Whole Striped Bass with Fennel and Tomatoes in a Roasting Bag

(color page 10)

You can use this technique for any large fish. You can also use different herbs, vegetables, or spices. A very simple method is to pour in ½ cup of white wine and slide a few sprigs of fresh dill in with the fish before sealing up the bag, or you can get more elaborate and include julienned vegetables such as leeks, turnips, and carrots or whole wild mushrooms or even sliced truffles.

Be certain that the fishmonger cuts all the fins off the fish, or they may puncture the roasting bag. If you don't have access to wild striped bass (in some states there's a moratorium on commercial sales of these fish), you'll probably have trouble finding one large enough for this recipe and may want to use one of the substitutes.

MAKES **4** MAIN-COURSE SERVINGS

one 4-pound striped bass, gutted, scaled, gills and fins removed

1 fennel bulb

¾ cup dry white wine

2 teaspoons coriander seeds

2 tablespoons extra-virgin olive oil

salt and pepper

4 tomatoes, peeled, seeded, and cut into ½-inch chunks

Scrape off any scales adhering to the fish and refrigerate. Cut the feathery green fronds off the fennel and reserve. Cut off the stalks at the top of the bulb and discard the stalks or save them for fish broth. Peel any tough, stringy fiber off the outside of the bulb with a vegetable peeler and then cut the fennel into 8 wedges. Simmer the wedges in a covered nonaluminum pan with the white wine, coriander seeds, olive oil, and salt and pepper over low heat until they soften but retain some crunch, about 20 minutes. Cool in the liquid.

Preheat the oven to 375°F. Rinse and dry the fish, season it with salt and pepper, and slide it into an oven roasting bag. If the fish is too large, you can cut off its head, but avoid this; a headless fish is much less dramatic.

Put all the ingredients from cooking the fennel—including any liquid—in the bag with the fish. Season the tomatoes with salt and pepper and put them in the bag along with the reserved fennel fronds. Push down along the bag to squeeze out excess air and seal the bag at one end with string.

Carefully place the bag with the fish in an oval baking dish or on a sheet pan (it's easiest to bake the fish on something you can take straight to the dining room) and bake for about 15 minutes per inch of thickness (e.g., 30 minutes for a 2-inch-thick fish).

Cut the bag open in front of the guests and serve everyone a piece of fish surrounded by a wedge of fennel, a few chopped tomatoes, and a spoonful of juices.

Substitutes Whole fish such as Arctic char, blackfish, black sea bass, coho salmon, grouper, ocean perch, red snapper, rockfish, sea trout, Spanish mackerel, weakfish

Fillet of Salmon en Papillote with Wild Mushrooms

(color page 16)

A fish fillet baked *en papillote* not only makes a dramatic presentation—the bag puffs up like a balloon—but also seals in the flavors and aromas of tasty and exotic ingredients such as wild mushrooms or truffles. I'm usually inspired to bake fish *en papillote* during the spring morel season or fall holidays, when I can justify including a few truffle slices.

Although the whole point of baking seafood *en papillote* is to let the guests open their own little bags so they catch a whiff of whatever's inside, it's awkward—and not very pretty—to eat the fish directly out of the bag. My own way around this is to set the bags on wide hot soup plates in front of each guest and then go around and cut them open on the sides with scissors (or just pass the scissors around) and then pull the bag away, sliding the fish right into each guest's bowl. Needless to say, this isn't practical with more than a few people.

continued

MAKES 4 MAIN-COURSE SERVINGS

one 2-pound center-cut salmon fillet, pin
　　bones and skin removed

salt and pepper

1 pound fresh wild mushrooms such as
　　morels, cèpes (porcini), hedgehogs
　　(pieds de mouton), or chanterelles,
　　rinsed and dried

2 tablespoons unsalted butter

1 shallot, finely chopped

1 small garlic clove, finely chopped

½ cup chicken broth (page 344) or fish
　　broth (page 343)

½ cup rainwater or Sercial Madeira or fino
　　sherry

2 tablespoons finely chopped parsley

1 black truffle, as large as you like
　　(optional)

1 egg white

Cut the salmon crosswise into 4
equal pieces. Fold under the thinner
stomach flap on each piece of salmon
so the salmon slice is the same thickness all the way across. Season the
slices with salt and pepper and refrigerate until needed.

If the mushrooms are extremely
large, cut them into 2-inch pieces, but
try to cut them so they retain some of
their original shape. Sauté the mushrooms in butter over medium to high
heat—don't let the butter burn—for
about 10 minutes. Sprinkle the mushrooms with the shallots and garlic
after about 5 minutes. If the mushrooms release liquid, continue cooking them until all the liquid
evaporates.

Pour the broth and Madeira into the
pan of mushrooms, sprinkle on the
parsley, and boil over high heat until
the liquids reduce by half. Let the
mixture cool and season it to taste
with salt and pepper.

Peel the truffle just before you're
ready to assemble the papillotes.
Chop the peelings and add them to
the mushroom mixture. Slice the truffle as thinly as possible with a paring
knife or vegetable slicer.

Preheat the oven to 450°F. Cut 4
squares of parchment paper about 12
inches on each side and place a slice of
salmon just one side to the center of
each square. Spoon on the mushrooms
and their cooking liquid and sprinkle
with the truffles.

Combine the egg white with a teaspoon of salt and beat it with a fork
for about a minute to loosen it. Brush
the egg white around the outside inch
of the squares and fold the squares
over, pressing against the egg white to
create a seal. Brush the outer part of
the squares a second time with egg
white and make a series of straight
folds to make a seal. Brush one last
time with egg wash and set the papillotes on a baking sheet. If you're using
aluminum foil, fold in the same way,
but don't bother with the egg whites.
Foil puffs up in the same way as
parchment paper.

Bake the papillotes until they puff
up, about 10 minutes per inch of
thickness. (Fish baked *en papillote*
cooks faster than most baked fish
because the fish actually steams.)
Immediately slide the papillotes onto
hot soup plates and serve.

Substitutes Fillets such as blackfish,
cod, halibut, lingcod, rockfish, sablefish, swordfish, tilefish, wolffish

BAKING FISH IN SALT

This is an excellent technique for sealing in a fish's flavor and scenting it
with sea salt. The salt doesn't come in
contact with the flesh of the fish
because the skin, which is left on,
forms a protective layer. Cracking
open a whole fish encased in salt also
makes a dramatic presentation for a
dinner party.

Arctic Char Baked in Salt

When I first saw this technique
demonstrated at a French cooking school, I thought it looked silly
and contrived—until I got a little
taste. The salt seals in the flavor of fish
better than any other technique I
know.

This recipe works especially well
with any fish from the salmon and
trout families, but I use Arctic char,
mainly because the char's 3-pound size
conveniently makes 4 servings. Almost
any large round fish can be baked
using this method.

Fish baked in salt must be completely coated with a ½- to ¾-inch-
thick layer of coarse salt on both
sides— usually about twice the
weight of the fish. The skin of the fish
must not peek through. Sea salt is
best, but you can also use the less-
expensive kosher salt.

The easiest way to enclose a
whole fish in salt is to use an oval baking dish a few inches longer and
wider than the fish, fill it with about a
third of the salt/egg white mixture
(the egg white helps the salt harden),
place the fish on top, pack on the rest

of the salt, and set the whole thing on a baking sheet in a 400°F oven. If you don't have an oval pan large enough to hold the fish, you can hold the salt in place on a baking sheet with a long strip of folded aluminum foil.

MAKES 4 MAIN-COURSE SERVINGS

one 3- to 3½-pound Arctic char, gutted, gills and fins removed

4 egg whites

½ cup cold water

6 to 7 pounds coarse sea salt or kosher salt

2 tablespoons vegetable oil (for aluminum foil method)

Preheat the oven to 400°F. Rinse and dry the fish thoroughly.

Whisk together the egg whites and the water and combine with the salt in a large mixing bowl. Work the mixture with your hands to distribute the water and egg whites through the salt.

Using a Baking Dish: Select a baking dish about 2 inches longer than the fish. Fill the baking dish about a third full of the salt mixture and place the fish on top. Cover the fish with the rest of the salt mixture and smooth the salt over with a spatula.

Using an Aluminum Foil Mold: Roll out a sheet of aluminum foil 2½ times the length of the fish. Fold the aluminum foil over itself lengthwise until you have a 3-inch-wide strip. Brush a baking sheet with oil and place the fish on top. Attach the 2 ends of the aluminum foil strip with a paper clip or by just pinching the top of one end over the other end. Place the aluminum foil around the fish and shape the foil so that it curves all around the fish with about 1 inch between fish and foil. Lift the fish off the baking sheet and fill the mold with about one third of the salt mixture—there should be a ½- to ¾-

inch-thick layer of salt. Place the fish on top. Spread the rest of the salt mixture over the fish and smooth its surface with a spatula.

Baking: Place the fish in the oven for approximately 40 minutes. The only way to know the fish is done is by inserting an instant-read thermometer through the layer of salt and measuring the temperature of the fish. When the fish reaches 135°F, take it out of the oven and serve immediately.

Serving: Bring the fish to the table on its baking sheet or on a large platter—something to catch flying salt—and crack it with a mallet or even a hammer. Pull back the salt layer, then peel off the skin with a fork. Serve on hot plates.

Substitutes Whole fish such as blackfish, grouper, ocean perch, red snapper, rockfish, salmon (especially smaller varieties), salmon trout, steelhead, striped bass

BAKING FISH IN PASTRY

A whole fish baked in pastry is one of the most dramatic and impressive things you can serve. To do it well, however, you must have enough patience to get the pastry-wrapped fish to look like a fish instead of a beached whale.

Almost any fish can be boned and skinned, wrapped in a thin layer of puff pastry, baked quickly, and then served in crosswise slices as though cutting it into steaks. One word of advice: use only fish that weigh 2 pounds or more. Smaller fish will overcook by the time the pastry is cooked thoroughly.

One of three kinds of pastry can be used for wrapping a whole fish—regular pie dough, puff pastry, and brioche. While pie dough is the easiest to make, I prefer the professional look of puff pastry or the satisfying buttery quality of brioche. Frozen puff pastry is available in fancy-food shops if you haven't mastered—or don't want to bother—making it yourself. When buying puff pastry, inspect the package to make sure that it has been made with butter and not margarine or anything hydrogenated. Whichever pastry you decide to use, remember that fish releases liquid as it cooks. This liquid then runs into the surrounding pastry and makes it soggy. The solution is to wrap something around the fish to absorb the liquid. Crêpes are used here, but you can also line the pastry with rice or chopped and cooked mushrooms.

You can use one of several approaches to preparing the fish. The classic method is to bone an ungutted fish through the back (see color page 27) and remove the innards, leaving a perfect boneless pouch. The fish can then be skinned by slicing the skin off in strips, but you can also leave the skin on. Any number of stuffings can be slid into the fish—from a simple sprinkling of chopped herbs to an elaborate mousseline (see "Mousses, Soufflés, and Other French Classics"). Another method that works well for fish that have already been gutted—such as salmon, large trout, or char—is to bone the fish from the belly side by sliding a sharp knife along each side just under the ribs and removing the spinal column and ribs in one piece (see color page 27). The easiest method is to buy a fish already boned—coho salmon is often sold this way—or to cheat and buy two 8-ounce fillets, place them on top of each other, with perhaps a little stuffing between, and wrap them in pastry, which can then be decorated like a whole fish.

CRÊPES

½ cup all-purpose flour

4 large eggs

¾ cup milk

½ teaspoon salt

4 tablespoons unsalted butter, melted

MAKES TEN 10-INCH CRÊPES

Whisk together the flour and eggs in a mixing bowl. Add just enough of the milk to make a smooth paste, stirring gently to eliminate lumps, then add the rest of the milk, the salt, and 3 tablespoons of the melted butter. Let the batter rest in the refrigerator for an hour.

Brush a 10-inch nonstick sauté pan with butter, heat the pan over medium heat, and ladle in just enough of the batter to cover the bottom of the pan. Cook gently for 2 to 3 minutes until the edges brown. Flip the crêpe over with a rubber spatula or by picking it up on the edge with your fingers. Cook it on the second side for about 2 minutes. Transfer to a plate.

This recipe makes more crêpes than you'll need for wrapping one fish. Crêpes can be kept for several months in the freezer if stacked with a sheet of wax paper between each crêpe and the whole thing wrapped tightly in plastic wrap and then aluminum foil.

❧

Rockfish in Puff Pastry

MAKES 4 MAIN-COURSE SERVINGS

one 2- to 2½-pound rockfish, scaled but ungutted, fins cut off with scissors, or two 8-ounce skinless boned rockfish fillets

salt and pepper

1 tablespoon chopped fresh tarragon or other fresh herb

four 10-inch crêpes

one 8-ounce sheet of puff pastry

1 egg

1 cup beurre blanc (page 333) or melted butter (optional)

Bone the fish through the back (see color page 27); remove the innards and all the bones, including the pin bones. If you wish, take the skin off the fish by cutting it off in strips with a sharp knife. Season the inside and outside of the fish with salt and pepper and sprinkle the chopped tarragon inside. If you're using fillets, season them with salt and pepper and sprinkle one with the chopped tarragon. Arrange the other fillet on top of the first. Wrap the boned fish or fillets in the crêpes.

Preheat the oven to 400°F. Roll out the sheet of puff pastry to about the thickness of 2 dimes (³/₃₂ of an inch), about 3 inches longer than the fish, and twice as wide as the fish plus 2 inches. (There must be enough extra pastry to completely enclose the fish and overlap.) In other words, if the fish (or fillets) is 10 inches long and 4 inches wide, the puff pastry should be 13 inches long and 10 inches wide. Arrange the fish in the center of the puff pastry. Fold one side of the pastry

up and over the fish—it should cover about two-thirds of the fish. Brush the top of the pastry with water, fold up the other side of the pastry, and press gently where it overlaps, forming a seal. Carefully turn the fish over, seal facing down, onto a baking sheet that has been sprinkled with cold water (the water prevents the bottom of the pastry from burning). If you want to make the pastry look like a fish, make scales by poking along the fish with a metal pastry bag tip or metal screw-top bottle cap pinched at one side. Score the tail and fins with a sharp knife. If you're uncertain of your technique, do what I often do and simply bake the fish without making scales so that it looks like a simple loaf.

Beat the egg with a fork in a small bowl with a teaspoon of salt. (The salt is important. It thins the egg mixture so that it goes on in a thinner and more even layer.) Brush the fish with the beaten egg mixture. Bake until the pastry browns, about 20 minutes, then turn the oven down to 300°F and bake for about 10 minutes more. Check the fish by inserting an instant-read thermometer through the side of the pastry—somewhere unobtrusive—to see if it has reached 135°F. Use a spatula to lift the fish off the baking sheet, if necessary scraping against the baking sheet to prevent the fish from sticking.

Present the whole fish on a platter at the table. If you've used a whole boned fish, cut off the tail and head; if you've used fillets, simply trim off an inch of pastry from the end. Serve everyone a 1-inch slice. Serve the beurre blanc in a sauceboat at the table.

Substitutes Whole fish or fillets such as Arctic char, blackfish, black bass, grouper, porgy, red snapper, sea trout, striped bass, weakfish

Coulibiac

SALMON BRIOCHE LOAF

Coulibiac was originally a Russian dish, but around the turn of the century it was lovingly adopted by the French, who made it richer and even more luxurious. This is obviously one of those dishes from the days when no one worried about fats and the more elaborate and rich the dish, the better. While many of these dated dishes aren't worth bothering about, I have to confess to a special fondness for coulibiac (sometimes spelled *koulibiac*).

This is a somewhat lightened version (but by no means low-cal). Older recipes always call for hard-boiled eggs (I've left them out) and insist on pouring melted butter through holes in the top of the pastry (definitely overkill). The rice (traditional) may seem bizarre, but it absorbs the juices from the salmon and keeps the brioche from getting soggy.

Coulibiac is best at an outdoor brunch or lunch and is delicious with rosé Champagne.

MAKES 8 LIGHT MAIN-COURSE SERVINGS

one 2-pound salmon fillet, pin bones and skin removed

2 pounds brioche dough

1 tablespoon unsalted butter, softened

2 cups cooked rice

salt and pepper

1 egg

Slice the salmon into 5-inch sections, each about ½ inch thick. This may mean leaving whole the sections near the tail and slicing crosswise through the thicker sections nearer the head end of the fillet so each section ends up being the same thickness.

Roll the brioche dough into a 12-inch square ⅓ inch thick. Cut in half to make two 6- by 12-inch rectangles. Place one of the rectangles on a buttered baking sheet.

Toss the rice with salt and pepper and spread half of it on the rectangle on the baking sheet, leaving about a ½-inch border. Arrange the slices of salmon fillet on top of the rice and season the salmon with salt and pepper. Spread the rest of the rice in an even layer over the salmon.

Beat the egg with a generous pinch of salt. Fold the sides of the bottom rectangle—the border with no rice—up around the fish and brush the underside of the folds with some of the egg wash. Don't be frustrated if the dough doesn't stay in place. Place the second brioche rectangle over this whole package and seal it over and underneath the first rectangle of dough, tucking it underneath so the seal doesn't show.

Cover the loaf with a moist towel and place it in a warm place (such as the oven with only the pilot light on or on top of the stove with the oven on low) for an hour. Preheat the oven to 375°F. Brush the coulibiac with the remaining egg wash and bake it until it's golden brown, about 30 minutes. If it turns brown sooner, turn the oven down to 325°F.

There are a few ways to tell when the coulibiac is done. You can tap it to see if it sounds hollow, stick a skewer in its side and make sure it comes out clean and not covered with raw dough, or insert an instant-read thermometer where the fish should be. The temperature should be 130°F, slightly less than normal because it will keep cooking as you're getting ready to serve the coulibiac.

Take the coulibiac to the table (or buffet) on a cutting board and slice it in front of the guests.

BRIOCHE

Brioche is basically a rich bread dough with eggs instead of water and butter incorporated into the dough before baking.

2 cups all-purpose flour

5 eggs

1 teaspoon salt

half a ¼-ounce envelope active dry yeast

2 tablespoons warm water

1 teaspoon sugar

½ pound (2 sticks) unsalted butter, cut into 8 pieces

MAKES 2 POUNDS

Combine the flour, eggs, and salt in a mixing bowl or in an electric mixer with a dough hook attachment. Knead the mixture by hand or in the mixer until the dough feels sticky to the touch yet pulls away from your fingers or the sides of the mixer bowl. Dissolve the yeast in the water with the sugar and work this mixture into the dough. (If the dough doesn't feel sticky, add a small amount of water; if it adheres to your fingers or the bowl without pulling away, add a little flour.) Work the pieces of butter, two at a time, into the dough until the butter completely disappears.

Put the dough in a large mixing bowl and cover with plastic wrap. Let rise in the refrigerator until it has doubled in volume, about 12 hours. Push the dough down with your hands to flatten it to its original size.

Brioche dough is best when allowed to rise for at least 12 hours in a cool place or in the refrigerator, but if you're in a hurry, double the amount of yeast and let rise in a warm place for a couple of hours, refrigerate for 1 hour, and flatten as directed.

Braising

Braising, cooking partially submerged in liquid, is one of the easiest and most versatile ways to prepare fish. Perhaps the most important advantage of braising is that the flavor of the fish ends up concentrated in the surrounding liquid, which is then easy to convert into a simple but tasty sauce.

Although both whole fish and fillets can be braised, there are advantages and disadvantages to both methods. The skin of a whole fish helps seal in its flavor, and fish looks great presented whole. However, most people don't know what to do with a whole fish when it arrives at the table, so you're stuck doing the carving.

Fillets are easier to deal with but don't look as dramatic at the table. One good trick is to have the fishmonger fillet a whole fish and save you the bones and head so you can throw together a quick fish broth to use as the braising liquid for your fillets. (Fish that is already filleted should be avoided anyway since it's often less fresh.)

BRAISING WHOLE FISH

When you buy whole fish, have the fishmonger clean it and scale it. Some cooks like to remove the head (I think there's something depressing about headless fish) to fit the fish in the pan.

When you get your fish home, take it to the sink and scrape off any remaining scales with the back of a kitchen knife, then rinse the fish thoroughly in cold water. Next find a vessel for braising that fits the shape and size of the fish as closely as possible so you don't end up having to use too much liquid. My favorite dishes for braising whole fish are oval porcelain or copper gratin dishes that are ovenproof and look attractive on the table. If you don't have either of these, you can use a sauté pan (preferably an oval one)—just make sure it will fit in the oven and has an ovenproof handle.

If you're braising a whole flatfish such as a flounder or sole, have the fishmonger clean the fish, remove the gills, trim off the fins, scale the bottom (the white side), and remove the skin on the top (black side). Or you can do this yourself (see color page 29). If the fish is large, you may have to braise it in a large roasting pan.

Preheat the oven to 425°F and lightly coat the bottom of the braising container with butter or olive oil. Sprinkle in some flavorful ingredients such as chopped shallots, garlic, or herbs (see chart on page 28) and

arrange the fish on top. If you're braising flatfish, the skinless dark side of the fish should be on top. Bring the braising liquid—water, white wine, etc.—to a simmer on top of the stove and pour it over until it comes halfway up the sides of the fish. Cover the fish loosely with a piece of lightly buttered aluminum foil and place it in the oven. The cooking time will depend on the fish's thickness; figure about 10 minutes per inch. Use a ladle to baste the fish every 2 minutes, working quickly so you don't let too much heat out of the oven. To tell if the fish is done, insert a knife along the dorsal fin between one of the fillets and the bones—the fillet should detach and look opaque rather than translucent where it touches the bone.

How you present whole fish at the table depends on whether you want to serve the braising liquid as is or convert it into a more substantial sauce. If you're serving the fish with the plain braising liquid, leave the fish in the cooking vessel to avoid breaking it up as you transfer it to a serving dish.

If you're converting the braising liquid into a sauce, strain the liquid into a saucepan. You can transfer the fish to a clean plate or platter before straining the cooking liquid, but the fragile cooked fish may end up on the kitchen floor. An easier method is to hold the fish in place in its cooking vessel—use a kitchen towel—and tilt it over a strainer set in a saucepan to capture the braising liquid. You then keep the fish warm while you're making the sauce. When the sauce is ready, just pour it back over the fish.

WHICH FISH TO BRAISE?

Braising works best with delicately flavored fish such as flatfish, members of the cod family, bass, porgies, snappers, rockfish, skate, salmon, and monkfish. Oily and strongly flavored fish such as bluefish and jacks should not be used because braising tends to concentrate the fish's flavor.

PRESENTING AND CARVING WHOLE BRAISED FISH

The easiest way to present a whole fish is to take it to the table in the dish it was cooked in, serve it on hot plates, and then ladle a spoonful of the cooking liquid or sauce over each serving. Most recipes suggest removing the skin before serving—this is easy to do; just peel it off with a fork—but it's up to you. I always peel the skin off fish with rubbery skin such as trout or grouper but leave it on fish with thinner skin such as sea bass or red snapper. In any case, the guests can always peel off their own.

BRAISING FILLETS

Braising a fish fillet can be as straightforward as dribbling on a little wine and baking for a few minutes, or it can be an elaborate affair with various reductions, herbs, thickeners, and garnishes. Braising is one of the best methods for cooking fish because the juices from the fish merge with the surrounding liquid to create a delicious sauce.

To braise fish fillets, preheat the oven to 425°F and arrange the fillets in a buttered pan or heatproof dish just large enough to hold the fillets so you don't have to use too much liquid. I usually use a sauté pan. Add

INGREDIENTS FOR BRAISING FISH

AROMATICS	BRAISING LIQUIDS	THICKENERS	GARNISHES AND FLAVORFUL FINISHES
shallots (minced)	water	cream	herbs (chopped cilantro, parsley, chives, tarragon, chervil, kaffir lime leaves, etc.)
garlic (minced)	white wine	unsalted butter (plain or flavored butters such as lobster, herb, or truffle butter)	
carrots (chopped, cubed, or jullienned, precooked in butter or simmered in braising liquid)	red wine		mushrooms (sliced, simmered in braising liquid, or sautéed)
	fortified wine (Madeira, sherry, port, etc.)	egg yolks	
	beer	flour (cooked in a roux or worked into a paste with an equal amount of butter)	shellfish (shrimp, crayfish tails, lobster medallions, mussels, oysters, clams—steamed or poached, cooking liquid incorporated into fish-braising liquid)
celery (chopped, cubed, or julienned, precooked in butter or simmered in braising liquid)	fish broth		
	cider	velouté sauce	
tomatoes (peeled, seeded, finely chopped—may also be added at the end)	cooking liquids from mussels, clams, lobster, crayfish, etc.	unsweetened coconut milk	
	tomato sauce	vegetable purees (asparagus, potato, roast garlic, bean, etc.); see "Sauces and Salsas, Condiments and Broths"	pearl onions (peeled, glazed)
mushrooms (sliced or quartered)	vegetable purees and juices		carrots (sliced, trimmed onto garlic clove shapes, or julienned—cooked in liquid or butter)
ginger (peeled, sliced, or grated)	unsweetened coconut milk	tomato puree	
		sorrel puree	asparagus tips (blanched)
lemongrass (finely chopped or sliced)		mayonnaise (such as aïoli)	truffles (sliced, julienned or chopped—simmered in sauce)
		Thai curries	
herbs (chopped thyme, marjoram, parseley, tarragon, chervil, etc.)		nut butters (cashew, peanut, almond, etc.)	tomatoes (peeled, seeded, chopped)
			Thai fish sauce
			fresh lemon or lime juice

enough liquid to come halfway up the sides of the fillets and place the pan on the stove over medium heat. As soon as the liquid begins to simmer, cover the pan loosely with a sheet of buttered aluminum foil and slide the fish into the oven. Beware—fish fillets cook quickly (about 10 minutes per inch of thickness), so they may need only a minute or two in the oven.

When the fillets are done, they'll be firm to the touch and no longer translucent—if you can't tell, cut into one. Once done, transfer them immediately to hot plates or wide bowls. Be careful; cooked fish fillets are very fragile. It is best to use a long, thin metal spatula and slide it lengthwise under the fillets. The cooking liquid can then be spooned over the fish or converted into a sauce using one of the following methods.

STEPS FOR BRAISING FISH

1. THE AROMATICS

Most recipes suggest adding some kind of chopped aromatic vegetable (see chart on page 28) to the pan before the fish is added to impart a flavor to the fish and the braising liquid. Because some ingredients—such as carrots or celery—are slow to release their flavor into the surrounding liquid, it is sometimes necessary to cook them first in a little butter or simmer them with the braising liquid before the fish is added.

Many cooks don't know when to add certain aromatic vegetables or flavorings. If the braising liquid is being strained after the fish is cooked, then ingredients such as mushrooms and tomatoes would be strained out and

wasted. Such ingredients are best added at the end as garnishes after the cooking liquid is strained. Other ingredients that might look unsightly in the sauce or be hard to eat, such as sliced ginger, lemongrass, or even shallots, can be strained out before finishing the sauce. But the decision about what to strain out and what to leave in is up to you.

2. THE BRAISING LIQUID

Almost any liquid can be used for braising. The best way to determine which liquid is the most appropriate is to consider the origins of the dish. French and Italian cooks are most likely to use white wine (although cooks in Normandy might use cider); German and Belgian cooks might use beer; and a safe and neutral bet is to use fish broth or water.

3. THE THICKENER

Once the fish has been cooked, the surrounding liquid can be served as is or strained and other ingredients added as flavors or thickeners. In classic French cooking (French cooks are very fond of braising fish because the technique lends itself well to making sauces), cream, butter, egg yolks, or combinations of all three are most often used to finish the braising liquid. In contemporary cooking lighter ingredients such as vegetable purees and yogurt are also used. In Thai cooking the braising liquid may be finished with red or green curry; in the Brazilian fish stew *vatapa* the braising liquid is finished with peanut or cashew butter and coconut milk.

4. THE GARNISH

Braised fish are sometimes garnished with shellfish, vegetables, or herbs. A garnish can be as simple as a pinch of chopped parsley added to the braising

liquid just before serving or as complicated as an assortment of lobster, mussels, and shrimp cooked separately and arranged around the fish.

Fillets of Sole Bercy

My guests are always convinced that this elegant and delicious dish took hours to make rather than the 15 minutes it requires. Although this classic French recipe is most often prepared with Dover sole, any firm-fleshed nonoily fillets will do.

In its simplest form sole Bercy is prepared by braising the fillets with a little shallot, parsley, and white wine or in a fish broth made from the fish head and bones. A little butter is stirred in at the end to give body to the braising liquid. The easiest approach is to put all the ingredients, including the butter, in the pan at once and then serve the fish in wide bowls with the brothlike braising liquid served around it. The more traditional method given here results in a thicker sauce.

MAKES 4 MAIN-COURSE SERVINGS

3 pounds whole sole, fluke, or flounder, filleted, head and bones reserved

1 onion, coarsely chopped

1 bouquet garni: 3 fresh thyme sprigs or ½ teaspoon dried, a small bunch of parsley, and a bay leaf tied up in string (or in cheesecloth for dried herbs)

½ cup dry white wine

2 shallots, finely chopped

2 tablespoons finely chopped parsley

2 tablespoons unsalted butter

1 tablespoon fresh lemon juice

salt and white pepper

continued

Prepare a fish broth: If the fishmonger hasn't already done it, remove the gills from the fish head with scissors. Then soak the head and bones in cold water for 30 minutes, changing the water every 10 minutes. Drain the head and bones and combine them in a pot with the onion, bouquet garni, wine, and enough water just to cover. Bring the broth to a slow simmer and simmer very gently for 30 minutes, removing and discarding foam with a ladle as it rises to the surface. Strain the broth through a fine-mesh strainer and discard the bones and vegetables. Reserve ½ cup and freeze the rest for another recipe. (If you don't want to bother making fish broth, just use the ½ cup white wine for braising the fish.)

Preheat the oven to 400°F. Sprinkle the bottom of a baking dish just large enough to hold the fillets in a single layer with the chopped shallots. Arrange the fillets side by side, attractive bone side up. Pour in just enough of the reserved fish broth or white wine to come halfway up the fillets.

Place the baking dish on the stove over medium heat (if the baking dish is glass, use a heat distributor such as a Flame-Tamer) until the liquid just begins to simmer. Loosely cover the baking dish with a sheet of aluminum foil. Immediately place the baking dish in the oven and braise for 2 to 10 minutes, about 10 minutes per inch of thickness.

When the fillets are done—a tiny piece cut into with a fork should pull away easily—carefully transfer them to hot plates and then strain the liquid left in the baking dish into a small saucepan. (If you're not bothered by the shallots, just make the sauce in the baking dish.)

Quickly boil the braising liquid down to about ⅓ cup—it should be lightly syrupy—and add the parsley.

Whisk in the butter over medium heat without letting the liquid boil. Add the lemon juice and season with salt and pepper to taste. Spoon the sauce over the fillets and serve immediately.

Substitutes Skinless fillets such as cod, drums, flatfish (flounder or sole), grouper, John Dory, lingcod, mahimahi, monkfish, orange roughy, pompano, porgy, rockfish, sea robin, snapper, tilapia, tilefish, walleye

❧

Braised Whole Red Snapper Dugléré

*T*his surprisingly contemporary nineteenth-century dish is part of my regular summer repertoire when I'm putting tomatoes in just about everything. I love serving it outside on a warm summer evening—it never fails to get oohs and aahs.

Whole fish is braised in almost the same way as fish fillets (see preceding recipe) except that it is basted several times after it goes into the oven to help it cook evenly. Many fish can be cooked in this nineteenth-century style, which simply means that some chopped tomatoes are added at the beginning along with some chopped shallots.

MAKES 4 MAIN-COURSE SERVINGS

two 1½ to 2 pounds or four ¾ to 1½ pounds whole red snappers or other lean round fish, cleaned and scaled

3 shallots or 1 medium onion, finely chopped

2 tomatoes, peeled, seeded, and chopped

¼ cup dry white wine

1 tablespoon fresh lemon juice

salt and pepper

2 tablespoons unsalted butter (optional)

Preheat the oven to 425°F. Rinse the snappers and dry them thoroughly with paper towels. Sprinkle the bottom of an oval or square gratin dish (a sauté pan will also work) with the chopped shallots and tomatoes.

Arrange the fish in the dish over the tomatoes and pour on the white wine. Set the dish on the stove over medium heat (use a heat distributor such as a Flame-Tamer under a glass or porcelain dish) until the wine comes to a simmer, about 5 minutes.

Place the fish in the oven and braise for about 10 minutes per inch of thickness (at the thickest part at the base of the head)—about 20 minutes for a 1½-pound fish. Baste the fish about every 3 minutes. Check to see if the fish is done by sticking a sharp paring knife into the back of the fish between the 2 fillets to see if the flesh can be pulled away from the bone. If the flesh is still translucent and clinging to the bone, the fish needs more cooking.

When the fish are done, you can sprinkle them with lemon juice and serve them directly from the oven in the baking dish or, if you wish, transfer them to a serving dish and boil down the braising liquid in a saucepan to thicken it slightly and concentrate its flavor. At this point the tomato sauce can be seasoned with salt and pepper and the optional butter whisked in to give it a richer flavor and silky texture. The sauce can then be poured over the fish or passed at the table.

Serving: If you're being informal and your guests know what they're doing, you can give each person an individual fish (assuming you've cooked 4 small ones) and let them do the skinning and filleting themselves. (Place the fish to each guest's left on a plate or dish of its own and place a clean heated plate in front of each guest. Give each guest an extra spoon for filleting.)

If you're not serving individual fish, you'll need to skin and carve the fish either in the kitchen or in the dining room in front of your guests (nerve-racking but more elegant).

Substitutes Whole fish such as black sea bass, croaker, drums, ocean perch, pickerel, rockfish, sea trout, striped bass, tilapia, walleye, weakfish

❧

Dover Sole Fillets with Red Wine Sauce

I'm fascinated with fish served in red wine sauce—the flavor of the sauce is deep and intriguing—and my guests are always pleasantly startled when I serve it at a dinner party. I call for Dover sole here because it has firm, meaty flesh that won't fall apart during the braising, but any firm white-fleshed nonoily fish will work well. Dover sole is sometimes hard to find (especially on the West Coast) and is never inexpensive. (Don't con-

fuse authentic Dover sole from the eastern side of the Atlantic with the variety of flounder sometimes sold as "Dover sole.") If you can't find Dover sole, use fillets of flounder or sole or any of the substitutes.

Although sole fillets can be braised directly in red wine—the wine simply poured over and everything slid into the oven—you'll have better results if you first make a red wine fish broth with the sole bones and heads.

When red wine is used to cook fish, the proteins in the fish clarify the wine so that the resulting broth is a murky brown instead of a deep red—but once the liquid is reduced, the deep color of the wine is restored.

MAKES **4** MAIN-COURSE SERVINGS

four ¾ to 1 pound whole Dover sole, filleted and skin removed, heads and bones reserved

1 large onion, chopped

1 bouquet garni: 3 fresh thyme sprigs or ½ teaspoon dried, a small bunch of parsley, and a bay leaf tied up with string (or in cheesecloth for dried thyme)

1 bottle of red wine (see box on page 33)

2 teaspoons all-purpose flour

2 teaspoons unsalted butter, softened

1 tablespoon finely chopped parsley

1 tablespoon good-quality red wine vinegar

2 teaspoons cognac or to taste (optional)

salt and pepper

Making the Red Wine Fish Broth: If the fishmonger hasn't already done it, remove the gills from the fish heads with scissors. Soak the fish bones and heads in cold water for 30 minutes. Drain and rinse the bones and heads and place them in a 4-quart pot with the onion, bouquet garni, and red wine. Bring slowly to a simmer and skim off any white foam with a ladle. Simmer gently for 30 minutes. Strain into a clean pot and simmer over medium

---

CLASSIC FRENCH RECIPES FOR BRAISED FISH

Although braising is a useful technique in any cuisine, the French have given us many wonderful braised fish dishes. These are a few of the most famous.

bercy: One of the simplest recipes for braising fish. Whole fish or fillets are braised with shallots, fish broth made with white wine, and parsley. A small chunk of butter is swirled into the braising liquid when the fish is done.

bonne femme: Whole fish or fillets are braised on a thin layer of chopped shallots and sliced mushrooms. Cream (sometimes whipped) is added to the reduced braising liquid, and the fish is then sauced and glazed under the broiler.

bordelaise: Prepared in the same way as Bercy except that red wine is used instead of white.

crécy: Prepared like Bercy, but carrot puree and a small amount of butter are whisked into the braising liquid as thickeners.

dugléré: Same as Bercy except chopped tomatoes are included.

foyot: Prepared in the same way as Bercy except that highly reduced broth (meat glaze) is added to the braising liquid.

thermidor: The same as Bercy except that the braising liquid is finished with a teaspoon or two of Dijon mustard.

véronique: The same as Bercy except that the braising liquid is finished with a teaspoon of orange curaçao (Grand Marnier actually works better) and ½ cup of peeled and seeded grapes.

heat until about 1 cup remains, about 30 minutes. Skim off any froth or scum that floats to the top of the broth.

Preheat the oven to 400°F. Arrange the fillets side by side—you should have 12 or 16—with the attractive bone side up in a gratin dish or baking dish just large enough to hold them in a single layer. Bring the reduced red wine fish broth back to a simmer if it has cooled and pour enough of it over the fillets to come halfway up their sides. Reserve any red wine broth you don't use.

Place the baking dish on the stove over medium heat—if the baking dish is glass, use a heat distributor such as a Flame-Tamer—until the liquid returns to a simmer. Loosely cover the baking dish with aluminum foil, immediately place the dish in the oven, and braise for about 5 minutes, about 10 minutes per inch of thickness.

When the fillets are done—a tiny piece cut into with a fork should pull away easily—carefully transfer them to hot plates using a long thin spatula and then pour the liquid left in the baking dish into a clean saucepan. (Or, if you've braised the fish in a sauté pan, just make the sauce right in the pan.)

If you've reserved any leftover red wine fish broth, combine it with the braising liquid from the fish and boil everything down until about ½ cup remains.

Make a *beurre manié* by kneading the flour and butter to a smooth paste with a fork (see box). Whisk the *beurre manié* into the simmering braising liquid. Whisk in the parsley, vinegar, and cognac. Simmer for 30 seconds—you'll see the liquid thicken—and season with salt and pepper to taste. If the sauce seems too thick, add a tablespoon or more of water to thin it to the consistency you like. Spoon the

---

Roux is a mixture of equal parts butter and flour that is stirred in a heavy-bottomed saucepan over medium heat for about 5 minutes, until the roux gives off a toasty aroma. Liquids to be thickened are whisked into the hot roux and simmered gently. Use approximately 4 teaspoons of roux to thicken 1 cup of liquid.

Literally "worked butter," *beurre manié* has been used for centuries as a last-minute thickener for sauces and stews. It's easy to make by just kneading equal parts of flour and butter into a paste with the back of a fork. The same amount of *beurre manié* can be used for thickening as roux. The only difference between a *beurre manié* and a roux is that a roux is cooked before it is used and a *beurre manié* is not.

---

sauce over the hot fillets and serve immediately.

Substitutes Firm-fleshed and moderately firm-fleshed skinless fillets such as blackfish, black sea bass, cod, drums, grouper, haddock, halibut, John Dory, lingcod, mahimahi, pompano, skate, striped bass

❧

Salmon Fillets with Red Wine

*T*his dish captures the essence of salmon in an intensely flavored red wine broth made from the salmon bones and head. The fish itself must be braised just before serving, but the time-consuming part—making the broth—can be done the day before.

MAKES 4 MAIN-COURSE SERVINGS

four 6- to 8-ounce pieces of salmon fillet, skin and bones removed, head and bones from an 8- to 10-pound salmon, gills removed from head and bones chopped into 4 sections with a cleaver

1 medium onion, chopped

1 carrot, chopped

one 6-inch piece of celery, chopped

3 garlic cloves, crushed

3 tablespoons olive oil

6 cups red wine

1 bouquet garni: 3 fresh thyme sprigs or ½ teaspoon dried, a small bunch of parsley, and a bay leaf tied up with string (or in cheesecloth for dried thyme)

salt and pepper

2 teaspoons good-quality red wine vinegar

2 tablespoons finely chopped parsley

Preparing the Red Wine Broth: In a 4-quart pot over medium heat, cook the salmon head and bones, onion, carrot, celery, and garlic in 2 tablespoons of the olive oil, stirring every few minutes to prevent sticking, until the vegetables have browned and the bones and head have completely fallen apart, about 20 minutes.

Add 1 cup of the wine and turn the heat up to high. Stir the mixture every couple of minutes until all the wine has evaporated. Watch closely so you don't burn the bottom of the pan. Add the rest of the wine and the bouquet garni. Simmer the mixture gently over low to medium heat for 30 minutes. Use a ladle to skim off any fat and froth that floats to the surface.

Strain the broth through a fine-mesh strainer into a 1-quart saucepan.

Reduce the broth over high heat until about a cup remains. Skim off any froth that floats to the surface.

Braising the Salmon Fillets: Preheat the oven to 400°F. Oil a sauté pan or baking dish just large enough to hold the salmon fillets in a single layer. Season the fillets with salt and pepper, arrange them in the baking dish, and pour on the broth. Heat the baking dish over high heat—use a heat distributor such as a Flame-Tamer if the dish is made of glass or porcelain—until the broth starts to simmer. Cover loosely with aluminum foil and slide into the oven.

Braise the salmon fillets for about 10 minutes per inch of thickness—you may have to cut into one to make sure it's cooked through—and transfer them to hot soup plates. Add the vinegar and parsley to the liquid left in the dish, season to taste with salt and pepper, and spoon the broth over the fish.

Substitutes Almost any full-flavored fish can be substituted; just be sure to save the heads and bones for making the sauce.

WHICH RED WINE TO USE?

Wine that is good for drinking is not necessarily the best wine for cooking. Cooking wine should be deeply colored and shouldn't be too tart. Wines from hot climates such as Spanish Rioja, Italian Merlot, California Zinfandel, and French Côtes-du-Rhône are best. Avoid tannic wines if you can (tannin is what makes some wines feel rough in your mouth) because the tannin will stain the fish with tiny purple specks. The best way to avoid tannin is to buy red wine with at least three or four years of bottle age.

USING THAI CURRY, THAI FISH SAUCE, AND COCONUT MILK

Thai curries, which unlike Indian curries are pastes rather than powders, can be whisked into a braising liquid, sauce, or broth for a quick Thai dish. Even though these curry pastes can be used alone, I almost always include Thai fish sauce and often coconut milk in the finished dish.

One of the easiest ways to use curry pastes for a quick Thai seafood dish is to braise fish (whole or fillets) or shellfish in wine, water, or a fish broth made from the head and bones and then whisk Thai fish sauce, coconut milk, and a couple of tablespoons of Thai curry into the braising liquid. The flavored braising liquid can then be served over and around the fish. Because Thai sauces are best served thin and almost brothlike, be sure to serve plenty of rice to absorb extra sauce. Thai curries can be bought in small cans and used as needed (keep what's left from opened cans in the freezer), or you can make your own.

Braised Striped Bass Fillets in Green Curry

Striped bass has a full enough flavor to hold up to a bold, hot Thai curry, but any firm-fleshed fish fillet will work. Coconut milk and fish sauce make the curry irresistible, but you can leave out the coconut milk for a completely nonfat dish. If you don't have all the herbs, just use more of one of the others. Be sure to serve this dish with plenty of rice.

MAKES 4 MAIN-COURSE SERVINGS

four 6- to 8-ounce striped bass fillets, skin and pin bones removed

salt and pepper

½ cup white wine, water, or fish broth (page 343)

¼ cup Thai fish sauce

½ cup unsweetened coconut milk

2 tablespoons canned or homemade green curry paste (page 340)

1 tablespoon finely chopped basil, preferably holy basil (see glossary)

1 tablespoon chopped fresh mint

1 tablespoon chopped fresh cilantro

Preheat the oven to 350°F. Arrange the striped bass fillets in a sauté pan just large enough to hold them in a single layer. Sprinkle with salt and pepper and pour on the wine.

Place the pan over high heat, and as soon as the liquid starts to simmer, cover loosely with aluminum foil and slide the pan into the oven. After about 5 minutes (10 minutes per inch of thickness), carefully cut into one of the fillets to see if it's opaque. Cook longer if still translucent.

Carefully transfer the fillets to hot soup plates (you need something deep to hold the runny sauce). Stir the rest of the ingredients into the hot liquid in the pan and bring to a simmer. Season to taste with salt and pepper or more curry or fish sauce, pour immediately over the fish, and serve.

Substitutes Skinless fillets such as blackfish, black sea bass, lingcod, ocean perch, red snapper, rockfish, skate, walleye, wolffish

Skinless steaks such as halibut, king mackerel, shark, swordfish

Individual Whole Flatfish with Mussel or Clam Sauce

Although I love eating mussels and clams in any form, it's really their briny broth that I can't resist. Mussel or clam broth is easy to convert into a simple sauce for fish or other shellfish. In this dish the mollusks are steamed open in white wine, and the briny cooking liquid they release is then used to braise the fish. The braising liquid is strained, quickly reduced, and served over and around the fish as a delicate broth. You can also thicken the braising liquid so it has a more saucelike consistency by whisking in cream or butter or something lighter such as a vegetable puree. The mussels or clams themselves are used to garnish the fish.

Although it's a nice touch to serve your guests each a whole fish and let them fillet it themselves, most people don't know how to tackle a cooked flatfish, so you might want to give a little demonstration at the table.

MAKES 4 MAIN-COURSE SERVINGS

four 1-pound flatfish such as sole, flounder, sand dab, or fluke

1 cup dry white wine

2 shallots or 1 medium onion, finely chopped

1 pound mussels, preferably small cultivated, scrubbed and beards removed, or 24 littleneck or Manila clams, scrubbed

1 tablespoon unsalted butter or olive oil

1 tablespoon fresh lemon juice

2 tablespoons finely chopped parsley

salt and pepper

Thickeners (optional):

¹⁄₂ cup heavy cream or

2 tablespoons unsalted butter or

1 tablespoon *beurre manié* (1¹⁄₂ teaspoons butter worked to a paste with 1¹⁄₂ teaspoons flour) or

¹⁄₄ cup garlic, potato, asparagus, or sorrel puree (page 128)

Depending on what kind of flatfish you're using, either remove the top dark skin by pulling it off or cutting it off with a sharp knife or—if the skin is relatively thin—leave it attached and simply have it scaled or scale it yourself (see color page 29). Scrape the bottom white side to remove any scales and remove the sharp fins with scissors. (Or ask your fishmonger to do all of this.) Rinse the fish in cold water.

Preheat the oven to 400°F.

In a 4-quart pot, bring the wine to a simmer with the shallots. Add the mussels or clams, cover, and steam until they open—about 7 minutes for mussels, 12 minutes for clams. Take the mussels or clams out of their shells, discard the shells, and reserve the meats. If the shellfish-steaming liquid is sandy, pour it slowly and carefully into a bowl, leaving the sand behind.

Arrange the flatfish—dark skin side up—in a buttered or oiled dish that closely fits it and pour on the shellfish-cooking liquid. (You may need to use one or more baking dishes to hold the fish.) There should be enough liquid to come halfway up the sides of the fish. If there isn't, add some water or fish broth.

Place the containers with the fish on the stove over medium heat until the liquid comes to a simmer. Loosely cover with aluminum foil and slide the fish into the oven. Braise for 5 to 12 minutes, about 10 minutes per inch of thickness. Carefully transfer the fish to individual platters or plates using a

large spatula. Keep the fish warm while you're preparing the sauce.

Strain the cooking liquid into a 2-quart saucepan and cook it down over high heat until ¹⁄₂ cup remains.

Thicken the sauce by whisking in any of the optional thickeners and bringing it to a quick simmer. You may have to adjust the consistency of the sauce by thinning it with water or by reducing it until it thickens. Don't make the sauce too thick.

Once the sauce has been thickened, add the lemon juice and parsley and season with salt and pepper to taste. Gently reheat the mussels or clams in the sauce—don't let it boil—and spoon the sauce and the mussels or clams over each fish. Serve immediately.

PANS FOR BRAISING FLATFISH

Finding a braising dish for flatfish such as whole sole or flounder is a little tricky. Although there is a piece of equipment called a *turbotière* designed especially for this job, it is probably not worth the expense unless you plan on putting it to frequent use or like to collect exotic cooking stuff. I usually use a square roasting pan, a square Pyrex dish, a large oval gratin dish, or an oval sauté pan. If you're cooking more than one fish at a time, you may need several dishes for braising.

Indian-Style Black Sea Bass Fillets with Yogurt Curry Sauce

Yogurt gives this dish a wonderful tang that goes especially well with curry. The best yogurt for thickening and flavoring a sauce for braised fish is labneh or drained yogurt.

MAKES 6 FIRST-COURSE SERVINGS

three 1-pound sea bass, filleted, bones and heads reserved

1 medium onion, chopped

1 bouquet garni: 3 fresh thyme sprigs or ½ teaspoon dried, a small bunch of parsley, and a bay leaf tied up with string (or in cheesecloth for dried thyme)

½ cup dry white wine

2 to 3 teaspoons curry powder to taste

1 tablespoon unsalted butter

3 tablespoons labneh or strained yogurt (see box on page 36)

2 tablespoons finely chopped fresh cilantro leaves

salt and pepper

Make a fish broth by soaking the fish bones and heads (gills removed) for 30 minutes in cold water, draining them, and then simmering them gently for 25 minutes with the onion, bouquet garni, white wine, and barely enough water to cover. Strain this fish broth and reserve.

Preheat the oven to 400°F. Arrange the fillets side by side, attractive bone side up, in a buttered gratin dish or baking dish just large enough to hold them in a single layer. Bring the fish broth back to a simmer if it has cooled and pour just enough over the fish to come halfway up the fillets. (Any leftover fish broth can be saved for another recipe.)

Loosely cover the baking dish with a sheet of lightly buttered aluminum foil. Place the baking dish on the stove over medium heat—if the baking dish is glass or porcelain, use a heat distributor such as a Flame-Tamer—until the liquid starts to simmer. Immediately place the baking dish in the oven for 4 to 10 minutes, and braise about 10 minutes per inch of thickness.

When the fillets are done—the flesh should separate when you cut into it with a fork—carefully transfer them to hot plates, keep them in a warm oven, and then strain the liquid left in the baking dish into a 2-quart saucepan. Boil down the cooking liquid until you have about ½ cup left.

In a small sauté pan, cook the curry powder in butter for about 30 seconds, until it just begins to smell fragrant. Stir the curry into the labneh in a stainless-steel bowl. Whisk the hot fish broth into the curry/labneh mixture and return the mixture to the saucepan. Add the cilantro, salt and pepper to taste, and gently reheat the sauce. *Don't let the sauce boil*, or the yogurt will curdle. Serve the sauce over or around the fish fillets.

Substitutes Firm- and moderately firm-fleshed skinless fillets such as cod, drums, grouper, John Dory, lingcod, mahimahi, monkfish, orange roughy, pompano, porgy, rockfish, sea robin, snapper, tilapia, tilefish, walleye

Braised Halibut Steaks with Tomato and Garlic Purees

(color page 9)

What I love about this dish is that it looks like a simple halibut steak served with a little tomato sauce, but the flavor of the sauce is so special and intense that guests are always surprised when they bite in.

Any firm-fleshed fish such as salmon, halibut, or swordfish can be used for this dish.

MAKES 4 MAIN-COURSE SERVINGS

four 6- to 8-ounce halibut, salmon, or swordfish steaks

2 shallots, finely chopped

1 tablespoon unsalted butter or olive oil

½ cup dry white wine

salt and pepper

1 tablespoon finely chopped parsley

¼ cup garlic puree (page 336)

½ cup stiff tomato puree (page 337)

2 teaspoons good-quality white wine vinegar

12 garlic cloves, peeled and blanched until soft

1 tomato, peeled, seeded, and cut into ¼-inch dice

continued

GETTING THE FISH OUT OF THE PAN

Cooked fish is fragile and can be difficult to get out of the pan it was cooked in. In most cases a large metal spatula will do the trick, but if the fish is especially large you may want to line the cooking container with a double layer of aluminum foil cut long enough to drape over the sides. When the fish is done, you can remove it by gripping the foil on both sides and lifting.

Another trick is to use a cake rack large enough to hold the fish but still able to fit in the baking dish. Bend down the legs with pliers so the rack rests flat against the inside of the braising pan. Tie string or wire in 2 places on each side of the rack to serve as handles. Braise the fish on the rack and just lift it out when it's done.

Preheat the oven to 400°F.

Rinse off the steaks and dry thoroughly with paper towels. Sprinkle the shallots in a buttered baking dish or sauté pan just large enough to hold the steaks in a single layer. Arrange the steaks over the shallots, pour on the wine, and season with salt and pepper.

Place the steaks on the stove over high heat, using a heat distributor such as a Flame-Tamer if you're heating them in a glass or porcelain baking dish. When the wine comes to a simmer, cover the steaks loosely with aluminum foil and slide them into the oven for 5 to 10 minutes, about 10 minutes per inch of thickness.

When the steaks are done (they'll be firm to the touch, but if you can't tell, cut into one) transfer them to hot plates with a spatula. Whisk the parsley, purees, vinegar, and garlic cloves into the hot wine. If the sauce seems too thin, boil it down slightly to thicken it. If it's too thick, stir in a little water. Season with salt and pepper to taste and spoon the sauce over the fish. Decorate each plate with the diced tomatoes.

Braised Tuna with Vegetables

THON À LA CHARTREUSE

(color page 13)

Provençal cooks are forever cooking fish *à la chartreuse*. The recipes are so varied, however, that it's almost impossible to define exactly what the term means other than it is cooking in the style of the Carthusian monks, an order known for austerity in things of the table—hardly in evidence here. What is consistent in all the recipes is the generous use of vegetables for braising and a green leafy vegetable—here spinach and Swiss chard but often lettuce—to accompany the finished fish. Cooking *à la chartreuse* is *not* cooking with Chartreuse liqueur.

In traditional versions of *thon à la chartreuse* the tuna is braised for well over an hour, which dries out the tuna. In this version the tuna is lightly pan-fried, the vegetables are thoroughly cooked separately, and the whole thing is assembled just before serving so the tuna stays moist and rosy pink. Everything except the last-minute reheating can be done earlier the same day. If you or your guests are squeamish about rare tuna, cook the tuna steaks for a minute or two more on each side.

MAKES 4 MAIN-COURSE SERVINGS

four 1- to 1½-inch-thick rounds of fresh tuna, preferably cut from near the tail, about 7 ounces each

salt and pepper

5 tablespoons olive oil

1 medium onion, sliced

4 medium carrots, finely sliced

2 garlic cloves, finely chopped

½ teaspoon dried savory or thyme or 4 small fresh sprigs

1 bay leaf

1 cup dry white wine

1 cup water

leaves from 2 large bunches of spinach, washed and cut into ¼-inch-wide strips

1 tightly packed cup sorrel leaves, coarsely chopped (optional)

1 bunch of Swiss chard, white stems cut out and leaves cut into ¼-inch-wide strips

Season the tuna on both sides with salt and pepper. In a heavy pot just large enough to hold the tuna steaks in a single layer, brown the steaks for 2 minutes on each side in 2 tablespoons of the oil over high heat. Transfer the steaks to a plate and discard the oil from the pot.

Add the remaining olive oil to the pot and cook the onion, carrots, garlic, and herbs over medium heat, stirring until the vegetables soften but are not browned—about 10 minutes. Pour on the white wine and water and simmer the vegetables gently, covered, for 15 minutes.

Cook the spinach in a pot of boiling water for 30 seconds. If you want to use the same water for cooking the chard, take the spinach out of the water with a skimmer. Rinse the spinach with cold water in a colander and gently squeeze out the excess water. Blanch the chard leaves in a large pot of boiling water for about 3 minutes, drain in a colander, rinse with cold water, and squeeze out the excess water.

Fifteen minutes before serving, bring the onion/carrot mixture to a slow simmer and arrange the tuna steaks in the pot. Cover the pot and simmer gently for 2 to 3 minutes, about 2 minutes per inch of thickness. Transfer the tuna steaks to hot soup plates. Stir the spinach, sorrel if you're using it, and Swiss chard into the simmering onion/carrot mixture. Simmer for about a minute and season to taste with salt and pepper. Ladle the vegetable mixture and broth over the tuna steaks and serve immediately.

LABNEH

Labneh, sold in Indian or Middle Eastern markets, is a yogurt so thick that it almost has the texture of cream cheese. It's especially useful for thickening braising liquids, soups, and fish stews and for its tangy flavor. You can make your own by draining plain yogurt for 3 hours or overnight in a coffee filter. One cup of plain yogurt makes about ¾ cup of drained yogurt after 3 hours and ½ cup of even stiffer yogurt (labneh) if allowed to drain overnight.

~

Braised Red Drum Fillets with Tomato Sauce

TRIGLIE ALLA LIVORNESE

*T*raditionally this recipe is made with whole fish, but since most people have a hard time grappling with a whole fish on their plate—especially when it's covered with sauce—I usually make this dish with fillets.

Triglie (also called *red mullet* or by their French name, *rouget*) are bright red Mediterranean fish with firm and very tasty flesh. They do sometimes show up in fish markets on the East Coast, but I never count on being able to find them and use red drum when I can find it or whatever firm-fleshed fillets or fish steaks look good at the market. Fillets or steaks should be at least ¾ inch thick, or they will overcook during the initial browning. Leave the skin on thin-skinned fillets such as red snapper, sea bass, or black bass, but remove it from thicker-skinned fish such as grouper or blackfish.

MAKES 4 MAIN-COURSE SERVINGS

four 6- to 8-ounce pieces of red drum fillet, skin and pin bones removed

salt and pepper

½ cup all-purpose flour for dredging

¼ cup olive oil

½ celery stalk, finely chopped

1 medium onion, finely chopped

2 garlic cloves, finely chopped

4 tomatoes, peeled, seeded, and chopped

2 tablespoons finely chopped parsley

Season the fillets with salt and pepper, dredge them in flour—pat off any excess—and brown them in half the olive oil over high heat for 1 to 2 min-

USING VEGETABLE PUREES TO THICKEN FISH SAUCES

Vegetable purees are light and delicious flavorings and thickeners for turning the cooking liquid from braised fish into a savory sauce. Vegetable purees can be used alone or combined with other ingredients such as yogurt, coconut milk, and small amounts of cream and butter.

Practically any vegetable can be cooked, pureed, and used as a thickener. You can sometimes get by using the same vegetable as a garnish for the fish. For example, you may want to serve asparagus tips with the fish and use the pureed stems to thicken the sauce, or you may want to use a mixture of tomato and garlic purees and then serve peeled and blanched garlic cloves and little squares of tomato right in the fish sauce.

Most vegetable purees can be made in a food processor, food mill, or blender, but for the smoothest texture, strain the puree through a drum sieve. If you don't have a drum sieve, you may have to combine the rough puree with the fish-braising liquid and then strain the whole thing through a fine-mesh strainer. Some purees, such as tomato puree, are best left slightly chunky; for these you can dispense with the straining.

The amount of vegetable puree you'll need to thicken the braising liquid from the fish will vary, but generally ¼ cup of puree will thicken ½ cup of liquid. Each recipe makes ¼ to ½ cup of puree. Vegetable purees will keep for up to 3 days in the refrigerator, although green vegetable purees will lose some of their color. They are best stored in a bowl with a small amount of oil spooned over the surface and then covered with plastic wrap. Vegetable purees can also be frozen for up to several months. I freeze them in plastic sandwich bags. For recipes, see "Sauces and Salsas, Condiments and Broths" (pages 329–344).

utes on each side. Be sure not to overcook the fillets. Set aside on a plate.

Prepare a light tomato sauce by cooking the celery, onion, and garlic in the remaining olive oil in a wide pot or sauté pan (the wider the pot, the more quickly the tomatoes will cook down into sauce) over medium heat for about 10 minutes, until the vegetables release their aroma but are not yet brown. Stir in the chopped tomatoes and cook the sauce over medium heat until it thickens, about 15 minutes. Stir in the parsley and season the sauce with salt and pepper to taste.

Preheat the oven to 375°F. Arrange the fillets in a gratin dish or baking dish just large enough to hold them in a single layer. Spread the hot sauce

over the fillets and bake for about 6 minutes. Serve immediately on hot plates.

Substitutes Fillets with skin on such as black sea bass, ocean perch, red snapper, rockfish, striped bass

Skinless fillets such as blackfish, grouper, lingcod

Steaks such as halibut, king mackerel, salmon, swordfish

Deep-frying

It wasn't until I was in my twenties, working in a Parisian restaurant, that I discovered I liked deep-fried seafood. Before that I had tasted only deep-fried scallops, oysters, and cod in inexpensive restaurants and in fish-and-chips places. The French version was a revelation because the seafood—tiny strips of Dover sole—was only lightly dusted with flour and then deep-fried in perfectly clean oil for only about 5 seconds. The sole was then carefully wrapped in absorbent towels so that hardly a trace of oil was left clinging to the fish.

Deep-frying—sometimes just called frying—is a method of cooking foods by completely submerging them in very hot oil. Deep-fried foods have gotten a bad reputation in recent years because they contain extra calories and fat from the frying oil. While it is true that they aren't diet foods, when cooked properly deep-fried foods absorb very little oil and can be surprisingly light.

EQUIPMENT FOR DEEP-FRYING

Pots: Choose a pot that is heavy enough so it won't slide around easily if you bump it. The size pot you'll need depends on the amount of deep-frying you do at one time and the size of the seafood pieces. Whatever size pot you do choose, make sure it is big enough to deep-fry when filled no more than half full of oil.

Electric Deep-fryers and Skillets: If you do a lot of deep-frying, you may want to invest in an electric deep-fryer or an electric skillet. The advantage of both is that they have their own stand or legs and have thermostats so you're not constantly adjusting the heat of the stove to keep the oil at the right temperature.

Woks: Chinese cooks prefer a wok for almost any kind of cooking, including deep-frying. A wok is perfect if you're frying small amounts of food because the food can be stirred around in the oil, helping it brown evenly without using too much oil.

Frying Baskets: Although a frying basket isn't absolutely essential, it will make your life much easier because a batch of seafood can be lowered and raised into and out of the oil all at once.

Spiders: These gadgets are well named because they look like spider webs with a long handle attached to one side. A spider is a great alternative to a frying basket if you're working with small amounts of seafood or deep-frying in something such as a wok that a basket won't fit into.

Slotted Spoons: These are suitable for frying small amounts of seafood but can be frustrating if you need to work quickly. A spoon will hold only a small amount at once and will also bring up too much oil when you reach in for the seafood.

Deep-fry Thermometer: While it is possible to judge the temperature of hot oil without a thermometer, you'll be less nervous, especially at the beginning, if you can measure the precise temperature of the oil.

OIL FOR DEEP-FRYING

Vegetable oils such as corn, peanut, canola, and safflower are the most commonly used for deep-frying because they're inexpensive, relatively unsaturated, and can sustain high temperatures without burning or smoking.

Because I dislike the taste and peculiar fishy smell of most vegetable oils, I usually prefer to deep-fry in "pure" olive oil. While no olive oil is cheap, that labeled "pure" is much less expensive than extra-virgin and only slightly more expensive than vegetable oil. (Don't use extra-virgin olive oil for deep-frying—the high heat will destroy its delicacy and you'll have spent a lot of money for nothing.)

How Much Oil to Use: Any time you deep-fry you'll want to use as little oil as possible—oil is expensive and can be a nuisance to store—but at the same time keep in mind that the more oil you use, the easier it is to control the temperature. Seafood added to a small amount of oil will cause the tempera-

1. Whatever you use for deep-frying—pot, wok, or electric deep-fryer—make sure it is heavy and set firmly on the surface so if you bump it accidentally it won't spatter hot oil.

2. Never fill the deep-frying container more than half full of oil.

3. If you're deep-frying on the stove, keep the pot on one of the *back* burners so you're less likely to bump into it.

4. Make sure the deep-fryer or deep-frying pot is completely dry before you put in the oil. Any traces of liquid will cause the oil to spatter.

5. Add pieces of seafood to the oil with a spoon, spider, or chopsticks, never with your fingers—oil could splash up and burn you.

6. Add seafood slowly. Don't add too much at once, or the oil may overflow. Test a few pieces at a time to get a sense of how much the oil froths up.

7. Have a box of baking soda handy in case the oil spills over and starts a grease fire. If a fire starts, pour on a lot of baking soda—don't skimp.

ture of the oil to drop, so the seafood may overcook while you're waiting for the oil to heat up again.

I use a minimum of a quart of oil for up to six servings and proportionately more for more servings.

Storing and Reusing Oil: Oil used in the amount suggested can be used twice, but when used a third time it starts to turn dark and take on a strong fishy flavor.

Let the once-used oil cool completely and strain it through a fine-mesh strainer—or a nylon stocking—into a clean container to eliminate minute particles, which burn and spoil the oil's flavor and color. Store the used oil in a tightly sealed bottle or jar in the refrigerator.

FRYING TEMPERATURES

Large pieces or whole fish should be fried at a lower temperature—around 350°F—while very small fish such as whitebait or baby eels and shellfish such as clams or oysters should be fried at a higher temperature, about 380°F.

Putting a whole fish or a large amount of seafood in a small amount of hot oil will lower the oil temperature. Because of this you should start the oil at a higher temperature than you'll actually need when deep-frying whole or large pieces of fish.

If you don't have a deep-fry thermometer you'll need to judge the temperature of the oil by sight and smell. The classic way to do this is to fry a piece of bread in the oil, but the bread tends to break up and leave burned crumbs in the oil. I prefer to take a small piece of the coated fish and put it in the oil. If the fish sinks, the oil is definitely not hot enough. If the fish floats and is surrounded by bubbling oil, the oil is probably near the right temperature. Watch the fish and see how long it takes for the coating to turn the right color. (This will depend on the coating—flour or flour-and-water batter should turn ever so slightly brown—while leavened batters and batters containing egg should turn a pale golden brown.) Very hot oil, appropriate for very small pieces of seafood, will begin to smoke slightly.

At this point you'll need to judge whether to raise or lower the temperature of the oil. You want to adjust the oil so the test piece of seafood turns the appropriate color in the same amount of time it will take the seafood to cook.

In other words, if you're cooking a whole fish, you will want the test piece to take about 8 minutes to brown. If you're frying tiny shrimp, the color should turn in 5 to 10 seconds.

FRYING TIME

Whole fish and large chunks of fish typically are done in 7 to 9 minutes per inch of thickness. Very small fish or shellfish or fish cut into goujonettes cooks in a few seconds. The only reliable way to judge frying times is to cook a few extra pieces of seafood and cut into them during the frying.

DEEP-FRYING COATINGS AND BATTERS

While most seafood can be deep-fried with no coating at all, one of the best things about deep-fried food is a crispy outer coating that gives the food a pleasant crunch and helps seal in flavor and juices.

Coatings for deep-fried foods can be very simple—seasonings and flour alone make one of the best—or more complicated, containing eggs, various seasonings, and sometimes bread crumbs.

FLOUR

One of the best and easiest ways to coat deep-fried foods is to season them with salt and pepper (and/or other spices) and then roll them in flour, patting off any excess. If you're deep-frying a lot of fish, one good method is to toss the pieces of fish in flour and then continue tossing the fish in a large medium-mesh strainer over a bowl. In this way the excess flour is eliminated quickly but not wasted.

Once deep-fried, flour-coated seafood has an almost imperceptible crispiness, and because the outer coating is so thin it absorbs very little oil. Never deep-fry flour-coated seafood until it turns brown. When fried properly, flour-coated seafood should have only the slightest hint of gold.

❧

Scrod Goujonettes with Green Peppercorn Sauce

*I*n French, a *goujon* is a minnow or very small fish. Goujonettes are thin strips that are cut from fillets and then deep-fried and served immediately—usually as a first course. In this recipe the goujonettes are served coated with a light and spicy green peppercorn sauce, but you can serve them with any sauce you like. Light mayonnaise and salsa are especially good.

You can also use any lean and nonoily firm-fleshed fish that you can conveniently cut into ¹/₃- by 3-inch strips. It's important that the fish be at least somewhat firm-fleshed, or it will fall apart when you're coating it with the sauce.

While any seafood is best deep-fried just seconds before it is served, the fish can be cut up earlier the same day and the sauce made an hour in advance. Don't flour the goujonettes until the oil is hot and you're ready to fry. Seafood floured in advance will stick together and make a tangled mess.

MAKES 6 FIRST-COURSE OR 4 LIGHT MAIN-COURSE SERVINGS

1½ pounds ¹/₃-inch-thick scrod fillets

1 cup dry white wine

2 shallots, finely chopped

1 cup heavy cream

1 tablespoon green peppercorns, packed in brine, drained, crushed with the side of a knife, and chopped

1 tablespoon fresh lemon juice

1 quart vegetable or pure olive oil for deep-frying

salt

¹/₂ cup all-purpose flour

fried parsley (see box)

Cut the fish fillets diagonally into 3- to 4-inch-long and ¹/₃-inch-wide strips. Refrigerate the strips, covered with plastic wrap, until needed.

Combine the white wine and shallots in a 10-inch sauté pan and simmer over low to medium heat until the wine has reduced by half. Whisk in the cream and simmer gently until the sauce starts to thicken, about 10 minutes. Stir in the peppercorns and lemon juice and simmer the sauce for about 3 minutes more, until it becomes quite thick. Season to taste with salt.

Heat the oil to 370°F in a heavy pot. (The oil should come between one third of the way and halfway up the sides—never more than halfway.)

Season the goujonettes with salt and roll them in flour. Place them in the largest strainer you have, set over a bowl. Toss the goujonettes in the strainer to eliminate excess flour.

Heat the sauce on low heat.

Fry the goujonettes, in 3 batches, for about 15 seconds per batch. Dump them onto a baking sheet coated with paper towels. Pat the goujonettes quickly to eliminate excess oil and toss them gently in the sauté pan with the sauce until each goujonette is lightly coated.

Arrange the goujonettes in small mounds on hot plates. Top each mound with a few sprigs of fried parsley.

Substitutes Fillets or steaks such as fluke, Dover sole, haddock, halibut, pollack, swordfish, other nonoily white-fleshed fish

---

FRIED PARSLEY

One of the classic garnishes for deep-fried fish is fried parsley. When parsley is fried—use the so-called curly parsley, not the flat Italian kind—it turns immediately crispy yet retains its fresh flavor.

To fry enough parsley for six servings of fried seafood, wash and dry a handful of tiny parsley sprigs. Make sure the sprigs are *completely* dry, or they'll spatter in the hot oil. When all the seafood has been fried, toss in the parsley sprigs—they'll make a frightening crackling sound—and fry for about 5 seconds. Quickly fish them out with a basket, spider, or slotted spoon, drain them on paper towels, and place them on top of the fried fish.

❧

Flour-Coated Fried Squid with Lemon and Tartar Sauce

*T*hese highly addictive squid make a great first course or hors d'oeuvre. My guests seem to have the most fun standing around in the kitchen sipping on cocktails and wolfing down squid as soon as I pull them out of the oil. Be careful if you're serving dinner afterward—people are likely to spoil their appetites.

I love fried squid—or any deep-fried seafood—served with homemade tartar sauce, but if you don't want to bother these squid are great with just lemon. In any case I always put out lemon wedges for the calorie-conscious.

continued

MAKES 6 FIRST-COURSE SERVINGS OR
HORS D'OEUVRES FOR 8

2½ pounds squid (1¼ pounds cleaned)

1 quart vegetable or pure olive oil for
   deep-frying

1 cup all-purpose flour

salt

fried parsley (see box on page 41), optional

2 lemons, cut into wedges

1 cup homemade tartar sauce (page 335),
   optional

Clean the squid as described on
page 222 and as shown on color page
19. Cut the tentacles in half through
the top and cut the hoods into ¼-inch-
wide rings.

Heat the oil to 370°F. Toss the squid
in the flour, patting it quickly to
remove excess flour, and gently lower
half the squid into the oil with a slotted spoon, spider, or fry basket. Fry
for about 45 seconds—stirring gently
so the squid fries evenly—and transfer the squid to a baking sheet covered
with paper towels. Repeat with the
rest of the squid. Sprinkle with salt

and place on individual plates or a
serving platter lined with a white
cloth napkin. Top with fried parsley.
Pass the lemon wedges and tartar
sauce.

STARCH-BASED BATTERS

FLOUR-AND-WATER BATTER

One of the most satisfying of all deep-
frying batters is a simple mixture of
flour and water, which is very light
and crispy and absorbs very little oil.
Seafood coated with flour-and-water
batter should be deep-fried only until
it turns a pale ivory color, never until it
browns. The usual proportions are one
part flour (by volume) to two parts
water. Flour-and-water batter should
be allowed to rest for at least 30 minutes before you use it to allow the
gluten to relax. Otherwise the batter
may shrink during frying and leave
pieces of the seafood exposed.

DEEP-FRYING COATINGS

Plain Flour	Very fragile coating that adheres to seafood
Flour-and-Water Batter	Very light; only slightly thicker than plain flour
Homemade Bread Crumbs	Light outer coating with no crunch
Japanese Bread Crumbs	Very thick outer coating but not oily; very crunchy and brittle
Fluffy Egg White Batter	Creates a sheathlike envelope—like a little package; only slightly crunchy
Club Soda Batter	Very light—much like flour-and-water batter—but with a delicate crunch
Baking Powder Batter	Light and very crunchy; a slightly tougher texture than club soda batter
Yeast Batter	Forms very brittle, crunchy crust; delicate breadlike flavor

BREAD CRUMBS

Bread crumbs make a delicate coating
for fried fish and shellfish, provided
the bread crumbs are fresh. The best
way to make fresh bread crumbs is to
cut the crusts off about 10 slices of
good-quality white bread, work the
slices in a food processor for about 30
seconds, and then work the crumbs
through a medium-mesh strainer. The
most common method for coating fish
and shellfish with bread crumbs is to
dip the seafood in beaten egg before
rolling it in bread crumbs (see page 19
for more about this method). I always
find that the egg imparts a strong taste
to fried fish, so I prefer to dip the fish
in flour-and-water batter before rolling
it in the bread crumbs.

JAPANESE BREAD CRUMBS

These packaged bread crumbs, called
hanayuki or "honey–wheat flour
crumbs," can be used to coat seafood
in the same way as fresh homemade
bread crumbs, but the effect is completely different. Homemade bread
crumbs leave fried foods with a very
delicate, fragile coating, whereas
hanayuki crumbs create a relatively
thick, very crunchy—and delightful—
outer crust.

LEAVENED BATTERS

Some of the best and lightest coatings
for deep-frying are made by incorporating air or carbon dioxide into the
batter before frying. Beaten egg
whites, baking powder, club soda,
beer, and yeast can all be used to produce this effect. While all of these batters can be used in the same way, each
produces a subtly different effect—
you'll probably want to experiment to
find the one you prefer.

Fluffy Egg White Batter: Prepare a
light flour-and-water batter by combining ¾ cup flour with 1 cup cold

water. Work the water into the flour slowly to eliminate lumps. Let the mixture rest for 30 minutes.

Shortly before you're ready to deep-fry, beat 3 egg whites with a teaspoon of salt in a copper bowl or in an electric mixer until the medium peak stage. If you're not using a copper bowl, add a pinch of cream of tartar to the egg whites before beating.

Fold the egg whites with the flour batter using a rubber spatula.

Club Soda Batter: This batter is very light and crispy. Because the carbon dioxide in the club soda dissipates quickly, this batter must be made at the last minute.

Starting with 1 cup, whisk just enough club soda into ¾ cup flour to make a smooth paste. Work the mixture as little as possible. Gently stir in the rest of the club soda. Use immediately. This method will also work with beer.

Baking Powder Batter: This very light and crispy batter is similar to club soda batter because the baking powder produces carbon dioxide as soon as it comes in contact with water.

Sift together ¾ cup flour with 2 teaspoons baking powder. Stir the mixture thoroughly so the baking powder is distributed throughout the flour. Just before deep-frying, use a whisk to quickly stir ½ cup of cold water into the flour to obtain a paste. Stir in ½ cup more water and use immediately.

Yeast Batter: This batter forms a slightly thicker crust than club soda or baking powder batter, but it's also extremely light and crispy because of the carbon dioxide produced by the yeast.

Slowly stir ¾ cup of warm (not hot) water into ½ cup of flour in a 2-quart mixing bowl to obtain a smooth paste. Stir in 1 teaspoon active dry yeast and let rise, covered with plastic wrap, in a warm place. When the batter has doubled in size—after about an hour—it is ready to use.

❧

Fried Cod

I worked out this recipe for fried cod after a trip to London that left me wanting to make the perfect fish and chips—made with fresh oil and a lighter batter. You don't have to use cod for this recipe; any thick and lean white fish will do. Try it with haddock, hake, tilefish, halibut, or pollack.

I usually serve this version of fried fish in a very informal fish-and-chips kind of way—usually for lunch or an early dinner with french fries, malt vinegar, and bottles of beer. It's worthwhile playing around with the concept and deep-frying vegetables such as sliced zucchini, small or quartered mushrooms, or even tomato slices, lightly coated in batter to serve with the fish. If you can't find malt vinegar, put a bottle of good wine vinegar on the table for people to help themselves. You can also serve fried fish with homemade tartar sauce (page 335).

MAKES 6 MAIN-COURSE SERVINGS

1 quart vegetable or pure olive oil for deep-frying

3 pounds cod, bones and skin removed, cut into 1-inch cubes

1 recipe yeast or club soda batter (page 43)

salt

malt vinegar

french fries

Heat the oil to 370°F. Preheat the oven to 200°F.

Fry the cod in 2 batches. Dip the chunks of cod into the batter using a long fork or chopsticks and carefully place them, one by one, in the hot oil.

Deep-fry for 3 to 3½ minutes—turn the pieces over after 1½ minutes—and transfer the fish with a basket, spider, or slotted spoon to a paper towel–covered baking sheet. Keep warm in the oven while you're frying the second batch. When all the fish is done, sprinkle it with salt.

Serve the fish in a napkin-lined (paper napkins add to the fish-and-chips atmosphere) basket or platter with french fries and let your guests help themselves.

Substitutes Fillets or boned steaks such as haddock, pollack, halibut, Dover sole, swordfish, tilefish, other lean whitefish

FRYING WHOLE FISH

If you find yourself wanting to deep-fry a whole fish, you must enjoy drama enough to overcome a healthy fear. Standing in front of a large pot of almost-smoking oil with a big slippery fish dangling from your hand indeed can be scary. I especially love Barbara Tropp's description, in her wonderful book *The Modern Art of Chinese Cooking*, of standing terrified in the corner of her kitchen and finally giving up and steaming the fish instead.

But a whole fried fish—especially something pretty like a red snapper—will be delicious and highly praised when you nonchalantly set it on the table.

While European and Asian cuisines all have their versions of fried fish, there is really little difference in the frying technique—the breading and presentation may differ, but most of the character is determined by the sauce.

The most important precaution when frying whole fish is not to fill the frying pot more than half full. You'll also need to use a relatively large amount of oil, or the fish—always rather large—

will cool the oil down too much at the beginning, preventing the skin from getting crispy. If you have one, an oval pot is best for frying whole fish. Most foods can be lowered into the hot oil with a spoon or basket, but because the skin of whole fish sometimes sticks and tears, it is best to lower the fish into the oil while holding it by the tail.

It's a good idea to wear a pair of gloves or to wrap your hand in a towel when deep-frying whole fish. And don't forget your apron.

⋄

Fried Sweet-and-Sour Red Snapper

I like to make this dish with red snapper because the skin is so pretty, but you can deep-fry any lean whole fish as long as it's the right size—I often use striped bass or black bass. It's most dramatic to deep-fry a 3- to 4-pound fish, but you'll need a lot of oil, and handling such a large fish can be cumbersome. You can also fry smaller fish—1 pound each—for individual servings, but unless you use an awful lot of oil you'll have to fry them one at a time while keeping the others warm. You'll also have to be sure your guests know what to do when confronted with their own whole fish; one large fish you can serve for them at the table.

The sauce can be made a day or two in advance, but the deep-frying has to be done just before serving.

MAKES **4** MAIN-COURSE SERVINGS

one 3- to 4-pound or four 1-pound red snappers, scaled, gutted fins and gills removed

vegetable or pure olive oil for deep-frying: about 3 quarts for a large fish, 1½ quarts for individual fish, or 1 quart for either with the skillet method (see box)

all-purpose flour for dredging

FRYING WHOLE FISH IN A SKILLET

If the idea of submerging a whole fish in a big pot of oil seems rather daunting, you may want to try deep-frying in only an inch of oil in a skillet.

The advantage of the skillet method is that you need much less oil, so it isn't quite as scary. One disadvantage is that the fish can easily stick to the bottom, so you need to hold it by the tail and move it back and forth for the first minute of frying to crisp the skin. A second disadvantage is that a whole fish will quickly bring down the temperature of a small amount of oil. So if you do use the skillet, you'll need to keep the stove on high to bring the oil temperature back up quickly.

Select a heavy iron or copper skillet, preferably oval. To avoid having to turn the fish over halfway through the cooking, baste the top with hot oil with a ladle.

For the Sauce:

2 garlic cloves, finely chopped

1 tablespoon grated fresh ginger

a 2-inch strip of orange zest (optional)

⅓ cup sherry vinegar or white wine vinegar

2 tablespoons dark soy sauce

2 tablespoons sugar

¼ cup dry sherry

¼ teaspoon dark sesame oil

1 teaspoon cornstarch dissolved in 1 tablespoon water

3 scallions, including green, finely sliced

Check the fish carefully and scrape off any stray scales—look especially along the belly of the fish near the tail. Score the fish by making 3 or 4 diagonal slashes all the way down to the bone on both sides of the fish. This helps the heat and oil penetrate and also makes the skin less likely to contract and tear. Pat the fish dry with paper towels and refrigerate until needed.

Prepare the sauce by combining all the ingredients except the cornstarch mixture and scallions in a small saucepan and simmering gently for 5 minutes to infuse the flavors. Stir in the cornstarch mixture and the scallions and simmer gently for 1 minute. Taste the sauce—you may need to add more vinegar or sugar to balance the relationship between sweet and sour.

Heat the oil to about 380°F. (The oil is started out especially hot because the whole fish will cool it about 10°F.) Roll the fish in the flour, carefully patting off any excess. Hold the fish by the tail directly over the oil and submerge just the head for about 10 seconds. Slowly lower the fish into the oil, taking about 1 minute altogether. This prevents the oil from bubbling up and overflowing and also gives the skin time to get crispy before it touches the bottom of the deep-fryer. Fry the fish for a total of about 7 minutes per inch of thickness at the thickest part. (A 1½-inch-thick fish will take about 10 minutes.)

Carefully take the fish out of the oil using 2 skimmers or spiders and transfer it to a baking sheet covered with a triple layer of paper towels. Pat the fish with paper towels to eliminate excess oil. Heat the sauce. Keep the fish warm in a 200°F oven if you're frying more than one fish. Serve the fish on a platter or on individual plates. Lightly coat each fish with 2 tablespoons of sauce. Serve the rest of the sauce in a sauceboat at the table.

Substitutes Whole fish such as striped bass, black sea bass, rockfish

SERVING FRIED FISH FILLETS IN BROTH

While in most cuisines fried fish is served with a sauce, Japanese cooks like to serve fried foods surrounded by a light but savory broth. The effect is very pleasant, the broth contrasting nicely with the crispiness of the fried fish and balancing some of the fish's richness.

Fried Fillets of Sea Bass in Japanese Broth

I first encountered a dish similar to this one in Shizuo Tsuji's wonderful book *Japanese Cooking: A Simple Art.* The trick is to serve this dish as soon as the fish comes out of the oil—it's imperative that the fish stay crispy even though it's surrounded by broth. The broth and vegetables, however, can be prepared earlier the same day (kept overnight, the vegetables will lose their color). This dish is best served as a first course—it doesn't look as elegant in large portions—in small Japanese pottery or lacquer cups with lids.

MAKES 4 FIRST-COURSE SERVINGS

two 6- to 8-ounce black sea bass fillets with skin, scaled

salt and pepper

1 quart vegetable or pure olive oil

all-purpose flour for dredging

For the Broth and Garnish:

2 cups dashi (page 343)

5 tablespoons mirin

6 tablespoons Japanese dark soy sauce

¼ cup sake (optional)

three 3-inch pieces of carrot, cut into fine julienne

9 snow peas, cut lengthwise into fine julienne

3 fresh medium shiitake mushrooms, stems discarded, caps thinly sliced

1 scallion, including green, thinly sliced

Preparing the Fillets: Carefully remove any scales still attached to the fillets and pull out any small bones. Cut the fillets in half so you end up with 4 vaguely square pieces. Using a very sharp knife, make 3 diagonal slashes on the skin side of the squares, cutting halfway through the flesh. Make 3 more diagonal slashes in the opposite direction. Season the squares with salt and pepper and refrigerate until needed.

Preparing the Broth and Garnish: Combine all the ingredients except the scallions in a small saucepan and simmer gently for 5 minutes. Stir in the scallions and remove from the heat.

Frying and Serving the Fish: Heat the oil to 370°F. Roll the sections of bass fillet in flour and pat off any excess. Fry the fish for about 4 minutes (7 minutes per inch of thickness) and place it on a plate covered with paper towels. Pat off any excess oil.

Heat the broth and garnish. Arrange the fish in lacquer or pottery bowls that have been warmed gently in the oven. Spoon the garnish over the fish and surround with the broth. Serve immediately.

Substitutes Fillets with their skin such as striped bass, red snapper, rockfish, ocean perch

Fried Monkfish in Ginger-Scented Broth

This dish reflects the Japanese fondness for cooking fish in 2 stages. In this recipe the monkfish—or other firm-fleshed whitefish—is floured lightly and deep-fried before being simmered in a ginger-flavored dashi. The effect is delicious and intriguing because the frying gives the fish a slightly crunchy outer coating and seals in the fish's juices.

This is a somewhat austere version—which makes it all the more striking, especially if you have pretty lacquer bowls—but you can make it more substantial by nestling a small mound of cooked *cha-soba* (green tea–flavored buckwheat noodles) in one side of the bowl or by adding a few pieces of blanched vegetable, such as snow peas, French green beans, or watercress leaves.

Although the broth for this dish can be made up to 3 days in advance, the actual cooking is a last-minute operation. Because deep-frying can be a nuisance, you'll probably want to serve this dish to at least 6 people at a time.

MAKES 6 MAIN-COURSE OR 10 FIRST-COURSE SERVINGS

2½ pounds monkfish tails or 2 pounds monkfish fillet or other delicately flavored firm whitefish, cut into 12 approximately 1-inch cubes (for main course) or 10 pieces (for first course)

vegetable or pure olive oil for frying

3 cups dashi (page 343)

6 tablespoons mirin

3 tablespoons Japanese dark soy sauce

2 tablespoons sake

2 teaspoons grated fresh ginger

salt and pepper

½ cup all-purpose flour

1 scallion, including green, chopped

If you're serving this dish as a main course, cut the fish into 12 cubes (2 per serving); for a first course, 10 pieces (1 per serving). Try to keep the pieces all the same size so they cook at the same time. Refrigerate until needed.

Heat the frying oil to 375°F.

continued

Boil the dashi until only 2 cups remain. Add the mirin, soy sauce, sake, and ginger and turn the heat down to keep the dashi at a slow simmer.

Season the fish pieces with salt and pepper and dredge them in flour. Pat off any excess flour and fry the pieces 3 or 4 at a time for about 2 minutes (for 1-inch cubes). Transfer them to a plate covered with a layer of paper towels.

When all the fish has been fried, arrange the pieces in warmed Japanese lacquer bowls and ladle on the simmering broth. Sprinkle with the scallion.

Substitutes Other firm white-fleshed fish such as blackfish, black sea bass, cod, haddock, halibut, lingcod, rockfish, skate, striped bass, tilefish

DEEP-FRYING FLAVORFUL MIXTURES OF FISH AND SHELLFISH

Some of the best of all deep-fried foods are flavorful mixtures of fish and shellfish that have been rolled into balls or flattened into cakes before being plunged into hot oil. Chinese cooks are famous for their ginger-scented shrimp balls, the French for their croquettes, and American cooks for crab cakes.

While there are plenty of good recipes for all sorts of deep-fried mixtures, you'll have a lot more fun just making them up with easy-to-find ingredients or when certain fish or shellfish drop in price. You may decide to adapt a favorite crab cake recipe and use lobster or scallops instead, or perhaps you have some leftover cooked monkfish and want to make some flavorful croquettes.

More likely than not you'll be able to substitute different seafood in your favorite recipe without changing anything else. But if you're starting out from scratch, here are a few guidelines:

1. Be consistent in your use of flavors. If you want Chinese flavors, use, for example, garlic, ginger, cilantro, soy sauce, and sesame oil; if you're making a French-style croquette, you may want to incorporate herbs such as tarragon and aromatic vegetables such as shallots or mushrooms. The same consistency should carry over to your choice of dipping sauces—don't serve a hot Chinese mustard sauce with a tarragon-scented croquette. Consistency, however, doesn't mean monotony. Don't repeat the seafood mixture flavors in the dipping sauce. The sauce should provide contrast.

2. Deep-fried mixtures require some kind of binder such as egg (sometimes just egg white) and a small amount of starch such as flour, cornstarch, bread crumbs, or béchamel sauce.

3. Shrimp balls and croquettes can be—and usually are—coated with a starch such as flour or cornstarch and sometimes with more exotic ingredients such as sesame seeds or broken-up noodles.

4. While any deep-frying is best done at the last minute, seafood croquettes, balls, and cakes can be formed and coated earlier the same day and kept in the refrigerator or carefully wrapped and frozen for several weeks. When frozen, thaw for an hour at room temperature before frying.

❧

Chinese Shrimp Balls

*T*hese savory little nuggets make a perfect cocktail party hors d'oeuvre. If you don't want to bother with rolling the shrimp balls in the broken vermicelli, just roll them in flour.

MAKES ABOUT 30 SHRIMP BALLS, HORS D'OEUVRES FOR 10

1 pound headless shrimp, peeled and deveined

1½ tablespoons grated fresh ginger

3 garlic cloves, finely chopped

2 scallions, including green, finely chopped

3 tablespoons finely chopped fresh cilantro

3 tablespoons dark soy sauce

¾ teaspoon dark sesame oil, preferably Japanese

2 tablespoons dry sherry

1 tablespoon cornstarch worked to a paste with 1 tablespoon cold water

a handful of Thai rice vermicelli (rice sticks) or Italian vermicelli in a pinch

1 quart vegetable or peanut oil

For the Mustard Sauce:

¼ cup rice vinegar, sherry vinegar, or white wine vinegar

¼ cup dry mustard

1 tablespoon sugar

2 tablespoons dark soy sauce

Preparing the Shrimp Balls: Chop the shrimp in a food processor for about 1 minute, stopping once or twice to scrape down the sides, or chop by hand until you have a stiff paste. Transfer to a mixing bowl and work in the rest of the ingredients except the noodles and oil with a wooden spoon until the mixture is stiff and smooth, after about 3 minutes of stirring.

Working in a large mixing bowl, break the noodles with your hands into about 1-inch lengths.

To form the shrimp mixture into balls, set a bowl of cold water next to the work area and wet your hands before you form each ball. Roll the shrimp mixture in your open palms into balls about 1 inch in diameter and then roll the shrimp balls in the broken-up noodles. Refrigerate (or freeze) until needed.

Preparing the Mustard Sauce: In a small mixing bowl, stir the vinegar into the mustard to form a thick paste.

Let sit for 15 minutes, then stir in the sugar and soy sauce. Stir for a couple of minutes to dissolve the sugar.

Deep-frying and Serving: Heat the oil to 320°F. Fry about 10 shrimp balls at a time for about 4 minutes, until golden brown. If they brown too quickly, turn down the heat under the oil. If they remain pale, turn it up.

Drain the shrimp balls on paper towels and arrange in a pyramid on a platter. Serve on a tray with the dipping sauce in a small bowl and a stack of cocktail napkins.

❧

Japanese-Style Lobster Balls

I make these savory little bites of deep-fried lobster paste during the summer when, on the East Coast at least, lobster sometimes drops to ridiculously low prices. If lobster is too pricey, you can use crabmeat or cooked firm-fleshed fish such as monkfish or swordfish.

You can serve lobster balls as an hors d'oeuvre—passed on a tray with a dipping sauce—but I prefer to stack them in dainty little pyramids in lacquer bowls and surround them with broth.

MAKES 30 ½-INCH LOBSTER BALLS,
6 FIRST-COURSE SERVINGS

For the Lobster Mixture:

meat from three 1¼-pound lightly cooked lobsters (14 ounces total)

1 tablespoon finely grated fresh ginger

1 garlic clove, finely chopped and crushed to a paste

1 egg, beaten

2 tablespoons Japanese dark soy sauce

2 scallions, including green, finely chopped

¼ cup light sesame seeds

1 quart vegetable oil or pure olive oil

For the Broth:

1 cup dashi (page 343)

¼ cup mirin

¼ cup dark soy sauce

1 small daikon (Japanese white radish)

1 scallion, including green, finely sliced

Making the Lobster Mixture and Forming the Lobster Balls: Combine the lobster, including any coral or tomalley, in the bowl of a food processor with the ginger, garlic, egg, and soy sauce. Puree for 2 minutes, twice scraping down any lobster adhering to the sides of the work bowl. Stir in the chopped scallion and transfer the lobster paste to a mixing bowl. Cover the mixture with plastic wrap and chill in the refrigerator for 1 to 2 hours.

Form the lobster paste into ½-inch balls by holding a small mound of the paste in your clenched fist and then gently squeezing so that the paste extrudes through your curled-over forefinger. Let the balls drop gently onto a baking sheet covered with the sesame seeds. Chill the whole sheet in the refrigerator for about 20 minutes to firm up the balls before trying to roll them in the seeds. Roll each of the balls in sesame seeds and place them on a wax paper–covered plate in the refrigerator.

Making the Broth and Grating the Daikon: Bring all the liquid ingredients to a slow simmer in a small saucepan.

Peel the daikon and shred it with a Japanese vegetable slicer or by slicing it very thinly on a slicer or mandoline and then cutting the slices into fine julienne with a chef's knife. You should end up with about 1½ cups shredded daikon.

Deep-Frying and Serving the Lobster Balls: Preheat the oven to 200°F and heat the oil to 370°F. Deep-fry the lobster balls in 3 batches of 10 for 2 minutes per batch. Drain immediately on a baking sheet covered with paper towels. Keep warm while the others are frying.

Place a small mound of daikon to one side in each of 6 warmed lacquer or pottery bowls. Arrange 5 of the lobster balls in a small pyramid in each of the bowls.

Add the sliced scallions to the simmering broth and carefully ladle the broth around the lobster balls. Serve immediately.

WRAPPING SEAFOOD IN RICE PAPER FOR FRYING

Southeast Asian and Chinese cooks are fond of wrapping seafood—shrimp is a favorite—in rice paper and then serving it fried with a dipping sauce. There seem to be hundreds of variations, some very simple, others almost frighteningly complicated with layers of stuffings and all kinds of chopped things folded around the seafood before it is wrapped. Fortunately even the simplest versions are very tasty and satisfying, so once you get used to working with rice paper you'll probably start inventing your own.

Rice paper comes in both rounds and triangles, but I usually use the rounds, 8 inches in diameter, because they're easier to track down. Look for cellophane packages of 50 in shops that sell Vietnamese products. The easiest way to soften rice paper is to spread it on a baking sheet, brush it with lightly sugared water (the sugar helps it brown), and give it about a minute to soften. You'll need to play around with the rice paper to get a feel for working with it. When you're starting out, don't moisten more than a couple of sheets at a time. Once the rice paper is soft, quickly use it to wrap whatever you're deep-frying.

Vietnamese Fried Shrimp Rolls

CHA GIO

In Vietnam *cha gio* has almost the status of a national dish. Most recipes for it are quite complicated and contain pork, cooked cellophane noodles, and sometimes ground beef. This version is greatly simplified, but because it's lighter you can serve it as an hors d'oeuvre or first course without worrying about spoiling appetites.

Shrimp rolls can be assembled earlier in the day and refrigerated, covered with plastic wrap, on a baking sheet, or they can be wrapped individually in plastic wrap and then aluminum foil and frozen for up to 2 months. Like most fried foods, shrimp rolls are best served right out of the hot oil, but this can be complicated, especially if you want to serve them all at once as a first course. An alternative is to keep them hot in a 200°F oven as you're making them.

MAKES 24 SHRIMP ROLLS, 8 FIRST-COURSE OR HORS D'OEUVRE SERVINGS

For the Shrimp and Stuffing:

36 medium shrimp, peeled, tiny tail shell left attached to 24, and deveined

2 tablespoons chopped fresh cilantro

2 tablespoons chopped fresh mint or basil

1 garlic clove, finely chopped

2 scallions, including 3 inches of green, finely chopped

2 shallots, finely chopped

2 tablespoons fish sauce, preferably Vietnamese, but Thai will do

½ teaspoon dark sesame oil

1 egg

1 teaspoon salt

pepper

¼ cup sugar

1 quart warm water

24 rice paper rounds (8-inch size)

1 quart peanut or vegetable oil

1 recipe nuoc mam (see box)

Butterfly 24 of the shrimp with the tail shell attached by cutting most of the way through the shrimp through the back and then spreading the shrimp open. Combine the remaining shrimp with the other stuffing ingredients in the bowl of a food processor. Process for 1 minute and reserve in the refrigerator in a covered bowl until needed.

Dissolve the sugar in the warm water. Gather together on a work surface a brush and baking sheet, the stack of rice paper, the shrimp filling, the whole shrimp, and the sugar water.

Arrange 2 rounds of rice paper in front of you on the baking sheet and brush each, on both sides, with the warm sugar water. Let sit for about a minute and fold the bottom of each round so that it comes about two thirds of the way up toward the top edge of the round. Place a teaspoon of filling about an inch up from the bottom fold and place a flattened butterflied shrimp over the filling so that just the tiny tail shell is sticking out over the fold. Place another teaspoon of filling on top of the shrimp and fold the top of the paper over the shrimp. Fold the paper from the right side over the shrimp and keep folding from the right until the shrimp is completely rolled up. Massage the shrimp rolls slightly to distribute the stuffing and so the paper forms a tight seal over the end of the shrimp.

Heat about 1 inch of oil in an iron skillet until the oil ripples slightly but doesn't smoke (325°F). Arrange 4 or 6 shrimp rolls in the oil—they should just fill the skillet when in a single layer and should be completely cov-

ered with oil. Fry the shrimp rolls for about 8 to 10 minutes, until golden brown, and drain on paper towels.

Serve the rolls with the nuoc mam for dipping.

VIETNAMESE DIPPING SAUCE

NUOC MAM

This is an almost universal sauce in Vietnamese cooking and can be quite addictive. I love to serve it with fried and grilled seafood.

While most versions of nuoc mam call for distilled white vinegar, I find that distilled vinegar has a sharp chemical smell. I substitute Japanese rice vinegar or sherry vinegar.

Nuoc mam will keep in the refrigerator for a week.

1 red Thai or red serrano chili, seeded and finely chopped

1 small garlic clove, finely chopped

¼ cup fish sauce, preferably Vietnamese, but Thai will do

2 tablespoons sugar

¼ cup rice or sherry vinegar

2 tablespoons fresh lime juice

MAKES 1 CUP

Crush the chopped chili and garlic with the side of a chef's knife or in a mortar and pestle and combine with the other ingredients. Stir for a couple of minutes to dissolve the sugar.

Seafood Samosas

(color page 4)

One favorite Indian fried food is the samosa—a triangular fritter usually stuffed with a spicy mixture of potatoes and herbs or ground meat. Even though I've never encountered seafood samosas in India or in my favorite New York restaurants, the idea seems like a natural. Samosas are delicious by themselves but really come into their own when served with an assortment of homemade Indian sauces and chutneys (see "Sauces and Salsas, Condiments and Broths").

In this version, invented one afternoon when I had some leftover cooked salmon, cooked seafood is broken up with a fork, combined with herbs and spices, and wrapped in pastry.

Most recipes for samosa pastry call for vegetable shortening, which gives a crust that is light and flaky but has a poor flavor. I've broken with tradition here and used butter. The trick to keeping the samosas light is to roll the dough out very thinly—no more than $1/16$ inch.

Samosas make a great hors d'oeuvre or first course at an Indian dinner. They can be made earlier in the day, fried up to 30 minutes before serving, and kept warm in a 200°F oven.

MAKES 30 SAMOSAS, 6 FIRST-COURSE OR HORS D'OEUVRE SERVINGS

For the Dough:

4 tablespoons unsalted butter

1 cup all-purpose flour

1 teaspoon salt

5 tablespoons cold water

all-purpose flour for rolling out dough

For the Filling:

1 pound leftover cooked fish or shellfish

2 tablespoons olive oil

2 medium onions, finely chopped

1 garlic clove, finely chopped

2 tablespoons grated fresh ginger

1 Thai or serrano chili, seeded and finely
   chopped

1 tablespoon ground coriander

1 teaspoon ground cumin

$1/2$ teaspoon ground cardamom

$1/2$ teaspoon ground cinnamon

$1/4$ teaspoon ground cloves

2 tablespoons finely chopped fresh cilantro

2 tablespoons finely chopped fresh mint

salt and pepper

1 quart vegetable or pure olive oil for
   deep-frying

Preparing the Dough: Food processor method: Combine all the ingredients in the food processor. Work the mixture using the steel blade until it forms a ball. Flatten the ball into a disk about $1/2$ inch thick and refrigerate it, wrapped in plastic wrap, for an hour.

Hand method: Cut the butter into $1/4$-inch cubes with a chef's knife or metal pastry cutter. Combine the butter with the flour and salt in a mixing bowl. Working quickly, take a small amount of the flour/butter mixture and crush it against the palm of one hand with the fingers of the other. When most of the cubes of butter have been flattened, pour in the cold water and quickly knead the mixture into a soft dough. Flatten the dough into a disk about $1/2$ inch thick and refrigerate it, wrapped in plastic wrap, for an hour.

Preparing the Filling: Chop the cooked fish or shellfish with a chef's knife on a cutting board until the fish is shredded or the shellfish is in approximately $1/4$-inch cubes. Refrigerate in a mixing bowl.

Heat the olive oil in a wide sauté pan over medium heat and stir in the onion, garlic, ginger, and chili. Cook gently until the onion turns translucent and then begins to brown slightly, about 15 minutes.

Stir in the ground spices—but not the fresh herbs—and cook, stirring, over medium heat for about 2 minutes, until you can smell their aroma. Remove from the heat and let cool for 15 minutes.

Stir the onion/spice mixture and chopped herbs into the chopped seafood. Season to taste with salt and pepper.

Filling the Samosas: Using your hands, shape and roll the dough into a cylinder about 1 inch by 12 inches. Slice the cylinder into 15 disks, each about $3/4$ inch thick. Reserve these disks, covered with plastic wrap, in the refrigerator.

Shape the stuffing into 30 small balls and reserve on a plate in the refrigerator. This is done in advance so you can work quickly while shaping the samosas.

Roll the disks, one at a time, into 6-inch-diameter circles about $1/16$ inch thick. You'll need a lot of flour on both the work surface and rolling pin because the dough tends to stick. As you roll out each disk, cut the disk in half so you end up with 30 semicircles.

Hold your left hand—palm facing up—over a semicircle placed on the work surface with the flat side of the semicircle facing away from you. Bring the left side of the semicircle up to the middle of your left hand and hold it in place with your left thumb. Wet the edge of the circle and pull the other side of the semicircle around with your right hand and seal it against the left side to form a triangular shape. Pinch with your fingers to seal the 2 edges together. Turn the triangle around so the closed point is facing you and put a ball of filling into the pouch formed by the triangle. Moisten the opened end and pinch closed. Flatten the samosas slightly between your hands and reserve on a floured plate.

Frying the Samosas: Heat the oil to 370°F in a heavy skillet and fry the samosas in 3 batches for 5 to 6 minutes, until golden. Place on a paper towel–covered baking sheet to absorb excess oil. Serve immediately or keep warm in a 200°F oven for up to 30 minutes. Serve with one or more relishes or chutney.

CROQUETTES

I like to make croquettes with leftover cooked fish or shellfish, which I usually combine with chopped leftover or freshly cooked vegetables. The principle behind making croquettes is simple: Small pieces of cooked seafood are bound together with a stiff sauce, usually a béchamel, and formed into balls, patties, or egg-shaped quenelles. The croquettes are then coated with bread crumbs, deep-fried, and served surrounded with a tangy sauce—kept light to counteract the richness of the croquettes. Tomato sauce, tangy mayonnaise variations such as tartar sauce, and delicately flavored broths can all be served with croquettes. One important factor in making croquettes is a béchamel sauce that is well flavored with herbs or spices. With this in mind it's easy to invent your own flavors by adding herbs such as chopped tarragon or cilantro or spices such as saffron or curry. Cooked vegetables such as carrots or mushrooms also provide flavor and make the croquettes less rich.

❧

Curry-Flavored Monkfish Croquettes with Pear Chutney

Monkfish is good in croquettes because of its firm texture once cooked, but any leftover firm-fleshed fish or shellfish will do. The sweetness of the chutney contrasts well with the spicy croquettes, but I also like to serve these with a simple tomato sauce made sweet and sour with sugar and wine vinegar.

Like other deep-fried foods, these croquettes should be deep-fried minutes before serving, but the croquettes themselves can be made earlier in the day—in fact they should be formed at least 2 hours before frying to help them hold their shape. While croquettes are traditionally coated with flour, egg, and bread crumbs, these are rolled in flour alone so they absorb less oil.

MAKES 18 CROQUETTES, 6 FIRST-COURSE SERVINGS

For the Curry Béchamel Sauce:

1 medium onion, finely chopped

5 tablespoons unsalted butter

4 tablespoons all-purpose flour

2 tablespoons good-quality curry powder

2 cups milk

salt and white pepper

pinch of cayenne pepper

very small pinch of freshly grated nutmeg

For the Pear Chutney:

2 unripe pears, peeled, cored, and cut into ¼ inch dice

¼ teaspoon ground cinnamon

½ teaspoon ground turmeric

2 tablespoons sugar

½ cup good-quality white wine vinegar

For the Filling and Coating:

1½ cups shredded cooked firm-fleshed fish fillets such as monkfish, salmon, sea bass, or striped bass (about 1 pound)

½ cup fresh bread crumbs

1 cup ¼-inch cubes of cooked vegetables such as carrots or mushrooms

all-purpose flour for dredging

1 quart vegetable or pure olive oil

Making the Curry Béchamel: In a 2-quart saucepan over low to medium heat, cook the onion in butter until the onion turns translucent, about 10 minutes. Add the flour and stir over medium heat for 2 minutes. Add the curry powder, stir for 1 minute more, and pour in the milk. Bring to a slow simmer—at which point the sauce should get very stiff—and whisk until smooth. Season to taste with salt, pepper, cayenne, and nutmeg. Cover the pot and let cool.

Making the Chutney: Combine all the ingredients in a 1-quart saucepan and simmer, covered, over medium heat for about 10 minutes, until the pear cubes soften slightly and release liquid. Uncover the pan, remove the pears with a slotted spoon, and reserve. Boil down the liquid in the pan until it turns into a light syrup, about 20 minutes. Stir in the reserved pear cubes and let cool.

Making the Filling, Shaping and Coating the Croquettes: Transfer the cooled béchamel to a mixing bowl and stir in the cooked fish, bread crumbs, and vegetables. Cover the mixture with plastic wrap and refrigerate for 1 to 2 hours. (The plastic wrap should actually touch the surface of the mixture—when plastic is stretched across the top of the bowl, the air insulates the mixture and it takes twice as long to cool.)

Coat a tray or baking sheet with a thin layer of flour. Shape the croquettes into 18 egg shapes using 2 tablespoons dipped each time in cold water. Start by dipping one spoon in cold water and spooning up a mound of croquette filling. Dip the second spoon and use it, turned upside down and facing the opposite direction, to smooth and shape the croquette mixture. Gently scoop the croquettes onto the floured tray. Refrigerate the croquettes until needed.

Coating, Deep-frying, and Serving: Within 15 minutes of deep-frying, roll the croquettes in flour. Pat them gently to eliminate excess flour.

Preheat the oven to 200°F and heat the oil to 350°F. Deep-fry the croquettes, 6 at a time, for about 5 minutes, until they turn golden brown. Keep the croquettes warm in the oven on a plate covered with paper towels. Serve on hot plates. Pass the room-temperature chutney in a small bowl at the table.

Grilling and Broiling

Whenever I bite into a piece of grilled fish, I wonder why I ever bother cooking any other way. The savory aroma and the crispy outer surface of a well-grilled fish make the minimal effort of grilling well worth it. While broiled fish will not have as much savor as a fish cooked over a grill, it's about as close as you can get on a rainy day.

Although grilling and broiling are similar techniques—in some parts of the United States the two words are used interchangeably—grilling is used here to mean cooking over, but not in contact with, the heat source. Broiling is cooking under the heat source.

GRILLING EQUIPMENT

Although some stoves come with gas or electric grills, most of us grill outdoors on a barbecue. An outdoor barbecue doesn't have to be complicated or expensive—a small enclosure of stacked bricks with a grill set on top works perfectly well. My favorite barbecue is an old hibachi with a heavy, slightly convex grill that allows rendered fat to move along the underside of the grill and drip over the sides rather than into the coals, where it would flame and leave soot on the food. These old round hibachis are expensive and hard to find, but the inexpensive rectangular ones are a suitable substitute.

Although there are dozens of barbecues to choose from—ranging in price from $6 to $600—you're best off with a grill made from thick metal, which will leave attractive grill marks on the fish and be less likely to stick than the thin chrome-plated grills used on most barbecues. I also recommend using a barbecue with a grill that can be raised or lowered so you can regulate its distance from the coals. While I don't recommend grilling food with a cover over the barbecue (it makes the food sooty), buying a covered barbecue may be worthwhile so you can use it for smoke grilling. Covering the barbecue when you're finished also extinguishes the coals so you can reuse them.

HEAT SOURCES

Although most of us use a wood-burning barbecue for grilling, there are gas and electric grills that make the process much simpler—no waiting for the coals to reach the right temperature, less cleanup, and more precise control of the heat. The first time I used a gas grill I was surprised by how well it worked and how much "grill" flavor the food had.

Despite the convenience of gas and electric grilling, grilling over wood is a satisfying ritual—it's the only time we get to cook with real fire—and a wood fire imparts a subtle and irresistible flavor to the food.

If you have no grill at all—a common situation for apartment dwellers—you can use a square cast-iron grill pan set on the stove. Be sure the pan is clean, lightly oiled, and very hot before putting on any food. Grill pans generate a lot of smoke, so open a window and don't be surprised if you set off the smoke alarm.

Selecting Charcoal or Wood: Because Japanese cooks favor charcoal that imparts little if any flavor to the food, the best-quality Japanese charcoal is a hot but slow-burning variety that produces hardly any smoke. European cooks in all but a few situations—grilling over vine cuttings in vineyards, grilling fish over dried fennel stalks—agree with the Japanese that too much smoke can spoil the flavor of grilled foods. Grills in professional European kitchens are often designed with ventilators to quickly suck away the slightest trace of smoke.

The American approach to grilling is somewhat different. Americans like the flavors that various woods such as hickory, fruitwoods, and mesquite impart to grilled foods. Lately I've seen wood chips for sale in fancy food stores at more than the price of potatoes!

If you decide on the "smokeless" approach to grilling, you can get by using most any charcoal, but you'll have better luck using real charcoal chips made from wood instead of briquets. Wood charcoal burns much hotter and lasts longer, and because it has a better aroma, you don't have to wait for any chemical odor to burn off. If you do use briquets, avoid the self-lighting kind and allow the charcoal to burn long enough to eliminate any chemical odors before grilling. Don't use charcoal lighter fluid.

If you want to scent your food lightly with the smoke from various woods, you'll save money by building a regular fire with briquets or inexpensive charcoal and then sprinkling hardwood chips on the hot coals just before grilling. Wait until the wood chips ignite and the flame dies down before grilling—never put food over a flaming fire. (Some recipes suggest soaking the wood chips in water before putting them on the fire, but I find they flare up anyway.)

Starting the Fire: For years I toyed around with kindling (admittedly still the most satisfying method), electric coil starters that threatened to blow fuses if left a minute too long, and liquid starter that left the food smelling like the airport. Finally I concluded that the best way to start a charcoal fire is to use one of those gadgets shaped like an oversized tin can with a handle on the side. The top three quarters of the cylinder are filled with charcoal, and the bottom quarter is stuffed with newspaper. The whole apparatus is then set in the bottom of the grill and the newspaper lit. It takes about 30 minutes for the coals to light completely, and then you just dump them out into the barbecue.

Once the coals are lit, I usually spread them out so that the heat is concentrated in the center or to one side of the grill (by making the bed of coals thicker or thinner accordingly) so I can position the fish on different sections of the grill to regulate the heat.

MARINATING FISH FOR GRILLING OR BROILING

Fish and shellfish can be marinated in the same way as meats to give them a characteristic flavor. Favorite marinade ingredients are herbs such as thyme, marjoram, and parsley; aromatic vegetables such as garlic, onions, and ginger; liquid ingredients such as lemon juice, vinegar, soy sauce, sake, and wine; and oil, especially olive oil.

Although marinades sometimes enhance the flavor of grilled fish, a marinade is certainly not essential. I often just rub fish to be grilled with a little olive oil—which in any case helps prevent sticking—and chopped fresh herbs. Acidic liquids such as lemon juice or vinegar tend to "cook" the fish—the fish takes on a matte appearance around the edges—and may cause it to stick to the grill.

Many recipes suggest basting fish with its marinade during grilling. Although this has the obvious advantage of flavoring the fish during cooking, it also has a couple of drawbacks: It may prevent browning by keeping the surface of the fish moist, and if the marinade contains fat such as olive oil or butter, it may cause the fire to flare up and give the fish a sooty flavor. I usually baste only large fish, when I'm not worried about there being enough time for the fish to brown properly.

GRILLING WHOLE FISH

A sizzling whole grilled fish makes an impressive sight. The simplest fish to grill are small, slightly oily fish such as fresh sardines, anchovies, mackerel, baby coho salmon, and herring. Because of their oil content, these fish rarely stick to the grill. Small fish can be nibbled at the table like corn on the cob or eaten whole, heads and all. Small fish can be placed directly on a hot grill and turned with tongs, but many cooks like to clamp the fish in square, hinged grills for easier turning. Most fish can also be placed in rows on skewers.

Remember that the smaller the fish, the higher the heat. If grilled over too high heat, large fish will blacken before they cook all the way through. If cooked too slowly, small fish will be overcooked and dry before they turn brown and crispy.

You can also grill larger whole fish such as sea bass, striped bass, red snapper, and even salmon, but you'll need to be especially careful to keep the fish from sticking or breaking when you turn it over.

One of the easiest ways to grill larger whole fish is to use a grilling basket. These look like fish-shaped cages—they come in different sizes—with a long handle at one end and hinges on the other. They have metal feet on each side so they can sit right in the grill among the coals. This eliminates the problem of trying to turn the fish without tearing its skin. (Sometimes the skin sticks to the grilling basket and tears anyway when you open the basket, but at least you can present the fish in the basket.)

Another method for grilling whole fish and preventing sticking is to leave the scales attached and then peel off the skin and carve the fish in front of your guests. The skin and scales seal in the flavor and keep the flesh juicy.

Another technique is to wrap the fish in grape leaves before putting it directly on the grill or in a grilling basket. If you don't happen to be grilling out in a vineyard, you can buy bottled grape leaves at stores selling Middle Eastern foods—they're used for wrapping dolmas. Be sure to rinse the leaves thoroughly in cold water to eliminate salt. Aluminum foil can be used in place of the grape leaves, but aluminum seals the fish so efficiently that the fish won't have any flavor of the grill but will taste, rather, like a fish that has been baked *en papillote*—not bad either.

GRILLING FISH FILLETS AND STEAKS

Fish steaks and fillets are easy to grill and make a delicious and casual outdoor barbecue. When grilling fish steaks and fillets, make sure they are at least $1/2$ inch thick so they'll have a chance to get crispy and flavorful before they overcook. Thinner steaks and fillets may also fall apart when you try to turn them. Tuna, swordfish, salmon, and halibut steaks are excellent grilled because the flesh is firm and holds together well.

When grilling fish steaks, always leave the skin attached. The skin helps seal in flavor and also helps the fish hold its shape. You can pull the skin away

---

HOW TO KEEP FISH FROM STICKING

1. Oily and richer fish such as tuna (steaks); salmon (steaks or fillets); fresh sardines, herrings, or anchovies (whole); eels (in sections or split down the middle); mackerel (whole or fillets) and bluefish (steaks, fillets, or whole) work best for grilling. The oil in these fish helps prevent sticking.

2. Nonoily fish such as red snapper, porgy, sea bass, and others can also be grilled but are best grilled in a grilling basket or with the scales left attached.

3. Make sure the grill is perfectly clean and very hot before placing the fish on it. A cool grill that warms along with the fish will stick to the fish.

4. Select a grill made of thick metal. The thin metal rods that form the grills on most barbecues don't retain enough heat, so they cool when you put the fish on and are more likely to stick.

5. Make sure the fish is perfectly dry. If you've marinated the fish in liquids such as wine or lemon juice, wipe these off completely before grilling.

6. Oil the fish and the grill lightly just before grilling. I use a paper towel for oiling the grill and a brush for oiling the fish. Don't use too much oil, or it will drip onto the coals and cause flare-up.

7. Be careful when using a spatula to turn the fish. A spatula can easily scrape against the bottom of the fish and cause it to tear. A better technique is to slide a long two-pronged fork (a professional sauté fork with two perfectly straight tines works best) under the fish—parallel with the grill rods—and then gently lift the fish in one or two places to detach it from the grill. It can then be flipped over by lifting with the fork and holding it with a spatula held over the *top* of the fish.

8. If you don't have grilling baskets and you're grilling fragile or nonoily fish, try using skewers or cut 1-inch-wide triple-thick strips of aluminum foil and slide them under the fish in two places. When it comes time to turn the fish, grip the strips and gently lift the fish and turn it on the grill.

---

before serving, but some skin such as salmon skin is delicious. In any case the guests can decide for themselves.

When grilling fish fillets, I usually leave the skin attached because it gets crispy and very tasty and helps seal in flavor. One problem, however, is that fish skin shrinks in contact with the heat and can cause the fillets to curl. You can prevent this by making a series of shallow diagonal slashes in the skin across the fillet. Make sure the grill is hot and the fish oiled to prevent sticking. If the skin does stick to the grill and tear, carefully turn over the

skinless fillet and forget about eating the skin. If you're careful, the flesh part of the fillet will remain intact.

USING SKEWERS FOR GRILLING OR BROILING

Skewers are useful for turning fish on the grill and are especially helpful when grilling smaller fish or fish pieces and shellfish such as scallops and shrimp.

Both metal and wooden skewers can be used. Metal skewers have the advantage of not burning up and letting the fish fall into the grill, but they get hot and therefore can be difficult to handle and aren't as pretty to look at as wooden skewers. Wooden skewers should be soaked in water for 30 minutes before they are used, and any exposed parts should be wrapped in aluminum foil to prevent burning Small pieces of fish arranged on wooden skewers should be placed right next to each other—with no exposed wood—or the skewer will burn and the whole thing will fall apart.

To thread whole small fish on skewers, slide one skewer sideways through the fish near the base of the head and another skewer near the tail so that the fish form a row perpendicular to the skewers. Don't try to skewer fish whole with only one skewer, or the fish will turn around on the skewer and be almost impossible to turn.

SUSPENDING THE FISH OVER THE GRILL

One foolproof method for preventing sticking is to skewer whole fish or fish fillets lengthwise with two long metal skewers and then set the ends of the skewers on the sides of the grill or prop them up on each side with a brick. In this way the fish never touches the grill but instead remains suspended directly over the coals. The fish should be skewered with two skewers so that it cooks flat and can be turned easily with the skewers.

CONTROLLING GRILL TEMPERATURE

With a little practice you'll learn to judge the temperature of the grill by watching the fish to see if it needs to cook over higher or lower heat. Always preheat the grill, which will help prevent sticking, and if the fish starts burning or the grill flares up after only 1 or 2 minutes, you'll need to raise the fish an inch or two more above the coals or lower the heat by

spreading some of the coals to one side of the grill so there's a thinner layer underneath the fish. If the coals keep flaring up, which is sometimes unavoidable with oily fish, lift off the grill with the fish and spray the coals—actually a thin stream rather than a spray—with water from a spray bottle. (Don't be tempted to spray the coals with the fish still on the grill—the spray loosens ash, which will cling to the fish.) If the fish just sits on the grill with no sizzling, dripping, or indication of cooking, you'll probably need to lower the grill—or, if the fish is in a grilling basket, move the coals into a small pile just underneath the fish.

While there are no hard-and-fast rules for regulating the temperature of the grill and deciding what temperature is right for each fish, medium-size whole fish (between 1 and 1½ pounds) or thick fillets (¾ to 1 inch) should be placed about 4 inches from the surface of the coals. Smaller fish such as fresh sardines should be placed very close to the coals, within an inch or two. Large fish—more than 2 pounds—should be grilled about 6 inches from the coals. Whole fish usually cook in about 10 minutes per inch at the thickest part. Steaks and fillets cook much faster, about 6 minutes total grilling time per inch of thickness over high heat and slightly longer over low heat. Whole fish and fish steaks should be grilled more on the side that will be visible when served. For example, if you judge the total grilling time of a whole fish to be 20 minutes, cook the first side for about 11 minutes and the second side for 9. The "presentation side" is always placed down on the grill first because the first surface to come in contact with the grill is less likely to stick and will have a cleaner look. Turn the fish only once—turning it more than this will only increase the risk of

sticking and will cause juices to run into the grill.

SAUCES FOR GRILLED FISH

Most of the time grilled fish doesn't really need a sauce—the crispy skin, well sprinkled with salt, serves as accent enough—except perhaps a little Tuscan green olive oil on the table for guests to help themselves.

Despite my usual purist approach, when I have more than a few guests I like to grill an assortment of the freshest fish I can find and then serve them with a collection of tart and savory sauces. Almost any sauce will do, but since grilled fish is surprisingly rich I avoid butter sauces and mayonnaises. The best sauces for grilled fish contain either lemon or lime juice or good vinegar to help them accent the flavor of the fish. See salsa verde, mint and cilantro yogurt pesto, tropical fruit salsa, tomato and avocado salsa, and tomato chutney in "Sauces and Salsas, Condiments and Broths."

❧

Grilled Whole Red Snapper

It amazes me how many elaborate fish preparations I run into in restaurants yet how rare it is to be able to order a perfectly fresh whole grilled fish served at the table. Whole grilled fish is not only one of my favorite ways of eating fish but one of my favorite methods of cooking fish at home. Some of my guests are startled to see me show up at the table with a whole fish resting on a platter, eager to show off my carving skills (gleaned from watching waiters in European restaurants).

Almost any whole fish can be grilled, but red snapper looks especially dramatic. I highly recommend using a grilling basket, but if you don't have one, leave the scales on the fish and skip the marinade. (A marinade has a hard time penetrating a fish with scales.)

Most recipes for grilled whole fish recommend making a series of deep diagonal slashes on both sides of the fish, ostensibly to help the heat penetrate. I find that the slashes cause the fish to lose juices and make it harder to serve, so I don't bother.

MAKES 2 MAIN-COURSE SERVINGS

one 1½- to 2-pound red snapper

salt and pepper

For the Marinade (optional):

1 garlic clove, finely chopped

3 tablespoons extra-virgin olive oil

1 tablespoon finely chopped fresh thyme or marjoram

If you're using a grilling basket, have the fishmonger scale the fish. When you get it home, go over it carefully and scrape off any remaining scales with the back of a knife. You may have to cut off the head so the fish will fit in the grilling basket. Put the fish in an oval dish with the combined marinade ingredients, if you're using them, about 2 hours before serving. Refrigerate and turn the fish over a couple of times so it stays well coated with marinade.

If you don't have a grilling basket, leave the scales on the fish and don't bother with the marinade. Season with salt.

If you're using a gas or electric grill, preheat the grill, set on high, for about 10 minutes before cooking. You can leave the cover on at this point, but you should remove it during the grilling. If you're using wood, start the fire about 45 minutes ahead. Leave the cover off at all times.

Wipe off any marinade clinging to the fish, which might cause the fire to flare up. If you're using a grilling basket, place the basket over the coals. If you're using the grill, place the unscaled fish about 4 inches above the coals. Grill the fish for about 10 minutes per inch of thickness at the thickest point. Turn the fish only once.

To see if the fish is done, insert a paring knife carefully into the back and gently pull the flesh away from the backbone. The flesh should pull away—but hesitantly—and appear moist. Don't cook the fish until it's flaky, or it will be dry.

Transfer the fish to a warm oval platter or dish. (In summer I usually warm the dishes by arranging them near the grill so I don't have to light the oven.) Serve the fish at the table on hot plates. Grilled vegetables are a nice accompaniment. I like to put a bottle of extra-virgin olive oil, some good sea salt, pepper, and some good vinegar on the table for guests to help themselves.

Substitutes Any whole medium or small round fish such as Arctic char, black sea bass, butterfish, jack, grouper, mackerel, mullet, ocean perch, pompano, rockfish, small salmon such as coho, sea trout, Spanish mackerel, striped bass, tilapia, trout (lake and brook), walleye, weakfish, whitefish, yellow perch

Grilled Fresh Sardines

(color page 11)

A crispy hot sardine fresh off the grill is one of the most satisfying and probably the healthiest of all snack foods—the Mediterranean equivalent of the hot dog. Unfortunately, they can be hard to track down in the United States, though occasionally local versions (actually small herring) show up in Pacific and Atlantic coast fish markets. Mediterranean sardines, flown in, also show up in fancier stores for a not-too-outrageous sum.

To the uninitiated, eating grilled sardines is somewhat of a mystery. My first attempt, at a tiny counter in Portugal, was met with good-natured laughter—as I tried to eat the sardine with knife and fork. A sardine should be eaten like corn on the cob—the rich fillets nibbled off the sides—or eaten whole, head and all. If you're worried about the reaction of your guests, you can cut off the sardine heads—a treat for the cat.

I like to serve grilled sardines for a small crowd—passing them on a platter at the table puts everyone in a festive mood.

This method works with any very small fish.

MAKES 6 FIRST-COURSE SERVINGS

3 dozen fresh sardines

3 tablespoons extra-virgin olive oil

salt and pepper

Clean the sardines by pinching the gills on both sides at the base of the head and pulling them out. Sometimes the innards will pull out with the gills, but if they don't, slide your finger along the belly cavity and pull out all the innards. Rinse the sardines in cold water while rubbing—to get rid of the scales—and wipe them with a towel. Any remaining scales will come off as the sardines are being wiped dry.

Toss the sardines in the olive oil but then wipe off the oil by sliding the sardines between your fingers—any oil left on will cause the fire to flare up. Grill over a very hot fire—make sure the grill has been preheated on the fire for a minute or two—with the sardines about 2 inches from the surface of the coals, for 2 to 3 minutes on each side. If the fire keeps flaring up, raise the grill a couple of inches. The sardines should be crispy and well browned. The sardines can be grilled directly on the grill and turned with tongs or grilled in a hinged square grilling basket. Season with salt and pepper.

Serve immediately on a platter or individual plates for people to help themselves with their fingers.

Substitutes Any small full-flavored fish such as anchovies, small herring (often called sardines anyway), baby mackerel, red mullet, smelts, sunfish, baby trout

Grilled Salmon Steaks

Salmon is wonderful on the barbecue because of its full flavor, firm texture, and festive color. It also has a high enough fat content that it won't dry out unless it's severely overcooked.

MAKES 6 MAIN-COURSE SERVINGS

six 1- to 1½-inch-thick salmon steaks with skin

2 tablespoons extra-virgin olive oil

salt and pepper

If you're using charcoal, build a fire about 45 minutes before you plan to start cooking. If you're using a gas grill, turn it on about 10 minutes ahead of cooking.

Toss the salmon steaks in half the olive oil. When the coals have completely ignited, spread them over a large enough area for the 6 steaks. Wait about 10 minutes so the coals end up coated with a fine layer of ash. Brush the grill with the remaining oil and set it about 6 inches from the coals. Give it about 5 minutes to heat up.

Season the salmon steaks with salt and pepper and place them on the grill. For 1-inch steaks, grill for 3 to 4 minutes on each side. If you're unsure whether the steaks are done, cut into one with a sharp paring knife; they should be served immediately on hot plates.

Substitutes Steaks at least 1-inch thick such as bonito, king mackerel, shark, sturgeon, swordfish, tuna, wahoo

Grilled Tuna Steaks with Tomato Broth and Saffron Aïoli

(color page 13)

Even jaded garlic eaters find it hard to resist the pungent flavors of grilled tuna slices surrounded by bright orange garlic- and saffron-scented broth. This dish requires a bit of preparation—all of which can be done earlier the same day—and a willingness to eat tuna almost raw. Tuna cooked all the way through is never as satisfying as tuna cooked like a rare steak, with a dark streak of red

down the middle. Just one bite always convinces even the most squeamish. When you're not up to grilling, this dish is also delicious made with pan-fried tuna steaks.

MAKES 4 MAIN-COURSE SERVINGS

four 6- to 8-ounce tuna steaks, ¾ to 1 inch thick, skin and dark meat removed

1 tablespoon olive oil

small pinch of saffron threads

1 tablespoon water

2 medium tomatoes, peeled

½ cup chicken broth (page 344), fish broth (page 343), or water

½ cup aïoli (page 334)

salt and pepper

Rub the tuna steaks with olive oil and refrigerate until needed. Combine the saffron threads with the water and let sit for 30 minutes or longer.

Cut the tomatoes in half crosswise. Place a strainer over a small bowl and squeeze the seeds out of each tomato half over the strainer. Work the tomato juice through the strainer with your fingers and discard the seeds that don't go through.

Finely chop the tomato halves and combine them with the tomato juice in a small saucepan. Cover the saucepan and cook gently over medium heat for 10 minutes.

Set the strainer again over the bowl, pour in the cooked chopped tomatoes, and let drain.

Whisking gently, stir the saffron threads, strained tomato liquid, and broth into the aïoli. Pour the mixture into a saucepan.

Season the tuna steaks with salt and pepper and grill them over a hot fire for 2 minutes on each side.

Heat the mayonnaise/broth mixture over medium heat while stirring until hot but not boiling. (Boiling will cause the egg yolk to curdle.)

Slice the tuna steaks into long strips and arrange them in rows in hot soup plates. Ladle the hot mayonnaise mixture into each plate so it comes halfway up the sides of the tuna slices. Place a mound of the chopped tomatoes from the strainer in the center of each plate. Serve immediately.

JAPANESE GRILLING TECHNIQUES

Japanese chefs, who are masters of the grill, use several techniques to make grilled foods especially savory. Unlike American and European cooks, who like to grill whole fish or large steaks and fillets, Japanese cooks grill fish in bite-size portions that are easy to handle with chopsticks. For this reason most Japanese grilled fish are arranged on skewers before grilling. The skewered pieces of fish can then be passed at the table—little kebabs, called *yakitori*—or, more formally, arranged on small serving plates or platters.

In Japan pieces of fish are almost always marinated before they are grilled, but unlike some Western grilled foods, the time spent in the marinade is relatively short—30 to 40 minutes. The marinade, called *yuan*, contains dark soy sauce, sake, and mirin (sweetened sake) in varying proportions depending on the time of year. In the winter months the marinade is sweeter (it contains a higher proportion of mirin) than in the summer, when sake and soy sauce predominate. *Yuan* is not only used as a marinade but is sometimes applied to the fish during cooking so that the pieces of fish become coated with a delicious sweet-and-savory glaze.

Salting is another technique often used by Japanese cooks to make fish firmer and more savory by eliminating moisture. Fish salted in this way is marinated with *yuan* with the soy sauce left out (which would make it too salty) or not marinated at all.

Yuan-Glazed Grilled Tilefish Fillets

I first read a version of this dish in Shizuo Tsuji's wonderful book *Japanese Cooking: A Simple Art.* Mr. Tsuji's version calls for red tilefish (*amadai*), but I've had good luck using the common tilefish found on the East Coast as well as large Spanish mackerel fillets and salmon fillets. I imagine that any firm-fleshed fish would work, but whatever kind of fillets you end up buying, make sure they are at least an inch thick so they can be cut into thick chunks.

The combination of sweet, salty, and smoky flavors makes these bite-size pieces of grilled fish hard to resist. In fact if you're serving this dish before dinner, don't serve too much, or your guests will spoil their appetites for the main course. While Japanese cooks are likely to serve this as a snack with drinks—the sweet-and-salty flavors are delicious with cocktails—or as one of many courses in a formal meal, I like to serve it with a salad and maybe a little rice for a light dinner. I also like to serve it with an assortment of little Japanese pickled plums or turnips. This dish should be started the day before it is served.

MAKES 4 FIRST-COURSE OR LIGHT MAIN-COURSE SERVINGS

1- to 1½-pound tilefish fillet with skin, scaled and pin bones removed
2 tablespoons coarse sea salt or kosher salt
1 tablespoon mirin
2 teaspoons sake or dry sherry
vegetable oil for the grill

Rub the tilefish fillet on both sides with the coarse salt to firm the texture. Place the fillet in a strainer set over a bowl and let drain in the refrigerator for 2 hours. Quickly rinse the salt off the fillet and pat dry with paper towels.

Cut the fillets crosswise into 12 equal pieces about 1 inch wide and 2 inches long.

If you're using charcoal, start the fire about 45 minutes before you're ready to start cooking.

Toss the mirin and sake with the pieces of fish and refrigerate for 30 minutes. Turn the fish around in the marinade every 10 minutes so the fish is coated evenly. Drain and wipe the fish dry with paper towels. Save the remaining marinade.

Skewer the pieces of fish on sets of 2 skewers to make them easier to turn. If you're using wooden skewers, soak them in water for 30 minutes; make sure the pieces of fish are touching each other when threaded, and wrap the ends of the skewers in aluminum foil to keep them from burning. Grill the fish, skin side down first, over medium heat—about 5 inches from the coals—for about 4 minutes. Turn the fish over and brush the crispy skin side with more marinade to give it a slight glaze. Grill for about 4 minutes more. Serve immediately on a small platter or small individual plates.

Substitutes Fillets with edible skin such as black sea bass, mackerel, mahimahi, rockfish, salmon, Spanish mackerel, striped bass, walleye

Salted and Grilled Salmon Fillets

*L*ightly coating fish with salt about 2 hours before cooking gives it a firmer texture, which makes it easier to grill in smaller pieces that might otherwise fall apart on the grill. This is a favorite technique of Japanese cooks, who like to serve fish in bite-size pieces that are easy to pick up with chopsticks. After salting, the salmon is soaked in sake, which helps eliminate the excess salt. If you have access to *sake kasu*—the dregs left in the bottom of the barrel used for making sake—use it instead of sake for a deeper flavor.

I like to serve these delicious morsels of salmon with slices of pickled ginger and perhaps a few Japanese pickled vegetables (such as shallots, yam slices, and plums), lemon wedges, or cucumber half-slices sprinkled with a little vinegar. Grilled miniature vegetables such as mushrooms or small onions also make a nice effect. The pickles and vegetables can be arranged on each plate or passed in little Japanese bowls at the table.

MAKES 4 FIRST-COURSE SERVINGS

one 1½-inch-thick piece of salmon fillet (12 ounces), cut from the head end of the salmon, skin removed

2 tablespoons coarse sea salt

½ cup sake or *sake kasu*

vegetable oil for the grill

For the Cucumber Garnish:

2 cucumbers, each about 8 inches long

1 tablespoon coarse sea salt

2 tablespoons Japanese rice vinegar or sherry vinegar

Wipe the salmon with paper towels and place it on a plate with the salt. Turn it around in the salt so it is well coated and place in the refrigerator for 1½ hours.

Peel the cucumber and cut it in half lengthwise. Scrape out the seeds with a tablespoon and discard. Slice each cucumber half into ⅛-inch-thick slices. Toss the slices in the salt for about 2 minutes—rub them until they are thoroughly coated and feel wet—and place the slices in the refrigerator in a colander set over a bowl for 30 minutes to drain. Squeeze the cucumber slices tightly in your fist to eliminate more water and place them in a bowl in the refrigerator.

Rinse the salmon under cold water to eliminate the salt clinging to its surface. Pat it dry with paper towels and place the salmon in a bowl with the sake for an hour. If the sake doesn't cover it completely, turn the salmon over after 30 minutes.

Drain the salmon and again pat it dry with paper towels. Oil the grill with vegetable oil and grill the salmon over very high heat about 4 inches from the coals for about 4 minutes on each side (3 minutes on each side for a 1-inch-thick fillet).

While the salmon is grilling, quickly squeeze the cucumber slices one more time and toss them with the vinegar. Carefully transfer the salmon, best-looking side up, to a cutting board. Cut the salmon in half lengthwise—just follow the natural division in the fillet—with a very sharp knife. Slice each strip of salmon crosswise into 10 thin slices. Arrange a small mound of cucumber and in another small mound 5 slices of salmon on each plate. Serve immediately.

Grilled Eels with Mussaman Curry

*E*els are particularly good here because they hold up well on the grill and there's little risk of overcooking them by then finishing them in a sauce. Salmon, tuna, and swordfish fillets or steaks cut into 1-inch cubes may also be used in this recipe. The eel sections suggested here contain bones but if you want, this recipe can also be made with boneless eel fillets (see color page 32).

This dish is very simple to make, especially if you buy a small can of Mussaman curry or already have some tucked away in your freezer. You can also make your own Mussaman curry following the recipe in "Sauces and Salsas, Condiments and Broths" or substitute other curries such as red or green.

This dish is best served with plenty of plain rice.

MAKES 6 MAIN-COURSE SERVINGS

three 2-pound eels or 6 pounds total smaller eels, skinned, cleaned or filleted

salt and pepper

¼ cup peanut oil

2 tablespoons Mussaman curry

1 cup unsweetened coconut milk

2 tablespoons finely chopped fresh cilantro leaves

Cut the eels into 3-inch lengths, season them with salt and pepper, and toss in 2 tablespoons oil.

Prepare the sauce by gently heating the curry in the remaining oil in a heavy pot over medium heat for about 5 minutes, until its fragrance fills the room. Stir with a wooden spoon to prevent burning. Stir in the coconut milk and cilantro and simmer for about 5 minutes.

Grill the eel over medium heat, about 5 inches from the coals, for 8 minutes or more, about 10 minutes per inch of thickness. Because eel is fatty, it may flare up, so arm yourself with a squirt bottle to put out any flames. When the eel is cooked, toss it in the hot sauce and serve on a platter or on hot plates.

Thai-Style Swordfish Satay

(color page 12)

Most of us think of satay as an exclusively Indonesian innovation, but in fact the technique of marinating and grilling on skewers is used throughout Southeast Asia.

Even though most satays are made with meat such as pork or beef, I've had great luck using firm-fleshed fish such as swordfish or tuna or with shellfish such as scallops or shrimp.

The trick to a successful satay is a very hot grill so that the fish browns without overcooking. Satays also get their own special character from being marinated and then served with a fiery sauce.

I've suggested the satay here as a first course, but to make it the focal point of an outdoor barbecue just double the quantities. Serve with a cucumber salad (see box).

MAKES 6 FIRST-COURSE SERVINGS

1½ **pounds swordfish steak, skin and bone removed, cut into 1-inch cubes**

For the Marinade and for Grilling:

2 **garlic cloves, finely chopped**

2 **Thai chilies, seeded and finely chopped**

2 **tablespoons Thai fish sauce**

juice of 1 lime

2 **shallots, finely chopped**

1 **tablespoon sugar**

2 **tablespoons peanut or vegetable oil**

For the Sauce:

3 **Thai chilies, seeded and finely chopped**

2 **shallots, finely chopped**

2 **teaspoons sugar**

juice of 1 lime

2 **tablespoons Thai fish sauce**

1 **cup unsweetened coconut milk**

¼ **cup creamy peanut butter without additives**

2 **tablespoons finely chopped fresh cilantro leaves**

Put the swordfish cubes in a mixing bowl with all the marinade ingredients except the oil. Toss thoroughly to distribute the ingredients evenly and refrigerate, covered, for 2 hours. Toss the cubes every 30 minutes to redistribute the marinade.

Drain the swordfish, discarding the marinade, and thread the cubes on 12 wooden or metal skewers so you'll have 2 skewers per serving. Soak wooden skewers for 30 minutes in water before using them; be sure the pieces of swordfish are touching each other when threaded, and wrap a small piece of aluminum foil around each end to prevent burning. Roll the skewered swordfish cubes in oil and refrigerate until you're ready to grill.

Whisk together all the sauce ingredients until smooth.

Grill the skewers of swordfish about 2 inches above a bed of extremely hot coals, turning once, for about 2 minutes on each side. Serve immediately on hot plates. Place a small bowl of sauce next to each place for dipping the fish.

CUCUMBER SALAD TO SERVE WITH SATAY

This simple sweet-and-sour salad is a perfect foil for the rich savors of a satay.

2 long hothouse cucumbers or 4 short regular cucumbers

2 teaspoons salt

1 Bermuda onion, thinly sliced

2 Thai chilies, seeded and finely chopped

2 tablespoons sugar

1 tablespoon Thai fish sauce

⅓ cup rice wine vinegar or sherry vinegar

MAKES 6 SERVINGS AS AN ACCOMPANIMENT TO SATAY

Peel the cucumbers, slice them in half lengthwise, scoop out the seeds with a spoon, and slice each half into semicircles about ⅛ inch thick. Toss with salt until the slices are well coated and let sit in a colander set over a bowl in the refrigerator for 30 minutes. Squeeze the cucumber slices in your hands to eliminate excess water. Combine the cucumber slices in a salad bowl with the sliced onion. Reserve, covered, in the refrigerator.

Stir together the remaining ingredients until the sugar dissolves. Toss the sauce with the salad just before serving. Serve the salad at the table for guests to help themselves.

GRILL SMOKING

Some cooks like their grilled foods to have a smoky flavor from wood and herbs. American cooks favor hickory, maple, fruitwoods, and mesquite, while cooks in the south of France prefer herbs or fennel branches added to the fire just before grilling. American-style barbecues with covers are useful for this kind of grilling because they help hold in the smoke. While some gas and electric grills allow you to cover the heat element with wood chips to give the foods a smoky flavor, most do not—you'll need to use a wood-burning barbecue. (For authentic hot and cold smoking, see "Marinating, Curing, and Smoking.")

It took me years of fumbling around to come up with a quick method for lightly smoking fish in the barbecue that doesn't leave the fish (or other food) covered with soot. The trick is to push the coals to one side so they're not directly under the food to be smoked.

Grill-Smoked Trout

*T*his technique can be used for almost any whole fish or fish steak, but trout is particularly good because it has a moderately high fat content—always good for grilling— and is easy to find very fresh. Since there is no rule about what kind of wood or herbs is best, part of the fun is experimenting with different flavors. To use this technique successfully you will need a grill with a cover.

MAKES 4 MAIN-COURSE SERVINGS

4 medium trout, cleaned

salt and pepper

1 tablespoon extra-virgin olive oil

vegetable oil for the grill

For Smoking:

2 cups wood chips such as hickory, maple, mesquite, fruitwood (apple, vine cuttings, etc.) or a handful of fresh rosemary or a bundle of dried fennel branches

Season the trout with salt and pepper and roll them in the olive oil. Refrigerate until needed.

Prepare a bed of coals with wood charcoal or briquets. When the coals are completely ignited and covered with a thin coating of ash, push the coals over to one side of the barbecue. Lightly coat the grill with vegetable oil. Put the wood chips on top of the coals.

Quickly wipe the oil off the trout and immediately place the trout on the grill on the opposite side of the coals—so no coals are actually under the trout. Cover the grill and at least partially close the vents to prevent the wood chips or herbs from flaring up. Grill the trout for about 5 minutes on each side (10 minutes total per inch of thickness). You may need to fiddle with the vents on the grill cover to keep the wood chips smoking (rather than flaring) without suffocating the coals.

Serve each guest his or her own trout.

Substitutes Small to medium whole fish with a moderate fat content such as salmon trout, baby coho salmon, small Arctic char, mackerel, Spanish mackerel, pompano, jacks

COATING GRILLED FISH WITH GLAZES AND PASTES

When fish is marinated before grilling, the marinade is usually discarded or brushed lightly on the fish during grilling. Some marinades are thick pastes that are applied to whole fish during cooking so the marinade forms a kind of crust or glaze. These pastes can be as simple as a coating of mustard or as complicated as the Indonesian and Indian spice mixtures given here.

Indonesian-Style Grilled Pompano

*P*ompano is my favorite fish for this dish, but any firm-fleshed whole fish will do. You can also use this technique for cooking firm-fleshed fish steaks and fillets from swordfish, tuna, halibut, or salmon.

MAKES 4 MAIN-COURSE SERVINGS

four 1-pound pompano, cleaned and trimmed

4 shallots, peeled

2 garlic cloves, peeled

2 Thai chilies or 4 jalapeño chilies, seeded

two 5-inch pieces of lemongrass, finely sliced

juice of 2 limes

one 14-ounce can unsweetened coconut milk

2 teaspoons grated fresh ginger

½ teaspoon ground turmeric

1 teaspoon ground coriander

1 tablespoon brown sugar

salt

Refrigerate the pompano until needed.

Chop together the shallots, garlic, chilies, and lemongrass into a paste. If you do this in a blender—by far the easiest method—add the lime juice and, if necessary, some of the coconut milk in increments to get the mixture to move around. Count on at least 15 minutes to chop the mixture by hand.

Combine the paste with the rest of the ingredients in a saucepan and boil the mixture gently, stirring every few minutes to prevent sticking, until it thickens to a thick paste, about 15 minutes. Season with salt to taste. The mixture should be quite salty. Let cool.

Smear both sides of the fish with the paste and let sit for 15 minutes.

Grill the fish over medium heat about 5 inches away from the coals for about 5 minutes on each side. When you've turned the pompano, brush more of the marinade on the cooked side. The grilled pompano should be crispy and golden brown.

Substitutes Medium or small full-flavored fish with moderate to high fat content such as other bluefish, jacks, small coho salmon, mackerel, mullet, Spanish mackerel, trout

❧

Indian-Style Grilled Tuna Steaks with Aromatic Spice Paste

Unlike most marinades, which are wiped off foods before cooking, Indian spice pastes can be left on during grilling so they form a light, savory crust. This spice paste is delicious on any firm-fleshed fish steak.

MAKES 6 MAIN-COURSE SERVINGS

six 1- to 1½-inch-thick (6- to 8-ounce) tuna steaks

2 Thai or serrano chilies, seeded and chopped

2 garlic cloves, chopped

1 small onion, chopped

1 tablespoon grated fresh ginger

1 teaspoon ground turmeric

10 saffron threads, soaked in 2 teaspoons water for 30 minutes

2 tablespoons fresh lemon juice

¼ cup unsweetened coconut milk

2 tablespoons chopped fresh cilantro leaves

salt

Trim any pieces of skin or bone from the fish. Refrigerate, covered with plastic wrap, until needed.

Combine all the remaining ingredients except the salt in a blender and puree the mixture to a smooth paste for about 2 minutes. Season the mixture to taste with salt. Spread the mixture over both sides of the tuna and marinate in the refrigerator for 30 minutes.

Gently transfer the tuna—so the paste doesn't fall off—to a preheated grill. Grill the tuna on both sides 1 to 2 inches above a bed of very hot coals. Remember that tuna will require only about 3 minutes on each side because it should be left rare in the center, while other fish steaks should be cooked all the way through, about 8 minutes per inch of thickness total cooking time. Serve immediately.

Substitutes Any full-flavored firm-fleshed steaks such as king mackerel, salmon, shark, sturgeon, swordfish

BROILING

Broiling is the simple indoor alternative to grilling—the words *broiling* and *grilling* are in fact often used interchangeably. Broiling is actually grilling upside down—a broiler simply grills from above instead of below.

Although broiled foods don't have the aromatic flavor of foods cooked outside on a wood grill, the main advantages of broiling are that most of us have an oven broiler and, because broiling creates little smoke, it can be done indoors. Another advantage is that any fat or oil that drips off the fish will just settle to the bottom instead of dripping down into the coals and making soot-producing flames. Finally, broiled foods are unlikely to stick.

Any fish that can be grilled can also be broiled. Many of the precautions are the same—a light oiling of the fish, careful control of the heat (by adjusting the distance of the fish from the heat source), and careful timing. Foods to be broiled should be placed on a sheet of oiled or buttered aluminum foil to keep the juices from running down into the broiler pan and making a mess. If you're broiling small whole fish—don't try to broil fish larger than 2 pounds—poke the fish about 20 times on each side with a pin. This creates minute holes in the skin and prevents it from blistering. If you're grilling fillets with the skin on, score the skin with shallow diagonal slashes about 1 inch apart so the skin won't contract and cause the fillets to curl. Always preheat the broiler for at least 5 minutes.

The best distance between the heat source and the fish depends on the thickness of the fish and the broiler's heat. As a general rule, a ½-inch-thick fillet should be broiled for about 2 minutes on each side, about 2 inches from the broiler heat. A fillet or whole fish 1 inch thick should be broiled about 4 inches away from the heat for about 4 minutes on each side. If you're broiling fillets with their skin, broil them for about two thirds of the total cooking time with the skin side up so the skin turns crispy. Because home broilers rarely produce as intense heat as restaurant broilers, you may not be able to achieve the crisp or brown outer surface produced in restaurants, especially when broiling thinner whole fish or fillets.

One of the easiest and tastiest tricks for enhancing broiled fish is to dollop each piece with herb butter and then spoon the melted butter over the fish after you arrange the fish on plates. The same sauces that complement grilled fish are good with broiled fish.

❧

Broiled Halibut Steaks with Tarragon Butter

When I first tasted fresh tarragon 20 years ago in a French country restaurant, I was instantly hooked. But when I returned to the United States, I couldn't find it in even the most sophisticated food shops. I tried growing it (I grew a Russian variety with no flavor; a second plant died), and dried tarragon had none of the excitement of fresh. Now fresh tarragon is usually available at fancy grocers; if you can't find it right away, I suggest you persist, because the results are worth it. The tarragon butter called for here is so intensely flavored that you won't need much, but if you're worried about eating too much butter the fish steaks can instead

be brushed with a little olive oil and the chopped tarragon sprinkled on before they are slid under the broiler.

MAKES 4 MAIN-COURSE SERVINGS

1 tablespoon olive oil
four 1-inch-thick 8-ounce halibut steaks
4 tablespoons tarragon or other herb butter (pages 329–331)
salt and pepper
lemon wedges

Cut a sheet of aluminum foil into 4 squares about 4 inches larger than the halibut steaks. Brush each square with olive oil and place a halibut steak in the middle. Fold up the edges of the aluminum foil so they come loosely up the sides of the halibut to capture the butter as it melts.

Preheat the broiler for 5 minutes. Place a tablespoon of tarragon butter in the middle of each steak and season with salt and pepper. Slide the halibut under the broiler with the top of the halibut about 2 inches from the heat source and broil for 4 minutes. Slide out the halibut and turn the steaks over with a spatula, being careful not to spill the butter that will have accumulated in the bottom of the aluminum foil. Broil for 4 minutes more.

Arrange the halibut steaks on hot plates and pour on the butter that has accumulated in each square of foil. Serve immediately.

Substitutes Firm-fleshed steaks or fillets such as bonito, cod, grouper, haddock, king mackerel, salmon, shark, swordfish, tuna (cook tuna for half as long as called for in the recipe), wolffish

QUICK BROILING

Most fish is broiled for several minutes on one side and then turned over so the cooking can continue on the second side. "Quick" broiling is a favorite technique in French restaurants, where thin slices of fish are broiled on one side only, either directly on the plate or on a baking sheet. Usually these thin slices are then brushed with a delicate sauce. The results can be delicious.

Careful timing of quick-broiled dishes is so important—the fish cooks in seconds—that if your broiler is on the bottom of your oven, you may have to get down on the floor so you can see the fish cooking.

Salmon with Hazelnut Aigrelette

(color page 16)

This dish is one of my favorite ways to eat salmon—the salmon is thinly sliced, broiled for just a few seconds, and brushed with a delicious and strikingly green hazelnut sauce. I was taught a dish similar to this during my apprenticeship at a three-star restaurant in the Burgundy region of eastern France.

Aigrelette means "a little sour" and can refer to any sauce containing vinegar or lemon juice. Strictly speaking, the *aigrelette* given here is a mayonnaise flavored with hazelnut oil. If you don't have any hazelnut oil, almost any homemade mayonnaise will work, provided it's well seasoned with salt and vinegar or lemon juice. *Aigrelette* sauce looks most dramatic when colored with green mustard such as Maille brand *moutarde aux fines herbes*, but a sharp-flavored mustard such as Grey Poupon Dijon also works well. Remember when tasting the sauce for seasoning that it should seem too salty and too acidic because it will be the salmon's only seasoning.

A certain amount of skill is required to cut the salmon into thin slices, but fortunately the fish can be sliced and the sauce prepared earlier in the day. Don't try to substitute other fish; only salmon has the high fat content needed to keep the dish moist.

MAKES 4 MAIN-COURSE OR 8 FIRST-COURSE SERVINGS

1½ to 2 pounds salmon fillet in one piece with skin

1 tablespoon flavorless oil such as safflower or canola

For the Aigrelette Sauce:

1 egg yolk

1 tablespoon mustard

1 teaspoon sea salt

½ cup flavorless vegetable oil such as safflower or canola

2 tablespoons sherry vinegar or white wine vinegar

2 tablespoons hazelnut oil or more to taste

1 tablespoon very finely chopped fresh chervil or parsley

Select four 10- to 12-inch or eight 8- to 9-inch ovenproof plates. Cut 4 or 8 squares of wax paper or aluminum foil large enough to cover each plate. Very lightly brush the paper or foil with oil.

Place one of the sheets of wax paper or foil oil side up over each plate. Slice the salmon into thin sheets with a very sharp flexible knife as you would slice smoked salmon (page 102) and arrange the sheets on the wax paper in the same way as they will appear on the plate—over the whole surface except for the rim. The least attractive side of the salmon slices should be

facing up on the paper so that it will end up facing down when inverted onto the hot plate.

Prepare the *aigrelette* sauce by combining the egg yolk with the mustard and salt and slowly working in the vegetable oil, either by hand or in a food processor. Slowly stir in the remaining ingredients. Taste the sauce and add more salt or vinegar if it's not fairly sharp.

Light the broiler and heat the plates in the oven. (If your broiler is part of the oven, leave the oven door open so the plates don't get too hot.)

Brush each hot plate very lightly with vegetable oil and quickly turn over the sheets of salmon onto each plate. Peel back the paper or foil and slide the plates—you'll probably have to do them one at a time—under the broiler. Rotate them so the salmon cooks evenly. The time needed to cook the salmon will vary considerably depending on how thinly you managed to slice it. Very thinly sliced salmon will cook in as little as 30 seconds, while thicker salmon—say ¼ inch—may take close to 3 minutes. You may need to cut carefully into the salmon every 30 seconds or so to make sure it is cooked properly. When the salmon is done, remove each plate, brush with a thin layer of *aigrelette* sauce, and serve immediately. (Or keep warm in the oven while you're finishing the last plates.)

Broiled Striped Bass Fillets with Mustard and Tomato Sauce

These broiled fillets are served with two tangy, sizzling sauces—a simple mustard sauce made of whole-grain mustard and cream and a tomato sauce made of cooked and pureed tomatoes. The tomato sauce is spooned under the fish and makes a striking red background for the mustard-glazed fish.

Like all quick-broiled fish, this dish must be done at the very last minute—while the guests are at the table. Fortunately, you can prepare the sauces in advance and arrange the fish on the baking sheet and keep it in the refrigerator until needed. Be sure to serve it as soon as it comes out of the oven, piping hot.

Don't worry if you don't have access to striped bass. Any firm, white-fleshed fish will do, but the fillets should be large enough that you can cut them into 3-inch squares. You can also serve this dish as a main course by doubling the quantities.

MAKES 4 FIRST-COURSE SERVINGS

two 8-ounce striped bass fillets, skin and small bones removed

2 tablespoons olive oil

For the Mustard Sauce:

1 tablespoon whole-grain mustard (*moutarde de Meaux*)

2 tablespoons crème fraîche or ¼ cup heavy cream, whipped

freshly ground white pepper

For the Tomatoes:

2 ripe tomatoes

salt and pepper

continued

Cut each fillet into two 3-inch squares. If the fillets are more than $\frac{1}{2}$ inch thick, butterfly them by cutting sideways almost all the way through with a sharp knife and folding them open so they end up between $\frac{1}{4}$ and $\frac{1}{2}$ inch thick.

Whisk together the mustard and the crème fraîche. Season to taste with pepper and refrigerate until needed.

Cut the tomatoes in half crosswise, squeeze each half to eliminate seeds, and chop coarsely. Cook the tomatoes over medium heat in a small saucepan, stirring every few minutes to prevent sticking. When the tomatoes have cooked down to a thick paste, after about 15 minutes, work them through a strainer with the back of a small ladle. Season the tomato sauce with salt and pepper to taste.

Light the broiler and heat large dinner plates in a 200°F oven. (If you have only one oven, leave the door open so the plates don't get too hot.) Arrange the fish fillets—most attractive side up—on a baking sheet brushed with olive oil and spread about $\frac{1}{2}$ tablespoon of mustard sauce on top of each fillet. Heat the tomato sauce on low heat or in a bowl in the microwave.

Slide the baking sheet under the broiler so the tops of the fillets are within 2 inches of the heat source. You may have to move the baking sheet around so each fillet cooks evenly. Broil until the sauce on each fillet sizzles and browns lightly, $1\frac{1}{2}$ to 3 minutes. (The fish cooks most of the way through under the broiler; the underside cooks on the plate.)

Spread the tomato sauce in a circle in the center of each of the hot plates. Place a hot fillet in the center of the sauce and serve immediately.

Substitutes Any pale firm-fleshed delicately flavored fillets such as black sea bass, cod, grouper, haddock, hake, John Dory, lingcod, mahimahi, ocean perch, rockfish, sablefish, skate, snapper, tilefish, wahoo, walleye, wolffish

Poaching

My first sight of a whole poached salmon was at a grown-up party when I was about 10 years old. The fish was covered from head to tail with sliced cucumber scales, and a pastry head and tail replaced the real things. I watched sadly as the guests gradually devoured it.

Poached fish needn't be as grandiose or elaborate as a whole salmon, and in fact poaching works for small chunks or single fillets as well as for whole fish. Poaching has the advantage of not interfering with the taste of delicately flavored fish, requiring no fats, and being quick and easy (although there are a few wonderfully complicated variations). Fish is poached by simmering it gently in just enough liquid to cover.

EQUIPMENT

The equipment you need depends on the size or number of fish you'll be poaching. The most practical and convenient piece of equipment for poaching fish is a fish poacher—an elongated pot with a lid and rack for holding the fish, available in various sizes for different-size fish. The advantage of a poacher is that the rack prevents the fish from falling apart when taken out of the poacher.

The disadvantages are that fish poachers are expensive—especially if you want more than one—and take up a lot of space in the kitchen. Unless you want to poach very large fish (e.g., a whole salmon) or poach fish often, you'll probably want to improvise a technique for using an ordinary pot or pan instead.

The easiest way to poach small fish (up to 12 inches) is to use a skillet, a small roasting pan, or, best of all, an oval sauté pan. What's important is that the pan fit the fish as closely as possible—so you'll need a minimum of poaching liquid—and that the sides be higher than the fish is thick so you'll be able to add enough liquid to cover.

When poaching fish in anything other than a fish poacher, the trick is getting the cooked fish out and onto a plate or platter. The best way to do this is to use a long wide spatula—like the kind you see in diners for flipping pancakes or hamburgers. When it's time to take the fish out of the poaching liquid, you just slide the spatula *lengthwise* under the fish and carefully lift it out.

Another almost foolproof method for getting poached fish out of the simmering liquid is to wrap each fish in a sheet of cheesecloth, leaving an inch or two of extra cloth at each end, and then tying the ends with string. The cheesecloth will help hold the fish together, and you'll be able to grab the cheesecloth at one end while taking the fish out of the liquid.

Poaching whole flatfish such as sole or flounder has its own problems. Because flatfish are wide, the fish may break if you try to lift it out with a spatula. The French, who seem to have a piece of equipment for every eventuality, have a special diamond-shaped fish poacher—a turbotière—designed specifically for flatfish. Assuming you're not running right out to pick up a turbotière, try setting a round cake rack in a skillet. The top of the cake rack should be about 1/2 inch from the bottom of the skillet. If it's higher than this, bend down the little legs with pliers. Tie two lengths of string at two places on each side of the cake rack to use as handles. When it comes time to poach the flatfish, set it on the cake rack and lower it into the pan of simmering liquid using the two string handles.

THE POACHING LIQUID

The first question most cooks ask when setting out to poach fish is what liquid to poach them in. This depends on the style of the finished dish and how much effort you're willing to expend. Many an evening I arrive home, fish in hand, only to slip my fish into a pan of simmering salted water. At more conscientious moments I may simmer a bay leaf, a sliced onion, a glass of white wine, and perhaps a sprig of thyme in the water for 10 minutes before adding the fish, but even these small refinements aren't essential. If I'm having company, I stick more to tradition and prepare a vegetable broth, a fish broth, or a Japanese-style poaching liquid.

Vegetable broth is the poaching liquid most often used in France and in most European countries. It's easy to make, and once you've used it for poaching fish you can save it to use again—it freezes well for months—or add it to a fish soup.

Fish broth can also be used to poach fish. It's similar to vegetable broth except fish bones and heads are included along with vegetables. I usually use fish broth only when I'm poaching fillets and can't bear to throw out the heads and bones.

Japanese cooks use combinations of flavorful ingredients—dashi, soy sauce, mirin, sake, and sometimes miso—to make distinctive and elegant fish dishes.

MAKING VEGETABLE BROTH FOR POACHING FISH

À LA NAGE METHOD

One of the best and easiest ways to poach fish is to make a simple broth with vegetables, herbs, and a little white wine. (Vegetable broth is often called *court bouillon,* which loosely means "quick broth.") Vegetable broth is used in one of two ways. In the first the vegetables are chopped and simmered in water for about 30 minutes, the broth is strained, and the vegetables are discarded. In the second method, *à la nage,* the vegetables are cut decoratively, and the fish is served in wide bowls surrounded by some of the vegetable broth and its vegetables.

Although recipes for vegetable broth usually give rigid directions for how much of each vegetable to use, I take a free-and-easy approach and rummage around in the refrigerator to use what I have on hand. A traditional court bouillon is made with carrots, onions, celery, and a bouquet garni, but I sometimes include a peeled clove of garlic or two, fennel, leeks, turnips, mushrooms (wild or cultivated, dried or fresh), various herbs (such as tarragon, cilantro, or dill), tomatoes (peeled, seeded, chopped), lemons or limes (peeled and sliced), fresh ginger (peeled and chopped), or saffron.

Whichever method you use, cut the vegetables approximately the same size so that they'll all cook at the same time. If you decide to serve the fish *à la nage,* you'll need to cut them more carefully than you might otherwise. This may be a simple matter of slicing the carrots into even rounds or of thinly slicing the onions. You can also get more elaborate and make lengthwise gouges in the carrots so that when you slice them they

have a decorative cogwheel shape. One of my favorite methods for serving fish *à la nage* is to finely julienne the vegetables and then serve them over and around the poached fish.

Basic Vegetable Broth for Poaching Fish

COURT BOUILLON

Vegetable broth is a light and refreshing alternative to fish broth, and when well made—with plenty of fresh vegetables—will impart a delicate and intriguing flavor to poached seafood. The broth can be used again and again—frozen between uses—and after several uses will transform itself into a full-flavored fish broth.

Some of the ingredients for vegetable broth are added in stages. Because the acidity of white wine causes vegetables to release their flavor more slowly, it is added only once the vegetables begin to soften. Pepper, when cooked for too long in simmering liquid, will turn harsh. It should be cooked for no longer than 5 minutes.

MAKES 6 CUPS

3 medium onions, sliced

2 carrots, sliced

2 celery stalks, sliced

a large bouquet garni: 4 fresh thyme sprigs or ¾ teaspoon dried, a medium bunch of parsley, and a large bay leaf tied up with string (or in cheesecloth for dried thyme)

6 cups water

2 cups dry white wine

10 black peppercorns, crushed (optional)

Combine the vegetables and bouquet garni in a 4-quart pot and add the water. Bring to a slow simmer and simmer gently, partially covered, for 20 minutes. Add the wine, simmer for 10 minutes more, and then add the crushed peppercorns if you're using them. Simmer for 5 minutes longer. Strain.

Salmon Fillets à la Nage with Julienned Vegetables

My guests always let out a sigh of delight when I set down soup plates of poached salmon, each slice half-covered with a bright tangle of julienned vegetables. Cutting the vegetables into fine julienne takes time, but the final arrangement of the salmon and vegetables on the plate isn't fussy at all; in fact the whole thing looks more inviting when the vegetables are tossed on in a spontaneous heap. This is one of few fat-free dishes that is so satisfying it doesn't leave me craving something richer.

Although this is a great method for cooking salmon fillets, it will work with practically any delicately flavored fish. Avoid strong-flavored oily fish such as bluefish and extremely fragile fish such as whiting.

The principle behind this dish is that a vegetable broth is prepared with julienned vegetables so that the vegetables can be used as a decorative garnish.

Buy salmon from the plump front or middle of the fillet—avoid the tail piece, which won't look as appealing on the plate.

Although this dish is somewhat time-consuming—julienning vegetables takes a while—the vegetable

broth can be made earlier the same day or even the day before.

MAKES 4 MAIN-COURSE SERVINGS

one 1¼-pound center-cut salmon fillet, skin removed

salt and pepper

2 medium leeks, including 1 inch of green

2 large carrots, peeled

1 medium turnip, peeled

1 celery stalk

1 bouquet garni: 3 fresh thyme sprigs or ½ teaspoon dried, a small bunch of parsley, and a bay leaf tied up with string (or in cheesecloth for dried thyme)

1 cup dry white wine

1 tablespoon finely chopped parsley

Pull the tiny bones out of the salmon fillet with tweezers, needlenose pliers, or a strong thumbnail. Cut the salmon crosswise into 4 sections. Fold under the thin stomach flaps so each section is of even thickness. Sprinkle with salt and pepper and reserve in the refrigerator.

Cut the leeks in half lengthwise and hold them under running water while flipping through the leaves to rinse out any sand. Cut the leaves 2 or 3 at a time into fine julienne. If the leaves are more than 4 or 5 inches long, fold them under to make them easier to julienne.

Julienne the carrots and turnip into 3-inch lengths. The easiest way to do this is first to slice them with a benriner cutter (a Japanese slicer) and then with a chef's knife.

Cut the celery stalk into 4-inch sections and julienne it as finely as possible.

Combine the julienned vegetables, bouquet garni, and just enough water to cover—about a quart—in a 4-quart pot. Simmer gently, partially covered, for 15 minutes. Add the wine and simmer for 10 minutes more. Strain the vegetable broth, reserving the cooked vegetables and broth.

About 10 minutes before you're ready to serve, put the cooked vegetables with ¼ cup of the broth in a covered saucepan over low heat.

Bring the remaining vegetable broth to a simmer in a sauté pan just large enough to hold the salmon in a single layer. (If the pan is too large, there won't be enough liquid to cover.) Gently slide the salmon into the simmering broth. If there's not enough liquid to cover, add just enough hot water to cover the salmon. Poach the salmon for 8 minutes per inch of thickness. (You can carefully cut into a piece with a paring knife and check the color, which should have just a

---

WHAT ABOUT THE SKIN?

When grilling, sautéing, or broiling, it is often best to leave the skin on whole fish or fillets as a crispy accent to the finished dish. Because poached fish skin takes on an unpleasant rubbery consistency, it is usually taken off before or after the fish is cooked.

When poaching whole fish, it is easiest to remove the skin immediately *after* the fish is poached. Just cut into the base of the head with a paring knife, peel back a fold of skin, and then pull it away with your fingers. It usually peels right off. Don't let the fish cool before removing the skin or it may stick and tear. For some dishes such as trout *au bleu*, the skin is left on so the diners can remove it themselves.

When poaching fillets, it's easiest to remove the skin *before* poaching.

---

trace of transparent bright orange flesh in the middle.)

Spread three quarters of the julienned vegetables in hot soup plates. Carefully arrange the salmon on the vegetables.

Add the chopped parsley to the simmering poaching liquid, season the liquid with salt and pepper, and ladle enough over the fish to come about a third of the way up the sides of the fish. Arrange the rest of the julienne over the fish.

Serve with knife, fork, and soup spoon.

Substitutes Any firm- or moderately firm-fleshed delicately flavored fillet or shellfish such as blackfish, cod, Dover sole, grouper, king mackerel, lingcod, ocean perch, pollack, rockfish, scallops, shrimp, striped bass, tilefish

---

HOW MUCH BROTH TO MAKE?

Unless you plan to make extra broth for freezing, you'll need to guess how much you need for a particular dish. The exact amount will depend on the shape of the fish and the container you're using for poaching. Usually a quart of broth is enough for a pound of fish. If you've made a batch of vegetable or fish broth and find that you don't have enough, just add a little extra water.

POACHING WHOLE SMALL FISH

AU BLEU

Poaching is an easy technique for cooking small whole fish such as trout, small sea bass or striped bass, or porgies, but serving whole fish can be tricky. Some guests don't even like to see the fish's head, much less contend with skinning and filleting their own cooked fish at the table. If you're unsure of your guests, don't serve whole fish. If you know your guests to be relatively adventurous, make a game of it and give a little tableside fish-filleting demonstration.

❧

Trout au Bleu

Once in a French restaurant in Vermont I asked if they could make me a trout *au bleu* (blue style). After all, they had trout on the menu (amandine, I think), and there was a lively stream running not so far away . . . But alas after a short negotiation the chef came out and admitted that all the trout had been frozen and shipped from a trout farm. You can't make trout *au bleu* from a frozen trout because for the trout to turn blue and curl in the characteristic way, it must be very fresh, almost alive.

Trout *au bleu* is made by poaching very fresh trout in vegetable broth containing vinegar. Traditionally the trout is then served with a hollandaise or rich butter sauce, but you can make the dish much lighter by serving it surrounded by a little of its own broth. Trout that is *very* fresh is slippery and should be almost impossible to hold. Your best bet is to buy it from

a store that has it live in tanks—and then rush home. When the trout is poached, the vinegar causes the slippery trout skin to turn blue.

The vegetable broth for trout *au bleu* can be made a day or two in advance, but cook the trout the same day you buy it.

MAKES 4 MAIN-COURSE SERVINGS

four 12-ounce very fresh trout, gutted

2 medium carrots, sliced into ⅛-inch rounds

2 medium red onions, very thinly sliced

1 celery stalk, thinly sliced

1 bouquet garni: 3 fresh thyme sprigs or ½ teaspoon dried, a small bunch of parsley, and a bay leaf tied up with string (or in cheesecloth for dried thyme)

1 cup good-quality white wine vinegar

1 tablespoon finely chopped parsley

1 cup hollandaise (page 335) or beurre blanc (page 333) (optional)

Wrap the trout in wax paper or plastic wrap as soon as you get them home. Don't wrap them in anything absorbent such as a towel, or you might damage the slippery skin.

Combine the vegetables and bouquet garni in a 4-quart pot. Add just enough water to cover. Simmer gently for 15 minutes, add the vinegar, and simmer for 10 minutes more.

Strain the hot broth into a sauté pan or roasting pan just large enough to hold the trout. Place the pan on the stove over medium heat. Quickly rinse the trout in cold water and slide them into the simmering broth. Adjust the heat to maintain a gentle simmer. If there isn't enough broth to cover the trout, baste them with a spoon or add just enough hot water to cover.

After about 7 minutes (8 minutes per inch of thickness at the thickest part), stick a paring knife into the back of one of the trout and try gently to pull the flesh away from the backbone. If the flesh sticks to the bone, poach the trout for a minute or two more. Keep testing until the trout are done.

Take the trout out of the broth with a long spatula and serve each guest a whole trout on a plate, oval gratin dish, or platter set to the side. Place a hot plate in front of each guest with 2 tablespoons for serving the trout. Add the parsley to a cup of the hot vegetable broth and serve it in a sauceboat at the table. Or, if you prefer, serve the hollandaise or beurre blanc.

MAKING FISH BROTH FOR POACHING FISH

I usually make fish broth only when I've had the fishmonger save me the head and bones after filleting a whole fish, but you can buy fish heads at an ethnic market as well. I also make a fish broth if I'm going to convert the poaching liquid into a sauce once the fish is cooked—fish broth has a fuller flavor than vegetable broth and will support stronger-flavored ingredients. See the recipe on page 281.

MAKING CLEAR FISH BROTH

One of the annoying things about fish broth is that it is usually cloudy. If you're enriching or thickening the finished poaching liquid with butter, cream, or vegetable purees (more about this later), a cloudy broth isn't a problem—the finished liquid will be opaque anyway. But if you want to present pieces of poached fish surrounded with a sparkling clear broth, you'll need to clarify the broth. There are three ways to do this:

1. Put the broth in a container in the refrigerator all day or overnight so the solid particles settle to the bottom. Carefully spoon out the top two thirds

of the broth, which should have gelled in the refrigerator and should be clear. Save the cloudy broth at the bottom for another recipe.
2. Strain the warm broth through a cloth napkin (well rinsed to remove traces of soap or bleach) or coffee filter.
3. Clarify the fish broth with egg whites as directed in the basic fish consommé recipe (page 281). Since I go through this process only for fancy dishes such as a seafood *pot-au-feu*, I like to fortify the flavor of the fish broth with extra fish during the clarification process.

❧

Fish and Shellfish Pot-au-Feu

*T*his is one of the most dramatically beautiful and colorful seafood dishes I've ever encountered. While a seafood *pot-au-feu* is a bit complicated to make, almost everything can be prepared in advance.

A traditional *pot-au-feu* is made by simmering cuts of meat and vegetables in water or broth for several hours and then serving a bowl of the broth followed by a plate of the poached meats and vegetables. Contemporary French cooks have stretched the *pot-au-feu* idea to include seafood. A seafood *pot-au-feu* is made by poaching different kinds of seafood in a clear broth and then serving everything together in wide soup plates. It's an elegant and versatile approach to cooking fish, and it's virtually fat-free.

In addition to different kinds of fish and shellfish, vegetables and herbs can also be included to make the *pot-au-feu* more substantial—so

you can serve it as a main course—and also to provide color.

MAKES 4 MAIN-COURSE SERVINGS

2 pounds assorted fish and shellfish (at least 3 kinds), such as scallops, sliced into ½-inch-thick disks; shrimp or crayfish, peeled and deveined; salmon, cut into 1-inch-thick squares or rectangles; fillets of red snapper, striped bass, etc., skin left on and scored to prevent curling, fillets cut into approximately 4-ounce sections; lobster medallions, live lobster precooked for about 6 minutes in a pot of boiling water, meat removed (2 pounds live lobster gives ½ pound meat); oysters, shucked; mussels or clams, steamed open, top shell removed

1 small fennel bulb

1 quart clear fish broth (this page)

4 scallions

salt

1 medium carrot, cut into fine julienne

1 large tomato

3 tablespoons finely chopped parsley or fresh chervil

Prepare the seafood, making sure you have the same number of pieces of each for each serving. Keep track of how many you have so when it comes time to serve you know how many pieces of each to put in the bowls.

Cut the stems and fronds off the fennel bulb. Save a few sprigs from the fronds to decorate the broth. Cut the bulb in half through the core. Cut 4 wedges out of each half, being sure to leave some of the core attached to each wedge so the wedges don't fall apart. Spread the wedges in a single layer in a nonaluminum pan with just enough broth to come halfway up their sides. Simmer the wedges, covered, over low to medium heat for about 20 minutes, until they soften but retain a little crunch. Drain, adding the braising liquid to the fish broth, and reserve.

continued

Trim the scallions, leaving about 2 inches of green. Simmer them for about 2 minutes in boiling salted water.

Simmer the julienned carrots for about 5 minutes in the clear fish broth/fennel-cooking liquid. Drain and reserve both broth and carrots.

Peel the tomato by plunging it into boiling water for about 15 seconds, quickly rinsing it in cold water and then pulling off the peel with a paring knife. Cut the tomato into wedges, push out the seeds with your finger, and cut away and discard the inner pulpy section from the inside of each wedge. Cut the outer part of the wedges into 1/4-inch cubes. Reserve.

Last-Minute Poaching and Serving:
Bring the clear broth to a gentle simmer in a sauté pan large enough to hold the seafood in a single layer. Place the vegetables in a pan or bowl covered with aluminum foil and slide them into a 250°F oven to warm for 15 minutes. Heat the tomatoes in a separate bowl. Slide the fish or shellfish into the simmering broth, putting thicker pieces in first. Fish or raw shellfish should be simmered for about 8 minutes per inch of thickness while precooked shellfish need only be heated in the simmering broth for about 15 seconds.

Arrange the seafood and vegetables in wide hot soup plates. Stir the chopped parsley or chervil and the tomatoes into the hot broth. Simmer for 30 seconds and carefully ladle the broth over and around the seafood. Serve immediately.

POACHING LARGE FISH

A fish poacher is almost essential for poaching large whole fish such as salmon. Large fish are poached in the same way as whole smaller fish except that they are started out in *cold* liquid while small fish are started in hot. A large fish plunged into simmering liquid will overcook on the outside and remain raw inside. Small fish, on the other hand, if started in cold liquid, will overcook by the time the liquid comes to a simmer.

Large poached whole fish are best served either hot or cold at buffets, where presenting the whole fish makes an impressive sight. If you're serving the whole fish on plates in the kitchen, you're better off poaching the fish in individual portions—it will be easier to control the cooking and easier to serve.

SERVING LARGE POACHED WHOLE FISH

As mentioned earlier, most people don't like the slippery texture of poached fish skin, so it is best to peel off the skin before serving. Follow the directions on page 67, but for a large fish don't bother peeling the skin off the underside, which would involve turning over the fragile cooked fish. Also gently pull out any remaining fins that run along the back of the fish.

You can set a whole poached fish on a buffet for guests to help themselves, but you'd be better off having someone serve—guests have a way of mangling a whole fish. The easiest way to carve a whole fish is to cut along the dark lateral line down to the backbone or ribs and then pull away the portions with two spoons. When the top side has been served, the whole head and spinal column can be gently pulled away and the fish from the "inside" served. The skin on the underside can be left clinging to the platter.

Whether to serve a whole fish hot or cold will depend on the season and the setting. A hot fish is best served in an atmosphere where it can be served quickly without getting cold. For a prolonged buffet, where the fish will have to sit for a half hour or more, a cold fish is better.

Poached Whole Salmon

When I really want to pull out all the stops to impress my guests, a whole poached salmon resplendent on a long oval platter (borrowed from a neighbor) is just the thing. This is one situation where you really will need a fish poacher—using another less stable method may leave you scraping the fish off the floor.

Most whole salmon weigh between 8 and 12 pounds, but the 10-pound size is the most common. If you're in a large city with several fish stores, it will pay to shop around for your salmon—some places charge twice as much as others.

MAKES 12 TO 15 MAIN-COURSE SERVINGS, TWICE AS MANY AT A BUFFET WITH OTHER FOODS

one 10-pound salmon (after gutting—most salmon is sold already gutted)

5 quarts fish broth (page 343) or vegetable broth (page 66)

Place the salmon in the fish poacher and add enough cold broth to cover. If you find you don't have enough broth, add water. Put the lid on the poacher.

Place the fish poacher on the stove—you'll need to use 2 burners—over medium heat. Check the poaching liquid after about 10 minutes.

When it starts to boil, turn down the heat to maintain a gentle simmer.

While the poaching usually takes somewhat longer, I start checking a 10-pound salmon 25 minutes from the time the poaching liquid comes to a simmer. To check for doneness, gently lift the poaching rack and insert an instant-read thermometer into the backbone next to the dorsal fins. It's best to get someone to help with this, but if there's no one around, set the rack with the salmon on a cutting board. The salmon is done when the thermometer reads 135°F. If you don't have a thermometer, insert a small paring knife along the backbone and peek in—the flesh should separate easily from the bone and should be pink instead of translucent red.

Drain the fish, peel off the top skin, and serve hot or cold.

Substitutes Large and attractive whole fish such as large drums, king mackerel, red snapper, large rockfish, large striped bass, tilefish

SAUCES FOR POACHED FISH

Because poached fish has a delicate and subtle flavor, it's delicious with a delicately flavored sauce. Making a sauce for poached fish can be approached in one of three ways:
1. You can serve a classic sauce such as a flavored butter, beurre blanc, hollandaise, mayonnaise, or vinaigrette (see "Sauces and Salsas, Condiments and Broths").
2. You can make a sauce out of the liquid used for poaching the fish.
3. You can use a combination of methods and combine a classic sauce with the fish-poaching liquid to come up with a light brothlike sauce.

CLASSIC SAUCES FOR POACHED FISH

While hot poached fish is best served with a butter-based sauce such as a beurre blanc, hollandaise, or a flavored butter or oil, cold poached fish can also be served with a homemade mayonnaise or vinaigrette. The mayonnaise variations and the vinaigrettes in "Sauces and Salsas, Condiments and Broths" are especially delicious.

MAKING BROTHLIKE SAUCES

One of the most elegant ways to serve fish is to combine some of the liquid used for poaching the fish with a classic sauce such as a beurre blanc, hollandaise, béarnaise, or mayonnaise. The result is a sauce with more body than a piece of fish served surrounded with its own poaching liquid (as in dishes served *à la nage*), but at the same time the sauce is much lighter than a classic butter sauce.

❧

Assorted Fish and Shellfish with Butter-Enriched Poaching Liquid

(color page 4)

While presenting a dish *à la nage* is a lean and attractive way to serve fish or shellfish, you can give the broth a deeper and more intriguing flavor by combining it with butter. Best of all, you can use combinations of flavored butters, which are in turn combined with the poaching liquid just before serving. I like to play around with bits of herb butter I have in the freezer.

In the version given here, the poaching liquid is combined with

parsley butter, lobster butter, and truffle butter. If you're not feeling this extravagant, substitute tomato butter for the lobster butter and morel butter for the truffle butter. Or just play around and use whatever butters you like.

Flavored butters should not be whisked directly into a large amount of the hot poaching liquid, or they may separate. It is better to whisk the butter into a few tablespoons of the hot poaching liquid over medium heat—in the same way as making a beurre blanc—and then combine this butter sauce with an equal part of the remaining poaching liquid.

MAKES 6 MAIN-COURSE SERVINGS

2 pounds assorted fish fillets and shellfish (a total of at least 3 kinds) such as scallops, lobster tails out of the shell, crayfish tails, shucked oysters

1 large carrot, cut into fine julienne

2 medium leeks, white parts only, cut into fine julienne

1 celery stalk, cut into fine julienne

1 medium turnip, peeled and cut into fine julienne

1 large bouquet garni: 4 fresh thyme sprigs or ³⁄₄ teaspoon dried, a medium bunch of parsley, and a large bay leaf tied up with string (or in cheesecloth for dried thyme)

1 cup dry white wine

2 tablespoons heavy cream

¹⁄₄ cup parsley butter (page 331) or unsalted butter

¹⁄₄ cup truffle butter (page 332), morel butter (page 331), or unsalted butter

¹⁄₄ cup lobster butter (page 330), tomato butter (page 332), or unsalted butter

salt and pepper

fresh lemon juice to taste

Cut the fish and shellfish into 6 pieces each for poaching. If some of the shellfish, such as the lobster or crayfish tails, has been precooked, these should be sliced and warmed gently in the poaching liquid just before serving.

Combine the julienned vegetables and the bouquet garni in a saucepan. Pour in the white wine and enough water just to cover, about 3 cups. Cover the pot and simmer the vegetables for about 25 minutes, until they retain only a slight crunch.

Strain the vegetables and reserve the liquid and vegetables separately until needed.

Bring ¼ cup of the reserved vegetable broth to a simmer in a 1-quart saucepan and add the heavy cream. Whisk the parsley and truffle butters or unsalted butter into the hot liquid over medium heat and then whisk in the lobster butter or the last of the unsalted butter. Keep this sauce warm.

Just before serving, poach or reheat the seafood in the vegetable broth. Chunks of raw seafood should be simmered gently for about 8 minutes per inch of thickness; precooked shellfish such as lobster medallions should be just heated through for 20 to 30 seconds. Reheat the julienned vegetables in a small amount of the vegetable broth. Arrange the seafood and vegetables in bowls or deep plates. Whisk ½ cup of the vegetable broth into the herb butter sauce and season to taste with salt, pepper, and lemon juice. Ladle the sauce over and around the seafood and vegetables.

Shrimp and Red Snapper Fillets en Bourride

*I*f you happen to be a lover of garlic, you'll love bourride. The genius behind this dish is that the garlic is worked into a homemade mayonnaise and incorporated into the dish just before serving so the garlic barely cooks, keeping all of its pungency.

Bourride is from Provence and is made by poaching fish fillets in a broth made with aromatic vegetables and the trimmings from the fish. When the fish is cooked, the poaching liquid is strained and whisked into an aïoli—a garlic mayonnaise—that binds it lightly and makes it explode with flavor.

Although a bourride requires some last-minute cooking, the fish broth and aïoli can be made earlier in the day.

MAKES 6 MAIN-COURSE SERVINGS

4 pounds whole red snapper, filleted, with or without skin, bones reserved

1½ pounds headless shrimp or 2 pounds with heads, which is preferable, peeled, shells and heads reserved

1 medium onion, coarsely chopped

1 bouquet garni: 3 fresh thyme sprigs or ½ teaspoon dried, a small bunch of parsley, a bay leaf, and a strip of dried orange rind tied up with string (or in cheesecloth for dried thyme)

branches and green fronds from a small fennel bulb

6 slices French bread from a large round or fat loaf, lightly toasted

2 cups aïoli (page 334)

salt and pepper

extra toast

Remove the gills from the fish heads and soak the bones and heads in cold water for 30 minutes.

Drain the fish bones and heads and combine them in a 4-quart pot with the shrimp shells and heads, onion, bouquet garni, and fennel branches. (The fennel greens can be saved to decorate the finished bourride and the bulb can be used in another recipe or cut into wedges, lightly braised in some of the fish broth, and used as a garnish.)

Add enough water to barely cover the fish bones, shrimp shells, and vegetables and simmer gently for 20 minutes. Strain the broth into a straight-sided sauté pan large enough to hold the fish fillets in a single layer.

About 10 minutes before serving, place a slice of the toasted French bread in the bottom of each serving bowl. Bring the fish broth to a simmer on top of the stove and carefully slide in the filleted fish. Poach the fillets for about 5 minutes (8 minutes per inch of thickness) and poach the shrimp for about 2 minutes. Place the pieces of fish over the bread in the serving bowls and the shrimp around it.

Finish the broth by placing a cup of the aïoli in a stainless-steel bowl and ladling 3 cups of the hot poaching liquid into the aïoli while whisking. (Any extra poaching liquid can be saved for another recipe.) Add salt and pepper to taste. Place the bowl of sauce over medium heat while whisking constantly to reheat the mixture. Don't let the sauce boil, or the egg yolks will curdle. Ladle the sauce over the hot poached fish and shrimp. Decorate with sprigs of fennel green.

Pass the remaining aïoli at the table along with the extra toasts.

Substitutes Whole firm-fleshed delicately flavored fish such as sea bass, striped bass, John Dory, rockfish, tilapia, or walleye. If you use a fish such as monkfish—traditional in a bourride—that provides little in the way of head or bones, you'll need to prepare a fish stock with bones from other fish. I prefer to leave the skin on fish for a bourride, but this is up to you. If you do leave the skin, make sure the fish has been scaled thoroughly.

GARNISHES FOR POACHED FISH

An assortment of poached fish fillets surrounded by colorful broth can be made even more dramatic by adding vegetables. Finely chopped herbs such as parsley, tarragon, chervil, or chives can be added to the broth at the last minute. Peeled, seeded, and chopped tomatoes placed on the fish fillets or casually arranged in the broth provide contrasting flavor and color. Sauces such as aïoli or beurre blanc–style butter sauces made with herb butter can be drizzled over the finished dishes—à la Jackson Pollock—to provide more color and flavor contrast.

Vegetables also make the dish more substantial and suitable as a main course. Try fennel wedges (braised in water and white wine), baby artichokes (simmered in water with a little lemon juice), sautéed mushrooms (wild or cultivated, sprinkled with Provençal herbs such as thyme, marjoram, or lavender flowers), French green beans (blanched), fresh fava beans (blanched), or baby peas (blanched).

JAPANESE TECHNIQUES FOR POACHING FISH

The Japanese approach to poaching fish is slightly different than the traditional European method of gentle simmering in aromatic liquid. In Japan a mixture of dashi, mirin, sake, and soy sauce is the liquid most often used for poaching. Japanese cooks like to use an *otoshibuta,* a wooden lid that fits inside the pan used for poaching and keeps the fish flat and submerged. In this way the fish can be poached using a higher heat—the liquid can actually boil—without the fish being tossed around and broken apart. This method also compresses the fish somewhat so it doesn't curl and so it can be poached in a minimum of liquid. Don't despair if you don't have an *otoshibuta;* just use a flat pan lid or plate slightly smaller than the pan you use for poaching.

Traditional Japanese recipes often suggest cooking fish in two stages—a preliminary blanching, broiling, or deep-frying followed by simmering. I bother with this two-stage process only if I'm feeling especially conscientious; it's easy to overcook the fish—especially if it's cut into small pieces—and I usually don't want to bother with two cooking methods.

Although exact amounts of dashi, mirin, soy sauce, and sake are given in each of these recipes, you'll probably want to do as the Japanese do and adjust the amounts according to taste. The need for adjustments will become more obvious as you become more familiar with Japanese ingredients.

Red Snapper Fillets Simmered in Sake-Flavored Dashi

It amazes me that I spent so many years making elaborate fish soups and stocks before I discovered the briny wood-smoked flavor of the simplest Japanese dashi. In this recipe the dashi is made heady and sweet with Japanese rice wine (mirin) and sake. You can use this method as a delicious and simple method for cooking almost any type of lean, firm-fleshed fish fillets. Be sure to keep the presentation simple. Relatively wide Japanese bowls—either porcelain or lacquer with lids—are the most elegant. If you're being strictly Japanese, you can garnish each bowl with a sprig of *kinome* (the leaf of the plant used for making sansho pepper; see glossary), but I usually settle for a flat parsley or chervil leaf or a tiny pile of chives cut into ¼-inch lengths.

MAKES 4 FIRST-COURSE SERVINGS

12 ounces red snapper fillet with skin, cut into 4 equal pieces

½ cup dashi (page 343)

¼ cup mirin (see glossary)

¼ cup sake

3 tablespoons Japanese dark soy sauce

4 *kinome*, parsley, or chervil sprigs or two 10-inch chives cut into ¼-inch lengths)

Inspect the fillets carefully and scrape away any scales adhering to the skin with the back of a knife. If your guests are fussy, you can pull out any remaining bones with tweezers or needlenose pliers. If you have 2 large fillets, cut them in half, keeping in mind the shape and size of your bowls. Make 2 diagonal slits about ¼ inch into the skin of each piece of fish.

Combine the liquid ingredients in a sauté pan (preferably one with straight sides) just large enough to hold the fillets in a single layer. Bring the liquids to a fast simmer, quickly arrange the fish—skin side up—in the simmering liquid, and place an *oto-shibuta*, flat lid, or plate directly on the fish. Continue simmering for about 5 minutes (about 8 minutes per inch of thickness).

Arrange the fish—skin side up—in warm bowls and turn the heat all the way up under the pan to reduce the poaching liquid slightly. After about 3 minutes, spoon about 3 tablespoons of the poaching liquid over and around each piece of fish. Decorate with the *kinome* or one of the substitutes.

Substitutes Fillets of fish with edible skin such as Atlantic croaker, black sea bass, mackerel, red drum, rockfish, striped bass

❧

Yellowtail Jack Fillets Simmered with Ginger and Daikon

Half the trick to impressing dinner guests is to present the food in the right bowls and serving dishes. The most beautiful Japanese pottery is gorgeous and frightfully expensive, but shops that sell to restaurants often have factory-made dishes for very lit-tle money. This recipe takes about 10 minutes to prepare, but if you serve it in Japanese pottery bowls your guests will be convinced you've labored for hours.

The shredded daikon or turnip served with this dish is a perfect foil for slightly oily and stronger-flavored fish. Unfortunately delicious yellow-tail jack is not always easy to find, but this method works with easier-to-find mackerel, herring, Spanish mackerel, kingfish, and other members of the jack family, especially pompano. The ingredients for this dish are similar to those used for poaching lean round fish except for the ginger and smaller amount of dashi. This results in a more assertive poaching liquid, which goes better with the bolder flavor of oilier fish.

This recipe contains shredded daikon, a large Japanese radish, which gives this dish an appealing crunch and bite. If you can't find daikon, use turnip or even carrot. To obtain the fine julienne you need for these veg-etables, I highly recommend using a benriner cutter (a Japanese slicer).

MAKES 4 FIRST-COURSE SERVINGS

four 3- to 4-ounce pieces of yellowtail, mackerel, or pompano fillet

one ½-inch piece of fresh ginger, peeled

¼ cup dashi (page 343)

2 tablespoons mirin

¼ cup sake

¼ cup Japanese dark soy sauce

one 1-inch piece of daikon, peeled, or 1 medium turnip, peeled, cut into fine julienne

1 scallion, including green, finely sliced

Make sure the fish is cut into 4 equal pieces, keeping in mind the size and shape of the serving bowls. I like to leave the skin attached to the fillets unless it seems really thick and rub-bery—you'll have to use your own judgment. If you do leave the skin on, make 2 diagonal slits in the skin of each piece of fish.

Slice the ginger as thinly as you can—again, a benriner cutter is best—and then cut the slices into fine juli-enne with a chef's knife.

Pour the liquid ingredients and gin-ger into a straight-sided sauté pan just large enough to hold the fish in a sin-gle layer. Bring the liquids to a brisk simmer and arrange the fish, skin side up, in the liquid. Place a flat lid or plate *inside* the pan to hold the fish flat and submerged in the liquid. Simmer the fish for about 5 minutes, depend-ing on its thickness.

Transfer the cooked fish to Japanese lacquer or porcelain bowls and place the bowls in a warm—not hot—oven. Spread the julienned daikon or turnip in the boiling liquid and boil rapidly for about 3 minutes to cook the daikon and reduce the poaching liquid.

Use a fork and spoon to arrange the daikon in small mounds next to each serving of fish. Toss the scallion into the poaching liquid and boil it for about 10 seconds. Spoon the poaching liquid over and around each serving of fish.

Panfrying

Panfrying—sometimes called just frying or sautéing—means cooking in a small amount of fat, usually in a sauté pan or skillet. Panfrying is one of the easiest and most straightforward methods for cooking fish: Heat a teaspoon or two of oil or butter in a pan, season the fish with salt and pepper, and cook the fish on the stove over medium heat, turning it over only once or, in the case of very thin fillets, not at all. When the fish is done, mop off any remaining fat with paper towels, then serve the fish alone or with any number of sauces.

CHOOSING THE RIGHT PAN

There are two things to look out for when selecting a pan for panfrying fish. The most important is to use a pan that won't stick—fish sticks easily and is fragile; if you try to turn it, it will tear. The easiest way around this is to use nonstick pans, which are easy to clean and require relatively little oil or butter. More traditional but equally good are properly seasoned cast-iron pans—less expensive and easier to find in different shapes and sizes. Avoid stainless steel and aluminum for panfrying fish—they stick like crazy. Second, select a pan that approximates the shape and size of the fish. If there are uncovered spots in the pan, the butter or oil is likely to burn there. If you're cooking whole fish or long fillets, the obvious solution is to use an oval fish pan, available in tin- or stainless steel–lined copper and in cast iron. The cast-iron pans work as well as if not better than copper (cast iron sticks less), but copper looks so great that you can take it right to the table.

WHAT FAT TO USE FOR BROWNING?

For panfrying I use either butter or olive oil, depending on the recipe or the character of the dish.

Butter imparts a wonderful flavor to panfried fish but burns at a fairly low temperature. If you're cooking fillets without skin (skin requires a higher temperature to make it crispy), if the fillets are at least ¹/₂ inch thick (thinner fillets require higher heat),

and your pan is exactly the right size to hold the fillets in a single layer, it's safe to use butter. When in doubt, use clarified butter (page 336) or oil, both of which burn at a much higher temperature than plain butter. Many recipes suggest cooking in a mixture of oil and plain butter, the idea being that the oil prevents the butter from burning. This is simply not true—butter burns at the same temperature whether or not it's combined with oil.

When using olive oil, use the less expensive "pure" instead of extra-virgin oil, which will lose its delicate flavor in the hot pan. Olive oil is easier to use than butter because olive oil never burns at the temperatures needed to cook fish.

I never cook with margarine—it gives the fish (and house) a peculiar smell—and only rarely do I use vegetable oil, which seems to make fish taste "fishy."

HOW MUCH BUTTER OR OIL TO USE?

The main purpose of butter or oil is to prevent the fish from sticking to the pan. If you're using a nonstick pan, 2 teaspoons is usually enough for a 10- or 12-inch pan. If you're using a cast-iron or copper pan, you'll need about 1¹/₂ tablespoons. Very little oil or butter is actually absorbed by the fish, and if you pat the cooked fish with paper towels, only a trace of fat will remain.

When fish is floured or breaded, butter or oil is absorbed into the coating, so you'll need to use up to three times as much.

HOW HIGH SHOULD THE HEAT BE?

The best temperature for sautéing depends on the thickness of the whole fish or fillets—the thinner the fish, the higher the heat. If a thick fish or fillet is panfried over heat that is too high, the outside may overbrown or even burn while the inside remains raw or under-cooked. When the heat is too low for a thin fish or fillet, the surface won't brown before the fish is cooked through. Also, because flour and bread crumbs brown at a much lower temperature than uncoated fish, coated fish should be browned over lower heat than uncoated fish.

COOKING TIMES

Sautéed fish fillets and steaks take approximately 8 minutes per inch of thickness to cook through. Whole fish take slightly longer, about 10 minutes per inch of thickness.

KEEPING THE FISH FROM STICKING TO THE PAN

Fish hardly ever attaches to a nonstick pan but will on occasion stick to even a well-seasoned cast-iron or a copper sauté pan. There are three tricks for minimizing sticking: (1) Make sure the fish is perfectly dry by patting it with paper towels just before putting it into the pan. (2) Add the oil or butter and make sure the pan is hot before sliding in the fish (the butter should froth and the oil should just start to ripple). (3) Move the sauté pan back and forth while adding the fish so the fish is moving over the surface of the hot pan for the first 5 or 10 seconds of cooking.

SAUTÉING VERSUS PANFRYING

Although these two terms are often used interchangeably (the term *sautéing* is gradually replacing the American *panfrying*), there is, strictly speaking, a difference. Usually when we say "sauté," we mean cooking in a small amount of fat. But *sauté* means literally "to jump" and when strictly defined refers to the method of tossing foods in a pan over high heat—literally making them jump.

While this technique would be a disaster for fragile fish such as fillets of sole, it's a great method for cooking firmer seafood such as blowfish, strips of skate, sliced squid, frogs' legs, or shellfish such as scallops or shrimp.

When sautéing, it's best to use a pan with gently sloping sides so that you can toss the seafood in the pan without using a spoon. Stirring the seafood with a spoon can break through a coating such as flour or bread crumbs and may cause the fish to stick together into tangled lumps. Tossing a hot pan of seafood can be intimidating at first, and you'll probably need a little practice to get the knack. Some people like to try it with beans or rice first. It's easiest to toss by jerking the pan quickly toward you—leaving it flat over the burner—so that the chunks of seafood bounce against the back of the inside of the pan and turn over. The same precautions that apply to panfrying hold true for sautéing. The pan should be very hot before adding the seafood, otherwise it will steam. The timing is somewhat trickier because seafood to be sautéed is often very small and cooks quickly. Your best bet is to just reach into the pan and test a piece to see if it's done.

COOKING FRAGILE FILLETS

Some fish fillets are so fragile that they break apart as soon as you try to turn them in the pan. A good way around this is to sauté the fillets on one side and then, instead of turning them over, put a cover on the pan so the top of the fillet steams.

WHAT ABOUT THE SKIN?

Whole round fish are almost always panfried with the skin on while certain flatfish are sautéed with the skin taken off one or both sides. With fillets the decision to remove or leave on the skin depends on the kind of fish. The skin of some fish—such as sole or flounder—is often removed simply because it contributes little flavor or texture, while that of swordfish or tuna is too tough and thus inedible. But the skin of fish like red snapper, sea bass, and striped bass is not only attractive to look at but turns pleasantly crispy when panfried.

If you decide to panfry fillets with the skin on, make sure the fish has been scaled properly; I inevitably have to scrape off a few stray scales when I get fillets home from the fishmonger. Another problem is that fish skin contracts with heat, causing the fillets to curl. Making shallow inch-long incisions in the skin will help prevent this, but the best method is to put the fillets in the pan skin side down and then immediately place a flat plate or lid over the fillets to prevent them from curling.

Because skin is best when it is well cooked and crispy, cook the fillets longer on the skin side than on the flesh side. Assuming about 4 minutes total cooking time for a 1/2-inch-thick fillet, I cook it for 3 minutes on the skin side and 1 minute on the flesh side.

SAUTÉING WHOLE FISH VERSUS FILLETS

Most of us sauté fillets because we don't want to deal with the bones in a whole fish, but fish cooked whole, on the bone, has a much finer flavor and will stay moister. If you want to sauté round fish, have the fishmonger scale and gut the fish, cut off the fins, and remove the gills. For flatfish, have the fishmonger pan-dress the fish by gutting, scaling, and cutting off the fins.

DEGLAZING THE PAN: MAKING A SAUCE

While Americans are usually satisfied with a simple unadorned fillet of fish, the French usually want a little sauce spooned over or around it. Many sauces can be prepared in advance and then served with the fish (see "Sauces and Salsas, Condiments and Broths"), but an easier method is to add a little flavorful liquid to the still-hot pan—

WHICH SIDE TO COOK FIRST?

Because fish is often fragile and can break apart when turned, always put the best-looking side facedown in the pan first so that you'll need to turn the fish only once.

If you're cooking fillets with the skin, cook the skin side first and present the fillets skin side up on the plate or platter. If you're cooking skinless fillets, cook the attractive bone side first (the skin side often has unsightly pink or gray coloration) so that the bone side is facing upward after the fillets have been turned in the pan.

called *deglazing*—and then make a little sauce to pour over the cooked fish.

One of the most popular methods for making sauces in the same pan used for cooking the fish is the meunière method, but it requires a large amount of butter. A more contemporary technique is to deglaze the hot pan with vinegar and make a hot vinaigrette.

❧

Panfried Red Snapper Fillets with Hot Sherry Vinegar and Herb Vinaigrette

Here is an example of how you can make a quick and lively sauce for any firm-fleshed fillet by deglazing the pan with good-quality wine vinegar. The plain extra-virgin olive oil can be replaced by Provençal herb-scented oil (page 92) if you wish.

MAKES 4 MAIN-COURSE SERVINGS

four 6- to 8-ounce fillets of firm fish such as red snapper (skin attached), sea bass (skin attached), salmon (skin attached or removed), tuna (skin removed), halibut (skin removed), or Dover sole (dark skin removed, light skin attached)

salt and pepper

2 to 4 teaspoons pure olive oil

3 tablespoons sherry vinegar

3 tablespoons extra-virgin olive oil

2 tablespoons mixed chopped fresh parsley, chives, and chervil (or 2 of the 3)

If you're leaving the skin attached to the fillets, scrape off any remaining scales. Season the fillets on both sides with salt and pepper.

Heat the pure olive oil in a sauté pan over medium heat, using the

smaller amount of oil for a nonstick pan. Add the fillets (see box) and adjust the heat according to their thickness (the thicker the fillet, the lower the heat). Cook for about 4 minutes altogether for a ½-inch-thick fillet, turning them halfway through the cooking time (or covering them if fragile), and transfer them to hot plates or a platter.

Wipe the cooked oil out of the sauté pan with a paper towel and add the vinegar, extra-virgin olive oil, and herbs. Bring the sauce to a rapid boil and season with salt and pepper to taste. If the sauce tastes too strongly of vinegar, boil it down slightly to evaporate some of the vinegar. If it tastes flat, add more vinegar. Spoon the boiling sauce over the fish and serve immediately.

COATING FISH WITH FLOUR: THE MEUNIÈRE METHOD

Coating fish with flour is an excellent way to make sure the surface of fish ends up crispy and golden brown. This works especially well for lean fish such as cod and flatfish, which benefit from the extra richness of the butter. One popular method using flour is the meunière method. To cook a fish or fish fillet *à la meunière* means to coat the fish with flour, panfry it in clarified butter, and then serve it with a sauce made of butter and lemon juice. Because many cooks today are averse to using so much butter, cooking *à la meunière* is less popular than it once was, but the technique is a good one, and the final melted butter can be left out and the fish served with lemon wedges and a little chopped parsley.

Trout Meunière

(color page 9)

I must have been four or five when my mother took me and my brothers into the mountains of California for a week of camping. We'd pitch a tent big enough for the whole family, and my mother would be up at dawn, rod and reel in hand, to fish for our breakfast. The trout would end up sizzling in bacon fat over an open fire. No trout has ever again tasted quite the same, but this recipe is for me as close as it gets.

MAKES **4** MAIN-COURSE SERVINGS

four 12-ounce trout, gutted

salt and pepper

½ cup all-purpose flour

4 tablespoons clarified butter (page 336)

2 tablespoons finely chopped parsley

2 tablespoons fresh lemon juice

4 tablespoons unsalted butter or extra-virgin olive oil (optional)

Rinse off and dry the trout. Season with salt and pepper and then dredge in flour. Pat thoroughly to shake off any excess flour.

Heat the clarified butter in a sauté pan, preferably oval, and place the trout in the hot butter. Cook over medium heat for about 4 minutes on each side, depending on their thickness. The trout skin should turn crispy and golden brown. Transfer the trout to a plate covered with paper towels, pat off the cooked butter, and arrange them on hot plates or on an oval platter. Sprinkle with parsley and lemon juice and serve.

If you're serving the trout with the traditional meunière butter, discard the cooked butter from the sauté pan, add the fresh butter, and heat it over medium heat until it froths. If you're using olive oil, just heat it until barely hot. Spoon the hot butter or oil over the trout and serve immediately.

Substitutes Small to medium round fish such as butterfish, Atlantic croaker, whiting, small snapper (such as vermilion snapper), porgy, sunfish, small sea bass, small striped bass, yellow perch, ocean perch, mullet, baby coho salmon, large smelts

Sole Meunière

This is one of those dishes that used to appear in almost every American or French restaurant serving fish. Now I hardly ever see it, probably because chefs like to try their hands at more "creative" dishes and people are scared off by fish cooked in butter. I'm not sure why—perhaps the butter seals in the flavor in some magical way—but sole meunière, made with whole fish, is one of the best seafood dishes imaginable.

This method will work with any flatfish, including Dover sole (the best), flounder, fluke, rex sole, and petrale sole. The tricks are to find flatfish that are perfectly fresh—the black side should be shiny, the fish stiff—and the right size. I sometimes serve small rex sole—about ½ pound each—as a first course and 1-pound flatfish per person as a main course.

Because flatfish take up a lot of room in the pan, you may need a separate nonstick or cast-iron sauté pan for each fish.

MAKES **4** MAIN-COURSE SERVINGS

four 1-pound flatfish

salt and pepper

½ cup all-purpose flour

4 to 6 tablespoons clarified butter (page 336)

2 tablespoons finely chopped parsley

2 tablespoons fresh lemon juice

4 tablespoons unsalted butter

Cut around the fish with a pair of heavy scissors, removing a ¼-inch-wide strip all around (see color page 30). Scrape off any scales clinging to the bottom white skin. If the top black skin is thick or scaly, peel it off for Dover sole (see color page 29) or cut off in strips for other flatfish (see color page 29). Season the fish with salt and pepper and then dredge in flour, patting thoroughly to shake off any excess flour.

Heat the clarified butter in sauté pans and place the fish in the hot butter. Cook over medium to high heat for 1 to 4 minutes on each side, about 10 minutes total cooking time per inch of thickness. The skin should turn crispy and golden brown. Transfer the sole to hot plates or a platter.

Sprinkle the fish with parsley and lemon. Discard the cooked butter left in the sauté pans and wipe them out with a paper towel. Add the fresh butter to one of the pans and heat over medium heat until the butter froths. Pour the hot butter over the fish and serve immediately.

MEUNIÈRE VARIATIONS

A number of classic variations of the meunière method can be made by tossing ingredients such as almonds or capers into the hot butter just before it is spooned over the fish. In addition to these classics, variations are easy to improvise. Try substituting herbs such as chervil, chives, or tarragon for the parsley. I sometimes sauté a few wild mushrooms such as morels, porcini (cèpes), or chanterelles in hot butter and then spoon them over and around the hot fish fillets. Chopped garlic and shallots can also be added to the butter at the end. So can baby artichokes, chunks of tomato, asparagus tips . . .

Amandine: From a very young age I remember studying the menus of expensive restaurants and dreaming about what went on inside. Trout amandine seemed always to be represented, as were beef Wellington and crêpes Suzette. There's no mystery to trout (or any fish) amandine—simply sprinkle lemon and parsley over the fish, heat slivered almonds in frothing butter in the sauté pan, and pour over the fish.

Grenobloise: Prepared in the same way as meunière, Grenobloise is different only in the capers added to the hot butter (or olive oil) just before it's poured over the fish and the few drops of wine vinegar sprinkled over the fish instead of lemon juice. The tangy capers are a perfect foil for the richness of the butter sauce.

SERVING WHOLE INDIVIDUAL FLATFISH

The easiest way to serve whole individual flatfish is just to put them on plates and set them down in front of each guest. Extra plates or bowls can then be passed at the table for guests to put their fish bones and heads on. A more elegant method is to set a clean hot plate in front of everyone and then serve each fish on its own plate or platter set to each diner's left. With this method the guests can fillet their own fish and transfer the fillets to their plates, leaving the bones on the serving plates.

Panfried Whole Fish or Fillets with Thai Ginger Sauce

*I*first read about a sauce similar to this one in Jennifer Brennan's wonderful book *The Original Thai Cookbook.* What first fascinated me about Ms. Brennan's recipe was her use of Chinese mushrooms and the juxtaposition of sweet-and-sour ingredients. I've adapted her recipe here so you can use it for sautéed fish fillets or whole fish such as red snapper, sea bass, or even small flatfish such as rex or petrale sole. The sesame oil is my own addition.

Whereas most meunière variations are prepared by cooking butter in the pan used to panfry the fish, in this recipe the browned fish is served with a sauce.

MAKES **4** MAIN-COURSE SERVINGS

For the Sauce:

10 medium dried Chinese mushrooms

1 cup hot water

¼ cup rice vinegar or sherry vinegar

¼ cup palm or granulated sugar

3 tablespoons dark soy sauce

2 tablespoons grated fresh ginger

1 small garlic clove, chopped and crushed to a fine paste

juice of 1 lime

½ teaspoon dark sesame oil, preferably Japanese

3 scallions, including green, finely sliced

For the Fish:

six 6- to 8-ounce fillets with skin from lean firm-fleshed fish such as striped bass, pin bones removed, or four 12- to 16-ounce whole fish, cleaned and scaled

salt and pepper

½ cup all-purpose flour

¼ cup peanut or vegetable oil

Preparing the Sauce: Rinse the mushrooms under cold running water and then soak them in the hot water for about 30 minutes. Remove and discard the mushrooms stems, slice and reserve the caps, and save the soaking liquid. Carefully pour the soaking liquid into a small saucepan, leaving behind any bits of grit or sand.

Add the sliced mushroom caps and the remaining ingredients to the mushroom-soaking liquid. Bring to a simmer and simmer very gently for about 10 minutes.

Cooking the Fish: Season the fillets or whole fish with salt and pepper and roll them in flour. Pat them thoroughly to shake off any excess flour.

In a nonstick pan, sauté the fish over medium to high heat in oil until crispy on both sides. Whole fish take slightly longer to cook (about 10 minutes per inch of thickness) than steaks and fillets (8 minutes per inch), so time the cooking accordingly. Quickly transfer to a baking sheet covered with paper towels and pat the fish to get rid of any clinging oil. Transfer again to heated plates, pour the sauce over each fish or fillet, and serve immediately.

Substitutes Fillets such as black sea bass, red snapper, croaker, porgy, tilapia, tilefish, rockfish

Small whole fish such as trout, baby coho salmon, small red snapper (such as vermilion snapper), croaker

Skate Wings à la Grenobloise

(color page 12)

Cooking *à la grenobloise* means simply cooking in butter and then serving with a sprinkling of hot vinegar, more butter (lightly browned in the pan used for cooking the fish), and a spoonful of capers. The tangy flavor of capers is a perfect accent to the delicate taste of skate, but any fish that can be prepared meunière can also be prepared *à la grenobloise.*

MAKES 4 MAIN-COURSE SERVINGS

1 large or 2 medium skate wings, about 3 pounds total, filleted and skinned (color page 24) (you should end up with 1½ to 2 pounds finished fillets)

salt and pepper

½ cup all-purpose flour

2 tablespoons clarified butter (page 336) or pure olive oil

2 tablespoons good-quality white wine vinegar

4 tablespoons unsalted butter or extra-virgin olive oil

2 tablespoons finely chopped parsley

2 tablespoons capers, preferably small

If you're using one large skate wing, cut each fillet into 2 pieces, cutting along the natural division between the ribs of flesh, to make 4 servings. Season them with salt and pepper and coat them with flour. Pat them thoroughly to eliminate excess flour.

Sauté the skate in the clarified butter over medium to high heat for about 3 minutes on each side. Arrange the skate on hot plates and sprinkle each serving with vinegar.

Discard the cooked butter, wipe out the pan with a paper towel, and add the fresh butter to the pan. Heat until the butter froths. (If you're using olive oil, heat it until barely hot; extra-virgin olive oil loses all its flavor when overheated.) Add the parsley and capers and toss them in the hot pan for a few seconds. Spoon the hot sauce over the skate wings and serve immediately.

BREADING AND CRUSTS

A perfectly breaded and cooked piece of fish is a delicious revelation to those who remember fish sticks or the breaded deep-fried fish served in mediocre restaurants. Several traditional methods are used for breading whole fish and fish fillets before sautéing. The simplest—meunière—involves a simple coating of flour, while fish breaded *à la parisienne* is dipped in beaten egg. Breading *à l'anglaise* consists of first coating the fish with flour, then dipping in a beaten egg mixture and coating with bread crumbs. A delicious Italian variation—*à la milanaise*—is the same as *à l'anglaise* except the bread crumbs are replaced by finely grated Parmigiano-Reggiano.

The trick to coating fish in bread crumbs is to make the bread crumbs yourself with good-quality white bread. Packaged bread crumbs have a stale flavor and are too hard. To make your own bread crumbs, cut the crusts off the bread and then process the slices in a food processor. Work the crumbs through a drum sieve or a large strainer so they end up very fine. If the bread crumbs are too coarse, they will absorb too much fat during sautéing, and the fish will end up greasy.

Remember that bread crumbs will absorb some of the fat used for sautéing, so be sure to use a cooking fat with good flavor. I stick to clarified butter or extra-virgin olive oil. Breaded fish can also be cooked in whole butter, but whole butter leaves tiny specks of milk solids on the surface of the fish, so it's preferable to use clarified butter. Don't keep cooking fillet after fillet in the same butter—bread crumbs fall off during sautéing, and unless you strain the butter after each batch of fish the bread crumbs burn and leave specks on the surface.

Don't bread fish in advance, or the breading will get soggy and separate from the fish.

SAUCES FOR BREADED FISH

Traditional recipes suggest using relatively thick sauces such as whipped compound butters or mayonnaise-based sauces such as tartar sauce, all in "Sauces and Salsas, Condiments and Broths." When more liquid sauces are poured over the breaded fillets, the breading absorbs the sauce and becomes soggy.

Because breading can add unwanted richness and precludes lighter sauces, some chefs bread only one side of the fillets and then serve them breaded side up with the sauce *around* the fillets instead of over them. In this way there is only half as much breading and the bottom of the fillet won't absorb the sauce on the plate.

Fillets of Sole Breaded à l'Anglaise with Watercress Sauce

This is a startlingly beautiful dish—golden brown breaded fillets surrounded by a bright green sauce—and the breading is especially light and delicate.

Although almost any sauce can be served with breaded fillets, this sauce illustrates how the fish bones and heads from the sole can be used to make a basic fish broth, which is in turn converted into a sauce by stirring in pureed watercress and mushrooms. The watercress can be blanched earlier in the day, but the sauce should be made within an hour of serving, or the mushrooms will cause it to turn dark.

MAKES 4 MAIN-COURSE SERVINGS

two 1½-pound sole, flounder, or other flatfish, filleted, bones and heads reserved

1 large onion, sliced

1 bouquet garni: 3 fresh thyme sprigs or ½ teaspoon dried, a small bunch of parsley, and a bay leaf tied up with string (or in cheesecloth for dried thyme)

1 cup dry white wine

leaves from 1 bunch of watercress

5 medium mushrooms

1 egg

salt and white pepper

½ cup all-purpose flour

½ cup bread crumbs made with 4 slices of good-quality white bread, crusts removed

4 tablespoons clarified butter (page 336) or extra-virgin olive oil

2 tablespoons heavy cream

Preparing the Fish Broth: Combine the sole bones and heads, onion, bouquet garni, and wine in a saucepan. Add as little water as possible to barely cover the bones. Simmer gently for 30 minutes, skimming off any froth that floats to the surface, and strain into a clean saucepan. Simmer the broth gently for about 20 minutes, until you have ¾ cup.

Preparing the Watercress and Mushroom Sauce: Blanch the watercress leaves in boiling water for 1 minute, drain them in a colander, and rinse with cold water. Squeeze the water out of the leaves.

Use a paring knife to cut off the bottom ¼ inch from the mushroom stems and put the mushrooms in a blender with the blanched watercress leaves. Turn the blender on low speed and add just enough of the cooled fish broth to get the mixture to turn around. Puree on high speed for 1 minute, add the rest of the fish broth, and strain through a fine-mesh strainer, using a ladle to force the sauce through. If necessary, thin the sauce with a little water so that it has the consistency of heavy cream. Set aside until needed.

Preparing the Breading: Whisk the egg with 1 teaspoon salt and 4 or 5 grinds of pepper. Coat the sole fillets with flour, pat off the excess, and dip the fillets in the egg. Hold the fillets in one hand over the bowl of egg and run your thumb and forefinger along the fillets to eliminate excess egg. Carefully place the fillets down in the bread crumbs so that only one side is well coated.

Cooking and Serving: Sauté the fillets over medium heat, breaded side down first, in clarified butter or olive oil for about 2 minutes on each side.

Heat the watercress sauce, stir in the cream, and season with salt and pepper to taste.

Place 2 fillets per serving, breaded side up, on hot plates. Carefully spoon the sauce around them, avoiding getting any of the sauce on the breading.

Round Fish Fillets à la Milanaise

Friends are always pleasantly startled when they bite into these fillets. What they expect to be a simple breading has a crisp but subtle flavor of Parmesan cheese.

Almost any delicate fish fillet is excellent when panfried with a light coating of Parmesan—as long as it's authentic Parmigiano-Reggiano. Substitutes, while less expensive, have a strong taste that is distinctly unpleasant with fish. They also tend to contain more moisture, so they can't be grated finely enough to provide a thin coating.

Because fish fillets coated *à la milanaise* have a full flavor, they demand an assertive sauce such as this chunky tomato sauce flavored with fresh basil.

MAKES 4 MAIN-COURSE SERVINGS

four 6- to 8-ounce round fish fillets such as striped bass, skin removed

20 fresh basil leaves

1 teaspoon extra-virgin olive oil

4 medium tomatoes, peeled, seeded, and coarsely chopped

salt and white pepper

1 large egg

¼ to ½ cup all-purpose flour

¼ to ½ cup finely grated Parmigiano-Reggiano

4 tablespoons clarified butter (page 336) or extra-virgin olive oil

continued

Remove any small bones remaining in the fillets with tweezers or a pair of needlenose pliers. Reserve in the refrigerator.

Sprinkle the basil leaves with the teaspoon of extra-virgin olive oil and chop them finely. Cook the tomatoes in a wide skillet over medium to high heat until the excess water evaporates and the mixture stiffens. Remove from the heat, stir in the chopped basil, and season with salt and pepper to taste. Reserve the sauce off the heat until ready to serve.

With a fork, lightly beat the egg with a large pinch of salt and pepper. Dip the fillets in the flour, pat off the excess, and then dip the fillets in the egg (bread one or both sides; you'll need the larger amounts of flour and cheese to bread both). Dip the fillets in the grated Parmigiano-Reggiano. Gently sauté the fillets in clarified butter over medium heat for about 3 minutes on each side.

When the fillets are done, transfer them to hot plates and surround with the heated sauce.

Substitutes Delicate firm-fleshed skinless fillets such as sea bass, blackfish, sea trout, tilefish, monkfish (cut into medallions), haddock, cod, pollack, Dover sole, John Dory, orange roughy, rockfish, ocean perch, walleye

More Breading Techniques

Many cooks have started experimenting with ground nuts or spice mixtures as flavorful alternatives to bread crumbs. Almonds, hazelnuts, pistachios, and macadamia nuts can all be ground in a food processor and used to coat fillets after their initial coating in flour and beaten egg. The ground nuts turn golden brown in the same way as bread crumbs and also contribute a distinctive flavor and texture of their own.

Dried mushrooms also make an interesting coating for fish. Dried morels, porcini (cèpes), or shiitake mushrooms can be ground very finely in a food processor and used as a light coating for fillets instead of flour.

One of the most extravagant—and delicious—"breadings" for fish is a finely chopped coating of black truffles.

Fish fillets can be flavored subtly by sprinkling them with ground spices such as cumin, coriander, or nutmeg in very small amounts. Spices such as saffron or finely chopped herbs such as tarragon or basil can also be stirred into the beaten egg mixture used to coat the fish.

USING BUTTER OR OLIVE OIL FOR PANFRYING

Because breading absorbs some of the fat used for panfrying, it's essential to use something flavorful such as butter or olive oil. In most recipes you'll need about 4 tablespoons so that the breading browns evenly. Although breaded foods are not for the diet-conscious—some absorption of fat is inevitable—only about 1 tablespoon of the 4 tablespoons called for remains in the finished dish.

Sautéed Salmon Fillets with Moroccan Spices

This light spice coating gives the salmon a unique flavor and is not as rich as breading. Don't coat the fish more than a couple of minutes before sautéing, or the spice flavor will take over.

MAKES 4 MAIN-COURSE SERVINGS

four 6-ounce salmon fillets with skin, pin bones removed

2 tablespoons coriander seeds

2 tablespoons cumin seeds

3 shelled cardamom pods

1½ tablespoons fennel seeds

¼ teaspoon cayenne pepper

2 egg whites

1 teaspoon pure olive oil

2 teaspoons salt

2 tablespoons unsalted butter or pure olive oil

Refrigerate the salmon fillets until needed. Grind the spices to a fine powder in a coffee grinder or spice grinder.

Beat the egg whites, 1 teaspoon olive oil, and salt together with a kitchen fork. Spread the ground spices on a plate. Dip the salmon fillets in the egg white mixture and then roll them around in the spice mixture until they are coated on both sides.

Heat the butter or olive oil over high heat in a sauté pan just large enough to hold the salmon. When the butter froths or the olive oil begins to ripple, gently slide the salmon fillets into the pan. Cook the fillets for 3 to 4 minutes on each side, a total of about 8 minutes per inch of thickness. Serve immediately on hot plates.

Substitutes Delicately flavored firm-fleshed fillets with skin removed such as John Dory, pompano, Dover sole, blackfish, lingcod, skate

Panfried Croaker Fillets with Porcini Dust and Chive Sauce

You don't need to search out croaker fillets to prepare this dish—any firm-fleshed not-too-strong fish will work. The real subtlety and deliciousness of this dish come from the mushrooms. Because the flavor of fish cooked with porcini dust is complex and intriguing, this is one of those dishes I serve when I have a very special wine to show off—especially a white Burgundy or red Côte de Beaune.

MAKES 4 MAIN-COURSE OR 8 FIRST-COURSE SERVINGS

For the Fillets:

eight 4-ounce croaker or other firm-fleshed fillets, skin and pin bones removed

½ cup milk

salt and pepper

¼ cup porcini dust (see box)

4 tablespoons unsalted butter

For the Chive Sauce:

½ cup dry white wine

1 shallot, finely chopped

1 cup heavy cream

2 tablespoons finely chopped fresh chives

salt and pepper

Dip the fillets in milk (so more of the porcini dust adheres to them) and season liberally with salt and pepper. Spread the porcini dust on a plate and press the fillets into it so they're well coated on both sides. Reserve in the refrigerator.

Prepare the chive sauce by gently simmering the white wine with the shallots until the mixture cooks down by half. Pour in the cream and continue simmering until the sauce thickens very slightly—it should have the consistency of cold heavy cream. Stir in the chives and simmer for about 1 minute. Season with salt and pepper to taste and reserve.

Sauté the fillets in butter for 2 to 3 minutes on each side (8 minutes total per inch of thickness). Spread the chive sauce on hot plates and place one or two fillets on each plate. Serve immediately.

Substitutes Small delicately flavored fillets or steaks such as sole or flounder, sea trout, tilefish, cod, pollack, halibut, salmon, walleye

---

PORCINI DUST

Porcini dust can be kept in a tightly sealed container in the freezer for up to 6 months.

⅛ **pound dried porcini (cèpes)**

MAKES ½ CUP

Place the porcini on a baking sheet in a 250°F oven for 30 minutes. Grind to a fine powder in a blender. Work the dust through a strainer to eliminate chunks not broken up by the blender. You can put what doesn't go through the strainer in the blender a second time.

Blowfish Fillets à la Provençal

I first encountered this dish in a restaurant in the south of France—but instead of blowfish, they used frogs' legs. I love frogs' legs, but they're hard to find and often very expensive. The blowfish fillets are every bit as satisfying but inexpensive. The secret to sautéing *à la Provençal* is the pungent mixture of parsley and garlic (and sometimes bread crumbs) called a *persillade.* When it's thrown generously into the sauté pan a minute before serving, the kitchen fills with the scent of garlic so that anyone in the vicinity instantly succumbs.

Blowfish is usually sold skinned but still on the bone. Because it has only one bone running down the middle, removing the two fillets is easy.

MAKES 4 FIRST-COURSE SERVINGS

1½ **pounds blowfish with bone**

2 **garlic cloves, finely chopped**

2 **tablespoons finely chopped parsley**

1 **tablespoon fresh bread crumbs (optional)**

salt and pepper

½ **cup all-purpose flour**

¼ **cup extra-virgin olive oil or unsalted butter**

Fillet the blowfish by running a sharp knife along each side of the center bone.

Prepare the persillade by crushing the chopped garlic into a paste with the side of a chef's knife on a cutting board. Combine it with the chopped parsley, and the bread crumbs if desired, in a small bowl.

continued

Season the blowfish fillets with salt and pepper and roll them in flour. Pat off the excess flour.

Heat the olive oil in a sauté pan over high heat and toss in the floured blowfish. Keep the pan moving so the fish doesn't have a chance to stick. Toss the fish, using a large spoon if you must, until it is lightly browned on all sides, about 5 minutes. Sprinkle on the persillade and continue tossing for about 1 minute more.

With a slotted spoon, distribute the blowfish fillets among hot plates. Serve immediately.

Substitutes Frogs' legs, sea scallops, bay scallops

ADDING HERB FLAVORINGS: À LA PROVENÇAL

One of the tastiest methods for flavoring sautéed fish and shellfish is to sprinkle them during cooking with flavorful herb or vegetable mixtures. French cooks are fond of cooking *à la Provençal* where a mixture called a *persillade*—finely chopped garlic, parsley, and bread crumbs—is sprinkled over sautéed foods about a minute before they are done. There are many variations on this theme, such as the Italian *con gremolata*, which uses a persillade with finely chopped lemon zest added. But don't stick to any prescribed mixture; it's more fun to play around with different chopped herbs such as thyme, marjoram, or oregano. Once I made a delicious mixture of lavender and garlic.

ADDING LIQUIDS TO SAUTÉED SEAFOOD

Although cooks are always saying things like "sautéed in white wine" or "sautéed with lemon juice," sautéed fish or shellfish should not come in contact with liquids such as water or wine or with moist vegetables such as tomatoes until the very end of cooking.

One often-used technique is to gently sauté small fish, shellfish, or slices of squid in butter or olive oil, draining off the cooked fat, and then add liquids such as wine, lemon juice, or chopped tomatoes just a minute or two before the end of cooking. This is a great technique because you end up with a little sauce and a kind of miniature seafood stew.

Squid in Stemperata Sauce

You can tell this is a typically Sicilian dish because of the combination of olives, raisins, vinegar, and pine nuts. Some versions of stemperata sauce contain tomatoes, but these are relatively modern since the tomato became popular in Italian cooking only in the nineteenth century. This dish is best served at room temperature as a first course. I like to serve it outside at a summer lunch with lots of red wine and a siesta to follow.

MAKES 6 FIRST-COURSE SERVINGS

2 pounds squid (1⅓ pounds cleaned), cleaned, cut into rings, tentacles left whole or cut in half (see color page 19)

2 tablespoons extra-virgin olive oil

2 garlic cloves, finely chopped

1 cup Italian or French green olives, pitted

¼ **cup pine nuts, toasted in a 350°F oven until pale brown, about 15 minutes**

¼ **cup dark raisins**

¼ **cup capers, preferably small, drained**

1 tablespoon finely chopped parsley

⅓ **cup good-quality white wine vinegar or sherry vinegar**

salt and pepper

Rinse and thoroughly dry the squid. In a medium sauté pan, heat the olive oil with the garlic over medium heat. As soon as you begin to smell the garlic, toss in the squid. Turn the heat up to high and toss the squid for about 30 seconds to keep it from sticking and to cook it evenly.

Add the rest of the ingredients and toss for about 1 minute more over high heat. Scoop the solid ingredients out of the pan into a serving bowl and boil down the liquid until you have about ¼ cup. Pour this liquid over the squid and toss.

Blackened Fish

Blackened fish is best in the summer, when strong direct flavors are welcomed—and you can leave the kitchen windows open so the kitchen doesn't fill up with smoke. Because the blackened flavor is so strong, I prefer to coat and blacken only one side of the fish and then to cook the other side more gently.

The seasoning mixture given here is similar to one used by chef Paul Prudhomme, but feel free to play around with other herbs and spices. This method works best with full-flavored firm-fleshed fish such as swordfish, tuna (which should be left undercooked), bluefish, salmon, and of course the original redfish (red drum).

The best pan to use for the blackening is a heavy iron skillet, which won't be damaged by high heat; use a nonstick pan to finish the cooking. Open the windows and be prepared to set off the smoke alarm.

Even though it's probably heretical to Cajun purists, I like to serve blackened fish with the spicy tartar sauce on page 335.

MAKES 4 MAIN-COURSE SERVINGS

four 6- to 8-ounce fish steaks or fillets, preferably more than ½ inch thick, skin removed

1 tablespoon finely chopped fresh or 1½ teaspoons dried thyme leaves

1 tablespoon finely chopped fresh or 1½ teaspoons dried marjoram or dried oregano

1½ teaspoons cayenne pepper

2 teaspoons salt

1 teaspoon freshly ground white pepper

¼ cup pure olive oil

If you're using fillets, pull out any small bones.

Thoroughly combine the chopped herbs, cayenne, salt, and pepper in a medium mixing bowl.

Heat an iron skillet over high heat until the metal takes on a dull, matte appearance, which indicates it is almost red-hot. Depending on your stove, this will take 5 to 10 minutes.

Coat the fillets on both sides with half the olive oil and then pat only one side with the herb mixture.

With the heat still on high, place the fillets in the pan, herb side down (they'll smoke like crazy) for about 2 minutes. Turn the fillets over into a second sauté pan—preferably nonstick—containing the rest of the olive oil, set over medium heat. Cook the fillets for 2 to 6 minutes more, depending on thickness.

Substitutes Red drum fillets from the Gulf of Mexico are the classic fish for blackening, but these have become difficult to find. Any firm-fleshed full-flavored fish will do. I avoid delicately flavored fish because the fish's flavor is completely masked by the blackening process. Try blackfish (without the skin), black sea bass, bluefish, catfish (without the skin), grouper (without the skin), lingcod, skate (without the skin), swordfish, walleye (without the skin)

GLAZING

Sautéed fish fillets are sometimes coated with a sweet mixture—usually containing honey, sugar, or Japanese sweet sake (mirin)—before they are sautéed so that the mixture forms a sweet glaze on the fish's surface. I'm especially fond of honey combined with herbs and chili pepper.

Honey- and Mustard-Glazed Swordfish Pavés

This honey and mustard glaze gives the swordfish a sweet and savory outer coating that catches even the most jaded guests by surprise. In French restaurants the word *pavé* (meaning "cobblestone") is sometimes used to describe a thick square steak. When I'm serving 4 or more people, I like to buy one very thick tuna or swordfish steak and then cut it into 4 thick, meaty chunks rather than serve 4 thin steaks.

MAKES 4 MAIN-COURSE SERVINGS

one 2-pound swordfish steak, ¾ to 1 inch thick

¼ cup honey

¼ cup Dijon mustard

1 tablespoon finely chopped fresh or 1½ teaspoons dried thyme leaves

½ teaspoon cayenne pepper

1 teaspoon salt

1 teaspoon black pepper

2 tablespoons vegetable oil or pure olive oil

Remove the skin and center vertebrae from the swordfish steak. Cut the steak in 2 directions so you end up with 4 thick sections.

In a mixing bowl, combine the rest of the ingredients except the oil. Turn the swordfish pavés around in the glaze until they are well coated. Sauté the pavés in oil over medium heat for about 3 to 4 minutes on each side (about 8 minutes total per inch of thickness). Serve immediately on hot plates.

Substitutes Thick firm-fleshed steaks such as halibut, king mackerel, tuna, shark, sturgeon

TERIYAKI SAUCE

Japanese cooks are fond of glazing fish steaks and fillets with teriyaki sauce. You can buy bottled teriyaki sauce, but it's easy to make with just a few Asian staples. This sweet-and-salty glaze is the perfect accent for dense firm-fleshed fish such as tuna, swordfish, marlin, and mako shark. You can also use a teriyaki glaze for relatively fatty round fish fillets such as salmon or yellowtail. Be sure to leave the skin on round fish fillets—it will turn sweet and salty and take on a delightful crispy texture. You can also leave the skin attached to flatfish fillets such as flounder or sole—just make sure the skin is well scaled. Teriyaki sauce is also used for grilling.

Sautéed Tuna Teriyaki

Fish being glazed with teriyaki sauce is sautéed in two stages: first in hot oil alone and then again with the teriyaki sauce. How long you cook the fish will depend on the type and your own tastes. I cook ¾-inch-thick tuna steaks for a total of 2½ minutes on each side so the tuna ends up almost completely raw in the middle, but if you don't like raw tuna, cook for a minute more on each side before adding the teriyaki sauce. Other fish such as swordfish, marlin, and shark are always better when cooked all the way through—about 3 minutes on each side for ¾-inch-thick steaks.

MAKES 4 MAIN-COURSE SERVINGS

two 12- to 16-ounce tuna steaks

2 tablespoons sake

2 tablespoons mirin

2 tablespoons Japanese dark soy sauce

2 tablespoons flavorless oil such as canola, safflower, or grapeseed

2 scallions, including green, finely chopped

Trim any strips of dark muscle off the tuna steaks with a sharp paring knife. Combine the sake, mirin, and soy sauce in a small bowl.

Heat the oil in a sauté pan over high heat until it barely begins to smoke. Slide in the tuna while moving the pan gently back and forth so the tuna doesn't have a chance to stick. Don't worry if the tuna is producing a lot of smoke—keep the heat on high. After 2 minutes, turn the tuna over and sauté on the other side for 2 minutes.

When the tuna is lightly browned on each side, transfer it to a plate and pat off any excess oil with a paper towel.

Pour out the burned oil and wipe the still-hot pan with a paper towel.

Let the pan cool for about 2 minutes—so the liquids won't spatter—and pour in the sake mixture. Boil the mixture down over high heat until it's reduced by about half. Slide the tuna back into the pan over high heat and let it sit in the boiling glaze for about 30 seconds. Turn the tuna over and repeat for 30 seconds on the second side.

Slice the tuna into strips and arrange them on plates (Japanese pottery looks great). Brush or spoon the remaining glaze left in the pan over each strip of tuna. Sprinkle on the scallions.

Sautéed Halibut in Teriyaki Broth

Many of the ingredients for this dish are the same as for fish coated with teriyaki glaze. The difference is that in this dish the glaze is thinned with dashi and the resulting broth is served around the fillets in a soup plate or, better yet, in a Japanese lacquer bowl. I like this dish best as a first course, but if you want to serve it as a main course, double the quantities.

MAKES 4 FIRST-COURSE SERVINGS

one 1-pound halibut steak, ¾ to 1 inch thick

3 tablespoons Japanese dark soy sauce

2 tablespoons sake

2 tablespoons mirin

¾ cup dashi (page 343)

2 tablespoons flavorless oil such as canola, safflower, or grapeseed

1 scallion, including green, finely chopped

Cut the halibut steak into 4 sections by cutting along the central bone (see color page 28). Take the skin off each of the sections and marinate them in

half of the soy sauce in the refrigerator for an hour.

Combine the remaining soy sauce, the sake, the mirin, and the dashi. Pat the halibut sections in paper towels. Heat the oil in a sauté pan until it begins to smoke and add the halibut. Sauté the sections for 3 to 4 minutes on each side, a total of 8 minutes per inch of thickness.

Take the halibut out of the sauté pan and pat off any traces of oil with paper towels. Pour the cooked oil out of the sauté pan and add the teriyaki mixture. Simmer for 30 seconds.

Arrange the halibut sections in bowls, pour on the broth—it should come halfway up the sides of the fish—and sprinkle on the chopped scallion. Serve immediately.

Substitutes Firm-fleshed skinless fillets can be sliced crosswise into sections the same thickness as the halibut steaks and cooked in the same way. Try blackfish, haddock, mahimahi, sablefish, salmon, swordfish, or tilefish.

FISH CAKES

Many recipes suggest that fish cakes be deep-fried, but unless I'm making a lot I prefer to panfry them so they don't absorb as much oil. Almost any stuffing can be shaped into a cake and lightly cooked in oil.

Sautéed Thai Fish Cakes with Dipping Sauce

You can make these fish cakes out of practically any kind of seafood. They're delicious made with crab, shrimp, or lobster, but the version given here makes a delicious and inexpensive standby. Most Thai recipes suggest deep-frying the cakes, but I prefer coating them with a little flour or bread crumbs and panfrying them in just a thin layer of oil. Fish cakes are also good steamed.

You can make the fish mixture and shape the cakes earlier in the day, but they're best cooked at the last minute. Keep the cooked cakes warm in a 200°F oven as you're sautéing.

MAKES 18 SMALL CAKES, 6 FIRST-COURSE OR HORS D'OEUVRE SERVINGS

For the Fish Cakes:

1½ pounds fillets of lean whitefish such as cod, halibut, or sea bass, skin and pin bones removed, cut into 2-inch chunks

3 Thai chilies, seeded and finely chopped

1 garlic clove, finely chopped

2 shallots, finely chopped

3 tablespoons finely chopped fresh cilantro

3 kaffir lime leaves, finely chopped

1 tablespoon Thai fish sauce

1 egg beaten with ¼ cup water

1 teaspoon salt

pepper

½ cup all-purpose flour or bread crumbs

¼ cup peanut or vegetable oil

For the Dipping Sauce:

2 Thai chilies, seeded and finely chopped

1 garlic clove, finely chopped

1 shallot, finely chopped

½ cup rice vinegar or sherry vinegar

1 tablespoon sugar

2 tablespoons Thai fish sauce

2 tablespoons creamy peanut butter without additives

Preparing the Fish Cake Mixture: Combine all the ingredients for the fish cakes except the flour and oil in the bowl of a food processor. Puree the mixture for about 2 minutes and

transfer it to a mixing bowl. If you don't have a food processor the ingredients can be chopped by hand. Count on 10 to 15 minutes if chopping.Cover with plastic wrap and refrigerate for about 2 hours so the mixture stiffens. Meanwhile, make the sauce.

Preparing the Sauce: Whisk together all the ingredients and let sit in a bowl in the refrigerator for at least an hour for the flavors to infuse.

Forming and Sautéing the Fish Cakes: Form the fish cake mixture into flattened balls by first dipping your hands in a bowl of cold water—this prevents sticking—and shaping the fish mixture between your palms. Spread a baking sheet with flour and arrange the fish cakes in rows on the flour. (Don't try to flour the cakes with your hands wet.) When all the fish cakes are formed (you should have 18 cakes about 1½ inches in diameter), roll them in the flour and pat them to remove excess. Arrange them on another baking sheet.

Heat the oil in a large sauté pan or skillet and sauté the fish cakes over low to medium heat for about 3 minutes on each side, until golden brown. Serve immediately on hot plates (or a platter if you're passing them as hors d'oeuvres) with a small bowl of dipping sauce on the platter or next to each place.

STIR-FRYING

There's hardly any difference between sautéing and stir-frying; in fact both are excellent methods for quick-cooking foods such as small chunks or strips of fish and vegetables. The only real difference between Western-style sautéing and Chinese-style stir-frying is the pan: The Chinese use a bowl-

shaped pan—a wok—and Western cooks use a skillet.

While the wok has certain advantages over a skillet—it's easy to keep the food moving in a wok so each piece cooks quickly and evenly—the best implement is what you're used to and feel handy with. I've made plenty of Chinese stir-fries in an iron skillet and an occasional dish of Provençal-style sautéed scallops in a wok.

The rules for stir-frying are much the same as when you're sautéing in a skillet. The wok should be set on a stand—so it stays straight—over medium to high heat with a tablespoon or two of oil. Finely chopped aromatic ingredients such as ginger, garlic, shallots, and onions can be added to the oil and given a minute or two to sizzle but not brown. This infuses the flavor of the aromatic ingredients in the oil so it ends up evenly distributed in the dish. Fish and vegetables can be added next and quickly tossed or stirred—I use a couple of chopsticks for stirring—so they don't have time to stick. When stir-frying combinations of fish, shellfish, or vegetables, you need to estimate the cooking times of each ingredient and put them in the wok at different stages. Whatever you decide to stir-fry, be sure to select seafood that won't stick to the pan or fall apart. My favorite candidates are shrimp, scallops (sea or bay), and cubes of firm-fleshed fish such as swordfish or monkfish. I also like to include crunchy vegetables such as snow or sugar snap peas, mushrooms (sliced or quartered vertically), asparagus tips, bok choy, and baby turnip greens.

Most stir-fried dishes are rushed to the table as soon as each ingredient is cooked through, but sometimes liquids such as broth or water are added to the stir-fry along with a thickener such as cornstarch or arrowroot so the fish and vegetables end up coated with a light sauce. Most stir-fried dishes are best served with plain boiled rice.

❧

Orange-Scented Stir-fried Shrimp

This is an adaptation of a scallop recipe in Barbara Tropp's wonderful book *The Modern Art of Chinese Cooking.* The scent of orange combined with the heat of the chilies and the cool crunch of water chestnuts is hard to resist. I sometimes serve this dish as a main course, but it's great as one of many courses in a Chinese meal. Shrimp is called for here, but any firm-fleshed shellfish or finfish will work.

MAKES 4 MAIN-COURSE SERVINGS

1½ pounds headless shrimp, peeled and deveined

2 tablespoons dry sherry or Chinese rice wine

1 tablespoon dark soy sauce

½ pound fresh water chestnuts or one 8-ounce can, drained

1 tablespoon cornstarch

½ cup chicken broth (page 344)

2 tablespoons peanut oil

two 3-inch strips orange zest, cut into very fine julienne

2 garlic cloves, finely chopped

1 tablespoon freshly grated ginger

½ teaspoon hot red pepper flakes

¼ pound snow peas, ends broken off

Marinate the shrimp in the sherry and soy sauce in the refrigerator for 2 hours.

If you're using fresh water chestnuts, rinse them thoroughly before peeling because they're often covered with mud. Peel them with a paring knife and slice them crosswise into ⅛-inch-thick disks. Rinse canned water chestnuts thoroughly under cold water, drain, and slice in the same way as fresh.

Work the cornstarch to a smooth paste with a tablespoon of the chicken broth and then stir the paste into the remaining chicken broth.

Heat the peanut oil in a wok or large iron skillet over medium heat. When the oil begins to ripple, stir in the orange zest, garlic, ginger, and hot pepper flakes. Stir for about 1 minute—the flavorings should sizzle but not brown—and toss in the shrimp and snow peas. Turn the heat up to high and stir or toss the mixture until the shrimp turns red, about 3 minutes. Pour in the chicken broth/cornstarch mixture and continue stirring over high heat until the liquids come to a boil and coat the shrimp and vegetables, after about 1 minute. Serve immediately.

USING THAI CURRIES FOR QUICK STIR-FRIES

Thai curries—either homemade (page 340) or out of a can—are great for finishing a quick stir-fry. If you include vegetables in the stir-fry, you can serve it with a bowl of rice for a quick and easy dinner. Most simple stir-fries I just leave alone and serve at the table in a large bowl or on a platter, but it's also easy to convert a stir-fry into a saucy Thai curry by adding a little broth or water and perhaps some coconut milk.

❧

Scallop, Shrimp, and Vegetable Stir-fry with Green Curry

This is one of my favorite don't-feel-like-cooking dishes. You can get by with canned Thai curry if you don't have any homemade on hand. Be sure to serve this dish with plenty of rice.

MAKES 4 MAIN-COURSE SERVINGS

¾ pound sea scallops, side muscle pulled away, cut into ⅓-inch-thick disks

1 pound medium or large shrimp, peeled and deveined

2 tablespoons peanut oil

⅓ pound small to medium mushrooms, quartered

⅓ pound snow peas, ends broken off, strings pulled away

2 tablespoons green curry paste (page 340)

salt

½ cup chicken broth (page 344) or water

1 cup unsweetened coconut milk

Dry the scallops and shrimp in paper towels. (Don't let them stay in contact with the paper towels, or they will stick.)

Heat the oil in a wok or heavy iron skillet or nonstick pan over high heat. Toss in the mushrooms and stir for about 4 minutes, until they brown lightly. Add the snow peas and the shrimp and scallops and continue to stir over high heat for about 3 minutes, until the shrimp starts to turn orange and the scallops start to turn opaque. Add the green curry and stir everything together—until well coated with curry—for about 1 minute. Sprinkle with salt. Arrange everything on plates or a platter, pour the chicken broth and coconut milk into the still-hot wok or skillet, and bring to a simmer. Ladle this sauce over the stir-fry.

Marinating, Curing, and Smoking

*B*efore we all had refrigerators and freezers, fish that needed to be saved for any length of time had to be prepared in some way to keep it from going bad. Salt, vinegar, lime juice, and smoke were all originally used as preservatives, but by happy coincidence many of the techniques used to preserve seafood also give us especially delicious seafood products. A lot of very good preserved seafood products are on the market—smoked salmon, marinated herring, salt cod to name a few—but the homemade versions are usually less expensive and often end up tasting better.

MARINATING SEAFOOD

Marinades are used for flavoring and sometimes for tenderizing or partially cooking raw seafood. Tougher seafood, especially shellfish such as octopus or squid, is sometimes soaked in a flavorful marinade before braising so that the marinade acts as a tenderizer while also contributing flavor. While marinated seafood looks cooked because it takes on an opaque appearance, the marinade rarely penetrates to the center of the seafood in the same way as heat, leaving the center virtually raw. The acid contained in certain foods such as limes causes the protein in seafood to denature in much the same way as egg whites turn opaque as they are heated.

Marinades are also used to flavor already fried or sautéed seafood such as escabeche.

SEVICHE

In South America and parts of Mexico, seviche is not just a seafood dish—it's practically a national pastime. Every town and village seems to have its own version, and seviche is such a regular part of the daily diet that everyone considers himself a connoisseur.

A seviche is a dish of raw seafood that has been marinated in lemon or lime juice, herbs, chilies, and aromatic vegetables for anywhere from a couple of minutes to several hours. The marinade tenderizes the fish, turning it from translucent to white and slightly opaque. While the result somewhat resembles cooked fish, the fish isn't *really* cooked—so you should take the same precautions when selecting fish for seviche as you would when serving raw fish (see Safety Tips, page 90).

Use whatever seafood is impeccably fresh and combine it with different herbs or vegetables following your own whimsy. Most seviche is made with raw fish or shellfish, but some kinds of shellfish must first be cooked at least partially, or they will either be too tough (octopus, squid), have an unpleasant texture, or be hard to extract from the shell (crab, lobster, shrimp).

INGREDIENTS FOR SEVICHE

Even though a seviche is often partly improvised (you never know what you're going to find at the fish market), certain guidelines will help you choose the right ingredients for your own version.

Herbs: Cilantro is the herb used most commonly in a seviche partly because of its almost magical affinity for hot chilies, another essential ingredient. Many people don't like the flavor of cilantro (it's an acquired taste), and even avid fans want a break now and then. In those cases you can substitute parsley (the flat-leaf Italian variety is best), dill, fennel greens, chives, chervil, thyme, marjoram, oregano, epazote, or even tarragon (which will give the seviche a French twist).

Chilies: A seviche should always include some hot chilies, although you can vary the amount to taste. Unless I'm serving people I know very well, I keep the seviche mild and then pass finely chopped chilies at the table. I usually use fresh serrano or jalapeño chilies, but you can also experiment with more exotic varieties or even dried chilies. If you want to keep the seviche distinctly mild but still want the color and flavor of chilies, use red, green, or yellow bell peppers with their skins charred (over a gas flame or under an electric broiler element, page 133) and scraped off.

Aromatic Vegetables: You'll always want to include at least one member of the onion family—try red onions, shallots, or scallions. I usually thinly slice the onions instead of chopping them so they give a little crunch to the whole concoction. And I almost always sneak in a little finely chopped garlic. Other possibilities include cooked and cubed sweet potatoes, avocados, tomatoes, olives (pit them yourself; never buy olives in a can), capers, corn kernels, lettuce (shredded), ginger (finely grated), peas, cucumbers, celery, and dozens of other ingredients.

Liquids: An acidic ingredient, usually lemon or lime juice but occasionally vinegar, is essential. I like to add a little dribble of extra-virgin olive oil or serve it on the table for guests to help themselves. Some recipes call for white wine, which can add a nice flavor— just make sure not to add too much (no more than half the quantity of citrus juice), or you'll dilute the acidity and the seafood won't "cook" or taste tangy enough.

A LITTLE TERMINOLOGY

brine: A concentrated solution of salt dissolved in water.

curing: Coating foods in preservative mixtures that usually include salt and sometimes sugar or submerging in brine to preserve and flavor.

escabeche: A method of sautéing or frying fish and then marinating it with herbs, aromatic vegetables, and an acidic ingredient such as vinegar or lime or lemon juice.

gravlax: A Scandinavian specialty made by curing fish, usually salmon, with salt, sugar, and herbs—especially dill.

seviche (also cebiche or ceviche): A Central and South American method of marinating raw seafood in lime or lemon juice with herbs and aromatic vegetables.

smoking: Exposing foods to wood smoke to flavor and (at least partially) preserve them. There are two kinds of smoking, hot and cold.

Mackerel Seviche

The poor underrated mackerel is one of my favorite fish because it's delicious, inexpensive, and, when available, usually very fresh. If you can't find mackerel (upscale fish stores often don't bother to carry it), any dense-fleshed saltwater round fish will work, provided it's impeccably fresh.

I used to recommend running home and making the seviche immediately after buying the fish, but unless you buy frozen fish or have some way of ascertaining that the fish contains no parasites, I now recommend freezing the fish for at least 24 hours at 0°F (see box) and then slowly thawing it out in the refrigerator. When you finally have your thawed-out fish in hand, prepare the other ingredients—squeeze limes, chop vegetables, etc. Seviche is best prepared only about an hour before serving but can be made up to 4 hours in advance.

This dish is a delicious opener to a warm-weather dinner.

MAKES 8 FIRST-COURSE SERVINGS

2½ pounds whole mackerel or Spanish mackerel, filleted and skin removed, or 1½ pounds tuna, swordfish, or king mackerel steaks, or 1½ pounds wahoo fillet

3 tomatoes, peeled, seeded, and cut into 1-inch chunks

1 tablespoon coarse salt

1 medium red onion, finely sliced

2 small garlic cloves, finely chopped

2 jalapeño chilies, seeded and finely chopped

2 serrano chilies, seeded and finely chopped (optional)

2 ripe avocados, preferably Haas (the kind with nubby skin), peeled, pitted, and cut into ½-inch cubes

1 cup fresh lime juice (from about 8 limes)

¼ cup extra-virgin olive oil

3 tablespoons chopped fresh cilantro

salt and pepper

Carefully go over the fish fillets or steaks. Remove any bones or skin and trim off any dark sections from the fish. Cut the fish into pieces about 1 inch long and ½ inch wide. Cover with plastic wrap and refrigerate.

Toss the tomato chunks with the coarse salt and place in a colander over a bowl to drain for 30 minutes.

One hour before serving, combine all the ingredients, including the fish, in a large decorative bowl and refrigerate. Just before serving, taste to make sure the seasoning is right. Serve on chilled plates at the table.

Mixed Shellfish Seviche

(color page 5)

Shellfish gives a wonderful texture to a seviche, but if you're including squid or crustaceans such as shrimp or lobster, you'll have to pre-cook them lightly in boiling water. This is a great dish for an outdoor buffet or for a family-style dinner. If you can't find some of the seafood, or if a particular variety is too expensive in your area, just substitute more of one of the others.

MAKES 8 FIRST-COURSE SERVINGS

1 gallon water

1 pound shrimp (1½ pounds if with heads)

three 1¼-pound lobsters or 1 pound crabmeat

1 pound squid, cleaned, tentacles cut in half through the base, hoods sliced into ¼-inch rings (see color page 19)

3 tomatoes, peeled, seeded, and cut into 1-inch chunks

1 tablespoon coarse salt

½ pound bay or sea scallops, small side muscle removed

1 cup fresh lime juice (from about 8 limes)

1 medium red onion, chopped

2 small garlic cloves, finely chopped

3 ripe avocados, preferably Haas (the kind with nubby skin), peeled, pitted, and cut into ½-inch cubes

4 jalapeño chilies, seeded and finely chopped

2 red bell peppers, skin charred and scraped off (page 133), cut into ¼-inch-wide strips

4 canned chipotle chilies, drained, seeded, and coarsely chopped

about 1 cup extra-virgin olive oil in a serving pitcher

¼ cup chopped fresh cilantro

salt and pepper

Bring the water to a boil in a big pot. Submerge the shrimp in the boiling water for 30 seconds, quickly remove with a skimmer or slotted spoon, and let cool. Remove the shrimp heads if the shrimp have them, peel, and devein if necessary.

Submerge the lobsters in the boiling water for 6 minutes—if there isn't enough water to submerge them completely, cover the pot so that those parts of the lobster not submerged will steam. Take out and let cool.

Blanch the squid in the boiling water for 30 seconds and quickly drain in a colander.

Toss the tomato chunks in coarse salt and drain in a colander set over a bowl for 30 minutes.

Take the lobsters out of the shell, slice the tails into ¼-inch-thick medallions, and cut the claw meat into cubes.

At least 1 hour before serving, toss together the seafood and the rest of the ingredients in a big decorative bowl. Season with salt and pepper to taste and toss gently. Refrigerate for at least 1 hour—but up to all day—and serve.

OTHER METHODS OF PRESENTING MARINATED FISH

While the seafood in a seviche is usually marinated for an hour or two, some seafood is marinated for only a couple of minutes before it is served.

One of the most delightful ways to serve fish is to slice it very thinly—in the same way as smoked salmon—and then marinate the fish right on the plate for just 20 or 30 minutes before serving.

Marinated Salmon with Capers and Herb-Scented Olive Oil

*I*f you don't happen to have a bottle of herb-scented oil around and don't want to make your own (it takes a week), substitute plain extra-virgin olive oil combined at the last minute with 3 tablespoons of chopped fresh herbs such as dill, parsley, tarragon, the green leafy parts of the fennel, chervil, or chives. Avoid using stronger herbs such as thyme, marjoram, oregano, or lavender because they will mask the flavor of the salmon—in the oil they become more subtle.

You can slice the salmon and put it on the plates earlier in the day—just cover the plates with plastic wrap and keep them in the refrigerator. The marinade, however, will need to be brushed on the salmon about 30 minutes before serving.

Although Atlantic salmon, almost all of which is farmed, rarely contains parasites, it is always safer to use fish that has been frozen (see box on page 90). This is absolutely true if you're using wild Pacific salmon, which is far more likely to contain parasites.

MAKES 8 FIRST-COURSE SERVINGS

½ cup Provençal herb-scented oil (see box) or 3 tablespoons finely chopped fresh tarragon, chervil, parsley, dill, basil, or fennel fronds combined with ½ cup extra-virgin olive oil

1½ pounds salmon fillet with skin, pin bones removed

20 black peppercorns

½ cup balsamic vinegar

2 teaspoons salt

1 tablespoon finely chopped chives

2 tablespoons capers, preferably small

Lightly brush the bottoms of eight 10-inch plates with some of the herb-scented oil or with plain extra-virgin olive oil.

Slice or pound the salmon fillet into ⅛-inch-thick slices (see box on page 93) and arrange the salmon on the oiled plates, covering as much of the plate—except the rim—as possible.

Crush the peppercorns by placing them on a cutting board and rocking a pot over them. Combine the peppercorns with the balsamic vinegar and salt in a small saucepan and boil the mixture over medium heat until ¼ cup remains. Strain through a fine-mesh strainer and discard the peppercorns. Let the sauce cool and stir in the chopped chives.

Gently whisk the remaining oil into the vinegar mixture. If you're not using the Provençal oil, whisk in the chopped herbs. Brush or lightly spoon the mixture over the salmon in a thin layer—you'll need about a tablespoon of sauce per serving. Chill the plates in the refrigerator for 15 minutes. Sprinkle a few capers over each plate and serve.

PROVENÇAL HERB-SCENTED OIL

about 20 fresh thyme sprigs

about 10 fresh marjoram sprigs

about 5 fresh oregano sprigs

about 20 fresh basil leaves

1-quart bottle of extra-virgin olive oil with ½ cup poured off to make room for the herbs

Wash the herbs and dry them thoroughly in paper towels. Push the herbs through the mouth of the olive oil bottle. Put the top on the bottle and store at room temperature for 1 week. To keep the oil longer, transfer it to the refrigerator.

Marinated Herring Fillets

(color page 12)

*M*arinated herring is easy to find in jars or at delicatessens, but it's always better when you make it yourself. Here the herring is marinated with fresh thyme and tarragon, though it's worthwhile to play around with other herbs such as dill, fennel, or basil. I like to serve marinated herring as a first course with crusty French bread, butter, and crisp white wine. You'll probably have leftovers for lunch or another dinner; the herring will keep for at least a week in the refrigerator.

MAKES 10 FIRST-COURSE SERVINGS

ten 12-ounce fresh herring, scaled and filleted

2 cups coarse salt

2 cloves

2 tablespoons white peppercorns

5 shallots, thinly sliced

3 carrots, thinly sliced

2 garlic cloves, finely chopped

1 tablespoon finely chopped fresh tarragon

2 tablespoons finely chopped parsley

½ teaspoon chopped fresh thyme or ¼ teaspoon dried

1 bay leaf

2 cups sherry vinegar or good-quality white wine vinegar

Rinse the herring fillets under cold water and dry them thoroughly. Roll the fillets in coarse salt and layer them in a nonmetal bowl. Refrigerate for 2 hours, turning the fillets over every 30 minutes.

Meanwhile, crush the cloves and peppercorns by placing them on a cutting board and rocking a saucepan over them. Combine the crushed cloves and peppercorns with the other ingredients in a nonmetal bowl and refrigerate.

Brush off the salt clinging to the herring fillets—but don't rinse the fillets—and put them in the bowl with the marinade. Make sure all the fillets are well covered with the marinade, cover the bowl with plastic wrap, and refrigerate for 24 hours. Serve right out of the refrigerator.

Safety Tip Fresh herring sometimes contain parasites called *herring worms.* To eliminate any risk of herring worms, freeze the herring fillets for at least 24 hours in a 0°F or colder freezer.

PICKLING ESCABECHE

Popular in the Mediterranean and South America and one of the most delicious ways of serving cold seafood, escabeche is made with marinated fish or shellfish that has been floured and sautéed or deep-fried. The principal marinade ingredient is usually vinegar, but some recipes use so much olive oil that the fish is completely submerged and will keep for over a month in the refrigerator.

One of the tastiest versions is the Venetian *sfogi in saor,* made with sole. Sometimes this dish calls for spices and pomegranate juice, reminiscent of Venice's link with the East. In Abruzzi, along Italy's Adriatic coast, *scapece* is fish that is first fried and then marinated in wooden barrels in saffron-scented wine vinegar. Sicily has several methods for preparing sardines *a beccafico*—most calling for pine nuts, raisins, vinegar, and herbs. Sardinia also has its own version of pickled fish, *scabecciu.*

The French too are fond of pickled fish, especially sardines marinated in

---

SLICING OR POUNDING

The best way to slice fish thinly is to use a long, thin, very sharp knife and cut off paper-thin slices starting from the tail and gradually working up to the head end of the fish (page 102).

Thinly slicing fish takes practice and can be frustrating the first time around. An easier method is just to slice the fish as thinly as you can, place each slice between two sheets of plastic wrap, and then gently pound them with the side of a cleaver until they have the thickness you want. This method also makes it easy to transfer the slices to plates—simply peel off the top layer of plastic, invert the bottom layer with the slice onto the plate, and peel off the plastic. Remember to place the least attractive side of the slice facedown on the plate.

---

olive oil, herbs, garlic, and vinegar, called escabeche. Spanish cooks also make a version of escabeche—called *escabetx* in Catalan—also with sardines and with perhaps a bit of rosemary not found in French versions.

I prefer to sauté the fish rather than fry it so I have to heat up less oil. Once the fish is cooked, I pour on hot wine vinegar and then add various herbs, spices, and aromatic vegetables, depending on whim and what I've found at the market. While most escabeche recipes call for relatively few ingredients, I like to include vegetables such as pearl onions, artichoke hearts, julienned carrots, or fennel wedges to make the dish more substantial and pretty. I almost always serve escabeche as a first course with plenty of crusty French or Italian bread and cool white wine.

Slightly oily fish such as mackerel, herring, tuna, trout, red mullet (rouget) or fresh sardines work best in escabeche, but almost any fish fillets will do except for flounder or so-called sole (except Dover sole), which will fall apart in the marinade.

Escabeche was probably invented as a means of preserving fish, but I think it is best served the same day it is made, when its flavors seem more delicate. It will, however, keep in a cov-

ered container in the refrigerator for at least three days.

Pickled fish dishes make lovely first courses or light main courses. In either case, be sure to serve them with plenty of crusty bread for mopping up the tangy marinade.

Sardines Escabeche

This is one of those dishes I first encountered in the south of France, sitting outdoors on a restaurant terrace, drinking too much white wine. The secret, I think, is to serve lots of crusty French bread for mopping up the marinade. This version is a little more complicated than the one I tasted in France—I've sneaked in some marinated vegetables—but feel free to leave out any or all except the red onion and garlic.

Sardines are abundant all along the Mediterranean, and sometimes imported fresh sardines are available, at least in East Coast fish stores. Most American sardines are actually herrings and work fine as well. If you can't find any of these, you can use another fish with a relatively high oil content such as mackerel, trout, or smelts. On the East Coast I sometimes find beautiful red imported Mediterranean rougets—I use them for this dish whenever I can. Fillet larger fish; gut and cook smaller fish whole.

This is one of the few seafood dishes that can be made up to 3 days in advance.

MAKES 6 FIRST-COURSE SERVINGS

18 to 30 fresh sardines, about 3 pounds, cleaned and scales rubbed off

salt and pepper

½ cup all-purpose flour

1 cup extra-virgin olive oil

1 medium red onion, thinly sliced

2 garlic cloves, peeled

⅔ cup sherry vinegar or good-quality white wine vinegar

2 bay leaves

½ teaspoon fresh thyme leaves or ¼ teaspoon dried

2 tablespoons finely chopped parsley

6 baby artichokes, outer leaves removed, tops trimmed (optional)

18 pearl onions, peeled (optional)

1 fennel bulb, cut vertically into 6 wedges (optional)

½ cup green French or Italian olives, pitted and coarsely chopped (optional)

Season the fillets or whole fish with salt and pepper and dredge them in flour. Be sure to pat off any excess flour.

Over medium to high heat, brown the fish for about 1½ minutes on each side in 2 tablespoons of the olive oil in a nonstick pan. Especially if you're using fillets, keep the fish slightly undercooked so they won't fall apart when stirred with the marinade. Transfer the cooked fish to a bowl or square casserole large enough to hold them in a single layer.

Wipe out the sauté pan and in 2 tablespoons more olive oil cook the

red onion and garlic over medium heat until the onion softens but remains crisp, about 8 minutes. Pour in the vinegar, bring to a simmer, and add the bay leaves and thyme. Simmer gently for 5 minutes, then pour in the rest of the olive oil and the chopped parsley. Pour this mixture over the fish. Let cool, cover with plastic wrap, and refrigerate for at least 2 hours but up to 3 days.

Prepare the remaining ingredients if desired. Cook the artichokes in boiling salted water in a nonaluminum pot for 15 to 20 minutes and then nestle them in the marinade with the fish.

Cook the pearl onions in a pot or pan just large enough to hold them in a single layer. Add enough water to come halfway up their sides, season them with salt and pepper, and cook over medium heat until all the water evaporates and the onions are coated with a light glaze, about 15 minutes. Nestle the onions in the marinade with the fish.

Season the fennel wedges and cook them in a single layer in a covered pot with just enough water to come halfway up their sides for about 15 minutes. Let cool and then nestle the wedges in with the fish.

Season the vegetables with salt and pepper and serve the escabeche with 3 pearl onions, a baby artichoke, and a fennel wedge on each plate. If you like, sprinkle each serving with the chopped olives.

Substitutes Fillets with skin such as Mediterranean rougets (red mullet), small mackerel or Spanish mackerel, trout (1½ pounds for 6 servings)

Whole fish such as anchovies, baby herring, smelts (3 pounds for 6 servings)

Mexican-Style Tuna Escabeche

*I*n all honesty I don't know if this dish is authentically Mexican, but it's gradually evolved from my experiments with Mexican ingredients. Tuna's full flavor and firm texture make it the perfect choice. I like to serve this dish as the main course for a summer lunch or dinner. This dish can be made up to 3 days in advance.

MAKES 6 FIRST-COURSE SERVINGS

2½ pounds fresh tuna steaks, skin and dark parts trimmed off

salt and pepper

1½ cups extra-virgin olive oil

1 medium red onion, thinly sliced

3 garlic cloves, finely chopped

2 jalapeño chilies, seeded and finely chopped

2 serrano chilies, seeded and finely chopped (optional; pass them at the table instead if desired)

1 teaspoon dried oregano, preferably Mexican, or 2 teaspoons finely chopped fresh

½ cup good-quality white wine vinegar

3 tablespoons finely chopped fresh cilantro

Season the tuna steaks with salt and pepper and brown them in 2 tablespoons of the olive oil in a skillet over high heat for about 2 minutes on each side. (The tuna will still be almost raw in the center but will "cook" in the marinade.) Transfer the tuna to a plate and let cool.

Wipe out the pan and add 2 tablespoons fresh oil. Cook the onion, garlic, and chilies over medium heat until the onions soften but remain crisp, about 8 minutes. Stir in the oregano, cook for 1 minute more, and then add the vinegar. Bring the vinegar to a slow simmer, turn off the heat, stir in the cilantro and the rest of the olive oil, and add a teaspoon of salt.

Slice the tuna, with the grain, into strips about ½ inch thick and arrange them in a single layer in a large bowl or square glass casserole. Pour on the vinegar mixture, cover with plastic wrap, and refrigerate for at least an hour before serving.

Substitutes Firm-fleshed full-flavored steaks or fillets such as mahimahi, shark, swordfish, wahoo

❧

Venetian-Style Marinated Cooked Pompano Fillets

SFOGI IN SAOR

Even though *sfogi* means "sole," American varieties of sole—which are really flounder—will fall apart if you fry them and then marinate them. Authentic Dover sole is the only sole you can really substitute—I've never seen the little Adriatic sole available in Venice for sale in the United States—but Dover sole is such an extravagance that I usually substitute pompano because of its firm texture and delicate flavor. Sturgeon, swordfish, and tuna will all work too, but pompano fillets remind me most of the sole tasted in Venice.

Some *sfogi in saor* recipes call for just onion, wine vinegar, and olive oil, but others, like this one, contain additional spices and pomegranate juice. Look for the juice at a health food store—some even squeeze it fresh—or substitute pomegranate molasses, sold in Middle Eastern groceries, diluted

with an equal quantity of water. If neither is available, leave it out.

MAKES 8 FIRST-COURSE OR 4 MAIN-COURSE SERVINGS

1½ **pounds pompano, John Dory, lingcod, blackfish, or yellowtail fillets or 2 pounds tuna, sturgeon, or swordfish steaks, bones and skin removed**

salt and pepper

½ **cup all-purpose flour**

¾ **cup extra-virgin olive oil**

1 **red onion, finely sliced**

¼ **teaspoon ground cinnamon**

⅛ **teaspoon ground cloves**

1 **teaspoon grated fresh ginger**

1 **teaspoon ground coriander**

½ **cup sherry vinegar or balsamic vinegar**

2 **fresh thyme sprigs**

⅓ **cup pomegranate juice or 3 tablespoons pomegranate molasses diluted with 3 tablespoons water (optional)**

2 **bay leaves**

2 **heaped tablespoons golden raisins**

2 **heaped tablespoons pine nuts toasted in a 350°F oven until pale brown, about 15 minutes**

Remove the skin and any bones from the fillets or steaks. If you have rather large fillets, cut them in half—crosswise on a diagonal—so you have at least 8 pieces. If you're using steaks, leave them whole until after they are cooked.

Season the fish with salt and pepper and dredge in flour. Pat off any excess flour—the coating on the fish should be very thin, or the whole thing will taste pasty—and brown the fish on both sides in ¼ cup of the olive oil in a nonstick pan over high heat. Take the fish out of the pan while it's just slightly underdone (3 minutes on each side per inch of thickness) and transfer it to a plate covered with paper towels to absorb the oil. If you're

using steaks, cut them into a total of 8 or 16 strips.

Wipe out the pan and gently cook the onion in the remaining olive oil over medium heat for about 10 minutes, until the onion slices start to turn limp but are not browned. Stir in the spices and continue stirring over medium heat for about a minute, until you smell the spices. Add the rest of the ingredients except the pine nuts and simmer gently for 5 minutes. Let this mixture cool for 5 minutes and season with salt and pepper to taste.

Arrange the cooked fish in a serving dish—I use an oval gratin dish—spoon on the cooked onion mixture, and sprinkle on the pine nuts. Season again with salt and pepper, cover with plastic wrap, and refrigerate for 8 to 48 hours. Take out of the refrigerator about an hour before serving.

CURING

Curing means coating fish or shellfish with salt and sometimes sugar or soaking it in brine. The salt and/or sugar draw out moisture and change the seafood's texture, making it denser and easier to slice into thin sheets. They also act as preservatives. The keeping qualities are usually secondary today; we value cured seafood mainly because it's delicious. Various herbs and spices can be included along with the salt to give cured seafood a special distinctive flavor.

Seafood with a high fat content is best for curing because the fat keeps the seafood from seeming dry even when the salt has removed most of its natural moisture. Salmon is a particularly good high-fat choice because of its deep flavor.

❧

Gravlax

This Swedish specialty is made by packing salmon fillets in salt, sugar, and dill (I sometimes substitute fresh basil or tarragon leaves) for 2 to 3 days. The finished salmon is then served in thin slices like smoked salmon, with crisp toasts, lemon wedges, and dill mustard sauce.

I usually use a whole salmon and serve it as the first course at a dinner party or brunch. This gives me plenty of leftovers, which will keep, tightly wrapped in plastic wrap, for 2 weeks in the refrigerator or indefinitely in the freezer. To make less, just buy 2 pieces of salmon fillet the same size and cut down the other ingredients proportionately. The curing time is the same regardless of the length or width of the fillets, but if the fillets are from the tail end and seem thin, cut the curing time in half. Don't use fillets without the skin—leaving the skin on the fillets makes slicing much easier. The larger the fillets, the easier they are to slice.

MAKES 5 POUNDS, ABOUT 20 GENEROUS FIRST-COURSE SERVINGS

two 2½-pound whole salmon fillets with skin

¾ cup coarse salt

¾ cup sugar

5 tablespoons coarsely chopped fresh dill or tarragon or 20 fresh basil leaves

lemon wedges

toast

unsalted butter

Use tweezers or needlenose pliers to carefully pull out any pin bones remaining in the salmon.

Stir the salt and sugar together in a mixing bowl. Roll out a sheet of aluminum foil about 4 inches longer than the salmon fillets and sprinkle on a quarter of the salt/sugar mixture. Place a fillet, skin side down, on the mixture and move the fillet around so the skin side is well coated. Sprinkle two thirds of the remaining mixture over the flesh side of the fillet—sprinkling less on the thinner tail end—and sprinkle on the dill or arrange the basil leaves in rows so they completely cover the fillet. Place the second fillet, flesh side down, over the first. Sprinkle the remaining salt/sugar mixture over the skin of the second fillet.

Wrap the salmon tightly in aluminum foil and place it on a platter or cutting board. Put a cutting board or something flat on the salmon to weight it slightly and refrigerate the whole thing for 48 hours, turning the salmon over every 12 hours.

When the salmon is finished curing, separate the fillets and quickly rinse off the salt/sugar mixture under cold running water. Pat dry with paper towels and serve in very thin slices in the same way as cold smoked salmon. Serve with lemon wedges and thin slices of toast and butter at the table.

SMOKING

Smoked seafood is not only one of the great delights of the table but also one of the most versatile. It can be served for breakfast, as an hors d'oeuvre at a cocktail party, or as a first course at dinner—even as dinner itself.

There are about as many kinds of smoked seafood as there are varieties of seafood. While almost anything from the sea can be smoked, fish and shellfish with a relatively high fat con-

tent take best to smoking—leaner fish and shellfish tend to dry out.

Two basic methods are used: Hot smoking cooks the seafood at the same time as it flavors it with smoke. Cold smoking uses cured seafood, and the smoke is cool enough not to cook the seafood.

Hot-smoked seafood usually looks opaque, while cold-smoked seafood looks almost shiny or translucent. Cold-smoked fish is usually served in thin slices; hot smoked seafood has to be served in larger pieces to prevent it from breaking apart.

HOT SMOKING

This is the easiest way to smoke seafood at home because it can be done without special equipment. And unlike cold-smoked seafood, hot-smoked seafood cooks in a relatively short time.

There are really three approaches to hot smoking. The first method, the same used for commercial hot-smoked fish, is to smoke the seafood long enough—usually several hours—so that it stays at an internal temperature of 180°F for at least 30 minutes. This kills most bacteria so that the smoked seafood will keep for up to a month in the refrigerator or indefinitely in the freezer. The disadvantage is that all but the oiliest seafood dries out and may acquire a very strong smoky taste.

A second method, my favorite, is to smoke the seafood until it reaches a temperature of 140°F—just hot enough to cook it through—and then serve it right out of the smoker. Seafood that has been hot-smoked in this way can also be kept, tightly wrapped in plastic, in the refrigerator for up to 2 days and served cold.

WHAT KIND OF WOOD TO USE?

Even though most woods can be used for smoking seafood, avoid resinous woods such as pine or eucalyptus. Not only might they flare up in the smoker, but they can give the seafood a strong acrid taste.

The best woods for smoking are fruitwoods and hardwoods. Apple, cherry, pear, and alderwood all give slightly different nuances to smoked fish. The best Scottish smoked salmon is made with oak barrels that were used for aging whiskey. (And the best whiskey barrels were first used for aging sherry.) Hickory, maple, and mesquite are also excellent for smoking but if not used carefully can give the seafood an overwhelmingly smoky taste—so use them sparingly. The best approach is to experiment with one or two woods and then stick with them until you learn to gauge smoking times and temperatures.

Wood for smoking is available in sawdust form or in chips. Sawdust is best for stovetop smoking or if your smoker has a hot plate. Wood chips are best to use if you're using an actual fire or bed of coals. Some recipes suggest soaking wood chips or moistening sawdust with water to get them to produce more smoke, but I've found that all this does is slow down the process, so I don't bother.

The last method consists of lightly smoking seafood without cooking it all the way through—just smoking it enough to scent it with smoke—and then immediately finishing the cooking using another method.

EQUIPMENT FOR HOT SMOKING

If you plan to do a lot of smoking or to smoke large whole fish or fillets, a home smoker might be worth the investment. In choosing among several brands and styles now on the market, you should watch for certain pitfalls. Don't buy a smoker that's too small. Think of the largest fish you're likely to smoke (a whole salmon fillet?) and buy accordingly. If you're smoking only a few fish or small fish, you can use one of the small stovetop smokers available at cooking equipment stores or use an improvised stovetop smoker following one of the methods given here. Avoid barbecue-type smokers, which stack the fish directly over hot coals and generate

too much heat. Smoking at too high a temperature causes the seafood to render fat, which drips down into the heat source, creating smoke with an unpleasant smell and taste.

My own hot smoker—bought out of a mail-order sporting goods catalog (see "Sources")—is a rectangular sheet-metal contraption about 3 feet high and 2 feet wide with a hot plate on the bottom and 3 shelves for holding the fish. It also has a little chimney sticking out of the top to release smoke. Its advantage is that I can closely control the cooking temperature by adjusting the knob on the heat plate and putting the seafood on an upper or lower shelf. This smoker is also easy to convert into a cold smoker.

HOT SMOKING WITH A BARBECUE

All you need to do to use a barbecue for smoking small whole fish is set it up so that any fat rendered doesn't drip into the coals and make smoke

and soot of its own. To do this, line the bottom of the barbecue with aluminum foil, build a charcoal fire, and when the coals are ready, push them to one side. Arrange the seafood over the side without coals, place a handful of wood chips on top of the charcoal, and put the lid on the barbecue. Look through the vents in the barbecue cover to make sure that the wood chips are smoldering and generating smoke instead of flaring up. If after 2 minutes the chips are still flaring up, close the vents halfway. Don't close the vents too much, or you'll suffocate the coals. If you're serving the smoked seafood right away, smoke it for about 10 minutes per inch of thickness—until it reaches an internal temperature of 140°F or looks done when you cut into it. If you want to preserve seafood for a week or more by smoking, smoke it until it reaches 180°F—stick an instant-read thermometer into its back—and then keep it at this temperature for 30 minutes.

STOVETOP HOT SMOKING (SKILLET METHOD)

My good friend author Sally Schneider first taught me a variation of this simple method whereby small amounts of seafood—up to about 4 servings—can be lightly hot-smoked in an iron skillet without smoking up the whole house. You'll need a large iron skillet with a lid from another pan and a circular cake rack just large enough to fit in the skillet.

When you're ready to smoke, heat the skillet over high heat for about 10 minutes, until it's extremely hot. (A sprinkling of sawdust on the pan should start smoldering right away.) Fold over a sheet of aluminum foil to form a double layer just large enough to cover the bottom of the skillet. Stab about 6 slits in the foil with a paring knife. Sprinkle the hot skillet with 3 tablespoons of sawdust and quickly place the aluminum foil over the bottom of the skillet. Set a lightly oiled cake rack over the pan, arrange the fish on the rack, and quickly cover the pan. Usually the fish is done after smoking for 20 minutes per inch of thickness, but you should start checking sooner—by cutting into the fish with a paring knife—because it's impossible to predict the exact heat of the smoker.

STOVETOP HOT SMOKING (WOK METHOD)

A wok can be used to smoke fish in almost the same way as the skillet method. In addition to a wok with a tight-fitting lid you'll need a circular cake rack that when placed in the wok is suspended at least 6 inches from the lowest part of the wok.

Make a double sheet of aluminum foil large enough to cover most of the bottom of the wok, but don't worry about covering every inch. Poke the foil in about six places with a paring knife.

When you're ready to smoke, heat the wok over high heat for about 10 minutes, until it's extremely hot. (A sprinkling of sawdust on the pan should start smoldering right away.) Sprinkle the wok with 3 heaped tablespoons of sawdust and quickly press the aluminum foil over the bottom of the wok. Set a lightly oiled circular cake rack in the wok, arrange the fish on the rack, and quickly put the cover on the wok. (If the cover doesn't rest flush against the wok—which will cause it to leak smoke—wrap the edges of the cover with aluminum foil for a tighter fit.) Usually the fish is done after smoking for 20 minutes per inch of thickness, but you should start checking sooner by cutting into the fish with a paring knife.

Hot-Smoked Salmon with Straw-Mat Potatoes

(color page 16)

I first encountered this dish when my brother ordered it in a Paris restaurant. I had expected the usual thin slices of cold smoked salmon—in fact I was a bit disappointed my brother hadn't ordered something more unusual—but what a surprise when it got to the table. The salmon was still hot—it had been smoked to order!—the slices were satisfyingly thick (about 1/3 inch), and instead of being served with toast the salmon was resting on crispy little straw-mat potatoes.

I've since made this dish using my home smoker, but you can also use a barbecue or the stovetop method. I like to serve this dish as a first course for my most special dinners, but you can also turn it into a lovely main course just by doubling the amounts, making the salmon slices thicker and larger. You may also want to serve a bowl of crème fraîche or sour cream at the table for guests to help themselves, but this isn't essential. This dish is also good made with fresh sturgeon.

MAKES 4 FIRST-COURSE SERVINGS

For the Straw-Mat Potatoes:

3 medium waxy white or red potatoes

6 tablespoons pure olive oil

6 tablespoons unsalted butter

salt and pepper

For the Salmon:

1 pound center-cut salmon fillet about
    1 inch thick, skin and pin bones removed

salt and pepper

crème fraîche or sour cream

Making the Straw-Mat Potatoes:
Peel the potatoes and cut them lengthwise into julienne about 1/8 inch on each side. The easiest way to do this is to slice the potatoes lengthwise into 1/8-inch slices on a vegetable slicer or mandoline and then slice the slices into julienne by hand. (The julienne attachment on inexpensive vegetable slicers cuts the potatoes too fine.) The julienne attachment on a French stainless-steel mandoline will also work. Soak the julienned potatoes in cold water for at least 5 minutes but up to several hours.

Drain the potatoes and dry them thoroughly—try putting them through a lettuce spinner in batches and then drying them with paper towels. (Don't leave them sitting on paper towels, or the paper will stick.)

Heat 3 tablespoons of the olive oil and 3 tablespoons of the butter in a nonstick pan. Put the pan over medium heat and when the butter starts frothing place half of the potatoes, in 2 mounds, in the pan. Press on each of the mounds with the back of the spatula to flatten them into 4-inch rounds. (This process is even easier if you make the potatoes one at a time in a small—4- to 6-inch diameter—nonstick pan). Season the potato pancakes with salt and pepper and cook over medium heat until the potatoes brown on the bottom, about 10 minutes. Gently flip the potatoes or turn them over gently with a spatula and brown for about 5 minutes on the other side. Repeat with the remaining potatoes so you end up with 4 pancakes. Keep each straw mat warm on a baking sheet in a 200°F oven while you make the others.

Smoking the Salmon and Serving:
With a long knife, slice sideways through the salmon so you have 2

slices each about ½ inch thick. Cut across each of these so you end up with 4 even, approximately rectangular pieces.

Just before serving, smoke the salmon slices for about 10 minutes in a hot smoker, barbecue, or stovetop smoker. Season the salmon with salt and pepper, place a potato straw mat on each hot plate, and set a piece of salmon on top. Serve immediately on hot plates. Pass a bowl of crème fraîche at the table for people to help themselves.

Smoked Shrimp and Tomatillo Soup

I love the tart flavor of tomatillos combined with hot chilies, and sometimes I like to cook them with chipotle chilies, which are smoked jalapeños. So combining tomatillos with lightly smoked shrimp seemed like a natural pairing.

This soup can be made up to 2 days in advance and kept in the refrigerator—just make sure the shrimp has been brought to a boil in the soup and the soup allowed to cool before refrigerating it.

MAKES 6 FIRST-COURSE SERVINGS

1½ pounds medium shrimp with heads or 1 pound without heads

1 quart chicken broth (page 344) or water

salt and pepper

2 tablespoons unsalted butter or olive oil

1 onion, chopped

3 garlic cloves, chopped

3 jalapeño chilies, seeded and chopped

1 pound fresh tomatillos, papery husks removed, coarsely chopped, or one 18-ounce can drained and coarsely chopped

2 tablespoons finely chopped fresh cilantro leaves

cayenne pepper (optional)

sour cream or crème fraîche

Peel and devein the shrimp. If the shrimp have heads, twist them off and crush with a rolling pin. Simmer the heads and/or shells, covered, in the chicken broth for 30 minutes, strain, and reserve. Season the shrimp with salt and pepper and smoke them for about 20 minutes in a hot smoker. (Don't worry if the shrimp aren't cooked through after 20 minutes; they'll finish cooking in the soup.) Reserve in the refrigerator.

Heat the butter in a 4-quart pot over medium heat and cook the onion, garlic, and chilies until the onion turns translucent, about 10 minutes. Add the tomatillos and reserved shrimp broth and simmer gently, covered, for 20 minutes.

Puree the tomatillo mixture in a blender for about 1 minute, then strain the mixture through a food mill or through a strainer using the back of a ladle into a clean pot. Stir the cilantro and smoked shrimp into the strained mixture. Thin the soup with a little broth or water if it seems too thick. Bring the soup back to a simmer and season with salt, and pepper or cayenne if it needs more heat. Serve immediately in hot bowls, passing sour cream at the table.

Hot-Smoked Trout

Smoked fish that isn't being eaten within 2 or 3 days must be cured with salt or brine before it is smoked to help extract moisture and create an unfavorable environment for bacteria

to grow. Brining also improves the flavor and texture of quick-smoked fish that you're planning to eat right away. Smaller whole fish (under 5 pounds) are most conveniently soaked for a few hours in brine, while larger whole fish or fish fillets are best rubbed with salt and sometimes sugar. Almost any whole fish can be hot-smoked, but the best fish for smoking are the oily varieties—besides trout, try mullet, Spanish mackerel, or eel.

The exact amount of smoking time needed will depend on how much smoke your smoker produces, the size of the fish, and how long you want to preserve the fish. For the light smoking to an internal temperature of 140°F that I prefer, I usually count on 1 hour per inch of thickness at the thickest part, the smoker at 180°F to 200°F. To preserve fish for a week or more, smoke it for twice as long at 200°F or more.

Preparing the Brine and Soaking the Fish: Soak the fish in a mixture of 1 gallon cold water and 3 cups kosher or sea salt (don't use table salt; it contains additives) for approximately 1 hour per pound of each individual fish (not total weight). Because different fish absorb salt at different rates, it is difficult to know exactly how long to leave a fish in the brine, so if you smoke the same kind of fish with any regularity, you'll probably want to make minor adjustments in the brining time.

Drying the Fish: After the soaking, let the fish dry for several hours so that a thin skin—called a pellicle—forms over the exposed flesh and helps seal in the fish's flavor: Quickly rinse the fish in cold water, pat them dry, and then hang them—by poking a hole in each fish near the base of the tail and inserting a loop of string—or lay it flat on racks in the open air for 3 to 6 hours, until you see that the pellicle has formed. People who live in clean places can hang their fish on a clothesline, but city dwellers must hang the fish indoors in front of a fan. (I place the fish on the rack of a turned-off oven and place a window fan, turned on low, facing the fish—this method also keeps the cat away.) While hanging helps seal in some juices, it's not an essential step. I am often too impatient and just smoke the fish as soon as it comes out of the brine.

Smoking: Place 2 cups of hardwood sawdust in a small metal skillet and place it on the hot plate in the smoker. Turn the hot plate to medium heat and hang the fish from the top of the smoker or arrange it on a rack. When

the sawdust starts to smolder, close the door to the smoker. After about 10 minutes, measure the temperature inside the smoker. (My smoker has a small hole, level with the fish rack, in which to insert an instant-read thermometer.) If it is not between 180°F and 200°F, adjust the hot plate accordingly. Smoke at this temperature for about 30 minutes, by which time the sawdust will be spent. (If at any time during the smoking you don't see smoke coming out of the air holes in the top of the smoker, sniff near the holes—the smoke should sting the inside of your nose.) Open the smoker, discard the ashes, and add another 2 cups of sawdust. Smoke for 30 minutes more. Repeat this process until the fish has smoked for the appropriate time.

IMPROVISING A LARGE HOT SMOKER

A barrel, an old refrigerator, or any large box made out of wood, metal, or even aluminum foil–lined cardboard can be used as a hot smoker. Just make sure that the container is tall enough—at least 3 feet—to keep the fish away from the heat source and wide enough (at least 2½ feet) so the heat doesn't cause the walls of a wooden or cardboard smoker to burn.

Once you've found a suitable container, cut some holes through the top to allow some of the smoke to escape and oxygen to seep in. Place an electric hot plate in the bottom of the smoker—you may need an extension cord—and use a small metal skillet to hold the sawdust.

Suspend a pole across the top of the smoker from which to suspend the fish. You may also want to attach a rack such as a cake rack near the top of the smoker for holding small items such as pieces of shrimp or scallops.

I also recommend inserting a meat thermometer in a small hole drilled or punctured—at the level at which the fish will hang—so you can monitor the temperature.

COLD SMOKING

Fish or shellfish smoked with cool smoke—at a temperature lower than 90°F—is called *cold-smoked*. Cold-smoked fish isn't actually cooked, so it has a denser and finer texture than hot-smoked fish—a texture that makes it easy to slice into thin translucent sheets. Because cold-smoked fish isn't actually cooked, it must first be cured with salt and sometimes sugar. As described earlier under "Curing," the salt and sugar have preservative, antiseptic properties, but the effect of curing on parasites is unclear, so most fish destined for cold smoking should be frozen first (page 90).

While cold-smoked fish is a preserved product and will keep better than fresh fish, cold-smoked fish is still perishable. I have kept cold-smoked salmon tightly wrapped in the refrigerator for two weeks, but you're better off eating most cold-smoked fish within seven days of smoking. Cold-smoked fish sold in vacuum packs will keep for at least a month and usually longer, but once the seal is broken the fish should be eaten within a few days. If you're not sure of the condition of a piece of smoked fish, give it a sniff—smoked fish that is too old will take on an unpleasant sour smell. Cold-smoked fish will keep for a month if tightly wrapped (first in plastic and then in aluminum foil) in a home freezer and for at least three months in a deep freeze at -20°F or less.

MAKING YOUR OWN COLD SMOKER

Most cooks are scared off by the idea of cold smoking their own seafood, partly because cold-smoking equipment is designed for commercial use and very expensive. Cold smoking may be time-consuming, but it in fact takes very little work. When you con-

THE CHEMISTRY OF SMOKING

Many cooks wonder if there is really much difference between hot-smoked fish and barbecued fish. True, smoked fish has more prolonged contact with smoke so that it takes on a smokier flavor, but other than that, what is the advantage of smoking fish for such a long time?

The answer lies in a chemical reaction between the smoke and the proteins in the fish. One of the components of wood smoke is formaldehyde, which when combined with gelatin (a protein found in fish and meat) prevents the gelatin from dissolving in water. This reaction gives the flesh of smoked fish a resiliency that barbecued fish doesn't have. Cold leftover barbecued fish will crumble if you try to cut it into thin slices, while both cold- and hot-smoked fish have a firmer texture and will hold together even in small pieces.

---

sider the price of cold-smoked fish, it's well worth the effort to put together your own smoker and smoke fish yourself.

First you must have access to an outdoor space (I use the roof of my apartment building) and of course a cold smoker. Start off with a hot smoker—a container with a hot plate and vents on top. Instead of smoking the fish inside the same container as the hot plate, however, you must pipe the smoke into a second container used for holding the fish.

My own hot smoker is a sheet-metal contraption with a 4-inch-diameter round hole in the top designed to house a small removable chimney. To convert it into a cold smoker I inserted a 4- by 18-inch section of stovepipe (cheap and easy to find at a hardware store) into the chimney hole, then an elbow pipe on the first length with a 24-inch length of pipe sticking sideways out of the elbow joint, another elbow (facing down) and a second 18-inch length of pipe facing down. I propped an oven rack on the inside of a large cardboard box (actually the box the smoker came in), placed the fish on the rack, and closed the top of the box. I cut a 4-inch hole in the top of the cardboard box,

inserted the end of the stovepipe, and sealed everything up with duct tape. Finally, I cut a little flap at the base of the cardboard box so the smoke could flow through the whole contraption.

If you don't want to buy a hot smoker (they cost about $120 and take up room), you can generate the smoke by using a hot plate in a wooden crate or an aluminum foil–lined cardboard box—the only thing you may need to buy is a hot plate.

❧

Hardwood-Cold-Smoked Salmon

Because cold-smoked salmon takes 2 days to cure and dry before it even goes into the smoker, I don't bother smoking small amounts. I usually buy an 8- to 10-pound whole salmon and fillet it (or have the fishmonger do it after I've selected the whole fish). Be sure to have the fishmonger trim off any rib bones, but don't worry about the pin bones—they're easier to pull out after the salmon has been smoked. Do *not*

remove the skin from the fillets, or the curing times will be thrown off and the smoked salmon will be almost impossible to slice. You'll end up with a lot of smoked salmon, so a good plan is to time the whole operation to lead into a big dinner party or brunch so that most of the salmon gets eaten right away. The alternative is to save one or both of the fillets in the freezer.

You should start preparing the salmon at least 3 days before you'll need to serve it. While the first steps—curing and drying—don't take much attention, count on hovering over the salmon during the smoking itself, which lasts about 5 hours. Each of the steps—curing, drying, smoking—is best done one right after the other, but if you need to you can store the salmon tightly wrapped in the refrigerator for up to 8 hours between steps.

The exact curing and smoking times will vary depending on the fat content and exact size of the fish, the temperature, the amount of smoke produced by your smoker, and of course your own tastes. I prefer salmon that has been smoked relatively lightly—so that I can taste the salmon and not just smoke—and lightly cured so the finished smoked salmon isn't too salty. If you smoke fish regularly, you'll no doubt make fine adjustments of your own.

one 10-pound whole salmon, filleted, scaled, and skin left on

2 cups kosher salt

2 cups sugar

Salt Curing (20 Hours): Follow the directions for gravlax (page 96), using only salt, refrigerating the salmon for 20 hours, turning it over after 10 hours.

continued

Sugar Curing (18 Hours): Unwrap the salmon, quickly rinse off the salt under cold running water, and pat the fillets dry with paper towels. Rinse off and dry the aluminum foil—you can use it for the next step.

Coat the fillets with the sugar in the same way as you did with the salt and refrigerate, weighted with a cutting board, for 18 hours. Turn the salmon over after 9 hours.

Drying (6 Hours): Unwrap the salmon, rinse it quickly with cold water, and pat it dry with paper towels. Place the salmon in front of a fan for 6 hours to air-dry it and cause a thin flavor-sealing film—called the pellicle—to form on its surface. The easiest way to do this is to place the salmon on a rack in the oven and set a fan, turned on low, on the open oven door facing the salmon.

Smoking (4 to 5 Hours): Set up the smoker and either place loops of string through the thin flaps near the head side of the fillets and hang the fillets from a horizontal pole inside the cold smoker or set the fillets on an oven rack propped up (on a milk crate, 2-by-4s, or a large metal pot) set upright inside the smoker.

Heat 2 cups of hardwood sawdust in a small skillet on the hot plate in the smoke generator (hot smoker) in the same way as for hot smoking. Make sure the hot plate is hot enough to generate smoke (you can check the amount of smoke by opening the small flap at the bottom of the smoke chamber) but not so hot as to overheat the smoke, which could cook the salmon. The easiest way to make sure the smoke isn't too hot is to feel the horizontal stovepipe near the smoke chamber side (the part holding the salmon), which shouldn't be any warmer than body temperature.

During the smoking process you'll need to check the smoker about every 30 minutes:

1. Make sure the sawdust is still generating smoke by looking through the flap into the smoke chamber. If you don't see or smell any smoke (the smoke should sting your nose when you sniff), open up the smoke generator. If the sawdust has turned into ash, discard the ash and add 2 cups more sawdust.

2. Make sure the smoke is circulating. Sometimes the sawdust asphyxiates and stops producing smoke. Leave the opening to the smoke generator cracked about ¼ inch to allow oxygen to enter. Leave the flap in the smoke chamber opened by about an inch so the smoke draws properly. If the sawdust still goes out, increase the size of the opening in the smoke generator and open the smoke chamber flap another inch or so.

3. Feel the stovepipe on the smoke chamber end to make sure it isn't any hotter than body temperature. (You can also stick an instant-read thermometer through the wall of the smoke chamber to keep the temperature below 100°F.) If the temperature is too high, turn down the hot plate. Check the sawdust to make sure that it hasn't turned into a bed of coals, which are much hotter. If the sawdust skillet is filled with coals, add another layer of sawdust and cut down the oxygen going into the smoke generator.

Final Drying (2 Hours): Place the smoked salmon on a rack in front of the fan and air-dry for 2 hours. You may want to do this outside or at least open all the windows, unless you don't mind your house smelling like smoke.

Serving: Slicing smoked salmon takes practice and can be frustrating at first. I love to proudly present a whole salmon fillet and slice it in front of my guests, but you might want to make your first slicing attempts in the kitchen, alone and unobserved.

The goal is to slice the salmon in the largest and thinnest sheets possible. The first step is to pull out the pin bones and trim off the pellicle with a long, flexible, razor-sharp knife. Place the salmon fillet on a cutting board that won't slide around while you're trying to slice. (I put a wet towel under the cutting board.) If you're right-handed, place the salmon tail end to your left. Hold the salmon in place with a fork held in your left hand. (Make sure the tines of the fork are pointing upward so you don't poke the salmon.) Start slicing in the middle of the salmon by keeping the knife flat against—almost parallel to—the salmon. The trick is to press down sideways on the knife—you should actually see the knife bend—so the side of the knife is pressing very firmly against the salmon but remains almost flat against it. As you're slicing—long and steady back-and-forth motions work best—keep looking at the knife blade *through* the transparent salmon to see how thickly you're slicing. Adjust the thickness of the slices by making very slight rotations with the knife handle. When you're ready to make your second slice, start about ¼ inch farther up toward the head end of the fillet so the second slice has the same length and thickness as the first. Lift the slices up with the knife and drape them over large plates or onto a platter.

OTHER COLD-SMOKED FISH

Almost any firm-fleshed fish with a relatively high fat content takes well to cold smoking. The technique for cold smoking smaller fish is the same as for smoked salmon except that smaller fillets are more convenient to cure by soaking in brine instead of rubbing in coarse salt. (The brine solution and curing times are the same as those for hot smoking, page 99.) I cold-smoke only fillets, never whole fish, which are very difficult to control. Fillets should be smoked for a minimum of 2 hours and up to 5 hours. I cold-smoke fillets from smaller fish such as mackerel, Spanish mackerel, trout, coho salmon, and pompano (and smaller jacks) for 2 to 3 hours.

❧

Assorted Cold-Smoked Fish with Blinis and Crème Fraîche

Blinis are one of the traditional accompaniments to caviar, but since most of us don't get to have caviar that often I also like to serve blinis with smoked fish. Blinis are moist and fluffy little Russian buckwheat pancakes that are especially light because they are leavened with both yeast and beaten egg whites. The yeast also gives them a delightful sour tang.

Blinis and smoked fish make a perfect brunch, light lunch, or first course in a fancy dinner. I like to serve them with champagne. Be forewarned: blinis are at their best served

with a lot of melted butter and crème fraîche, so diets are out.

The blini batter should be allowed to rise with the yeast for about 3 hours before serving. The egg whites should be beaten and folded into the batter within 30 minutes of cooking and serving the blinis. Because blinis are best served right out of the skillet onto the plate, it's sometimes fun to make them right in front of the guests and let the guests serve themselves fish, crème fraîche, and butter. If you want to serve everything together at the table, you'll have to keep the blinis in a 200°F oven until you have enough. However you decide to serve, arrange the thinly sliced smoked fish on wide plates in a single layer and serve the melted butter—make sure it's hot—in a sauceboat.

You can serve as few or as many varieties of smoked fish as you like. I often serve only smoked salmon.

MAKES 6 BRUNCH, LUNCH, OR GENEROUS FIRST-COURSE SERVINGS

For the Blinis:

1 cup milk

¼-ounce envelope active dry yeast

2 teaspoons sugar

½ cup buckwheat flour

½ cup all-purpose flour

4 eggs, separated

⅓ teaspoon salt

pinch of cream of tartar (if you don't have a copper bowl)

4 tablespoons unsalted butter, melted

For the Accompaniments:

1½ pounds assorted thinly sliced smoked fish such as salmon, sturgeon, or mackerel

1 cup crème fraîche or sour cream

1 cup (½ pound) unsalted butter, melted

½ cup (¼ pound) salmon roe or caviar (optional)

Preparing the Blinis: Heat the milk until it feels only slightly warm to the touch. Combine a quarter of the milk with the yeast and the sugar in a small mixing bowl. Put the bowl in a warm place.

Combine the buckwheat and all-purpose flours in a mixing bowl. Using a small whisk, stir in just enough of the milk to work the flour into a smooth paste. When you've smoothed out all the lumps, stir in the rest of the milk, the egg yolks, and the yeast mixture. Cover the bowl with plastic wrap and let rise in a warm place until the mixture has approximately doubled in volume, 2 to 3 hours.

Beat the egg whites with the salt until the egg whites are fluffy and stiff. If you're not using a copper bowl, add a pinch of cream of tartar to the egg whites before beating. Fold the egg whites into the yeast mixture with a rubber spatula.

Brush a nonstick pan or griddle with melted butter and ladle about 3 tablespoons of batter to make a 4-inch-diameter blini. Depending on the size of your pan, you should be able to make between 3 and 6 at a time. Cook the blinis over medium heat, in the same way as pancakes, until bubbles form on the uncooked surface and begin to burst. Then turn the blinis over with a spatula and cook them for 2 minutes more. Keep the blinis warm in the oven as you make them. Figure a total of 3 blinis per guest.

Serving: If your guests have yet to be initiated into blini eating, you may want to serve yourself first to provide a little demonstration. (I sometimes find that guests are shy and won't serve themselves enough.) I start with a couple of blinis, then 2 or 3 tablespoons of melted butter, a couple of slices of smoked fish, a big dollop of crème fraîche, and, last, a spoonful of caviar.

DRIED AND SALTED FISH: STOCKFISH AND SALT COD

I never understood the Mediterranean fondness for stockfish and salt cod (with so much fresh seafood available, why eat fish preserved in salt?) until I first sampled a *brandade* (a mixture of salt cod and mashed potatoes) smeared over slices of crusty bread in the south of France. Salt cod and stockfish may smell strong, but when properly soaked and combined lovingly with olive oil or cream they become surprisingly delicate.

The difference between the two is that salt cod has been salted and dried, while stockfish has only been allowed to dry in the open air. While many a connoisseur swears that stockfish should be used instead of salt cod for certain traditional recipes, stockfish is hard to find and work with (see box).

Mediterranean cooks prepare salt cod and stockfish using several distinct methods. One of the favorites is to beat or pound the desalted salt cod into a paste and combine it with various combinations of olive oil, vinegar, herbs, and potatoes. Another popular approach is to cut the soaked salt cod or stockfish into small pieces and then simmer them in broth for a rich soup or gratinlike sauced dish. The best pieces of salt cod are sometimes cooked in large pieces—almost like fish steaks—and then served as you would fresh fish, usually with a full-flavored sauce.

HOW TO BUY AND PREPARE SALT COD AND STOCKFISH

Salt cod is sold as fillets, either skinless or with the skin. I prefer skinless and always look for the thickest pieces—so-called loins—instead of tail pieces. Because salt cod turns gray as it ages, I always look for fillets that appear white or that even have a silvery sheen. My favorite cod is not completely dry and is sold vacuum-packed.

Stockfish is always rock-hard, but again I look for the thickest and whitest pieces.

Salt cod and stockfish should be soaked in cold water to soften them and/or remove their salt. Salt cod fillets should be soaked for 36 hours, salt cod with skin for 48 hours (peel the skin off after soaking), and stockfish for 72 hours. Change the water every 4 hours for salt cod and every 6 hours for stockfish. Refrigerate the soaking cod during the last half of the soaking; it becomes perishable once it loses its salt.

PUREED AND CREAMED SALT COD DISHES

Dishes of pureed salt cod and stockfish show up all over the Mediterranean, from the lagoons of Venice to the Portuguese coast. The Venetians are justifiably proud of their version—*baccalà mantecato*—a creamy mixture containing milk, a good amount of garlic, olive oil, anchovies, and parsley. *Baccalà mantecato* is traditionally served as a first course with a wedge of polenta, but I like to serve it on little toasts or even crackers as an hors d'oeuvre. The best-known salt cod puree is the Provençal *brandade de morue,* made in much the same way as the Venetian version except that potatoes are sometimes (not always) included along with a little heavy cream. Another favorite creamy salt cod mixture is from Lisbon—*bacalhau à lisbonense*—and contains eggs and matchstick potatoes cooked separately and folded into the mixture near the end of preparation.

Once you've soaked and simmered the salt cod or stockfish, the trick remains how best to shred it into the special consistency so essential to these traditional dishes. Older recipes suggest a mortar and pestle or meticulous shredding with a fork, one of my books on Venetian cooking says to use a butter churn, and a few modern books suggest a food processor. I admit I've come to rely on the food processor—but not the metal blade, which will turn the cod into a stiff and dense puree. Use the small white plastic blade, meant for kneading bread, instead.

Pureed salt cod mixtures can be served as is, mounded on hot plates and served with baskets of crusty bread (or polenta), but because most of these mixtures are quite filling and strongly flavored, many cooks like to serve the salt cod mixture before meals, spread on little croutons as an hors d'oeuvre.

Venetian Creamed Salt Cod or Stockfish

BACCALÀ MANTECATO

If you serve this salty and very garlicky hors d'oeuvre at a cocktail party, make sure everyone tries it at least once—the uninitiated may otherwise be driven from the room by their garlic-reeking fellow revelers.

This recipe makes rather a lot, but since salt cod and especially stockfish take so long to soak, I like to make extra and then either freeze any leftover finished mixture or use it to make gratins or little pancakes. When I first make this mixture, I serve it with crackers or little croutons as an hors d'oeuvre.

MAKES 16 HORS D'OEUVRE SERVINGS

1 pound center-cut salt cod or stockfish fillet

1 quart milk

3 garlic cloves, finely chopped and crushed to a paste with the side of a knife or in a mortar and pestle

1½ cups extra-virgin olive oil

leaves from 1 large bunch of flat-leaf parsley, finely chopped at the last minute

salt

crackers or thin slices of baguette, toasted

Soak the salt cod as described at the beginning of this section.

Gently simmer the drained cod in milk in a stainless-steel pot for 15 minutes. Remove from the heat, take out the cod—don't throw out the milk—and pull off and discard any pieces of skin or bone.

Puree the cod in a food processor, using the small white plastic blade, until you obtain a stiff paste, about 30 seconds. Transfer the cod to a mixing bowl and stir in the garlic. Using a wooden spoon, slowly work in the olive oil until the mixture is light and fluffy. If you've added all the olive oil and the mixture still seems stiff and dense, work in a little of the milk until the baccalà has the consistency of fluffy mashed potatoes. Stir in the parsley and add salt to taste.

If the baccalà has cooled off, place the mixing bowl over a small pot of boiling water and stir constantly or reheat the baccalà in the microwave—it should be very warm, but not burning hot.

❧

Lisbon-Style Salt Cod or Stockfish

BACALHAU À LISBONENSE

This is one of my favorite ways to cook salt cod and one of the few I can eat just with a fork. This dish gets part of its delicacy from eggs and, heresy of heresies, a small amount of heavy cream (my own addition). I like to serve this dish at lunch with bread and a salad for my more adventurous friends. While bacalhau à lisbonense is traditionally served in the style of scrambled eggs, I like to fashion it into small pancakes and serve them straight out of the pan—strangely, the flavor reminds me of salmon eggs.

MAKES 4 MAIN-COURSE SERVINGS

1 pound center-cut salt cod or stockfish fillet

1 large onion, finely chopped

1 garlic clove, finely chopped

1 cup pure olive oil

2 large Idaho potatoes, soaked in cold water

4 eggs, beaten

½ cup heavy cream

¼ cup finely chopped parsley

½ cup extra-virgin olive oil

salt

Soak the cod as described at the beginning of this section. Pick over the cod and remove and discard any pieces of skin or bone.

Puree the cod for about 15 seconds in a food processor fitted with the small plastic blade. Transfer the cod to a mixing bowl.

In a small sauté pan, stir the onion and garlic in 3 tablespoons of the pure olive oil until they turn translucent but not brown, about 10 minutes. Stir this mixture into the cod.

Cut the potatoes lengthwise into ⅛-inch-thick slices and slice each into ⅛-inch matchsticks. (It's best to use a vegetable slicer for the slicing and a chef's knife for the julienning.) Heat the remaining pure olive oil in a skillet or heavy pot until the surface of the oil ripples slightly. Panfry the potatoes for about 7 minutes, until they cook through and turn very pale golden brown. Scoop out the potatoes with a slotted spoon—leaving the oil behind—and gently stir the potatoes into the cod mixture.

Stir the eggs, cream, parsley, and all but 2 tablespoons of the extra-virgin olive oil into the cod mixture. Season with salt to taste.

Heat the remaining extra-virgin olive oil in a skillet or nonstick pan and pour in the cod mixture. Stir the mixture over medium heat—as though making scrambled eggs—until it thickens slightly but remains creamy. Immediately spoon out onto hot plates and serve. If you wish, the cod/potato mixture can also be shaped into little pancakes and cooked in butter or olive oil.

USING LEFTOVER CREAMED COD

Creamed cod mixtures make great little pancakes, which can be served as a first course for a simple dinner or as a light lunch. If your leftover mixture doesn't contain eggs, stir in a beaten egg or two—you'll need to experiment a little—and fashion the cold cod mixture into pancakes about 3 inches across. Pat the pancakes with flour and refrigerate until you're ready to sauté them.

I suppose purists would insist that the cod pancakes be cooked in olive oil, but I like to cook them gently on both sides in plenty of butter and then serve more butter at the table.

COOKING LARGE PIECES OF SALT COD

In this era of frozen and air-freighted foods, sitting down to a plate of salt cod will probably seem eccentric and anachronistic. But lovers of flavorful foods will be much happier eating a chunk of robust salt cod served in a flavorful sauce than many of the insipid "fresh" fish fillets found at the store.

Salt cod also has the advantage of being firm-textured, even after soaking, so it won't fall apart even after the heartiest treatment. One of the most popular Mediterranean methods is to flour the cod, sauté it in olive oil, and then stew it or bake it for 15 minutes—a process that would cause many fresh fish to fall apart. And because salt cod has a full flavor, it tastes good with robust Mediterranean ingredients.

∾

Salt Cod with Peppers, Tomatoes, and Eggplant

BACALAO EN SAMFAINA

My favorite description of *samfaina* came from a famous Catalan food writer, whom Colman Andrews quoted as calling it "a kind of baroque *sofregit*." A *sofregit* is the Catalan equivalent of the Italian sof-fritto or the French mirepoix, mixtures of aromatic vegetables cooked in some kind of fat—oil, butter, pork or duck fat—that form the base for many a stew, soup, or sauced dish. *Samfaina* is almost identical to the Provençal ratatouille, and in the same way as a ratatouille the vegetables can be cut to different sizes or even pureed after cooking to make a delicious sauce.

A number of interpretations of this dish are served mostly in Catalonia but also in the rest of Spain—each region claims its own to be the only authentic version—but I never follow any one too carefully. In fact you can give this dish an entirely different character by substituting marjoram, oregano, rosemary, or a combination of these herbs for the thyme.

Unlike most fish dishes, this can be made a day or two in advance and reheated gently. I like to serve it with rice or sautéed potatoes.

MAKES 4 MAIN-COURSE SERVINGS

1½ pounds salt cod, soaked (page 104)

½ cup extra-virgin olive oil

1 medium onion, finely chopped

1 teaspoon finely chopped fresh thyme leaves or ½ teaspoon dried

4 garlic cloves, finely chopped

2 bell peppers, preferably 1 red and 1 yellow, but green will do, charred, peeled, (page 133), seeded, and cut into ¼-inch cubes

2 medium zucchini, cut into ¼-inch cubes

½ medium eggplant or 1 narrow Italian-style eggplant, peeled and cut into ¼-inch cubes

6 medium tomatoes, peeled, seeded, and chopped

½ cup dry white wine

salt and pepper

all-purpose flour for dusting

Drain the salt cod, remove any pieces of skin or bone, and cut into 4 pieces.

Heat ¼ cup of the oil in a large heavy pot or skillet and stir in the onion, thyme, and garlic. Cook the mixture over medium heat for about 5 minutes and stir in the rest of the cubed vegetables. Turn the heat up to high and stir the vegetables until they release their liquid and then dry out again, about 15 minutes.

Meanwhile, stew the tomatoes in a second large pot over medium heat until they cook down to a thick sauce, about 25 minutes. Stir in the wine and simmer for 5 minutes more. Combine the tomato sauce with the cubed vegetables, season the mixture with salt and pepper to taste, and reserve.

Season the cod with salt and pepper and coat with flour, patting off any excess. Brown the cod in the remaining oil in a skillet or nonstick pan over medium to high heat. Transfer to a baking dish—an oval gratin dish looks best—and spread on the vegetable mixture. Bake in a 350°F oven for 30 minutes. Serve immediately on hot plates.

Steaming

The techniques of steaming, braising, and poaching are so closely related that much of the preparation, sauce making, and final presentation of the finished dish is the same. Whereas poaching and braising involve cooking fish in direct contact with liquid, fish to be steamed is suspended above a boiling liquid so that only moist air—steam—actually touches the fish.

The most important advantages of steaming are that nothing distorts the fish's natural flavor and steamed fish holds its shape better because it is not moved in and out of a simmering liquid. There is, however, a common misconception that steaming somehow seals in a fish's juices so that the fish retains more of its nutrients. Regardless of how fish is cooked, it releases juices. So the best way to make sure that no nutrients are lost is to transform the juices released by the fish into some form of sauce.

The best gadget for steaming fish is a couscousière (designed, obviously, to cook couscous), which looks like a large double boiler with little holes punched in the bottom of the upper pot. Buy a large one—at least 12 inches across—to accommodate whole fish, but don't spend a lot of money to get a heavy-duty version. Another good choice is a similar Chinese metal steamer. Either way, make sure it has a domed rather than a flat lid. Steam that condenses on the underside of a domed lid will drip down the insides of the pot rather than down onto the food.

Inexpensive Chinese bamboo steamers with lids are also excellent for steaming fish—and any other part of your meal since you can stack the steamers on top of one another and place different foods in each.

A fourth choice is to improvise by inserting a round metal cake rack in the bottom of a pot. Or simply invert a small heatproof mixing bowl in the bottom of a pot and set a plate over it to steam the fish on the plate. You can also use tin cans—the thin kind for tuna are best—with both ends cut out, arranged around the bottom of a pot to prop up a plate.

To steam large whole fish you'll need a fish poacher with the rack propped up on a couple of ramekins or small plates so there is room for the steaming liquid. Once you've rigged your fish poacher in this way you may find that the rack handles are sticking out too high and the lid won't fit. You can bend them down with a pair of pliers, but be careful not to do what I did and snap them off. (My fish poacher rack is suspended with string.)

Steaming with one of those little folding metal steamer baskets is difficult unless you're cooking only one or two pieces of fish.

STEAMING TECHNIQUES

In its simplest form steaming is so straightforward that little can go wrong. Just make sure the steamer lid is on tight, use high heat, and make sure the steaming liquid doesn't run dry and the bottom of the pot burn. Remember also to tilt the lid away from you when taking it off the steamer, let the steam disperse for a minute before reaching into the steamer, and use oven mitts to avoid painful burns.

Although steaming is a simple technique, there are tricks for taking best advantage of it. One method is to flavor the steaming liquid with herbs, spices, or vegetables so that the steam subtly scents the fish. Another approach is to use only a small amount of liquid for steaming the fish—again, taking care not to let it run dry—so the fish's juices end up in the liquid and are easy to concentrate into a sauce. You can then flavor and finish the steaming liquid as for braised or poached fish. Chinese cooks like to surround a whole fish with a concentrated sauce, usually one based on soy sauce, and then rely on condensed steam to form on the underside of the bamboo lid and drip down over the fish, diluting the sauce. The Japanese prefer to leave any flavorful ingredients or natural juices undiluted and so cover the fish with plastic wrap or aluminum foil.

One of the easiest ways to steam fish and shellfish is to use a technique the French call *étuver*. *Étuver* means to cook tightly covered with little or no liquid and few or no other ingredients, so that foods release their own juices, which vaporize and in turn cause the food to steam. The simplest application of this method, which I like to call *sauté-steaming*, is to cook fish fillets or small shellfish such as scallops or shrimp in a very small amount of liquid in a covered sauté pan.

❧

Sauté-Steamed Striped Bass Fillets

This is an everyday 5-minute dish that can masquerade as something you've labored over for hours. All but most strong-tasting fish such as bluefish can be used. Sauté-steaming is in fact an excellent method for cooking fragile fillets. Any sauté pan will work for this method, but nonstick pans are the safest bet.

MAKES 4 MAIN-COURSE SERVINGS

four 6- to 8-ounce striped bass fillets, skin and small bones removed

salt and pepper

¼ cup dry white wine

1 tablespoon finely chopped fresh parsley, chervil, or tarragon

2 teaspoons fresh lemon juice

2 tablespoons unsalted butter

Season the fish fillets on both sides with salt and pepper.

Measure the white wine into a sauté pan, preferably nonstick, with a tight-fitting lid, just large enough to hold the fillets in a single layer. (If the fillets are unusually large, you may have to use 2 pans.) Place the sauté pan over high heat until the wine begins to steam and quickly arrange the fillets, most attractive side up, in the hot wine. Rapidly move the pan back and forth for a few seconds to prevent the fillets from sticking.

Cover the pan, lower the heat to medium, and cook for a little less than 8 minutes per inch of thickness to avoid overcooking. Check by cutting into one of them at the thickest part to see if the flesh is white and opaque.

With a long spatula, gently transfer the cooked fillets to hot plates. You should have 1 to 3 tablespoons of liquid left in the pan. Add enough water to make about 5 tablespoons, bring the liquid to a simmer, and quickly whisk in the parsley, lemon juice, and butter. Bring the sauce to a quick simmer and immediately remove from the heat. Season with salt and pepper to taste and spoon over the fillets.

Substitutes Skinless fillets such as blackfish, flatfish, haddock, John Dory, mahimahi, pompano, red snapper, rockfish, tilefish, walleye

❧

Assorted Steamed Fish and Shellfish in Thai-Spice-Scented Broth

Steaming is well suited to Thai cooking because the ingredients are so aromatic that they gently perfume the fish with an irresistible lemony flavor. Almost any kind of fish or shellfish can be steamed over water or fish broth flavored with aromatic Thai ingredients. You can prepare this dish with just one or as many different kinds of fish as you like. I find that three different types of seafood—maybe a piece of red snapper or sea bass fillet, a sea scallop, and a jumbo shrimp per serving—are interesting to eat and look at without making the dish overly complicated. When buying shellfish such as scallops or shrimp by weight, be sure to buy multiples of 4 so you can give the same amount per serving. You can also steam a whole fish using this method.

This dish is easy to set up in advance. Only the steaming itself needs to be done at the last minute.

MAKES 4 MAIN-COURSE SERVINGS

2 pounds seafood: assorted fish fillets and shucked or peeled shellfish such as shrimp, sea scallops, or bay scallops

2 cups water

a 4-inch piece of lemongrass from the white end, finely chopped

2 kaffir lime leaves, sliced into fine strips

1 garlic clove, finely chopped

1 or 2 Thai chilies to taste, seeded and finely chopped

1 shallot or small onion, finely chopped

1 tomato, peeled, seeded, and coarsely chopped

1 tablespoon softened unsalted butter

2 tablespoons finely chopped fresh
cilantro

2 tablespoons fresh lime juice (from
1 lime)

2 tablespoons Thai fish sauce or to taste

salt and pepper

Trim the fish and shellfish and divide them into 4 equal portions.

Combine the water, lemongrass, lime leaves, garlic, chilies, shallot, and tomato in the bottom of a steamer. Bring to a boil on the stove and then turn down the heat and keep at a gentle simmer for 5 minutes to give the flavors a chance to infuse into the liquid.

Brush the steamer rack with softened butter and arrange the thickest pieces of fish and shellfish on top of the steamer rack. Put the steamer rack on the base, cover tightly, and turn the heat to high. Steam the fish and shellfish for 8 minutes per inch of thickness—adding pieces of fish according to their thickness—so everything is done at once. (Be careful of the hot steam when reaching into the steamer.)

Remove the steamer lid and arrange the fish and shellfish in hot soup plates. Add the cilantro, lime juice, and fish sauce to the steaming liquid. Simmer for 1 minute.

Season the fish with salt and pepper and spoon the liquid from the bottom of the steamer over and around the fish.

❧

Chinese Steamed Sea Bass with Scallions, Ginger, and Black Beans

(color page 10)

This is a brightly flavored dish made in the traditional Chinese way—condensed steam mingles with the savory flavorings to make a light

sauce. Almost all Chinese and Japanese recipes for steamed fish suggest cutting deep slashes along the sides of the fish to help the steam penetrate. I've found that the heat penetrates well anyway, so I usually don't bother.

MAKES 4 MAIN-COURSE SERVINGS

one 3- to 4-pound or two 1- to 1½-pound whole round fish to fit your steamer, scaled and gutted

1 tablespoon preserved black beans

2 tablespoons dark soy sauce

3 tablespoons Chinese rice wine or Spanish dry sherry

1 teaspoon Japanese dark sesame oil

½ teaspoon sugar

a 1-inch piece of fresh ginger, peeled

2 scallions, including green, cut into 1-inch lengths

Thoroughly rinse the fish inside and out. Scrape off any scales left by the fishmonger.

Rinse the black beans in a strainer for about 1 minute under cold running water and chop coarsely. Combine the beans with the soy sauce, rice wine, sesame oil, and sugar in a small bowl.

Slice the ginger into ⅛-inch-thick rounds and then into fine julienne.

Place the fish on a plate with a deep enough rim to hold the soy sauce mixture and any juices released by the fish. Pour on the soy sauce mixture and sprinkle the fish with the ginger and scallions.

Bring a quart of water to a rolling boil in the base of the steamer, set the plate in the top, and cover tightly. Steam for 8 minutes per inch of thickness.

Turn off the heat, remove the lid, and let the steam dissipate for a minute before reaching in and pulling out the plate. Be careful not to tilt the plate and spill the sauce. Make sure the fish is done by inserting a paring knife along the backbone; you should

be able to pull the flesh gently away from the bone.

Serve the fish at the table, spooning the sauce, ginger, and scallions over each portion.

Substitutes Whole fish such as black sea bass, grouper, monkfish (whole tails), large porgy, red snapper, rockfish, sea trout, Spanish mackerel, striped bass, tilapia, trout, walleye, weakfish

Vietnamese-Style Whole Steamed Striped Bass

To make eating a whole fish easier for my guests, I bone the fish and stuff it through the back. To do that you need scaled but ungutted fish, which is bound to elicit a funny look from your fishmonger. I never try to make this dish for more than 4 people because I have only 2 steamers that will hold 2 fish each.

MAKES 4 MAIN-COURSE SERVINGS

four 1-pound whole fish such as striped bass, scaled but ungutted

8 dried Chinese (shiitake) mushrooms, soaked for 30 minutes in just enough hot water to cover

1 medium carrot, julienned

2 leeks, julienned

2 teaspoons grated fresh ginger

1 garlic clove, finely chopped

2 tablespoons peanut or vegetable oil

2 tablespoons finely chopped cilantro

3 tablespoons unsweetened coconut milk

2 tablespoons Thai or Vietnamese fish sauce

about 20 fresh mint leaves, coarsely chopped

salt and pepper

continued

Preparing the Fish: Bone and gut the fish through the back (see color page 27). Pull the pin bones out of the fillets by working from the inside of the cavity. Rinse the cavity thoroughly and set on a plate, covered with plastic wrap, in the refrigerator.

Preparing the Stuffing: Cut off and discard the mushroom stems or save them for broth. Thinly slice the caps and reserve.

Sauté the carrot and leek julienne with the ginger, garlic, and mushrooms in the peanut oil over medium heat for about 15 minutes, until the vegetables soften but don't brown.

Transfer the vegetable mixture to a bowl and stir in the cilantro, coconut milk, fish sauce, and mint. Season to taste with salt and pepper and let cool.

Stuffing and Steaming the Fish: Spread the stuffing in the fish cavities and steam the fish on their sides over boiling water for about 20 minutes (10 minutes per inch of thickness). Carefully transfer the fish to hot plates. Serve each guest a whole fish with an extra plate for heads and bones.

Substitutes Whole fish such as black sea bass, grouper, large porgy, red snapper, rockfish, Spanish mackerel, tilapia, trout, walleye

❧

Japanese Steamed Red Snapper Fillets

Japanese cooks typically steam seafood in individual serving bowls so the bowls can be taken out of the steamer and set right down in front of each guest. In many cases the bowls are covered tightly or a cloth napkin is tied around the steamer lid to prevent condensation from diluting the flavorings. Once the seafood is done, a brothlike sauce—usually some variation of *dashi*—is added to each bowl, or each diner is given one or two little bowls of sauce for dipping.

Although there are many strictly traditional recipes, you'll probably want to assemble ingredients according to whim and what's available. This recipe is adapted from Shizuo Tsuji's *Japanese Cooking: A Simple Art.*

This dish looks best in small Japanese-style porcelain or lacquer bowls. The food can be arranged in the bowls up to several hours before serving.

MAKES 4 FIRST-COURSE SERVINGS

one 12-ounce red snapper fillet with skin

salt

2 ounces dried soba noodles, preferably green *cha-soba* **(a round pile about ¹⁄₂ inch thick)**

2 quarts boiling water

4 fresh shiitake mushroom caps, cut in half, rinsed, and dried

1¹⁄₂ cups dashi (page 343)

5 tablespoons mirin

5 tablespoons Japanese dark soy sauce

1 loosely packed cup dried bonito flakes

2 quarts water

1 sheet pretoasted nori (see glossary), cut into fine julienne with scissors

1 scallion, including green, finely chopped

Carefully inspect the red snapper and scrape off any remaining scales. Pull out any bones with needlenose pliers and carefully cut the fillet into 4 pieces. Make 2 shallow slits diagonally in the skin of each piece. Sprinkle with salt. Refrigerate until needed.

Cook the soba noodles in the boiling water for 6 to 8 minutes, until *al dente.* Pour into a colander, rinse with cold water, and drain thoroughly.

In each of the bowls, arrange a small mound of noodles to one side. Nestle the fish next to the noodles and arrange 2 mushroom cap halves decoratively next to the fish and noodles. Sprinkle the ingredients in each bowl with a tablespoon of dashi. Cover each bowl tightly with plastic wrap or aluminum foil and keep the bowls in the refrigerator until needed.

Prepare the broth by bringing the remaining dashi to a boil with the mirin and soy sauce. Stir in the bonito flakes and immediately take the pan off the heat. Let sit for 1 minute and strain through a fine-mesh sieve.

Put the water in the steamer and bring to a rolling boil. Arrange the bowls in the top of the steamer, cover, and cook over high heat for about 15 minutes for ³⁄₄- to 1-inch-thick fillets. (This method takes slightly longer than steaming fish directly because the plastic wrap protects the fish from the heat.)

While the fish is steaming, bring the broth to a gentle simmer. Turn off the heat, take off the lid—let the steam dissipate for a minute—and remove the bowls. Peel off the plastic, ladle in the broth, and decorate with the julienned nori and scallions.

Substitutes Lean round fish fillets such as blackfish, black sea bass, lingcod, ocean perch, rockfish, striped bass, walleye

Sauté-Steamed Sea Scallops with Herbs and White Wine

Scallops are perfect for sauté-steaming because they have a firm texture and don't stick easily. This method will also work with firm-fleshed fish such as monkfish or salmon. I recommend using a nonstick pan.

This is a very simple recipe—chopped fresh herbs and a little butter are added to the liquid left in the bottom of the pan and poured over the scallops as a sauce—but you can use any of the ingredients or techniques for finishing braising liquids.

MAKES 4 FIRST-COURSE SERVINGS

1 pound sea scallops

salt and pepper

¼ cup dry white wine

2 tablespoons finely chopped parsley, chervil, or chives or a combination

2 tablespoons unsalted butter

Trim off and discard the small muscle running up the side of each scallop. Cut the scallops into ¼-inch-thick disks and season with salt and pepper.

Put the wine and the scallops in a nonstick sauté pan just large enough to hold the scallops in a single layer. (If you don't have a large enough pan, divide the sauce ingredients into 2 pans.) Cover the pan with a tight-fitting lid and place the pan over high heat for 2 minutes. Turn off the heat and let the pan sit—don't remove the lid—for 1 minute.

Remove the lid and quickly arrange the scallops in a single layer on hot plates. Over medium heat, whisk the herbs and butter into the liquid left in the pan. Season the sauce with salt and pepper to taste and spoon a thin layer over the scallops.

USING LEAVES AS WRAPPERS

One of the delights of Southeast Asian cooking is the tradition of wrapping foods in leaves and then steaming them in little packets. Whenever I serve individual portions of wrapped seafood, my guests act as though they have just received a little gift.

Various leaves can be used as wrappers, but banana leaves are by far the most popular in Southeast Asia. Bandan leaves, which are thinner and more ribbonlike, are also popular and can be found in most Asian groceries in the United States. In a pinch you can also use blanched cabbage leaves.

Thai Steamed Salmon Fillet Packets

I like to use salmon here because it's easy to find and has a full flavor that holds up to the pungent curry flavors, but it wouldn't be traditional in Thailand and almost any other fish will do. Be sure to cut the fillets into even pieces so they will cook evenly.

If you prefer, you can make the packets half the size and serve them as a first or even a middle course in an elaborate dinner. You can make the salmon packets earlier in the day, but serve them within 10 or 15 minutes of steaming.

MAKES 6 MAIN-COURSE SERVINGS

2½ pounds center-cut salmon fillet, skin and pin bones removed

3 tablespoons homemade (page 340) or canned red curry paste

3 tablespoons finely chopped fresh basil

3 tablespoons finely chopped fresh mint

2 tablespoons finely chopped fresh cilantro

1 tablespoon creamy peanut butter

3 tablespoons unsweetened coconut milk

1 tablespoon Thai fish sauce

salt and pepper

2 cups water

six 12-inch square sections of banana leaves or 6 large cabbage leaves blanched in boiling water for 2 minutes and rinsed

Making the Salmon Packets: Cut across the salmon fillet until you have 6 rectangles. Fold the stomach flap under each rectangle so they are of even thickness. Reserve in the refrigerator.

Work the remaining ingredients except the leaves into a paste in a small mixing bowl. Season to taste with salt and pepper.

Spread the banana leaf squares on a work surface and spread a third of the paste mixture on each leaf. Set a piece of salmon on top and spread the top of the salmon with another third of the mixture.

Fold the leaves over so they completely wrap and cover the salmon. If the leaves don't hold together, tie them around the salmon with string.

Steaming: Bring the water to a boil in the bottom of the steamer and steam the packets for about 8 minutes per inch of thickness of the salmon squares.

When the packets are done—you may have to sneak into one and cut into the fish to judge doneness—arrange them in hot soup plates. Whisk the remaining paste into a cup of the steaming liquid left in the bottom of the steamer. Slit open the top of each packet with a sharp knife and ladle the flavored broth into each packet in the bowls. Serve immediately.

Using the Microwave

As a cooking purist fascinated with the old rather than the new (I've always wanted to cook on a hearth), I didn't succumb to buying a microwave until a couple of years ago, when a friend told me they were good for heating plates. My skepticism has gradually worn down so that I now occasionally use the microwave for cooking.

My microwave finds the most use during the summer, when I don't want to light my big gas oven and heat up the apartment. With a little ingenuity the microwave can be used for almost any kind of cooking, but I find it most useful for braising and steaming small amounts of seafood, never more than four servings and usually no more than two. I usually resort to the microwave when I'm feeling lazy.

One of the drawbacks to cooking with a microwave is that microwaves don't heat evenly. This isn't a problem if you're heating up a cup of soup, because you can stir the soup once or twice to redistribute the heat evenly. But for solid ingredients—a whole fish for instance—this results in food that is raw on one side and overcooked on the other. A couple of microwave innovations, specifically the little turntable that rotates the food while it is heating, have alleviated this problem somewhat but not enough so that a large piece of seafood will cook evenly.

The best way to cook seafood in the microwave is in a covered container with liquid. In this way the fish is cooked evenly by the hot liquid and the steam it produces instead of by the microwaves themselves. Leaving the fish covered in its container for a minute or two after cooking gives the heat a chance to distribute itself, so the fish ends up cooked evenly. Once the fish is taken out and placed on hot plates, the juices remaining in the dish can be poured over the fish as a light sauce or manipulated in the same way as the liquids from any braised fish (page 28). In fact any of the liquids used for braising seafood on the stove or in the oven can be used for cooking in the microwave.

MICROWAVE EQUIPMENT

Because metal of any sort cannot go into a microwave, you may need to improvise containers for cooking in the microwave or invest in some of the equipment designed specifically for microwave cookery. My choices, however, are microwave-safe glass, porcelain, or Corning Ware casseroles with lids.

Microwave ovens have become very sophisticated and have all sorts of computerized controls, none of which I've ever been able to figure out. Just make sure the oven is powerful enough—at least 700 watts—and has a turntable. (Otherwise you'll have to give the dish of seafood a quarter turn three times during the cooking.)

❧

Salmon Fillets with White Wine, Butter, and Parsley

This has to be the absolute easiest way to cook fish and, as much as I hate to admit it, one of the best. The salmon releases savory juices that mingle with the butter and white wine to form a light and delicious sauce that can be spooned over the salmon once it's placed on plates. This method lends itself to almost infinite improvisation. Try substituting sherry, hard cider, peeled and chopped tomatoes, or even water for the white wine. Omit the butter or replace it with extra-virgin olive oil or an herb butter. Sprinkle chopped herbs over the fish before cooking. Lightly precook aromatic and decorative vegetables such as pearl onions, baby carrots, or fennel wedges and then heat and serve them with the fish. Almost any fish fillet or steak will work using this method.

MAKES 2 MAIN-COURSE SERVINGS

1½ tablespoons unsalted butter

two 6-ounce center-cut salmon fillets, about 1½ inches thick at the thickest part, skin and pin bones removed

2 tablespoons dry white wine

1 tablespoon finely chopped parsley

salt and pepper

Butter a square microwave-safe casserole with lid with a third of the butter. Place the salmon in the casserole—fold the stomach flaps under the salmon fillets so the fillets are of even thickness—and sprinkle with the wine. Dot the salmon with the remaining butter. Sprinkle on the parsley, salt, and pepper.

Set 2 wide soup plates in the microwave. Cover the casserole and place it in the microwave on top of the plates. Heat on high for 5 minutes (less if the fillets are thinner than 1½ inches). If your microwave does not have a turntable, give the casserole 3 quarter turns, one every minute, so the salmon cooks evenly. Remove the casserole and let sit for 2 minutes—don't open it—before serving the salmon.

Use a spatula to transfer the fish to hot plates. If you wish, peel the skin off salmon steaks, but I usually don't bother. Spoon on the liquid left in the casserole and serve immediately.

Substitutes Steaks such as Atlantic pollack, cod, halibut, king mackerel, shark, swordfish, tuna (cut cooking times in half)

Skinless fillets such as Atlantic mackerel, bass (black sea, striped, and fresh), blackfish, flatfish, lingcod, mullet, ocean perch, red snapper, rockfish, sablefish, sea robin, Spanish mackerel, wolffish

❧

Microwave Seafood Stew

The microwave is great for quick cooking of shellfish such as clams and mussels—and for this recipe you dirty only a couple of dishes. I heat the plates by putting them in the microwave at the same time as the stew.

MAKES 2 MAIN-COURSE SERVINGS

¼ cup chicken broth (page 344) or water

¼ cup dry white wine

½ pound headless large shrimp, peeled and deveined

¼ pound sea scallops, small side muscle pulled off, cut into ¼-inch-thick disks if large

1 dozen littleneck or Manila clams or cultivated mussels, scrubbed

½ pound firm-fleshed fish such as halibut or swordfish, cut into 1½-inch cubes

½ cup heavy cream (optional)

1 tablespoon finely chopped parsley

salt and pepper

Place 2 wide soup plates in the microwave.

Combine the broth and wine in a microwave-safe casserole. Put the lid on the casserole and place the casserole on the soup plates in the microwave. Heat on high for 3 minutes, until the liquids come to a simmer.

Remove the casserole lid and put the seafood in layers in and over the hot liquid, starting with the shrimp, then adding the scallops, and finally the clams or mussels. Cover the casserole and cook on high for 3 minutes. Quickly take off the lid, add the cubes of fish, cover again, and cook for 2 minutes more. Remove the lid, pour in the heavy cream, and sprinkle with parsley. Cover and cook for 2 minutes more. Remove the casserole and let sit, covered, for 2 minutes. Remove the lid and gently poke around in the casserole to make sure all the fish is done. If some of the fish is undercooked, cover the casserole and cook for 1 minute more. Otherwise, scoop the seafood out with a slotted spoon into the hot bowls, pour on the hot liquid, and serve.

A NOTE ABOUT COOKING TIMES

Unlike regular ovens, which will cook eight pieces of fish in about the same time it takes to cook two pieces, microwave ovens cook more slowly when they contain more food. So you can't predict cooking times based on the thickness of the fish alone, and if you double or halve the amounts given in a recipe, the cooking times will be different. If you use the microwave a lot, it might be worth consulting a book on the subject such as Barbara Kafka's *Microwave Gourmet*.

Three-flavored Bay Scallop Gratins
page 163

**Steamed Lobster Medallions
with Saffron, Tomatoes, Basil, and Thyme**
page 173

Lobster and Scallop Chat
page 258

Lobster Risotto
page 186

Steamed Lobster with Coconut Milk and Thai Spices
page 175

Brazilian Shrimp Stew
page 200

Thai Curry-Marinated Barbecued Shrimp
page 195

Sautéed Shrimp with Parsley and Garlic
page 193

Filleting a Whole *Flatfish*

1. Cut off the tail.

2. Remove the ventral and dorsal fins (the fins that run along the sides of the fish), the pectoral fins (small fins at the base of the head), and anal fins (near the rear of the fish's belly).

3. Use kitchen shears to cut out the gills under the flap at the base of the fish's head. Discard the fins and gills.

4. Cut along the base of the head, down to the backbone, with a sharp flexible knife.

5. Make cuts into the fish all around, about ¼ inch in from the sides. Cut down just to the backbone, not through it.

6. With the fish's head facing away from you, cut down to the backbone along the line that separates the two fillets (the lateral line).

7. Press the knife against the backbone so the blade rests flat. Slide the knife under the fillet to your left in long swiping motions, moving from head to tail. Repeat until you've detached the fillet. (Right-handed people should cut to their left; left-handed people should cut to the right.)

8. Turn the fish around so the head is facing you and remove the fillet to your left (to the right if you're left-handed).

9. Turn the fish over and remove the bottom (white-skinned) fillets in the same way.

10. Remove the skin by cutting between the skin and flesh with a sharp flexible knife and then moving the skin back and forth sideways while pulling, always keeping the knife blade flush against the skin.

11. If you're using the fish bones to make fish broth, use a knife to detach the viscera at the base of the head. Remove the viscera with your fingers.

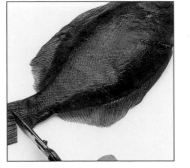

1

2

3

4

5

6

7

8

9

10

11

Boning a Whole *Flatfish*

1

2

3

4

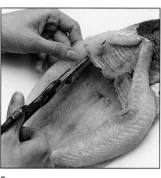
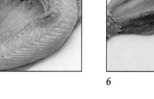
5

6

1. Prepare the fish as shown on color page 29. Scale the white skin if rough to the touch. Remove the black skin. Cut between the two fillets with a long flexible knife. Slide the knife under the fillet to your left in a long sweeping motion until fillet is separated from backbone but still attached to the rest of the fish on one side.

2. Turn fish around so head faces you and repeat with other fillet to expose entire backbone.

3. Cut through the backbone where it joins the head and tail and at two places in between so that it is broken in four places.

4. Slide a long knife along the underside of each section of back-bone, detaching the bones from the bottom fillets.

5. Cut along each side of the backbone sections with kitchen shears, detaching the bones.

6. The finished fish should form a pouch for stuffing.

Serving a Whole Cooked *Flatfish*

1

2

3

4

5

6

1. Pull away the small bones along each side of the fish with a large fish or cake knife. Leave bones in the pan.

2. Cut gently between the two fillets on top of the fish and slide the fish knife under the fillet closest to you, separating it from the backbone.

3. Gently lift off the fillet and transfer it to a hot plate. Repeat with the other fillet.

4. Press down on the backbone where it joins the head and separate the head from the backbone with a large knife and fork. Repeat with the tail.

5. Slide the fish knife under the backbone and gently lift it off.

6. Gently separate the two bottom fillets with the large knife and fork; gently transfer the bottom fillets to a hot plate or platter.

Skinning and Sectioning an *E e l*

1. If the eel is alive, grip it by the neck with a kitchen towel and rapidly strike its head against a hard surface. Make a shallow cut all around the base of the head with a small sharp knife.

2. Peel the skin back about ¼ inch all around the base of the head with a pair of pliers.

3. Grip the skin with a towel held in your right hand and the head with a towel held in your left hand and pull so the skin peels back completely away from the eel.

4. Cut along the underside of the eel starting at the base of the head. Pull out and discard the viscera. Rinse the eel thoroughly under cold running water.

5. Cut the eel into sections with a strong knife.

1

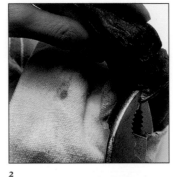

3

5

4

Boning an *E e l* Through the Back (Butterflying)

1. Kill the eel by striking its head firmly against a hard surface. Don't skin. Starting along the back at the base of the head, cut along the right side of the backbone all the way down to the inside of the belly.

2. Repeat on the left side of the backbone until the backbone and viscera are completely exposed.

3. Cut the backbone away from the head and tail with kitchen shears. Remove. Pull out any viscera and rinse out the eel. Use a sharp knife to scrape out any viscera clinging to the inside.

1

2

3

Preparing Seafood to Serve Raw

Because cooking eliminates the most delicate flavors of the freshest seafood, the most subtle differences among various types can be discerned only when the seafood is eaten raw. Despite what many people believe, raw seafood is much milder and more delicate than cooked. Those who have tried raw seafood sometimes end up preferring it to cooked.

If you've never tried raw seafood, I recommend that you go to a good Japanese restaurant with friends, sit at the sushi bar so you can see the whole process, and order a single piece of tuna sushi, one of the mildest in flavor and softest in texture. Have a sake or beer while you wait. Once you've tasted the tuna sushi, you'll probably want to try other fish or shellfish. At this point you may want to entrust yourself to the sushi chef.

The raw fish served at Japanese restaurants is in fact usually so impeccable that when serving it at home I buy it from a market that caters to Japanese clientele and prepares and sells fish exclusively for eating raw. When buying sashimi-grade fish in a Japanese market, be prepared to spend a lot of money. The best tuna—called toro*—costs approximately four times what a slice of yellowfin will cost at the regular fish market. If you can't find a Japanese market, talk to a trusted fishmonger about ordering sashimi-grade fish or, if you live near the ocean and feel confident about being able to buy perfectly fresh fish, buy fish from your regular fishmonger. Wherever you buy it, I recommend freezing it for at least 24 hours to kill parasites. Fish that is to be eaten raw must have no fishy odor; it should be either completely odorless or have only a slight aroma of the sea.*

SASHIMI

Sashimi is simply raw fish that has been sliced artfully and presented in small bowls or plates or on a wooden platter or tray. In a traditional and formal Japanese meal individual kinds of raw fish are presented in tiny bowls, each with its own garnish, early in the meal, before cooked and hot foods. In Japanese restaurants in the United States several varieties of raw fish are sometimes served together on a wooden platter or tray. At family gatherings in Japan there is sometimes only one kind of fish—often tuna—cut into rectangles or cubes and piled on a platter for the guests to dive at with chopsticks. If you decide to serve sashimi at home, don't buy inferior fish just to create a dramatic effect; you're better off serving only one or two kinds of perfect quality than five that are less than perfect.

Other than the seafood itself, not much is required for serving sashimi. You can make do with little plates and bowls, but if you like serving sashimi more than once in a while, invest in some small Japanese dishes or the wooden trays used in Japanese restaurants. Be sure to buy Japanese-style chopsticks, which are much shorter than the Chinese type.

SASHIMI AND SUSHI SAUCES, CONDIMENTS, AND GARNISHES

While Japanese cooks serve sashimi with a variety of specially prepared sauces, garnishes, and condiments, only three are essential: soy sauce, wasabi (very strong powdered horseradish), and pickled ginger. Kikkoman dark soy sauce is excellent and easy to find, but be sure you buy the kind labeled "naturally brewed." Wasabi is sold powdered in cans and need only be stirred with an equal volume of cold water about 15 minutes before serving. You can make your own pickled ginger (see box), but it's also available in jars in most supermarkets. When serving sashimi or sushi, place a small cone of wasabi somewhere on the tray or bowl and the soy sauce in a small individual dish. The diners then work a small amount of the wasabi into the soy sauce with chopsticks. The amount of wasabi to use is a matter of taste— some diners don't use any at all. Pickled ginger is also placed in a small mound on the sashimi tray or in a small dish for the diners to serve themselves.

The Japanese are also fond of understated accompaniments to raw fish, the most common one being shredded daikon (Japanese white radish), but shredded carrot or even turnip will work in a pinch. Ideally, use the julienne attachment on a Japanese vegetable slicer (benriner cutter) and nestle the shredded vegetable in a small mound next to the slices of raw fish on the platter or in the small bowl. Garnish the sashimi with a sprig of something green, traditionally a heart-shaped *shiso* leaf, which has a delicate cinnamonlike flavor. Use shiso leaves if you live near a good Japanese grocery, but keep in mind that the spirit of

Japanese cuisine is to use what's available and in season. I play around with different decorations, such as a piece of cucumber with the skin cut like a comb and fanned out slightly, a few sprigs of fennel frond or dill, or sometimes even a simple sprig of Italian parsley or watercress.

SLICING AND CUTTING FISH FOR SASHIMI

Fish for sashimi is sliced in four basic ways. The most common method is to slice a rectangular section of fish into small rectangular slices. This method is best for large fish such as tuna that can be bought cut in the necessary rectangular shape. A second common method is simply to slice fish fillets on a bias so the resulting slices are more or less rectangular but less regular. The other two cuts are the cube cut, used for very soft fish such as skipjack tuna, and the thread cut, which consists of cutting very small fillets lengthwise into strips.

Fish for sashimi or sushi should be sliced to the correct thickness. Softer fish such as tuna should be cut relatively thickly—about ¼ inch—while firmer-fleshed fish such as Japanese red snapper should be cut about half as thick. Very firm fish or seafood such as squid or cuttlefish should be sliced paper-thin or into strips using the thread cut.

KINDS OF SEAFOOD FOR SASHIMI AND SUSHI

While almost any fish or shellfish can be eaten raw if perfectly fresh, most finfish should be frozen before they are eaten to eliminate the risk of parasites. In addition to fish that are commonly available locally, you're liable to encounter certain Japanese favorites at the sushi counter or the Japanese fish market. Many of these fish have been

PICKLED GINGER FOR SASHIMI AND SUSHI

If you live near an Asian market, you might be able to find young ginger, which has pale skin and a more delicate flavor and texture. A good trick for peeling ginger is to scrape it with a spoon; the peel comes right off. Pickled ginger lasts for several months in the refrigerator.

> ½ **pound ginger, preferably young, peeled and sliced paper-thin with a benriner cutter**
>
> 1 **tablespoon coarse salt**
>
> 1¼ **cups good-quality rice wine vinegar**
>
> 3 **tablespoons water**
>
> ¼ **cup sugar**

MAKES 2 CUPS

In a small mixing bowl, rub the ginger with the coarse salt until you don't feel the texture of the salt, for about 3 minutes. Place the ginger in the mixing bowl and refrigerate for several hours or overnight.

Squeeze the ginger slices to extract as much liquid as you can and place them in a clean jar. Combine the vinegar, water, and sugar in a small saucepan. Bring the mixture to a simmer over high heat, stirring quickly to dissolve the sugar. Pour this mixture over the ginger. Let cool slightly, seal the jar, and marinate in a cool place for at least 4 days before using.

frozen on Japanese fishing boats or have been aquacultured in or around Japan and are air-shipped to the United States so they are available only in Japanese restaurants or fish shops.

CLAMS

The Japanese are fond of several clams that are rarely eaten in the United States. The large siphon of geoduck clams (*mirugai*) is a delicacy when thinly sliced and served as sushi or sashimi. Japanese red clams (*aoyagi*) are frozen and imported from Japan. They are tasty and beautiful to look at but can be quite tough.

EEL (*unagi*)

Because it is always served already cooked—broiled with a savory sauce—eel doesn't really count as raw seafood, but broiled or grilled eel is such a delicacy and is a part of so many sushi platters that I've included it here. While theoretically it's possible to make your own *unagi* using American eel, American eel doesn't have the same rich and delicate flavor as the eels specially cultivated in Japan. So if you're serving *unagi* at home, count on buying it already prepared at a Japanese market, where it won't be cheap. *Unagi* is best cut into 3-inch-long sections and served as sushi with a strip of nori tied around as decoration and to hold the eel in place.

FLUKE (*hirame*)

Fluke often shows up in Japanese markets and restaurants in the late fall and early winter. Because raw fluke has a firm texture, the skinless fillets should be cut rather thinly, about $1/8$ inch. Most fluke fillets are somewhat thin, so to get large enough slices for both sushi and sashimi it is best to slice them on a slight diagonal and on a sharp bias.

If you make sashimi with any regularity, you're probably going to get bored with the standard garnishes of shredded daikon or carrot. One of my favorite ways to serve sashimi is in a series of miniature courses in tiny Japanese bowls, all of them different. Next to each mound of raw fish I like to serve a different little savory or crunchy vegetable or condiment. A few of my favorites are thin slices of cucumber seasoned with vinegar, sugar, and salt, blanched spinach or watercress seasoned with a few drops of sesame oil and sprinkled with sesame seeds, very thin cooked somen noodles cut into 1-inch lengths, reconstituted dried wakame seaweed dribbled with a little rice vinegar, and cubes of tofu decorated with a few very thin rings of sliced scallion. A treasure trove of colorful and savory garnishes can also be found on the pickle shelf of a good Japanese grocery. It's worth experimenting with several kinds and arranging the pickles, thinly sliced, next to each small mound of raw seafood.

MACKEREL (*saba*)

Mackerel is one of the most delicious of all fish when eaten raw, but it must be handled very carefully as soon as it is caught or it will lose flavor. Most of the mackerel sold in the United States at sushi bars or in Japanese fish stores has been frozen and flown in from Japan. Skinless mackerel fillets—with the silvery membrane left attached to the skin side—should be sliced on an angle between $1/8$ and $1/4$ inch thick.

OCTOPUS (*tako*)

This is another example of cooked seafood that is often served as a piece of sushi or on a sashimi platter. While most of the octopus sold in Japanese restaurants or shops is a special Japanese variety, you can cook frozen octopus, slice it—about $1/8$ inch thick—and serve it on sushi or as sashimi.

ROE

The Japanese are fond of many delicious kinds of fish and shellfish roe that are unfamiliar to Americans. If you're making sushi using a runny roe such as salmon roe, wrap a strip of nori around the rice to keep the roe from running off. Various kinds of roe can be served in small mounds as sashimi.

Cod Roe: This roe is specially treated so it ends up being bright red and quite soft. It has a somewhat strong flavor but is deliciously reminiscent of the sea. Cod roe can be sliced into lengthwise strips about $1/4$ inch thick and attached to a mound of sushi rice with a strip of nori. Cod roe can also be served as sashimi.

Flying Fish Roe (*tobiko*): These tiny bright orange eggs are common in most Japanese restaurants and, especially when compared to other kinds of roe, quite inexpensive. Tobiko is usually served on sushi, held in place with a ribbon of nori.

Herring Roe (*kazunoko*): These bright yellow strips of roe are beautiful to look at when ribboned onto a mound of rice with a strip of nori. They are also very expensive. Herring roe has a delicate cucumberlike flavor and a surprisingly firm texture. Unfortunately herring roe can be very salty. Some of the salt can be eliminated by soaking the roe in cold water for 2 hours and then patting it dry.

Salmon Roe (*ikura*): This is the best known and one of the most delicious roes. Salmon roe is served raw as a part of a sashimi platter—usually atop slices of fish—or on sushi. Don't buy pasteurized salmon roe in jars, but try to find fresh lightly salted roe that has been kept refrigerated.

Sea Urchin Roe (*uni*): This is one of the best of all foods to encounter on a plate of sashimi or sushi. Because *uni* has to be perfectly fresh to be good, I wouldn't risk buying it except in the best Japanese fish stores or restaurants. If you're lucky enough to find fresh sea urchins still in the shell, you can remove the roe yourself (see color page 18). Sea urchin roe can be presented on top of sushi or in a small mound as sashimi. Don't bother buying frozen *uni*.

SALMON (*sake*)

Salmon makes delicious sashimi and sushi but should never be eaten raw without first being frozen for at least 24 hours. Salmon should be sliced between ⅛ and ¼ inch thick.

SQUID (*ika*)

The kind of squid destined for eating raw is not the squid typically sold in American fish stores but a special species imported, usually frozen, from Japan. Japanese squid is large, and only the white thick body is sold for sashimi and sushi. It should be sliced very thinly and scored lightly on one side to tenderize it slightly. Japanese squid is not to everyone's taste because of its rubbery, somewhat sticky texture.

TUNA

Most tuna species can be served raw as sashimi or sushi, but in Japanese restaurants yellowfin and bluefin tuna are named and sold according to their fat content. The most commonly sold tuna at sushi bars is a relatively lean cut of yellowfish called *maguro*. Cuts of tuna with a higher fat content—taken from the bluefin tuna—are sold as *chutoro* (moderately high fat content) and *otoro* (high fat content). These are more expensive than *maguro*, with *otoro* being the most expensive of all. *Otoro* is very pale, almost white because of its high fat content, and has a deep yet delicate flavor and a melting texture.

Tuna for sashimi is usually sold in 1-inch-thick rectangular sections that make it easy to slice. Buy a rectangle about 1 inch wide for sashimi and 2 inches wide for sushi. Slice the tuna across the grain and at a slight diagonal into ¼-inch-thick rectangles 1½ to 2 inches long for sashimi and 2½ inches long for sushi. These tuna rectangles should be arranged together—like falling dominos—on a sashimi platter or bowl.

YELLOWTAIL (*hamachi*)

This richly flavored delicate member of the jack family is a favorite for sashimi and sushi. In the United States yellowtail is available only as skinless fillets, although a silvery skinlike membrane should be left on one side. Slice the fillets with the knife at an angle into ⅛-inch-thick slices. Yellowtail slices can be presented together and falling over slightly or arranged in a flower pattern when presented as sashimi.

PONZU SAUCE

For some kinds of very thinly sliced fish served as sushi or sashimi the traditional soy sauce and wasabi are too strong. Ponzu sauce, which contains citrus juice, is lighter and better for more delicate fish.

You can buy ponzu sauce in jars, but it's much better homemade. Of all Western citrus fruits kumquats taste the most like Japanese lemons, but if you're not up to squeezing kumquats, use lime juice instead. Ponzu sauce keeps well for a year in the refrigerator and is said to improve after a month or two.

> **1 cup fresh kumquat or lime juice (from about 8 limes)**
>
> **1 cup Japanese dark soy sauce**
>
> **¼ cup mirin**
>
> **½ ounce bonito flakes (half a 1-ounce package)**
>
> **a 4-inch length of konbu**

MAKES 2 CUPS

Combine all the ingredients in a covered glass container and let sit in the refrigerator for 2 days. Strain and store in the refrigerator in a tightly covered jar.

SUSHI

(color page 15)

When most people think of raw fish, they think of sushi, raw seafood combined with seasoned rice. The most common type of sushi—*nigiri-sushi*—is made by placing a strip of raw fish or shellfish over a hand-shaped mound of seasoned rice. The other most popular form of sushi is *maki-sushi*, which is raw fish rolled up with seasoned rice in a sheet of nori. These rolls are then sliced and served in bite-size rounds.

SEASONED VINEGAR FOR SUSHI

Even though some sushi chefs have their own, sometimes secret, recipe for seasoned vinegar, this simple version is delicious and perfectly satisfying. You'll end up with more than you need for one recipe of sushi, but seasoned vinegar lasts forever out of the refrigerator.

**1 cup good-quality Japanese rice
   vinegar**
½ cup sugar
¼ cup salt

MAKES 1¾ CUPS

Combine the ingredients in a small saucepan and heat over medium heat while stirring until the sugar and salt dissolve. Let cool. Store in a glass bottle with a tight-fitting lid.

❧

Seasoned Rice for Sushi

Sushi rice should always be made using Japanese medium-grain rice; don't try making it with other varieties.

The method for cooking sushi rice is similar to other rice-cooking methods except that less liquid is used and the lid mustn't be taken off the pot until the rice is completely cooked and has had time to cool somewhat. The cooked rice is sprinkled and tossed with vinegar flavored with salt and sugar.

MAKES 7 CUPS COOKED RICE, ENOUGH FOR 60 INDIVIDUAL PIECES OF *NIGIRI-SUSHI* OR *MAKI-SUSHI*, ABOUT 4 MAIN-COURSE SERVINGS

3 cups Japanese medium-grain rice
3 cups cold water
6 tablespoons seasoned vinegar (see box)

Rinse the rice 6 or 7 times in cold water until the water is perfectly clear. Drain the rice and combine it with the water in a heavy 4-quart pot with a tight-fitting lid.

Place the uncovered pot over high heat. When the water approaches a simmer, after about 10 minutes, cover the pot and turn the heat down to medium-low. Cook the rice for 10 minutes without removing the cover at any point. Turn the heat down to very low and cook for 10 minutes more, again not removing the cover at any point. Turn off the heat—still without opening the pot—and let the rice rest for 15 minutes.

Turn the hot cooked rice into a large glass or stainless-steel bowl (tradition calls for using a wooden bowl) and sprinkle with the seasoned vinegar. Cut into the rice with a sideways motion using a wooden spatula or wooden spoon, while tossing, for about 5 minutes to separate the rice kernels and get the rice to cool. Don't overwork the rice, or you'll make it too sticky. Cover the rice with a damp towel and let cool to room temperature, for about 15 minutes.

❧

Nigiri-sushi

(color page 14)

To make *nigiri-sushi*—a strip of fish or a mound of fish roe on a small mound of rice—to professional standards takes years of apprenticeship, but very presentable sushi—attractive enough to impress guests—can be learned in an afternoon.

MAKES 60 PIECES, ABOUT 4 MAIN-COURSE SERVINGS

**2 pounds assorted perfectly trimmed raw
   fish, raw shellfish, or fish roe**
1 recipe seasoned rice (this page)
3 tablespoons powdered wasabi
3 tablespoons cold water
**1 or more sheets of nori for roe or long
   strips of fish that need to be ribboned
   onto the rice mounds**

Slice the fish into strips of appropriate length and thickness, following the guidelines under the individual fish headings. If you have a piece of fish you're uncertain about, cut the strips long enough—about 2½ inches—so they barely hang over the edges of the rice mounds. Bite into a slice of the fish to determine the right thickness. If the fish is difficult to chew, you've probably cut it too thick; if the strip feels mushy in the mouth or doesn't seem to have enough taste,

Nori is a variety of dried seaweed that looks somewhat like dried black paper. If you're shopping in a Japanese grocery, you'll probably encounter about 20 brands. Be sure to buy nori that has been already roasted—it should say so somewhere on the package. Look for the darkest nori you can find, which will be black or very dark green and will probably be slightly more expensive than paler brands.

it's probably too thin. In any case the thickness of the fish slices should range between $1/16$ and $1/4$ inch. Don't slice the fish all at once—I usually slice only one kind at a time—and keep it covered with plastic wrap in the refrigerator until you're ready to start constructing the sushi.

Once the fish is ready, prepare the wasabi by combining the powder with the cold water in a small glass or stainless-steel bowl to obtain a stiff paste. Turn the bowl over on the counter until you're ready to use the horseradish, or you'll find yourself sneezing as you make the rice mounds.

If you're using fish roe or long strips of *unagi* (cooked eel), you'll need to cut some nori ribbons to hold the seafood in place. For dry ingredients such as strips of *unagi* or herring roe, use a pair of sharp scissors to cut nori strips $3/8$ inch wide and 4 inches long. These strips are moistened on one end and wrapped under and over the sushi mounds to hold the seafood in place—you'll need 1 strip per sushi mound. If you're making sushi with wet or runny roe such as salmon roe, you'll need to cut strips of nori 1 inch wide and 7 inches long for wrapping

around the rice mound to keep the roe from running out.

As you're forming the rice mounds, wet your hands each time with cold water to prevent the rice from sticking to them. If your hands are too wet, the rice will fall apart, and if they aren't wet enough the rice will stick to your hands. The best approach is to dip 2 fingers in a bowl of cold water and then rub your hands together to moisten the entire surface of both hands.

If you're right-handed, scoop out a mound of rice about the size of a Ping-Pong ball ($2/3$ ounce) with your right hand. While holding the rice cupped in your right hand, lift up a strip of fish between the thumb and forefinger of your right hand and place it across your left hand, where the fingers join the palm. With the forefinger of your right hand—and while still holding on to the rice—take a tiny dollop, $1/4$ to $1/3$ teaspoon, of wasabi and smear it along the length of the fish strip. Place the mound of rice over the strip of fish and press gently against the top of the rice with your right forefinger and second finger to get the rice to cling to the fish. Gently clasp the sushi between your right thumb and forefinger and second finger and turn it over in your left hand so the fish is on top. Press the sides of the sushi between your right thumb and forefinger to further shape the rice and to get the fish to pull down slightly over the sides. Curl up the fingers of your left hand so that the sushi is well nestled in place and then press on the top of the sushi with the forefinger and second finger of your right hand while also pressing against one end of the sushi with the thumb of your left hand. Curve the fingers of your right hand slightly while shaping the sushi so the surface of the fish curves slightly down over

the rice. Rotate the sushi around on your left hand and again press against the sides and top of the sushi to help shape and compress it (see color page 14).

Once you've formed the *nigiri-sushi*, and especially if the fish or shellfish threatens to fall off the rice, you can wrap it with a narrow strip of nori moistened on the bottom, ends pinched together.

When making *nigiri-sushi* with fish roe you'll need to form a small mound of rice without any fish and press it down slightly with your fingers so it ends up being slightly flattened. When you've shaped the rice mound, wrap it with a wide strip of nori—moisten one end of the nori to help seal it—to form a container for the roe. Carefully spoon the roe in the opening formed by the nori.

Maki-sushi

(color page 14)

MAKES 10 ROLLS, 60 PIECES, ABOUT 4 MAIN-COURSE SERVINGS

five 7- by 8-inch sheets of nori

3 tablespoons powdered wasabi

3 tablespoons cold water

1 recipe seasoned rice (page 119)

$1\frac{1}{2}$ pounds assorted trimmed raw fish or shellfish (you can use end pieces and trimmings)

Because the raw seafood for *maki-sushi* is rolled up inside the rice, the pieces don't have to be as presentable. I sometimes make both *nigiri-sushi* and *maki-sushi* and use the best parts for *nigiri-sushi* and the trimmings for the *maki-sushi*.

To make *maki-sushi* you'll need a small bamboo mat called a *sudare* (see "Sources"), which is used to roll up the rice in the sheet of nori.

To make *maki-sushi,* start by cutting the sheets of nori in half by folding them in 2 directions so they snap or by cutting with sharp scissors. You will end up with 10 rectangles measuring 4 by 7 inches. Cut the fish into ½- by 7-inch strips. You may have to improvise and use smaller strips, smaller pieces, or fish trimmings to fill the sushi rolls, but the seafood in the center of the rolls should end up being about ½ inch thick. Combine the wasabi powder with the cold water in a small bowl until you obtain a stiff paste; reserve.

Unroll the *sudare* with the end directly in front of you and place a sheet of nori, shiny side down, so that the nori runs lengthwise from right to left with its edge about an inch from the front end of the *sudare.* Wet your hands by dipping 2 fingers in a bowl of cold water and quickly rubbing your hands together and with your right hand grab a ball of rice about the size of a tennis ball. Spread the rice in an even layer over the nori, but leave about a ¼-inch border uncovered along the side of the nori nearest you and about ¾ inch on the side farthest from you. Make a well running the length of the rice by pressing gently with your fingers. Scoop up a dollop—about ½ teaspoon—of wasabi with your right forefinger and spread it along the entire length of the well. Arrange the strip(s) or pieces of seafood in the well so they run the entire 7-inch length of the rice.

Lift the *sudare* on the end nearest you and gently roll it over the sushi roll, lifting the nori until the end of the nori nearest you is almost directly above the backside of the sushi roll.

Press straight down, gently, on the *sudare* to compact the rice. Lift up the top end of the *sudare* and roll the sushi slightly forward so the seam is on the bottom. Press firmly down on the *sudare* and squeeze it on both sides to hold it together in a roll. Unroll the *sudare* and set the sushi roll to the side. Repeat this process until you end up with 10 rolls.

Slice the rolls, 3 at a time, in half with a sharp chef's knife. Slide the knife carefully through the sushi roll without exerting too much pressure, which would cause the roll to split or tear. Keep the knife blade parallel with the work surface and use a gentle sawing motion to cut each of the sushi roll halves into thirds so each roll makes 6 rings. Set the rings on a platter or plate in the refrigerator until you're ready to serve (see color page 14).

REVERSE-ROLLED SUSHI

For decorative effect rolled sushi can be prepared with the rice instead of the nori on the outside. The technique is the same as for making *maki-sushi* except that the sushi rice is spread completely over the sheet of nori—no border of nori is left exposed—and the rice-covered nori turned onto a moist towel, rice side down. A dollop of wasabi is spread lengthwise in a line along the center of the sheet of nori, and the seafood is placed along this center line. The towel is then lifted so that the roll folds over itself and is pressed down in the same way the *sudare* is pressed when making regular *maki-sushi.* Once the sushi roll is completely rolled up, the *sudare* is placed over the whole assembly—including the towel—and pressed against the roll to compress the rice. The sushi roll is then unwrapped and sliced as for regular *maki-sushi.*

SUSHI HAND ROLLS

TEMAKI-SUSHI

These little sushi rolls look a little like black ice cream cones. They're easy to make because all you need are some sheets of nori, seasoned rice, and bits and pieces of raw fish or vegetable such as cucumber. You won't need a *sudare.* I sometimes use raw fish trimmings and little pieces of vegetable to improvise sushi hand rolls when I'm preparing a sushi meal and the guests are standing around ravenously waiting for dinner.

To make hand rolls you'll need to cut standard-size sheets of nori in half (with scissors or by folding the sheets in half and pinching) so you end up with 4- by 7-inch rectangles. To make the hand rolls, place a small mound of rice—about 50 percent larger than the Ping-Pong-ball–size lump used for *nigiri-sushi*—on the nori rectangle, slightly left of center. Flatten the rice slightly with wet fingers and place other ingredients such as thinly sliced cucumbers, pieces of raw fish or shellfish, shiso leaves, watercress leaves, shredded carrot, chopped scallions, shredded daikon, avocado slices, salmon roe, etc., on top of the rice. Roll up the nori starting with the left corner so you end up with the ingredients enclosed in a cone. Hand rolls don't lend themselves to any kind of formality—just hand them to guests as they're standing around.

Shellfish

Mussels

It wasn't until my first trip to France that I encountered an enormous bowl of black, gaping steamed mussels—to be scooped and gobbled up using one of the shells as a spoon. Now I know of few meals as satisfying as a bowl of mussels served with some crusty French bread and a glass of white wine.

The delicious briny broth that mussels release as they cook adds to their wonderful versatility. Mussels can also be lightly broiled on the half shell, deep-fried, stuffed, tossed into salads, or even grilled, and their broth can be used as the base for an almost infinite variety of soups, seafood stews, and sauces.

Although there are many species of mussels, only two show up regularly in American markets. The most common and reliable is the common mussel or "blue" mussel (a misnomer since this mussel is black), Mytilus edulis. More recently, beautiful blue-green mussels (Perna canaliculus) from New Zealand, somewhat more expensive, have shown up. These can be prepared in the same way as blue mussels, but because they're somewhat larger they are well suited for stuffing and baking.

SELECTING MUSSELS

Unless I'm serving them stuffed, baked, or broiled, I always look for cultivated mussels, which are rarely over 2 inches long. Cultivated mussels can be cleaned with a simple rinsing because there are no barnacles or grit attached to the shells and they rarely contain any sand. Cultivated mussels also have a more delicate flavor than their wild cousins.

Make sure the mussels you choose are not gaping wide open. If the mussels are just slightly opened (¼ inch or so), tap two of them together—they should close within 30 seconds. If you still have doubts, give the mussels a sniff—they should smell like a clean beach.

STORING, SORTING, AND CLEANING MUSSELS

The first rule: Don't store mussels in plain water; it will kill them. While some especially sandy mussels may benefit from a couple hours of soaking in salt water (½ cup salt to 1 quart water), most of the time—especially with cultivated mussels—this isn't necessary. Mussels should be stored in a bowl in the refrigerator, covered with a wet towel so they don't dry out.

Clean mussels by brushing them with a stiff kitchen brush under cold running water to eliminate any grit or sand. Pull out the beard—the little tuft of hairs sticking out the side of the mussels—by pinching it between thumb and forefinger and giving it a yank. If it's stubborn, you may have to grab it with a kitchen towel.

While you're scrubbing the mussels, keep an eye out for dead ones. Some mussels will feel light because there's nothing in them, while others may feel heavy because they're full of mud. The best system for getting rid of dead mussels is to firmly push the shells sideways in opposing directions with your thumb and forefinger. If the mussel is dead, the shells will fall apart in your hand.

Mussels should not be cleaned—or at least the beard shouldn't be pulled out—more than several hours before they are cooked, or they will die and spoil.

COOKING TECHNIQUES

STEAMING

Except for the occasional dish that requires mussels to be shucked raw, most mussel recipes begin with steaming the mussels open in a little liquid in a covered pot over high heat for 5 to 10 minutes. Use a pot in which the mussels will come no more than three quarters up the sides to give the mussels room to open. Always discard any mussels that have not opened.

Almost any liquid can be used, but the one you use will help determine the character of the finished dish. French cooks are likely to use white wine, while Italian cooks may start out with a flavorful mixture of olive oil and tomatoes. In a pinch I've used water or beer.

In the simplest steamed mussel dishes the delicious broth is served over the mussels in bowls. In more elaborate dishes the mussels are taken out of their shells and the cooking liquid is flavored or enriched with additional ingredients. In other dishes the mussels are steamed open simply to get them out of their shells before they're fried, grilled, broiled, or served cold in salads. This leaves you the broth, which you can freeze and use later in fish soups and sauces.

ARE MUSSELS SAFE?

Because mussels filter large amounts of water to extract their food, they tend to accumulate toxins and so are particularly vulnerable to pollutants. Mussels are also susceptible to "red tides," which contain large concentrations of a plankton that makes mussels poisonous.

Fortunately mussel beds are carefully monitored, and it's unlikely that any mussel you buy is going to make you sick. Going out and collecting your own mussels is a different story: Make sure you know the local waters. If you have any doubts, call your local health department or shellfish control agency. I also don't recommend eating any mussel raw.

HOW MANY TO SERVE?

Mussels are usually sold by the pound, and when I'm serving steamed mussels as a first course in an informal meal I count about ½ to ¾ pound per person. Depending on the size of the mussels, this can mean anywhere from about 9 to 18 mussels. When serving steamed mussels as a main course, I usually serve 1½ pounds per person.

When serving broiled mussels as a first course, I serve 6 medium to large mussels per person.

❧

Steamed Mussels with White Wine and Parsley

MOULES À LA MARINIÈRE

This is one of those dishes I would happily eat several times a week if I weren't always preoccupied with experimenting with and tasting new dishes. Because the best part of this dish is soaking up the broth with crusty French bread, be sure to use bread with a firm crust—sourdough is particularly good. Save this dish for informal occasions, when your guests won't hesitate to use their hands for dipping into the mussel broth.

Traditional recipes for *moules à la marinière* call for swirling butter into the hot mussel broth just before serving, but if you're watching your fat intake the broth is perfectly satisfying without it.

MAKES 8 FIRST-COURSE OR 4 MAIN-COURSE SERVINGS

6 pounds mussels, preferably small cultivated

2 cups dry white wine

3 shallots, finely chopped

1 Turkish bay leaf

2 fresh thyme sprigs or ½ teaspoon dried

3 tablespoons finely chopped parsley

¼ pound unsalted butter (optional)

pepper

Wash and sort the mussels, pulling off any pieces of protruding beard.

Combine the wine, shallots, bay leaf, and thyme in a 10-quart pot and bring to a slow simmer over medium heat. Simmer for about 5 minutes, then add the mussels, cover the pot, and turn the heat up to high.

When steam starts to shoot out from under the lid, turn the heat back down

to medium. Leave the pot on the heat for 5 minutes more. Shake the pot—holding down the lid with a kitchen towel—to redistribute the mussels. Put the pot back on the heat for 2 minutes more. Take off the lid and check to see if all the mussels have opened. If not, replace the lid and cook for 2 minutes more.

Remove the lid, wait a minute for the steam to dissipate, scoop the mussels out of the pot with a large spoon or skimmer, and place them in hot bowls, discarding any unopened mussels. If the liquid in the bottom of the pan is sandy, carefully pour it into a clean saucepan, leaving any sand or grit behind. Add the chopped parsley to the hot broth, whisk in the butter if desired, and season with pepper. Heat the broth for a minute or two and ladle it over the hot mussels. Serve slices of crusty bread at the table.

❧

Steamed Mussels with Thai Green Curry

Soon after I made my first batch of Thai curry paste I was spooning it over and into anything I could think of. Two weeks of Thai-inspired meals ensued—including these mussels. This dish is mildly hot with an exotic lemony flavor, but in no way is the taste of the mussels overpowered.

I serve these mussels in deep bowls with their soupy sauce poured over them. I also like to set a bowl of jasmine or basmati rice in the middle of the table. Count on wetting your fingers and using a lot of napkins.

MAKES 8 FIRST-COURSE OR 4 MAIN-COURSE SERVINGS

½ cup dry white wine

6 pounds mussels, preferably New Zealand or small cultivated

one 14-ounce can unsweetened coconut milk

3 tablespoons canned or homemade green curry paste (page 340)

juice of 2 limes

Combine the wine and mussels in a 10-quart covered pot and put over high heat until steam starts shooting out from under the lid. Shake the pot every couple of minutes with the lid held down with a kitchen towel to redistribute the mussels. When the mussels have opened, after about 10 minutes, scoop them out into large individual hot bowls, discarding any unopened mussels. Carefully pour the liquid in the bottom of the pot into a 2-quart saucepan so that any sand or grit is left behind in the large pot. If there's a lot of sand, strain the cooking liquid through a fine strainer or through a coffee filter.

Bring the mussel broth to a boil and stir in the coconut milk. Whisk in the green curry paste and lime juice.

Ladle the brothlike sauce over the mussels. Pass any extra sauce in a sauceboat at the table.

Italian-Style Steamed Mussels with Garlic and Sometimes Tomatoes

COZZE ALLA MARINARA

(color page 4)

Italians have a couple of mussel dishes that end with the words *alla marinara*. In the simplest version, *cozze alla marinara*, only a little chopped parsley and garlic are added to the liquid, while more elaborate versions contain tomatoes and olive oil. Both are delicious served as is or as pasta sauces—*pasta alle cozze in bianco* without tomatoes, *pasta alle cozze con i pelati* with tomatoes.

The Venetian *zuppa de peòci* is really *pasta alle cozze in bianco* except that the mussels and juices are ladled over slices of bread instead of pasta.

Without Tomatoes

MAKES 4 FIRST-COURSE SERVINGS

2 garlic cloves, finely chopped

3 tablespoons finely chopped parsley

½ cup dry white wine or water

3 pounds mussels, preferably small cultivated

pepper

1 pound fresh or ½ pound dried linguine or other pasta or 4 thick slices of Italian bread (optional)

Crush the chopped garlic into a paste in a mortar and pestle or with the side of a chef's knife on a cutting board. Combine the garlic paste in a bowl with the chopped parsley.

Bring the wine to a rapid boil in a pot large enough to hold the mussels. Cover the pot and steam the mussels.

When the mussels have opened, after about 10 minutes, scoop them out into hot bowls, discarding any unopened mussels. If the mussel cooking liquid is sandy, carefully pour it into a saucepan, leaving the sand behind, or strain it through a fine-mesh strainer. Add the parsley and garlic mixture to the hot broth, simmer it for about 1 minute, and ladle it over the mussels. Season the mussels with pepper.

Put a thick slice of bread in the bottom of each bowl before adding the mussels if desired. Or serve them over pasta: Reduce the mussel broth until only a cup remains and then, if you wish, whisk in ¼ cup virgin olive oil or butter before pouring it over the cooked pasta.

With Tomatoes

MAKES 4 FIRST-COURSE SERVINGS

¼ cup virgin olive oil

2 garlic cloves, chopped

3 tomatoes, peeled, seeded, and chopped, or 1½ cups drained, seeded, and chopped canned tomatoes

3 pounds mussels, preferably small cultivated

½ cup dry white wine or water

3 tablespoons finely chopped parsley

pepper

½ pound dried vermicelli (optional)

Heat the olive oil and garlic over medium heat in a 4-quart pot for about 5 minutes. When the garlic starts to smell fragrant, add the tomatoes and simmer for about 10 minutes, stirring every minute or two, until the mixture starts to thicken.

Put the mussels in the pot with the wine. Cover and steam for about 10 minutes over medium to high heat until the mussels open. Scoop the mussels into hot bowls, discarding any unopened ones, and carefully pour the mussel steaming liquid into the tomato sauce, leaving any sand behind. Quickly simmer the tomato sauce until it thickens slightly and ladle it over the mussels. Sprinkle with parsley and grind on some pepper.

If you want to serve the mussels over pasta, you may need to reduce the broth to thicken it slightly. You also may want to make things less messy—if less picturesque—by taking the mussels out of the shells and stirring them into the sauce at the last minute before pouring it over the pasta.

STEPS FOR IMPROVISING STEAMED MUSSEL AND CLAM DISHES

prepare the mussels/clams: Wash, sort, and remove beards.

decide on a steaming liquid: Water, white wine, beer, hard cider, and dashi are just a few possibilities.

steam the mussels/clams: Steam open the shellfish in a covered pot. If the resulting liquid contains sand, carefully pour the liquid into a clean container, leaving the sand behind, or strain it through a fine-mesh strainer or through a triple layer of cheesecloth or a clean, well-rinsed cloth napkin or a coffee filter.

add herbs to the cooking liquid: Herbs, chopped or tied into a bouquet garni, give a delicious flavor to the mussel or clam juices. Parsley, chervil, tarragon, chives, mint, cilantro, thyme, bay leaves, sage, rosemary, marjoram, and oregano are some possibilities. Simmer the herbs in the cooking liquid for at least 2 minutes to give them time to infuse their flavors.

add aromatic vegetables to the steaming liquid: Aromatic vegetables such as onions (finely sliced or chopped), shallots (chopped), carrots (sliced or cut into decorative cubes or julienned), celery (sliced, cut into cubes, or julienned), garlic (peeled, left whole, or chopped), ginger (sliced or chopped), galangal (sliced), lemongrass (finely sliced), chilies (seeded and chopped), and kaffir lime leaves (left whole or chopped) can be simmered in the steaming liquid several minutes before adding the mussels or clams. In this way the vegetables have time to cook and impart their flavors

to the liquid by the time the mussels or clams are done. The vegetables can be left in or strained before serving the mussels or clams.

add spices: Spices such as saffron or curry can be stirred into the steaming liquid before or after the mussels or clams are cooked.

add other flavorings: Thai fish sauce, soy sauce, mirin, sake, miso, and tomatoes (peeled, seeded, chopped) can all be stirred into the steaming liquid before serving.

add thickeners: Starches such as roux (cooked flour and butter), cornstarch, or arrowroot (worked to a paste with cold water, stirred into simmering cooking liquid) are sometimes added to the cooking liquid to thicken it. This is especially useful when a thick sauce is needed to coat the shellfish on the half shell for baking or broiling. You can also thicken the liquid with vegetable purees such as sorrel (see recipe at right).

add enricheners: Rich ingredients such as heavy cream, crème fraîche, unsalted butter, mayonnaise, and unsweetened coconut milk can be added to the cooking liquid to give it a richer flavor and texture.

presenting the cooked mussels /clams: On the half shell (coated with sauce made from reduced cooking liquid); in broth (cooking liquid is left unreduced and hence thin)—mussels and clams served in broth can be left in or taken out of their shells.

Mussels with Sorrel Sauce

I'm nuts about combining sorrel with shellfish, probably because the natural tartness of the sorrel leaves goes so well with the briny flavors of the sea. In this dish pureed sorrel and a small amount of cream are added to the hot liquid to give it texture and tang, and the resulting sauce is spooned into the hot mussels on the half shell.

MAKES 4 FIRST-COURSE SERVINGS

1 pound fresh sorrel including stems, coarsely chopped
1 cup dry white wine
3 shallots, finely chopped
1 bunch of parsley, finely chopped
2 pounds small cultivated mussels
½ cup heavy cream
salt and pepper

Place the sorrel in a small pot while stirring over medium heat until it turns gray and releases liquid, in about 3 minutes. Puree the sorrel in a blender or food processor and work it through a food mill or a strainer.

Combine the wine, shallots, and parsley in a pot large enough to hold the mussels when they open. Bring the mixture to a simmer, add the mussels, and cover the pot. Turn the heat to high and start checking the mussels after 5 minutes. When they have opened, take the pot off the heat and discard any unopened mussels. Remove and discard the top shells and arrange the mussels on their half shells on a baking sheet covered with a sheet of crumpled aluminum foil to keep the mussels flat.

If the cooking liquid from the mussels is sandy, carefully pour it into a 2-

quart saucepan, leaving sand and grit behind. Boil down the cooking liquid until about ½ cup remains. Whisk the sorrel puree and cream into the liquid. Cook over medium heat for about 5 minutes, stirring until the sauce thickens. Season the sauce with salt and pepper and spoon it into each mussel. Place the whole tray of mussels in a 300°F oven for 5 minutes and serve immediately.

❧

Cold Mussels with Herb Mayonnaise

MAKES 6 HORS D'OEUVRE OR FIRST-COURSE SERVINGS

2 pounds mussels (3 dozen or more)

1 cup dry white wine

½ cup homemade mayonnaise (page 333) made with half virgin olive oil, half canola oil

1 tablespoon finely chopped fresh chervil or parsley

1 tablespoon finely chopped fresh chives

1 tablespoon wine vinegar such as sherry or balsamic

Steam the mussels in the white wine in a covered pot for about 10 minutes, until they open. Discard any unopened mussels. Strain or decant the mussel-cooking liquid into a clean saucepan and simmer until only ¼ cup remains.

Take the top shell off the mussels and arrange the mussels on a baking sheet covered with crumpled aluminum foil to hold the mussels flat.

Whisk together the mayonnaise, reduced liquid, and herbs and let sit for at least 20 minutes to give the herbs time to infuse into the mayonnaise. Season to taste with some or all

of the vinegar, but be careful not to make the sauce too thin. Arrange the mussels in their half shells and warm them in a 250°F oven for 15 minutes. Spoon the sauce over each mussel and serve on the half shell. The mussels can also be tossed in the cold mayonnaise and be served as a salad.

MUSSEL SOUPS

The only difference between a plate of steamed mussels and a bowl of mussel soup is the proportion of liquid to mussels. The easiest way to make a mussel soup is just to toss the mussels into a pot of simmering broth about 10 minutes before serving. A more sophisticated approach consists of steaming open the mussels, flavoring the cooking liquid with herbs and vegetables, and adding the mussels—either out of their shells or on the half shell—just before serving.

In less calorie-conscious days soups were often given a rich velvety texture with a lot of cream, butter, or egg yolks. Nowadays soups are better thickened with vegetable purees or pureed fish or left alone so they have a light brothlike consistency.

French-Style Mussel Soup with Basil and Saffron

MOULES AU PISTOU

There's something magical about the combination of saffron with the sealike flavors of shellfish. This soup, inspired by pistou—the basil-scented vegetable soup from the south of France—is thickened with flavorful vegetables and pureed fish. The result is astonishing.

MAKES 6 FIRST-COURSE SERVINGS

4 pounds whole lean fish, cleaned, filleted, skin removed, heads and bones reserved

1 medium onion, chopped

2 cups dry white wine

1 bouquet garni: 3 fresh thyme sprigs or ½ teaspoon dried, a small bunch of parsley, and a bay leaf tied up with string (or in cheesecloth for dried thyme)

4 pounds mussels, preferably small cultivated

3 leeks, including 1 inch of green, finely sliced

1 carrot, finely sliced

3 tomatoes, cut in half crosswise, seeds squeezed out, and chopped

leaves from 1 large bunch of fresh basil

1 garlic clove, finely chopped and crushed to a paste

5 tablespoons extra-virgin olive oil

small pinch of saffron threads, soaked for 15 minutes in 1 tablespoon water

salt and pepper

6 slices of toasted French bread

Remove the gills from the fish heads (see color page 26) and rinse the heads and bones thoroughly in cold water. Make a fish broth by combining the fish bones and heads with the onion, white wine, bouquet garni, and enough cold water to barely cover in a 4-quart pot. Bring to a slow boil and simmer for 30 minutes. Strain. Discard the solids and reserve the broth.

Put the mussels in a large pot, pour in a cup of the fish broth, cover the pot, and steam over medium heat until the mussels open, 5 to 10 minutes. Take out the mussels, discarding any that haven't opened, and combine the liquid with the rest of the fish broth (strain or decant it if necessary to remove sand). Take the mussels out of the shells, discard the shells, and reserve the mussels.

Bring the fish broth to a simmer in a 4-quart pot and add the fish fillets, leeks, carrot, and tomatoes. Cover and simmer gently for 40 minutes. Strain the broth into a clean pot. Puree the solids that won't go through the strainer in a food processor and then work them through a food mill into the broth. Discard the solids that don't go through the food mill. If you don't have a food mill, work the fish puree as well as you can through a strainer with the back of a ladle.

Make a pistou by tossing the basil leaves with the crushed garlic and a tablespoon of the olive oil—to prevent them from turning black—and chopping them very finely with a chef's knife or in a food processor or blender. If you chop the basil by hand, add the rest of the olive oil after chopping. If you're using a food processor or blender, combine all the olive oil with the basil leaves and garlic at the beginning. (Miniature food processors and the small processor attachments that fit on blenders are especially good for this.)

Bring the broth to a simmer and add the mussels and saffron with its soaking liquid. Place a slice of toasted bread into each soup bowl. Stir the pistou into the soup, season with salt and pepper, and ladle immediately into the hot bowls.

Fish for Pureed Fish Soups Soft-textured fish are especially good for making pureed soups. Use cod, flatfish, rockfish, sea bass, sea trout, less expensive snappers, or weakfish

---

THICKENING MUSSEL-COOKING LIQUID

roux: *Moules à la poulette*, a classic French mussel dish, provides a perfect example of how roux can be used to thicken and convert mussel-cooking liquid into a sauce. To make *moules à la poulette*, make a roux with 3 tablespoons flour and 2 tablespoons butter for every 2 cups mussel-cooking liquid and whisk the liquid into the hot roux. Add 2 egg yolks (stir a little hot liquid into the beaten yolks first) and 2 tablespoons unsalted butter and stir the sauce over low heat—just enough to thicken it slightly without letting it boil. Arrange the mussels in their half shells and spoon the sauce into each shell. *Moules à la poulette* takes well to all kinds of variations, such as a teaspoon or two of curry cooked with the roux.

cream: Boil the mussel-cooking liquid down to about a quarter of its original volume, then add an equal amount of heavy cream (e.g., 1 cup of liquid reduced to ¼ cup, mixed with ¼ cup cream) and reduce until thickened (to about ⅓ cup). You can make dozens of different sauces by adding chopped fresh herbs, pureed tomatoes, curry, saffron, finely chopped mushrooms, etc.

mayonnaise: Whisk a little of the mussel-cooking liquid into homemade mayonnaise (page 333) flavored any way you like—with herbs, garlic, curry, saffron, truffle juice, oils (including nut oils), tomatoes, capers, and so on. Don't serve the mussels too hot, or the mayonnaise will separate.

Mussel and Garlic Soup

This soup is a must for garlic lovers—it contains almost a whole head per serving—but is surprisingly mild and will be enjoyed by nonfanatics as well. The flavor of the mussels is a perfect accent to the garlic, which makes a creamy fat-free thickener. This version contains fresh sage, but it's just as good with fresh thyme or marjoram.

MAKES 6 FIRST-COURSE SERVINGS

4 pounds mussels, preferably small cultivated

7 cups chicken broth (page 344) or fish broth (page 343) or water

6 heads of garlic, broken into cloves, unpeeled

3 fresh sage leaves tied into a bouquet garni with 1 small bunch of parsley and a bay leaf

juice of 1 lime or lemon

salt and pepper

6 slices of toasted crusty bread

Steam the mussels in 2 cups of the broth in a covered pot until they open, 5 to 10 minutes. Scoop out the mussels, discarding any that haven't opened, check the liquid for sand (strain or decant if necessary), and combine the liquid with the rest of the broth. Put the garlic and bouquet garni in the pot with the liquid, cover, and simmer slowly about 40 minutes until the garlic is soft—the cloves can easily be crushed against the inside of the pan with a spoon.

Meanwhile, take the top shells off half of the mussels—leaving about 40 mussels on the half shell—and take the remaining mussels completely out of the shells. Discard the extra shells.

Work the garlic broth through a food mill or push it through a strainer with the back of a ladle so the garlic pulp falls into the broth. Add the lime juice and season the broth with salt and pepper. Heat the mussels (both those on the half shell and those completely out of the shell) in the broth.

Place the bread slices in wide hot soup bowls and ladle in the soup. Distribute the mussels on the half shell evenly among the bowls.

Curried Mussel Soup with Red Lentils and Yogurt

*T*his creamy-textured soup, thickened with quick-cooking, delicate-flavored miniature red lentils, has very little fat. If you can't find the lentils at a health food store or Middle Eastern or Indian market, the soup will still be good with regular brown lentils.

MAKES 6 FIRST-COURSE SERVINGS

2 pounds small cultivated mussels

1½ cups dry white wine

1 medium onion, chopped

½ teaspoon fresh thyme leaves

2 garlic cloves, chopped

2 tablespoons unsalted butter

2 teaspoons good-quality curry powder

1 cup water

½ cup red lentils, rinsed

2 tablespoons chopped fresh cilantro

1½ cups plain yogurt

pepper

cayenne pepper (optional)

6 tablespoons extra yogurt or crème fraîche for garnish

Steaming Open the Mussels: Put the mussels and white wine in a 4-quart pot with a tight-fitting lid. Cover the pot and place it over medium heat for 5 to 10 minutes, until the mussels open. Remove the lid, let the mussels cool, and take them out of their shells, discarding the shells and any unopened mussels and reserving the mussels and steaming liquid. (If the liquid is sandy, decant it carefully into another container, leaving the sand behind.)

Preparing the Flavor Base and Lentil Mixture: Gently cook the onion, thyme, and garlic in butter in a 4-quart pot over medium heat until the onion turns translucent, about 10 minutes. Add the curry powder and stir for 1 minute more, until you can smell the curry. (Don't overdo it, or the curry may burn.) Add the lentils, the steaming liquid, and the water. Cover the pot and simmer over low heat for 25 minutes, until the lentils are very soft. If the lentils run dry at any point during the cooking, add another cup of water.

Finishing the Soup: Let the lentil mixture cool for about 10 minutes and then puree it in a blender or food processor with half of the reserved mussels.

Work the pureed mussel mixture through a fine-mesh strainer (the back of a ladle works best for this) into a clean 4-quart pot. Stir in the rest of the mussels, the chopped cilantro, and the yogurt and bring the soup to a slow simmer. If the soup seems too thick, thin it with broth or water. Season to taste with pepper and cayenne if you like it spicy. Serve in hot bowls and garnish each serving with a dollop of yogurt.

STUFFED MUSSELS

There are two ways to stuff mussels. The easiest method is to steam them open (save the liquid for a sauce or another recipe or reduce it and integrate it into the stuffing or sauce), remove the top shell, and slide a stuffing under each mussel on the half shell. A sauce made from the steaming liquid or an herb butter (garlic- and parsley-flavored snail butter is especially good) can then be dolloped on each mussel and the mussels heated briefly just before serving in a very hot oven or under the broiler.

A second method, more traditional and more time-consuming, is to partially open the raw mussels with an oyster knife, push the stuffing in through the side of the shell, tie the shells together with a short length of string, and steam the mussels in a little white wine for about 10 minutes. One of the shells is then pulled off the mussels, leaving the plump stuffed mussel sitting on the half shell. Typically the mussels are then dolloped with a little butter or a sauce made from the steaming liquid and reheated briefly in the oven or under the broiler.

Mussels Stuffed with Spinach and Garlic

*A*lthough this dish takes time to prepare, it's one of the most elegant and tasty mussel dishes I know. I recommend using medium to large mussels for this dish, or the stuffing process is liable to get tedious. Buy a few extra mussels in case there are any bad ones or you break a couple forcing in the stuffing. The time-con-suming part—stuffing and tying the mussels—can be done up to 4 hours before serving.

MAKES 4 FIRST-COURSE SERVINGS

leaves from 2 large bunches of spinach, stems removed

2 quarts boiling water

2 garlic cloves, finely chopped

2 tablespoons extra-virgin olive oil

salt and pepper

24 medium to large mussels (about 1½ to 2 pounds)

½ cup dry white wine

1 cup heavy cream

Blanch the spinach leaves in the boiling water for 30 seconds. Drain the leaves in a colander and rinse immediately with cold water. Squeeze the excess water out of the spinach—but not so hard as to squeeze out the flavor—and chop it coarsely.

Crush the chopped garlic to a paste in a mortar and pestle or on a cutting board with the side of a chef's knife. Combine the garlic with the spinach in a mixing bowl. Stir the olive oil into the spinach and season with salt and pepper.

Stick a small knife into the side of the mussels and twist so the mussel opens on the side by about ⅓ inch. Push a couple of teaspoons of the stuffing into each mussel with the han-dle of a fork. When all the mussels are stuffed in this way, tie each one closed with a short length of cotton string.

Put the mussels in a pan or pot with a tight-fitting lid, preferably just large enough so the mussels fit in a single layer. Pour in the wine, cover, and steam over medium heat for 10 min-utes. Turn off the heat and let cool for 5 minutes. Cut the strings off the mus-sels and pull one of the shells off each mussel.

Boil down the liquid left in the pot until only about ½ cup is left. Add the heavy cream and boil again, stirring, for about 5 minutes, until the sauce thickens slightly. Season with pepper. Preheat the oven to 350°F.

Just before serving, arrange the mussels on a baking sheet covered with crumpled aluminum foil to keep them as level as possible and carefully spoon a little sauce over each one. Warm in the oven for 8 minutes. Serve immediately on individual plates. Pass the extra sauce in a sauceboat at the table.

A less time-consuming method is to steam open the mussels without stuff-ing, put a spoonful of stuffing on each half shell, arrange the mussels on top, prepare the sauce, and finish and pre-sent the dish in the same way.

COLD MUSSELS AND MUSSEL SALADS

I once had a restaurant where we used so much mussel-steaming liquid for our fish sauces that we were forever inventing cold mussel dishes to use up the mussels. I've given a couple of the best versions here, but you'll probably have more fun making them up as you go along. Both of these recipes suggest putting the mussels and the sauce in the half shells, but if you like the mus-sels can be tossed together with the sauce and served as a salad.

❦

Cold Mussels in Salsa

This salsa combines all my favorite Mexican ingredients—cilantro, lime juice, garlic, chipotle chilies, jalapeño chilies, and grilled poblano chilies. This salsa is so good you don't have to limit yourself to serving it with mussels—it's great with a bag of tortilla chips or on grilled fish or meats.

MAKES 6 FIRST-COURSE SERVINGS

36 medium to large mussels (about 2¼ to 3 pounds)

½ cup water

1 garlic clove, finely chopped

2 poblano chilies, peeled, seeded, and chopped (see box on page 133)

1 small onion, finely chopped

juice of 2 limes

2 tablespoons finely chopped fresh cilantro

2 jalapeño chilies, seeded and finely chopped

4 canned chipotle chilies (usually they come packed in adobo sauce), drained, seeded, and finely chopped

1 tomato, peeled, seeded, and chopped

2 tablespoons extra-virgin olive oil

salt

In a covered pot large enough to hold the opened mussels, steam the mussels in the water for 5 to 10 min-utes. Save the liquid for another recipe, take the mussels out of the shells, and discard half the shells and any unopened mussels.

Crush the garlic to a paste in a mor-tar and pestle or on a cutting board with the side of a chef's knife.

Combine all the ingredients in a mixing bowl, season to taste with salt, and let sit in the refrigerator for at least 2 hours.

Just before serving, stir the salsa and spoon about a teaspoon into each mussel shell, place a mussel on top, and spoon on another teaspoon or two of salsa. Serve chilled.

PEELING CHILIES AND BELL PEPPERS

To peel chilies or peppers, you must completely char their thin, shiny skin. This is best done over hot coals, which lightly scent the chilies, but unless you're barbecuing anyway it's more convenient to use a gas or electric stove.

If you're using a gas stove, simply place the chilies right on the burner over a medium to high flame. Turn the peppers over with tongs every 2 to 3 minutes, until they are completely blackened. If you start to see any traces of white ash, remove the chilies from the heat.

If you have an electric stove, bend a wire coat hanger and set it on the electric burner so the chilies are kept about 1/8 inch away from the electric coils. Turn the heat on high and blacken them on each side. Or halve the peppers and char them, skin side up, under the broiler.

When the chilies are blackened, wrap them in a plastic bag and let cool for 15 minutes. Pull away the blackened skin and, if necessary, quickly rinse the chilies under cold water to eliminate specks of blackened peel.

The softened chilies can then be slit in half down the middle and the seeds scraped out.

❧

Cold Mussels in Herb and Caper Sauce

The trick to this dish is to use a lot of fresh herbs and a fair amount of good wine vinegar to give the sauce the necessary tang. The sauce—a homemade mayonnaise—is a hybrid of traditional tartar, gribiche, and rémoulade sauces.

MAKES 6 HORS D'OEUVRE OR FIRST-COURSE SERVINGS

36 medium to large mussels (about 2 1/4 to 3 pounds)

1/2 cup water

1/4 cup vegetable oil

1 egg yolk

1/2 cup extra-virgin olive oil

3 tablespoons drained capers, coarsely chopped

10 small sour gherkins (cornichons), chopped

1 tablespoon Dijon mustard

1/4 cup finely chopped fresh herbs such as tarragon, chervil, chives, parsley, basil, or a combination

2 tablespoons good-quality wine vinegar such as sherry or Champagne or more to taste

salt and pepper

In a covered pot large enough to hold the opened mussels, steam the mussels in the water for 5 to 10 minutes, until they open. Take the mussels out of the shell. Discard half the mussel shells and any unopened mussels and save a little of the liquid in case you need to thin the sauce (freeze the rest).

Prepare a mayonnaise by slowly working the vegetable oil into the egg yolk and then slowly stirring in the olive oil. You can also start the mayonnaise in a miniature food processor, but stir in the olive oil by hand. For some inexplicable reason, hard beating turns extra-virgin olive oil bitter.

Stir the rest of the ingredients into the mayonnaise. If the mayonnaise seems too thick, stir in a tablespoon or two of the mussel-cooking liquid.

Put a teaspoon of the sauce into each mussel shell and put the mussel on top. Put another teaspoon of sauce on top of the mussels. Serve cold.

FRYING MUSSELS

I like meals that involve passing around platters of food because helping each other gets guests relaxed and talking. Another way to break the ice is to serve finger food, such as a plate of fried mussels placed in the center of the table.

Several kinds of coatings can be used for the mussels, but my favorite is a simple flour-and-water batter. I also sometimes include mussels in an assorted tempura. Whichever breading you decide to use, you must first steam the mussels open in a little water or white wine.

Fried mussels can be served unaccompanied—skewered with a toothpick, they make a great cocktail party hors d'oeuvre—but at the table I usually serve lemon wedges or this simple sauce, a homemade mayonnaise lightened with a little whipped cream.

❧

Fried Mussels with Curry Mayonnaise

MAKES 6 FIRST-COURSE OR
HORS D'OEUVRE SERVINGS

1½ cups water

½ cup all-purpose flour, sifted

36 medium mussels (about 2 pounds)

½ cup vegetable oil

1 egg yolk

juice of ½ lemon

½ cup extra-virgin olive oil

1 tablespoon good-quality curry powder or
  to taste

½ cup heavy cream (optional)

salt and pepper

1 quart vegetable or pure olive oil

1 bunch of curly parsley, large stems
  removed, thoroughly dried

Prepare a batter by slowly whisking 1 cup water into the flour in a small mixing bowl. Strain this mixture into a bowl, cover, and let it rest.

Meanwhile, in a covered pot large enough to hold the opened mussels, steam them in ½ cup water for 5 to 10 minutes, until they open. Discard any unopened mussels and save the liquid for another recipe. Or reduce it down to 2 tablespoons and add it to the mayonnaise.

Make a mayonnaise by slowly whisking the vegetable oil into the egg yolk by hand or in a miniature food processor. Stir the lemon juice and all but 2 tablespoons of the olive oil into the mayonnaise. If the mayonnaise starts to get too thick, stir in a tablespoon or two of the mussel-cooking liquid to thin it to a workable consistency.

In a small sauté pan, gently heat the curry powder in the remaining olive oil until it starts to froth slightly and give off its aroma, no more than 2 minutes. Be careful not to overdo it—curry burns easily. Stir this mixture into the mayonnaise.

If you're using the cream, whip it until it holds its shape but not until it is too stiff, and fold it into the mayonnaise with a rubber spatula.

Season the sauce with salt and pepper to taste and a few drops more lemon juice if needed. You can make the sauce several hours before the mussels are served, but be sure to cover it, keep it in the refrigerator, and give it a quick stir before serving.

Just Before Serving: Heat the frying oil to 350°F. Dip the mussels in the batter—I use chopsticks or 2 wooden skewers or toothpicks for this—and gently drop them one by one into the hot oil. Fry the mussels for about 1 minute, take them out with a slotted spoon or spider, and drain them on a cloth towel. Stand back when frying the mussels, they crackle and spatter.

Arrange the hot mussels on a folded cloth napkin on a plate. Sprinkle with salt. Throw the sprigs of parsley into the hot oil and fry for about 5 seconds. Remove, drain on a towel, and gently scatter on top of the mussels. Give everyone a small plate and serve the sauce in a bowl or, if you're being more formal, in individual dipping bowls.

Clams

Clam chowder, clam bakes, stuffed clams, fried clams, and raw clams, all done up in various regional guises, are a part of the American tradition.

Where you live will usually dictate what you can get, but of the dozens of existing varieties, normally only one or two kinds will be available at one time and place. Fortunately one kind can almost always be exchanged for another in recipes.

ATLANTIC CLAMS

There are four major categories of Atlantic clams: hard-shell, soft-shell, surf clams, and razor clams.

HARD-SHELLS, ALSO CALLED QUAHOGS, PRONOUNCED KO-HOGS
(Mercenaria mercenaria)

Even though these are the best known of the Atlantic clams, they are rarely sold by the name hard-shell or quahog but instead are sold according to size.

The smallest quahogs, called *littlenecks*, are about 1½ to 2¼ inches across and weigh roughly 2 ounces each. (You'll get from 7 to 10 per pound.) Even though they are the smallest, littlenecks are the most expensive, probably because they are the most tender and have the sweetest flavor. If you like raw clams, littlenecks are best. Littlenecks are also excellent when steamed or cooked into soups, but most cooks use larger clams because they are less expensive by weight and you end up with fewer to shuck.

Medium-size quahogs (2¼ to 3 inches across, 5 to 7 clams per pound) are called *cherrystones*. Cherrystones can be eaten raw or cooked in the same way as littlenecks. They are also the perfect size for stuffing. They are slightly less expensive than littlenecks.

Large quahogs (over 3 inches across, 2 to 4 clams per pound) are called *chowder clams*. Chowder clams are the most practical for making soup because relatively few clams are needed and they're inexpensive. Chowder clams, however, don't have the delicate briny flavor of littlenecks or cherrystones. *Mahogany clams* (*Arctica islandica*), also known as *ocean quahogs*, which have maroon shells and orange-colored meat, are about the same size as chowder or cherrystone clams and are used in the same way—mostly for their meats. They are harvested offshore in deeper ocean waters, while hard-shell clams are harvested in shallower bays and coastal waters.

When buying quahogs, make sure the shells are firmly closed. If any of the clams gape slightly, give them a squeeze—they should close back up.

SOFT-SHELLS, ALSO CALLED STEAMERS, FRYERS, OR LONG-NECKS
(Mya arenaria)

Soft-shell clams are best recognized not by their shells (they have hard shells, albeit thinner and more fragile than quahog shells) but by the necklike siphon that protrudes from the side of the shell.

Soft-shells have 3- to 4-inch-long oval shells. Because soft-shell clams can't close once they're out of the water (the neck gets in the way), they're liable to contain sand and are more perishable than hard-shell clams. To check for freshness, touch the siphon—it should pull in slightly. Once you get the clams home, soak them in a bowl of cold salted water (1 cup salt to 3 quarts water) for a couple of hours or overnight to get them to purge themselves of sand. While much of the time soft-shell clams are steamed open and the meat scooped out as they're being eaten, there are times when they need to be shucked raw. Just slide a clam knife or kitchen knife under the clam's top shell and then again along the bottom shell to detach it. Pull away the membrane and layer of skin coating the clam's neck (see color page 18).

SURF CLAMS, ALSO CALLED BAR CLAMS (Spisula solidissima)

These are the large white clams that are strewn along Atlantic beaches after a storm. Surf clams are larger (often up to 8 inches wide) than hard-shell clams and are too large to cook or serve whole. You're probably not going to find surf clams at your local fish market because most of them are processed and frozen or canned for use in chowders or for frying. Most of the fried clams offered in American restaurants are surf clams that have been cut into strips.

RAZOR CLAMS (Ensis directus)

Razor clams (see color page 8) are easy to recognize because they look exactly like what they're called: old-fashioned straight razors, about eight to the pound. Unless you hunt them yourself—a challenging and hazardous process of digging and grabbing (it's easy to cut yourself on the shells)—you're unlikely to have an opportunity to serve razor clams. I do occasionally see them in my favorite Chinese fish stalls—where I snatch them up—but never in more upscale places.

Like soft-shells, razor clams gape slightly, which makes them quite sandy. They should be soaked in salted water (1 cup salt per 3 quarts of water) for a couple of hours or overnight in the refrigerator before cooking and then carefully rinsed—I run my finger carefully along the inside to force out any sand. Razor clams can be steamed in the same way as quahogs and soft-shell clams, or they can be shucked, sautéed, and simmered in white wine and served as a soup or little stew. Because razor clams are quite tough, they are best simmered for about an hour to make them tender. They can also be steamed open, finely chopped, and added to soups and chowders.

PACIFIC CLAMS

Four kinds of Pacific clams—Pacific littlenecks, Manila clams, geoducks, and horse clams—are sold regularly in the United States, but if you're lucky enough to find the less common native Pismo and butter clams, be sure to snap them up.

LITTLENECKS (Protothaca staminea)

This is one of the most common Pacific coast clams, although its popularity is being outrun by the Manila clam. Don't confuse Pacific littleneck clams with the unrelated small Atlantic quahog that goes by the same name.

Pacific littlenecks can be steamed in the same way as Atlantic clams, but they tend to be slightly tougher.

MANILA CLAMS, SOMETIMES CALLED JAPANESE CLAMS (Tapas semi decussatus or Venerupis japonica)

These delicious clams are not native to the American Pacific coast but have rapidly become one of the most important Pacific species. Although Manila clams can grow quite large, the tastiest are about 1 inch wide and are sold by the pound. Manila clams can be eaten raw and are especially good when steamed.

GEODUCKS, PRONOUNCED GOOEY-DUCKS (Panopea abrupta)

These are the most bizarre-looking of all clams (and perhaps of all foods). They are similar in appearance to soft-shell clams—with an oval shell and protruding siphon—but can be 10 times as large. The siphon alone can be up to 3 feet long with the shell adding another 8 inches.

Although geoducks occur only in the Pacific Northwest, I've seen them in East Coast fish markets, where they are kept alive in tanks. The section of meat surrounding the belly can be used in soups or stews, but the siphon is tough and is best peeled and pounded into slices and then fried or sautéed. The siphon is also excellent—blanched for 1 minute, peeled, and thinly sliced—for sushi.

BUTTER CLAMS (Saxidomus giganteus)

These are one of the few native varieties still found with any regularity in the Pacific Northwest. Butter clams are usually sold from 2 to 4 inches wide. Smaller butter clams can be eaten raw on the half shell, but larger ones are better for stuffing or making into soups in much the same way as quahogs.

WESTERN JACKKNIFE CLAMS (Tagelus californianus)

These clams are similar to Atlantic razor clams (*Ensis directus*) but are slightly shorter and broader. Because the meat of the western jackknife is somewhat tough, it is most often fried.

COCKLES

Even though cockles belong to a different family from clams, they can be cooked in the same way and have a very similar flavor. Because most cockles are smaller than clams, some people consider them a nuisance to eat, but cockles have such an intense briny flavor and look so pretty on the plate that to me they are well worth the effort. Cockles are found on the North Atlantic Coast, but those I see most often in the United States are from New Zealand (*Austrovenus stutchburyi*), with pronounced ridges and a lovely green tint on one side.

SERVING RAW CLAMS

Littleneck clams are delicious served raw on the half shell, but be sure they've come from a reliable source. If you've harvested them yourself, check with the local health department or shellfish control agency to make sure they've come from unpolluted waters.

SHUCKING

For most recipes clams can be steamed open in a small amount of liquid, but when serving raw clams, you have to shuck them. Unlike oysters, which do a good job of hiding where the two shells join, shucking clams is a relatively straightforward process.

Scrub the clams thoroughly with a small brush under cold running water. To shuck a clam, hold it in the palm of your hand and slide a table knife or clam knife (a knife with an easily gripped handle and a thin but not sharp blade) in between the two shells. (Don't use a sharp kitchen knife!) Once you get the knife blade in between the two shells, rotate the clam until you get the knife around to the hinge. Cut through the hinge without sliding the knife straight through the clam, or you'll cut the clam in half. Slide the knife along the underside of the top shell, detaching it from the clam. Pull off and throw away the top shell. Slide the knife under the clam nestled in the bottom shell to detach it (see color page 18). It's a good idea to shuck clams over a bowl to catch any juices—this fresh clam juice can be sprinkled back over the clams or used for cooking. Serve raw clams with lemon wedges.

GETTING RID OF THE GRIT

Clam recipes abound with suggestions for getting rid of sand and grit trapped inside. While the easiest way is to soak them overnight in the refrigerator in salted water, most hard-shell clams have so little sand that I rarely bother—I just thoroughly scrub the *outside* of the clams.

Clams such as razor clams, soft-shelled clams, and geoducks, whose shells gape open, are inevitably filled with sand and must be encouraged to cleanse themselves before cooking. Stir 1 cup salt into 3 quarts cold water (make enough solution to cover the clams) until the salt dissolves. Soak the clams in the salt water overnight—or at least for a couple of hours—in the refrigerator.

Some writers suggest adding cornmeal to the salt mixture to entice the clams to better cleanse themselves, but I haven't found this makes any difference.

Steamed Clams

One of the easiest and tastiest ways to cook clams is to steam them in a pot with a small amount of flavorful liquid. As the clams open, their juices fall into the steaming liquid and leave an intensely flavored broth that can be served with the clams and mopped up with crusty French bread. This briny broth can also be converted into a soup or reduced slightly and served as a sauce. The steaming liquid can be flavored with herbs, aromatic vegetables such as garlic or shallots, or spices (curry and saffron are especially good) and enriched with butter, cream, coconut milk, or flavored mayonnaise.

Almost any clam can be steamed using the same technique, but remember if you're using soft-shell clams let them sit in salt water for a couple of hours before cooking to get them to flush out sand.

MAKES 4 FIRST-COURSE SERVINGS

1 cup dry white wine

2 tablespoons finely chopped parsley

1 garlic clove, finely chopped

2 dozen littleneck, soft-shell (steamer), Pacific littleneck, or Manila clams

Steaming the Clams: Bring the wine, parsley, and garlic to a simmer in a 6-quart pot with a tight-fitting lid. Add the clams, cover, and simmer for 10 to 15 minutes, until all the clams have opened. Scoop the clams into a bowl and keep them warm in a 150°F oven.

If the liquid in the pot is sandy, pour it slowly into another pot—leaving the sand behind—or strain it through cheesecloth or a clean cloth napkin.

continued

Serving the Clams: Once the clams have been steamed open, there are many ways to serve them. The easiest is just to scoop them into hot bowls, pour on the hot broth, and serve with plenty of crusty bread. The clam broth can also be converted into a sauce by boiling it down to half its original volume, adding 1/3 cup of heavy cream, and boiling the sauce again for a minute or two until it thickens slightly. The sauce can then be poured over the clams or served at the table in a sauceboat for people to help themselves. The clams can also be taken out of their shells and served directly in the sauce in hot soup plates or miniature cassoulettes (see box).

CASSOULETTES

It's sometimes hard to make a miniature shellfish stew look presentable because most of us don't have small enough bowls. The French have come up with an implement called a *cassoulette*—not to be confused with a cassoulet—to solve this problem. A cassoulette usually looks like a miniature pot with a lid and handle and is made of either silver or copper. In restaurants the cassoulettes are usually presented on small plates, and the lid is lifted off and set to one side in front of the diner.

A Traditional Clam "Bake"

*T*his is an adaptation of a traditional clam bake that you prepare in your kitchen instead of setting out to the nearest beach. Needless to say it is not as picturesque as the traditional version, but all you need to pull it off are 2 or 3 Chinese bamboo steamers, cheap and easy to find in any Chinese market. You'll need 1 steamer per 2 servings, so if you want to make more than the 4 servings called for here you'll need more steamers and stove space.

MAKES 4 MAIN-COURSE SERVINGS

24 littleneck or soft-shell clams

Four 1¼-pound lobsters

12 very small red new potatoes, washed but not peeled, cut in half lengthwise

8 golf-ball-size white onions, cut in half lengthwise

4 ears of corn, husked

1 pound sausage such as linguiça or kielbasa, cut into 4 pieces

1 cup (½ pound) unsalted butter, melted

2 lemons, cut into wedges

If you're using littleneck clams, scrub them under cold running water. If you're using soft-shell clams, soak them for at least 2 hours but as long as overnight in a quart of water in which you've dissolved 1/3 cup salt.

Fill 2 large pots—with rims that the bamboo steamers will just fit over—with about 4 inches of water. Bring the water to a boil.

Kill the lobsters by cutting lengthwise through the underside of their heads with a chef's knife. Don't cut all the way through the top of the head.

Distribute the ingredients—except the butter and lemon—equally

between the two bamboo steamers and place the bamboo steamers on the pots. Cover the steamers with their lids and steam for about 12 minutes.

Serve everything on hot platters with the butter and lemon passed at the table.

THE UNOPENED-CLAM CONTROVERSY

It's common to see recipes that recommend throwing out any clams that don't open after steaming. I don't recommend this. Clams that don't open are rarely bad but are just particularly tenacious. Instead I take clams out of the pot as they open so the more stubborn ones get more time to cook. If I get tired of waiting around for one clam to open—15 minutes is about the limit—I just take it out and pry it open with a knife.

If you've got a bad clam in your bunch—a rare occurrence—you'll probably discover it when you're scrubbing the clams. A bad clam will open and usually fall apart while you're handling it—and its smell will leave no doubt that it is bad.

SERVING SOFT-SHELL CLAMS

The small siphon protruding from the side of the shell of a soft-shell clam is covered with a gritty black sheath. The easiest way to deal with this membrane is to pick the clam up by the siphon and pull away the sheath as you eat the clam. But if you're serving the clams already in a sauce, pull off this part before stirring the clams into the sauce.

CLAM SOUPS AND CHOWDERS

While any dish containing a reasonable amount of liquid and eaten with a spoon qualifies as a soup, defining chowder is a subject of almost endless controversy. Most people do agree that onions, potatoes or corn, pork, and milk or cream must enter the pot at some point, but participants in the discussion rarely agree on finer points, such as whether flour can be used instead of the more traditional bread crumbs, the acceptability of wine, and if bacon is better than butter. The controversy grows even more heated among aficionados of New England and Manhattan chowders, who are forever claiming one is better than the other. The vehemence of the controversy always strikes me as a little silly especially since so many "authentic" versions of clam chowder—usually in establishments known for their excellent seafood—are so disappointing. Often these chowders are overly thickened with flour and have a milky flavor that masks the briny metallic flavor of the clams.

Such arguments are of little importance to the intuitive cook who might add corn or tomatoes when in season or extra potatoes during the winter, when there is need for something more substantial or to make the most of a limited number of clams. I sometimes use heretical ingredients (tarragon, chervil, parsley, curry, saffron . . .), which turn the soup into something else entirely.

The purpose of a clam soup—chowder or otherwise—is to show off the flavor of clams while stretching and accenting their flavor with other ingredients. Most recipes start with shucked raw clams, but this is such a nuisance that I almost always opt for steaming the clams open in a flavorful liquid—usually white wine—and then using the steaming liquid as the base for the soup. If the soup is a chowder, onions are added at some point but must first be softened in fat. (Traditionally rendered cubes of salt pork are used, but the only salt pork I can find always seems to have a vaguely soapy flavor, so I avoid it and use butter or bacon fat.) Cubed or sliced potatoes are added after first being simmered in water, milk, or the clam-cooking liquid. Most recipes include milk, but I use water or fish broth and a proportionately smaller amount of heavy cream, which is less likely to curdle and interferes less with the clam flavor.

The choice of clams is of course central to making good chowder. I almost always use quahogs because they're easy to find on the East Coast, but Manila clams and soft-shells work every bit as well. Chowder clams (the largest quahogs) are the cheapest but not always available. The smaller cherrystones or littlenecks make the best chowder but are more expensive. Cockles make wonderful chowder but can get expensive.

Clam chowder is traditionally served with soda crackers to be broken up and added to the soup. You may also want to try little croutons sautéed in butter.

❧

New England Clam Chowder

MAKES 10 GENEROUS FIRST-COURSE SERVINGS

3 cups water or fish broth (page 343)

1 cup dry white wine

1 bouquet garni: 3 fresh thyme sprigs or 1½ teaspoon dried, 1 bay leaf, and 1 small bunch of parsley tied up with string (or in cheesecloth for dried thyme)

8 dozen littleneck or cherrystone clams or 2 dozen chowder clams (about 8 pounds)

¼ pound sliced bacon or 3 tablespoons unsalted butter

3 medium onions, chopped

3 medium potatoes (2 pounds), peeled and cut into ½-inch dice

2 cups heavy cream

pepper

crackers or croutons

In a 6-quart pot, bring the water and wine to a simmer with the bouquet garni. Add the clams, cover the pot, and steam until the clams have opened, 12 to 15 minutes for chowder clams, 7 to 8 minutes for smaller clams. Pry open any clams that are still closed (see box on page 138). Take the clams out of the shells; reserve the clams and discard the shells. If you're using chowder clams, chop them into ½-inch pieces. Carefully pour the clam-cooking liquid into another container to eliminate sand or strain it through a triple layer of cheesecloth or a clean kitchen towel.

If you're using bacon, cut across the slices so you end up with 1-inch strips. Cook the strips in a 4-quart pot until they render their fat and barely begin to crisp. Take out the strips and reserve.

Gently cook the onions in the bacon fat until they have softened but not browned, about 20 minutes. Pour in the clam-cooking liquid, add the potatoes, and simmer gently until the potatoes soften—they'll be easy to crush with a spoon against the inside of the pot—about 20 minutes.

Five minutes before serving, add the reserved clams, the bacon, and the cream to the simmering soup. Season with freshly ground pepper—the chowder probably won't need salt. Ladle into hot bowls and serve with crackers or croutons.

⌇

Japanese-Style Clam Consommé

This delicate soup combines the sealike flavor of clam-steaming liquid with a broth made from Japanese konbu, a dried seaweed that is one of the fundamental flavors in Japanese cooking. This soup is understated, in a typical Japanese way, so that the flavor of the clams isn't lost or distorted under a barrage of strong-tasting ingredients.

Traditional versions of this soup call for *udo,* a celerylike vegetable, and *yuzu* rind, a kind of Japanese citrus fruit. Both are easily found at Japanese groceries, but an asparagus tip or a strip of julienned celery is an easy substitute for the *udo,* and a tiny strip of julienned kumquat or lemon zest can replace the *yuzu.* I've also used 2-inch strips of Chinese chives, tiny mushroom slices, a single Italian parsley leaf, or a thin strip of tomato. Again, it is the shape and almost imperceptible flavor of the ingredients that are important here. (See the glossary for information on unfamiliar ingredients.)

This soup looks best in Japanese bowls with lids coated on the inside with black lacquer (or, these days, plastic).

MAKES **4** FIRST-COURSE SERVINGS

12 littleneck or 20 smaller clams such as Manila (3 to 5 clams per serving)

an 8-inch strip of konbu

1 quart cold water

1 stalk of *udo,* cut into julienne, or 12 asparagus tips or other decorative vegetable

a 1½-inch strip of *yuzu* or kumquat zest or lemon zest, cut into 6 fine julienne strips

Scrub the clams under cold running water. Wipe the konbu strip quickly with a very lightly moistened towel. Combine the konbu with the cold water in a 4-quart pot. Bring the water to a simmer over low to medium heat so it takes about 15 minutes to come to a boil. Reach in with a fork and take out and discard the konbu as soon as the water starts boiling. Put the clams into the liquid, cover the pot, and simmer gently for 8 minutes. Start checking the clams and remove and reserve those that have opened. Replace the lid and continue steaming until all the clams have opened. Remove the clams and carefully pour the clam-steaming liquid into another container to eliminate sand or strain it through a cloth napkin or cheesecloth.

Blanch the *udo* in boiling water for 1 minute. If you're using asparagus, blanch it somewhat longer, about 3 minutes. Rinse either in cold water and drain.

Arrange 3 or 5 clams, the *yuzu,* and the *udo* in each soup bowl. Bring the clam broth to a full boil, ladle it into each bowl, and serve immediately.

Littleneck Clams in Black Bean–Scented Broth

MAKES **4** GENEROUS FIRST-COURSE SERVINGS

48 littleneck clams

1 tablespoon Chinese preserved black beans (preferably Yang-Jiang or Moc Chun brand)

¼ cup dry sherry

1 teaspoon grated fresh ginger

½ Thai chili or 1 jalapeño chili, seeded and finely chopped

1 small garlic clove, chopped

¼ teaspoon Japanese dark sesame oil

2 teaspoons dark soy sauce

1 tablespoon sherry vinegar

½ teaspoon sugar

One ⅛-inch-thick slice of prosciutto, fat trimmed off, cut into 1- by ⅛-inch strips

½ cup cold water

2 cups fish broth (page 343) or water

½ cup heavy cream

2 scallions, finely chopped

Scrub the clams under cold running water.

In a small bowl, soak the black beans in the sherry for 15 minutes to soften the beans. Combine the beans, their soaking liquid, the ginger, chili, garlic, sesame oil, soy sauce, vinegar, and sugar in the bowl of a miniature food processor or blender and puree for 1 minute; reserve.

Soak the prosciutto in the cold water for 5 minutes and drain, discarding the water.

Steam the clams in a covered pot in the fish broth until they all open, about 10 minutes. Take the clams out of the shells and discard the shells. Carefully pour the clam-cooking liquid into a clean saucepan, leaving any sand in the bottom of the pot. Add the prosciutto, black bean mixture, cream, and chopped scallions to the steaming liquid. Bring to a slow simmer and simmer gently for 5 minutes. Stir the reserved clams into the soup and ladle into hot bowls.

CLAM SAUCES

Clams and the liquid they release during cooking are often used as a base for sauces—from familiar favorites such as linguine with clam sauce to subtle Japanese and French sauces for grilled or sautéed fish. The secret behind all these sauces is the deeply flavored braising liquid released by the clams while they're being steamed open. The liquid from clams captures the flavor of the ocean with none of the strong sometimes fishy flavor of fish broth or bottled clam juice.

Once clams have been steamed open and the steaming liquid has been incorporated into a sauce, the clams can be served as an integral part of the sauce (in or out of their shells) or saved for a salad or a light first course.

Clam sauces can be thick or thin depending on how much you decide to reduce the clam-cooking liquid and whether or not you decide to use a thickener such as flour, cream, butter, egg yolks, or vegetable purees. For a great number of dishes it isn't neces-

---

CLAM SAUCE WITH CREAM

I sometimes prepare a richer and more formal version of the recipe by taking the clams completely out of their shells, adding a cup of heavy cream to the clam-cooking liquid, reducing the sauce until it thickens, and leaving out the pasta. This clam "stew" can then be served in small bowls or miniature silver or copper pans with lids that the French call *cassoulettes*. Because clams out of their shells don't amount to much, I usually add vegetables such as lightly creamed spinach, pearl onions, or blanched whole peeled garlic cloves.

---

sary to serve a thick sauce—the clam sauce can be served almost as a broth—but some dishes require a thicker sauce that will cling to the clams.

The easiest way to prepare a clam sauce is to steam open the clams in a small amount of liquid such as wine or water. When the clams have all opened, the liquid is strained or carefully poured into another container to eliminate sand. Flavorful ingredients and sometimes thickeners are then added to the clam liquid to convert it into a sauce.

❧

Linguine with Clam Sauce

This simple version of clam sauce is made by flavoring clam-cooking liquid with garlic, parsley, and a little olive oil.

MAKES 4 FIRST-COURSE OR 2 MAIN-COURSE SERVINGS

4 pounds littleneck or Manila clams, well rinsed and scrubbed

½ cup water

4 garlic cloves, finely chopped

¼ cup olive oil

¼ cup finely chopped parsley

pepper

Two 9-ounce packages of fresh linguine or ½ pound dried

In a 4-quart pot, steam the clams in the water until they all open, about 10 minutes. Scoop out the clams and remove the top shell from each one.

Gently cook the garlic in olive oil in a saucepan for 4 minutes and carefully pour in the clam-cooking liquid, leaving the sand behind in the pot.

Add the parsley and season with freshly ground pepper to taste. Put the clams in the sauce and cover to keep warm.

Boil and drain the pasta, divide among hot bowls, and ladle on the clams with their sauce.

SERVING CLAM-COOKING LIQUID AS A LIGHT SAUCE

The cooking liquid from steamed clams has such a delicious and intense flavor that many chefs use it as the base for delicate fish and shellfish sauces. Although many sauces benefit from a little cream or butter, clam-cooking liquid is so full-flavored that it can be used as a brothlike sauce without adding fat.

In this version of clam sauce the clam-cooking liquid is flavored with finely chopped fresh herbs and served around sautéed or grilled fish or shellfish. I tasted one especially memorable version in a New York seafood restaurant, where thinly sliced sea scallops were arranged on a wide plate and surrounded with this delicate sauce. The flavor of the sauce can be given extra nuance by using different liquids—wine, water, dashi, hard cider, etc.—to steam open the clams. The clams themselves can be served along with the sauce (in or out of their shells) or saved for another dish. Although this version is finished with chopped chives, it's worth experimenting with other herbs such as tarragon, parsley, and chervil.

❧

Sea Bass Fillets with Clams and Chive-Scented Broth

This is an example of how clams can be steamed open to make a light and delicious brothlike sauce for fish. You can make a fish broth out of the sea bass head and bones and use it to steam open the clams, but the clams release such a flavorful broth that making a fish broth isn't really necessary. In this recipe the sea bass fillets are braised in the clam juices, but you can cook fish any way you like and use the sauce given here.

MAKES 6 MAIN-COURSE SERVINGS

Six 8-ounce sea bass fillets, skin and pin bones removed

2 pounds littleneck or Manila clams

½ cup water, wine, dashi (page 343), hard cider, or fish broth (page 343) made from sea bass heads and bones

3 tablespoons finely chopped fresh chives

pepper

Reserve the sea bass fillets on a plate in the refrigerator. Preheat the oven to 350°F.

In a 4-quart pot, steam the clams with the liquid for about 10 minutes, until all the clams open. Scoop out the clams, remove the top shells from half the clams, and take the remaining clams out of the shells entirely. Reserve the clam-cooking liquid.

Arrange the sea bass fillets in a pan just large enough to hold them in a single layer—you may need to use 2 pans—and carefully pour on the clam-cooking liquid, leaving behind any sand or grit. Place the pan on the stove over medium heat. When the liquid surrounding the fillets comes to a gentle simmer, cover the pan loosely with a sheet of aluminum foil and place the pan in the oven.

When the fish is done—after about 8 minutes per inch of thickness at the thickest part—gently transfer the fillets to hot soup plates with a long spatula. Add the chives and reserved clams to the clam liquid remaining in the pan and simmer for 1 minute more. Season to taste with freshly ground pepper and ladle the clams and broth over and around the fillets.

Substitutes Blackfish, flatfish fillets, monkfish, salmon, tilapia, tilefish, rockfish, walleye

BAKED CLAMS

Baked clams are delicious served straight out of the oven, piping hot. There's an almost limitless variety of stuffings and sauces that can be placed in the shell with the clams so that it's easy to make up your own versions.

Baked clams can be passed on platters as a delicious hot hors d'oeuvre or arranged on individual plates as an elegant first course.

Most recipes for baked clams suggest shucking the raw clams, discarding the top shells, placing some sort of stuffing under the clams in the shell, and then topping with a flavored butter, olive oil, sauce, or perhaps some bread crumbs before baking. I prefer to steam open the clams—so I don't need to shuck them—and then incorporate the liquid they throw off into the sauce or herb butter.

Once you've steamed the clams open you can flavor the liquid they release with herbs or aromatic vegetables such as garlic or shallots. I usually add some heavy cream to pull together the flavors and to thicken the sauce and then arrange the clams on a baking sheet covered with a layer of aluminum foil that I've crumpled up and unfolded again. The clams, once embedded slightly into the foil, stay flat so the sauce doesn't run out during the baking.

KEEPING BIVALVES FLAT FOR BAKING AND SERVING

One of the problems with serving hot mussels, clams, and oysters is keeping them flat on the plate or platter so the sauce doesn't run out of the shell. If you're lucky, you'll be able to get fresh seaweed—which is often used for packing oysters—from the fishmonger. A sprig or two of the seaweed can then be arranged on the plates as a support for the shellfish. Many recipes recommend serving and baking oysters, mussels, and clams on a bed of coarse salt. Coarse salt does the job, but some of the salt inevitably gets on your fingers and sneaks its way into the sauce. A sheet of crumpled aluminum foil works well for baking but looks ugly on a plate or platter. If you serve baked bivalves often, it might be worth investing in escargot plates, which have indentations for holding the snail shells and will do the trick with other shells as well.

Clams Baked with Garlic and Parsley

MAKES 6 FIRST-COURSE SERVINGS

36 littleneck or cherrystone clams,
   scrubbed and rinsed

½ cup dry white wine

6 garlic cloves, finely chopped

3 tablespoons finely chopped parsley

1 cup heavy cream

salt and pepper

Steam the clams in the wine in a covered pot for about 10 minutes, until they all open. Scoop the clams out of the pot and remove and discard the top shells. Carefully pour the steaming liquid into a clean saucepan, leaving behind any sand. Crush the chopped garlic into a paste with the side of a chef's knife on a cutting board or in a mortar and pestle and add it, along with the parsley, to the clam liquid. Boil the clam liquid down to about half its original volume and add the cream. Continue boiling the sauce—keep a close watch so it doesn't boil over—until it thickens slightly. Season to taste (it's probably salty enough already) with freshly ground pepper.

Preheat the oven to 400°F. Arrange the clams in their bottom shells on a sheet of crumpled aluminum foil on a baking sheet. Spoon enough sauce into each clam to fill up the shells. Bake for about 5 minutes—until the sauce bubbles up—and serve immediately with little forks or spoons.

Spanish-Style Baked Clams

ALMEJAS AL HORNO

This dish makes a delicious opening to an informal dinner (the clams are a bit messy if people are dressed up), but I like best to pull the clams out of the oven and serve them in the kitchen while my guests are standing around having drinks.

The stuffing for these clams contains typically Spanish flavors—garlic, olive oil, grilled peppers, and sherry—but most characteristic are the little strips of ham. Spanish cooks use one of many of their own delicious Serrano hams, but if you can't find Serrano ham use an unsmoked cured ham such as Italian prosciutto—the less expensive ends if you can find them. Like many Spanish recipes, this dish starts out with a *sofrito* of onions, garlic, and tomatoes. This stuffing is also great with mussels.

MAKES 6 FIRST-COURSE OR 12 HORS D'OEUVRE SERVINGS

36 littleneck or cherrystone clams

½ cup dry sherry or white wine

⅓ pound prosciutto, cut into ⅛-inch slices,
   slices cut into 1- by ⅛- by ⅛-inch strips

6 garlic cloves, finely chopped

1 medium onion, finely chopped

5 tablespoons extra-virgin olive oil

3 medium tomatoes, peeled, seeded, and
   coarsely chopped

3 tablespoons finely chopped parsley

pepper

fresh lemon juice to taste

Steam the clams in the sherry or white wine for about 10 minutes, until they all open. Scoop the clams out of the pot and pull off and discard the top shells. Carefully pour the steaming liquid into a clean container, leaving any sand behind in the pot.

Eliminate the salt in the strips of proscuitto by soaking them in just enough cold water to cover for 5 minutes and then draining and throwing out the water. In a wide sauté pan over medium heat, cook the garlic and onions in the olive oil for about 10 minutes, until they soften and release their aroma. Don't let them brown. Add the tomatoes and the clam-cooking liquid and turn up the heat to high. Cook for about 15 minutes, stirring every minute or so with a wooden spoon, until the clam liquid and the liquid released by the tomatoes evaporate completely. Stir in the drained ham strips, the parsley, freshly ground pepper, and lemon juice to taste. Preheat the oven to 350°F.

Slide a sharp knife under each clam to detach it from the bottom shell—to make them easier to eat—and arrange the clams on an ovenproof serving dish covered with a sheet of crumpled aluminum foil (to keep the clams flat) and spoon the stuffing over each one. Bake the clams for 10 minutes and serve immediately with small forks or spoons.

CLAM STEWS

This is one of my favorite ways to serve clams and one of the best ways to show off their intense sealike flavor. If you've made a clam soup, clam stews are easy; they just contain less liquid.

Although a basic clam stew makes a lovely first course or light main course, it's easy to round out and make more elaborate with other ingredients such as herbs and vegetables. I especially like to serve clams with beans (as do the Italians and Spanish), artichokes, wild mushrooms, chopped fresh parsley or basil, fresh tomatoes, tiny French green beans, or, around the winter holidays, truffles.

❧

Clam Stew with Beans, Artichokes, and Wild Mushrooms

(color page 8)

The combination of beans and clams may sound bizarre for those of us who grew up on baked beans or have enjoyed cassoulet, but a taste will reveal that there's nothing incongruous about the match. If you can find them, use fresh beans such as cranberry (borlotti) beans or fava beans (which have to be peeled twice), but if you're using dried beans, use borlotti, Great Northern, or white kidney beans (cannellini). I use whatever wild mushroom is in season, but if you can't find fresh wild mushrooms, this dish is delicious with dried porcini or morels.

MAKES 4 FIRST-COURSE SERVINGS

1 cup dried beans such as borlotti, Great Northern, or cannellini, rinsed and soaked in 1 quart cold water for 3 hours, or 1½ cups shelled fresh beans

1 pound fresh wild mushrooms, rinsed and dried, or 2 ounces dried morels or porcini

9 fresh baby or 4 large artichokes, trimmed and cooked (see box) or 9 bottled baby artichokes, rinsed

2 tablespoons extra-virgin olive oil

2 pounds littleneck or Manila clams, rinsed and scrubbed

½ cup dry white wine

½ cup heavy cream

2 tablespoons unsalted butter

1 tablespoon finely chopped parsley

salt and pepper

If you're using dried beans, cook them in a covered pot in their soaking water for about an hour, until they have completely softened. If you're using fresh beans, cook them in a 4-quart pot half full of boiling water for about 10 minutes, until they are soft but still retain the slightest crunch. Drain both fresh and dried beans in a colander. If you're using dried beans, reserve their cooking liquid. Rinse fresh beans under cold water, but don't rinse cooked dried beans.

If you're using dried mushrooms, soak them in just enough water to cover until they soften, about 30 minutes. Squeeze out the water and reserve the mushrooms. (The soaking liquid should be strained and cooked down with the clam-cooking liquid.) If the fresh or dried mushrooms are large, cut them into quarters.

Cut large artichoke bottoms into 6 wedges each, medium artichoke bottoms into 4 wedges, and baby artichokes in half; toss with the olive oil and reserve.

In a 4-quart pot, steam the clams in the white wine until they all open, about 10 minutes. Scoop out the clams, take half of them out of the shells, and reserve.

Carefully pour the clam-steaming liquid into a clean 4-quart pot, leaving any sand behind. Add the mushrooms, artichokes, reserved clams, drained beans, and cream. Cover the pot and slowly bring the ingredients to a simmer over medium heat. Stir in the butter and parsley and season to taste with salt and pepper. Spoon out into hot bowls and serve immediately.

———

PREPARING ARTICHOKES

To prepare artichokes for soups and stews, you must remove the tough outer leaves and, if the artichokes are large, the hairy choke.

If you're using baby artichokes, cut off the top third of the leaves and trim the fibrous outer skin off the stalk with a sharp paring knife or vegetable peeler. Rotate the artichoke against the blade of a sharp paring knife to remove the outermost layer of leaves. Rub each artichoke with a lemon half until you're ready to cook.

If you're using large artichokes, cut off the stalk and the top third of the artichoke. Rotate the artichoke against the blade of a sharp knife—keeping the blade perpendicular to the base—until you've removed the outer layer of leaves and exposed the pale green leaves at the base. Trim off the leaves adhering to the bottom of the artichoke. Cut the remaining leaves off the artichoke just above the base. Rub the base with a lemon half.

Trimmed or "turned" artichokes should be cooked in water containing the juice of a lemon and a tablespoon of olive oil in a non-aluminum pot until they can be penetrated with a sharp knife but still retain some of their texture, about 20 minutes. Baby artichokes can be served as is or cut into sections. When serving the bottoms of large artichokes, scoop out the choke with a spoon.

———

Razor Clam Fricassee

Unlike most shellfish, which can be eaten lightly steamed or even raw, razor clams have the consistency of rubber bands unless they're simmered gently for over an hour. The long cooking is worth the effort because razor clams have a delicious flavor—brought out in this simple recipe that lends itself to all sorts of last-minute improvisations. I sometimes use vermouth or sherry instead of white wine and shallot instead of garlic. Be sure to have plenty of crusty bread on hand for soaking up the broth. You can also serve this dish over pasta in the same way as linguine with clam sauce (page 141). I always save the shells to show my guests what they're eating.

MAKES 4 FIRST-COURSE SERVINGS

24 razor clams
1 cup salt
3 quarts cold water
3 garlic cloves, finely chopped
1 cup dry white wine
2 tablespoons finely chopped parsley
3 tablespoons unsalted butter
salt and pepper

Rinse the razor clams in cold water. Dissolve the salt in the cold water and pour it over the clams. Let the clams soak for at least 2 hours but preferably overnight in the refrigerator to eliminate sand.

Shuck the clams by sliding a sharp knife along the inside of each shell. When you get the clams out of the shell, cut away and discard the brown clump of digestive apparatus on the side of each clam. Put the clams in a small pot with the garlic and wine. Bring to a slow simmer, cover the pot, and cook for an hour and 15 minutes. Check the pot every 15 minutes to make sure the liquid isn't threatening to run dry. If so, pour ½ cup water into the pot.

Add the parsley, simmer for a minute longer, and whisk in the butter. Season with salt and pepper and serve in hot little bowls.

CLAMS: IN OR OUT OF THE SHELL?

When serving steamed clams as part of a delicate fish stew, over pasta, or in a soup, you may want to take the clams out of the shells to make them easier to eat. While this is convenient, some of the drama and beauty of the dish is lost. A good compromise is to take *half* of the clams out of the shells—discarding the shells—and arrange these extra clams in the top shells of the other clams. In this way there are half as many clam shells to contend with, and each shell contains a bonus.

Clam Risotto

RISOTTO DI VONGOLE

Some people are put off by the unassuming look of risotto, but once tasted, risotto makes instant converts. One mistake is to serve risotto as an accompaniment to other dishes. Because of its particular delicacy and richness, it is best served as a first course, unadorned. Short-grain risotto rice absorbs the flavor of the liquid it's cooked in, so the trick to making a good risotto is to cook the rice in the flavorful liquid released by shellfish, especially bivalves such as clams or mussels.

When making any kind of risotto, don't try to substitute American rice—Italian rice is essential to give the finished risotto its characteristic creamy texture. Of the Italian varieties, Arborio, Vialone Nano, and Carnaroli are the best.

MAKES 6 FIRST-COURSE SERVINGS

4 dozen littleneck or 4 pounds Manila clams or cockles, rinsed and scrubbed
1 cup dry white wine
1 quart water
1 medium onion, finely chopped
½ pound unsalted butter
2 cups Italian short-grain rice
salt and pepper

In a large pot, steam the clams in the wine until they open, about 8 minutes. Scoop out the clams and take the clams out of the shells and reserve.

Strain the clam-steaming liquid or carefully pour it into a bowl, leaving behind any sand.

Bring the water to a slow simmer in a saucepan.

In a heavy 4-quart pot, gently cook the chopped onion in 2 tablespoons of the butter for about 10 minutes, until the onion softens. Add the rice, stir for a minute to coat the rice with butter, and add half of the clam-cooking liquid. Cook the rice over medium heat, stirring every minute or two, until all the liquid has been absorbed. Add the rest of the clam-cooking liquid and continue cooking and stirring until it is absorbed. Add a cup of simmering water to the rice and stir continuously with a wooden spoon until all the liquid has been absorbed. At this point you'll need to start tasting the rice to know when it's done—the rice should be cooked through but mustn't be mushy, and the risotto itself should have a creamy, runny consistency. Add the hot water $1/2$ cup at a time until the risotto is done (you probably won't use all the water). Risotto usually takes from 20 to 30 minutes to cook.

When the rice is done, stir in the remaining butter and the reserved clams. Season with salt and pepper to taste. Serve immediately on hot plates.

❧

Fried Clams

Soft-shell clams are best for frying, but frying is also an excellent method for geoducks, some razor clams, and surf clams, which tend to be tough when cooked using other methods.

Most traditional recipes call for a coating of eggs, flour, and bread crumbs. I prefer using a lighter batter such as club soda batter or yeast batter—or just coating the clams in flour—and then serving the clams with a homemade tartar sauce.

I don't usually serve fried clams as part of a formal dinner—the timing is too tricky, and I hate being in the kitchen frying at the last minute—but prefer to fry clams with guests in the kitchen eating the clams as soon as I take them out of the hot oil. Sometimes I can even get the guests to help shuck.

Clams must of course be fried at the very last minute, but you're best off buying the clams the day before and soaking them in salt water to get rid of sand.

MAKES 8 FIRST-COURSE OR 4 MAIN-COURSE SERVINGS

4 dozen (about 4 pounds) soft-shell clams

$2/3$ cup salt

2 quarts cold water

1 quart pure olive oil or canola oil

1 recipe club soda or yeast batter (page 43)

1 recipe tartar sauce (page 335)

Scrub the clams thoroughly under cold running water. Dissolve the salt in the cold water. Put the clams in a bowl, cover with the salt water, and refrigerate overnight or at least for a couple of hours.

Within 4 hours of frying, shuck the clams into a bowl. Soft-shell clams are easy to shuck because the shell is already partially open. Just slide a knife along the underside of the top shell—don't cut into the middle or you'll damage the clam—and then again along the surface of the bottom shell. Make a slit along the "neck" of each clam and peel off the black membrane (see color page 18). (Unlike for steamed clams, when this membrane is left attached for guests to peel off as they go along, for fried clams it must be removed because coated in batter it's hard to remove.) Arrange the shucked clams on a kitchen towel and pat dry with a second towel.

When you're ready to fry, heat the oil to 370°F in a heavy pot or skillet. Fry the clams 6 at a time by dipping them in the batter and then transferring them to the oil with 2 chopsticks. Fry until golden brown, about 2 minutes. Be careful; they spatter.

Transfer the clams to a plate covered with paper towels. Pat off excess oil and serve immediately with a bowl of tartar sauce.

Oysters

To some the oyster has the mythical status of truffles or rare vintage wine. This may be in part because of the oyster's reputation as an aphrodisiac, but it could certainly be based on its flavor alone. The oyster has a flavor like no other food, and each variety tastes slightly different, from briny and metallic to mild and buttery.

Unfortunately for those who prize them, oysters' cost usually matches their culinary standing. From a fast food of the 1930s—in some places you could make a cheap evening out of a few dozen oysters and a bottle of beer—they've become a chic luxury now sold by the piece instead of the dozen so that every bite reminds us of their price.

Because oysters adapt well to different temperatures, they can be found in the wild as far north as Greenland and as far south as Cape Horn. Most oysters sold in Europe are farmed, while most American oysters are harvested in the wild. On our shores they're harvested from Maine to the Gulf coast and from Seattle to southern California.

Because oysters pick up the flavor of their surroundings, most oysters are named after where they are harvested. But the dozens of varieties of oysters grown in and around the United States are actually taken from only four species. In general, oysters grown in more northern, colder waters have a sharper, brinier flavor, while oysters grown in warmer waters tend to be milder.

OYSTER VARIETIES

ATLANTIC OYSTERS (Crassostrea virginica)

Until recently Atlantic oysters—native to American waters—were the most common oysters sold in the United States. Although their shape and size vary, Atlantic oysters are elongated and have a relatively smooth top shell.

PACIFIC OYSTERS

There are two species of Pacific oysters—*Crassostrea gigas*, the so-called *Japanese oyster* originally imported from Japan and New Zealand, and the miniature Olympia oyster, *Ostrea lurida*, a native of the Northwest.

Today the most common Pacific oyster is the Japanese oyster, which grows all along the Pacific coast. Japanese oysters range in size from the miniature kumamoto to the very large "Pacific" oyster. (The "Pacific" oyster is a particular variety of Japanese oyster—it doesn't refer just to oysters grown on the Pacific coast.)

The Pacific coast's indigenous oyster, the Olympia oyster (*Ostrea lurida*), is still a rarity despite efforts to encourage its return to its native habitats after long dissemination from pollution. Even if these efforts are successful, Olympia oysters will always be expensive. They take four years to grow to marketable size, which isn't much larger than a quarter.

FLAT OYSTERS (Ostrea edulis)

These delicious European natives are flat and round and are farmed on both the Atlantic and Pacific coasts. In the United States flat oysters are usually called *Belon oysters* after the region near the mouth of the Loire River in France where these oysters are traditionally cultivated. Although flat oysters are considered to have a finer flavor than all the other varieties, an oyster's flavor has far more to do with where it grows than the actual species. The best American "Belons" come from Maine and northern California, where the cold water gives them a delicious briny, almost metallic flavor. Although the actual oyster contained in the shell is usually quite small, it has an intense flavor that makes these oysters well suited for oyster stews and cooked dishes as well as for eating on the half shell.

SELECTING AND STORING OYSTERS

The more oysters you eat, the more you'll learn to recognize your favorites. I'm a fan of briny oysters, so I usually buy northern varieties from Cape Cod, Maine, or Canada or West Coast oysters that are cultivated in relatively cold water and thus have a similar flavor to North Atlantic oysters.

When you buy oysters, make sure the shell is tightly closed. Unlike clams or mussels, which are usually all right if they gape a little, oysters must be tightly sealed or they will dry out. Watch also how the oysters are displayed. They should be kept flat on a bed of ice or in a refrigerator—if they're left topsy-turvy in bags, their briny juices will run out. Some oysters even come packed in boxes with indented sheets of egg carton cardboard to keep them flat during shipping.

When you get your oysters home, arrange them in the refrigerator on a baking sheet or platter so they stay flat. Make sure they are upright with the flat shell on top. Never soak oysters in water in the way that is sometimes recommended for getting the sand and grit out of mussels and clams. Depending on how fresh they are to begin with, oysters will keep for up to a week in the refrigerator, but I always try to use them as soon as possible.

SHUCKING OYSTERS

Some fish merchants will shuck oysters for you, which is a convenience if you're going straight home and plan to serve the oysters within a couple of hours. Oysters also come already shucked in cans with transparent lids. I've never been a fan of oysters already out of the shell—they never seem to have the sealike taste of fresh shucked oysters—but if you're cooking a soup or stew, canned oysters are easier to deal with and will do in a pinch.

If you're buying oysters to use in a day or two, you'll need to shuck them at home within a few hours of serving. Until you get the knack, shucking oysters can be a frustrating ordeal. Some are relatively cooperative, while others have you struggling to find a way into the shell.

Many oysters are covered with grit and mud, so the first step is to scrub them with a stiff brush under cold running water. When it comes time to snap the oysters open, you'll need a couple of kitchen towels and an oyster knife or an old table knife (*not* a sharp kitchen knife). Some cooks also like to use a church key–style can opener.

The trick to opening oysters is to find the best place to sneak in with the knife between the two shells. It may take a little time to develop your eye, but you'll soon be able to see where the shells join. Most oysters—flat oysters are the exception—are best opened by inserting the oyster knife or can opener into the hinge and then pushing down on or twisting the handle to loosen the top shell. You may have to twist the knife back and forth to bore into the shell. Once the top shell lifts slightly—you'll feel it give—slide the oyster knife along the bottom of the top shell to detach the muscle. Remove and discard the top shell. Be careful to keep the knife blade flush with the underside of the top shell. Otherwise you may cut into the oyster itself and damage it. When opening oysters, arrange a folded kitchen towel under the oyster while you're working to keep it from slipping. Right-handed professional oyster shuckers like to hold the oyster in a towel in their left hand and the knife in their right, but I find it easier to set the oyster on a folded towel on the work surface. Whichever approach you use, make sure that the hand holding the oyster is protected by a couple layers of towel. If you're using a table knife instead of an oyster knife, hold the knife with a towel to make it easier to grip (see color page 17).

Once you've removed the top shell, you may find grit or pieces of broken shell inside the oyster. Reach around and under the oyster with your forefinger to pull out any debris. If the oysters seem particularly gritty, hold each oyster sideways under cold running water for a second or two to rinse out the grit. Stick your finger under the oyster and lift it slightly so the water can run under and around. I know this sounds as if you're rinsing away the

MIGNONETTE SAUCE

The French love oysters. When the cool weather sets in around October, crates of oysters start appearing on the sidewalk in front of cafés and restaurants. Different prices are posted for oysters to take away and oysters served *à l'intérieur*. Raw oysters in France are served with a small sauceboat of sauce mignonette. The word *mignonette* is used in the kitchen to mean crushed pepper. You can buy crushed pepper, but it will be more aromatic if you crush it yourself by placing a tablespoon of peppercorns on a cutting board and then crushing them with the bottom of a saucepan.

Since most people use only about a teaspoon per oyster, a little goes a long way.

3 tablespoons crushed black peppercorns

3 tablespoons finely minced shallots

²/₃ cup good-quality white wine vinegar

MAKES 1 CUP

Combine the ingredients in a glass or stainless-steel bowl. Cover with plastic wrap and store at room temperature overnight. Mignonette sauce will keep for months in the refrigerator.

oyster's flavor, but in fact it has little effect—the oyster shell immediately fills again with the oyster's own tasty brine. Oysters can be served as they are—European style with the oyster still attached to the bottom shell—or you can make life simpler for your guests and run a knife along the inside of the bottom shell, cutting through the abductor muscle, and serve the oysters already detached.

SERVING RAW OYSTERS

Raw oysters make an elegant first course for the most formal dinner, but they can also be served as the beginning of a simple meal at home. There's something festive about a tray of raw oysters—the sight of them always cheers me up in much the same way as the neck of a Champagne bottle sticking out of an ice bucket.

When serving oysters as a first course for a formal meal I usually figure on 6 per person, but sometimes I serve as many as 18 and then serve something simple as the "main" course to follow.

Raw oysters are served differently around the world. In restaurants in France they are arranged on a tray of ice set on a stand in front of the diner. Beneath the stand are placed a plate of brown bread, a little tub of butter, lemon wedges, and a sauceboat filled with sauce mignonette (see box). In the United States oysters are served with lemon wedges and in New Orleans with Tabasco. Although I usually prefer oysters unadorned, I did once taste a delicious version where each oyster had been anointed with *one* drop of Pernod and another where each oyster had a dollop of caviar on top.

One problem with serving oysters is getting them to sit flat on the plate. Many recipes recommend using coarse salt as a bed for the oysters, but I always end up making a mess with salt falling off the shell. Try to get your fishmonger to give you a little seaweed—often used for packing oysters—and then arrange a few strands of seaweed on each plate to hold the oysters upright. You can also heap crushed ice on a tray and have people help themselves, but this is a bit of a nuisance. You can also use shredded red cabbage, which is attractive and inexpensive.

GRILLING OYSTERS

Grilled oysters are really just oysters that are heated on top of the barbecue until they open. While they don't end up scented in the same way as other grilled foods, there's no shucking involved, and guests have fun grilling their own.

Adjust the grill so it's about 6 inches away from the bed of hot coals and just set the oysters upright on the grill. In about 3 minutes the oysterlids will loosen so they're easily pulled off. Lift the oysters off the grill with a kitchen towel and slide a regular table knife along the underside of the top shell to detach it. Set the oysters on a tray and let the guests help themselves. But don't keep the oysters waiting—it's better to keep the guests hovering hungrily around the barbecue. I put out lemon wedges, Tabasco sauce, sauce mignonette, and, if I'm feeling conscientious, this salsa:

Salsa for Oysters or Chips

MAKES 3 CUPS, ENOUGH FOR ABOUT 4 DOZEN OYSTERS

3 medium tomatoes, peeled, seeded, and chopped

1 garlic clove, chopped and crushed to a paste with the side of a chef's knife

2 poblano chilies, roasted (page 133), peeled, seeded, and chopped

2 jalapeño chilies, seeded and chopped

1 medium onion, chopped

juice of 2 limes

salt to taste

continued

Combine all the ingredients and let sit for at least 2 hours before serving. This salsa can be made up to a day in advance and kept in the refrigerator.

PREPARING HOT OYSTERS

Some people like only raw oysters, and others will eat only cooked. M.F.K. Fisher divided oyster lovers into three categories, "those loose-minded sports who will eat anything, hot, cold, thin, thick, dead or alive, as long as it is *oyster;* those who will eat them raw and only raw; and those who with equal severity will eat them cooked and no way other." I for one love little more than a plate of raw oysters except perhaps for a plate of hot oysters or a little oyster stew.

Hot oysters can be served in their shells or out of their shells as individual servings of soup or stew. Whichever method you use, it's essential to get rid of any grit and pieces of shell that may be attached to the shucked oyster. The best way to do this is to shuck the oyster into a bowl, thoroughly scrub its shell, lift the shucked oysters, place them on a clean kitchen towel—a paper towel will work only if you work very quickly—and place a second towel on top. In this way pieces of grit and sand will adhere to the towels when you lift off the oyster. Don't leave the oysters sitting on the towel for more than a minute or so, or their juices will leach out into the towel. Meanwhile, strain the oyster juices through a fine-mesh strainer into a clean bowl. The oysters can now be cooked by gently heating them in their strained juices or in some other liquid such as cream. Don't let the liquid boil, or the oysters will shrink to practically nothing—the edges of the oysters should just curl up slightly, and

the liquid should only approach the barest simmer.

In some hot oyster recipes the oyster-cooking liquid is discarded or saved for another recipe and another sauce is prepared for serving over or around the oysters. In other recipes the oyster-cooking liquid is reduced—sometimes after being combined with wine, shallots, or other ingredients—and used as the base for a sauce.

An almost unlimited number of sauces can be used for hot oysters. Some of the best are made by cooking down the liquid and then flavoring it with herbs, spices, or condiments such as mustard. Other sauces are hollandaise, which can be flavored with herbs, chopped tomatoes, saffron, and other spices; homemade mayonnaise, which is especially good when flavored with garlic; and cream sauces made by reducing heavy cream and flavoring it with mustard, white wine, shallots, or other aromatic vegetables.

Oysters can also be stuffed by placing various mixtures in the bottom

---

WHEN TO EAT AN OYSTER

In most parts of the world oysters are eaten in the fall and winter, the cooler times of the year. This habit started in prerefrigeration days, when eating oysters out of season—the old axiom is never to eat an oyster during a month that doesn't have an *r* in its name—could be risky indeed.

Nowadays a raw oyster slurped down on a hot August afternoon isn't likely to cause a problem, but many summer oysters are in fact less tasty because the oysters may be spawning. Spawning oysters are usually less sweet and sometimes have a milky appearance that makes them less appetizing.

---

shell under the hot oyster. Some of my favorite stuffings are lightly creamed spinach or sorrel; chopped tomatoes, cooked down to eliminate their moisture; chopped mushrooms, lightly creamed and cooked down until dry; chopped or finely julienned leeks; and other vegetables such as shallots, celery, or carrots, cut into cubes and cooked gently in butter until soft.

Hot Oysters with Saffron Hollandaise

(color page 6)

No one I've ever encountered—including me—can get enough of these oysters. Although I usually serve them as a first course for my most special dinners, they're great as the main course for a quiet evening at home. They can also be passed on a platter as an hors d'oeuvre at a cocktail party.

Although this dish requires some last-minute cooking, the oysters can be shucked and the spinach blanched earlier the same day.

MAKES **4** GENEROUS FIRST COURSE OR LIGHT MAIN COURSE SERVINGS

24 medium oysters
Two 10-ounce bunches of spinach
salt and pepper
1½ cups hollandaise (page 335)
¼ teaspoon saffron threads, soaked for 15 minutes in 1 tablespoon water
¼ cup heavy cream
paprika

Shuck the oysters into a bowl and discard the top shells. Scrub the bottom shells under running water and arrange them on a baking sheet covered with crumpled aluminum foil.

Pick the oysters out of the bowl and arrange them on a clean kitchen towel. Pat them with a second towel and place them in a 2-quart saucepan—all the grit and sand should be left adhering to the towels. Strain the oyster liquid in the bowl through a fine-mesh strainer into the saucepan with the oysters. Reserve in the refrigerator.

Clean the spinach, remove and discard the stems, and blanch the leaves for 30 seconds in boiling salted water. Drain the spinach in a colander and quickly rinse it under cold running water to cool it. Gently squeeze it in bunches to eliminate excess water. Reserve on a plate.

About 20 minutes before you're ready to serve, preheat the oven to 250°F. Prepare the hollandaise and stir in the saffron and its soaking liquid. Heat the oyster shells in the oven.

Boil the cream in a small saucepan until it gets very thick and stir in the spinach. Continue stirring over medium heat until the spinach is hot. Season lightly with salt and pepper.

Put the saucepan containing the oysters over medium heat until the oysters just begin to curl around the edges, about 3 minutes. Remove the oyster shells from the oven and preheat the broiler. Put a spoonful of hot spinach on each oyster shell. Lift the oysters out of the saucepan with a spoon and arrange them in the shells over the spinach. (The oyster liquid in the saucepan can be frozen and saved for fish soups.) Spread a tablespoon of saffron hollandaise over each oyster.

Broil the oysters for about 30 seconds, until the hollandaise bubbles up slightly. Sprinkle with paprika and serve immediately.

Hot Oysters with Leeks and White Wine Sauce

This is a takeoff on that tastiest of French dishes, oysters with Champagne sauce. Since most people don't want to open a bottle of Champagne to throw into a sauce, I've adapted the recipe for white wine with almost equally fabulous results. Don't, however, use inexpensive sparkling wine. You'll get more for your money using a good still wine— one with a lot of tangy acidity and an austere fruitiness is perfect. I usually use a Muscadet or an Alsatian pinot blanc, neither of which is terribly expensive and both of which you can serve *with* the oysters as well. These oysters can be served on individual plates as a first course or passed on a platter as an hors d'oeuvre.

MAKES 4 FIRST-COURSE OR 8 HORS D'OEUVRE SERVINGS

24 medium oysters

2 leeks

1 tablespoon unsalted butter

salt and pepper

1 cup white wine

1 cup heavy cream

Shuck the oysters into a bowl and discard the top shells. Scrub the bottom shells under running water and arrange them on a baking sheet covered with crumpled aluminum foil to keep them flat. Set aside. Pick the oysters out of the bowl and arrange them on a clean kitchen towel. Pat

them with a second towel and place them in a 2-quart saucepan—all the grit and sand should adhere to the towels. Strain the oyster liquid in the bowl through a fine-mesh strainer into the saucepan with the oysters. Reserve in the refrigerator.

Cut off and discard all but about an inch of pale green from the leeks. Slice the leeks in half lengthwise and rinse out any sand. A couple of leaves at a time, slice the leeks lengthwise into fine julienne. In a small saucepan over medium-low heat, cook the julienned leeks in butter until they are completely soft, about 20 minutes. Don't let them brown. Season lightly with salt and pepper and distribute in the bottom of each oyster shell. Preheat the oven to 250°F.

Heat the oysters in their own liquid over medium heat until their edges barely begin to curl, about 3 minutes. Remove the oysters from the cooking liquid with a slotted spoon and place an oyster over the leeks in each shell. Add the wine to the oyster liquid and boil down the mixture until only about ½ cup remains. Add the cream and reduce again until the sauce thickens slightly—you'll end up with about a cup of sauce.

Heat the oysters in the oven for 10 minutes, spoon 2 teaspoons of the sauce over each oyster, and slide the oysters under the broiler for about 30 seconds. Serve immediately.

Oysters with Truffle Sauce

(color page 6)

I admit this is hardly a practical recipe for a typical dinner, but I'm including it because these oysters may very well be the most delicious things I've ever tasted.

MAKES 6 FIRST-COURSE SERVINGS

36 medium oysters
1 medium black truffle (about 1 ounce)
1 cup dry white wine
1¼ cups heavy cream
salt and pepper

Shuck the oysters into a bowl and discard the top shells. Scrub the bottom shells under running water and arrange them on a baking sheet covered with crumpled aluminum foil to keep them flat. Set aside. Pick the oysters out of the bowl and arrange them on a clean kitchen towel. Pat them with a second towel and place them in a 4-quart saucepan—all the grit and sand should adhere to the towels. Strain the oyster liquid in the bowl through a fine-mesh strainer into the saucepan with the oysters. Reserve in the refrigerator.

Within an hour of serving, peel the truffle with a paring knife and finely chop and reserve the peels. Finely slice the truffle with a benriner cutter (a Japanese slicer) or a paring knife, stack the slices, a few at a time, and cut them into fine julienne strips and reserve.

Heat the oysters over medium heat until their edges barely begin to curl, about 3 minutes. Take the oysters out of their cooking liquid with a slotted spoon and place an oyster in each shell. Add the wine to the oyster-cooking liquid and heat until only ½ cup remains. Add the cream and reduce again until the sauce is just thick enough to coat the back of a spoon—you'll end up with about a cup of sauce. Add the julienned truffles and the chopped peels and let the sauce sit off the heat for 5 minutes.

Preheat the oven to 250°F. Season with salt and pepper to taste.

Heat the oysters in the oven for 10 minutes. Spoon 2 teaspoons of sauce over each oyster—making sure that each oyster gets some julienned truffle—and slide the oysters under the broiler for about 30 seconds, just long enough for the sauce to bubble up slightly. Arrange 6 oysters on each plate and serve immediately.

Oysters with Ancho Chili Sauce

(color page 6)

T hese hot and spicy oysters make a great first course, a platter of hors d'oeuvre, or even a whole meal. This recipe calls for a mixture of ancho chilies (dried poblano chilies) and chipotle chilies (smoked jalapeño chilies), but if you can't find one or the other it's fun to fool around with combinations of different chilies—it's hard to go completely wrong.

MAKES 6 FIRST-COURSE OR 12 HORS D'OEUVRE SERVINGS

3 dozen oysters, shucked
2 ancho chilies
1 small onion, chopped
2 garlic cloves, finely chopped
2 canned chipotle chilies, drained and finely chopped
½ teaspoon ground cumin
2 tablespoons olive oil
4 medium tomatoes, peeled, seeded, and chopped
¼ cup finely chopped cilantro
juice of 1 lime
salt and pepper

TRUFFLES

Truffles are funguslike growths that attach themselves to the roots of trees, usually oak trees. Because they grow underground, they have to be sniffed out by trained dogs or pigs. Truffles are not beautiful to look at—black truffles look like black golf balls and white truffles like misshapen clumps of gray clay—but we love their aroma and flavor, not their appearance.

While there are dozens of species of truffles, only three varieties show up in American markets. White Italian truffles are the most expensive, are in season in November, and are usually shaved raw over cooked foods, especially pasta; black Perigord French truffles are also extremely expensive, have a much different flavor, and are used in cooked dishes; summer truffles are brownish black and sell for about a third the price of Perigord truffles.

Unless you manage to find fresh truffles, you're best off buying frozen truffles rather than canned. This may mean buying more than you need for one recipe, but truffles keep well in the freezer for several months. It is also sometimes possible to buy truffle pieces for less money than whole truffles (see "Sources").

Earlier in the Day: Shuck the oysters into a bowl and discard the top shells. Scrub the bottom shells under running water and arrange them on a baking sheet covered with crumpled aluminum foil to keep them flat. Set aside. Pick the oysters out of the bowl and arrange them on a clean kitchen towel. Pat them with a second towel—all the grit and sand should adhere to the towels. Place them in a 4-quart saucepan. Strain the oyster liquid in the bowl through a fine-mesh strainer into the saucepan with the oysters. Reserve in the refrigerator.

Soak the ancho chilies in just enough warm water to cover for 15 minutes, until they are soft. Cut them down the middle, remove the seeds, and chop them finely.

In a 2-quart saucepan over medium heat, cook the onion, garlic, chopped ancho and chipotle chilies, and cumin in olive oil for about 10 minutes, until everything softens. Add the tomatoes and cook for about 15 minutes, until the mixture is almost dry. Stir in the cilantro and lime juice and season to taste with salt and pepper.

Just Before Serving: Heat the oyster shells in a 250°F oven for 10 minutes.

Heat the oysters in their liquid in a 2-quart saucepan over medium heat. As soon as the liquid barely begins to simmer around the edges and the oysters curl slightly, about 3 minutes, remove the oysters with a slotted spoon and put an oyster in each of the hot shells.

Place a teaspoon of sauce over each oyster, turn the oven up to 300°F, and heat the oysters for 5 minutes. Serve immediately.

OYSTER STEWS AND SOUPS

Judging from descriptions in turn-of-the-century American novels, oyster stews—on the East Coast at least—were once common everyday fare. And any decent cookbook from before World War II would not have been complete without a serious discussion of how to make a good oyster stew.

Because oysters have such a full flavor that they release into the surrounding cooking liquid, they are well suited for stews. Unlike meat stews, however, they are cooked for just a couple of minutes—long enough to heat the oysters through. Traditionally the medium is heavy cream or butter, which is diluted by the oyster liquid to become a rich soup more than a thick stew. If you want your oyster stew to be thicker, lift out the cooked oysters with a slotted spoon and quickly boil down the stewing liquid, reheating the oysters in the liquid just before serving.

❧

Oyster Stew

The oysters for this stew can be shucked earlier the same day, but the stew itself has to be made at the very last minute—almost when the guests are seated. Be sure to serve oyster stew with plenty of crunchy French bread or, in the American tradition, with soda crackers.

MAKES 4 MAIN-COURSE OR 6 FIRST-COURSE SERVINGS

3 dozen oysters, shucked and liquid saved
1 cup heavy cream
2 tablespoons very finely chopped parsley
salt and pepper

Shuck the oysters into a bowl and discard the shells. Pick the oysters out of the bowl and arrange them on a clean kitchen towel. Pat them with a second towel and then lift them off and place them in a 4-quart saucepan so that all the grit and sand is left adhering to the towels. Strain the oyster liquid left in the bowl through a fine-mesh strainer into the saucepan with the oysters. Reserve the oysters in the refrigerator until shortly before serving.

Heat the oysters over medium heat until the liquid barely simmers around the edges of the pan and the oysters shrink and curl every so slightly, about 3 minutes. Lift the oysters out of the liquid with a slotted spoon and reserve them in a bowl. Cook down the oyster liquid over high heat until only about 1/4 cup remains. Add the cream and boil for about 5 minutes, until the liquid is just slightly thickened. Stir in the parsley and reserved oysters and gently reheat the oysters for a minute over medium heat, being careful not to let the liquid boil. Season with salt and pepper and serve immediately in hot bowls.

OYSTER STEW VARIATIONS

The beauty of oyster stew is that its simplicity lends itself to whimsy and last-minute creativity in the kitchen.

Sometimes I make oyster stew less rich by thickening the oyster liquid with a small amount of vegetable puree made from potatoes, celeriac, or spinach (boil, drain, and sieve or puree in a blender), using only half the amount of heavy cream as for a traditional oyster stew.

I also like to vary the texture of oyster stew by combining the oysters with cooked vegetables such as pearl onions, lightly creamed spinach, button mushrooms (or wild mushrooms such as morels or porcini), asparagus tips, or even carrots or turnips turned into decorative shapes.

It's hard to improve on the flavor of oysters, but curry, saffron, or herbs such as finely chopped tarragon, chervil, or parsley added to the oyster liquid near the end of cooking accent the flavor of the oysters.

Curried Oyster and Vegetable Stew

You can use the recipe for this delicious stew as a model for almost any combination of vegetables and oysters. The flavor of oysters is great with vegetables—and the combination is striking to look at.

MAKES 4 MAIN-COURSE OR 6 FIRST-COURSE SERVINGS

3 dozen oysters

30 pearl onions, peeled

1 teaspoon sugar

salt and pepper

4 tablespoons unsalted butter

2 large carrots, peeled, cut into 1-inch sections

½ pound small or button mushrooms

¼ cup water

2 teaspoons good-quality curry powder

¼ cup dry white wine

¼ cup vegetable puree (optional)

½ cup heavy cream

leaves from 2 bunches of spinach, washed, blanched for 1 minute, rinsed under cold water in a colander, water squeezed out

Earlier in the Day: Shuck the oysters into a bowl and discard the shells.

Pick the oysters out of the bowl and arrange them on a clean kitchen towel. Pat them with a second towel and then lift them off and place them in a 4-quart saucepan so that all the grit and sand is left adhering to the towels. Strain the oyster liquid left in the bowl through a fine-mesh strainer into the saucepan with the oysters. Reserve the oysters in the refrigerator until shortly before serving.

Place the pearl onions in a sauté pan just large enough to hold them in a single layer. Sprinkle them with half the sugar and some salt and pepper and add a tablespoon of butter. Pour in enough water to come halfway up their sides. Partially cover the pan and simmer the onions until all the liquid evaporates and they're covered with a light glaze, after about 15 minutes. Set aside.

Cut the carrot sections lengthwise in half or in thirds depending on their thickness. Snap out the woody inner core by cutting into it on each side with a paring knife. Glaze the carrots with the remaining sugar, a tablespoon of butter, enough water to come halfway up their sides, and salt and pepper in the same way as the pearl onions. Set aside.

Just Before Serving: Unless the mushrooms are very small, cut them into quarters, leaving the stems attached. Simmer the mushrooms in the water in a covered nonaluminum saucepan for 10 minutes. Set aside.

In a small sauté pan, heat the curry in a tablespoon of butter for about 1 minute, until you're just able to smell it.

Heat the oysters in their own liquid until the liquid barely starts to simmer and the oysters just start to curl around the edges, about 3 minutes. Remove the oysters with a slotted spoon and transfer them to a clean

bowl. Add the wine to the oyster-cooking liquid and simmer gently for 5 minutes. Whisk in the vegetable puree if desired, the cooking liquid from the mushrooms, the curry mixture, and the cream and bring back to a simmer.

Heat the cooked vegetables in their respective containers on the stove or in the oven for 8 minutes in a 300°F oven. Heat the spinach in the remaining butter in a small pan on the stove.

Add the oysters to the sauce and heat gently for 1 minute.

Serving: Arrange the hot spinach in a loosely packed mound in the center of hot wide soup bowls. Ladle the sauce and the oysters over and around the spinach. Arrange the hot vegetables on each serving—but so they don't *look* arranged. Serve immediately.

OYSTER SOUPS

Because the only real difference between a soup and a stew is the amount of liquid, any stew recipe can be converted into a soup and vice versa. The occasional problem with oyster soups is that too much liquid dilutes the flavor of the oysters and the soup tastes insipid. There are a couple of ways around this problem, the first and most important being the oysters themselves. The tastiest oysters are not necessarily the largest; in fact the opposite is sometimes true. My favorite oysters for making soups are the little Belons from Maine or California—they don't have much bulk, but three or four in a bowl of soup will give the soup an intense oyster flavor. If you can't find Belons—few of us can be so choosy—try to use Pacific oysters or oysters from the North Atlantic such as those from Cape Cod or Prince Edward Island (Malpeques).

Another factor is the choice of liquid. One of my favorites is fish broth, which you just might have in the freezer if you've gotten into the habit of taking home the head and bones when you have a fish filleted.

Another trick is not to limit your soup to oysters alone. Mussels provide plenty of liquid when they're steamed open and the flavor of mussel broth makes a nice blend with oysters. And one of the best broths to use as a base for oysters is miso soup.

❧

Oyster and Mussel Soup

MAKES 6 FIRST-COURSE SERVINGS

2 dozen oysters

2 cups fish broth (page 343) or chicken broth (page 344)

1 cup dry white wine

3 shallots, finely chopped

2 pounds cultivated mussels

2 tablespoons all-purpose flour

2 tablespoons unsalted butter

½ cup heavy cream

2 tablespoons finely chopped fresh chives or parsley

salt and pepper

Shuck the oysters into a bowl and discard the shells. Pick the oysters out of the bowl and arrange them on a clean kitchen towel. Pat them with a second towel and then lift them off and place them in a bowl so that all the grit and sand is left adhering to the towels. Strain the oyster liquid left in the bowl through a fine-mesh strainer into the bowl with the oysters. Reserve the oysters in the refrigerator.

Combine the fish broth, wine, and shallots in a pot large enough to hold the mussels. Bring the liquids to a simmer, add the mussels, and cover the pot. Start checking the mussels after about 5 minutes. When they've all opened, remove the pot from the heat.

Take the cooked mussels out of their shells, discarding any unopened ones and the shells. Check to see if there is any sand in the bottom of the pot. If there is, carefully pour the broth into another pot, leaving the sand behind.

Work the flour and butter to a smooth paste with the back of a fork on a small plate. Bring the mussel-cooking liquid to a simmer and whisk in the butter-and-flour paste. Simmer the mixture for 1 minute—the soup should thicken slightly—and add the shucked mussels, the oysters with their liquid, the cream, and the chives. Bring the soup to a bare simmer and season with salt and pepper to taste. Serve immediately.

❧

Oyster and Miso Soup with Shiitake Mushrooms

Miso soup makes a versatile backdrop for almost any fish or shellfish, but it's especially good for oysters because the flavor of the oysters, unlike more delicate flavors, which might be lost, isn't covered up by the miso. Chopped chives are called for here, but other decorative herbs, lemon or lime or kumquat zests (the Japanese use the rind of *yuzu*, a tart little lemon), and miniature vegetables can be used instead. This soup looks gorgeous in black lacquer bowls.

MAKES 4 FIRST-COURSE SERVINGS

20 small oysters, shucked

2 tablespoons brown miso or 1 tablespoon red miso mixed with 1 tablespoon white miso

3 cups dashi (page 343)

4 medium shiitake mushrooms, stems removed, caps thinly sliced

2 tablespoons finely chopped fresh chives

Cut the oysters away from the bottom shells, discard the shells, and carefully pick over the oysters to eliminate grit. If the oysters seem especially gritty, place them on a clean kitchen towel and pat them with a second towel so any grit adheres to the towels. Strain any liquid released by the oysters through a fine-mesh strainer and reserve.

In a small bowl, combine the miso with about 2 tablespoons of the dashi and work the mixture into a smooth paste.

Heat the remaining dashi in a saucepan and add the sliced mushroom caps. Simmer gently for 5 minutes. Whisk in the miso paste and add the oysters, the strained oyster liquid, and the chives. Simmer for 30 seconds more and serve immediately in hot bowls—preferably little Japanese lacquer bowls with lids.

Cream of Oyster Soup

I first encountered this soup in a restaurant in Paris. While the soup captures the essence of oysters—and what could be better?—it was presented with a flare that made it even more spectacular. After ladling the soup into hot bowls, the waiter spooned tiny croutons and lovingly placed a dollop of caviar in the middle of each bowl. I make the soup at home without the caviar.

MAKES 6 FIRST-COURSE SERVINGS

¼ cup short-grain rice such as Arborio, Carnaroli, or Vialone Nano

1 cup milk

1 cup water

10 medium cultivated mushrooms, perfectly white with closed caps, rinsed and sliced

2 dozen small to medium oysters, preferably briny oysters such as Malpeque, Cape Cod, Maine Belon, or Pacific

1 cup heavy cream

sea salt and freshly ground white pepper

18 very thin slices of baguette, cut in half and toasted

1 tablespoon unsalted butter, melted

1 tablespoon very finely chopped parsley

2 ounces sevruga or osetra caviar (optional)

Combine the rice, milk, water, and mushrooms in a heavy 4-quart pot and simmer gently, covered, for 25 minutes, until the rice has turned mushy. Don't worry about overcooking the rice. (Bite into a grain; there should be no hint of mealiness.)

Meanwhile, shuck the oysters into a bowl, being sure to save all the liquid. Carefully pick over the oysters to eliminate grit. If the oysters seem especially gritty, place them on a clean kitchen towel and pat them with a second towel so any grit adheres to the towels. Strain any liquid released by the oysters through a fine-mesh strainer and reserve.

Add the oysters and reserved oyster liquid to the rice mixture and bring to a simmer. Simmer for 2 minutes. Let cool for 5 minutes and puree the mixture in a blender for about 1 minute, until smooth. (Be careful pureeing hot mixtures in the blender: never fill the blender more than a third full and start out by pulsing the mixture with short, quick pulses to prevent the hot liquid from shooting out the top.)

Work the soup through a food mill and again through a fine-mesh strainer (use the back of a ladle to work the mixture through the strainer) into a clean pot. Add the heavy cream and season with salt and pepper to taste.

Brush each crouton with melted butter. Place a tiny pinch of parsley on top of each crouton.

Bring the soup to a gentle simmer. If it seems too thick, thin it with a little milk or water and adjust the seasoning. Ladle into hot bowls. Arrange the croutons, parsley side up, on top of the soup in each bowl. In front of the guests, dollop a spoonful of caviar in the center of each bowl.

Fried Oysters

I was never much of a fan of fried oysters—the flavor of the oysters themselves was always masked in a heavy batter—until I tried them in a Chinese restaurant in San Francisco that was famous for its seafood. The trick, I realized, was to use freshly shucked oysters—not out of a can or jar—and to fry the oysters with a very light batter. My favorite is club soda batter.

Traditionalists insist that fried oysters be served only with lemon wedges, but in addition I like to serve a sauce or two.

Except for shucking the oysters, very little can be done in advance—the oysters must be fried at the very last minute.

MAKES 4 FIRST-COURSE SERVINGS

1 quart olive oil or vegetable oil

2 dozen oysters, shucked and shells discarded

1 recipe club soda batter (page 43)

lemon wedges and/or dipping sauce for Thai fish cakes (page 86) or gribiche sauce (page 334)

Heat the olive oil in a heavy iron skillet until it ripples (375°F) and barely begins to smoke.

Dip each oyster in the batter and then fry in the hot oil until they puff and turn golden brown, about 30 seconds. Take the oysters out of the oil with a slotted spoon or a spider and drain them on paper towels for a few seconds. Serve the oysters in little mounds on individual hot plates. Pass lemon wedges and either or both sauces.

Scallops

Scallops are the most popular of all bivalves, probably because they come already shucked and they're plump, meaty, and easy to eat. Although there are dozens of species, American cooks are likely to encounter only three kinds—sea scallops, bay scallops, and calico scallops. All are found on the Atlantic coast of the United States, but because some domestic sources are drying up, scallops are also being imported from places like Peru, Iceland, Japan, and China. Sea scallops are also being cultivated in California as are pink and spiny (singing) scallops in Puget Sound. Very similar cooking methods can be used for all three types.

SCALLOP VARIETIES

SEA SCALLOPS (Placopecten megallanicus, American; and Pecten maximus, European)

American sea scallops are the scallops most often seen in our fish stores, but because they are usually sold already shucked, most Americans have never seen a whole sea scallop in the shell. The shells, usually about 8 inches wide but as wide as 12 inches, have two little wings at the base near the hinge. Depending on the species, scallops may have variegated strips fanning out along the top shell or may be almost perfectly smooth. The scallop shell most of us have seen is the symbol for Shell Oil.

A freshly shucked sea scallop contains a lot more than the average consumer probably wants to think about. Other than the large white abductor muscle—what we think of as the scallop—the shell contains red female roe, white male reproductive glands (yes, scallops are hermaphrodites), 50 little eyes for avoiding predators, gills, and a set of digestive apparatus. On American fishing boats everything is thrown overboard except the abductor muscle, while in Europe the red female ovaries and/or male reproductive glands are left attached. This may have to do with more than American provincialism—European scallops have bright red roe, while the American scallop's roe is often an unappetizing dirty orange. (European sea scallops, *Pecten max-imus*, are now being cultivated in California and have the same bright red roe I've seen attached to scallops in Europe.) Shucked sea scallops are usually about an inch across and ¾ to 1½ inches high.

Because sea scallops are almost always shucked at sea and usually on boats that stay out for up to 10 days at a time, they are rarely perfectly fresh and can develop a strong odor. Scallops also have a tendency to lose water, and it's common practice to soak them for several hours in water containing tripolyphosphate to increase their bulk and help preserve them. (This is catastrophic when the scallops are sautéed, because the water runs out as soon as the scallop gets hot.) Wholesalers sell scallops labeled "wet," which have been soaked and are less expensive, and "dry," which have not been soaked—but retailers aren't yet required to pass this information on to their customers. Soaked scallops often look pure white and have a shiny appearance, while scallops that haven't been soaked vary in color from white to ivory to pinkish orange. Soaked scallops also seem to merge together into a single mass, while non-soaked scallops remain separate. Scallops are also sold "quick frozen." Because quick-frozen scallops are frozen immediately after they are shucked instead of being kept in a ship's hold for up to 10 days, they often have a fresher taste than "fresh" scallops.

One way to be sure you're getting perfectly fresh scallops is to buy them in the shell. Scallops in the shell are not easy to find, and when you do find them they're expensive—but they're well worth it. Look for live scallops in the shell in Chinese markets—the Chinese are sticklers for freshness—or in an upscale market that is likely to carry exotic seafood. You can also try ordering scallops in the shell from your regular fish purveyor. Sea scallops in the shell usually gape slightly. This is normal provided they close slightly when pinched and have a fresh odor.

BAY SCALLOPS (Argopecten irradians)

These smaller cousins of sea scallops are the most delicate and sweetest of all American scallops. Bay scallop shells are usually from 2 to 3 inches wide, and the meat is about ½ inch across and ¾ to 1 inch thick.

Bay scallops are harvested on the Atlantic seaboard from October through March with the peak in late fall. They are usually sold only in East Coast fish markets during this period and tend to be quite expensive. Bay scallops can often be found for sale alive, in the shell.

CALICO SCALLOPS (Argopecten gibbus)

Unfortunately these miniature scallops are rarely seen in their beautiful shells but are sold already shucked. Usually calico scallops are sold as bay scallops even though they are much smaller and have less flavor. (Shucked calico scallops look like baby marshmallows.) Much of the natural delicacy of the calico scallop is lost in the shucking process—the scallops are lightly steamed to loosen the shell, which leaves the meat partially cooked. Shucked calico scallops are easy to recognize because they are pale white and opaque around the edges and very small.

STORING AND
SHUCKING LIVE SEA
AND BAY SCALLOPS

Live scallops in the shell should be used within a day or two of purchase because they die quickly out of water. If you're not using them right away, keep them in a bowl covered with a wet towel in the refrigerator. Don't soak them in water and don't shuck them until an hour or so before serving.

Both sea and bay scallops are easy to shuck because the shells are already partially open. Slide a sharp paring knife along the inside of the top shell, pull off and discard the shell (unless you need ashtrays), and repeat the process with the bottom shell. When you've gotten the scallop out of the shell, pull off or cut away the membrane surrounding the "scallop" (the muscle) and discard the rest (see color page 17). The bright orange roe surrounding the scallop "eye" has long been popular with Europeans, but because roe tends to accumulate toxins it should be eaten only if the scallops are cultured. With your fingers, pull off the small white muscle that wraps partially around each eye.

RAW SCALLOPS

For lovers of raw shellfish the sweet delicate flavor of sea or bay scallops is hard to beat, but most Americans have never eaten scallops this way, probably because they're only occasionally available alive in the shell. You can have the fishmonger shuck them as long as it's within a couple of hours of serving, but since it's easy to do I usually opt for shucking scallops myself—sometimes in front of the guests.

The easiest way to serve raw scallops is to slice them into ⅛- to ⅙-inch-thick disks and arrange them unadorned on chilled plates. I usually serve lemon wedges in a small bowl and put a salt grinder filled with sea salt on the table for guests to season them as they wish. I always encourage my guests to try at least one with neither salt nor lemon. Raw scallops can also be served Japanese style with a simple dipping sauce such as soy sauce with wasabi (page 116) or ponzu sauce (page 118).

MARINATED SCALLOPS

Because of their sweet flavor and soft texture, scallops are excellent when lightly marinated in a tangy sauce. Although marinated scallops look like they've been cooked (they turn slightly opaque), the same precautions should be taken when eating raw shellfish.

Scallops are best marinated in delicately flavored liquids such as very fine extra-virgin olive oil or lemon juice which won't obscure their natural sweetness.

SCALLOP SAFETY

Although you should be sure of your source before eating any shellfish, scallops are probably the safest shellfish to eat raw. Most of the danger in eating raw shellfish stems from the fact that shellfish filter large amounts of sea water to obtain nutrients, and bacteria, viruses, and toxins tend to accumulate in this filtration apparatus. The filtration apparatus in scallops is, however, discarded, and only the abductor muscle, where few toxins accumulate, is eaten.

FAKE SCALLOPS

My students are always asking me if the scallops I'm serving are real or if they've been "manufactured" from skate or shark. I don't know where this legend originated—there are probably restaurants out there that have tried such sneaky tricks—but it's hard to imagine its being worth the effort. First of all, skate flesh with its striated surface looks nothing like scallops. Shark looks a bit like scallop flesh, but if you look closely it doesn't fit the bill either. If you get your scallops home and still have doubts, check for the tiny white muscle that should be adhering to the side of the scallop.

Sea Scallops Marinated in Citronette

These scallops are marinated in the simplest of sauces—a vinaigrette made with lemon instead of vinegar. Feel free to experiment with different vinegars, oils, and herbs.

The only tricky part of this recipe is slicing the scallops very thinly. Arm yourself with a very sharp and fairly long slicing knife. If you still have trouble, put the scallops in the freezer until they stiffen—in about 20 minutes—take them out of the freezer one at a time, and immediately slice them before they have time to soften.

MAKES 4 FIRST-COURSE SERVINGS

8 to 12 large sea scallops (12 ounces), preferably freshly shucked

3 tablespoons best-quality extra-virgin olive oil

1 tablespoon lemon juice

salt, preferably freshly ground sea salt, and white pepper

2 tablespoons fresh chervil leaves or finely chopped fresh chives or other herbs

With your fingers, pull off the small white muscle on the side of each scallop. Using a very sharp knife, slice the scallops into ⅛-inch-thick disks by pressing down on the top of the scallop with the fingers of your left hand (assuming you're right-handed) and shaving slices off the top.

Gently stir together the olive oil, lemon juice, salt, and pepper. Brush chilled wide plates with a thin layer of sauce. If you're using chives, add them to the remaining sauce.

Arrange the scallop slices—you should have about 15 slices per serving—on the chilled plates and brush

---

them with the citronette sauce. If you're using chervil leaves, arrange them decoratively over each plate. Chill the plates in the refrigerator for 15 minutes and serve.

Scallop Seviche

Seviche is popular throughout South America, in parts of Mexico (where it's called *cebiche*), and in Central America. It is one of my favorite ways to eat shellfish, and it works especially well with scallops. Because the ingredients are full-flavored and would obscure the delicate flavor of freshly shucked scallops, the preshucked sea, bay, or calico scallops available at most fish stores work well in this dish.

Although lots of different ingredients can go into a seviche, in addition to salt only three are essential: fresh cilantro, lime or lemon juice, and some kind of hot chili. Other ingredients such as orange juice, scallions, garlic, saffron, olives, tomatoes, oregano, avocados, onions, shallots, and miscellaneous herbs can all be added to a seviche with delicious if not strictly authentic results. (See page 89 for more seviche ideas.)

MAKES 4 FIRST-COURSE SERVINGS

1 pound sea, bay, or calico scallops

juice of 3 limes

3 tablespoons chopped fresh cilantro

2 jalapeño chilies or 1 serrano chili, seeded and finely chopped

salt and pepper

If you're using sea or bay scallops, remove the small white muscle that wraps partially around each scallop and slice the scallops into disks about

¼ inch thick. Bay scallops, unless they are unusually large, can be left whole. Calico scallops should always be left whole.

Combine the scallops with the other ingredients and chill in the refrigerator for 20 minutes. Serve on small chilled plates or in wide glasses such as champagne coupes.

❧

Sautéed Scallops

Scallops can be a little tricky to sauté because, especially if they've been soaked in tripolyphosphate solution, they contain a lot of water, which runs out as soon as the scallops get hot. The result is that they end up simmering in their own juices instead of browning. One way around this is to make sure the scallops are perfectly dry and to sear them in a very hot pan—preferably nonstick—and not overcrowd the pan. Another method is to dip each end of the scallops in flour before placing them in the hot pan. Avoid getting flour on the sides of the scallops or the flour will remain raw. If you can't fit the scallops into the pan in a single layer, sauté them in 2 stages or use 2 pans.

Sautéed scallops must be served piping hot, right out of the pan. Slice them into disks, brown them for about a minute on each side, sprinkle with salt and pepper, arrange them on very hot plates, and serve immediately.

One easy way to make a sauce is to sauté chopped garlic and parsley in olive oil or butter for about 30 seconds in the sauté pan and then pour this hot mixture over each plate. Another method is to heat a dollop of flavored butter or oil in the sauté pan and pour

it over the scallops. Whatever you do, you'll need plenty of French bread for guests to mop up the melted herb butter or basil oil.

MAKES 4 FIRST-COURSE SERVINGS

2 tablespoons pure olive oil

8 to 12 large sea scallops (12 ounces), small white muscle removed, cut into ⅓-inch disks

salt and pepper

For the Sauce:

¼ pound unsalted butter or ½ cup extra-virgin olive oil

**2 garlic cloves, finely chopped and crushed to a paste combined with 3 tablespoons finely chopped parsley
or ½ cup Montpelier butter
(page 331) or basil oil (page 254)**

Divide the olive oil between two 10- or 12-inch sauté pans, preferably nonstick, and heat the pans over high heat until the oil starts to smoke. Dry the scallops on paper towels (don't let them sit on the towels, or they will stick) and arrange them quickly in a single layer in the pans. Brown the scallops over high heat for 1 minute on each side. Sprinkle with salt and pepper and transfer immediately to hot plates.

Pour the burned oil out of the pans and wipe one of them clean with a paper towel. Put the unsalted butter and the garlic and parsley mixture into the clean pan and heat over high heat until the butter melts and the garlic sizzles. Spoon this hot mixture over the scallops and serve immediately. If you're using a compound butter or basil oil, simply heat it in the sauté pan and spoon it over the scallops.

COOKING IN LIQUID: POACHING, BRAISING, AND SAUTÉ-STEAMING

One of the most delightful ways to serve scallops is surrounded with a light sauce made from their own cooking liquid. In this case the released liquid that is anathema to sautéing is coaxed out deliberately by cooking over low heat or covering the pan. Then, if you're lucky enough to have perfectly fresh scallops, a tiny piece of butter, a pinch of chopped fresh herbs, a few drops of lemon juice, or a swirl of heavy cream will be enough to transform the liquid into an appealing but not overwhelming sauce. The liquid released by the scallops most of us can get will have less delicacy and finesse, so you can add fuller-flavored ingredients: tomatoes, basil or tarragon, or sorrel puree.

The French method—*étuver*—I call it *sauté-steaming*—of gently cooking scallops in a covered pan with no or very little liquid is an excellent way to collect the pure unadulterated juices from the scallops, but because you end up with very little liquid you'll be able to prepare only a small amount of very tasty sauce. If you want more liquid—and more sauce—you're better off poaching or braising the scallops in court bouillon, fish broth, or dashi. You can also use the cooking liquid from clams, mussels, or oysters and either use the cooked shellfish for another recipe or include them in a mixed stew with the scallops.

When poaching or braising scallops, choose a pan that holds the scallops in a single layer so that the amount of liquid is kept to a minimum—in this way the scallop flavor is diluted as little as possible. The easiest way to deal with irregularly sized scallops is to slice them all into disks about ½ inch thick. When I occasionally encounter very large scallops, I leave them whole and serve only one or two per person—they're very dramatic.

Cooking scallops in liquid leaves you with infinite possibilities for enriching, flavoring, and garnishing the broth or sauce. I sometimes include lightly cooked vegetables such as spinach (blanched, liquid squeezed out), mushrooms (wild or cultivated, sautéed or simmered along with scallops in poaching or braising liquid), sorrel (lightly stewed, leaves left whole, and the liquid released added to the scallop-cooking liquid or pureed and used as a thickener), chopped fresh tomatoes (lightly stewed, added to the cooking liquid just before serving), or baby carrots and turnips (glazed and arranged with the scallops just before serving).

In classic French cooking the scallops are poached or braised in fish stock, the resulting liquid is thickened with flour, and the resulting sauce is enriched with cream. The scallops are then arranged in their shells (perhaps on a bed of cooked mushrooms), the sauce is spooned over and the whole thing is sprinkled with bread crumbs and browned under the broiler. This is a heavy-handed approach for today's eaters, and in contrast some cooks serve scallops surrounded with the unadulterated hot poaching or braising liquid. Such a purist approach is effective if the scallops are spectacular, but most cooks (including me) can't resist sneaking in extra flavorings such as chopped fresh herbs or light enrichers such as cream, butter, or coconut milk. An especially elegant and tasty approach is to make a scallop roe butter and whisk it into the sauce (see box on page 162).

Sauté-Steamed Scallops with Shallots, White Wine, and Fines Herbes

I use this delicate method when I track down perfect scallops still in the shell. I'm always surprised by the ease of preparation and the subtle sophistication of the flavors—and so are my guests.

MAKES 4 FIRST-COURSE OR 2 MAIN-COURSE SERVINGS

8 to 12 large sea scallops (about 12 ounces), small white muscle removed, cut into ¹/₂-inch disks

salt and pepper

1 teaspoon unsalted butter for cooking

2 tablespoons dry white wine

3 tablespoons any combination of finely chopped parsley, chervil, and chives

2 tablespoons unsalted butter or scallop roe butter for sauce (optional)

Dry the scallops with paper towels and season them with salt and pepper. Over low to medium heat, melt the teaspoon of butter in a nonstick sauté pan just large enough to hold the scallops in a single layer. Arrange the scallops in the pan, pour in the white wine, and cover. Cook over medium heat for 3 minutes and check the scallops; there should be more liquid in the pan than when you started, and the scallops should be opaque around the edges. Using a slotted spoon, quickly arrange the scallops on hot plates with deep rims or wide soup bowls. Keep the plates in a 200°F oven while preparing the sauce. Add the herbs to the liquid in the pan and whisk in the butter if desired. Simmer the sauce, stirring, for 1 minute. Season with salt and pepper and pour over the scallops.

Braised Scallops with Tomatoes and Fresh Basil

MAKES 4 FIRST-COURSE OR 2 MAIN-COURSE SERVINGS

8 large sea scallops (about 12 ounces), small white muscle removed, cut into ¹/₂-inch disks

salt and pepper

10 fresh basil leaves

2 teaspoons olive oil

1 cup court bouillon (page 66) or fish broth (page 343)

2 ripe tomatoes, peeled, seeded, and finely chopped

Dry the scallops with paper towels and season with salt and pepper.

Toss the basil leaves in olive oil to prevent them from turning black and chop them finely.

Arrange the scallops in a pan just large enough to hold them in a single layer. Bring the court bouillon to a simmer and pour it over the scallops—it should just come up to the top of the scallops. Place the scallops over low to medium heat and barely simmer for 3 minutes.

Transfer the scallops to wide bowls or plates with deep rims—keep the plates warm in a 200°F oven. Add the tomatoes to the pan and bring to a simmer. Stir in the chopped basil, simmer for 1 minute more, and season with salt and pepper. Ladle over and around the scallops.

Poached Scallops with Saffron and Lobster Butter

When I was living in Paris, scallops were always sold freshly shucked and still had their roe—which looks like a bright orange tongue. The roe can be eaten along with the rest of the scallop, but it's also delicious pureed with butter in a food processor and whisked into the poaching liquid just before serving (see box).

Since scallops with roe are hard to find in the United States, I often use lobster butter instead of the scallop roe butter I used in Europe. If you're cooking lobster and making the lobster butter the same day, it will be easy to turn this dish into a combined scallop and lobster stew by gently reheating the chunks of shelled lobster for 1 to 2 minutes in the scallop-braising liquid. Sea urchin roe butter can also be used. Another elegant touch is a tiny spoonful of caviar on each scallop.

Remember that braising differs from poaching in that the scallops are cooked in only enough liquid to come halfway up the sides of the scallops.

MAKES 4 FIRST-COURSE OR 2 MAIN-COURSE SERVINGS

8 large sea scallops (about 12 ounces), small white muscle removed, cut into ¹/₂-inch disks

salt and pepper

¹/₂ cup court bouillon (page 66) or fish broth (page 343)

¹/₄ cup heavy cream

small pinch of saffron threads, soaked in 1 tablespoon water for 15 minutes

3 tablespoons lobster butter (page 330), scallop roe butter (see box), or sea urchin roe butter (page 234)

2 tablespoons fresh lemon juice

2 tablespoons finely chopped fresh chervil or parsley

Dry the scallops with paper towels and season with salt and pepper.

Arrange the scallops in a pan just large enough to hold them in a single layer. Bring the court bouillon to a simmer and pour it over the scallops—it should just come halfway up the sides of the scallops. Place the scallops over medium heat until the liquid starts to steam, cover the pot, and barely simmer for 3 minutes.

Transfer the scallops to wide bowls or plates with deep rims and keep them warm in the oven.

Whisk the cream and saffron along with its soaking liquid into the liquid left in the pan, turn the heat on high, and boil for about 2 minutes, until the liquids have cooked down slightly. Whisk in the shellfish butter, lemon juice, and chervil. Season with salt and pepper to taste. Ladle the sauce over and around the scallops.

SCALLOP SOUPS

There's very little difference between poaching scallops and making a soup. For soup the broth must be full-flavored, but you don't have to worry about using too much liquid. A flavorful liquid base for the soup can be prepared entirely in advance and the scallops added a minute or two before serving.

Scallops in Hot-and-Sour Thai Broth

To make this versatile soup, start by preparing a basic Thai broth (*gaeng prik*) and then add scallops to the hot broth about 2 minutes before serving. The broth is so versatile that you can substitute shrimp, lobster, or even strips of chicken or pork. *Gaeng prik* is spicy—if you or your guests are sensitive to heat, cut back on the chilies. See the glossary for information on Asian ingredients.

COOKING WITH SCALLOP ROE

If you manage to find fresh scallops with the bright red roe still attached, you can cook the roe along with the rest of the scallop or convert it into scallop roe butter and then use it as a sauce. Scallop roe butter freezes well for up to 2 months and can be used in other recipes.

Made by pureeing the roe with an equal amount of butter in a food processor and straining, it can be whisked into hot scallop sauces, stewing liquids, or soups as a delicate and flavorful finish. Because most roe curdles if allowed to approach the boil, a roe butter should be whisked into the hot, but not boiling sauce, off the heat. Scallop roe butter can also be served, melting, on top of grilled or sautéed sea scallops or other fish or shellfish.

Avoid using scallop roe from wild scallops or if the roe is a dingy brown.

MAKES 6 FIRST-COURSE SERVINGS

For the Scallops:

1 pound sea scallops, small white muscle removed, cut into ¼-inch disks

For the Broth (Gaeng Prik)

6 cups chicken broth (page 344) or fish broth (page 343)

4 Thai chilies or 6 jalapeño chilies, seeded and finely chopped

3 garlic cloves, finely chopped

2 shallots, finely chopped

a ¼-inch slice of galangal (optional)

4 kaffir lime leaves

a 6-inch piece of lemongrass, thinly sliced

3 tablespoons tamarind paste dissolved in ½ cup hot water and strained or the juice of 2 limes

5 tablespoons Thai fish sauce

1 scallion, finely chopped

¼ cup finely chopped fresh cilantro leaves

½ cup unsweetened coconut milk (optional)

Place the scallops on a plate, cover with plastic wrap, and refrigerate.

Bring the chicken broth to a slow simmer and add the rest of the ingredients except the cilantro, coconut milk, and scallops. Simmer gently for 10 minutes. When you're ready to serve, add the cilantro, the coconut milk if desired, and the scallops. Simmer for 2 minutes more and serve in hot bowls.

SCALLOP GRATINS

Scallops gratinéed in their shells have long been a French staple, but unfortunately the scallops were usually overcooked and masked in layers of white sauce, cheese, mushrooms, and bread crumbs. On the other hand it's a pleasant experience for guests to be served scallops in the shell and hopefully in the scallops' *own* shells and not shells bought at the corner cooking boutique.

Gratins have always lent themselves to improvisation and usually consist of a makeshift filling—typically made with vegetables—that is arranged under and around the scallop meat in the shell and a sauce or dusting of cheese or bread crumbs to protect the scallops from the direct heat of the broiler while at the same time encouraging the formation of a savory crust. I sometimes cheat and instead of browning the scallops under the broiler simply heat them in the oven, leaving the scallops slightly undercooked and more delicately flavored.

THREE-FLAVORED BAY SCALLOP GRATINS

(color page 1)

Although there's no need to serve all 3 gratins at once, serving 3 bay scallops, hot in their own shells and each flavored in a different way, makes an elegant and very tasty first course or hors d'oeuvre. If you're serving only one or two of these gratins, you'll need to double or triple the recipes accordingly. Each of these scallop dishes can be prepared and assembled up to 3 hours before serving.

❧

Bay Scallops with Mushrooms

MAKES 6 INDIVIDUAL SCALLOPS

¼ pound fresh mushrooms

1 shallot, finely chopped

1 tablespoon unsalted butter

1 tablespoon finely chopped parsley

2 tablespoons heavy cream

salt and pepper

6 bay scallops in the shell, shucked, shells reserved

Preheat the broiler. Chop the mushrooms coarsely by hand or in a food processor, being careful not to puree them.

Cook the shallot in butter in a sauté pan over medium heat for about 3 minutes. Add the chopped mushrooms, turn the heat up to high, and cook, stirring occasionally, until they dry out, about 10 minutes. Stir in the parsley and cream and season with salt and pepper to taste. Simmer for a minute or two, until the mixture stiffens.

Arrange the scallop shells on a baking sheet covered with crumpled aluminum foil to keep the shells flat. Spoon half the mushroom mixture into each shell, making sure each shell has the same amount.

Place the scallops over the mushroom mixture in each shell, spread on the remaining mushroom mixture, and sprinkle with salt and pepper.

Slide the baking sheet under the broiler for about 3 minutes, until the mushroom mixture begins to bubble. Serve immediately.

Bay Scallops with Spinach and Saffron Cream

MAKES 6 INDIVIDUAL SCALLOPS

6 bay scallops in the shell, shucked, shells reserved

1 quart water

salt

leaves from one 10-ounce bunch of spinach, washed

6 tablespoons heavy cream

pepper

tiny pinch of saffron, soaked in 1 tablespoon water for 30 minutes

continued

Wash and dry the scallop shells and place them on a baking sheet covered with crumpled aluminum foil to keep the shells flat. Make sure the baking sheet will fit under the broiler. Reserve the raw bay scallops in the refrigerator.

Bring the water to a rolling boil in a 4-quart saucepan, add a tablespoon of salt, and toss in the spinach leaves. When the leaves have "melted," about 30 seconds, drain them in a colander and rinse them quickly under cold running water. Gently squeeze the leaves into a ball to remove excess water. Slice the ball of leaves to shred the spinach.

Just before serving, preheat the broiler and heat 1 tablespoon cream in a small sauté pan until it reduces by half and becomes quite thick. Stir the shredded spinach into the cream over medium heat to warm the spinach. Season the spinach with salt and pepper and arrange it in the scallop shells. Place a bay scallop in the center of the spinach.

In the saucepan used to heat the cooked spinach combine the remaining cream with the saffron and its soaking liquid. Simmer the mixture until it thickens slightly, about 3 minutes. Remove from the heat, season with salt and pepper to taste, and spoon the saffron cream over each scallop.

Slide the baking sheet under the broiler for 2 to 3 minutes, until the saffron cream starts to bubble.

Bay Scallops with Smoked Salmon and Balsamic Vinegar Sauce

MAKES 6 INDIVIDUAL SCALLOPS

6 bay scallops in the shell, shucked, shells removed

2 tablespoons plus 1 teaspoon extra-virgin olive oil

2 teaspoons balsamic vinegar

salt and pepper

1 thin slice of smoked salmon (about 1 ounce), cut into very thin 1-inch shreds

1 teaspoon finely chopped fresh chives

In a small bowl, combine 2 tablespoons of the olive oil with the vinegar, a little salt and pepper, and the smoked salmon.

Just before serving, put the shells on a baking sheet covered with crumpled aluminum foil so the shells stay flat. Preheat the broiler. Arrange the scallops in their shells and spoon on the smoked salmon mixture. Season lightly with salt and pepper and slide under the broiler for about 3 minutes, until the tops of the scallops turn opaque. Decorate each scallop with a tiny pinch of chives. Serve immediately.

GRILLED SCALLOPS

Grilled scallops are fun and easy to serve at an outdoor barbecue, and grilling gives the scallops a lovely smoky flavor.

In the same way as all small pieces of fish and shellfish, both sea and bay scallops should be threaded on skewers so they don't fall through the cracks in the grill.

Any of the methods suggested in the grilling chapter can be used for scallops, but here are a few additional suggestions. Both of the recipes given here can also be adapted for broiling.

Scallop Yakitori

I like to serve these yakitori the way the Japanese do, as an hors d'oeuvre, usually with cocktails. The scallops end up with a sweet and smoky flavor that perfectly complements their own natural sweetness.

MAKES 6 HORS D'OEUVRE OR FIRST-COURSE SERVINGS

15 medium sea scallops or 30 large bay scallops

1 recipe yakitori sauce (see box on page 165)

Japanese seven-spice mixture (shichimi)

Soak 12 wooden skewers in water for 30 minutes to help prevent them from burning.

Pull off and discard the small white muscle that runs up the side of each scallop. If you're using sea scallops, cut them in half crosswise so you end up with 30 disks. Marinate the scallops in the yakitori sauce for 15 minutes. Carefully skewer 5 bay scallops or sea scallop disks with 2 skewers to make the scallops easy to turn on the grill. Make sure the scallops are close together so no wood remains exposed. Pour the yakitori sauce onto a plate.

Grill the scallops over hot coals for about 1 minute on each side and then dip them in the yakitori sauce on the plate. Grill the scallops again for 1 minute on each side and dip once more in yakitori sauce. Grill for 30 seconds more on each side and serve immediately. Let guests season their scallops to taste with the seven-spice mixture.

YAKITORI SAUCE

¼ **cup sake**

6 **tablespoons Japanese dark soy sauce**

2 **tablespoons mirin**

1 **tablespoon sugar**

MAKES ¾ CUP

Combine the ingredients in a small saucepan and bring to a slow simmer. Simmer gently for 1 minute. Let cool. Yakitori sauce will keep in the refrigerator for several weeks.

Scallop Kebabs with Mint and Cilantro Yogurt Pesto

*T*hese simple kebabs include only the scallops, but the mint and cilantro pesto is also delicious on hot vegetables. Feel free to add pearl onions, peeled garlic cloves (blanched or roasted until slightly soft), tomato wedges, strips of chilies or whole small chilies, or mushrooms (tossed in olive oil).

MAKES 6 FIRST-COURSE SERVINGS

1½ **pounds medium to large sea scallops or large bay scallops**

juice of 1 lemon

1 **tablespoon pure olive oil**

salt and pepper

1 **recipe mint and cilantro yogurt pesto (page 338)**

Soak 12 wooden skewers in water for 30 minutes to help prevent them from burning.

Pull off and discard the small white muscle wrapped around each scallop. If you're using large sea scallops, cut them in half crosswise so you end up with at least 30 disks. Toss the scallops in the lemon and olive oil and marinate for 15 minutes. Dry the scallops in paper towels, season them with salt and pepper, and carefully skewer 5 bay scallops or sea scallop disks with 2 skewers. Make sure the scallops are close together so no wood is exposed.

Grill the scallops over hot coals for 3 to 4 minutes on each side. Serve immediately and pass the mint and cilantro yogurt pesto at the table.

Lobster

Lobster's delicious flavor and thick meaty flesh make it a coveted delicacy all over the world. It's not cheap these days, but it hasn't always been so prized. Lobster was so common in 18th-century Maine that it was used for fertilizer. In 19th-century Europe it had none of the cachet of oysters, the luxury food of the day, and was thought to be rather a poor man's food.

CLAWED LOBSTERS

There are two species of clawed lobster, the American or northern lobster (*Homarus americanus*) and the European lobster (*Homarus gammarus*). Although gourmets like to quibble about which is better, the two clawed species are virtually the same. The European version has slightly darker coloring—sometimes bordering on blue—while the American lobster is more typically orange and black.

People cooking in America will rarely encounter a European lobster because they are scarce and aren't exported to North America. On the other hand, American lobsters are exported in large numbers to Europe, where there isn't enough lobster to go around.

SPINY LOBSTERS

The obvious difference between the familiar American lobster and spiny lobsters (and the closely related rock and thorny lobsters) is that spiny lobsters don't have claws. Spiny lobsters also have very long antennae and a rougher and usually harder shell.

Various species of spiny and thorny lobsters are found in the United States—especially along the southern Atlantic coast and the coast of California—but, unlike whole American lobsters, are sold only locally or are frozen and sold as lobster tails. Although gourmets may argue over which is tastier, I always opt for a fresh local product instead of one that has been flown from thousands of miles away or frozen.

FROZEN LOBSTER TAILS

Most of the frozen lobster tails sold in the United States actually come from rock or spiny lobsters rather than the so-called true American lobster.

Frozen lobster tails have a tougher texture than live American lobster, and of course there is no tomalley or coral to use in soups or sauces. Frozen lobster tails, however, are convenient, and because you're not paying for the head section, they are often good bargains.

Frozen lobster tails can be thawed out in the refrigerator or in the microwave or can be cooked in their frozen state.

Like so many shellfish, frozen lobster tails are marketed according to sizes ranging from 2 to 24 ounces.

Spiny lobsters and spiny lobster tails are commercially designated as *warm-water* (from Florida, the Caribbean, and Brazil) or *cold-water* (from New Zealand, Australia, and South Africa). Cold-water species are considered better than warm-water species and usually cost more. Also, the larger the tail, the higher the price per pound. Live spiny, rock, and thorny lobsters can all be cooked in the same way as American lobsters.

EUROPEAN SPINY AND THORNY LOBSTERS

Two major species—the spiny lobster (*Palinurus mauritanicus*) and the thorny lobster (*P. elephas*)—are found in the Mediterranean and the Eastern Atlantic, where they sell for almost the price of European lobster. Like the European lobster, these species never make it to the United States because they are already more expensive in Europe than our own American lobster. Once cooked, it is difficult to tell the difference between regular lobster and a European spiny or thorny lobster.

FLORIDA SPINY LOBSTER

This lobster (*Panulirus argus*), also called *Caribbean lobster*, is found not only off the coast of Florida but throughout the Caribbean and along the East Coast of South America. Other than locally, it is rarely sold alive but is frozen whole or sold as tails. The flavor and texture are similar to those of American or northern lobster.

CALIFORNIA SPINY LOBSTER
(Panulirus interruptus)

Although of less commercial importance than its Florida cousin, California spiny lobster—found along the coast of southern California and western Mexico—is enjoyed locally.

AUSTRALIAN AND NEW ZEALAND ROCK LOBSTER (Jasus edwardsii and jverreauxi)

These species, along with others from New Zealand and Australia, are another major source of frozen lobster tails marketed in the United States. Because they are cold-water species, they are more flavorful and slightly more expensive than warm-water varieties.

SOUTH AFRICAN ROCK LOBSTER OR CAPE CRAYFISH (Jasus lalandii)

These lobsters are often sold in the United States in the form of frozen lobster tails. Because, like Australian and New Zealand varieties, they are considered cold-water species, they are slightly more expensive.

BRAZILIAN SPINY LOBSTER (Panulirus llaevicauda)

This species is caught in the Caribbean and off the coast of Brazil and the rest of the East Coast of South America. It is often marketed in the United States as frozen lobster tails.

SELECTING LOBSTERS

With the exception of lobster tails, which are always frozen, lobster should always be bought alive. I always try to buy lobster from a place that has them in tanks—and preferably one that does a thriving business so I'm reasonably assured that the lobsters haven't been in the tanks too long. Lobsters that have lived too long in tanks tend to lose weight and contain less meat so that when you crack open a claw it will be half empty.

However you buy your lobster, make sure that it's feisty. When you pick it up—by grasping it on each side of the head—the tail should flap indignantly. If the tail and claws sag or there is foam coming out of the head, look for another lobster.

Lobsters commonly range in size from 1¼ pounds (smaller sizes are illegal) to 2 pounds, but occasionally large specimens show up that weigh up to 20 pounds. Unless I'm planning to serve whole lobsters to hungry guests (for whom I'll buy 2-pounders), I buy the smallest lobsters because they're the least expensive and just as tasty as the larger ones.

Places that do a large lobster business usually sell lobster "culls." Culls are missing one claw or have one very small claw and are sold for less. I use culls for soups or stews when there's no need to present a whole lobster.

Lobster lovers are forever debating the merits of male versus female lobsters, some claiming that the flesh of one is better than that of the other. I've never really figured this out, but for some dishes, such as stews calling for lobster coral, it's essential to have female lobsters. It's easy to tell the difference between a male and female lobster: turn the lobster over so you're looking at the underside of the tail. Starting at the end of the tail, follow the pairs of small hind legs lining each side of the tail until you're looking at where the tail joins the head section.* At the base of the head section there are two small pointed legs. On the male lobster these are hard and bony, while on the female they are very soft and flexible. If you're unsure, when you're buying the lobster, ask someone to show you (see color page 23).

STORING LOBSTER

It's best to cook lobster the day you buy it, but you can keep it alive in the refrigerator for a day or two by wrapping it in several sheets of newspaper soaked in cold water. If the paper dries out, rinse it with cold water.

*The lobster body breaks into only two sections: the familiar meaty tail sold separately at fish markets and restaurants and the rest, which I call the head (technically called the thorax but given various names by different food writers). See color page 23.

BOILING

The easiest and most popular method for cooking lobster is to plunge the live lobsters into a pot of boiling water. Although it's hard to go wrong with this method, there are two things to look out for. First, be sure to use enough water—at least a gallon for the first lobster and a quart more for each additional lobster. If there isn't enough water, the lobsters will bring down the water temperature and make it difficult to determine the correct cooking time. Another common pitfall is overcooking. Some recipes suggest cooking the lobster for 20 minutes for the first pound—a culinary catastrophe. For my own enjoyment I cook a 1¼-pound lobster for 5 minutes and then about 2 minutes more for every additional pound. Properly cooked lobster should be slightly translucent, and the coral—if there is any—should still be dark green. If all the coral has turned orange and hard, the lobster is overcooked. If I'm afraid my guests will think translucent lobster meat is raw, I cook it for 8 minutes and an extra 2 minutes per pound, no more. Either way, don't actually *boil* the lobsters, or the flesh may toughen. The water should be at a rolling boil when you add the lobsters, but then the water will stop boiling. Leave the pot on high heat, and as soon as the water starts to reboil, turn down the heat so the lobsters actually *poach.*

SERVING BOILED LOBSTER

The easiest way to serve a boiled lobster is to cut it in half lengthwise, pull out and discard the grain sac in each side of the head near the front (see color page 22), and crack the claws. You can use a cracker for the claws, but it's easier to whack them on the thorny side with an old knife, so the knife goes in about ¼ inch, and then twist the knife from side to side. The claw shell will snap right open. If you want to make it even easier on your guests, take the claw meat out yourself and arrange it on the split tail halves. If you don't want to split the tail, cut through the membrane on the underside of the tail with scissors to make it easier for your guests to extract the meat.

I've never been terribly fond of the American habit of serving lobster with melted or clarified butter and prefer to put a bottle of good extra-virgin olive oil and a plate of lemon wedges on the table for guests to help themselves. Or if I'm being fancy I make a hollandaise sauce. I also like this little tarragon sauce.

Boiled Lobster

MAKES 4 MAIN-COURSE SERVINGS

**Four 1½-pound (or larger) live lobsters
2 gallons water**

Bring the water to a boil in a pot large enough to hold the lobsters.

Rinse the lobsters under cold water and quickly slide them into the boiling water. Cover the pot and simmer gently until the lobsters turn completely red, in about 6 minutes.

Drain in a colander and serve immediately with melted butter, extra-virgin olive oil, or the Tarragon Cream Sauce below.

Tarragon Cream Sauce for Lobster

MAKES 1 CUP, ENOUGH FOR 4 LARGE LOBSTERS

**1 tomato, peeled, seeded, and finely chopped
½ cup heavy cream
1 tablespoon chopped fresh tarragon, basil, parsley, or chives
1 tablespoon fresh lemon juice
salt and white pepper**

Combine the tomato, cream, and tarragon in a 2-quart saucepan. Cook the mixture over medium heat until the sauce thickens slightly, about 15 minutes. Keep a close eye on it and whisk every minute or two to keep the cream from boiling over or turning grainy.

Stir in the lemon juice and season with salt and pepper to taste. Serve in a sauceboat at the table.

HOW TO KILL A LOBSTER?

My students are always presenting me with theories about how best to kill a lobster humanely. One common suggestion is to start the lobsters in cold water and gradually heat the water so that the lobsters don't squeak when they're added to the water. If anthropomorphism is any guide, I personally would want to get it over with fast, whether I screamed or not.

In a more scientific vein, a lobster probably suffers least when the brain is quickly cut in half before cooking. Hold the lobster on a cutting board. Quickly stab the lobster in the head—an inch behind the eyes—with a chef's knife held straight up and down. Drive the knife all the way down to the cutting board and then move it forward so the front part of the head is cut in half. The lobster may still flap around a bit, but technically it should be dead. This method does, however, cause the lobster to lose some of its juices. (See color page 23.)

BROILING AND BAKING

I've never been crazy about broiled lobster because the lobster always seems to overcook on the side facing the broiler flames and all the juices run out if I try to turn the lobster over. I've had much better luck baking lobsters: The lobster cooks more evenly, and the juices are held in by the shell. Occasionally I do use the broiler to quickly brown the inside surface of the tails when they're coated with a sauce.

A popular method for preparing lobster for the oven or broiler is to crack the claws and then cut halfway into the tail from the underside, fanning open the tail but leaving the back shell intact and the lobster tail partially split open. Again, I find that this method causes the lobster tail to cook unevenly and to dry out. I prefer cutting the lobster completely in half, removing the grain sac—now split into two gritty halves at the very front of each side of the head—and then laying the halves, flesh side up, on a baking sheet. I snap off the claws where they join the body and stick them in the oven about 8 minutes before the rest of the lobster so they finish cooking at the same time. I don't crack the claws until I'm ready to serve, so the juices stay inside. I also brush the tails with melted butter, olive oil, or some kind of sauce during bakingto keep them from drying out and to add flavor.

Baked Lobster

This is one of my favorite methods when I'm home alone or with close friends and don't want to fool around with fancy sauces. For big eaters, buy 2-pound lobsters and bake the claws and the bodies a few minutes more than called for here.

MAKES 4 MAIN-COURSE SERVINGS

Four 1¼-pound lobsters

4 tablespoons unsalted butter, melted, or ¼ cup extra-virgin olive oil

salt and pepper

lemon wedges

Preheat the oven to 400°F. Rinse the lobsters under cold running water, place them on a cutting board, and split them in half lengthwise with a chef's knife. Start by pushing the knife straight down into the head and then moving the knife forward (see box on page 169), splitting the head in two; repeat at the tail end. Remove and discard the grain sac in each side of the head and snap off the claws where they join the body.

Place the claws on a baking sheet and bake them for 8 minutes. Arrange the split lobsters, flesh side up, on the same sheet so the flesh side rests perfectly flat and no juices will run out onto the baking sheet. (If you can't get the lobster halves to rest flat, crumple and uncrumple a sheet of aluminum foil and place it on the sheet to hold them in place.) Brush the lobster with melted butter or olive oil and bake for 10 minutes, so the claws bake for a total of 18 minutes and the rest of the lobster for a total of 10 minutes. Brush the lobster with butter or olive oil once more during baking.

Crack open the claws, take out the meat, and arrange it on the lobster halves placed on hot plates. Brush everything one more time with melted butter or olive oil. Sprinkle with salt and pepper. Serve lemon wedges at the table.

❧

Lobster Thermidor

This is one of those dishes that became a culinary cliché and fell out of vogue. I rank it as one of my favorite out-of-vogue dishes (along with crêpes Suzette) and find that my guests like it too.

In this somewhat lightened version, a mixture of mustard and crème fraîche replaces the original flour-thickened sauce. Heavy cream can also be used, but it's harder to keep inside the lobster because it is runnier than crème fraîche. The lobster is cooked mostly in the oven and then finished under the broiler. If your oven and broiler are separate, preheat both.

MAKES 4 MAIN-COURSE SERVINGS

Four 1¼-pound lobsters

½ cup crème fraîche or heavy cream

1 tablespoon Dijon mustard

Preheat the oven to 400°F. Rinse the lobsters under cold running water, place them on a cutting board, and split them in half lengthwise with a chef's knife. Start by pushing the knife straight down into the head and then moving the knife forward (see box on page 169), splitting the head in two; repeat at the tail end. Remove and discard the grain sac in each side of the head and snap off the claws where they join the body.

Place the claws on a baking sheet and bake them for 8 minutes. Arrange the halves flesh side up on the baking sheet so the flesh side rests perfectly flat and no juices will run out onto the sheet. (If you can't get the tails to rest flat, crumple and uncrumple a sheet of aluminum foil and place it on the sheet to hold the tails in place.) Whisk together the cream and mustard in a small bowl and carefully spoon half to three quarters of the mixture over the lobster tails. Bake the lobster tails for 7 minutes. Take the claws out of the oven—they will now have been baking for 15 minutes—and take the meat out of the shells.

Take the lobster tails out of the oven and spoon on the rest of the mustard/cream mixture. Slide the baking sheet under the broiler with the lobster about 2 inches away from the heat. Broil the lobster until the mustard/cream sauce begins to brown and bubble, about 1 minute. Arrange the shelled lobster claws on top of the lobster tails. Serve immediately.

LOBSTER SAUCES

An almost infinite number of sauces can be used for coating a piece of hot or cold cooked lobster. While classic French sauces such as hollandaise, beurre blanc, and mayonnaise can all be used for lobster, the best sauces incorporate the flavor of the lobster into the sauce. There are three sources of lobster flavor: The broken-up lobster shells can be simmered in liquid with herbs and aromatic vegetables to make a flavorful liquid base; the lobster shells can also be cooked in fat and the fat separated to make a bright orange and intensely flavored lobster butter or oil; the tomalley and coral, which can be strained and whisked into the sauce just before serving.

In older recipes lobster sauces are usually thickened with flour, but today they are more likely thickened with cream or butter or incorporated into a hollandaise-style sauce. Very light, broth-like sauces that contain little or no fat are also sometimes served with lobster. Liquids such as fish broth, the steaming liquid from mussels, or broth from steamed lobster can all be used as the base for a lobster sauce.

LOBSTER GRATINS

A gratin is a dish that has been baked or lightly broiled so a savory crust forms on its surface. Most lobster gratins are prepared by lightly steaming or poaching the lobsters, taking the meat out of the shell, coating the lobster meat with a sauce (often a sauce made out of the lobster shells), and then quickly baking or broiling the dish so a crust forms but the lobster doesn't overcook. Gratins can be quite elaborate because the lobster can be cooked lightly earlier in the day or the night before so there's plenty of time to make a sauce out of the shells.

There are several ways to present a gratin. My favorite is to present the shelled lobster tails—cut in half lengthwise and lightly coated with sauce—in a gratin dish and then serve the tails on hot plates at the table. This never fails to impress guests. A more formal method is to arrange the lobster—either half tails or medallions—on individual plates and then slide each plate under the broiler to lightly brown the sauce directly on each plate.

Lobster Gratin with Lobster Hollandaise

This dish is so delicious but also so rich that I wait to serve it until the holidays, when my guests forget about their diets. The truffle is great, but the dish is still fabulous without it.

The trick to this dish is to prepare a flavorful broth, boil it down to concentrate its flavor, and then add it to a hollandaise sauce. The lightly cooked lobster meat—taken out of the shell—is then covered with the sauce and quickly baked.

MAKES 4 MAIN-COURSE OR 8 FIRST-COURSE SERVINGS

Four 1¼- to 1½-pound female lobsters (see color page 23 to tell the difference)
1 teaspoon good-quality wine vinegar such as balsamic or sherry
½ cup plus 1 teaspoon cognac or good brandy
3 tablespoons olive oil
2 shallots, finely chopped
1 garlic clove, finely chopped
1 cup dry white wine
3 tomatoes, peeled, seeded, and chopped
½ cup chicken broth (page 344) or fish broth (page 343)
3 egg yolks
¾ cup (6 ounces) clarified butter (page 336)
3 tablespoons lobster butter (optional; page 330)
1 small black truffle, finely chopped (optional)
1 tablespoon finely chopped parsley
salt and pepper

Rinse the lobsters under cold running water and kill them by cutting their heads in half lengthwise with a large chef's knife (see box on page 169). Twist off the tails and claws and scoop the coral and tomalley out of the heads and tails into a strainer set over a bowl containing the vinegar and 1 teaspoon cognac. Work the tomalley and coral through the strainer with the back of a wooden spoon or with your fingers. Reserve the strained coral and tomalley in the refrigerator. Remove and discard the grain sac in each side of the head (see color page 23).

In a 6-quart or larger pot over medium heat, cook the lobster parts in olive oil for about 5 minutes, stirring every minute or so. Sprinkle them with the shallots and garlic halfway into the cooking. Pour on the white wine and cognac and add the tomatoes and broth. Cover the pot and simmer for 5 minutes more, stirring the lobsters around to redistribute them after about 3 minutes. Remove and reserve the lobster meat and put the shells back in the pot. Break the shells up with a handleless rolling pin on end, cover the pot, and simmer gently for 30 minutes. Strain this liquid and boil to reduce it to $\frac{1}{4}$ cup. Allow to cool.

Slice the tail meat in half lengthwise and reserve, covered, along with the shelled claws, in the refrigerator.

In a heavy saucepan—preferably one with sloping sides (called a *windsor pan*)—whisk the yolks with the reduced lobster shell liquid over medium heat until the mixture becomes foamy and thickens; be careful, though, not to let it boil, or it will curdle. Remove the pan from the heat and slowly whisk in the clarified butter, the lobster butter and truffles if desired, the reserved coral and tomalley mixture, and the parsley. Season with salt and pepper to taste.

Arrange the claws and the tails, flat side down, in hot buttered gratin dishes just large enough to hold them in a single layer. Coat them thoroughly with the hollandaise sauce and slide under the broiler for 30 seconds to 2 minutes, until the sauce blisters and browns lightly. Serve immediately in the dining room on hot plates.

STEAMING

When a lobster is boiled, it releases flavorful juices into the boiling water. Most of the time these juices are thrown out with the cooking water. If, on the other hand, a small amount of liquid is used to steam the lobster, the juices from the lobster drip down into the steaming liquid so that the liquid can be converted into a sauce. The resulting sauce captures the briny flavor of the lobsters.

A large pot with a tight-fitting cover is best for steaming lobsters—you won't need a steamer. Lobsters are best steamed whole by placing them in a covered pot containing already-boiling liquid. If death by steaming seems inhumane, kill the lobsters first (see box on page 169).

Once you've steamed the lobsters, you can present them in several ways. The most obvious and easiest is just to crack the claws and serve the lobsters whole or cut them in half lengthwise and serve them in the same way as boiled lobsters. The meat can also be served taken out of the shell (see color page 22).

SAUCES FOR STEAMED LOBSTER

Once the lobsters have been steamed, the liquid in the bottom of the pot should be strained and then flavored or thickened. I usually take one of two approaches. The first is to reduce the steaming liquid in a saucepan, add a few tablespoons of chopped herbs such as parsley, chervil, or tarragon, and then finish the sauce with a small amount of heavy cream or butter. In the second—fat-free—approach, the strained steaming liquid isn't reduced but just flavored directly with chopped herbs, spices such as saffron or curry, or chopped aromatic vegetables such as tomatoes, garlic, or chilies. It is then poured over and around the lobsters in hot soup plates.

KEEPING LOBSTER TAILS FROM CURLING

One problem with steaming (and boiling) lobsters is that the tails curl up in the pot. This makes it difficult if you're presenting the whole lobsters on a platter or if you're taking the lobster out of the shell and slicing it into even medallions. One way to keep the lobsters from curling is to tie a long flat knife or skewer along the lobsters' undersides with a piece of string. The lobsters can also be tied together in pairs—so the tails remain straight—but this makes the tails take longer to cook. If you're killing the lobsters and twisting off their tails before cooking, the easiest way to keep the tail straight is to insert a short wooden skewer through the length of the tail, just below the underside.

Steamed Lobster with Parsley Cream Sauce

MAKES 4 MAIN-COURSE SERVINGS

Four 1¼- to 1½-pound lobsters

1 cup dry white wine

2 tablespoons finely chopped parsley or chervil

½ cup heavy cream

salt and pepper

Rinse the lobsters under cold running water.

Bring the white wine to a rapid boil in a pot large enough to hold the 4 lobsters. Put the lobsters in the pot and cover with a tight-fitting lid. Steam the lobsters over high heat for 4 minutes. Shake the pot—without removing the lid—to redistribute the lobsters and steam for 4 to 6 minutes more, depending on the size of the lobsters.

Take the lid off the pot, let the steam dissipate, and take out the lobsters. Strain the liquid in the bottom of the pot into a saucepan and reduce over high heat to about ¼ cup. Add the herbs and cream and simmer for about 1 minute more until the sauce thickens slightly. If you're using a fat-free approach, don't reduce the liquid or add the cream—just simmer the herbs in the cooking liquid for about 30 seconds. Season either version to taste with salt and pepper.

Snap off the lobster claws, remove the meat, and cut the lobster in half lengthwise. Remove the grain sac from each half of the head and arrange the lobster halves, flesh side up, on hot plates. Arrange the claw meat on top of the shells. Serve immediately. Pass the sauce in a sauceboat at the table.

TAKING THE LOBSTER MEAT OUT OF THE SHELL

In many of the simplest lobster recipes, the guests take the lobster out of the shell themselves, but in more elaborate and formal dishes, the meat is extracted before it is served. The tail can then be cut in half lengthwise, left whole, or sliced into medallions.

To take the meat out of the tail, twist the tail away from the lobster head and snap off the bottom flap at the end of the tail. Set the tail on its side and press gently with the heel of your hand until you hear a crunching sound. Don't press too hard. Hold the tail in a kitchen towel with the underside facing you and pull the sides apart. The underside will split open. Push the tail meat out through one end.

Remove the meat from the claws by gently wiggling the small pinchers from side to side and then pulling back so that the small piece of cartilage embedded in the claw will pull out. Hold the claw on a cutting board with the thorny underside facing up. Hack into the shell about ¼ inch with an old knife and twist sideways. The shell should crack in two.

Remove the meat from the small joints by crushing gently with the side of a knife and cutting them open with a pair of kitchen scissors. (See color page 22.)

Steamed Lobster Medallions with Saffron, Tomatoes, Basil, and Thyme

(color page 1)

The magic of basil, tomatoes, and saffron gives this lobster dish a typically Mediterranean aroma and flavor, and the bright red of the lobster tail never fails to impress. It's a great dish for summer.

Although this dish does take some time to prepare, you can make the sauce, slice the medallions in advance, and then gently reheat the medallions—covered with aluminum foil on a baking sheet—in a 200°F oven just before serving.

MAKES 4 MAIN-COURSE OR 8-FIRST COURSE SERVINGS

Four 1¼- to 1½-pound lobsters

1½ cups dry white wine

10 fresh basil leaves

1 teaspoon olive oil

3 tomatoes, peeled, seeded, and chopped

small pinch of saffron threads

½ teaspoon fresh or ¼ teaspoon dried thyme leaves

Place 4 wide soup plates in a 200°F oven. Rinse the lobsters under cold running water and slide a skewer along the underside of each tail or tie a knife to each tail with string to keep the tails straight.

Bring the wine to a rapid boil in a pot large enough to hold the 4 lobsters. Put the lobsters in the pot and cover with a tight-fitting lid. Steam over high heat for 4 minutes. Shake the pot—without removing the lid—to redistribute the lobsters and steam for 4 to 6 minutes more, depending on the size of the lobsters. When the lobsters have turned completely red, they are done. Take the lid off the lobster pot, let the steam dissipate, and take out the lobsters. Take the lobster meat out of the shells (see color page 22) and slice each of the tails into 5 medallions (or 6 if you're serving 8 people a first course). Leave the claw meat whole. Reserve the lobster meat, tightly covered with aluminum foil, on a baking dish.

Sprinkle the basil leaves with a teaspoon of olive oil to keep them from turning black and chop them finely.

Strain the lobster-steaming liquid into a small saucepan and add the tomatoes, basil, saffron, and thyme.

Shortly before serving, heat the lobster meat in a 200°F oven for about 10 minutes.

Bring the flavored lobster broth to a slow simmer and season to taste with salt and pepper. Arrange the lobster medallions and claws in the hot soup plates and ladle in the hot broth. Serve immediately.

❧

Lobster à la Nage

Lobster à la nage (loosely translated as "in the swim") is lobster that has been simmered in an aromatic vegetable broth (a court bouillon) and then served surrounded or topped with the cooked vegetables from the broth. Because the vegetables used for making the broth end up as part of the final dish, they should be cut carefully into decorative shapes such as even slices, cubes, or julienne. The liquid itself, after it's been used to cook the lobsters, can then be flavored with chopped herbs or combined with a rich sauce to create a creamy broth that can be served around the lobster.

In traditional recipes for lobster à la nage, the lobsters are cooked completely submerged in vegetable broth, but in this version a relatively small amount of vegetable broth is used so the lobsters actually steam rather than poach.

Lobster à la nage is one of the lightest ways to serve lobster. The time-consuming part—preparing the vegetables and making the broth—can be done the day before.

MAKES 4 MAIN-COURSE SERVINGS

Four 1¼- to 1½-pound lobsters

2 medium leeks, including 1 inch of green

2 large carrots, peeled

1 medium turnip, peeled

1 celery stalk

1 bouquet garni: 3 fresh thyme sprigs or ½ teaspoon dried, a small bunch of parsley, and 1 bay leaf, tied up with string (or in cheesecloth for dried thyme)

1 quart water

1 cup dry white wine

salt and pepper

1 tablespoon finely chopped parsley or chervil

Rinse the lobsters and store in the refrigerator until needed.

Cut the leeks in half lengthwise and hold them under running water while flipping through the leaves to rinse out any sand. Cut the leaves lengthwise 2 or 3 at a time into fine julienne. If the leaves are more than 4 or 5 inches long, fold them over to make them easier to julienne.

Julienne the carrots and turnip into 3-inch lengths. The easiest way to do this is to slice them with a benriner cutter (a Japanese slicer) and then with a chef's knife.

Cut the celery stalk into 4-inch lengths and julienne it as finely as possible with a chef's knife.

Combine the julienned vegetables, bouquet garni, and water in a 4-quart pot. Simmer gently, covered, for 15 minutes. Add the wine and simmer for 10 minutes more.

Strain the vegetable broth—reserving the cooked vegetables—into a pot large enough to hold the lobsters.

Cooking the Lobsters: About 15 minutes before you're ready to serve, heat the cooked vegetables over low heat in a covered saucepan with ¼ cup of the broth and bring the rest of the vegetable broth in the large pot to a simmer. Kill the lobsters by cutting the front half of their heads in half lengthwise with a large chef's knife (see box on page 169) and put them in the pot of simmering vegetable broth. Don't worry if there isn't enough liquid to cover the lobsters. Cover the pot and simmer for 6 to 8 minutes. Reach into the pot with a long spoon after 3 or 4 minutes of cooking to redistribute the lobsters.

Take the lobsters out of the pot, split them in half, and remove and discard the grain sacs. If you want to make it easier on your guests, take the meat out of the claws and arrange it on top of the split lobsters.

Arrange the lobsters in wide soup plates and scatter the hot julienned vegetables over the lobsters. Season the hot broth with salt and pepper to taste, strain it, and ladle it over the lobsters. Sprinkle the lobsters with chopped parsley.

Serve with knife, fork, and soup spoon.

Steamed Lobster with Coconut Milk and Thai Spices

(color page 2)

This delicately flavored dish is easy to prepare because the whole lobsters are simply steamed with Thai herbs and flavorings and the cooking liquid quickly turned into a sauce with a little coconut milk. Since this dish calls for only half a can of coconut milk, freeze the rest in a plastic container with a tight-fitting lid. (See the glossary for information on Asian ingredients.)

The easiest way to serve this dish is to make the sauce and slice the lobster tails in advance and then gently reheat the lobster on a baking sheet covered with aluminum foil in a 200°F oven for about 10 minutes. The lobster tails can also be cut in half lengthwise and served in the shell.

MAKES 4 MAIN-COURSE OR 8 FIRST-COURSE SERVINGS

Four 1¼- to 1½-pound lobsters

1 garlic clove, finely chopped

1 shallot, finely chopped

2-inch piece of lemongrass, finely sliced

1 cup water

1 Thai or jalapeño chili, seeded and finely chopped

1 kaffir lime leaf

2 tablespoons fresh lime juice

1 tablespoon Thai fish sauce

2 tablespoons finely chopped fresh cilantro

half a 14-ounce can unsweetened coconut milk

Rinse the lobsters under cold running water and kill them by inserting a large knife through their heads and quickly moving it forward so the front part of the head is cut in two (see box on page 169). Slide a small wooden skewer through the bottom of each of the lobster tails to keep them straight.

Combine the garlic, shallot, and lemongrass with the water in a pot large enough to hold the lobsters. Bring the water to a rapid boil over high heat, put the lobsters in the pot, and cover tightly. Steam the lobsters over high heat for 4 minutes. Shake the pot—without removing the lid—to redistribute the lobsters and steam for 4 to 6 minutes more, depending on the size of the lobsters. Take the lobsters out of the pot and take the meat out of the shells. Or you can cut the lobster tails in half, leaving the meat in the shell.

Strain the steaming liquid into a small saucepan and add the rest of the ingredients. Simmer gently for about 4 minutes.

If you've taken the meat out of the shell, slice the lobster tails into 5 medallions each (or 6 if you're serving the lobster as a first course) and arrange them and the claws in the hot soup plates. Ladle in the hot brothlike sauce.

LOBSTER STEWS

Lobsters stews taste intensely of lobster because the lobster's flavor is drawn out by simmering the shells in liquid. This liquid is then converted into a sauce used to coat the stew. Lobster stews also lend themselves to various refinements such as adding assorted vegetables—or even fruits—which make the stews beautifully colorful and stretch the flavor of the lobster. One advantage of lobster stews is that they can be made with lobster culls—lobsters missing a claw—which are less expensive.

A lobster stew is prepared by simmering the cut-up lobster in a small amount of flavorful liquid. In most recipes the lobster is cooked in oil or butter along with chopped-up aromatic vegetables—usually onions, carrots, celery, and garlic—before the liquid is added.

The simplest and most traditional way to present a lobster stew is to serve the lobster pieces in the shell, surrounded with the stewing liquid. This is fun and informal, but you'll make a mess getting the lobster out of the shell—a bib might be well advised.

In more sophisticated lobster stews the lobster is cooked lightly (until it turns red), the meat is taken out of the shell, and the shells are broken up and cooked in the stewing liquid to extract their flavor. The stewing liquid is then strained, sometimes thickened and/or flavored with other ingredients, and served as a sauce for the lobster and the other ingredients in the stew.

INGREDIENTS FOR LOBSTER STEWS

One of the best-known lobster stews is lobster *à l'Américaine*. In this classic French dish the cut-up lobster is cooked in a little butter and oil and sprinkled with chopped shallots and garlic before it is simmered with fish broth, chopped tomatoes, and cognac. Typically the sauce is then bound with flour, cream, butter, or a combination of all three. Further refinements include stirring in lobster butter made from the lobster shells and whisking in the lobster and coral taken out of the lobster as soon as it is killed.

The method for preparing lobster *à l'Américaine* can be adapted for use with different liquids, aromatic vegetables, herbs, and spices to come up with different lobster stews. An example of this easy adaptability is lobster Newburg, which is prepared in the same way as lobster *à l'Américaine* with Madeira and cream substituted for the tomatoes and cognac. Lobster *à l'Orientale* is lobster *à l'Américaine* with curry powder added to the stewing liquid. The same approach can be used to prepare lobster dishes with ingredients from different parts of the world. The one principle to remember is not to obscure the flavor of the lobster with too many strong-flavored ingredients.

PREPARING THE RAW LOBSTERS

Rinse the lobster, kill it by inserting a knife into its head, and twist off the tail and legs where they join the head (see color page 23).

SAVING THE LOBSTER CORAL AND TOMALLEY (optional)

Most female lobsters contain coral—the ovaries and egg sacs—in both the heads and tails. Lobster coral can be tricky to work with—it's very perishable and curdles quickly if overheated—but nothing will give a lobster stew such an intensely delicious lobster flavor. Whisk it into the stewing liquid just before serving.

To save the lobster coral and tomalley, put a teaspoon of wine vinegar and a teaspoon of cognac (or brandy or whiskey) in a mixing bowl. Place a strainer over the bowl. Reach into the head and tail and scoop out as much coral and tomalley as you can into the strainer and work them through the strainer with the back of a small ladle and eventually with your fingers. When all the coral and tomalley have been worked through the strainer, cover the bowl with plastic wrap and refrigerate until needed. (Lobster coral must be used the same day it is taken out of the lobster; if stored longer, it will sour.) (See color page 23.)

COOKING THE LOBSTER

If you're presenting the cooked lobsters in medallions, insert a wooden skewer along the underside of the tails to keep them straight. If you're serving a whole or half lobster tail curled up on itself, don't bother with the straightening.

In a wide pot, cook the cut up lobsters in a single layer in 2 to 3 tablespoons of oil or butter over medium to high heat until they turn red, about 10 minutes. Take out the lobster parts, set them on a plate, and add chopped flavorful vegetables such as onions, shallots, garlic, or lemongrass to the hot fat. (If the oil or butter has burned, pour it out and add fresh.) Cook the vegetables over low heat for about 10 minutes—the exact time will depend on the vegetables and how they've been cut—until they soften and release their flavor.

COOKING THE LOBSTER SHELLS

Take the lightly cooked lobster meat out of the shells, split the head in half, and remove and discard the grain sac. Put the shells and head in the pot with the cooked vegetables. Nestle a bouquet garni in with the shells (it usually contains thyme, parsley, and a bay leaf, but sometimes other herbs such as tarragon or marjoram are used instead of the thyme). Add liquid such as water, white wine, Madeira, cognac, or fish, chicken, or meat broth or wet ingredients such as tomatoes. (Tomatoes are almost always helpful because of their color.) Simmer the shells, covered, in the liquid for about 30 minutes. Break up the shells during the cooking with a cleaver held on end or a handleless rolling pin. Strain the cooking liquid into a saucepan, pressing hard to get all the liquid out of the shells and vegetables (see box).

FINISHING THE LOBSTER-STEWING LIQUID

Unless you want to keep the stew very light—surrounded with the almost souplike cooking liquid—you'll probably want to cook down the liquid to concentrate its flavor and thicken it slightly. You may also want to add a thickener such as flour (kneaded with butter), cream (reduced with cooking liquid until it thickens), butter, coconut milk, or vegetable purees such as potato, garlic, or corn.

FLAVORING THE LOBSTER SAUCE (optional)

Many European and American recipes suggest adding flavorings such as saffron, curry, or freshly chopped herbs

---

BREAKING UP AND STRAINING LOBSTER SHELLS

My favorite method for breaking up lobster shells is to use the end of a European (handleless) rolling pin or a cleaver held up on end. If you don't have either of these, wrap the shells in a towel and break them up with a mallet or hammer.

Lobster shells that have been simmered in liquid should be strained through a fine-mesh strainer so no fragments of shell get into the sauce. Because fine-mesh strainers are expensive and easily damaged by the shells, it's best to strain the mixture through a coarse strainer first. I like to use a professional cone-shaped perforated strainer (sometimes called a *china cap*) and ram the shell mixture down with the end of a rolling pin to extract the most liquid. I then strain this liquid through a fine-mesh strainer (sometimes called a *chinois*).

such as parsley, chervil, or tarragon, while Asian recipes may include lemongrass, fish sauce, and exotic spices. Any of these ingredients will add nuances to the sauce, but don't add so much of any one of these ingredients that you mask the flavor of the lobster.

ADDING LOBSTER BUTTER (optional)

Lobster butter (page 330), which can be made from the lobster shells even after they've been cooked in liquid, can be swirled into the sauce shortly before serving. Lobster butter has a strong flavor, so use it sparingly. A tablespoon is usually plenty to flavor a cup of sauce. In any case, don't follow any recipe blindly, but add lobster butter gradually to taste.

ADDING LOBSTER CORAL AND TOMALLEY (optional)

To prevent the lobster coral from curdling, combine about a tablespoon of heavy cream per lobster with the strained coral and tomalley and then combine the coral mixture with the sauce just before serving by whisking half of the hot sauce into the cold coral mixture. Return the heated coral mixture to the pan with the sauce and heat gently while whisking over low heat. The dark coral should turn the sauce a murky green color. Heat the sauce, whisking, over low heat until the murky color turns to a bright orange. Immediately remove from the heat.

COMBINING VEGETABLES WITH LOBSTER STEWS JUST BEFORE SERVING

Often the only differences among lobster stews are the vegetables added at the end. Vegetables are a good way of stretching the expensive lobster flavor in a stew. In most recipes the vegetables are cooked separately and then added to or arranged with the lobster upon serving. I like to use glazed pearl onions, small mushrooms (preferably wild, sautéed or cooked lightly in some of the lobster-cooking liquid), small mounds of lightly creamed spinach, baby artichokes, baby carrots, baby turnips, asparagus tips, French green beans, and fava beans.

PRESENTING THE LOBSTER STEW

If you need to reheat the lobster, don't let it boil for even a second, or the lobster will curl up and toughen. It's easier to reheat the lobster in the oven: Slice the tail into medallions or lengthwise in two, arrange the tail meat and claws on a buttered baking sheet, cover with aluminum foil, and then slide the pan—along with the plates—into a 200°F oven about 15 minutes before serving. The vegetables and lobster can then be arranged on the hot plates and the sauce carefully poured over and around. Unless you're serving a lobster stew with the meat in the shell, the stew will look better and be easier to handle if you put it on plates or in wide soup bowls in the kitchen.

Lobster
à l'Américaine

Despite its name, lobster à l'Américaine is decidedly French. French food writers always seem a bit uncomfortable about the name (this is too good a dish to attribute to Americans), so many insist the name is really lobster à l'armoricaine, named after a region in Brittany. This doesn't make much sense either because tomatoes (an important ingredient) are not grown in Brittany. Regardless of who gets the credit, lobster à l'américaine, which gets its flavor from slowly simmering the lobster shells with wine, cognac, and tomatoes, is magnificent. If you want to incorporate lobster coral, use only female lobsters and follow the preceding directions.

MAKES 4 MAIN-COURSE SERVINGS

Four 1¼- to 1½-pound lobsters

3 tablespoons olive oil

2 shallots, finely chopped

1 garlic clove, finely chopped

1 cup dry white wine

½ cup cognac or brandy

4 tomatoes, peeled, seeded, and chopped

½ cup chicken broth (page 344) or fish broth (page 343)

½ cup heavy cream

4 tablespoons unsalted butter

2 tablespoons lobster butter (optional; page 330)

2 tablespoons finely chopped parsley

salt and pepper

Cutting Up the Lobster (see color page 22): Rinse the lobster under cold running water. Kill the lobster by inserting a knife into its head (see box on page 169). Hold the lobster firmly by the back of the head with one hand and the base of the tail with the other and quickly twist off the tail. Snap off the claws where they join the head. Cut the head in half and remove and discard the grain sac. (If you're serving the tails cut into medallions, insert a wooden skewer along the underside of the tails to keep them straight.)

Cooking the Lobster: Heat the olive oil in a pot large enough to hold the lobster pieces in a single layer. Sauté the lobster pieces in the hot oil, with the pot covered, stirring every few minutes, until they turn red, about 10 minutes. Transfer the lobster to a bowl.

Preparing the Stewing Liquid: Add the shallots and garlic to the hot oil and stir over medium heat for about 5 minutes. Add the wine, cognac, tomatoes, and broth.

Take the lobster meat out of the shell as shown on color page 22 and put the shells in the pot with the other ingredients. Break up the shells with a cleaver or rolling pin and simmer gently for 20 minutes.

Strain the liquid in the pot first through a coarse strainer and then through a fine-mesh strainer into a saucepan. Reduce the sauce by about two thirds, until you have about ½ cup left.

Whisk in the cream and reduce the sauce again until it has the consistency you like. I recommend leaving it on the light side—about the consistency of cold heavy cream. Whisk in the unsalted butter, the lobster butter if desired, the parsley, and salt and pepper to taste. Bring to a simmer and immediately remove from the heat.

Serving the Lobster: Preheat the oven to 200°F and gently reheat the pieces of lobster covered with a sheet of aluminum foil on a buttered baking sheet. The lobster tails can be cut in half lengthwise or in medallions and arranged decoratively in flat plates or soup plates lightly coated or surrounded with the sauce. I like to serve the lobster with plenty of boiled rice.

❧

Lobster Medallions with Morels and Saffron

This is one of those dishes where 2 elegant and tasty ingredients make a perfect match. The rich smoky flavor of the morels enhances the delicate complexity of the lobster and its sauce, made with Madeira and lobster coral.

Fresh or dried morels are equally satisfying in this dish. If you're buying dried morels, select fairly large ones. If you're buying fresh morels, make sure they aren't wet—it's OK if they're a little dried out—and smell them to make sure they aren't mildewed.

This is an elaborate dish, but everything can be done earlier the same day except for incorporating the coral into the sauce and reheating the morels and lobster.

MAKES 4 MAIN-COURSE OR GENEROUS FIRST-COURSE SERVINGS

Four 1¼- to 1½-pound female lobsters

1 teaspoon good-quality wine vinegar such as sherry or balsamic

1 teaspoon cognac or brandy

½ pound fresh morels or 1 ounce dried

1 cup Madeira or dry white wine

2 tablespoons olive oil

2 tablespoons unsalted butter

2 shallots, finely chopped

1 garlic clove, finely chopped

3 fresh thyme sprigs or ¼ teaspoon dried

3 tomatoes, peeled, seeded, and chopped

1½ cups chicken broth (page 344) or water

½ cup heavy cream

small pinch of saffron threads, soaked in 1 tablespoon water for 30 minutes

2 tablespoons finely chopped parsley

salt and pepper

Rinse and kill the lobsters (see box on page 169), remove the tails and claws, and split the head—being sure to remove the grain sacs. Strain the coral and tomalley into a bowl containing the vinegar and cognac. Refrigerate. Insert a skewer along the underside of each of the lobster tails.

If you're using fresh morels, rinse them quickly under cold water and dry them immediately with paper towels. If you're using dried morels, rinse them quickly under cold water and soak them in the Madeira or white wine for 30 minutes. Squeeze the morels—saving any wine that drips out—and set them on a plate. If the wine is full of sand, let it settle and carefully pour it into a clean bowl, leaving the sand behind.

Cook the lobster parts in olive oil over medium heat in a pot just large enough to hold them in a single layer. Cover the pot and keep turning the lobster parts over every couple of minutes until they have all turned red, about 10 minutes.

Take the lobster out of the pot, let it cool, and take the meat out of the shell as explained in the box on page 169 and shown on color page 22. Slice each of the tails into 5 medallions and reserve in the refrigerator.

Add the butter, shallots, garlic, thyme, and lobster shells to the pan used for cooking the lobster and cook, stirring, over medium heat for about 5 minutes. Add the tomatoes, Madeira, any liquid drained off from the morels, and the broth. Break the shells up with a cleaver or rolling pin. Cover the pot and simmer gently for 20 minutes, reaching in every few minutes to stir and break up the shells some more.

Strain the lobster-shell mixture first through a coarse strainer, then through a fine-mesh one into a saucepan. Reduce the liquid to about ¾ cup, add the morels, and simmer gently, covered, for 5 minutes. Scoop the morels into a bowl with a slotted spoon. Add the cream to the liquid in the pan and reduce it until it has the consistency of cold heavy cream—not too thick. Whisk a ladleful of this hot cream mixture into the reserved coral mixture. Take the saucepan off the heat to allow the sauce to cool slightly and then whisk the coral mixture into the sauce. Set the sauce aside without reheating.

Just Before Serving: Heat wide soup plates, the morels (covered with aluminum foil in a bowl), and the lobster (on a buttered baking sheet, covered with foil) in a 200°F oven for 15 minutes.

Stir the saffron with its soaking water and the parsley into the reserved sauce. Whisk the sauce over low heat until the coral turns it bright orange. Don't let the sauce approach the boil, or the coral will curdle. Season to taste with salt and pepper.

Lightly coat the bottom of each plate with sauce and arrange the lobster pieces and morels on top. Spoon over any remaining sauce.

LOBSTER SOUPS

Most lobster soups are made in much the same way as stews—the lobster is cooked lightly, the meat is taken out of the shells, and the shells are used to make a broth to which the lobster meat is added shortly before serving. Herbs, vegetables, and spices can be added to a lobster soup to give it a particular flavor or character.

❧

Lobster Bisque

Lobster bisque, once the hallmark of expensive French restaurants, is less appreciated than it once was, probably because bisques are quite rich. This is a pity, for lobster bisque, when well made, captures the essence of lobster and ends up tasting more like lobster than lobster itself.

A lobster bisque is prepared in almost the same way as lobster *à l'Américaine*, except that more liquid is used and a bisque is thickened with either rice or bread crumbs. Recipes vary—some suggest pureeing some of the lobster meat, while others add the lobster, cut into chunks, just before serving. Some versions add lobster butter and a large amount of unflavored butter, while still others, such as this one, suggest incorporating the lobster coral.

If you incorporate the raw lobster coral, which is very perishable, into the soup just before serving, this recipe must be made the same day it is served. An alternative method is to leave the coral in the lobster at the beginning so that it cooks along with the other ingredients. This way you can make this soup up to 3 days in advance.

Three 1¼-pound female lobsters

2 tablespoons plus 1 teaspoon cognac or brandy

1 teaspoon good-quality wine vinegar such as sherry or balsamic

½ cup Italian short-grain rice such as Arborio, Carnaroli, or Vialone Nano

5 cups fish broth (page 343) or chicken broth (page 344)

1 medium onion, finely chopped

1 carrot, finely chopped

½ celery stalk, finely chopped

1 garlic clove, chopped

2 tablespoons unsalted butter

2 cups dry white wine

1 bouquet garni: 3 fresh thyme sprigs or ½ teaspoon dried, a small bunch of parsley, and a bay leaf tied up with string (or in cheesecloth for dried thyme)

½ cup heavy cream

4 tablespoons lobster butter (page 330) or unsalted butter

pinch of cayenne pepper

salt

Rinse the lobsters, kill them by inserting a knife in their heads (see color page 23), and twist off their tails. Snap off the claws where they join the head. Split the head in two and pull out and discard the grain sac from each half. Pull the coral and tomalley out of the tail and head. Work the coral and tomalley through a fine-mesh strainer into a bowl containing 1 teaspoon cognac and the vinegar. Refrigerate until needed.

Cook the rice, covered, in a small saucepan with half the broth until it has completely softened—in fact overcooked—about 30 minutes.

Cook the chopped vegetables in butter over medium heat in a pot large enough to hold the lobsters. When the vegetables have softened but not browned, about 8 minutes, put in the lobster pieces, 2 tablespoons cognac, the white wine, the remaining broth, and the bouquet garni. Cover the pot and simmer gently until the lobster pieces have turned a deep red, about 10 minutes. Turn off the heat, let the lobsters cool (out of the broth), and remove the meat from the lobsters as shown on color page 22.

Put the lobster shells in the pot with the vegetables and break up the shells with the end of a European (handleless) rolling pin or a cleaver held up on end. Cover the pot and simmer gently for 20 minutes. Strain the mixture first through a coarse strainer and then through a fine-mesh one into a clean pot and discard the shells. While the lobster shells are simmering, cut the lobster meat into small dice and reserve.

Puree the rice with any broth left in the pot in a blender for about 1 minute. Combine with the lobster mixture and strain the soup through a fine-mesh strainer.

Whisk the cream into the coral mixture. Bring the soup to a gentle simmer and whisk in the lobster butter. Whisk the soup into the coral/cream mixture, return everything to the pot, and heat the bisque gently without letting it boil. Add cayenne, the diced lobster, and salt to taste.

AVOIDING CANNED CHICKEN BROTH

Canned chicken broth works for most soup recipes or in recipes where the liquid ingredients aren't cooked down. In recipes calling for a lot of salt or that have you reducing (boiling down) liquids to concentrate their flavor, canned broth should be avoided because it's too salty. This is also true of "low-sodium" versions.

❧

Cold Lobster Soup with Cucumbers and Dill

*B*ecause lobster is least expensive in the summer, I often end up serving it in salads or cold soups. Almost any lobster soup can be served cold, but it should be thinner than if you were serving it hot. For a cold lobster bisque, for example, use only half the rice.

Here a flavorful lobster broth is served over a cold gazpacholike cucumber soup and the lobster medallions and claws are arranged on top—a luxurious and elegant first course to be served in small quantities.

The lobster broth is flavored with dill, but you can substitute tarragon, mint, or chives. Each part of this soup can be made a day ahead and the final presentation put together just before serving.

MAKES 8 FIRST-COURSE SERVINGS

For the Cold Lobster Broth:

Four 1¼ -pound female lobsters

2 tablespoons plus 1 teaspoon cognac or brandy

1 teaspoon good-quality wine vinegar such as balsamic or sherry

1 medium onion, finely chopped

1 carrot, finely chopped

½ celery stalk, finely chopped

1 garlic clove, chopped

2 tablespoons unsalted butter

2 cups dry white wine

3 cups fish broth (page 343), chicken broth (page 344), or water

½ cup heavy cream

2 teaspoons finely chopped fresh dill

For the Cold Cucumber Soup:

2 long European cucumbers or 4 regular cucumbers

2 teaspoons salt

¼ teaspoon cayenne pepper or 2 teaspoons Tabasco sauce

For Finishing the Soup:

1 tablespoon finely chopped fresh chives

Preparing the Lobster Broth: Kill the lobsters by splitting the head in two lengthwise with a chef's knife (see color page 23). Discard the grain sac in each half of the head, snap off the claws, twist off the tails, and strain the coral and tomalley into a bowl containing 1 teaspoon cognac and the vinegar. Reserve the tomalley and coral mixture in a bowl covered with plastic wrap in the refrigerator. Insert a skewer along the bottom of the lobster tails to keep them straight.

Cook the vegetables in butter in a 6-quart pot over medium heat for 10 minutes, until they soften. Add the lobster pieces, 2 tablespoons cognac, and the wine. Cover the pot and simmer gently, stirring every couple of minutes, until the lobster parts all turn red, about 10 minutes. Remove the lobster parts and take the meat out of the shells as shown on color page 22. Return the shells to the pot with the vegetables and wine and break them up with a handleless rolling pin or a cleaver held up on end. Pour in the broth, cover the pot, and simmer for 20 minutes, crushing the shells every now and then with the rolling pin or cleaver. Strain the shell mixture first through a coarse strainer (to get rid of the shells that can damage a delicate strainer) and then through a fine-mesh strainer into a saucepan. The shells can be discarded or saved in the freezer for making lobster butter.

Boil down the lobster broth over medium heat until only 2½ cups remain. Stir in the cream, bring to a slow simmer, and whisk the broth into the coral mixture. Return the broth/coral mixture to the saucepan over low heat and whisk until the sauce turns orange. Don't let the sauce boil, or it will curdle. Stir in the dill and chill the soup over ice or in the refrigerator.

Slice the lobster tails into 4 or 6 medallions each, cover with plastic wrap, and refrigerate until needed.

Preparing the Cucumber Soup: Peel the cucumbers and cut them in half lengthwise. Scoop out the seeds with a small spoon. Finely dice the cucumbers by hand or in a food processor—not so finely that they turn into puree. Toss the cucumbers with the salt and drain them in a colander set over a bowl in the refrigerator for about 30 minutes. Squeeze small handfuls of the cucumbers to eliminate juice and salt. Season the cucumbers to taste with cayenne and refrigerate until you're ready to serve.

Presenting the Finished Soup: Stir the cucumber "soup" and spread it evenly in chilled wide soup plates. Carefully place a small ladleful of the chilled lobster broth in the middle of each bowl. Arrange the lobster medallions around the broth and the claws in the middle. Place a tiny pinch of chopped chives on top of each lobster medallion.

❧

Indian Lobster Soup with Red Lentils, Coconut Milk, and Spinach

*E*ven though I don't know if there is an authentic Indian soup just like this one, this soup does have the flavor of many authentic Indian dishes and also captures the flavor of the lobster.

MAKES 8 FIRST-COURSE SERVINGS

2 medium onions, chopped

3 garlic cloves, chopped

2 Thai chilies, seeded and finely chopped

2 tablespoons peanut or vegetable oil

2 tablespoons ground coriander

1 teaspoon ground cumin

1 teaspoon ground turmeric

1 teaspoon ground fenugreek

1 tablespoon paprika

⅛ teaspoon ground cloves

¼ teaspoon ground cinnamon

6 tomatoes, peeled, seeded, and chopped

3½ cups water, chicken broth (page 344), or fish broth (page 343)

Four 1¼-pound lobsters, preferably female, heads halved lengthwise and grain sacs discarded, claws and tails removed but not cracked

½ cup red lentils or yellow split peas, rinsed

2 cups water

1 cup plain yogurt

½ cup heavy cream

leaves from 1 bunch of spinach, blanched in boiling water for 30 seconds, rinsed with cold water, drained, and coarsely chopped

2 tablespoons finely chopped fresh cilantro

salt

Up to a Day in Advance: Cook the onions, garlic, and chilies in peanut oil in a 4-quart pot over medium heat for about 10 minutes, stirring occasionally, until the onions turn translucent. Add the ground spices and stir over medium heat for about 2 minutes, until you can smell the fragrance of the spices. Stir in the tomatoes and simmer very gently, covered, over low heat for about 20 minutes. Remove from the heat.

While the tomatoes are cooking, bring the 3½ cups water to a rapid boil in a pot large enough to hold the lobsters. Rinse the lobsters, put them in the pot (there won't be enough liquid to submerge them), and cover tightly. Steam for 8 minutes, uncover, remove from the heat, and let cool for about 10 minutes.

Combine the lentils with 2 cups of water in a 4-quart pot and simmer gently, covered, for about 30 minutes, until the lentils are completely soft, even overcooked.

Remove the meat from the lobsters as shown on color page 22, cut it into ½-inch cubes, and reserve in the refrigerator. Break up the lobster shells with a heavy chef's knife, rolling pin, or cleaver and return the broken-up shells to the pot with the lobster-steaming liquid. Cover the pot and simmer gently for about 20 minutes to extract the flavor from the shells. Strain this broth first through a coarse strainer and then through a fine-mesh strainer into the tomato/spice mixture. Discard the shells.

Puree the cooked lentils and their cooking liquid together with the tomato/spice mixture in a blender.

Just Before Serving: Whisk together the yogurt and cream and stir it into the pureed lentil/tomato/ spice mixture. Stir in the reserved lobster meat, chopped spinach, and cilantro. Season with salt to taste and serve immediately in hot bowls.

LOBSTER CONSOMMÉ This is one of those dishes that I prepare for only the most formal occasions. I don't know why this is exactly (lots of dishes are more complicated to make), but there's something 19th century and refined about consommé and even more refined about lobster consommé.

Lobster consommé can be approached in one of two ways. You can prepare a rich consommé with either fish or meat and simply garnish it with slices or cubes of cooked lobster, or you can prepare a flavorful broth with the lobster shells and coral and then clarify it. This latter method is the more complicated, but it's the only way of actually working some of the lobster flavor into the bouillon. I sometimes take a third approach and serve lobster consommé cold and lightly gelled and then make a creamy vinaigrette with the lobster shells and coral, which is then spooned over the consommé either in the kitchen or by the guests.

Whichever approach you take, use the richest broth you can afford to make (in time or money).

❧

Cold Lobster Consommé with Coral Vinaigrette

*I*f you want to serve this consommé hot, skip the vinaigrette, which would just cloud a hot consommé, and combine the reserved coral with the clarification mixture.

Because of the lobster coral, which is very perishable, this con-

sommé has to be prepared the day it is served. But the most time-consuming component—the beef broth—can be prepared days ahead and kept in the refrigerator or prepared weeks ahead and frozen. Or substitute chicken broth, which cooks in half the time of beef broth, or fish broth, which cooks even faster.

MAKES 8 FIRST-COURSE SERVINGS

For the Beef Broth:

4 pounds beef shanks, cut into 2-inch-thick rounds

6 tablespoons olive oil

2 medium carrots, sliced

2 medium onions, sliced

1 celery stalk, sliced

2 garlic cloves, crushed

2 cups dry white wine

1 bouquet garni: 3 fresh thyme sprigs or ½ teaspoon dried, a small bunch of parsley, and a bay leaf tied up with string (or in cheesecloth for dried thyme)

For the Clarification:

Three 1¼-pound female lobsters

1 teaspoon cognac or brandy

1 teaspoon good-quality wine vinegar such as balsamic or sherry

5 egg whites

2 tomatoes, seeded and chopped

1 small bunch of parsley, coarsely chopped

1 tablespoon fresh tarragon leaves

salt

For the Coral Vinaigrette:

1 teaspoon wine vinegar

1 teaspoon cognac

½ cup heavy cream

3 tablespoons sherry vinegar or more to taste

1 tablespoon finely chopped fresh herbs such as parsley, chives, or tarragon

salt and pepper

For Finishing the Consommé:

1 tablespoon finely chopped fresh chives

Preparing the Beef Broth: Brown the beef shanks on both sides in half the olive oil in a heavy pot over high heat. If the pot isn't big enough to hold them in a single layer, brown them in 2 batches. Take out the shanks and replace the burned oil with fresh. Cook the vegetables over medium heat for 15 minutes, until they soften. Put the shanks back in the pot over the vegetables, pour in the wine, and boil over high heat until the wine completely evaporates—be careful not to overdo it and burn the juices. (This step may take 20 minutes or so, but it's important because it causes the meat to release its juices, which in turn lightly caramelize on the bottom of the pot, creating more flavor. This method also causes any fat to separate from the liquid—fat that would cloud the broth.) When the wine has evaporated, pour in enough cold water to cover the meat by 1 inch and bring to a slow simmer. Skim off any fat or froth with a ladle and nestle the bouquet garni under one of the shanks. Simmer very gently for 5 hours, adding water as needed to keep the meat covered. Strain the broth and skim off any fat that has floated to the surface—you should end up with about 2 quarts of broth. The easiest way to do this is to refrigerate the broth and take off the congealed fat with a spoon. (The meat from the shanks is great served cold and makes a wonderful ravioli stuffing, shredded and flavored with plenty of fresh marjoram.)

Preparing the Lobster and Clarifying the Beef Broth: Bring the beef broth to a simmer in a pot large enough to hold the cut-up lobsters. Using a ladle, skim off any froth that floats to the top.

Kill the lobsters (see box on page 169), break them into pieces, and slide a skewer into the tails to keep the tails straight (see box on page 172). Strain the coral and tomalley into a bowl containing the cognac and vinegar and refrigerate. Simmer the lobster parts in the covered pot with the simmering broth for 5 minutes. If the lobster parts aren't completely covered with broth, stir them around every minute or two with a spoon so they cook evenly. Take the lobster out of the broth with a slotted spoon and let cool. Remove the broth from the stove.

Take the lobster meat out of the shells as shown on color page 22. Wrap the shells in a towel and break them apart with a rolling pin. Combine them with the egg whites, tomatoes, parsley, and tarragon (and the coral mixture if you're serving the consommé hot) in a large mixing bowl. Work the mixture with your hands to break up the egg whites. Pour half of the warm broth (not hot) over the lobster-shell mixture and then return the mixture to the pot. Whisk the mixture vigorously to distribute the egg white mixture into the broth. Bring the broth to a slow simmer and simmer gently for 30 minutes, repositioning the pot on the burner so each area of consommé ends up getting the same amount of heat. The egg white mixture should have coagulated into a solid mass surrounded with perfectly clear consommé.

Carefully strain the consommé through a fine-mesh sieve and again through a cloth napkin or triple layer of cheesecloth. Season with salt to taste. Cool in the refrigerator or over a bowl of ice, which will work more quickly.

Preparing the Coral Vinaigrette: Combine all the vinaigrette ingredients except the salt and pepper with the strained chilled lobster coral and whisk the mixture in a saucepan (preferably one with sloping sides) over medium heat until the coral turns orange. Don't let the mixture boil. Let the sauce cool and season to taste with more vinegar (if needed), salt, and pepper. Keep covered in the refrigerator with plastic wrap until needed.

Finishing and Serving the Consommé: If the consommé has set, heat it just enough to melt it and stir in the chopped chives. Arrange the lobster tails—cut into medallions—and the claws in the bottom of soup bowls. You can ladle on the warm consommé and place the bowls in the refrigerator until the consommé sets or just scoop the gelled consommé into the bowls over the lobster. Serve the coral vinaigrette in a sauceboat at the table.

LOBSTER IN ASPIC

Few people realize that an authentic aspic can delicately capture the flavor of some of our favorite foods and, when well made, has a delicate melt-in-your-mouth texture. Except for the fact that it is sometimes used to coat foods, aspic is virtually the same as cold consommé. The simplest aspic—so-called natural aspic—is simply clear broth that has been allowed to set. When the broth is full-bodied, you won't need to add much or any gelatin—the natural gelatin will be enough. And in fact the only mistake you can make is to add large amounts of commercial gelatin. Aspic should barely hold together when chilled so

that it will melt in the mouth without any hint of rubberiness.

The easiest way to serve lobster in a natural aspic is to make the preceding consommé, use it to line individual molds, arrange pieces of lobster inside each aspic-lined mold, and then fill the molds with the barely set aspic. I usually include other ingredients such as pieces of cooked artichoke, cooked mushrooms, or truffles to make the texture and color more interesting and to add a little crunch.

❧

Individual Lobster Aspics with Artichokes and Chervil

If you can, serve these in a garden under an arbor or in a candlelit dining room so that the aspic catches the light and glitters.

This recipe calls for the coral vinaigrette from the preceding recipe, which means you have to cook the lobsters the same day. To make the aspics a day or two ahead, just leave the coral in the lobsters at the beginning and forget about the sauce; it isn't essential.

To make this dish you'll need 8 individual molds such as ½-cup dariole molds (shaped like large cocktail jiggers) or ½-cup ramekins. Because of their subtle and complex flavor, I serve these aspics with the most special wines I can afford at the moment—especially well-aged Champagne, Chablis, or Meursault.

continued

MAKES 8 FIRST-COURSE SERVINGS

1 recipe plain lobster consommé (preceding recipe)

2 tablespoons finely chopped fresh chervil or parsley

salt

4 large artichokes

1 tablespoon olive oil

juice of 1 lemon

meat from 3 lobsters used to prepare the consommé

1 small black truffle, cut into ¼-inch cubes (optional)

1 recipe coral vinaigrette (preceding recipe)

Put the consommé on the stove to simmer, carefully skimming off any foam that floats to the top. When the consommé has cooked down by half, after about 40 minutes, remove from the heat, stir in the chervil, season with salt to taste, and let cool. When the consommé is no longer hot, refrigerate it until it is well chilled but not set.

Prepare artichoke bottoms as described on page 144 and simmer them in a nonaluminum pot in a large amount of water containing the olive oil and all but a teaspoon of the lemon juice until they are just slightly firmer

than boiled potatoes for potato salad, about 20 minutes. Pour them into a colander and let cool, then carefully pull out the choke with a spoon. Or just cook the artichokes whole (maybe serve them the night before) and eat your way down to the hearts. Cut the artichoke bottoms into ⅓-inch cubes and toss them with the remaining lemon juice.

Slice the lobster tails into thin medallions and cut the claws into ¼-inch cubes. Reserve in the refrigerator.

Hold the molds upright in a tray of ice water and line the bottoms of the molds with an ⅛-inch coating of aspic. You can also line the sides, but this gets tedious.

Arrange the pieces of lobster, artichoke, and truffle in the lined molds. Chill the remaining consommé in a bowl set over ice until the consommé is cool but not set. Fill the molds with the consommé. Chill the molds in the refrigerator for 3 hours to set the aspic.

When you're ready to serve, dip the molds in a bowl of hot water and unmold them onto chilled plates. Serve the vinaigrette at the table or put a small spoonful on each plate.

LOBSTER SOUFFLÉS

The easiest way to make a lobster soufflé is to treat it in the same way as most other savory soufflés—by making a stiff béchamel and folding it with pieces of cooked lobster and beaten egg whites. A second method is to make a mousseline—made by working cream into the pureed raw lobster—and bake in a well-buttered and floured soufflé mold. I'm not crazy about either method—the béchamel method doesn't capture the flavor of the lobster, and the mousseline method is tedious with just so-so results.

My favorite approach is to make a flavorful broth with the lobster shells as though I were making a bisque or a lobster stew and then thicken the reduced broth with flour and the lobster coral. This flavorful mixture is then folded with beaten egg whites and pieces of cooked lobster meat and baked in buttered and floured soufflé dishes. Older recipes suggest splitting the lobster in two lengthwise and then baking the soufflé in the shell, but I've never been able to get it to look right and prefer just serving the soufflés in individual molds.

USING COMMERCIAL GELATIN

If you find that your finished consommé doesn't set firmly enough once it is well chilled, you can continue to simmer it to concentrate the gelatin further, though you may end up with less consommé than you need—albeit with more concentrated flavor. Alternatively, you can add packaged gelatin to the warmed consommé. The problem is that you must be very careful not to add too much, and it's sometimes hard to judge how much natural gelatin is already in the consommé. My favorite solution is to gently warm 1 cup of the consommé and dissolve in it half the amount of gelatin recommended on the package (¾ teaspoon or ½ envelope gelatin). I then chill this mixture, and if it's too rubbery when set or not set enough, I adjust the amount of gelatin I add to the remaining consommé. Packaged gelatin should be soaked for 30 minutes in a tablespoon or two of cold water before it is incorporated into hot liquids.

Individual Lobster Soufflés

MAKES 6 FIRST-COURSE SERVINGS

Three 1¼-pound female lobsters

2 tablespoons plus 1 teaspoon cognac
or brandy

1 teaspoon good-quality wine vinegar
such as balsamic or sherry

1 medium onion, finely chopped

1 carrot, finely chopped

½ celery stalk, finely chopped

1 garlic clove, chopped

2 tablespoons unsalted butter

2 cups dry white wine

3 cups fish broth (page 343), chicken broth
(page 344), or water

2 heaped tablespoons all-purpose flour

2 tablespoons lobster butter (page 330) or
unsalted butter

½ cup heavy cream

3 tablespoons softened unsalted butter for
the molds

3 tablespoons all-purpose flour for the
molds

2 quarts water

10 egg whites

pinch of cream of tartar (unless you're
using a copper bowl)

Kill the lobsters by splitting the head in two lengthwise with a chef's knife as shown on color page 23. Discard the grain sac in each half of the head, snap off the claws, twist off the tails, and strain the coral and tomalley into a bowl containing 1 teaspoon cognac and the vinegar. Reserve the tomalley and coral mixture in a bowl covered with plastic wrap in the refrigerator.

In a pot large enough to hold the lobsters, cook the vegetables in butter over medium heat for 10 minutes—until they soften. Add the lobster parts, 2 tablespoons cognac, the wine, and the broth. Cover the pot and simmer gently until the lobster parts all turn red, 8 to 10 minutes. Remove the lobster parts and take the meat out of the shells as shown on color page 22. Return the shells to the pot with the vegetables and break them up with the end of a handleless rolling pin or a cleaver held on end. Cover the pot and simmer the lobster broth for 20 minutes. Strain first through a coarse strainer and then through a fine-mesh strainer and reserve. Cut the cooked lobster meat into ½-inch cubes and reserve.

In a 2-quart saucepan, whisk together the flour and lobster butter over medium heat for about 3 minutes to make a roux. Whisk in the reserved lobster broth. Reduce this lobster sauce over medium heat until only 1 cup remains. Stir in the cream and reduce again to a cup. Whisk the sauce into the coral mixture and return it to low heat while whisking until the sauce turns orange. Don't let the sauce boil, or it will curdle. Remove the sauce from the heat to let it cool slightly while you prepare the molds and beat the egg whites.

Preheat the oven to 400°F. Brush six 10-ounce soufflé or charlotte molds with softened butter and coat them with flour. Turn the molds upside down and tap them to shake out any excess flour—but be sure the molds are completely coated. Don't touch the inside of the molds at any point. Refrigerate the molds.

Bring the water to a boil. Beat the egg whites to stiff peaks, adding the cream of tartar before beating if you're not using a copper bowl. Fold the lobster sauce with the egg whites. Sprinkle on the pieces of lobster while folding and completely fill the molds with the mixture. Smooth the surface, make a small moat around the outside with your thumb, and place the soufflés in a rectangular pan. Pour in the boiling water—it should come at least a third of the way up the sides of the molds—and bake the soufflés until they've risen about 1½ inches above the rim of the mold, 15 to 20 minutes. Serve immediately.

JUDGING DONENESS

It is sometimes hard to tell when a soufflé is ready to take out of the oven. Because soufflés rise differently depending on what they contain—soufflés containing rich ingredients tend to rise less—it's difficult to judge doneness by how much the soufflés have risen.

One method is to gently jiggle the soufflé back and forth and see if it holds firm or if it seems to be liquid underneath. Because soufflés are less delicate than people usually think, it's also safe to open the oven, stick a knife into the side of one of the soufflés, and peek inside to see if it is done. But remember, soufflés should be very moist and airy inside. If you try to cook them all the way through, they will fall and taste dry.

Lobster Risotto

(color page 2)

Seafood risotto is very popular in Italy, but the closest version to a lobster risotto is made with Mediterranean spiny lobster (langoustine) rather than authentic lobster from the Atlantic coast. In the United States I like to make risotto out of Maine lobster. In most Italian versions the spiny lobster is precooked, cut into chunks, and stirred into the rice. Although there's certainly nothing wrong with risotto made in this way, very little of the creature's flavor actually makes it into the rice.

In this version a flavorful broth is made out of the lobster shells and then used to cook the rice. The lobster coral and meat are incorporated into the risotto just before serving.

Although the risotto itself must be prepared just before serving, the lobster broth and coral mixture can be made earlier in the day. Serve this risotto Italian style—as a first course—not as an accompaniment or side dish.

MAKES 6 FIRST-COURSE SERVINGS

Two 1¼-pound female lobsters

2 tablespoons plus 1 teaspoon cognac or brandy

1 teaspoon good-quality wine vinegar such as balsamic or sherry

1 medium onion, finely chopped

1 carrot, finely chopped

½ celery stalk, finely chopped

1 garlic clove, chopped

¼ pound unsalted butter

2 cups dry white wine

2 cups fish broth (page 343) or chicken broth (page 344)

1 small onion, finely chopped

2 cups Italian short-grain rice such as Vialone Nano, Arborio, or Carnaroli

salt and pepper

Kill the lobsters by splitting the heads in half lengthwise with a chef's knife (see box on page 169). Twist off the tails and claws and discard the grain sac from each half of the head. Remove the tomalley and coral from inside the tails and heads and strain it into a bowl with 1 teaspoon cognac and the vinegar and reserve, covered with plastic wrap, in the refrigerator.

In a pot large enough to hold the lobsters, cook the vegetables in 2 tablespoons butter over medium heat for 10 minutes—until they soften. Add the lobster parts, 2 tablespoons cognac, the wine, and the broth. Cover the pot and simmer gently until the lobster parts all turn red, 8 to 10 minutes. Remove the lobster parts and take the meat out of the shells as shown on color page 22. Return the shells to the pot with the vegetables and break them up with the end of a handleless rolling pin or a cleaver held on end. Cover the pot and simmer the lobster broth for 20 minutes. Strain the broth first through a coarse strainer and then through a fine-mesh strainer and reserve. Cut the cooked lobster meat into ½-inch cubes and reserve.

Gently cook the small onion in 3 tablespoons butter in a heavy 4-quart pot for about 10 minutes, until it's translucent but not browned. Stir in the rice and ½ cup of the lobster broth. Continue stirring over medium heat until the lobster broth is absorbed. Keep repeating this process, adding the lobster broth ½ cup at a time, for about 20 minutes, until all the broth has been absorbed. If you've run out of broth before the rice has softened, stir in some water. (A cup of Arborio rice absorbs about 3 cups of liquid.) When the rice is ready, remove it from the heat and stir in the remaining 3 tablespoons butter, the lobster meat, and the coral mixture. Season with salt and pepper to taste and serve immediately on hot plates.

COLD LOBSTER AND LOBSTER SALADS

Cooked lobster combined with salad greens, lightly cooked vegetables, or other seafood is perfectly satisfying when tossed with a light vinaigrette or mayonnaise but much more dramatic in a cold sauce made out of the lobster shells and coral. There are several ways to prepare a cold lobster sauce. One of the easiest is the coral vinaigrette on page 187, but an even deeper-flavored and more elaborate sauce can be made by cooking the lobster shells with wine and aromatic vegetables, reducing this cooking liquid to ¼ cup, and then adding it to the coral vinaigrette. As a third method, you can prepare a light mayonnaise, flavor it with reduced lobster-shell-cooking liquid and/or lobster coral, and then whisk it over the heat just long enough to cook the coral and turn the mayonnaise orange. Finely chopped herbs can then be added to the mayonnaise for flavor and extra color, and the mayonnaise can be thinned to the right consistency with a little vinegar or lightened with whipped cream. You can also make a simple and cholesterol-free vinaigrette by gently cooking the lobster coral from 4 female lobsters in ½ cup olive oil—until the oil turns red—and then straining the oil and using it to make a vinaigrette. Cooked and strained tomato puree can be added to any of these sauces to round out the flavor and intensify the natural orange color of the lobsters.

Cold Lobster with Coral Sauce and Basil Pesto

This is an elegant and simple way to serve lobster, and because of the sauce the lobster flavor is very intense. The green basil pesto looks dramatic swirled into the pink lobster sauce and gives the dish a special fragrant vitality. Other fresh herbs such as mint or cilantro can also be used to make the pesto.

Each element for this dish can be prepared the day before and everything then assembled at the last minute. In this recipe the lobster is cooked less than usual so that it stays tender and slightly translucent.

MAKES 4 GENEROUS FIRST-COURSE SERVINGS

Four 1¼-pound female lobsters

½ cup dry white wine

½ cup water

For the Coral Vinaigrette:

1 teaspoon wine vinegar

1 teaspoon cognac

½ cup heavy cream

3 tablespoons sherry vinegar or more to taste

1 tablespoon finely chopped fresh herbs such as parsley, chives, or tarragon

salt and pepper

20 large fresh basil leaves

3 tablespoons extra-virgin olive oil

salt and white pepper

1 teaspoon finely chopped fresh chives or parsley

Kill the lobsters, separate the tails and claws from the head, and split the head in half, being sure to discard the grain sac as shown on color page 23.

Remove and save the coral for the vinaigrette and slide a skewer into the underside of each lobster tail. Steam the lobster parts in a covered pot with the wine and water until the lobster turns red, about 8 minutes.

Strain the lobster-cooking liquid into a saucepan and reduce it to ¼ cup. Prepare the coral vinaigrette, adding the reduced lobster-cooking liquid while cooking the other ingredients.

Preparing the Coral Vinaigrette: Combine all the vinaigrette ingredients except the salt and pepper with the strained chilled lobster coral and whisk the mixture in a saucepan (preferably one with sloping sides) over medium heat until the coral turns orange. Don't let the mixture boil. Let the sauce cool and season to taste with more vinegar (if needed), salt, and pepper. Keep covered in the refrigerator with plastic wrap until needed.

Sprinkle the basil leaves with a teaspoon of the olive oil to keep them from turning black and chop them very finely with a knife or in a miniature food processor. If you're using a food processor add a tablespoon or two of water to the basil leaves to get them to turn around. Combine the chopped leaves with the rest of the oil in a small mixing bowl.

Take the lobster meat out of the shells as shown on color page 22 and cut the tails into neat medallions. Season the lobster with salt and pepper.

Coat the bottom of chilled plates or soup plates with the coral vinaigrette. Use a teaspoon to swirl or lightly dollop the basil pesto over the coral sauce. Arrange the lobster medallions and claws over the sauces and place a tiny pinch of chopped chives on each medallion.

Grilled Vegetable and Lobster Salad

For this simple salad vegetables are grilled and combined with cooked lobster tails and claws just before serving—an irresistible summer main or first course. The sauce can be as simple as some extra-virgin olive oil combined with a little wine vinegar or an elaborate lobster coral vinaigrette. Just be sure it is thin enough so that it doesn't mask the color of the vegetables. To make this dish a little more sophisticated, sprinkle each vegetable with a different chopped fresh herb. Fresh leafy greens can also be tossed with the grilled vegetables.

The quantities given for the assembled vegetables are based on using at least 5. If you choose fewer, increase the amounts proportionately.

MAKES 4 MAIN-COURSE OR GENEROUS FIRST-COURSE SERVINGS

Four 1¼-pound lobsters, female if you're making coral vinaigrette

½ cup dry white wine

½ cup water

5 tablespoons of an appropriate sauce such as lobster coral vinaigrette (this page), a simple vinaigrette (just olive oil, wine vinegar, salt, and pepper), plain mayonnaise (page 333), or mayonnaise flavored with lobster coral

assorted vegetables: 20 pearl onions (peeled), ½ pound small cultivated or wild mushrooms, 20 asparagus tips (blanched for 1 minute in boiling water), 4 large artichoke hearts or 20 baby artichokes (outer leaves trimmed), or 20 bottled artichoke hearts, ½ pound *haricots verts*, 1 medium zucchini (cut into small chunks or lengthwise strips), 1 narrow Italian-style eggplant, 1 small bunch of escarole, 1 medium head of radicchio, etc.

continued

extra-virgin olive oil to coat the vegetables

fresh chopped herbs to taste

finely chopped garlic to taste

salt and pepper

small handful of tiny chervil sprigs
  (optional)

Kill the lobsters by splitting their heads in half with a chef's knife (see box on page 169). Twist off the tails and snap off the claws. Discard the grain sac from each half of the lobster heads. Remove and save the coral and tomalley for the vinaigrette and slide a skewer into the underside of each of the lobster tails. Steam the lobster parts in a covered pot with the wine and water until the lobster turns red, about 8 minutes.

Strain the lobster-cooking liquid into a saucepan and reduce to $1/4$ cup. Prepare the coral vinaigrette (see page 187), adding the reduced lobster-cooking liquid while cooking the other ingredients.

Marinate the vegetables in the oil with herbs and garlic for 1 to 2 hours.

Season with salt and pepper to taste.

Take the lobster meat out of the shells as shown on color page 22 and cut the tails into neat medallions.

Grill the vegetables over charcoal shortly before serving. While the vegetables are still hot, toss them with the sauce. Toss the lobster medallions and claws in the same sauce. Arrange the vegetables and lobsters on plates, decorate with chervil, and serve immediately.

Shrimp

There are thousands of varieties of shrimp, but most are so small that they are more likely to be eaten by whales than people. Of the several hundred around the world that people do eat, only a dozen or so appear with any regularity in the United States. But new varieties are constantly showing up because Americans eat much more shrimp than is caught by American fishermen, and we're constantly looking for new sources.

I haven't listed every kind of shrimp sold in the United States because even if you know about the different species it's very hard to tell them apart. Much of this confusion comes from the habit of naming shrimp by color—pinks, whites, and browns—when in fact a pink shrimp can be white, a brown shrimp gray, and so forth. If you're a regular customer at a particular fish store, the fishmonger will probably appreciate your curiosity and help you out. Most shrimp come in clearly labeled boxes, so if need be you can ask the fishmonger to show you the box.

TROPICAL SHRIMP

Most of the shrimp eaten in the United States are members of the family Penaeidae (tropical shrimp), which is a group of relatively large shrimp that usually live in warm shallow water.

GULF OF MEXICO WHITE (Penaeus setiferus)

These shrimp are harvested off the Carolina and Florida coasts down to the Gulf of Mexico and are usually considered the best shrimp available in the United States. They have a full nut-like flavor and firm texture. Other species—including some farmed varieties—can be called white shrimp, but the tastiest are wild and are sometimes called Mexican whites, although wild Gulf of Mexico white shrimp are also harvested by American fishermen.

GULF OF MEXICO PINK (Penaeus duorarum)

These high-quality shrimp are harvested along the coast of the Carolinas and Florida and in the Gulf of Mexico. They are also available farmed. They are pink or pale orange when raw. Some consider these to be the premium domestic shrimp. They are less common than white or brown shrimp.

GULF OF MEXICO BROWN (Penaeus aztecus)

Sometimes called just brown or northern brown, these shrimp are popular in Texas, which is also their major producing state. Although I've been perfectly satisfied with brown shrimp, they are usually somewhat less flavorful and firm than their white or pink cousins and sometimes have a taste of iodine. Their shells are usually brownish gray and have a groove on the carapace. Brown shrimp are a good alternative to pink or white shrimp when price is important.

CHINESE WHITE (Penaeus chinensis)

As the name implies, these shrimp come from China, where most of them are farmed. Chinese whites are sometimes less firm than Gulf of Mexico shrimp and are likely to be somewhat watery and less flavorful. Much of this, however, has to do with the way the shrimp have been handled rather than actual variations among species. Fortunately the quality of these shrimp is improving, so they may soon rival Gulf of Mexico shrimp. Chinese whites are less expensive than Gulf of Mexico shrimp.

BLUE SHRIMP (Penaeus stylirostris)

Although the shells of these shrimp often have a slightly blue hue, they are easily confused with Gulf of Mexico whites. To add to the confusion, blue shrimp are often marketed as West Coast whites or Mexican whites, the same name often used for Gulf of Mexico whites. Blue shrimp are harvested off the Pacific coast of Mexico. They have a full flavor and firm texture.

WEST COAST WHITE (Penaeus vannamei)

Sometimes called Ecuadorean, Mexican white, or white leg, these shrimp look similar to Gulf of Mexico whites but, because many have been farmed, may be less flavorful. These shrimp are farmed in Ecuador and Central America and are found wild on the Pacific coast of Mexico, Central America, and parts of South America.

BLACK TIGER (penaeus monodon)

This is at least one shrimp that is easy to recognize. It is well named because it is distinctively darker than other shrimp—almost black—with yellow markings, so it looks striped. Black tiger shrimp grow up to 13 inches long, but most found in markets in the United States are considerably smaller, about 25 per pound. Most of the black tigers imported into the United States have been farmed in Thailand or Indonesia, Taiwan, China, and environs, but they live in the wild all the way from Japan west to East Africa. Black tigers usually have an excellent flavor, but they can be inconsistent. Many people consider the black tiger bland and a less expensive alternative to the higher-priced whites or pinks.

DON'T JUDGE A SHRIMP BY ITS COLOR

One way to tell the difference among varieties is to feel for a small groove that runs along the back of the last segment of carapace nearest the tail. Pinch along the back of the carapace with your thumbnail and forefinger nail to see if you can find the groove. White shrimp have no groove; pink and brown shrimp do. Pink shrimp have a small dark red spot between the third and fourth segments of the carapace; browns do not.

COLD-WATER SHRIMP

These shrimp are usually smaller and swim in deeper water than tropical shrimp. They are members of the family Pandalidae.

NORTHERN PINK SHRIMP (Pandalus borealis or P. jordani)

Don't confuse these with pink Gulf of Mexico shrimp, which are larger and paler. These deep-water shrimp are bright red and are harvested in northern waters all over the world—from Norway to Maine to Alaska. The West Coast variety, *P. jordani*, is caught from Washington to Alaska, while the East Coast variety, *P. borealis*, is caught all the way from Cape Cod to Greenland and over to Norway. The two varieties taste almost the same. Although these shrimp are smaller than Gulf of Mexico shrimp, on the East Coast at least, they are often available fresh with their heads in Chinese markets. They are also sold frozen as smaller shrimp and as "popcorn" shrimp in family restaurants.

GIANT SPOT (Pandalus platyceros)

These are the largest of cold-water shrimp—sometimes called *prawns* or Alaska spot—and are caught on both sides of the north Pacific. Although most giant spots are caught in Alaskan waters, they are sometimes found as far south as Monterey Bay. One of the advantages of spot shrimp is that they are often marketed with the flavorful roe left attached to the shell. Whenever I encounter this, I carefully pull off and save the roe and whisk it into the sauce. Spot shrimp often lack the crunchy texture of Gulf of Mexico shrimp.

ROCK SHRIMP (sicyonia brevirostris)

In most parts of the country—other than in Florida, where they are caught locally—these delicious little shrimp are

sold without their heads and already peeled because the shells are tough and hard to remove. Although rock shrimp are small, they have a firm texture and a delicious lobsterlike flavor.

FRESHWATER SHRIMP

Although there are dozens of varieties of freshwater shrimp and closely related shrimp that prefer brackish water, most of these shrimp are sold only locally and rarely marketed on any grand scale. There is one exception, the giant river prawn (*Macrobrachium rosenbergii*), sometimes called the *Hawaiian blue prawn*, found wild in Malaysia but now farmed all over the world, including the Caribbean, Hawaii, and Southeast Asia. These beautiful prawns have bright blue tails and long blue legs and antennae. They are usually sold frozen, although on the East Coast and in Hawaii they are sometimes available fresh the day after they're harvested. Freshwater shrimp grow very large and very quickly but don't have as satisfying a flavor and texture as tropical (penaeid) shrimp.

SHRIMP, PRAWNS, AND SCAMPI

In parts of the United States and in Great Britain the word *prawn* is used for all shrimp except tiny cocktail shrimp, which are usually called *bay shrimp*. In other parts of the United States only very large shrimp are called *prawns* with all others called simply *shrimp*. On the East Coast everything is just called *shrimp* except freshwater prawns, which are called simply *prawns*.

Scampi is a Venetian word for Dublin Bay prawns (sometimes called lobsterettes, langoustines, or langostinos), which are more closely related to lobsters than to shrimp.

SAND SHRIMP

This family of shrimp—Crangonidae—has very little importance in the United States but is very much appreciated in Europe. One small variety (*Crangon crangon*) is the small crunchy *crevette grise* popular in France and Belgium, where it is sold already cooked—shell and all—as an accompaniment to a platter of oysters. In England these are called *brown shrimp*, but they have no relation to Gulf of Mexico brown shrimp. A similar species, *Cragon franciscorum* (gray shrimp), is found on the California coast and for years was the "bay shrimp" popular in San Francisco.

BUYING SHRIMP

FRESHNESS: Most shrimp sold in the United States have been frozen, so unless you live near the Gulf coast or in areas where there are local shrimp, you're probably not going to find fresh shrimp. Fortunately most shrimp freezes well and loses little of its original flavor or texture. The problem with frozen shrimp can begin at the retail level. Most shrimp is frozen while very fresh and sold to retailers in 5-pound or 2-kilo (4.4-pound) blocks. (This is net weight; the actual weight of the blocks including the ice is 6 to 7 pounds.) The fishmonger then thaws out the block and puts the shrimp in the display case. Once shrimp is thawed out, it quickly deteriorates, so after it has spent more than two or three days in the display case it will start to take on a stale ammonia or fishy smell. One solution to this problem is to ask to smell the shrimp before you buy it and refuse it if there is any odor. Another sign of deterioration—called *melanosis*—is the appearance of black spots along the sides of the shrimp or at the base of the head if the shrimp still have their heads.

Because any shrimp you buy is likely to have been frozen anyway, you're best off buying shrimp while it is still frozen and thawing it as you need it. One of the easiest ways to use shrimp is to buy individually frozen shrimp (called *IQF*) which is sold in 1- or sometimes 5-pound bags in supermarkets. You can then keep the shrimp in the freezer for up to a couple of months and reach in and take out shrimp as you need them. Remember to keep shrimp tightly wrapped (first in plastic wrap and then aluminum foil) to prevent freezer burn. Shrimp is also sold in whole frozen 5-pound (or 2-kilo/4.4-pound) blocks, which you can thaw all at once or keep in the freezer and thaw as you need it by dipping the block in cold water and peeling the partially thawed shrimp away until you have enough. If you do buy a 5-pound block, count on using it within two months. Most home freezers aren't cold enough to keep it much longer without the shrimp slowly deteriorating. When buying a block of frozen shrimp, be sure of whether you're getting the 5-pound or 2-kilo (4.4-pound) size.

SIZE: Shrimp sold at the fish store are usually given ambiguous size names such as *jumbo, large,* and *medium.* Although these names give you a sense of the shrimp's size, they're not used consistently. The retailer, on the other hand, buys shrimp according to the number of shrimp per pound (or occasionally per kilo). On every box of shrimp there is a range of numbers—usually with a spread of four—such as 36–40, which indicates there are between 36 and 40 shrimp per pound. Very large shrimp are sometimes sold as U/20 or U/15, meaning that there are fewer than 20 or 15 shrimp per pound. Very small shrimp are sometimes sold as ov/70 or ov/80, meaning that there are more than 70 or 80 per pound. These numbers are useful not only because they're a consistent measure of shrimp size but also because they allow you to quickly convert between weight and numbers of shrimp. (Some recipes specify a number of shrimp, others a weight.) In some cities these names won't correspond to the number sizes given here (which is why it is better to buy by number), and some of these names won't be used at all. Medium, large, and jumbo are the most common sizes.

LOOKING OUT FOR CHEMICALS

Shrimp is sometimes dipped in a solution of sodium bisulfite to prevent deterioration and the development of melanosis (also called *black spot*), which stains the shell and even the meat with black rings. If too much sodium bisulfite is used (some say *any* is too much), it will give unpeeled shrimp a rough or sandpapery feel.

Already-peeled shrimp is sometimes dipped in a solution of sodium tripolyphosphate (STP), which prevents moisture from seeping out of the shrimp, which would lower its weight. STP sometimes gives a slippery feel or soapy taste to the shrimp.

Although the use of these additives seems to be on the wane (more shrimp are now advertised as "additive free"), the only way to be certain is to ask your fishmonger to show you the box.

This list shows the relation between size names and numbers, but don't count on accuracy and consistency at the fish store:

U/12: **Super-colossal**
U/15: **Colossal**
16/20: **Super-jumbo**
21/25: **Jumbo**
26/30: **Extra-large**
31/35: **Large**
35/40: **Medium**
40+: **Cocktail or salad**

STYLES OF SHRIMP

Head Removed, Shell on, Not Cooked (wholesalers call these green headless): This is the way most shrimp are sold. Most uncooked shrimp tails* are gray to pale pink. Although I always recommend buying raw versus cooked shrimp, raw shrimp should be considerably cheaper than cooked because of the weight loss that occurs during cooking.

Shrimp with Heads: I always prefer to buy shrimp with the heads still attached because I enjoy snapping the heads off grilled shrimps and sucking out the juices. I also like to use the heads to flavor sauces and soups (more about all this later). Depending on where you live, buying shrimp with the heads may be difficult. Try an Asian market or a cooperative fishmonger who will order them for you (my fishmonger is used to my weird requests). Remember when buying shrimp with the heads that you need almost twice as much by weight to get the same number of tails. If you have shrimp with heads but aren't planning to use the heads in your

*As for lobster, shrimp bodies are made up of just heads and tails, the tail being what we see most commonly in stores and on our plates and the head being the rest.

recipe, you can keep them, tightly wrapped, in the freezer for at least a month for use in other recipes. One disadvantage of buying shrimp with heads is that they are more perishable; so make sure they're fresh to begin with and use them right away.

Peeled Raw Shrimp: Shrimp are often sold already peeled. This can be a boon if you're in a hurry, especially if you're using smaller ones. But because you pay more for the peeling, it may be worth buying larger shrimp and peeling them yourself. Undeveined peeled shrimp are designated *PUD* (peeled, undeveined), while deveined shrimp are called *P&D* (peeled and deveined).

Cooked Shrimp: Shrimp are sometimes sold already cooked, and very small shrimp are almost never available in any other form. Usually cooked shrimp have already been shelled and sometimes already deveined. Sometimes, but not always, the tiny tail shell is left attached (these are called *cocktail shrimp*). I hardly ever buy cooked shrimp because I want the juices that the shrimp release during cooking to end up in whatever I'm making. But if you're in a hurry and need to throw together an emergency shrimp salad or cocktail, you can find cooked and frozen IQF shrimp in the freezer section of the supermarket. It's better to buy them frozen and thaw them out yourself than to buy them already thawed.

Live Shrimp: You're lucky if you live where you can net your own shrimp or can buy them off the boat while they're still wiggling. When I occasionally find live shrimp in tanks in Chinese markets in New York, I rush them home and toss them into a sauté pan or onto a hot grill.

YIELDS: Remember that shrimp with heads lose more than half their whole

weight by the time the head is removed and the rest of the shrimp is peeled and deveined. Shrimp lose even more weight when they are cooked (see chart below).

SHRIMP YIELDS

WHOLE RAW SHRIMP WITH HEADS
1 pound
100%

SHRIMP WITH HEADS REMOVED, UNPEELED
.6 pound (9 oz.)
60%

PEELED SHRIMP
.4 pound (7 oz.)
44%

COOKED TAILS
1 main-course serving (6 oz.)
37%

If a recipe calls for 1 pound shrimp with shells but without heads, you can substitute one of the following:

1⅔ pounds (1 pound 10 ounces) shrimp with heads
¾ pound (12 ounces) peeled shrimp
⅔ pound (10 ounces) peeled and cooked shrimp (assuming precooked shrimp works in the recipe)

HOW MUCH TO SERVE: This of course depends on your guests' appetites, but I calculate 2 to 3 ounces of peeled cooked shrimp per person as a first course and about 6 ounces for a main course. Remember that depending on how you buy your shrimp you'll need to buy more to get these amounts. In other words, you'll need to buy almost a pound of shrimp with the heads on or ½ pound of peeled shrimp for one large main-course serving (6 ounces).

PREPARING SHRIMP FOR COOKING

The easiest way to prepare shrimp is just to rinse and dry them. Once they're cooked, guests twist off the heads (if there are any) and peel the tails. This is certainly the tastiest way to serve grilled or sautéed shrimp because the shell seals in all the flavor and keeps the shrimp moist. The only disadvantage of this method is that many guests don't want to deal with the peeling—which may leave spotted shirts and blouses in its wake—and some guests are horrified by seeing shrimp with the heads on. So when deciding whether to peel or not to peel, consider your guests and how the shrimp are being served. You may want to leave simple grilled or sautéed shrimp unpeeled, while you're better off peeling shrimp that are going to be covered with messy sauce or broth.

Another forever-asked shrimp question is whether the shrimp should be deveined, and if so, on which side? I never bother with the minuscule little "vein" (actually a digestive tube) on the concave side of the shrimp, and as far as the convex side is concerned, I cut into a few of the shrimp and look at the vein. If it's thick and black, I devein; if it's thin and white, I leave it

in. Of course if you're serving shrimp in the shell, the guests will decide for themselves.

There are a couple of ways to devein a shrimp. I first peel all the shrimp, then make a slit along their backs with a paring knife, and then go through them and pick out the veins under cold running water. (You can slide the pointed end of a can opener along the opening to help dislodge the vein.) Some cooks like to cut through the shell with a sharp pair of scissors, thus removing the shell and making the slit at the same time, but I find this takes too long. Some cooks like to use a curved plastic gadget, called a *shrimper*, that slides under the shell and removes vein and shell in one swoop. This is the fastest method of all but leaves the back of each shrimp a bit ragged. So I use the shrimper only if the shrimp are being disguised in some way—cut up or covered with sauce or soup. See color page 24.

SAUTÉING

One of the easiest ways to cook shrimp is to heat a little butter or oil in a sauté pan—if you use a nonstick pan, a teaspoon or two is enough—and toss or stir the shrimp over high heat. The seasoning can be as simple as a little salt

and pepper, but you can also add chopped garlic or shallots and chopped fresh herbs such as basil, marjoram, or thyme.

Usually I sauté shrimp in the shells and let the guests peel their own (I use extra-large or jumbo shrimp to avoid frustration). My favorite way to serve the shrimp is to wait until the guests are seated (sautéed shrimp must be served very hot) and serve the shrimp in the center of the table on a hot platter so guests can help themselves. When the shrimp are done, I give each guest a little finger bowl to wipe up. For dressier occasions I peel the shrimp before sautéing and arrange them on hot plates, but shrimp always have more flavor when cooked in the shell.

Sautéed Shrimp with Parsley and Garlic

(color page 3)

This simple recipe can also serve as a model for sautéing shrimp with herbs. Here the shrimp are flavored with a paste of crushed garlic, finely chopped parsley, and sometimes bread crumbs called a *persillade*, but you can replace the parsley with other herbs such as thyme, marjoram (use smaller amounts for these), or basil. Once I even used lavender. The aroma of the fresh garlic as it coats the hot shrimp is irresistible, but you can also replace the garlic—try finely chopped shallots, lemongrass, or chilies, alone or in combination.

continued

BRINING SHRIMP

Brining enhances the flavor and crunchy texture of shrimp by drawing out excess moisture. To brine 2 pounds of shrimp, dissolve 1 cup sea salt and ½ cup sugar in 2 cups hot water. Add a tray of ice cubes and stir until cold (refrigerate longer if necessary). Soak peeled shrimp in the brine for 30 minutes in the refrigerator or unpeeled shrimp for 1 hour. Drain, rinse, and dry the shrimp.

To prevent the herb and garlic mixture from burning in the hot oil, add it during the last 30 seconds of sautéing. Both the garlic and parsley must be very finely chopped (in fact the garlic is crushed into a paste) so that they release their flavor quickly.

MAKES 4 FIRST-COURSE SERVINGS

1 pound extra-large or jumbo headless shrimp or 1²/₃ pounds with heads

2 garlic cloves, finely chopped

2 tablespoons finely chopped parsley

2 tablespoons extra-virgin olive oil

sea salt and pepper

If you're serving the shrimp in the shell, rinse them off and refrigerate until needed. If not, peel and devein them.

Prepare the persillade by crushing the garlic to a paste with a mortar and pestle or on a cutting board with the side of a chef's knife and combining it with the parsley in a small mixing bowl.

Heat the olive oil in a sauté pan over high heat until the oil begins to ripple slightly. Toss in the shrimp and stir or toss over high heat for 2 to 3 minutes—until the shrimp are completely red—and add the persillade. Toss or stir for 1 minute more—still over high heat—season with salt and pepper, and serve immediately.

❧

Shrimp with Tomato Sauce, Saffron Aïoli, and Pesto

I invented this dish by combining three of my favorite ingredients: garlic, basil, and tomatoes. The trick, though, is to keep the colors and flavors separate and dynamic in 3 different sauces—pesto, garlic mayonnaise, and tomato sauce—and partially combine them only at the last minute.

Most of the work for this dish can be done in advance. Only the sautéing and cooking the tomato must be done at the last minute.

MAKES 8 FIRST-COURSE OR 4 MAIN-COURSE SERVINGS

2 pounds jumbo or extra-large headless shrimp, peeled, deveined if desired

25 fresh basil leaves

6 tablespoons olive oil

¼ cup cold water

½ cup saffron aïoli (page 334)

4 medium tomatoes, peeled, seeded, and chopped

salt and white pepper

Rinse the shrimp and refrigerate until needed.

Puree the basil leaves in a blender with ¼ cup of the olive oil and the water. Cover this light, very green sauce and reserve at room temperature. (Don't try to make the basil sauce more than 2 hours in advance, or it will lose flavor and color.)

Thin the aïoli with about a tablespoon of water so that it is just slightly thicker than heavy cream. Reserve.

Cook the chopped tomatoes in a wide nonstick sauté pan over medium heat until they thicken slightly into a

light sauce, about 10 minutes. Season with salt and pepper to taste.

Sauté the shrimp in the remaining 2 tablespoons olive oil for about 3 minutes, until they have completely turned red. Season with salt and pepper.

Immediately arrange the shrimp on hot plates and carefully spoon the tomato sauce over and around them. Wipe out the pan used for sautéing the shrimp with a paper towel and use the pan to heat the basil sauce quickly. Spoon the basil sauce and the aïoli around and partially over the shrimp. Serve immediately.

GRILLING / BROILING

Grilling or broiling shrimp is a snap because, unlike some shellfish, shrimp never stick to the grill. The only thing you need to be careful of is overcooking. One of my favorite ways to grill shrimp for a party is to build a bed of hot coals, adjust the grill about 4 inches from the top of the coals (shrimp cook quickly and must be served piping-hot), and let the guests cook their own. I buy the biggest shrimp I can find so no one gets frustrated with the peeling and the shrimp don't fall through the spaces in the grill.

You can also grill peeled shrimp, which aren't as tasty as shrimp cooked in the shell but are easier to eat. If you're grilling small shrimp—small enough to fall through the spaces in the grill—cook them on skewers. Just be sure, if you're using wooden skewers, to presoak them in water for 30 minutes and keep the shrimp touching each other on the skewers so the wood doesn't burn and to wrap the ends of the skewers in aluminum foil so the ends don't burn.

Broiling is even easier than grilling. Just spread aluminum foil over the broiling pan, rub it with a little olive oil, and broil the shrimp, about 4 inches away from the heat, for about 2 minutes on each side. The shrimp are done as soon as the shells—or the flesh—turn red.

MARINADES: While most of the time I just season shrimp with a little sea salt and pepper, it's easy to give shrimp a little extra zest by tossing it in a marinade before grilling. Unpeeled shrimp should be marinated for about an hour, but for peeled shrimp 15 minutes is often long enough. Usually I throw a marinade together with what I have in the refrigerator or what herbs are growing on my apartment building roof, but here are a few of my favorite mixtures (enough for 2 pounds shrimp):

Soy Sauce and Garlic: Combine 3 tablespoons Japanese dark soy sauce with 1 peeled and finely chopped garlic clove and a teaspoon chopped fresh or ½ teaspoon dried thyme or marjoram. Don't salt the shrimp when using this marinade—the soy sauce is salty enough.

White Wine, Thyme, Olive Oil: Combine 3 tablespoons dry white wine with 1 teaspoon chopped fresh or ½ teaspoon dried thyme or oregano and 1 tablespoon extra-virgin olive oil.

Lemongrass, Shallot, Chilies, Wine, Thai Fish Sauce, Cilantro: Finely chop a 3-inch piece of lemongrass and combine it with 1 finely chopped shallot, 1 or 2 finely chopped Thai chilies or jalapeños, 2 tablespoons white wine, 1 tablespoon Thai fish sauce, and 2 tablespoons chopped fresh cilantro.

Thai Curries: Thai curries, which can be made at home (see "Sauces and Salsas, Condiments and Broths") or bought in small cans, make excellent marinades for shrimp, other shellfish, and firm-fleshed fish.

❧

Thai Curry–Marinated Barbecued Shrimp

(color page 3)

Thai curry, smeared over shrimp, scallops, or chunks of swordfish just before grilling, gives the seafood a hot, spicy, and slightly crisp outer crust. Recipes usually call for either red or green Thai curry, but I find the two virtually interchangeable. You can buy good-quality Thai curry in jars or cans in Asian markets, but I prefer to make my own. These shrimp are great served straight off the grill as an hors d'oeuvre—they're wonderful with cocktails.

MAKES 12 HORS D'OEUVRE SERVINGS

2 pounds jumbo or extra-large headless shrimp, peeled, deveined if desired

juice of 2 limes

3 tablespoons red or green Thai curry paste (page 340)

Toss the shrimp with the lime juice and curry paste in a mixing bowl and refrigerate for 1 hour.

Arrange the marinated shrimp on skewers. (Use 2 skewers for each row of shrimp so they stay flat when you turn them over on the grill.) Grill on a hot barbecue for about 2 to 3 minutes on each side. Pass immediately on hot plates or on a platter.

SHRIMP SOUPS

Shrimp make delicious soups and keep their shape, flavor, and texture, unlike some kinds of fish, which fall apart if cooked for a second too long. Shrimp do cook quickly, though, and should be thrown into the soup just before serving and then simmered in the soup for only 2 or 3 minutes. The most flavorful recipes start out with a soup base made with the shrimp heads, but you can add shrimp to almost any basic seafood soup or even vegetable soup. The fish or shellfish corn and poblano chili soup on page 281 is particularly good when made with shrimp.

SAVING SHRIMP HEADS AND SHELLS

Shrimp heads and shells make an excellent flavorful broth (page 201), so when you're preparing a recipe that doesn't call for them, save the shrimp heads and shells for use in soups and sauces. Tightly wrapped, they will keep in the freezer for at least a month.

Miso Soup with Shrimp

Miso (fermented soybean paste) comes in dozens of shades and varieties. You can use brown miso as an all-purpose miso, but see the glossary for more information on the various types.

Except for adding the shrimp at the end, this soup can be made up to 3 days in advance. I like to serve it in Japanese lacquer bowls.

continued

MAKES **4** FIRST-COURSE SERVINGS

12 large headless shrimp, peeled, deveined if desired

1 quart dashi (page 343)

¼ cup brown miso or 2 tablespoons white miso combined with 2 tablespoons brown or red miso

12 flat-leaf parsley leaves or watercress leaves or ½-inch pieces of scallion green

Prepare the shrimp and refrigerate until needed.

Bring the dashi to a simmer. In a small mixing bowl, work the miso to a smooth paste with about 3 tablespoons of the dashi. Whisk this mixture into the simmering dashi.

Distribute the parsley leaves in warmed bowls. Toss the shrimp into the simmering dashi and leave it just long enough to turn red, about 1 minute. (Remember, the shrimp will keep cooking in the bowls.) Arrange 3 hot shrimp in each of the bowls, ladle in the soup, and serve immediately.

❧

Aromatic Thai Shrimp Soup

Most Thai shrimp soups are made by simmering together aromatic vegetables with exotic flavorings such as lemongrass, kaffir lime leaves, and galangal (see glossary). The result is an irresistible spicy, pungent, and sour broth, but the soup itself has little shrimp flavor. This version starts with an aromatic broth made with the shrimp heads (or just the shells) for a much deeper shrimp flavor. The popular classic Thai soup *tom yam gung* is made in much the same way but without the shrimp head broth or the coconut milk (see box).

MAKES **4** FIRST-COURSE SERVINGS

1½ pounds large shrimp with heads or ¾ pound headless shrimp

3 medium shallots or 1 medium onion, chopped

2 garlic cloves, chopped

2 tablespoons peanut or vegetable oil

2 tomatoes, chopped

3 Thai or serrano chilies, seeded and finely chopped

¼-inch-thick slice of galangal

4-inch piece of lemongrass, finely chopped

3 kaffir lime leaves

¼ cup Thai fish sauce

¼ cup fresh lime juice, from about 2 limes

One 14-ounce can unsweetened coconut milk

2 tablespoons chopped fresh cilantro

If you're using shrimp with the heads, twist the heads off and peel the rest. If you're using headless shrimp, simply peel them. Reserve the shrimp heads and/or shells. Devein the shrimp if they need it and reserve in the refrigerator. If you have shrimp heads, chop the heads and shells in a food processor for 30 seconds. If you're using only shells, don't bother with the food processor.

Cook the shallots and garlic in peanut oil in a 4-quart pot over medium heat until they start to turn translucent, about 10 minutes. Add the chopped shrimp heads and/or shells and turn the heat up to high. Stir with a wooden spoon until the shrimp heads and/or shells turn orange, about 3 minutes. Add the tomatoes and enough water to cover, about 2 cups. Cover the pot and simmer the heads and/or shells gently for 20 minutes over medium-low heat. Strain the broth into a clean pot. Push down hard to extract as much broth and flavor from the heads and shells as possible.

Add the rest of the ingredients—except the peeled shrimp—to the broth and simmer gently for 5 minutes. Stir in the reserved shrimp, simmer for 2 minutes more, and serve.

HOT-AND-SOUR SHRIMP SOUP *TOM YAM GUNG*

This simple and delicious Thai classic soup is made with the same ingredients as the Aromatic Thai Shrimp Soup, only the coconut milk and shrimp heads are left out and a small amount of chicken broth is added.

To prepare *tom yam gung*, reserve the headless shrimp in the refrigerator. Cook the shallots and garlic in the vegetable oil in a 4-quart pot over medium heat for about 5 minutes. Add 3 cups of chicken broth (page 344) and the tomatoes (which need to be peeled) and simmer, covered, for 20 minutes. Strain into a clean pan, bring to a simmer, and add the chilies, galangal, lemongrass, and lime leaves. Simmer, covered, for 5 minutes and add the reserved shrimp and the rest of the ingredients except the coconut milk. Simmer for 2 minutes and serve immediately in hot bowls.

Shrimp Bisque

I've always loved eating and making bisques because more than any other dish they capture the pure flavor of shellfish. A shrimp bisque is made by adding a thickener (usually cooked rice) to a broth made from the shrimp heads and then finishing the soup with the pureed shrimp. You can also finish the soup with shrimp butter.

MAKES 8 FIRST-COURSE SERVINGS

4 pounds large shrimp with heads

For the Shrimp-Head Broth:

1 medium onion, chopped

2 tablespoons unsalted butter

4 tomatoes, chopped

1½ quarts chicken broth (page 344), fish broth (page 343), or water

For Finishing the Bisque:

½ cup short-grain rice such as Arborio, Carnaroli, or Vialone Nano

4 tablespoons unsalted butter or shrimp butter (page 330)

1 cup heavy cream

salt and cayenne pepper

¼-inch croutons cooked in butter

Twist off the heads and peel the shrimp. Reserve the heads and shells and chop them for 30 seconds in a food processor. Devein the shrimp if necessary and refrigerate until needed.

Cook the onion in butter in a 4-quart pot over medium heat until it turns translucent, about 10 minutes. Add the chopped shrimp heads and shells, the tomatoes, and the broth. Cover the pot and simmer gently for 30 minutes.

Strain the shrimp broth, discard the solids that don't go through the strainer, and reserve the broth.

Combine 2 cups of the shrimp broth with the rice in a small saucepan. Cover the pot and simmer the mixture gently, for about 30 minutes, until the rice is completely cooked—in fact overcooked and mushy.

Cut 8 of the shrimp into ½-inch pieces and reserve to garnish the soup.

Puree the rice mixture, butter, and remaining shrimp in a blender or food processor for 2 minutes. Combine the mixture with the rest of the shrimp broth.

Bring the shrimp broth/rice mixture to a simmer, whisk in the cream, and strain through a fine-mesh strainer into a clean pot. Bring the soup back to a simmer, add the shrimp cubes, and season with salt and cayenne to taste. If the soup seems too thick, you may have to dilute it slightly with a small amount of broth or water. Serve in hot bowls and sprinkle with croutons.

SHRIMP STEWS

As for stews made of other shellfish—except octopus, squid, whelk, and conch—shrimp stews are simmered just long enough to barely cook the shrimp through. Essentially they are shrimp soups with a smaller amount of thicker, more concentrated liquid.

The shrimp can be simmered directly in a flavorful liquid or marinated and sautéed first, with or without chopped garlic, shallots, ginger, or other ingredients. The liquid can be thickened or enriched with butter, cream, or something else or just left as is. One of the most delicious ways to make a shrimp stew is to begin with a shrimp broth made out of the heads and shells and then add ingredients according to the national character you wish to impart; see the chart on page 198 for ideas.

Thai Shrimp with Red Curry and Pineapple

*T*his dish is easy to make, light, and satisfying. Be sure to serve lots of rice—preferably jasmine or basmati—to soak up the delicious sauce. See the glossary for information on Asian ingredients.

MAKES 4 MAIN-COURSE OR 6 FIRST-COURSE SERVINGS

1½ pounds large or extra-large headless shrimp, peeled, deveined if desired

1 tablespoon finely chopped garlic

1 tablespoon finely chopped lemongrass

1 tablespoon vegetable oil

2 kaffir lime leaves

One 14-ounce can unsweetened coconut milk

3 tablespoons red curry paste (page 340)

3 tablespoons Thai fish sauce

¼ cup fresh lime juice (from about 2 limes)

½ fresh pineapple, peeled, cored, and cut into small wedges (about 2 cups), or one 20-ounce can pineapple wedges, drained

2 tablespoons finely chopped fresh cilantro

Toss the peeled shrimp with the garlic and lemongrass in a mixing bowl and refrigerate for 2 hours.

Heat the vegetable oil in a large nonstick sauté pan over high heat. Toss or stir the shrimp in the hot oil until they begin to turn red, about 2 minutes. Reserve in a bowl. Stir the rest of the ingredients except the pineapple and cilantro into the same pan. Whisk the mixture over high heat to break up and distribute the curry paste. When the sauce comes back to a simmer, stir in the pineapple, cilantro, and reserved shrimp. Bring to a simmer over high heat. Serve on a hot platter or on hot plates.

INGREDIENTS FOR SHRIMP STEWS AND SOUPS

	MARINADES	COOKING FAT	AROMATIC INGREDIENTS*	LIQUIDS (FOR SIMMERING SHRIMP)	FLAVORFUL INGREDIENTS SIMMERED IN LIQUID	THICKENERS/ FLAVORFUL FINISHES	ENRICHENERS	GARNISHES
THAI	Chopped lemongrass, garlic, shallots, Thai curry pastes, Thai chilies, fish sauce	Peanut oil, coconut oil	Same as marinade ingredients; also kaffir lime leaves, cilantro	Water, broth, coconut milk, Thai fish sauce, shrimp head broth	Kaffir lime leaves, cilantro, mint, holy basil, tomatoes, pineapple, straw mushrooms, snow peas, cucumbers	Green, yellow, red Thai curries	Coconut milk	Chopped scallions, peanuts, cilantro
CHINESE	Ginger, garlic, scallions, rice wine or sherry, soy sauce	Peanut oil, vegetable oil	Same as solid marinade ingredients, sugar	Rice wine or sherry, soy sauce, sesame oil	Crispy vegetables such as snow peas, green beans, water chestnuts	Cornstarch		Chopped scallions
BRAZILIAN	Garlic, vinegar, chilies, cumin, cilantro	Dende oil, peanut oil, butter	Onion, garlic, chilies (habañero, mirasol, jalapeño), achiote oil	Coconut milk, tomatoes, beer, wine, shrimp head broth, lemon juice	Dried shrimp, ginger	Ground peanuts or cashews, cornstarch	Coconut milk	Chopped cilantro, parsley, dill
FRENCH	White wine, lemon juice, olive oil, parsley, chervil, tarragon, bay leaves,	Butter, olive oil	Shallots, garlic, onions, carrots, celery (mirepoix)	White wine, vermouth, cider, tomatoes, fish broth, shrimp head broth, clam or mussel cooking liquids	Green vegetables including green beans, spinach, Swiss chard; root vegetables (usually julienned or "turned" into shapes)	Flour (roux), cornstarch, arrowroot, vegetable purees, butter, reduced cream, egg yolks	Cream, butter	Chopped parsley, chervil, chives, tarragon, etc.
ITALIAN	White wine, vermouth, garlic, onion, olive oil, oregano, marjoram, bay leaves, mint, fennel	Olive oil, butter, rendered pancetta	Onions, garlic, pancetta, ham, tomatoes, herbs (soffrito); fennel	White wine, vermouth, tomato sauce, fish broth, shrimp head broth, mussel or clam cooking liquids	Dried porcini mushrooms, green vegetables, fennel	Flour, vegetable purees	Cream	Chopped parsley, basil (chopped or worked into a pesto), oregano, mint
INDIAN	Turmeric, ginger, chilies, carom seeds	Ghee, vegetable oil	Onions, garlic, poppy seeds, cumin, coriander, paprika, chilies, ginger, cardamom, cinnamon, curry leaves	Coconut milk, yogurt, tomatoes, shrimp head broth	Almonds, tamarind	Ground poppy seeds, vegetable (especially bean and lentil) purees, ground nuts (especially almonds)	Cream	Chopped cilantro, chilies
SPANISH/CATALAN	Olive oil, thyme, garlic	Olive oil, rendered pork fat	Catalan sofregit, Castilian sofrito: onions, leeks, tomatoes; fresh and dried hot peppers	Water, fish broth, shrimp head/shell broth, wine, Pernod, cognac (brandy), rum, sherry (or vi ranci)	Artichokes, green beans, tomatoes, cinnamon, allspice, paprika, peas, mushrooms, potatoes, rice, saffron, white beans, fava beans	Toasted bread, picada (sauce made of bread, peppers, garlic, parsley, and ground hazelnuts or almonds), romesco (similar to picada but with vinegar)	Olive oil (usually contained in one of the sauces above)	Chopped parsley, pitted olives, toasted pine nuts, raisins

* Added before or during sautéing/stir-frying

Indonesian Stew

SAMBAL UDANG

*I*f you glance quickly through this recipe, you'll see that it's very similar to many Thai recipes in that the shrimp is simmered in an aromatic liquid containing lemongrass and kaffir lime leaves. There are, however, some significant differences. A Thai or Vietnamese sauce is likely to be finished with chopped mint, cilantro, or basil leaves, while in Indonesian cooking these herbs are used far less often. Instead notice that ground coriander *seeds* are used here, along with ginger (less common in Thai recipes), tomatoes, kemiri nuts, and salam leaves (the last 2 being the most characteristic of Indonesian cooking). See the glossary for information on any unfamiliar ingredients.

This dish is really meant to be served in small quantities along with lots of other little dishes, but I've given quantities for a Western-style main course. To serve the shrimp as a first course or Indonesian style, cut the recipe in half.

This dish is best made with whole shrimp so the shrimp heads can be ground up with the *bumbu*—the basic flavor mixture used as the starting point in most Indonesian dishes. The complicated part of this dish—the stewing liquid—can be made earlier in the day and the shrimp then heated in the liquid just before serving—with plenty of rice.

MAKES **4** MAIN-COURSE SERVINGS

2½ **pounds medium or large shrimp with heads or 1½ pounds headless shrimp**

3 **shallots, coarsely chopped**

3 **Thai chilies, seeded and coarsely chopped**

2 **garlic cloves, coarsely chopped**

5 **kemiri nuts or macadamia nuts**

2 **teaspoons shrimp paste (optional)**

2 **teaspoons ground coriander**

3-**inch piece of lemongrass, finely sliced**

2 **kaffir lime leaves, coarsely chopped**

¼-**inch-thick slice of galangal, coarsely chopped**

2 **tablespoons peanut or vegetable oil**

2 **tablespoons tamarind paste or ¼ cup fresh lime juice (from about 2 limes)**

¼ **cup boiling water if using tamarind**

2 **teaspoons palm or granulated sugar**

2 **salam leaves (optional)**

3 **tomatoes, chopped**

1 **cup unsweetened coconut milk**

salt

If you're using shrimp with heads, remove and reserve the heads. Peel the rest, reserving the shells, and devein if necessary.

Prepare a *bumbu* by combining the shrimp shells and heads (if you have them) in the bowl of a food processor with the shallots, chilies, garlic, kemiri nuts, shrimp paste, coriander, lemongrass, kaffir lime leaves, galangal, and peanut oil. Process for about 2 minutes, until you have a coarse paste.

Using a wooden spoon, work the tamarind paste with the boiling water. Strain the mixture and reserve the liquid. Discard what doesn't go through the strainer.

Heat a sauté pan or an iron skillet over medium heat and stir in the *bumbu*. (If you've included the shrimp paste, be sure to open the windows.) Stir the *bumbu* for about 5 minutes, until it sizzles and—because of the shrimp shells—turns orange.

Stir in the strained tamarind paste and the rest of the ingredients except the salt. Simmer gently for 20 minutes and strain first through a coarse strainer or food mill and then through a fine strainer into a 4-quart pot.

Heat the stewing liquid just before serving and add the shrimp. Simmer the shrimp for about 3 minutes, season with salt to taste, and serve on hot plates or a platter.

Brazilian Shrimp Stew with Coconut Milk and Cashews

VATAPA

(color page 3)

I fell in love with this stew in a Brazilian restaurant in New York. Except for the absence of Thai fish sauce, the flavors are reminiscent of Thai cooking but with a subtle complexity of their own.

One way to make a *vatapa* is to make a concentrated broth with the shrimp heads and then use this broth in the stew. If you can't find shrimp with the heads, do as the Brazilians and use ground dried shrimp. Dried shrimp do in fact give the stew a bit of exotic zest. If you don't live near a market specializing in South American products, you should be able to find dried shrimp in most Asian markets. Buy small dried shrimp—they're less expensive—and choose shrimp that are pink rather than brown. This recipe calls for ¼ cup ground dried shrimp. Because it's hard to make this small amount in a food processor, I usually make twice as much and store it in the freezer—where it keeps indefinitely—until I need it. If you can't find dried shrimp, it's still worth making this shrimp stew.

Thanks to food processors, this dish is easy to prepare. Because the shrimp is added at the end, the whole stew can be prepared earlier in the day and the shrimp simmered in the stew a few minutes before serving.

MAKES 6 MAIN-COURSE SERVINGS

3½ **pounds shrimp with heads, heads and shells removed and reserved, or 2 pounds medium headless shrimp, peeled, shells reserved, deveined if desired**

2 **tablespoons peanut or vegetable oil**

1 **onion, finely chopped**

2 **garlic cloves, finely chopped**

2 **tablespoons freshly grated ginger**

2 **serrano or 3 jalapeño chilies, seeded and finely chopped**

¼ **cup ground dried shrimp (optional)**

4 **tomatoes, chopped**

3 **cups water**

1 **cup (half a 14-ounce can) unsweetened coconut milk**

3 **tablespoons all-natural cashew butter or peanut butter**

2 **tablespoons finely chopped fresh cilantro**

6 **tablespoons fresh lime juice (from about 3 limes)**

salt and pepper

Refrigerate the shrimp until needed. If you have shrimp heads, chop them in a food processor for 30 seconds. If you have just shrimp shells, don't bother with the chopping. Combine the chopped shrimp heads or shells with the oil in a heavy 4-quart pot and add the onion, garlic, ginger, chilies, and the dried shrimp if you have it. Stir this mixture over medium heat for about 10 minutes, until the shrimp heads or shells turn red. Don't let anything brown.

Add the tomatoes and water to the shrimp shell/head mixture and bring to a gentle simmer. Cover the pot, simmer for 30 minutes, and strain through a fine-mesh strainer into a clean 4-quart pot. Discard the solids

that don't go through the strainer.

In a small mixing bowl, whisk about ½ cup coconut milk into the cashew or peanut butter until the mixture is smooth. Whisk this mixture into the strained shrimp shell mixture along with the rest of the coconut milk.

Just before serving, bring the shrimp broth to a gentle simmer and stir in the reserved peeled shrimp, cilantro, and lime juice. Simmer gently for about 3 minutes. Season with salt and pepper to taste. Serve with rice.

❧

French-Style Shrimp Stew with Fines Herbes, Spinach, and Sorrel

CREVETTES AUX FINES HERBES À L'OSEILLE

*I*n typical French fashion most of the ingredients in this dish act as a backdrop for the flavors of the shrimp. Finely chopped fines herbes—equal parts chervil, parsley, chives, and tarragon—stirred into the sauce near the end of cooking are the only accent to the underlying flavor of shrimp. If you don't have access to all 4 fines herbes, just use more of the others.

In this dish the cooked shrimp is arranged on small mounds of lightly creamed spinach and sorrel. (If you can't find sorrel, just leave it out.) You can also use other leafy greens such as Swiss chard or finely julienned vegetables such as leeks, carrots, or turnips, cooked gently in butter. Although this recipe is kept simple to illustrate a basic technique for cooking shrimp, assortments of cooked vegetables such as mushrooms (cultivated or wild), baby squash, carrots, or turnips can be

added to the dish to make it more elaborate. Different herbs such as dill, marjoram, or mint and spices such as saffron or curry can also be used.

Most of the dish can be prepared earlier the same day. Only the herbs need to be chopped and the shrimp added just before serving.

MAKES 6 FIRST-COURSE SERVINGS

2½ **pounds large shrimp with heads, heads and shells removed and reserved, or 1½ pounds headless shrimp, peeled, deveined if desired**

1½ **quarts chicken broth (page 344), fish broth (page 343), or water**

1 **medium onion, chopped**

2 **garlic cloves, chopped**

2 **tablespoons unsalted butter**

3 **tomatoes, peeled, seeded, and chopped**

½ **cup heavy cream**

leaves from 1 large bunch of spinach

salt and pepper

1 **large handful of sorrel leaves**

2 **tablespoons shrimp butter (page 330) or unsalted butter**

2 **tablespoons fresh lemon juice**

1 **teaspoon finely chopped fresh tarragon**

1 **teaspoon finely chopped fresh chervil**

1 **teaspoon finely chopped fresh chives**

1 **teaspoon finely chopped fresh parsley**

Puree the shrimp heads and/or shells in a blender for about 1 minute with just enough of the broth or water to get the mixture to turn around and form a coarse wet paste.

Cook the onion and garlic in butter in a 4-quart pot over medium heat until they turn translucent, about 10 minutes. Add the shrimp head paste and the remaining broth or water. Cover the pot and simmer gently for 30 minutes. Strain through a fine-mesh strainer into a clean 4-quart pot. Boil down the broth until only 1 cup remains. Add the tomatoes and all except 2 tablespoons of the cream and simmer for about 10 minutes, until the mixture has the consistency of cold heavy cream. Whisk every couple of minutes to prevent the cream from turning granular. Set the sauce aside.

Blanch the spinach leaves in boiling water for 30 seconds. Drain the leaves in a colander, rinse with cold water, squeeze out the excess water, and set aside on a plate. Boil down the remaining 2 tablespoons heavy cream in a small saucepan until the cream gets very thick. Season the cream with salt and pepper and stir in the cooked spinach and raw sorrel leaves. Stir over medium heat until the sorrel melts and the spinach is hot, about 2 minutes.

Bring the shrimp sauce to a gentle simmer and stir in the reserved shrimp. Heat the mixture over medium heat until all the shrimp turns red, about 3 minutes. Arrange the spinach/sorrel mixture in small mounds in the center of hot soup plates. Spoon on the shrimp—if you like, arrange it in a pinwheel pattern over the spinach. Whisk the shrimp butter, lemon juice, and herbs into the shrimp sauce and simmer for 1 minute. Season with salt and pepper to taste and spoon carefully over and around the shrimp.

Italian-Style Shrimp Stew

This simple garlicky shrimp stew typifies the light and full flavors of Italian cooking. You can make the sauce for this dish as thick or thin as you like by adjusting the amount of broth you add—in fact, you can serve it as a soup.

MAKES **4** FIRST-COURSE SERVINGS

1½ **pounds large headless shrimp, peeled, deveined if desired**

4 garlic cloves, finely chopped

¼ **cup extra-virgin olive oil**

3 tomatoes, peeled, seeded, and chopped

1 cup fish broth (page 343), chicken broth (page 344), mussel- or clam-cooking liquid, shrimp-head broth (below), or water

2 tablespoons finely chopped parsley

salt and pepper

Reserve the shrimp in the refrigerator until needed. In a small sauté pan, gently cook half the garlic in half the olive oil for about 2 minutes, until the garlic releases its fragrance. Don't let the garlic brown. Stir in the tomatoes and broth and boil the mixture down until it has the thickness you like, but usually to the consistency of a med-ium-thick sauce, which will take about 20 minutes.

Sauté the shrimp and the rest of the garlic for about 3 minutes (until the shrimp turn orange) in another sauté pan in the remaining olive oil. Pour in the tomato sauce, sprinkle with the chopped parsley, and simmer for 1 minute. Season with salt and pepper to taste. Serve on hot plates or over pasta.

Shrimp-Head Broth for Shrimp Soups and Sauces

This basic broth, made by chopping shrimp heads in a food processor and simmering them in broth or water, makes a great base for shrimp sauces, stews, and soups. I save shrimp heads and shells in the freezer until I accumulate enough to make a batch of broth. The broth will keep in the refrigerator for 3 days and in the freezer for several months.

MAKES **2** QUARTS

2 pounds shrimp heads and shells (from about 4 pounds shrimp)

1 medium onion, chopped

2 tablespoons unsalted butter

2 tomatoes, chopped

1½ **quarts chicken broth (page 344), fish broth (page 343), or water**

Place the shrimp heads and shells in a colander and rinse under cold running water. Process in a food processor for about 30 seconds, until the heads are coarsely chopped.

Cook the onion in butter in a 4-quart pot over medium heat until it turns translucent, about 10 minutes. Add the ground shrimp heads, tomatoes, and broth. Cover the pot and simmer gently for 30 minutes.

Strain the mixture through a food mill or large regular strainer and then through a fine-mesh strainer.

Indian-Style Shrimp Stew

I first read about this dish in Julie Sahni's book *Classic Indian Cooking* In this version a rich and spicy coconut sauce is prepared in advance and the peeled shrimp simmered in the sauce just before serving. You'll end up with a lot of sauce for relatively few shrimp, so be sure to serve with enough basmati rice to soak it up. If you have shrimp with heads, I highly recommend using them to make a flavorful broth to use as the base for this stew.

continued

MAKES 6 FIRST-COURSE SERVINGS

1½ pounds large headless shrimp, peeled, deveined if desired, or 2¼ pounds large shrimp with heads, heads and shells removed and reserved

1 large onion, finely chopped

2 garlic cloves, finely chopped

2 tablespoons grated fresh ginger

2 Thai or serrano chilies or 3 jalapeño chilies, seeded and finely chopped

3 tablespoons unsalted butter

2 tablespoons ground coriander

1 teaspoon ground fenugreek

1 tablespoon paprika

1 cup shrimp-head broth (page 201), fish broth (page 343), chicken broth (page 344), or water

One 14-ounce can unsweetened coconut milk

2 tablespoons finely chopped fresh cilantro

Juice of ½ lemon

salt and pepper

Reserve the peeled shrimp in the refrigerator until needed.

Cook the onion, garlic, ginger, and chilies in butter in a heavy 4-quart pot over medium heat until the vegetables turn translucent and begin to brown, about 12 minutes.

Stir the coriander, fenugreek, and paprika into the hot vegetable mixture and cook for 2 minutes more, until you can smell the spices. Pour in the broth and boil over high heat until the liquid reduces by about half.

Stir the coconut milk into the vegetable/spice mixture, bring to a simmer, and add the reserved shrimp, cilantro, and lemon juice. Simmer for about 3 minutes, season with salt and pepper to taste, and serve immediately.

FRYING AND STIR-FRYING

Shrimp are excellent when coated with any of the batters in the deep-frying chapter, but I particularly like the Indian version given here.

Indian-Style Marinated Deep-fried Shrimp

*I*ndian cooks are great fans of deep-fried seafood and give their fish and shellfish a special character with spicy marinades and a fragrant batter made with chickpea flour and more spices. While traditional Indian chickpea batter is always delicious, my own preference is to lighten it with some all-purpose flour and more liquid than is traditional.

Serve these shrimp as a first course or as a cocktail-party hors d'oeuvre with one of the chutneys in "Sauces and Salsa, Condiments and Broths."

MAKES 6 FIRST-COURSE OR HORS D'OEUVRE SERVINGS

1½ pounds (about 30) large or extra-large headless shrimp, peeled (leave the tiny tail shell attached) and deveined

For the Marinade:

1 garlic clove, finely chopped

1 tablespoon grated fresh ginger

1 Thai or serrano chili, seeded and finely chopped

1 tablespoon chopped fresh mint or cilantro

2 teaspoons olive oil

For the Batter:

¼ cup chickpea flour

¼ cup all-purpose flour

2 tablespoons ground coriander

2 teaspoons ground cumin

1 teaspoon cayenne pepper

2 teaspoons salt

1 cup cold water

For Frying:

1 quart olive oil or vegetable oil

Toss the shrimp with the marinade ingredients in a mixing bowl. Cover with plastic wrap and refrigerator for 1 to 3 hours.

Combine the flours, spices, and salt in a mixing bowl. Whisk in half the water and gently stir the batter until you obtain a smooth paste. Stir in the rest of the water. Cover the bowl and let sit at room temperature for 1 to 3 hours.

Heat the oil to 350°F in a heavy 4-quart pot. Hold the shrimp by the tail, dip them in the batter, and gently lower them into the hot oil. Fry for 2 to 3 minutes in batches of 6 to 8, flip the shrimp over, and fry for 2 minutes more, until they're golden brown on both sides. Transfer to a plate covered with paper towels to drain. Serve immediately.

Shrimp Stir-fry with Cashews and Chinese Vegetables

*T*his dish starts out as a stir-fry but ends up as a light stew with the shrimp simmered in a mixture of soy sauce and rice wine, lightly thickened with only enough cornstarch to give the sauce a light consistency. Try to find fresh water chestnuts—once canned they retain their texture but little of their flavor.

Although this is a last-minute dish, all the raw ingredients can be prepared in advance, so the final cooking takes only about 5 minutes. I serve this dish with bowls of steamed rice.

MAKES 4 MAIN-COURSE SERVINGS

1½ pounds large headless shrimp, peeled, deveined if desired

3 tablespoons Chinese dark soy sauce

3 tablespoons Chinese rice wine or sherry

1½ teaspoons dark sesame oil

1 teaspoon grated fresh ginger

1 garlic clove, finely chopped and crushed to a paste

16 fresh water chestnuts or one 8-ounce can rinsed and drained

8 medium dried Chinese (shiitake) mushrooms, soaked for 30 minutes in just enough hot water to cover, or 8 fresh shiitake mushrooms, stems removed, caps sliced

1½ teaspoons cornstarch blended with 3 teaspoons water

2 tablespoons peanut oil

½ cup cashews, lightly toasted in a 350°F oven for 10 minutes

¼ pound snow peas

Toss the shrimp with the soy sauce, rice wine, sesame oil, ginger, and garlic in a mixing bowl and refrigerate for 1 hour.

If you're using fresh water chestnuts, rinse them off thoroughly—they're often covered with mud—and peel them with a sharp paring knife. If you're using canned water chestnuts, drain and rinse them under cold water. Cut the water chestnuts into quarters and reserve.

If you're using dried mushrooms, take the mushrooms out of their soaking liquid and squeeze out any water. Cut off and discard the mushroom stems and slice the mushroom caps.

Drain the shrimp, reserving the marinade. Combine the cornstarch paste with the reserved marinade.

Heat the peanut oil in a wok or cast-iron skillet over high heat. When the oil just begins to ripple and barely smoke, toss in the shrimp, water chestnuts, sliced mushroom caps, cashews, and snow peas.Stir the mixture over high heat—you can use chopsticks or a wooden spoon—until the shrimp turns red on both sides, about 3 minutes. Pour in the marinade/cornstarch mixture and stir for 1 minute more. Serve immediately on hot plates.

Crab

When I was a child in San Francisco, Dungeness crab, served cold with mayonnaise, was one of my family's favorite meals. Somehow the messy cracking and sucking on shells created the relaxed atmosphere of a picnic. I've since traveled and savored many a shellfish, but perhaps because of the memories, crab remains my favorite.

Out of the thousands of species of crab that occur worldwide, Americans eat only several varieties. For the most part the crabs you eat depend on where you live. New Englanders enjoy rock crab, Jonah crab, and blue crab; Floridians feast on stone crab claws and a variety of land crabs; and Dungeness crab has always been the West Coast favorite. Today fresh crabs are flown here and there, so the tastier varieties can be found almost anywhere.

ALASKAN AND ANTARCTIC CRABS

KING CRAB

There are several species of these huge (up to 25 pounds) delicious crabs. The best known is the red king crab (*Paralithodes camtschaticus*), which is preferred over blue king crab (*P. platypus*) and brown or deep-water king crab (*P. brevipes*) only because it's bigger and has chunkier meat. A more distantly related crab, the golden crab (*Lithodes aequispina*), can also be sold, along with the other species, as king crab. Most of the time all these crabs are marketed simply as "king crab."

Unless you live in Alaska, it's almost impossible to find king crab other than in a can or frozen. Although I usually avoid frozen shellfish, king crab legs are an exception. They usually come already split lengthwise, so the meat—unlike that of so many other crabs—is easy to get at. Unlike most crabs, which have 10 appendages, king crabs have only 8 (6 legs and 2 claws). King crab legs are meatier than the claws, so if you're buying king crab, try to get all legs or at least a fair proportion (three legs to one claw). Don't let anyone foist off only claws. In the same way as shrimp, king crab is sold according to size, with a range of 9 to more than 28 legs per 10-pound box. It's unlikely that the fishmonger will post these numbers, but remember that smaller legs should be less expensive—a fair-sized leg should weigh about ½ pound and a big leg as much as a pound.

The centolla crab, also known as the southern king crab (*Lithodes antarcticus*), is closely related to Alaskan king crab except that it's found in the Southern Hemisphere from Chili to Antarctica. Although almost indistinguishable from its northern cousins, southern king crab cannot be marketed in the United States as king crab. You may find it, however, under its Spanish name, *centolla*.

Because king crab legs and claws have already been cooked, they should just be heated through before being served hot.

SNOW CRAB

Although snow crabs are only distantly related to king crabs, the two are often confused, probably because both come from Alaska. A much closer relative of the snow crab, also in the spider crab family (Majidae), is the sea spider, sometimes called the *thornback crab*, one of the most popular crabs in Europe.

Although snow crab meat is delicious, it is less popular than king crab because the legs are thin and the meat can be difficult to get out of the shell. Most of the time snow crab legs are sold already split, so getting the meat out of the shell isn't a problem anyway. Snow crab claws are also sold with half of the shell removed for easy eating. Snow crabs are also a source of crabmeat and are a less expensive alternative to king crab.

Three species of snow crabs—*Chionoecetes oplio, C. bairdi,* and *C. tanneri*—are most important in the United States. Because they all have a similar flavor, it isn't important to know how to distinguish them except that *C. bairdi* is usually larger. *C. oplio* is sometimes harvested off the East Coast of Canada and is sold under the name "queen crab."

As snow crabs grow older, they sometimes develop black patches on their shells and have a browner, less appealing appearance. These are often a bargain because people incorrectly assume that the meat of these crabs is less tasty.

PACIFIC COAST CRABS

DUNGENESS CRABS (Cancer magister)

These are the most popular crabs on the West Coast. Although Californians usually assume that most Dungeness crabs are harvested near San Francisco, Dungeness crabs are found from Mexico to Alaska with most of the catch coming from the coasts of Oregon and Washington.

You can find live Dungeness crab in season, but it is almost always sold already cooked so that the shell has turned from brown to red. For this reason a favorite San Francisco tradition is to serve Dungeness crab cold—so it isn't cooked twice—with homemade mayonnaise.

Cooking Dungeness Crab: If you are lucky enough to get your hands on a live Dungeness crab, your best bet is to throw it into a pot of boiling water until the shell turns red, about 8 to 10 minutes. You can also steam crab in a bamboo steamer or couscousière. For some

recipes, those that involve stir-frying or cooking in sauce, the live crab should be cut up alive. Always scrub the crab with a small brush and rinse it thoroughly before throwing it into the pot.

Cleaning Cooked Dungeness Crab (see color page 21): Grip the legs with one hand (use a towel if the crab is hot) and the top shell with the other. Push down on the legs and pull up on the shell until the shell comes off. Reach into the shell with your index finger and pull out and reserve any yellow "butter'' (actually fat and edible organs). Discard the shell or wash it for presenting crab salads. Unfold, twist off, and discard the "apron" on the bottom of the crab. Turn the crab over and pull off and discard the gills that cling to the shell above the legs. Pull out and discard the white length of intestine that runs along the back as well as the small mouth section. Cut the body in half lengthwise with a strong chef's knife. Snap the claws off the body and crack them gently with a rolling pin or the back of a cleaver. The crab "mustard" (or "butter") from the shell and body can be served at the table along with everything else or worked into a sauce.

ATLANTIC COAST CRABS

BLUE CRAB (callinectes sapidus)

This is by far the most popular crab on the Atlantic coast, where it is found from Massachusetts all the way down to the Bahamas with the bulk of the catch made off the coast of Virginia and in Chesapeake Bay. Eating whole blue crabs can be frustrating for the inexperienced, who must work hard to get at a small amount of delicious meat. For those who are more skilled

or less lazy this isn't a problem. Or the problem can be avoided entirely by cooking blue crabs in soups—which have all the flavor from both meat and shell and require no effort to eat.

Blue crab aficionados are divided in their preferences for male or female crabs. Virginians usually prefer males (in Maryland called *jimmies*), which usually contain more meat, while New Yorkers prefer females (when immature called *she-crabs,* when mature called *sooks*)—in part because of a large Chinese population that insists on crabs with roe. (In New York it is illegal to harvest crabs with visible roe, but most female crabs contain roe on the inside.) It's easy to tell the difference between males and females by looking at the small flap—the "apron"—on the crabs' underside. The male apron is thin and pointed, while the female's is rounded.

Cleaning Blue Crabs for Soups and Sauces (see color page 20): I used to recommend that blue crabs destined for soups or sauces be cleaned and cut up while still alive. This was before I encountered a particularly ferocious batch that wouldn't let me get near them. Now I plunge my crabs into boiling water for about 30 seconds to kill them, quickly drain them in a colander, and then rinse them under cold running water. This quick boiling also makes the crabs easier to clean by loosening grit and dirt that cling to the crabs' shells.

After you've plunged the crabs into boiling water for 30 seconds, drain them in a colander and rinse them under cold running water for about 5 minutes. Brush the crab—especially the underside behind the legs—with a scrub brush. Rinse the crabs thoroughly. Unfold, twist off, and discard the crab's apron. With one hand, press down on one side of the top shell from the underside and pull up on the center and leg sections until the two come apart. Pull the gills ("dead man's fingers") off each side of the center section and discard. Twist off the legs and claws and remove and discard the spongy sand bag from behind the crab's eyes. Cut the center section in half with a chef's knife. Of course if you're serving whole steamed or boiled crabs, except for the initial brushing your guests or family will have to do all of this themselves—after the crabs have been cooked.

Cooking Whole Blue Crabs: The easiest way to cook blue crabs is to throw them into a big pot of boiling water and simmer them for about 6 minutes. While many people add spice mixtures (such as Old Bay) to the water, I don't spend a lot of time (or money) on flavoring it or turning it into an elaborate vegetable broth as recommended by some recipes. Whole blue crabs can also be steamed until they turn red, in 8 to 10 minutes.

Eating Whole Blue Crabs: Alan Davidson, in his book *North Atlantic Seafood*, claims to be able to extract the meat from a cooked blue crab in 4 minutes, while local experts manage in 40 seconds. I come in a dismal third at a little over 7 minutes. A cooked crab is eaten in the same way it is cleaned, except that diners should be given bibs (I don't have bibs, so I hand out long aprons) and nutcrackers or small mallets—I use an upholstery hammer. I like to serve homemade tartar sauce, but melted butter and lemon wedges are more typical.

SOFT-SHELL CRABS: I once thought these were a completely different species of crab until someone explained that blue crabs periodically

shed their hard outer shell and for six hours or so have only a soft shell. If the crabs are taken out of the water during this period, they will stay alive for several days and the shell won't harden.

Although soft-shell season is fairly long—from May to September—soft-shell crabs are always quite expensive, and each year they seem to be smaller and pricier than the year before. The great advantage of course is that soft-shell crabs can be eaten whole, "shell" and all. Always buy soft-shell crabs alive.

Cleaning Soft-shell Crabs (see color page 18): Soft-shell crabs should be cleaned immediately before they are cooked. Rinse them under cold running water and brush them off with a small brush if they seem muddy. Twist off and discard the apron. Curl back the pointed side of one side of the top shell to expose the gills. Pull these off. Repeat on the other side. Cut across the front of the crab about ¼ inch behind the eyes and mouth and squeeze out the small sac that hides behind the mouth. Cook immediately.

Cooking Soft-shell Crabs: Although they are sometimes deep-fried, my favorite way to cook soft-shells is to sauté them in hot oil. I don't like to poach or steam soft-shells because the outer shell loses its delightful crispiness.

ROCK CRAB (Cancer irroratus)
AND JONAH CRAB (Cancer borealis)

Although both of these crabs are distinctly different species, it is sometimes difficult to tell them apart. They are generally larger than blue crabs but smaller than Dungeness crabs. The males are usually about 7 inches across, while females usually measure around 5 inches. They are light to dark brownish red, depending on where

they are caught—the farther north you go, the darker they get. Although both of these crabs are found along the Atlantic coast all the way from Nova Scotia to Florida, they aren't usually sold in upscale fish stores or in supermarkets. I usually find them in Spanish or Chinese markets, where they are almost ridiculously inexpensive. Although not usually as meaty as Dungeness crabs, rock and Jonah crabs have a delicious flavor. They can be cleaned, cooked, and served the same way as Dungeness crab.

CARIBBEAN, GULF, AND FLORIDA CRABS

STONE CRABS

There are more than 900 species of crabs from the higher stone crab family (Xanthidae), but only one species, the southern or Florida stone crab (*Menippi mercenaria*), is eaten with any regularity in the United States. I was shocked the first time I saw stone crab claws for sale, because I assumed that the whole crab had been sacrificed for two claws. In fact one of the delicious claws is snapped off the live crabs and the crabs thrown back in the water and given another year or two to grow another, albeit smaller, claw.

Most stone crab claws are sold cooked (the meat is hard to get out raw) and ready to eat. Unless you're in Florida, where you can eat them hot right out of the pot, I recommend eating stone crab claws cold with a little mayonnaise or in salads so they aren't heated twice, which can dry them out. Stone crabs are in season in Florida from November to May and all year in the Gulf.

CARIBBEAN LAND CRABS OR BLUE LAND CRAB (Cardisoma spp.)

You're unlikely to encounter these crabs anywhere other than their native habitats, Florida and the Caribbean— but if you do they're well worth eating. Their flavor is very similar to that of the Atlantic blue crab.

SMOOTH CORAL CRAB (Carpilius corralinus): Related to the southern stone crab, this smooth-shelled orange-tinted crab is sold in Caribbean markets.

CRABMEAT

Many recipes call for crabmeat. If you're a purist or have access to an abundance of fresh crabs, you may want to boil or steam the crabs and take out their meat yourself. Dungeness crab yields about 25 percent meat, while blue crab yields closer to 15 percent, so you'll need four to seven times the weight of whole crab to crabmeat.

Although markets that sell crabmeat rarely go into any detail about its grade or what crab it is from, it doesn't hurt to ask a few questions and show your eagerness to be informed. Crabmeat is sold wholesale in several grades, with different names and grading systems used for different crabs.

Much of the crabmeat sold in the United States comes from cooked Atlantic blue crabs. The meat is sold in three grades: The best grade is composed of large chunks from the body and is called *lump, jumbo,* or *backfin;* the second-best grade consists of smaller pieces of body meat and is called *flake;* the least-desirable grade is the brownish claw meat. Cocktail claws have the meat still in the shell, but the front part of the shell has been removed so the meat is easy to pull out. Crabmeat is

usually pasteurized to stretch its shelf-life; if you can find it, just picked very fresh unpasteurized crabmeat has a more delicate flavor.

You can also buy Dungeness crabmeat, which needless to say is very expensive. The grading system for Dungeness crab is somewhat different, with the leg meat—sometimes called "fry-legs"—being the most expensive, followed by "broken leg meat," with "body meat" coming in last.

Other crabs such as snow crab, king crab, and deep-sea red crab (*Geryon quinquedens*) are also picked and the meat is sold. Usually the size of the chunks (the larger the better) and color (the whiter the better) are general indicators of quality and price.

SOUPS AND SAUCES

Smaller crabs such as blue crabs can be broken up and cooked so that flavor is extracted from their shells, while larger crabs such as Dungeness crabs have such hard shells that no amount of boiling and pounding will get much flavor out of the shell. Although already picked crabmeat can be stirred into a soup at the last minute, the best crab soups start out with crabs broken up while they're still alive. Delicious sauces can also be made from whole crabs in the same way as soups but using less liquid.

❧

She-crab Soup

I, a northerner, hesitate to give a recipe for this South Carolina favorite, but I've come up with such an intensely flavored interpretation that I can't resist including it here.

Traditional recipes for this soup call for picked crabmeat and either canned or cooked crab roe along with a goodly amount of milk and cream. My own version is based on a tasty broth made from live blue crabs.

MAKES 8 FIRST-COURSE SERVINGS

12 blue crabs, preferably female
1 medium onion, finely chopped
½ celery stalk, chopped
½ teaspoon chopped fresh thyme or
  ¼ teaspoon dried
3 tablespoons pure olive oil
6 cups chicken broth (page 344) or water
¼ cup all-purpose flour
4 tablespoons unsalted butter
1 cup heavy cream
Tabasco sauce
1 pound fresh lump crabmeat
salt and pepper

Clean and break up the crabs as shown on color page 20.

In a pot large enough to hold the crabs, cook the onion, celery, and thyme in olive oil over medium heat until the onion turns translucent, about 10 minutes. Add the broken-up crabs and break them up further with the end of a European (handleless) rolling pin or a cleaver held up on end, stirring, for about 5 minutes more.

Pour in the broth, cover, and simmer gently for 30 minutes, breaking up and stirring the shells every 10 minutes. Strain and reserve the crab-cooking liquid through a regular strainer—push down hard with a wooden spoon to extract all the juices—and discard the shells. Strain the soup a second time through a fine-mesh strainer or triple layer of cheesecloth.

Make a roux by cooking the flour and butter in a 4-quart pot over medium heat for about 10 minutes, until the flour smells toasty.

Pour the reserved crab-cooking liquid into the hot roux while whisking. Bring the soup to a simmer while whisking to break up the roux. Simmer for about 5 minutes to get rid of the flour taste.

Just before serving, stir in the heavy cream, Tabasco, and crabmeat. Bring the soup to a simmer, season with salt and pepper to taste, and serve immediately in hot bowls.

Crab Sauce for Steamed, Braised, or Sautéed Fish

Atlantic blue crabs can be used to prepare a delicious sauce for sautéed, braised, or poached fish. When you're braising whole fish or fish fillets, you may want to braise the fish in concentrated crab broth and then finish the sauce with a small amount of cream or butter. This sauce is a lot of work, but you will end up with a concentrated almost indescribably delicious essence of crab.

The method for preparing a crab sauce is the same as for making the preceding she-crab soup—the crabs are broken up and simmered in broth or water—except that less liquid is used and the crab broth is boiled down (reduced) to concentrate its flavor. As in most crustacean soups and sauces, I like to add chopped tomatoes to give a slight sweetness to the sauce and to reinforce the natural red of the crabs.

This sauce has a light, creamy, almost brothlike texture. If you want a thicker sauce, reduce it to the consistency you like, but remember you'll end up with proportionately less sauce.

You can make the concentrated crab broth earlier in the day.

MAKES 1½ CUPS SAUCE, ENOUGH FOR 6 TO 12 SERVINGS

6 female blue crabs

1 medium onion, finely chopped

½ celery stalk, chopped

2 garlic cloves, crushed

½ teaspoon chopped fresh or ¼ teaspoon dried thyme

3 tablespoons olive oil

1 quart chicken broth (page 344) or water

4 tomatoes, seeded and chopped

2 tablespoons cognac

½ cup heavy cream

1 tablespoon crab or other crustacean butter (page 330) or unsalted butter

1 tablespoon finely chopped parsley or chervil

salt and white pepper

Clean and break up the crabs as shown on color page 20. In a pot large enough to hold the crabs, cook the onion, celery, garlic, and thyme in the olive oil over medium heat until the onion start s to turn translucent, about 10 minutes. Add the broken-up crabs and break them up further with the end of a cleaver or handleless rolling pin.

Pour in enough broth to cover the crabs (about 1 quart) and add the tomatoes. Cover the pot and simmer gently for 30 minutes, smashing on the crabs from time to time to break up the shells and get them to release their flavor into the surrounding liquid.

Strain the crab-cooking liquid with a regular strainer into a saucepan, pushing hard with the back of a wooden spoon to extract all the liquid. Discard the crab shells.

Add the cognac to the crab broth and boil the mixture down until about 1½ cups remain. Pour in the cream

and simmer the sauce, whisking every minute or so, for about 10 minutes, until the sauce has the texture of cold heavy cream. Strain the sauce through a fine-mesh strainer. Whisk in the butter and parsley and season with salt and pepper to taste.

SAUTÉING

Most crabs don't take well to sautéing because the heat has difficulty penetrating the shell and the crab ends up coated with hot oil, making it difficult to eat. Soft-shell crabs are the exception.

Sautéed Soft-shell Crabs

Soft-shell crabs are one of those foods best served as simply as possible. Sautéing is ideal because it enhances the delightful crispiness of the outer shell while the crab stays juicy on the inside.

Soft-shell crabs vary in size from 2 to 5 inches. Depending on their size, I serve 3 or 4 as a main course and 1 or 2 as a first course. Usually I don't bother serving a sauce, but if I'm being festive I sometimes make one or more of the salsas in "Sauces and Salsas, Condiments and Broths."

MAKES 6 TO 8 FIRST-COURSE OR 4 MAIN-COURSE SERVINGS

12 to 16 live soft-shell crabs

½ cup all-purpose flour

¼ cup olive oil

salt and pepper

continued

Clean the crabs as shown on color page 20 within an hour of serving. Ten minutes before you're ready to serve, toss the crabs in flour in a large mixing bowl. Pat them gently to eliminate excess flour.

Heat the olive oil in a sauté pan large enough to hold the crabs in a single layer or use 2 pans. When the oil starts to ripple, gently slide the crabs, top shell down, into the pan. Move the pan back and forth for a few seconds while adding the crabs to prevent them from sticking.

Cook the crabs over medium-high heat for about 3 minutes on each side. Keep lifting the crabs up to check how they are browning—the flour should brown and turn crispy, but be careful not to let it burn.

Transfer the crabs to a plate covered with paper towels. Pat them gently with paper towels to eliminate excess oil. Season with salt and pepper and serve immediately on hot plates.

❧

Sautéed Crab Cakes

(color page 5)

Crab cakes are one of those dishes that make me think of old-fashioned American restaurants with sawdust on the floor and big steins of beer. Like so many of my favorite seafood goodies, crab cakes have gotten expensive so it's worthwhile to learn to make them at home.

Crab cakes are often fried, but I'm always much happier when they are sautéed gently in butter. Crab cakes can be breaded in any number of ways—with bread crumbs is a favorite—but again I think they're lighter when dusted lightly with flour. Crab cakes are most delicious when

served with a tangy homemade mayonnaise, such as gribiche or tartar sauce, but a plate of lemon wedges will do in a pinch. Crab cakes can be made earlier in the day.

MAKES 8 CRAB CAKES, ENOUGH FOR 4 FIRST-COURSE OR LIGHT MAIN-COURSE SERVINGS

1 pound lump crabmeat

4 slices of white bread, crusts removed, or 6 tablespoons fresh bread crumbs

2 eggs

¼ cup milk

2 teaspoons salt

pepper

¼ teaspoon cayenne pepper

3 tablespoons finely chopped parsley

½ cup all-purpose flour

¼ cup unsalted butter

lemon wedges

tartar or gribiche sauce (pages 335 or 334)

Pick through the crabmeat to eliminate any stray pieces of shell or cartilage.

Put the bread in a food processor or blender for about 30 seconds to break it up into crumbs.

Beat the eggs with the milk, the salt, about 5 grinds of the pepper mill, and the cayenne in a mixing bowl. Stir in the crab, bread crumbs, and parsley.

Form the crab mixture into 8 patties and gently roll them in flour. Pat off most the flour so only a thin layer adheres to the cakes.

Gently heat the butter in a nonstick sauté pan or skillet large enough to hold the crab cakes in a single layer (or use 2 pans or cook the cakes in batches, keeping them warm in a 200°F oven).

Gently sauté the crab cakes for about 4 minutes on each side. Pat off the excess butter with a paper towel and serve immediately on hot plates with lemon wedges and/or a sauce.

BAKING, BROILING, OR MICROWAVING KING CRAB LEGS

These techniques work best for king crab legs. When buying king crab legs, remember that they have already been cooked before being flash-frozen, so just thaw and heat them through. It's better to buy king crab legs still frozen than already thawed so they won't have any time to lose freshness.

If you're using a microwave, the legs can be thawed and heated at the same time. Otherwise the best way to thaw them is to leave them at room temperature for about 2 hours or in the refrigerator overnight.

Legs that have been split lengthwise are best thawed and brushed with melted butter or extra-virgin olive oil, seasoned with salt and pepper and perhaps some chopped herbs such as thyme or marjoram, and broiled for about 3 minutes.

Whole cracked legs are best thawed and then baked in a 350°F oven for 8 minutes.

Whole or split king crab legs can be thawed in the microwave by wrapping them in a damp towel and cooking on high for about 2 minutes. They can also be thawed and heated through at the same time by keeping them in the microwave for a total of 4 minutes. The best way to know when the legs are done is to reach in and feel when they're hot. (In the microwave the actual thawing and cooking time will depend on how many legs you heat at once.)

BRAISING

Although live crabs are sometimes broken into several sections and simmered, shell and all, in liquid or sauce, I find this more trouble than it's worth. Getting the meat out of a crab can be difficult enough without having the crab pieces covered with a sticky sauce. Unlike lobster, crayfish, or shrimp, which have softer shells that release their flavor into the surrounding liquid, most large crabs have hard shells that contribute little to the cooking liquid. Smaller crabs such as Atlantic blue crabs do have pliable shells, but there is still the trouble of getting the meat out of the shell.

Because of these factors, I prefer to prepare the sauce with whole blue crabs and then use the sauce to gently reheat lump crabmeat. If you want your sauce to have a full crab flavor, you'll have to use smaller crabs, such as Atlantic blue crabs, and prepare the crab sauce for steamed, braised, or sautéed fish on page 209.

ᘒ

Atlantic Crab Stew

Once you've made the crab sauce, assembling this light but hearty stew takes only a few minutes. In this version mushrooms and tomatoes are added for extra color and flavor and to vary the texture—but almost any vegetable will do. I sometimes use freshly blanched peas, asparagus tips, or little French green beans. Buy the largest pieces of crabmeat you can find. This stew is more intensely crab flavored than any dish I've ever tasted. I like to serve it with plain rice.

MAKES 6 FIRST-COURSE OR LIGHT MAIN-COURSE SERVINGS

1 recipe crab sauce for fish (page 209)

1 pound lump crabmeat

1½ pounds wild or cultivated mushrooms, rinsed and dried

3 tablespoons pure olive oil

salt and pepper

6 tomatoes, peeled, seeded, and coarsely chopped

2 tablespoons finely chopped parsley or chervil

fresh chervil sprigs for decoration (optional)

Prepare the crab sauce. Carefully pick through the crabmeat and discard any stray pieces of shell or cartilage.

If the mushrooms are more than 2 inches in diameter, cut them into quarters. Sauté the mushrooms in olive oil in a saucepan over high heat until they brown lightly, about 8 minutes. If they release liquid, keep sautéing until the liquid evaporates. Season with salt and pepper and set aside.

In a separate sauté pan, heat the tomatoes over high heat, stirring, until the liquid they release completely evaporates, about 20 minutes. Season with salt and pepper.

Add the crab sauce, tomatoes, and parsley to the mushrooms and stir over medium heat until the mixture is hot. Stir in the crabmeat, stir over the heat for a minute more, and place the stew in mounds on hot plates. Decorate each mound with a sprig of chervil if desired.

Crayfish

As a child I first encountered crayfish in a nearby California lake. Compared to the wary trout, crayfish were an easy catch—a piece of hot dog tied to the end of a string did the trick—and a neighbor from New Orleans paid 15 cents per crayfish, a good price even now. It wasn't until years later in France, where crayfish are a supreme and costly delicacy, that I tasted one for myself, in an elaborate dish with chicken and cream. I now eat crayfish in all their many guises.

Crayfish, or "crawfish" as they are called in the southern United States, look like miniature lobsters (usually about 3 to 4 inches long) and swim in streams, lakes, and sometimes in brackish water but never in the open sea. (Don't confuse crayfish with spiny lobsters, sometimes called crayfish, or with lobsterettes, saltwater crustaceans about the same size as crayfish.) Once available only in Louisiana and some parts of California and the Northwest, live crayfish are now sold in most parts of the United States.

Although shelled crayfish tails are available packaged, most of the crayfish flavor is in the shells and head. So if you want to cook anything more elaborate than a simple crayfish salad, you'll need to buy whole crayfish. Whole crayfish are sometimes available frozen but most of the time you'll need to buy live crayfish.

CRAYFISH VARIETIES

Of the more than 400 species of crayfish found around the world, about 250 are North American. Most of the American species are similar in appearance and differ only in size. Only three species are sold with any regularity in the United States: red swamp crayfish (*Procambarus clarkii*) from the Louisiana delta, white river crayfish (*Procambarus acutus*) from northern Louisiana, and Pacific crayfish (*Pacifastacus leniusculus*) from California and Oregon. Of these three the red swamp crayfish is a favorite because it is usually slightly larger than the other two and turns a beautiful bright red when cooked. But since it's unlikely that any more than one variety of crayfish is going to be sold at one time in one place, you're not going to be able to pick and choose.

BUYING AND STORING CRAYFISH

The main thing to look for when buying crayfish is to make sure they are all alive. In most places you'll have to trust the fishmonger to pick through them for you, but if the crayfish are out in the open you can select your own. Hold them face down by the sides (near where the claws join the body) so they won't be able to pinch—dead ones will hang limp, and live ones will squirm.

When you get your crayfish home, cover them in a bowl with a wet towel and keep them in the refrigerator. Don't try to keep them for more than 24 hours.

YIELD

There are between 15 and 20 crayfish per pound. Whole crayfish yield between 15 percent and 20 percent meat. You'll need 3 pounds live crayfish to obtain a cup (½ pound) of crayfish tail meat. When I'm making crayfish for a crowd, I sometimes fill out the recipe with packaged crayfish tails and buy only enough live crayfish to make a tasty broth or sauce and for decoration.

PREPARING CRAYFISH FOR COOKING

Many old French recipes call for pulling out the crayfish intestines while the crayfish are still alive. It is true that the intestine can be unsightly in the same way as a shrimp "vein," but it's so easy to remove once the crayfish is cooked that I never bother with the medieval disemboweling

SOFT-SHELL CRAYFISH

Soft-shell crayfish that have shed their hard outer shells in the same way as soft-shell crabs have begun to appear on the market in vacuum-packed plastic containers. You can eat the whole crayfish except for the gastroliths, two hard calcium stones held in reserve for growing a new hard shell. To remove the gastroliths, snip off the eyes and snout with scissors and squeeze the head to pop out the stones.

process. I do admit to being cold-hearted when it comes to the actual cooking and usually toss the living crayfish into boiling water or wine or hot oil. If this seems too barbaric, the crayfish can be killed shortly before cooking in the same way as lobsters, by quickly cutting the fronts of their heads in half with a sharp knife.

When you're ready to cook your crayfish, spread them on a counter and quickly sort through them to get rid of any dead ones. (Don't put them in a sink full of water, which will give them a decided tactical advantage.) Put the live crayfish in a colander, rinse them with cold water, and let them drain for a minute or two.

SERVING WHOLE CRAYFISH

Although the easiest way to cook and serve crayfish is to throw them in a pot of boiling water, simmer them for about 5 to 8 minutes, and serve, most cooks add flavorings such as vegetables, herbs, or spices to the boiling liquid. A Creole version of boiled crayfish can be made by stirring 2 or 3 tablespoons of Creole spices—usually available in jars—into the boiling water, while a Scandinavian version may contain a large bunch of dill. French versions on the same theme are likely to contain aromatic vegetables (carrots, onions, celery), herbs such as tarragon, chervil, or parsley, and either white or red wine. Most of the time the crayfish are then served, hot or cold, in their cooking liquid. In more complicated variations the cooking liquid can be boiled down to concentrate its flavor or flavored and enriched with additional herbs, butter, or cream. Whatever flavors you decide to use, the technique is the same.

EUROPEAN AND AUSTRALIAN CRAYFISH

European species of crayfish have become so rare in Europe that most crayfish served in restaurants come from the United States. The largest European crayfish (*Astacus astacus*) is the beloved *patte rouge* (red claw) crayfish of France's finest restaurants. Unfortunately these "red claw" crayfish are almost fished out or decimated by disease, so they are found only rarely on menus and, as far as I know, never for sale on the open market. Another European variety, *Astacus leptodactylus*—the French call this one a *patte blanche*—comes from Eastern Europe and along with American crayfish is the variety eaten by most Europeans.

Three Australian varieties of crayfish are worth mentioning. Although as of yet none of these is available in the United States, they're so enormous and apparently delicious that they will no doubt eventually show up. Despite its name, the Murray lobster (*Astacopsis gouldi*) is actually a crayfish—the largest crayfish in the world, weighing up to 12 pounds. It is found on the Australian island of Tasmania and occasionally in eastern Australia. To add to the confusion there is also the Murray River crayfish (*Euastacus armatus*), which is the second-largest crayfish in the world—up to 20 inches long—and also found in Tasmania and mainland Australia. A second runner-up, the marron (*Cherax tenuimanus*), weighs up to 6 pounds and is one of Australia's favorites. The marron is the mostly likely candidate for exporting to the United States because it has been farmed successfully in Australia since 1976. Australians call crayfish *yabbies*.

Boiled Crayfish

This is a basic recipe that can be adapted to your own preferred style. For a French version (*à la nage*), include the white wine; for a Scandinavian version, use the dill; and for a Creole version, whisk in the spices. Whatever version you do prepare, your guests will have fun picking the meat out of the tails and sucking the juices (the tastiest part) out of the heads. The broth, which will be left in the bottom of the bowl, is fun to mop up with crusty French bread. The broth can be prepared a day or two in advance.

MAKES 6 FIRST-COURSE SERVINGS

6 pounds live crayfish

1 celery stalk, finely sliced

1 medium carrot, peeled, finely sliced

1 medium onion, peeled, finely sliced

1 large bouquet garni (about 3 inches in diameter) of fresh herbs, including dill, tarragon, parsley, chervil, basil, marjoram, or thyme or any combination, tied into a bundle with string

10 cups water

2 cups white wine or 3 tablespoons Creole spice mixture

juice of 2 lemons

sea salt and cayenne pepper (optional)

Sort through the crayfish and throw out any dead ones. Rinse off the crayfish and keep them, covered with a wet towel, in a large bowl in the refrigerator.

Simmer the vegetables and bouquet garni in the water in a covered pot large enough to hold all the crayfish for 45 minutes. If you're using the wine, pour it into the pot after 30 minutes. If you're using the Creole spice mixture, whisk it into the broth

halfway through the cooking. You can add the crayfish directly to the boiling broth or—for slightly dressier occasions—strain the broth and discard the vegetables before using the broth to boil the crayfish.

Bring the broth—strained or not—to a rapid boil, throw in the crayfish, cover the pot, and boil until all the crayfish turn at least partly red (some species of crayfish never turn completely red), 5 to 8 minutes. Stir the crayfish with a long spoon halfway into the cooking so that those above the boiling liquid are turned under into the liquid. When the crayfish are done, scoop them into deep wide bowls. Add the lemon juice, salt, and cayenne to taste to the broth. Ladle the hot cooking liquid over the crayfish. You can also chill both crayfish and broth and serve this dish cold. Or you can quickly boil down the cooking liquid by half to concentrate its flavor—keeping the crayfish warm in the oven—before pouring it over the crayfish in the bowls.

HOW TO GET THE MEAT OUT OF A CRAYFISH

To the uninitiated eating a whole crayfish can be a daunting experience. I got my first lesson from a patient waiter in a Parisian restaurant while, it seemed, the whole dining room looked on.

Compared to some creatures—crab, for instance—eating a crayfish is quick and easy and clearly worth the effort. The first step is to twist off the tail. If you're working in the kitchen, you can take the meat out of the tail by cutting along one side of its underside with scissors and then just pulling away the sides of the tails so the meat pops out. If you're at the table and unequipped with scissors, you can take the meat out of the tail by pinching the sides of the tail until you feel a gentle crunch. You then pull on the sides of the tail, and the meat should pop right out. If you want to devein the tail—I don't bother if I'm eating the crayfish myself—just push the top of the back to one side so that the meat tears and reveals the "vein." If the vein is black, just pull it out. Suck the juices out of the head.

Some crayfish claws are so small that you may not want to bother with them, but if so, just snap them in half and suck out the meat (see color page 23).

Crayfish Stew with Tomatoes, Sorrel, and Vegetables

This brightly colored and subtly flavored miniature stew is prepared in the same way as simple boiled crayfish except that finely julienned vegetables are used for the broth, which is then boiled down to concentrate its flavors. The concentrated broth is then combined with a small amount of heavy cream and crayfish butter. The tomatoes add color and flavor, and sorrel adds a pleasant tang, but you can substitute other herbs and vegetables depending on whim and season. Tarragon, dill, or mint can replace the sorrel, and vegetables such as baby peas (lightly blanched), spinach (blanched), haricots verts (blanched), blanched baby asparagus tips, or, the ultimate treat, chopped black truffles can replace or augment the sorrel. You can julienne the vegetables with a chef's knife, but a benriner cutter (a Japanese slicer) will make it a lot easier.

You can make this dish all in one day, but if you cook crayfish with any regularity it's probably most convenient to save the shells in the freezer and to make crayfish butter when you accumulate a pound or two so you don't have to make it each time.

Because crustacean butters are so similar in flavor you can also get by substituting lobster or shrimp butter. If you haven't any of these and don't want to bother making crayfish butter, substitute plain unsalted butter.

MAKES 4 FIRST-COURSE OR 2 LIGHT MAIN-COURSE SERVINGS

36 live crayfish (about 2 pounds)

1 leek, including 1 inch of green, cut in half lengthwise and sand rinsed out

2 medium carrots, peeled, cut into 3-inch lengths

1 turnip, peeled

1 cup dry white wine

1 bouquet garni: 4 fresh thyme sprigs or ½ teaspoon dried, a small bunch of parsley, and a bay leaf, tied up with string (or in cheesecloth for dried thyme)

1 cup water

½ cup heavy cream

½ tightly packed cup sorrel leaves (about ¼ pound), finely chopped (optional)

1 medium tomato, peeled, seeded, and chopped

1 tablespoon fresh lemon juice

3 tablespoons crayfish butter, other crustacean butter (page 330), or unsalted butter

salt and pepper

Rinse the crayfish in a colander and reserve in the refrigerator. If you're keeping the crayfish for more than a few hours before cooking, cover them with a wet towel.

Cut the leek into fine julienne—2 or 3 leaves at a time—with a chef's knife. If the leaves are more than 3 inches long, fold them end to end to make them easier to julienne.

Slice the carrots lengthwise—about ⅛ inch thick—on 4 sides until you reach the core. Discard the core. Cut the slices into fine julienne. Thinly slice the turnip and cut each slice into julienne.

In a 4-quart pot, combine the julienned vegetables with the wine, bouquet garni, and water. Cover the pot and simmer gently for 25 minutes, until the vegetables are soft but not mushy. Remove the vegetables and bouquet garni with a slotted spoon; reserve the vegetables and discard the bouquet garni. Bring the vegetable broth to a simmer, toss in the crayfish, cover the pot, and simmer for about 5 to 8 minutes, depending on size, until the crayfish turn at least partially red. (Some species never turn bright red in the same way as lobsters.) Stir them once to submerge those not covered by liquid.

Take the crayfish out of the broth and reserve one per serving for decorating the plates. Pull the vein out of the tail by tugging gently on the piece of shell at the very end of the tail—the vein should pull right out. Take the tail meat out of the shells and reserve both meat and shells. Use the heads and shells to make crayfish butter or, if you already have some crayfish butter on hand, freeze them for another recipe or for another batch of butter.

Bring the vegetable broth to a rapid boil and cook it down to about 1 cup. Add the cream, stir in the sorrel, tomato, and lemon juice, and simmer for 1 minute. Whisk in the crayfish butter and season with salt and pepper to taste.

Heat the julienned vegetables and crayfish tails in separate saucepans by stirring each with 2 tablespoons of the creamy broth. Mound the vegetables in the center of wide soup bowls and arrange the crayfish tails around them. Place a whole cooked crayfish on each plate for decoration. Ladle in the hot broth.

MAKING BROTH AND BUTTER FROM SHELLS AND HEADS

Many recipes use crayfish tails, either packaged or prepared fresh, in various stews, étouffées, and jambalayas. Crayfish tails are delicious little morsels of meat, but paradoxically most of the crayfish's flavor is actually in the head and shells. There are several ways to get the flavor out of the crayfish head and shells. One method, popular in Louisiana, is to reach into the head with a spoon and scoop out the coral and yellow fat—called the *heptopancreas*. Another, used in France and in Louisiana, is to make a flavorful broth from the broken-up crayfish head and shells.

I usually opt for the second method because it provides an intensely flavored broth that can be used in soups and stews or cooked down and turned into a sauce. The crayfish heads and shells can be broken up with a rolling pin in the same way as shrimp and lobster shells, or they can be ground in a food processor. The food processor does a better job of extracting the crayfish's flavor, but you have to be careful not to puree the shells too finely or the resulting liquid will turn muddy and have to be strained several times, the last time through a cloth. You should also avoid grinding crayfish claws in a food processor, or their hard shells may damage the blade.

Another method for getting flavor out of crayfish shells and heads is to prepare crayfish butter (page 330). An ideal if somewhat complicated approach is to make crayfish broth with one batch of shells and crayfish butter with another batch and incorporate both into the same dish.

Fillet of Grouper with Crayfish Sauce

This is one of those old-fashioned French dishes that most of us never taste anymore—it's been replaced with foods lighter and quicker to prepare. But when I look down on my plate and see the bright orange sauce and the delicate crayfish tails and then take a bite, the beauty of rich and subtle French food comes back in a flood of memory. I like to serve this dish at my best dinners with the best Burgundy I can afford.

While French cooks would probably use Dover sole, that's expensive and hard to find in the United States. It's best to substitute a firm-fleshed delicate-tasting white fish such as grouper.

The crayfish sauce makes the flavor of a small number of crayfish go a long way—the same concept behind several French dishes, including *poulet aux écrevisses*, a chicken stewed in crayfish sauce and served covered with crayfish tails. The sauce is time-consuming but can be made the day before.

MAKES 6 MAIN-COURSE SERVINGS

42 live crayfish (about 2½ pounds)

one 5-pound whole grouper or other firm white-fleshed fish, filleted and skin removed, fillets cut into a total of 6 portions, heads and bones reserved

For the Fish Broth:

heads and bones from fish

1 medium onion, chopped

1 celery stalk, chopped

1 carrot, chopped

1 bouquet garni: 3 fresh thyme sprigs or ½ teaspoon dried, a small bunch of parsley, and a bay leaf tied up in string (or in cheesecloth for dried thyme)

4 medium tomatoes, chopped

1 cup dry white wine

For Cooking the Crayfish and Crayfish Shells:

2 tablespoons olive oil

1½ cups heavy cream

For Finishing the Sauce:

1 tablespoon cognac

2 tablespoons crayfish butter (page 330) or unsalted butter

1 tablespoon finely chopped parsley or other fresh herbs such as chervil, tarragon, chives, or dill

1 tablespoon fresh lemon juice

salt and pepper

For Cooking the Fish:

1 to 2 tablespoons unsalted butter or olive oil

Sort through the crayfish to make sure they're all alive. Rinse them in a colander and keep in the refrigerator. If you're keeping the crayfish for more than a few hours before cooking, cover them with a wet towel.

Prepare a fish broth by gently simmering the fish heads and bones, vegetables, bouquet garni, tomatoes, wine, and barely enough water to cover for about 30 minutes, until the bones and heads fall apart. Use a ladle to skim off froth and scum that floats to the top. Strain the fish broth into a pot and reserve.

While the fish broth is cooking, heat 2 tablespoons olive oil in a pot large enough to hold the crayfish. When the oil begins to smoke, pour in the crayfish and stir with a wooden spoon. Cover the pot, lower the heat to medium, and steam the crayfish until they turn at least partly red, 5 to 8 minutes. During the steaming, stir the crayfish once or twice to redistribute them.

Remove the lid and let the crayfish cool. Set aside 6 of the largest crayfish for decorating the plates. Devein, remove, and reserve the tail meat of the remaining crayfish, being sure to save the tail shells along with the heads. Snap the claws away from the heads, crack them with a rolling pin, and reserve. If the claws seem big or you're very conscientious, remove and reserve the meat (keep the claw shells separate from the other shells).

Place all the crayfish shells except the claws or claw shells in a food processor with enough of the reserved fish broth to get the shells to move around freely—if your food processor is small, you may have to do this in 2 batches. Puree the shell/fish broth mixture for about 30 seconds and combine the mixture with the cream, 2 cups of the reserved fish broth, and claw shells in a 4-quart pot. Any remaining fish broth can be saved for another recipe. Simmer the mixture gently for 45 minutes and strain through a fine-mesh strainer into a saucepan. Add the cognac and boil the sauce down to about 1 cup, until it has a silky, saucelike consistency. Whisk in the crayfish butter, stir in the herbs and lemon juice, and season with salt and pepper to taste. Just before serving, heat the reserved crayfish tails in the sauce.

Sauté the grouper fillets in butter or olive oil over medium to high heat for about 4 minutes on each side (8 minutes per inch of thickness altogether) and arrange on hot plates or on a platter. (The fillets can also be braised in the remaining fish broth and the braising liquid incorporated into the sauce.) Coat the fillets lightly with the sauce and garnish with the crayfish tails. Decorate the plates or platter with the reserved whole crayfish.

Substitutes Fillets such as black drum, blackfish, blowfish, cod/scrod, cusk, Dover sole, haddock, hake, halibut, John Dory, kingclip, lingcod, mahimahi, monkfish, ocean pout, orange roughy, red drum, sea robin, skate, striped bass

❧

Crayfish Étouffée

To cook something *à l'étouffée* is to steam it in a tightly covered container with relatively little liquid—literally to suffocate it. Despite the word's French roots, the American étouffée is a Cajun innovation, best appreciated in Louisiana and Texas. Although étouffée recipes are the subject of constant dispute, the many variations share certain elements. All are thickened with a lightly cooked roux (not the dark roux used for gumbos), and all contain onion, garlic, celery, and green bell peppers. Most are also finished with chopped parsley or perhaps a little chopped scallion, and some, but not all, are flavored with prepared seasonings such as Worcestershire sauce, Tabasco sauce, or Beau Monde seasoning mixes, cayenne, or paprika. A few contain tomatoes.

Because étouffée recipes usually call for chicken or fish broth or even water, the stew itself has little crayfish flavor. For this reason I like to make a flavorful broth from crayfish heads and tails and use it as the base for the stew. Because this approach is also somewhat labor-intensive, I augment the live crayfish with prepared and peeled crayfish tails.

Crayfish étouffée can be made a day or two ahead and reheated gently. Serve with plenty of rice.

MAKES 6 MAIN-COURSE SERVINGS

3 pounds live crayfish and 2 cups crayfish tail meat

1 quart water

4 medium tomatoes, seeded and chopped

1 quart chicken broth (page 344), fish broth (page 343), or water or just enough to cover

1 medium onion, finely chopped

1 green bell pepper, finely chopped

2 garlic cloves, finely chopped

1 teaspoon fresh or ½ teaspoon dried thyme leaves

4 tablespoons unsalted butter

4 heaped tablespoons all-purpose flour

2 tablespoons finely chopped parsley

2 tablespoons fresh lemon juice

Tabasco sauce

salt and pepper

Rinse the live crayfish thoroughly in a colander and drain. Bring the water to a rapid boil in a pot large enough to hold all the crayfish. Pour the crayfish into the boiling liquid and cover the pot tightly. Cook the crayfish over high heat for about 5 to 8 minutes, until they've all turned at least partly red. Stir the crayfish every couple of minutes so they cook evenly.

Take the crayfish out of the pot with a skimmer, leaving the cooking liquid in the pot. Twist off the tails, devein, and remove the meat, saving the shells.

Put the crayfish shells and tomatoes in the pot with the water used to cook the crayfish. Spend about 10 minutes crushing the shells with the end of a cleaver or European (handleless) rolling pin. Simmer the shells gently for 45 minutes.

Strain the shell-cooking liquid first through a coarse strainer and then through a fine-mesh strainer. (The shells can damage the fine-mesh strainer.) You should end up with 3 cups of liquid. If you have more, boil the crayfish broth down to 3 cups; if you have less, add broth or water to stretch it to 3 cups.

In a heavy 4-quart saucepan over medium heat, cook the onion, bell pepper, garlic, and thyme in the butter, stirring every few minutes with a wooden spoon, until the onions turn translucent, about 10 minutes. Stir in the flour and cook for 5 minutes more. Stir in the crayfish broth and simmer gently for 10 minutes. Stir in the parsley, lemon juice, and all the crayfish tails. Season with Tabasco, salt, and pepper to taste. Serve with steamed rice.

CRAYFISH SOUPS

Most crayfish soups are made in the same way as crayfish sauces and stews: a broth is made by simmering the crushed crayfish shells and bodies; the broth is thickened with roux, bread crumbs, rice, or vegetable purees such as potato, corn, or squash; and the soup is enriched lightly with cream or butter (sometimes crayfish butter). Herbs and spices are then added to give the soup its final character. Crayfish bisque is one of the most popular crayfish soups. You can make a classic crayfish bisque by substituting crayfish for the shrimp in the recipe on page 197 or make the potato-thickened crayfish soup that follows.

Cream of Crayfish, Potato, and Leek Soup

I'm a great lover of bisques, and even though this soup is similar to a bisque—the only difference is that potatoes are used instead of rice or bread crumbs—it seems smoother and more delicate. You can make the soup up to 2 days in advance.

MAKES 8 FIRST-COURSE SERVINGS

6 pounds live crayfish

6 cups water

4 medium tomatoes, seeded and chopped

4 medium leeks, halved lengthwise, sand rinsed out, chopped

1½ pounds (about 4 medium) potatoes, preferably Yukon gold but russets will do, peeled and coarsely chopped

1 cup heavy cream

salt, pepper, and cayenne

Rinse the live crayfish thoroughly in a colander and drain. Bring the water to a boil in a pot large enough to hold all the crayfish. Pour in the crayfish, cover the pot, and simmer until the crayfish have all turned at least partly red, 5 to 8 minutes. Remove the pot from the heat, uncover, and let cool.

Devein and peel the crayfish tails, saving the cooking liquid. Put all the crayfish shells and the tomatoes in the pot with the water used to cook the crayfish. Spend about 10 minutes crushing the crayfish shells with the end of a cleaver or European (handle-less) rolling pin. Gently simmer the shells, covered, for 45 minutes.

Strain the shell-cooking liquid first through a coarse strainer and then through a fine-mesh strainer. (The shells can damage the fine-mesh strainer.) If, after straining, the liquid is murky or gritty, strain it through a cloth napkin or a triple layer of cheesecloth. Discard the shells. You should end up with about 6 cups of crayfish broth.

Combine the broth with the leeks and potatoes in a 4-quart pot and simmer gently for about 25 minutes, until you can crush the potatoes against the inside of the pot with a spoon. Work the soup through a food mill with the finest attachment or puree it in a blender or food processor for about 30 seconds and strain it.

Stir the cream and crayfish tails into the soup, bring to a slow simmer, and season with salt, pepper, and cayenne to taste. If the soup is too thick, thin it with a little water or milk.

Squid, Cuttlefish, and Octopus

American eating habits have come a long way since I first saw (with horror) an octopus for sale while walking around Chinatown with my mother in the 1950s. Squid was the first of the many-tentacled creatures to be adopted by the American public and is now sold even in fast-food places. Octopus has begun to appear on the menus of trendy restaurants and will no doubt be standard fare in family restaurants before too long. Cuttlefish is still somewhat hard to find, but this is probably because it has to be imported, not because it inspires primal fears.

These three sea creatures are lumped together because they are all cephalopods (Greek for "head-foot"); that is, they all have conical or cylindrical heads and 8 or 10 tentacles. All cephalopods produce ink, which they use as a smoke screen to escape attackers. Cephalopods come in a variety of sizes from tiny squid and octopus little more than an inch long to horror-movie-size giant squid as long as 70 feet. Fortunately the larger of these creatures never makes it to market.

SQUID

After years of relative obscurity and confinement to truly ethnic restaurants, squid is now so popular that it's a regular pizza item and fried squid rings are sold in chain restaurants. Squid's popularity is undoubtedly due in part to the fact that it's cheap and plentiful. Whole squid typically costs one fifth of the price of whole red snapper and other premium fish and yields up to 70 percent edible flesh, 18 percent of which is protein.

Although there are dozens of species of squid, only three are sold with any regularity in the United States—Atlantic long-finned squid (*Loligo pealeii*), Atlantic short-finned squid (*Illex illecebrosus*), and California or Pacific squid (*Loligo opalescens*). Although California squid has the best reputation, I am equally happy with both Atlantic and Pacific varieties.

Much of the squid that is sold as fresh has actually been frozen and thawed before it is put in the display case. Fortunately neither the flavor nor the texture of squid is altered by freezing, but you should be sure that thawed squid hasn't been out too long. The most reliable method of judging freshness is smell—there should be a delicate ocean smell—but the squid should also look shiny and firm, not sagging like a deflated balloon. The thin dull membrane covering the squid should be gray rather than pink or purple; pink or purple coloration indicates that the squid is less than perfectly fresh.

CLEANING SQUID

Cleaned squid bodies (hoods) and tentacles are often sold in upscale fish markets at about twice the price of uncleaned squid. Although cleaned squid saves time, if you like shopping in ethnic markets—where things are cheaper and there's always something new to discover—you'll have to buy squid whole, uncleaned.

To clean a squid, just reach into the hood and pull everything out—or push it out by slicing a knife along the outside of the squid—including the transparent plasticlike quill running along the inside. Cut off the tentacles just below the eyes with a sharp knife. Save the tentacles and throw out the rest of the innards. Rinse out the inside of the hoods under cold running water. Pull the thin gray membrane off the outside of the hood—you may have to scrape it with the back of a paring knife to help get it off. Cut off and save the 2 small wings on the side of the hood (see color page 19).

CUTTING SQUID INTO RINGS

To cut squid into rings before cooking, just slice the hoods into ¼-inch-wide rings with a sharp knife. Unless they are very small, cut the tentacle clusters in half through the top. Rinse out any grit trapped in the top ring where the tentacles join. Rinse both the hood slices and tentacles under cold running water and dry them thoroughly with cloth or paper towels. (Don't let squid touch paper towels for more than a few seconds, or the towels will stick and be impossible to remove.)

USING SQUID INK

Many Mediterranean dishes include squid ink to color the sauce a distinctive black and to give it a deeper sealike flavor. If you're using the squid ink, remove the innards carefully so as not to damage the small silver-gray sac located near the top of the squid's hood. Carefully cut these sacs away from the rest of the innards and save them, covered with a tablespoon of water, in the refrigerator until needed. Unlike cuttlefish (see below), which have larger ink sacs filled with a very thick and powerful ink, squid ink is paler and there's less of it.

COOKING SQUID

Squid has the undeserved reputation of being tough. It is true that it turns rubbery and chewy when cooked improperly. The trick is to cook squid either a very short time (no more than 2 minutes) or a very long time (no fewer than 30 minutes). The best techniques for cooking are deep-frying, sautéing, grilling, and stir-frying. The best slow cooking technique is braising, especially in wine.

DEEP-FRYING SQUID

Squid is usually deep-fried after its hood has been cut into small rings and the tentacles, if they are large, are cut in half through the top of the cluster. Because the squid pieces are small, the cooking oil should be hot—360°F to 370°F—and the cooking time just long enough to turn the outer coating crispy but leave the squid pale, almost white. Don't deep-fry squid until it turns brown, or it will be overcooked. My favorite coatings for squid are plain flour and the club soda batter on page 43.

Deep-fried Squid Rings and Tentacles

I love serving these at a cocktail party or in a big bowl in the middle of the table as the opening for a casual dinner party. Especially if my guests don't know each other, the reaching and nibbling seems to loosen everybody up. The easiest way to serve deep-fried squid is to squeeze some lemon juice over the hot squid or pass lemon wedges at the table. You can also serve tartar or gribiche sauce (pages 335 or 334) or Thai dipping sauce (page 86), but be careful if you have a big dinner planned that the guests don't fill themselves up. Fried parsley also makes a decorative touch.

The squid can be cut up, washed, and dried in advance, but don't try flouring it until the last second or it will all clump together.

MAKES 6 HORS D'OEUVRE SERVINGS

2 pounds whole squid or 1¼ pounds cleaned

1 quart pure olive oil or vegetable oil

¾ cup all-purpose flour

salt

lemon juice or wedges

a handful of curly parsley leaves, washed and perfectly dry

Clean the squid and cut it into rings as shown on color page 19.

Heat the oil to 360°F in a heavy pot or iron skillet. If you don't have a thermometer, put a floured squid ring in the hot oil. It should immediately float to the top and be surrounded by bubbles, but if it browns before 45 seconds, turn down the heat.

Toss the squid in the flour and then toss in a strainer to get rid of excess flour. Deep-fry the squid in 3 batches—large batches will cool the oil or cause it to overflow—and quickly drain the hot squid on paper towels.

Arrange the squid on a hot plate and sprinkle with salt. Sprinkle the squid with lemon juice or serve with a small plate of lemon wedges. Fry the parsley in the hot oil—stand back—for about 5 seconds, quickly drain it on paper towels, and arrange it over the squid. Serve immediately.

SAUTÉING AND STIR-FRYING

The easiest and quickest way to cook squid is to sauté or stir-fry it in butter or oil for no more than 2 minutes. If you're stir-frying squid with vegetables or other ingredients that take longer than 2 minutes to cook, get the other ingredients started and add the squid for the last 2 minutes of cooking.

One of the simplest and most delicious ways to sauté squid is to gently cook a little chopped garlic in butter or extra-virgin olive oil and then stir the squid rings and tentacles in the hot butter or oil for about 1 minute, until the squid loses its sheen. Many squid recipes start out this way and then call for other ingredients such as tomatoes, chopped herbs, or olives. Whatever recipe you follow, remember not to cook the squid for more than 2 minutes. If necessary, take the squid out of the pan while cooking the other ingredients and reunite everything a few seconds before serving.

Sautéed Squid with Garlic and Parsley

Once you get used to this easy method you can substitute other ingredients such as shallots for the garlic or basil for the parsley. If squid isn't sautéed in a large enough pan, it will steam rather than sauté, so this recipe is best done in 2 pans.

MAKES 4 FIRST-COURSE SERVINGS

1½ pounds whole squid or 1 pound cleaned

3 tablespoons extra-virgin olive oil

2 garlic cloves, finely chopped

2 tablespoons finely chopped parsley

salt and white pepper

If the squid isn't cleaned, clean it as described at the beginning of this chapter and cut it into ¼-inch rings. Cut the cluster of tentacles in half. Dry the squid on cloth towels. (Paper towels will stick and tear.)

Heat the olive oil in a large sauté pan and stir the garlic into each pan. Turn the heat up to high and watch very carefully so as not to brown the garlic. When the garlic begins to sizzle, add the squid all at once, equally divided between the pans. Stir the squid over high heat for about 1 minute, sprinkle on the parsley, and sauté for 30 seconds more. Sprinkle with salt and white pepper to taste.

Arrange the squid on hot plates with a slotted spoon. If the squid has released liquid into the pan, quickly boil the liquid down until it starts to turn oily. Spoon this flavorful liquid over the squid and serve immediately.

Sautéed Squid with Garlic, Tomatoes, Basil, and Black Olives

This delicious little squid stew is prepared by quickly sautéing squid in extra-virgin olive oil, keeping the squid warm, and making a light tomato sauce in the still-hot pan. The squid is then reheated gently in the sauce. Whatever you do, don't use canned California olives, which have little taste.

MAKES 4 FIRST-COURSE OR LIGHT MAIN-COURSE SERVINGS

1½ pounds whole squid or 1 pound cleaned

2 tablespoons extra-virgin olive oil

1 garlic clove, finely chopped

salt and pepper

2 tomatoes, peeled, seeded, and chopped

10 fresh basil leaves

½ cup good-quality Mediterranean black olives, pitted and coarsely chopped

Clean the squid if you're using whole squid and cut it into rings as shown on color page 19.

Heat the olive oil in a large sauté pan and stir in the garlic. Turn the heat up to high and watch very carefully so the garlic doesn't brown. When the garlic begins to sizzle, add the squid all at once. Stir or toss the squid over high heat for about 1½ minutes. Sprinkle with salt and pepper to taste and transfer the squid with a slotted spoon to a hot plate. Keep the squid warm in a 200°F oven.

continued

Put the tomatoes in the hot pan used for sautéing the squid and turn the heat up to high. Roll the basil leaves up on themselves and slice them into thin shreds. Boil the tomatoes for about 3 minutes and then stir in the basil and olives. The sauce will still be quite runny. Season the sauce with salt and pepper to taste and stir the squid into the sauce. Stir over high heat for about 30 seconds and spoon out into hot soup plates.

❧

Vietnamese-Style Squid Stir-fry

(color page 11)

I don't know if such a dish really exists in Vietnam. I derived the recipe while working with two of my favorite Vietnamese cookbooks, Binh Duong and Marcia Kiesel's *Simple Art of Vietnamese Cooking* and Nicole Routhier's *The Foods of Vietnam.* Part of the secret to this dish is the slightly sweet Vietnamese sauce, nuoc mam. See the glossary for information on Asian ingredients.

MAKES 4 FIRST-COURSE OR LIGHT MAIN-COURSE SERVINGS

1½ pounds whole squid or 1 pound cleaned, cut into rings (see color page 19)

2 garlic cloves, finely chopped

3 tablespoons nuoc mam (page 48)

2-inch piece of lemongrass, finely chopped

2 tablespoons peanut or vegetable oil

2 red Thai chilies or serrano chilies, seeded and finely chopped

2 scallions, including green, finely sliced

3 tablespoons finely chopped fresh cilantro

3 tablespoons finely chopped fresh mint

Toss the squid in a mixing bowl with the garlic and nuoc mam and let sit in the refrigerator for about 45 minutes.

Drain the squid, reserving the sauce that runs off.

Heat the lemongrass in the oil in a wok or large sauté pan over high heat. When the lemongrass starts to sizzle—don't let it brown—add the squid all at once. Stir the squid over high heat for about 30 seconds. Add the rest of the ingredients except the reserved sauce and stir for about 30 seconds more. Pour on the reserved sauce and heat for about 30 seconds, until it comes to a simmer. Spoon the squid with its sauce onto hot plates and serve immediately.

SQUID STEWS

Squid benefits from stewing since after 2 minutes of cooking it toughens and then needs at least 30 to 40 minutes of additional cooking to begin to soften again. A squid stew usually starts out with a light cooking in oil or butter followed by prolonged and gentle simmering in liquid.

Italian cooks start out by cooking a flavorful *soffrito* of onions, celery, garlic, and tomatoes; Catalan cooks a *sofregit* of onion, carrot, garlic, and parsley; and French cooks a simple mirepoix of chopped onion or leek, carrot, and celery. Flour is often sprinkled into the cooking vegetables to thicken the braising liquid. Full-flavored liquids such as red wine, tomatoes (peeled and seeded), or a broth made from blue crab are the best match for squid's assertive flavor. Vegetables of various sorts can be cooked separately and heated in the stew or added directly to the stew and cooked along with the squid. Baby artichokes

(cooked separately), fresh peas (tossed into the stew 10 minutes before serving), fennel wedges (braised separately in water and olive oil, combined with the stew 2 minutes before serving), and mushrooms (wild or cultivated, sautéed, poured over the stew just before serving) are a few possibilities for turning a squid stew into a surprisingly elegant main course.

Squid shrinks considerably in a stew, so count on using almost twice as much per serving as you would for sautéed or fried squid.

❧

Tomato Squid Stew with Artichokes, Pearl Onions, and Garlic

I love to make full-flavored seafood dishes and then add lots of different vegetables to stretch the flavor of the seafood, lighten the dish, and make it more colorful.

This is just one example of the many squid stew variations that can be made using a few simple techniques. The only thing that makes this particular squid stew time-consuming to prepare—but also what makes it so good—is the artichoke, onion, and garlic garnish. Since the garnish isn't intrinsic to the cooking or to the final flavor of the dish (garnishes rarely are), one or more of the components can be left out or other ingredients substituted depending on whim, season, and ambition.

This entire stew can be made earlier the same day or even the day before and reheated at the last minute.

MAKES 4 MAIN-COURSE SERVINGS

3 pounds whole squid or 2 pounds cleaned squid, hoods cut into ¼-inch rings and tentacles left whole

1 small onion, finely chopped

1 teaspoon fresh thyme or marjoram leaves or ½ teaspoon dried

5 tablespoons olive oil

4 tomatoes, peeled, seeded, and chopped

1 cup dry white wine

20 garlic cloves, peeled

12 baby artichokes or 4 large artichokes

juice of 1 lemon

20 pearl onions, peeled

salt and pepper

1 tablespoon finely chopped parsley

Thoroughly rinse and dry the squid rings and tentacles on cloth towels. (Paper towels will tear and stick unless you work very quickly.)

In a pot large enough to hold the squid, cook the onion and thyme in 2 tablespoons of the olive oil over medium heat. When the onion turns translucent, after about 10 minutes (don't let it brown), add the squid. Stir the squid over medium heat for about 2 minutes and add the tomatoes, wine, and garlic. Bring to a simmer over medium heat. Cover the pot and leave barely at a simmer over the lowest heat for 45 minutes or transfer the pot, once the liquid has come to a simmer, to a 300°F oven and bake for 45 minutes to an hour.

While the squid is cooking, cut the top two thirds off the artichokes, trim the dark leaves off the bottoms and sides, and put the artichokes in a non-aluminum pot with the lemon juice, a tablespoon of olive oil, and enough water to cover generously. Simmer the artichokes until they have the texture of a firm boiled potato when poked through the bottom with a knife, in about 15 minutes for baby artichokes or 30 minutes for large artichokes.

Drain and let cool. If you're using large artichokes, carefully pull out the choke with a tablespoon and cut the artichoke bottoms into 5 wedges each. Trimmed baby artichokes can be left whole or cut in half. Toss the cooked artichoke bottoms or baby artichokes in a tablespoon of olive oil.

Put the pearl onions and remaining olive oil in a small pot just large enough to hold the onions in a single layer. Add enough water to come halfway up the onions, partially cover the pot, and simmer the onions for about 15 minutes, until all the water evaporates and leaves them coated with a light glaze.

Uncover the squid and pour it into a colander or strainer set over a pot. Boil the liquid down until 1 cup remains and reheat the artichokes, pearl onions, and drained squid in the reduced liquid. Season with salt and pepper to taste. Spoon the squid stew into hot soup plates and sprinkle each plate with chopped parsley.

GRILLING

It wouldn't have occurred to me to grill squid, which toughens and dries out quickly, had I not read about it in Shizuo Tsuji's wonderful book *Japanese Cooking: A Simple Art.* In Mr. Tsuji's version the squid is sprinkled with black sesame seeds before grilling, while in other versions the finished squid is sprinkled with chopped *kinome* leaves, a kind of Japanese pepper. Because *kinome* leaves are hard to come by in the United States, I substitute chopped chives.

There are a couple of tricks to grilling squid so it doesn't toughen or curl. The first is to open the squid hoods and cut them into squares or rectangles about 2 to 3 inches on each

side and then score the squares on the inside of the hood with a gridlike pattern and then again diagonally, on the outside surface of the hoods. The trick is to score *almost* halfway into the squid, but no more, or you'll cut all the way through. The second trick is to skewer the squid rectangles twice to prevent them from curling.

Although grilled squid has a place in a traditional Japanese meal, I like to serve it as a simple hors d'oeuvre or first course. If you don't happen to be grilling and don't want to fire up the grill for this one dish, the squid rectangles can also be sautéed in hot vegetable oil while being held down with a heavy pot so they don't curl.

Japanese-Style Grilled Squid

MAKES 6 HORS D'OEUVRE OR LIGHT FIRST-COURSE SERVINGS

18 large squid

5 tablespoons Japanese dark soy sauce

3 tablespoons sake or dry white wine

2 tablespoons mirin or 2 teaspoons sugar dissolved in 2 tablespoons water

1 tablespoon chopped *kinome* leaves or fresh chives

Clean the squid as described earlier in this chapter, saving the tentacles for stuffings. Scrape the membrane off the hoods and carefully cut down one side of each hood and unfold. Cut 1 or 2 rectangles from each hood. (In a formal Japanese meal the rectangles must be perfectly squared, but for more ordinary circumstances they needn't be perfect.) Save the trimmings for stuffings. Rinse the rectangles thoroughly with cold water and, using a very sharp paring or filleting knife, score them with a series of fine incisions in 2 directions—about ⅛ inch between cuts—on the inside, making the cuts parallel to the sides of the rectangles. Score the front side of the rectangles in the same way, but make the cuts diagonal rather than parallel with the sides. Don't cut more than halfway into the squid on either side during the scoring or you'll cause the squid to fall apart.

Combine the soy sauce, sake, and mirin in a mixing bowl and marinate the squid rectangles in the mixture for 30 minutes.

Skewer the squid rectangles in rows on 2 metal skewers running along each side. Run the skewers through in several places as though you were sewing. Pat the squid rectangles dry.

Arrange the grill about 1 inch away from the surface of a bed of very hot coals or from the broiler heat source. Place the squid on the grill or under the broiler and cook for 2 minutes. Turn over and cook for 2 minutes more. Slide out the skewers and sprinkle with the chopped *kinome* or chives. Slice the rectangles into strips about ½ inch wide. Serve immediately.

STUFFED SQUID

Squid hoods are natural receptacles for stuffings, and squid tentacles provide flavor, texture, and bulk for the stuffing itself. Once the squid hoods are stuffed—the ends are held closed with wooden skewers or sewn together with thread—they can be braised using any of the same variations that work for a squid stew. The stuffing itself can be as simple or elaborate as you like, but remember that since the flavor of squid is by no means delicate—yet delicious nonetheless—you're better off staying

away from delicately flavored herbs or fancy shellfish such as lobster or crayfish. My stuffings are usually last-minute improvised affairs often made from vegetables left over from last night's dinner held together with an egg and a few bread crumbs and flavored generously with garlic and fresh herbs such as thyme or marjoram. If I'm trying to impress, I might add a few chopped shrimp or mussels, as in the following recipe. Remember when stuffing squid to fill the hoods only three-quarters full—the hoods shrink as they cook and if overstuffed may tear or burst open.

❧

Braised Squid Stuffed with Mussels and Vegetables

This rustic and savory dish can be made entirely with inexpensive ingredients, but you don't need to limit yourself to the ones suggested here. Squid bodies make a great receptacle for all kinds of improvised stuffings, including those made from leftover seafood and vegetables. The mussels play a dual role by contributing to both the braising liquid and the stuffing. Other shellfish can be used in the same way—crab is especially good—by preparing a flavorful braising liquid with the shellfish shells, heads, or bodies and then using the cooked shellfish in the stuffing.

MAKES 6 FIRST-COURSE SERVINGS

6 very large squid or 12 large squid (about 2½ pounds whole squid or 1½ pounds cleaned)

2 shallots, finely chopped

2 garlic cloves, finely chopped

2 cups dry white wine

2 pounds mussels, preferably small cultivated, sorted and scrubbed

For the Stuffing:

1 medium onion, chopped

2 fresh sage leaves, chopped

2 tablespoons pure olive oil

1 cup cooked spinach (about two 10-ounce bunches), water squeezed out, chopped

½ cup fresh bread crumbs

1 egg, lightly beaten

salt and pepper

For the Sauce:

2 tomatoes, peeled, seeded, and coarsely chopped

¼ teaspoon saffron threads, soaked in 1 tablespoon water for 30 minutes

2 tablespoons finely chopped parsley

4 tablespoons unsalted butter (optional)

Clean the squid as described earlier in the chapter if necessary, reserving the tentacles and carefully removing the purple membrane from the hoods.

Preparing the Mussels: Combine the shallots, garlic, and wine in a pot large enough to hold the mussels. Bring to a simmer, add the mussels, and cover the pot. Turn the heat up to high and steam the mussels for 5 to 10 minutes, until they have all opened. Discard any unopened mussels. Take the lid off the pot and let the mussels cool. Take the mussels out of the shells and discard the shells. Gently pour the liquid in the pot into a small bowl, leaving any sand or grit behind in the pot.

Preparing the Stuffing: Coarsely chop the squid tentacles and cook the onion, sage, and tentacles in the olive oil over medium heat until the onions turn translucent, about 10 minutes. Let the mixture cool and stir in the spinach, bread crumbs, and egg. Coarsely chop the mussels and add them to the stuffing. Stir the stuffing thoroughly and season with salt and pepper.

Stuffing the Squid: Stuff the hoods about three-quarters full, leaving room for the stuffing to expand and the hoods to contract. Close the hoods with half or a third of a wooden skewer—toothpicks aren't long enough—or sew them closed with needle and thread.

Braising: Preheat the oven to 300°F. Arrange the stuffed squid in a casserole with a tight-fitting lid that will hold them close together in a single layer. Stir the tomatoes and saffron with its soaking liquid into the mussel-cooking liquid and pour this mixture over the squid. Heat the casserole on the stove until the liquid comes to a boil. Cover the casserole and bake for 1 hour, checking after about 15 minutes. The liquid should be at a bare simmer. If it isn't moving at all, turn the oven up to 350°F; if it's boiling, turn the oven down to 250°F.

When the squid are ready, transfer them to a hot plate and keep them warm in the oven. Pour the liquid in the casserole into a saucepan and boil it down until only 1 cup remains. Off the heat, whisk in the parsley and the butter if desired. Take the skewers or thread out of the squid, and arrange the squid on hot soup plates. Ladle over the sauce and serve immediately.

Vietnamese-Style Stuffed Squid

Vietnamese cooks often include noodles in their stuffings in much the same way as European cooks like to use rice or bread crumbs as a starchy filler and a way of lightening or stretching a rich stuffing.

Squid makes a convenient and natural receptacle for all kinds of stuffings. In fact when I have leftover cooked fish I sometimes turn it into a stuffing and run out to buy some squid to use as a holder. Shrimp is used in this recipe, but almost any kind of fish or shellfish will work. Already-cleaned squid are of course easiest to use, but if you have the energy, clean the squid yourself and include the chopped tentacles in the stuffing. These squid can be stuffed earlier in the day and then cooked just before serving.

My favorite way to cook these squid is to grill them over wood coals, but if this isn't practical they can also be lightly sautéed and baked. See the glossary for information on Asian ingredients.

MAKES 6 FIRST-COURSE OR 12 HORS D'OEUVRE SERVINGS

12 large squid (about 4 pounds whole or 2½ pounds cleaned)

½ ounce dried cellophane noodles, soaked in cold water for 30 minutes, drained (about ½ cup after draining), and squeezed dry

1 pound headless medium shrimp, peeled and deveined

3 garlic cloves, finely chopped

3 shallots, finely chopped

3 tablespoons Thai fish sauce

3 tablespoons finely chopped fresh cilantro

3 tablespoons finely chopped fresh basil, preferably Asian holy basil type

3-inch piece of lemongrass, finely sliced, then finely chopped

1 egg, lightly beaten

½ teaspoon salt

2 teaspoons sugar

pepper

3 tablespoons peanut or vegetable oil

fresh mint or cilantro sprigs

Preparing the Stuffing and Stuffing the Squid: If you're using whole squid, clean the squid as shown on color page 19 and reserve the tentacles.

Cut the cellophane noodles into approximately ½-inch lengths.

Chop the shrimp into small but irregular dice, about ¼ inch on each side, by hand or in a food processor. Chop the squid tentacles to about the same size as the shrimp. Combine the shrimp and squid in a mixing bowl with the noodles and add the rest of the ingredients except the oil and mint sprigs. Stir the mixture until all the ingredients are well distributed.

Fill each squid hood about three-quarters full of stuffing—don't overfill them, or they may burst when cooked—and close each hood with a piece of wooden skewer (break skewers into thirds; toothpicks are too small).

Cooking the Squid: If you're grilling the squid, brush them lightly with oil, season them with salt and pepper, and grill them about 2 inches away from a bed of medium-hot coals for about 6 minutes on each side.

continued

If you're baking the squid, brown them lightly on both sides in oil in a heavy skillet and then slide the whole skillet into a 375°F oven for about 12 minutes.

Carefully slice the squid hoods crosswise into about 4 slices each—not too thin, or they'll fall apart—and arrange them on individual hot plates. Garnish each plate with a sprig of mint or cilantro.

CUTTLEFISH

Cuttlefish, sometimes called *sepia*, isn't found in American waters and must be imported from Europe. The most common cuttlefish, *Sepia officinalis,* is similar to squid but larger—its body is much fatter and rounder than squid's—and it has a much larger ink sac containing a deeper-colored ink than either squid or octopus.

Despite the claims of a number of food writers, cooked cuttlefish is almost indistinguishable from squid, except perhaps for the fact that its hood is slightly thicker and meatier. In Europe, where cuttlefish is almost as common as squid, the two are often used interchangeably. In the United States the only reason to pay five times as much for cuttlefish (when you can find it) is to use its abundant ink, which can be used to flavor and color stews and sauces. The cuttlefish ink sacs can also be saved in the freezer and used as needed to color and flavor risotto or pasta.

Cuttlefish are prepared for cooking in almost the same way as squid except that they are slit down the side to facilitate removing the innards and ink sac—so the hood must then be sliced into strips rather than rings. The cuttlebone, analogous to the transparent featherlike strip found in squid hoods, is opaque and more bonelike

and can be hard to remove unless it is cut out with a knife. Cuttlefish is cooked exactly the same way as squid except that it requires a slightly longer cooking time.

CUTTLEFISH STEWS

Typically cuttlefish is cut into strips and cooked lightly in butter or olive oil before being stewed with liquid ingredients such as wine or chopped tomatoes. When the cuttlefish is tender, after 40 minutes to an hour, the ink, diluted with a little water, is stirred into the sauce.

❧

Venetian-Style Cuttlefish Stew

SEPPIE COL NERO

On a recent trip to Venice I did my best to avoid the ubiquitous tourist-trap places and instead hunted out restaurants that serve authentic Venetian cooking. In my quest to sample genuine Venetian cuisine I ran into this wonderful dish in both the most chic and expensive restaurants and the cheap little hole-in-the-wall places. Amazingly, the cheap and expensive versions were almost identical and equally good.

Typically *seppie col nero* is served with rectangles of grilled polenta and in some places with the traditional Venetian white polenta. When I don't want to bother with polenta, I serve rice.

When working with cuttlefish, wear an apron you don't mind staining. This dish can be prepared earlier the same day and reheated just before serving.

MAKES 4 MAIN-COURSE SERVINGS

2½ **pounds whole cuttlefish**

1 **onion, finely chopped**

2 **garlic cloves, finely chopped**

2 **tablespoons extra-virgin olive oil**

2 **medium tomatoes, peeled, seeded, and chopped**

1 **cup dry white wine**

salt and pepper

Cut down one side of the cuttlefish hoods and remove the cuttlebone. Carefully pull out the innards and discard everything except the silver-black ink sac found near the top of the hood. Reserve the ink sacs in the refrigerator in a small glass covered with a tablespoon of water. Rinse out the inside of the cuttlefish hoods and cut the hoods crosswise into ¼-inch-wide strips. Rinse again and reserve.

In a pot large enough to hold the cuttlefish, cook the onion and garlic in the olive oil over medium heat until the onion starts to turn translucent, about 10 minutes. Stir in the cuttlefish strips and cook for 5 minutes more. Stir in the tomatoes and continue cooking, uncovered, over medium heat for about 15 minutes—until all the moisture from the tomatoes has evaporated.

Add the wine, bring to a gentle simmer, and cook, covered, over low heat or in a 300°F oven for about 40 minutes. To test for doneness, reach into the pot and taste a piece of cuttlefish to make sure it is tender—cook longer if needed.

When the cuttlefish is tender, scoop it out of the pot with a slotted spoon and reserve in a bowl. Boil down the cooking liquid in the pot until only about 1 cup remains. Put the ink sacs in a small strainer and work the ink through the strainer into the cooking liquid. Put the cuttlefish back in the pot and reheat the stew while stirring. Season to taste with salt and pepper. Serve on hot plates.

OCTOPUS

When you consider that our first introduction to the beast was probably in a horror movie and not on the dinner table, it's little wonder that octopus has yet to become an American staple. Any initial aversion to octopus is worth overcoming, though, because it's delicious and versatile and, unlike squid or cuttlefish, can be served in large meaty chunks.

Although there are several species of octopus, those found in the United States (the Atlantic coast *Octopus vulgaris* and the Pacific *Octopus dofleini*) are so similar that you needn't worry about searching out one or the other.

BUYING OCTOPUS

In the United States octopus is usually sold raw and often frozen. Cooked octopus, which is fine for salads or cold dishes, is easy to recognize because it is purple and the tentacles have usually curled. Fresh or frozen raw octopus has a gray or pale blue cast. Most octopus found in fish stores weigh about 2 pounds and look surprisingly small (especially compared to what's pictured in horror movies).

BABY OCTOPUS

Mediterranean cooks often concoct stews and soups with baby octopus. Because they're often hard to find, I take advantage of the appearance of baby octopus whenever I see them in New York, usually at Spanish or Italian markets.

When baby octopus are extremely small—an inch or less long—they can be cleaned by hammering them gently with a rolling pin to loosen the viscera and rinsing them quickly in cold water. Baby octopus are cooked whole in the same way as squid.

CLEANING OCTOPUS

Most of the octopus sold in the United States has already been cleaned, but if a fisherman friend gives you an uncleaned one or you find a fresh octopus in an ethnic market, you must cut off the head just above the eyes and turn it inside out. The viscera and various organs are attached to the inside of the head and can easily be detached and removed with a knife. Then you need only rinse the head, which you can cut up and cook with the rest of the octopus. Cut the eyes away from the rest of the octopus body and discard. Remove the "beak" from the main body of the octopus by turning the octopus upside down and pressing against the underside of the base—where the eyes were cut off—so that the hard beaklike substance can be pushed through the hole and discarded. The insides of the suckers of fresh octopus are sometimes clogged with mud, so you may have to knead the octopus under cold running water to clean out the suckers.

COOKING OCTOPUS

There are two basic approaches to cooking octopus. The first, popular in Japan, is to tenderize the octopus by rubbing it with grated daikon and then cook the octopus for just a few minutes. Because octopus cooked in this way still has a chewy texture, it is usually sliced thinly and marinated in a light but savory sauce. In Europe octopus is simmered for up to 2 hours so that it becomes meltingly tender.

Japanese-Style Cold Octopus in Vinegar Sauce

*I*n a traditional Japanese meal this cool and refreshing dish is likely to be served along with raw fish or with assorted bowls of other Japanese foods. I like it too much to limit it to Japanese meals, so I sometimes serve it as a light and savory opener to others. I like to serve cold blanched watercress seasoned with a little sesame oil in the same bowl.

If you can't find a small enough octopus, buy a large one and freeze what you don't use.

MAKES 6 LIGHT FIRST-COURSE SERVINGS

1 pound daikon (Japanese radish)

one 1- to 1½-pound octopus, cleaned (see color page 19)

salt

3 bunches of watercress

½ teaspoon dark sesame oil, preferably Japanese

For the Vinegar Sauce:

juice of 1 lemon

1 tablespoon mirin or 2 teaspoons sugar dissolved in 2 teaspoons water

3 tablespoons Japanese dark soy sauce

¼ cup dashi (page 343) or water

Peel the daikon and grate it by hand or in a food processor. Put the grated daikon and octopus in a large nonmetal mixing bowl. Knead the daikon into the octopus for about 10 minutes and let sit for 30 minutes more. Rinse the octopus with cold water.

Bring enough water to cover the octopus to a boil in a large pot. Add a handful of salt. Stick a fork through the top of the octopus to hold on to it while it's being dipped in the water.

continued

Submerge the octopus in the water for 1 minute, then pull it out and let it cool for 1 minute. Repeat this process once more and then gently simmer the octopus in the salt water for 5 minutes more. Remove the octopus and let cool in the open air. Don't rinse with cold water, which may toughen it.

While the octopus is cooling, blanch the leaves and smallest stems from the watercress bunches in a pot of boiling salted water. Drain in a colander, immediately rinse with cold water, cool, squeeze out the excess water, and refrigerate until needed. Toss with the sesame oil and season with salt to taste.

Cut the tentacles away from where they join near the top of the octopus and slice them on a bias as thinly as you can with a very sharp knife. The octopus slices should be no more than ⅛ inch thick. For formal Japanese meals the curly ends of the tentacles aren't used, but I always include them.

Stir together the sauce ingredients. Arrange a small mound of watercress to the side in each of 6 small—preferably Japanese pottery or lacquer—bowls. Arrange the octopus slices next to the watercress mounds. Spoon over enough of the sauce to come about ½ inch up the sides of the octopus.

❧

Red Wine Octopus Stew

Octopus takes on a melting meat-like texture when stewed for a couple of hours in red wine, and the resulting red wine sauce has the same richness and full flavor as the liquid from a meat stew. The octopus itself loses all of its chewiness yet remains firm and meaty.

This stew can be served plain or garnished with separately cooked vegetables. The version given here is served with mushrooms and blanched whole garlic cloves. Baby artichokes, olives, coarsely chopped tomatoes, sautéed zucchini, pearl onions, baby carrots, or turnips can be substituted.

Like most stews, octopus stew is better made the day before. I like to serve it with buttered noodles.

MAKES 6 MAIN-COURSE SERVINGS

two 2½-pound octopuses, cleaned

2 bottles full-bodied red wine

4 garlic cloves, chopped

2 medium onions, coarsely chopped

2 medium carrots, coarsely chopped

5 tablespoons olive oil

1 bouquet garni: 4 fresh thyme sprigs or 1 teaspoon dried, a bunch of parsley, and a bay leaf, tied up with string (or in cheesecloth for dried thyme)

3 tablespoons unsalted butter

3 tablespoons all-purpose flour

1 pound wild or cultivated mushrooms

salt and pepper to taste

30 garlic cloves, peeled, simmered for 20 minutes, and drained

3 tablespoons finely chopped parsley

Submerge the octopuses in a large pot of boiling water for 5 minutes. Drain, cool, and cut the tentacles and center section into 3-inch lengths or chunks. Toss the octopus chunks with the red wine and chopped garlic and marinate for 2 hours at room temperature or overnight in the refrigerator.

In a pot large enough to hold the octopus, cook the onions and carrots in 2 tablespoons of the olive oil over medium heat until the onion turns translucent, about 10 minutes. Add the octopus chunks with the red wine and garlic and nestle the bouquet garni in with the octopus. Bring the wine to a gentle simmer and cover the pot. Keep the stew at the gentlest simmer on the stove over low heat or in a 300°F oven. If you're cooking the octopus in the oven, be sure to bring it to a simmer on the stove first.

When the octopus is cooked, after 2 hours, strain the cooking liquid into a 4-quart pot. Pick the octopus out of the strainer and press down on the vegetables left in the strainer to extract all the liquid. Discard the vegetables and bouquet garni. Simmer the liquid until only 3 cups remain, skimming off with a ladle any fat or scum that forms on the surface.

On a small plate, work the butter and flour to a smooth paste with the back of a fork.

Cut the mushrooms into quarters if more than an inch in diameter and sauté them in the rest of the olive oil until well browned. Season with salt and pepper to taste.

Whisk two thirds of the butter and flour paste into the simmering red wine sauce and check the consistency; the sauce should be just thick enough to coat a spoon. If it's too thin, whisk in the rest of the butter/flour mixture. Stir in the octopus, mushrooms, and whole garlic cloves. Season with salt and pepper to taste. Spoon onto hot plates or into a serving dish and sprinkle with parsley.

Warm Bean and Octopus Salad

I got the idea for this dish from a
plate of beans with seafood I had
once in Tuscany. Use the best olive oil
you can find and serve with plenty of
dry white wine.

MAKES 6 FIRST-COURSE SERVINGS

one 2-pound octopus, cleaned

1 small red onion, finely chopped

1 garlic clove, finely chopped

½ to ¾ cup extra-virgin olive oil

**1 cup cannellini or navy beans, rinsed and
    soaked in 3 cups water for 3 hours or
    overnight**

2 sage leaves, preferably fresh

2 teaspoons salt

juice of 2 lemons

3 tablespoons chopped parsley

pepper

Submerge the octopus in a pot of
boiling water for 5 minutes. Drain the
octopus and let it cool. Cut the tentacles into 2-inch lengths and the center
section into 1-inch square chunks.

In a heavy pot large enough to hold
the beans and octopus, cook the onion
and garlic in 2 tablespoons of the olive
oil over medium heat until the onions
turn translucent, about 10 minutes.
Pour in the beans with their soaking
liquid, the sage, and the octopus.
Bring to a slow simmer, partially
cover the pot, and simmer very gently
for 2 hours. If necessary, add water

from time to time to keep the beans
barely covered. Gently stir the beans
every 30 minutes, scraping against the
bottom of the pot, to prevent sticking.
Be careful, however, not to stir too
much—especially near the end of
cooking—or the beans will turn to
mush. After the beans have cooked for
1 hour, add the salt. If there seems to
be a lot of water left in the pot after an
hour and half of cooking, remove the
lid so it evaporates; the finished beans
should be quite dry.

Pour the hot beans and octopus into
a mixing bowl, stir in the lemon juice,
parsley, and the remaining olive oil
to taste, and let cool. Season to taste
with pepper and, if necessary, more
salt. Serve slightly cool or at room
temperature.

Unusual Shellfish

LOBSTERETTES

Although these lobsterlike shellfish are rarely sold by this name, it is probably the least confusing name for what are sometimes marketed as prawns, Dublin Bay prawns, langoustines, and scampi. Lobsterettes look vaguely like freshwater prawns—they have long forelegs and antennae—but they live exclusively in salt water. Their flavor is reminiscent of both lobster and shrimp.

In Europe, lobsterettes (*Nephrops norvegicus*, often sold under their French name, *langoustine*) are so expensive that few, if any, end up being exported. Fortunately, New Zealand lobsterettes (*Metanephrops challengeri*), sold as "scampi" or "langoustines," are beginning to show up in the United States—and while they're never cheap, they cost half as much as their European cousins and are equally delicious.

COOKING LOBSTERETTES

Lobsterette claws contain so little meat that only the tails are eaten. Twist them off and prepare them in the same way as shrimp. Because I hate to see so much of the beautiful lobsterette go to waste, I sometimes leave it intact so my guests have the pleasure of seeing the whole creature. I do, however, carefully peel the shell off the tail before serving because lobsterette shells are tough and sometimes hard to remove. An alternative is to facilitate shelling by cutting through the membrane on the bottom of the tail with scissors before serving.

Be careful not to overcook lobsterettes; their meat quickly dries out. The simplest way to cook lobsterettes is to boil them whole for about 3 minutes and shell the tail just before serving. The whole lobsterettes can also be split lengthwise and the small grain sac pulled out of each side of the head (in the same way as for lobster) and then sautéed for about 3 minutes or broiled for 2 to 3 minutes. Lobsterette tails can also be taken out of the shell and sautéed in the same way as shrimp—very simply with a few herbs scattered over or finished with a sauce. Shelled lobsterette tails should be sautéed for only about 1 minute. Cooked lobsterette tails can also be served in salads.

❧

Baked Lobsterettes

*T*his is my favorite way to serve lobsterettes because they come sizzling hot out of the oven and there's no struggle getting the meat out of the shell. Use the biggest lobsterettes you can find and make sure your guests are ready, forks in hand, when you rush these from kitchen to dining room.

MAKES 4 FIRST-COURSE SERVINGS

16 whole lobsterettes

2 tablespoons melted unsalted butter or olive oil

sea salt and pepper

Preheat the oven to 400°F and brush the lobsterettes with melted butter or olive oil. Place them facedown, flat on a baking sheet—not on their sides—and bake in the oven for 8 to 10 minutes, until the tail turns deeper red and you can smell the delicious fragrance when you open the oven door.

Turn the oven down to 200°F. Quickly take the lobsterettes out of the oven one by one and with small scissors cut through the membrane on the bottom of the tail, being careful not to damage the meat. Pull the shell sideways away from the tail meat—using a towel—and twist it around to detach it from the rest of the body, leaving the tail meat attached.

Arrange 4 lobsterettes on each heated plate. Brush the tails with butter or olive oil, sprinkle with salt and pepper, and serve immediately.

LANGOSTINOS

Because of their similar name, langostinos are often confused with lobsterettes (langoustines) and the much larger spiny lobster (Fr. *langouste*). To compound the confusion, langostinos are sometimes sold in the United States as "scampi" (the true Dublin prawn), which they are not. Langostinos are only distantly related to either of these and are members of the family Galatheidae, actually a kind of crab.

Although there are many species of langostino, the only one marketed with any regularity—*Pleuroncodes monodon*—comes from Chile, where it is sold as *langostino colorado*. Langostinos are commonly between 8 and 10 inches long—they look like stubby crayfish with wrinkled tails—but like so many other crustaceans all of their edible meat is in the tail, which is smaller (about an inch long) and squatter than that of most crayfish. Whole langostinos rarely show up in the United States but are sold as frozen tails, either shelled or unshelled.

Shelled langostino tails can be cooked in the same way as shrimp.

SLIPPER LOBSTERS

Although these odd-looking creatures occur along the coast of North Carolina down to Florida, I've never seen them for sale in the United States. They do have a somewhat offputting appearance with a flattened flaplike head that takes up half the animal. Although ignored by American cooks, slipper lobsters have long been appreciated in Mediterranean countries and at least until recently (their numbers are decreasing) were an essential ingredient in a bouillabaisse.

Besides the ignored American varieties, *Scyllarides nodifer* and *Scyllarides aequinoctialis*, several species of slipper lobsters are eaten in various parts of the world. There are two main European species, the larger *Scyllarides latus*, which grows to about a foot and

a half, and the smaller *Scyllarus arctus*, which grows to about half that size. The French call them *grande cigale* and *petite cigale* (large and small sea crickets). Australians are big fans of slipper lobster, which they call *bugs*. There seems to be a growing market for their favorites, the Moreton Bay bug (*Thenus orientalis*) and the slightly smaller Balmain bug (*Ibacus peronii*). A similar species, *Scyllarides squammosus*, is fished and sold in Hawaii.

Slipper lobster tails can be prepared in the same way as shrimp or lobster.

MANTIS SHRIMP

Despite their name (*Squilla mantis*), mantis shrimp are not shrimp, nor do they even belong to the group of decapods (10-legged) of which shrimp are just some of the many members. Mantis shrimp look somewhat like flattened-out shrimp with heads at both ends—it takes a second to see what's front and what's back. Although they get up to 10 inches long, those sold in Mediterranean countries are rarely longer than 6 inches.

Mantis shrimp can be cooked in the same way as shrimp and freshwater prawns. They can be found on both the Pacific and Atlantic coasts of the United States but are marketed only in Hawaii and occasionally in ethnic markets elsewhere.

SEA URCHINS
(color page 8)

Americans, unless they frequent Japanese or French seafood restaurants, show little interest in eating sea urchins. The French, on the other hand, will pay almost the price of a dozen oysters for a single sea urchin.

Of the several species of sea urchins sold in the United States, most are sold according to their color—green, purple, or black—and sometimes as short-spined and long-spined. Because the actual color rarely corresponds to the name, this system only adds to the confusion. "Black" sea urchins, found in the Caribbean and off the coast of Florida, actually appear white because of their white spines, while green sea urchins (*Strongylocentus droebachiensis*), found along both the Atlantic and Pacific coasts, have only a subtle green cast. California also has a large purple urchin that grows up to 10 inches in diameter.

Most sea urchins are served raw with the top half cut off with a pair of scissors. Only the female roe or male gonads are eaten, but depending on the time of year these can constitute as much as 20 percent of the sea urchin's weight—not such a bad deal. The flavor of sea urchins varies depending on the time of year and the sea urchin's freshness. The best sea urchin roe tastes slightly sweet and reminds me of a cross between oysters and milk chocolate. Unfortunately, some sea urchin roe has an unpleasant taste of iodine—so it's a good idea to sample before you buy. The sea urchin roe sometimes packaged in little wooden trays doesn't have the delicate flavor of roe taken fresh out of the shell.

Sea urchin roe can also be used in cooking. The French make sea urchin soufflés, and I've even seen a recipe for sea urchin ice cream, but my favorite method is to puree the roe with equal parts butter in a food processor and whisk this sea urchin butter into fish and shellfish sauces as a flavorful finish. So much sea urchin roe is now shipped to Japan that it has become one of the Northeast's most important commercial species.

WHELK AND CONCH

Whelks and conch (pronounced KONK) are members of the class of sea snails (Gastropoda, meaning "stomach-foot") because they creep along the ocean floor with a muscular and usually edible foot, dragging their shell with them. Other than their shared status as snails and the fact that they are often confused, whelks and conch are only distantly related.

Most of the several whelks found in the United States are sold along the Atlantic coast, but this may be because of a large Italian population that has long appreciated them. One of these whelks, the common or waved whelk (*Buccinum undatum*), is the most popular in Europe and often shows up in ethnic markets on the American Atlantic coast, where it is found as far south as New Jersey. Common whelks are typically 1½ to 3 inches long and have a distinct spiraling appearance with the shell coming to a sharp point at one end. My own fondest memories of these whelks are on seafood platters in French restaurants, where they are pulled out of the shell at the table with an oyster fork and eaten whole except

for the thin bonelike plate that protects the entrance to the shell. The easiest way to cook common whelks is to simmer them in salted water or vegetable stock for 5 minutes and let them cool in the liquid. If you have friends or family who are unused to eating sea snails (most of us), you may want to cook the whelks lightly—just long enough to get them out of the shell—and then chop them to use in soups, or braise them in the same way as octopus or squid (in the same way as squid, they get tough at first and then start to tenderize after 30 minutes of cooking).

The best-appreciated whelks in the United States are the channeled whelk (*Busycon canaliculata*) and the knobbed whelk (*Busycon carica*), which are sold in East Coast Italian neighborhoods as scungilli. Both of these whelks are larger (6 to 8 inches) and more elongated than common whelks. The outside of their shells is a dull gray with orange coloration on the inside. Knobbed whelks differ from channeled whelks only in that they have little knobs on the rings near the widest part of the shell. Scungilli are usually sold out of the shell and often lightly precooked.

The most important species of conch, the queen conch (*Strombus gigas*), is found off the coast of Florida and in the Caribbean, where it is prepared and eaten in the same way as the larger whelks except that the extracted animal is sometimes parboiled to eliminate compounds that have on occasion caused vomiting. Because conch meat is very tough, it is often finely chopped and incorporated into soups and chowders. Conch is easy to recognize because its classic-shaped shell—pink and elongated with a series of spikelike appendages—is so often used for decoration.

ABALONE
(*Haliotis* spp.)

The abalones that I remember while growing up in California were relatively large—9 or 10 inches in diameter—and were as appreciated for their shells (they were popular as ashtrays) as for their meat. We ate them only occasionally as a rare extravagance in seafood restaurants on Fisherman's Wharf in San Francisco, where they were usually the most expensive food on the menu.

Also called California abalone (*Haliotis rufescens*), red abalone is becoming increasingly rare, and because harvesting is closely regulated it's very unusual to find it for sale alive, in the shell. Smaller abalone are farmed in California and Hawaii and harvested in Alaska.

Anatomically, abalones are made up almost entirely of a giant and very strong foot that makes it difficult to pull them off anything they happen to be clinging to, but once you have one in hand, getting it out of the shell is a straightforward process of cutting around the inside of the shell until the abalone pops out. The dark fringe, dark

---

TAKING WHELKS AND CONCHS OUT OF THE SHELL

Common whelks are always cooked in the shell and pulled right out with a small fork, whereas channel whelks, knobbed whelks, and conch are sometimes taken out of the shell while raw.

The traditional method for removing a raw whelk or conch from the shell is to make a hole in the spiral front of the shell in the third row from the center with a hammer and screwdriver. You then wiggle a sharp paring knife around in the hole to detach the muscle, allowing you to pry out the whelk or conch by wedging a knife under the bony disk (operculum) covering the entrance.

I never really got the knack of the hammer method and find it much easier just to dunk the whole whelk or conch in boiling water for 3 minutes and then pull the animal out with a fork.

Whichever method you use, once you get the animal out, cut off the operculum and scrape off the skin and intestines.

skin, and intestine should then be trimmed off. Depending on the abalone's size, you can then slice it very thinly (⅛ inch) and eat it raw or lightly flour and sauté it in butter for no more than a minute. Abalone is similar to squid in that you must cook it for a very short time or a very long time. One Japanese dish involves steaming the abalone in its shell, well doused with sake, for 2 to 3 hours and then cleaning and trimming it once it is cooked.

Abalone of indifferent quality is available in cans, but the already-pounded frozen abalone found in Japanese and Chinese markets is quite good. Abalone is never cheap in any form.

❧

Abalone Medallions with Parsley Sauce

When I'm lucky enough to get my hands on fresh abalone, I like to cook it in the simplest possible way so that nothing gets in the way of its delicate flavor. Whatever you do, don't cook the abalone for more than a minute.

MAKES 4 FIRST-COURSE SERVINGS

2 large abalones shelled, dark fringe, skin, and intestine removed

salt and pepper

4 tablespoons unsalted butter

2 tablespoons dry vermouth or white wine

1 tablespoon very finely chopped parsley

Slice the abalones into a total of twelve ⅛-inch-thick slices. Just before cooking, season the abalone slices with salt and pepper and sauté them in butter—you may need to use 2 pans—over low to medium heat for 30 seconds on each side.

Transfer the abalone slices to hot plates and add the vermouth and parsley to the hot pan. Bring the liquid in the pan to a quick simmer, season with salt and pepper to taste, and dribble the sauce over the abalone slices. Serve immediately.

GOOSENECK BARNACLES

Few people have ever heard of, much less seen, this odd-looking but delicious shellfish. Those of us who are familiar with them are most likely to have encountered them in Portugal or Spain, where they're served—at a staggering price—as a tapa under the name *percebes*.

While the gooseneck barnacle (*Mitella cornucopia*) is becoming harder to find in Europe, Americans are just discovering their own supply in the Pacific Northwest, most of which ends up being shipped off to Spain. Because gooseneck barnacles like to cling to rocks and to the face of cliffs, they are difficult to capture. This in addition to their rarity means they're always expensive.

Gooseneck barnacles are easy to cook (just toss them into boiling salted water for 5 minutes and serve them warm) and are best served with a buttery sauce such as a beurre blanc containing a hint of garlic. They have a thin leathery skin, which is easy to peel off as you go.

PERIWINKLES

This is another one of those foods that most Americans would probably never see without having first encountered them on foreign travels. In France they're often served as a light—and sometimes frustrating—first course under the name *bigorneaux*. They are so small they have to be hooked out of their tiny shells with a pin—or, in fancier places, a two-tined fork—but despite their size they have a very pleasant peppery flavor. Although most restaurants leave the diners to fend for themselves, I do remember a fabulous oyster ragout that had been garnished with the tiny little periwinkles, which no doubt had been picked out of their shells by the lowest kitchen apprentice.

Periwinkles (*Littorina littorea*) were not found on American shores until the first part of this century, when they immigrated on the hull of a ship from Europe. I find them in ethnic markets in New York but haven't seen them anywhere else.

Wash the periwinkles in a colander under cold running water as soon as you get them home and then sort through them by making sure their entrances are tightly closed and covered with a hard little disk, the operculum. If you have any doubts, give them a sniff—if they smell like anything other than ocean, throw them out.

Periwinkles should be cooked for no more than 3 minutes because if they're even slightly overcooked they'll break apart as you're trying to get them out of the shell. The easiest way to cook them is just to toss them into boiling water spiced up with a little cayenne, but I like to cook them in a wide sauté pan with just enough concentrated court bouillon to come halfway up their sides, spoon them into hot bowls, pour on their cooking liquid—generously buttered—and serve the whole concoction with plenty of crusty bread. When eating periwinkles, be sure to pull off the hard operculum.

〜

Periwinkles in Court Bouillon

*B*y now my friends are used to encountering something weird when they come over for dinner, but if your friends aren't, warn them—"Oh, I'm so glad you can come...we're starting out with the most wonderful little sea snails"—and then serve a main course that you're sure everyone will eat.

MAKES 4 FIRST-COURSE SERVINGS

1 pound periwinkles, well rinsed and sorted

1½ cups court bouillon (page 66)

1 tablespoon finely chopped fresh chives

3 tablespoons unsalted butter (optional)

salt and pepper

Spread the periwinkles in a pot or pan large enough to hold them in a single layer. Pour on the court bouillon, the chives, and the butter, bring to a boil, and cover the pot. Simmer the periwinkles for about 3 minutes. Season the cooking liquid with salt and pepper to taste and spoon the periwinkles and broth into hot soup plates. Serve immediately with plenty of crusty French bread.

Combining Seafood

One of the most interesting ways to cook fish and shellfish is to combine them in various soups, stews, and sauces. Once you've learned to cook a few different types of fish and shellfish, it becomes simple to combine them and coordinate their cooking so that everything ends up being cooked at the same time.

One of my favorite approaches to combining seafood is to prepare a shellfish soup or stew with bivalves such as mussels or clams and one or more crustaceans such as lobster or crayfish. The mussels or clams are steamed open, and the resulting liquid is used to steam the lobster or crayfish. The mixed shellfish is then served in the concentrated steaming liquid. You can elaborate on this approach by making a broth with the crustacean shells, by incorporating various butters, herbs, thickeners, garnishes, and enricheners, constructing and inventing as you go along, carefully balancing the flavors of the different shellfish and other ingredients. Another excellent way to combine shellfish and finfish is to make a shellfish stew or soup and then use it as a sauce and garnish for a sautéed fish steak or fillet. This is an elegant method for stretching the flavor of expensive shellfish such as lobster.

IMPROVISING SHELLFISH SOUPS AND STEWS

Decide first on the best way to cook each of the individual elements and then how best to assemble them. The easiest approach is to toss various shellfish and fish into a pot of simmering liquid such as wine, water, or fish broth and cook the whole thing until all the seafood is done. The problem with this method is that seafoods all have different cooking times and react differently to various cooking techniques. For example, much of the flavor of crustaceans is contained in the shells, so it's worth lightly precooking lobsters, crayfish, or shrimp and then extracting flavor from their shells by making a concentrated broth or shellfish butter. Long-cooking seafood such as squid or octopus need to be simmered for perhaps hours before quick-cooking shellfish such as mussels and oysters can be added.

What's most fascinating about a mixed seafood stew is the interplay of flavors that comes about as each seafood releases juices into the shared cooking liquid. The careful manipulation of this cooking liquid into a deeply flavored and texturally satisfying sauce is for the cook one of the kitchen's most gratifying processes.

To learn best how to cook the various kinds of shellfish, refer to individual chapters.

SHELLFISH

Mussels, Clams, Cockles: When combining mussels and other bivalves for a fish soup, stew, or sauce, cook the bivalves first and then use the resulting briny steaming liquid to cook other fish or shellfish. Mussels, clams, and cockles are best steamed open in wine, fish stock, or other liquid flavored with chopped garlic, shallots, lemongrass, herbs, etc. Another approach is simply to add mussels, clams, or cockles to a soup or stew during the last 10 minutes of cooking.

Lobsters, Crayfish, Crabs: These crustaceans can be cooked in a soup or stew in one of three ways. The easiest method is simply to toss the whole or cut-up shellfish into a simmering seafood soup or stew about 10 minutes before the end of cooking. The second method consists of lightly steaming the shellfish, removing the meat, and adding the meat to the seafood soup or stew about a minute before serving. A third method consists of lightly cooking the crustaceans, removing the meat from the shell, and then making a flavorful broth from the crustacean shells. This broth can then be used to cook other seafood and to reheat the crustacean meat at the last minute.

Shrimp: The easiest way to incorporate shrimp into a seafood soup or stew is simply to toss the shelled and deveined shrimp tails into the simmering soup or stew about 5 minutes before serving. A more complicated but more satisfying approach is to buy shrimp with heads and make a flavorful shrimp-head broth, which can be used as the liquid base for cooking the shrimp tails and other shellfish.

Squid, Cuttlefish, Octopus: Because they need to be cooked longer than other seafood, squid, cuttlefish, and octopus should be simmered until done in white or red wine or fish or vegetable broth and the richly flavored cooking liquid then used to cook other seafood. The cooked squid, octopus, or cuttlefish can then be reheated gently in the finished soup or stew just before serving.

Oysters: Oysters can be poached in a finished soup, stew, or sauce 30 seconds to a minute before serving, or they can be precooked gently in their own liquid and this briny liquid combined with other shellfish-cooking liquid. The cooked oysters can then be reheated gently at the very end in the soup, stew, or sauce. Remember never to let oysters boil.

Sea Urchins: Sea urchin roe is usually added to a soup or stew in the form of sea urchin butter, but it is possible to gently warm the bright-colored lumps of roe in a shellfish stew just before serving.

THICKENERS

Roux: Shellfish-cooking liquids can be thickened by whisking them into hot roux and gently simmering.

Cream: Cream can be added to shellfish liquids to lightly enrich them and round out their flavors. The cream can also be reduced with the shellfish-cooking liquid until the mixture thickens.

Butter: Butter can be whisked into the cooking liquid just before serving as a thickener and to give a silky texture to sauces.

Egg Yolks: Shellfish-cooking liquid can be combined with egg yolks and the mixture cooked gently until it thickens. Egg yolks are rarely used alone, but usually in combination with cream or butter. Sometimes egg yolks are used to make a hollandaise-type sauce by whisking them with the shellfish-cooking liquid and then adding butter.

Vegetable Purees: Vegetables can be simmered with shellfish-cooking liquid until they soften and the whole mixture then pureed, or a vegetable puree can be prepared separately and whisked into the shellfish-cooking liquid as a thickener. Tomatoes are the most common of these thickeners, but other vegetables such as garlic, mushrooms, potatoes, root vegetables, and green vegetables are also used.

Shellfish and Fish Roe: Roe from shellfish such as lobster, scallops, sea urchins or fish roe from salmon or even sturgeon (caviar!) can be whisked into shellfish-cooking liquids to give them texture and flavor. Most of the time shellfish or fish roe is worked with butter or cream to prevent the roe from curdling or hardening when it comes in contact with the hot shellfish-cooking liquid. Most shellfish or fish roe should never be allowed to boil.

Mayonnaise: Homemade mayonnaise makes an excellent thickener and flavoring for a shellfish soup or stew. The hot shellfish-cooking-liquid is whisked into the mayonnaise and the mixture reheated just before serving. The most famous dish using this technique is the French bourride, made by whisking the poaching liquid from fish into a garlic mayonnaise, aïoli.

Bread Crumbs: Lightly toasted bread was a popular thickener in medieval cooking, before the discovery of roux. There are vestiges of its use in today's Mediterranean cooking, the most famous being the addition of rouille (traditional versions are made with bread crumbs) to a bowl of bouillabaisse.

Rice: Cooked and pureed rice is one of the classic thickeners for bisque. Because it releases more starch and is a more efficient thickener, I prefer to use Italian short-grain rice instead of the more common long-grain rice.

FLAVORINGS

Herbs: While some herbs are used more than others, almost any herb can be used to flavor a shellfish soup, stew, or sauce. When to add an herb to a shellfish soup or stew depends on the herb. So-called herbes de Provence—thyme, marjoram, oregano, lavender—have a high oil content (to protect them from the hot climates where they usually grow) that allows them to release their flavor slowly during long cooking. For this reason these herbs are often added—tied up with string or in cheesecloth in a bouquet garni—at the beginning of cooking. These herbs also dry well, a distinct advantage for those of us who don't always have access to fresh herbs. The flavor of more delicate herbs such as mint, cilantro, basil, and the so-called fines herbes—parsley, tarragon, chervil, and chives—cooks off quickly once heated. These herbs are best chopped and added to a hot dish within a minute or two of serving. These delicate herbs take poorly to drying.

Wines: Many shellfish are steamed in wine as the first step in preparing a soup or stew. The best wines for cooking shellfish are usually very dry wines with a good amount of acidity to give the necessary tang to the cooking liquid. In some cases—especially with crustaceans—you may want to use a slightly sweet or deeper-flavored wine such as Sauternes, Madeira, or sherry. For squid and octopus, full-bodied red wine is usually the best.

Spirits: Cognac has long been a classic ingredient in shellfish stews and bisques, especially those made with lobster. While there is a very special affinity between cognac and the flavor of crustaceans, it is worthwhile experimenting with other spirits such as Armagnac, whiskey, Calvados (apple brandy from Normandy), unsweetened fruit eaux-de-vie such as kirsch or framboise, and even grappa (*marc* in French).

Spirits should always be added to a soup or stew at least several minutes before the end of cooking and the liquid then simmered to cook off the alcohol. The flavor of some spirits such as that of eaux-de-vie, however, is so fleeting that a few drops of these liquors have to be added within a minute of the end of cooking. Other spirits, especially those that have been aged in wood (and as a result are brown rather than clear), can be added earlier since their flavor won't cook off as fast.

GARNISHES

Most of us think of a garnish as a sprig of parsley or some small decoration that has very little to do with the character of the final dish. In European cooking the garnish refers to foods—usually vegetables—that are combined with the finished dish shortly before serving. A typical French garnish for a red wine meat or seafood stew might contain sautéed mushrooms, pearl onions, and little strips of bacon; an Italian garnish would perhaps include chopped tomatoes, fennel wedges, or artichokes; in Thailand, pineapple wedges might be used.

Adding vegetables to a shellfish soup or stew adds color and texture to the finished dish and is also a good way of stretching the flavor of expensive ingredients. Almost any vegetable can be added to a shellfish stew or soup once the vegetable has been cut into an appropriate shape and size (vegetables for soups need to be smaller so they can be eaten with a spoon). It is important, however, to give some thought to how the vegetable should be cooked. For mushrooms (especially wild ones) and truffles, for example, it's best to simmer the vegetable directly in the shellfish-cooking liquid so the vegetable's flavor works its way into the liquid. Other vegetables are best cooked separately and stirred into or tossed over the stew at the last minute.

Artichokes: Baby artichokes are best precooked in a large pot of simmering water and then sautéed in a little olive oil or butter or simply reheated in the soup or stew. Larger artichokes should be trimmed (turned), precooked, the choke removed, and the bottoms cut into wedges.

Green Vegetables: Most green vegetables such as green beans, peas, asparagus tips, fresh fava beans, broccoli, spinach, and others are best cooked quickly, uncovered, in a large pot of boiling salted water and rinsed quickly in a colander under cold water. A few green vegetables such as sorrel are best cooked directly in a little butter and the liquid they release incorporated into the stew or soup. Cooked green vegetables can be reheated directly in the soup or stew or be sautéed in a little oil or butter.

Root Vegetables: Sliced or cubed root vegetables such as carrots or turnips are delicious and look great in a shellfish soup. They are equally delicious in a stew, but their shape can be difficult to make look attractive—sliced or cubed turnips or carrots look somehow too geometric next to the organic shapes of shellfish. For this reason professional chefs often shape root vegetables into softer-edged olive or garlic-clove shapes—a time-consuming technique both to learn and to execute. An easier method is to julienne root vegetables and lightly cook them in butter or olive oil. Baby root vegetables such as turnips, carrots, or pearl onions can be left whole and lightly glazed in a little water or butter before being stirred into the stew just before serving.

Mushrooms: Sautéed or braised mushrooms—especially wild mushrooms—are one of the easiest and most delicious vegetables to serve with shellfish soups and stews. Mushrooms can be sautéed in olive oil or clarified butter over high heat or simmered in some of the shellfish-cooking liquid so their flavor ends up in the sauce or broth. Mushrooms should be stirred into or tossed over soups and stews just before serving.

A NOTE ABOUT CREAM AND BUTTER

While Americans are eating less cream and butter than ever before, there's nothing that enhances the flavor of shellfish as well as these rich dairy products. The good news is that very little is needed. Usually 1 tablespoon of heavy cream or ½ tablespoon of butter (each 50 calories or about 5 grams of fat) per serving is enough to give a dish that indefinable suavity and richness. But if you want to avoid them altogether, you can omit them entirely from most recipes.

❧

Oyster and Sea Urchin Stew

I like this little stew because it's quick and easy to prepare, it's elegant and understated, and it's absolutely bursting with the flavor of the sea. Be sure to taste your sea urchins before embarking on this dish to make sure they have a delicate sweet ocean flavor and not the strong iodine taste they sometimes take on. Serve this stew in small soup plates, cassoulettes, or, better yet, in the cleaned-out sea urchin shells. I like best to serve this dish as a first course for a special dinner.

The oysters and sea urchins can be shucked and the spinach blanched earlier in the day.

MAKES 4 FIRST-COURSE SERVINGS

16 oysters

8 sea urchins or ½ cup sea urchin roe

leaves from 1 bunch of spinach

1 teaspoon fresh lemon juice

5 tablespoons heavy cream

salt and white pepper

2 teaspoons finely chopped fresh chives or parsley

Shuck the oysters into a bowl and refrigerate. Discard the shells.

Cut into the top of the sea urchins and then around the sides with a strong pair of scissors. Carefully spoon out the orange or yellow roe and reserve it in a small bowl in the refrigerator. If you're serving the stew in the sea urchin shells, scrub them thoroughly and dry them in a 200°F oven. (See color page 18.)

Blanch the spinach leaves in boiling water for 30 seconds, rinse them in a colander under cold running water, squeeze out the excess water, and reserve.

Warm the oysters in their liquid in a saucepan over medium heat until the liquid barely begins to simmer at the edge of the pan and the oysters begin to curl around the edges, about 3 minutes. With a slotted spoon, transfer the hot oysters to a clean kitchen towel or clean napkin so any grit will pull off the oysters and cling to the towel. Strain the oyster-cooking liquid through a fine strainer into a clean saucepan.

Add the lemon juice and 4 tablespoons of the heavy cream to the oyster liquid and simmer gently for about 5 minutes, until the mixture has the consistency of cold heavy cream. Meanwhile, simmer the remaining tablespoon of cream in a small pan until it thickens. Season with salt and pepper and add the spinach. Stir for a minute over medium heat to heat the spinach. Arrange the spinach in a small mound in the center of each soup plate or sea urchin shell.

Gently stir the chives, oysters, and sea urchin roe into the oyster sauce and heat gently—without boiling—for about 30 seconds. Arrange the oysters and roe around and over the spinach. Make sure everyone gets 4 oysters. Spoon over the sauce. Serve immediately.

Mussel and Lobster Stew

This deep-flavored dish is a simple and delicious way to serve lobster. The mussels and lobster combine to create a complex and exciting taste of the sea, and this dish is more economical but just as satisfying as serving lobster alone.

I like to serve this dish as a first course, but it also makes a great main course with the quantities doubled. Most of the cooking has to be done at the last minute, but the mussels can be steamed earlier in the day and both mussels and steaming liquid kept in the refrigerator until needed.

MAKES 4 FIRST-COURSE SERVINGS

1 cup dry white wine

2 shallots, finely chopped

2 pounds small cultivated mussels, scrubbed and sorted

two 1¼-pound live lobsters

½ cup heavy cream

1 tablespoon lobster butter (page 330) or unsalted butter

1 tablespoon finely chopped parsley

salt and white pepper

Bring the wine to a simmer with the shallots in a covered pot large enough to hold the mussels. Add the mussels, cover the pot, and simmer over medium-high heat until all the mussels open, 5 to 8 minutes. Remove the lid, discard any unopened mussels, and let the rest cool slightly. Take the mussels out of the shells; discard the shells and reserve the mussels and cooking liquid.

Rinse the lobsters under cold water and cut them in half lengthwise. Remove and discard the grain sacs and snap off the claws. Arrange the lobster claws and tails (flesh side up)

in a pot or pan large enough to hold them in a single layer. Carefully pour the mussel-steaming liquid over the lobster—leaving behind any sand— and place the pan over high heat. As soon as the liquid comes to a boil, cover the pot with a tight-fitting lid. Steam the lobsters for 6 minutes.

Remove the meat from the lobster claws and tails and arrange it in hot soup plates. Keep the plates warm in a 200°F oven. Add the cream to the liquid left in the lobster pan and boil it down until about 1 cup remains. Whisk in the lobster butter and parsley. Season the sauce with salt and pepper to taste. Gently reheat the mussels in the sauce for about 30 seconds and arrange them over and around the lobster in the bowls. Spoon on the sauce.

Lobster, Crayfish, and Shrimp Stew with Green Vegetables

This is one of those elaborate and delicious dishes that I serve at my most special dinners. A lot of shopping and preparation is involved and so I rarely make this dish for fewer than six, but fortunately most everything can be done in advance and then reheated gently before serving. The vegetables are essential to lightening the dish and giving it color. I've chosen some of my favorites for this version, but follow your own whims and buy what looks good at the market. You can serve this dish as a first course—by halving the quantities— but it's a hard act to follow.

MAKES 6 MAIN-COURSE SERVINGS

three 1¼-pound live lobsters

3 tablespoons pure olive oil

1½ pounds (2 dozen) live crayfish

6 jumbo shrimp, preferably with heads

1 medium onion, finely chopped

2 garlic cloves, finely chopped

1 celery stalk, finely chopped

4 tomatoes, seeded

1 bouquet garni: 4 fresh thyme sprigs or ½ teaspoon dried, ½ bunch of parsley, and a bay leaf, tied up with string (or in cheesecloth for dried thyme)

1 cup dry white wine

1 cup chicken broth (page 344) or water

¼ cup cognac or good brandy

¼ pound green beans, preferably thin French *haricots verts*, ends broken off

leaves from 1 bunch of spinach

1 fennel bulb, trimmed and cut into wedges

salt and pepper

½ cup heavy cream

2 tablespoons lobster or crayfish butter (page 330) or unsalted butter

2 tablespoons finely chopped parsley

Rinse the lobster, cut it up, leaving the tail whole (see color page 23), and sauté it in olive oil over medium to high heat along with the crayfish and shrimp. Unless you have a very large pan, you may have to sauté in stages. After 2 minutes, cover the pan and turn down the heat. When all the shells have turned red—after about 5 minutes more—take the shellfish out of the pan with a slotted spoon and add the onion, garlic, and celery. Cook gently for about 10 minutes. Take the shellfish meat out of the shells, reserving the meat and putting the shells back in the pot.

Break the shells up with the end of a handleless rolling pin or with a cleaver held up on end. Add the tomatoes, bouquet garni, wine, chicken broth, and cognac. Cover the pot and simmer gently for 20 minutes. While the shell mixture is simmering, devein the shrimp and crayfish tails and cut the lobster tails into 4 medallions each. Arrange the shellfish on an ovenproof plate and cover with aluminum foil. Refrigerate until just before serving.

Blanch the green beans in a pot of boiling salted water until they lose most but not all of their crunch, take them out of the water with a strainer or slotted spoon, and use the same water to blanch the spinach. Rinse both vegetables under cold water and drain in a colander. Cook the fennel wedges in a single layer with just enough water to come halfway up their sides in a covered sauté pan over medium heat for about 20 minutes. When all the vegetables are cooked, season them with salt and pepper and arrange them on a baking sheet. Cover the baking sheet with aluminum foil.

Strain the shellfish shells over a saucepan, pushing hard on the strainer with a ladle to extract all the liquid. Boil down the liquid until about a cup remains. Add the cream and whisk in the lobster butter and parsley. Season with salt and pepper to taste.

Just before serving, preheat the oven to 200°F and heat the vegetables and shellfish for 15 minutes. Heat the sauce. Arrange the vegetables and shellfish in hot soup plates and spoon the sauce—which should have a very light, almost brothlike consistency—over and around. Serve immediately.

RED WINE SHELLFISH STEWS AND SOUPS

Fuller-flavored shellfish such as octopus or squid are often best when simmered in red wine, which holds up to their stronger flavor. Red wine is also best used in slow-cooking dishes so that its tannin and acids have time to cook off. It's easy to combine octopus, squid, and cuttlefish in the same dish because their flavors are similar and they cook in much the same way. Try making the octopus with red wine on page 230 and then adding cleaned squid or cuttlefish halfway into the cooking. If you're using cuttlefish, you can stir in the ink just before serving so you'll end up with a dramatic jet-black stew. A soup can be made the same way except that you'll need to use more liquid and the ingredients should be cut into smaller pieces.

Red wine can also be used as the base for shellfish stews and soups containing quick-cooking shellfish such as clams, mussels, or lobster, but red wine should be cooked for about an hour to soften its tannin and acidity before these quicker-cooking shellfish are added. For this reason I sometimes prepare a red wine squid or octopus stew or soup and then use it as the base for shellfish stews, soups, or sauces.

Red Wine Octopus and Clam Stew

(color page 16)

For this dish the rich and flavorful red wine stewing liquid from octopus stew is used to steam open clams so the liquid takes on an even more intense seafood flavor. Various vegetables—cooked separately—can be added to this stew just before serving. My favorites are fennel and baby artichokes, but you can substitute sautéed mushrooms, glazed pearl onions, or sliced carrots.

You can cook the octopus in red wine 2 or 3 days in advance, but the vegetables need to be prepared and the clams steamed just before serving.

I usually serve this stew as a light main course, but you can halve the quantities and serve it as an opener.

MAKES 6 MAIN-COURSE SERVINGS

two 2-pound octopuses, cleaned

1 medium onion, coarsely chopped

1 medium carrot, coarsely chopped

2 garlic cloves, crushed and peeled

1 fennel bulb, top stalk chopped, leafy frond and bulb reserved

6 tablespoons extra-virgin olive oil

1 bouquet garni: 4 fresh thyme sprigs or ½ teaspoon dried, ½ bunch of parsley, and a bay leaf tied up with string (or in cheesecloth for dried thyme)

2 bottles full-bodied red wine

18 baby artichokes, outer leaves trimmed off

3 to 4 dozen littleneck, Manila, or other small clams, scrubbed

2 tablespoons finely chopped parsley

salt and pepper

Submerge the octopuses in a large pot of boiling water for 5 minutes. Drain them, let them cool, and cut the tentacles and center section into 2-inch lengths or chunks.

In a pot large enough to hold the octopuses, cook the onion, carrot, garlic, and chopped fennel stalk (you should have about ½ cup) in 2 tablespoons of the olive oil over medium heat until the onion turns translucent, about 10 minutes. Add the octopus and stir for 5 minutes more. Nestle the bouquet garni in with the octopus and pour in the wine. Bring the wine to a gentle simmer and cover the pot. Keep the stew at the gentlest simmer on the stove over low heat or in a 300°F oven for 2 hours.

Meanwhile, cut the fennel bulb through the base into 6 even wedges. Arrange the wedges in a pot just large enough to hold them in a single layer. Sprinkle with 2 tablespoons of the olive oil and add enough water to come halfway up their sides. Cook, covered, over low to medium heat for 20 minutes, until the fennel softens but retains some of its texture. Using a nonaluminum pot, cook the whole baby artichokes in the same way, using the remaining olive oil, cooking for about 15 minutes. Season both vegetables with salt and pepper.

When the octopus is cooked, strain the cooking liquid into a 4-quart pot. Pick the octopus out of the strainer and press down on the vegetables to extract all the liquid. Discard the vegetables and bouquet garni. Simmer the cooking liquid until only 1½ cups remain, skimming off with a ladle any fat or scum that forms on the surface.

Put the cooking liquid in a pot with the clams. Cover the pot and steam the clams open over high heat—they should all open in 10 to 12 minutes.

Reheat the octopus with the clams in the clam cooking liquid and place the braised fennel and artichokes in heated soup plates. Add the parsley to the red wine broth and season with salt and pepper to taste. Pour the broth over and around the vegetables and shellfish.

SHELLFISH POT-AU-FEU

A traditional pot-au-feu is a slowly simmered pot of meat and vegetables, half stew, half broth. The broth is served as a first course and the meats after. In France during the 1970s restaurant chefs began naming new and sophisticated dishes after traditional favorites. Pot-au-feu was one of the first to succumb to this confusing but picturesque trend. In the modern interpretation of the pot-au-feu the ingredients are not limited to meat and vegetables (here enter shellfish), and the solid ingredients are sliced (or in some way cut into manageable pieces) and presented in

wide soup plates, partially immersed in flavorful broth rather than being served in two separate courses. To complicate matters further, some chefs prepare each of the elements of the pot-au-feu using a different technique such as grilling, poaching, or even frying. The one remnant of the traditional pot-au-feu is that the solid ingredients are presented in a clear broth rather than in a sauce. Because no fat is used in the cooking, the so-called modern pot-au-feu is a perfect dish for the diet-conscious.

Pot-au-feu variations are almost limitless. The easiest approach is to undercook each of the shellfish, prepare a clear broth from the shells and/or cooking liquids, and then gently reheat the liquid and shellfish just before serving.

❧

Pot-au-feu of Scallops, Clams, and Shrimp

Although almost any shellfish or fish can be used in a pot-au-feu, you'll still need certain types for the broth. If what you choose has no broth-making possibilities, you may have to use a broth you've frozen ahead of time.

Although this is an elaborate dish, a lot of the work can be done earlier the same day—including preparing the broth, peeling and deveining the shrimp, and steaming open the clams.

MAKES 6 MAIN-COURSE SERVINGS

1 pound sea scallops (about 12 large or 18 small), preferably freshly shucked

18 extra-large or jumbo shrimp, preferably with heads

½ cup dry white wine

1 quart fish broth (page 343), chicken broth (page 344), or water

18 to 30 clams or cockles (3 or 5 per serving depending on size)

3 tomatoes, seeded and chopped

1 small onion, chopped

2 large leeks

3 egg whites

1 small bunch of flat-leaf parsley

2 medium carrots, cut into fine julienne

1 turnip, peeled and cut into fine julienne

salt and white pepper

2 teaspoons olive oil

If you're using large scallops, cut each one into 3 disks. Small scallops can be left whole. Reserve in the refrigerator.

Peel the shrimp, twist off the heads, and simmer heads and/or shells in the wine and broth in a covered pot for 30 minutes. Crush the heads and/or shells with the end of a handleless rolling pin or a cleaver held on end every 10 minutes during the simmering. Strain the broth through a fine-mesh strainer and discard the shells.

Simmer the clams in the shrimp-shell broth in a covered pot until the clams open, about 10 minutes. Remove the clams with a slotted spoon and reserve in the refrigerator. Let the cooking liquid cool; reserve.

Poach the peeled shrimp in the clam/shrimp-shell broth for about 2 minutes, until they just turn orange. Reserve on a plate, covered, in the refrigerator.

Stir together the tomatoes, the onion, the chopped greens from one of the leeks, and the egg whites in a mixing bowl. Set aside 18 parsley leaves and coarsely chop the rest of the bunch—including the stems—and combine with the tomato/egg-white mixture. Whisk the cooled shellfish broth into the egg-white mixture. Bring this mixture to a slow simmer over medium heat in a saucepan. Simmer gently for 30 minutes, until the solids have coagulated into a single mass, and strain through a fine-mesh strainer. Reserve.

Cut the whites from both leeks into fine julienne and simmer the julienned vegetables in the clear broth in a covered saucepan until barely tender, about 20 minutes. Season the broth with salt and white pepper to taste.

Sauté the scallops in olive oil in a nonstick pan over very high heat for 3 to 4 minutes, until no longer translucent. Remove and pat the scallops with paper towels to eliminate any oil clinging to their surface.

Arrange the hot julienned vegetables in wide soup plates. Gently reheat the clams and shrimp in the hot broth and arrange all the shellfish around the vegetables in the bowls. Heat the reserved parsley leaves in the clear broth. Ladle the broth over all and serve immediately.

COMBINING FINFISH AND SHELLFISH

It's easy to add pieces of filleted fish to shellfish soups and stews as long as you keep in mind that finfish are often quicker cooking and more fragile then shellfish. For this reason stews or soups that include finfish are almost entirely cooked before the fish is added. Occasionally when raw fish is added to a simmering soup or stew, froth and scum will float to the surface and should be skimmed off with a ladle.

Another approach to combining fish and shellfish is to use the shellfish-cooking liquids to make a sauce for the fish and use the shellfish themselves as the garnish. Even though some of these combinations can get very complicated, they can also be as simple as a sautéed fish fillet topped with a few steamed clams and the clam-steaming liquid.

❧

Salmon Fillet with Oysters

You can use almost any fish for this dish provided it is firm-fleshed and has a delicate flavor. This dish is one of my favorite quick and easy dishes that is sublimely delicious and looks like I've labored for hours. If you can, use smallish briny-flavored oysters. If you buy the oysters the day you're cooking, have the fishmonger shuck them for you. As soon as you get them home, shuck them out of their bottom shells into a bowl, cover with plastic wrap, and refrigerate. You can cook the salmon any way you like, as long as you cook it just before serving. I find the easiest method is to bake it. Although this dish has to be cooked at the last minute, you'll have the oysters already shucked and the salmon cut in advance.

MAKES 6 MAIN-COURSE SERVINGS

one 2½-pound piece of center-cut salmon fillet, skin and pin bones removed

1 tablespoon olive oil

18 oysters, shucked

½ cup dry white wine

1 shallot, finely chopped

2 tablespoons finely chopped parsley, chervil, and chives in any combination

½ cup heavy cream

salt and pepper

Cut the salmon crosswise into 6 equal strips, each between 1 and 1½

inches wide. Brush a baking sheet and the pieces of salmon with olive oil. Arrange the salmon on the baking sheet, making sure the pieces don't touch. Fold the belly flap under each salmon strip so the strips are of the same thickness along their entire length. Preheat the oven to 400°F.

Spoon the oysters onto a clean towel and pat gently with a second towel so any grit attached to the oysters clings to the towels. Simmer the wine with the shallots in a small saucepan over medium heat for 10 minutes and add the oysters. Heat the oysters gently until their edges curl slightly, about 1 minute. The oysters should be hot but mustn't simmer. Take the oysters out of the liquid with a slotted spoon and place them in a small bowl. Add the herbs and cream to the shallot/white wine mixture and simmer the sauce over medium heat for about 5 minutes, until it thickens slightly and takes on the consistency of cold heavy cream.

Meanwhile, sprinkle the salmon fillets with salt and pepper and place them in the oven for 8 minutes for 1-inch-thick fillets. The salmon is done when a white liquid forms on its surface and it feels firm to the touch.

Arrange the salmon on hot soup plates. Reheat the oysters in the sauce and season with salt and pepper to taste. Spoon the oysters (3 per serving) and sauce over the salmon and serve immediately.

Substitutes Blackfish, black sea bass, cod, cusk, Dover sole, halibut, grouper, skate, striped bass, wolffish

Pompano Fillets with Lobster Sauce and Lobster Medallions

Pompano comes to mind for this recipe because it has a very similar texture to the Dover sole most likely to be used in fancy French restaurants, but any delicately flavored firm-fleshed fish fillet can be used. The basis for this recipe is the lobster *à l'Américaine* recipe. If you have the bones and head from your fish, cook them with the lobster shells to make the sauce.

You can cook the fish any way you like—I usually sauté it because sautéing is easy, but grilling the fish would provide an elegant contrast of flavors. Purists would probably braise the fillets in the lobster sauce, but the choice is yours.

This is an elaborate dish that I'm likely to serve at only my most special and extravagant dinners. And since such dinners involve breaking the bank anyway, I occasionally splurge and gently simmer a sliced black truffle in the lobster sauce 5 minutes before serving. You can control the consistency of the sauce by reducing it more or less. A traditional sauce should be thick enough to coat the fish, but my own preference is to keep the sauce relatively thin and brothlike and serve it *around* the fish in a soup plate.

The ingredients given here are for a large amount—8 main-course servings—because it seems like a nuisance to prepare the lobster for a few people. If you want to serve this as a first course, cut the quantities in half.

MAKES 8 MAIN-COURSE SERVINGS

1 recipe lobster *à l'Américaine* (page 177)

sixteen 3-ounce or eight 6-ounce pompano fillets

2 tablespoons unsalted butter

salt and pepper

Slice each lobster tail into 4 to 6 medallions depending on the size of the tails. (You may not be able to place the same number of medallions on each serving, but you can make up the difference with the claws.) Arrange the claws and sliced tails on an ovenproof plate. Cover with aluminum foil and place in a 200°F oven for 15 minutes.

Gently heat the lobster sauce. Sauté the fillets in a nonstick pan in butter and season with salt and pepper to taste. Transfer the fillets to a hot plate covered with paper towels to absorb the butter. (Any butter left clinging to the fillets will float up into the sauce and look oily.)

Quickly arrange the fillets on hot plates or soup plates and ladle the sauce over and around. Arrange the lobster medallions and claws on top of the fillets. Serve immediately.

Substitutes Blackfish, black sea bass, cod, cusk, Dover sole, halibut, grouper, skate, striped bass, wolffish

Seafood in Other Guises

Salads

Soups

Stews

Pasta and Rice Dishes

Mousses, Soufflés,
and Other French Classics

Sauces and Salsas,
Condiments and Broths

Salads

When I make salads, I never follow a recipe exactly, and most of the time I don't even know what I want to end up with. The process usually consists of picking up something green, fresh, and crunchy at the market and then rummaging around in the refrigerator until I figure out what to combine. Fish and shellfish leftovers are great because they can be used in so many ways. Sometimes they get cut into cubes and end up tossed with a little olive oil, some chopped parsley (for freshness and color), a few cubes or slices of celery or onion (for flavor and crunch), and a little lemon juice. At other times large chunks or slices of leftover fish are tossed with salad greens and maybe sprinkled with capers or a few croutons and served as a summer main course. Some fish ends up on large plates, thinly sliced, brushed with olive oil, and dotted with finely chopped fresh herbs such as chives or tarragon.

Although the best salads always seem to be last-minute improvised affairs, this probably isn't a reliable approach if you're trying to plan a meal for a crowd. You can still improvise, but it will help to have a few basic approaches in mind and then combine ingredients and techniques following your own whim and inspiration.

TOSSING FISH AND SHELLFISH WITH LEAFY GREENS

One of the easiest seafood salads is made by tossing hot or cold fish or shellfish in a green salad just before serving—a great technique for turning a simple piece of grilled or sautéed fish into a complete meal. Salad greens seem to lighten fish or shellfish, making these salads perfect for summer main courses.

Use full-flavored greens that will match and accent the flavors of the fish or shellfish. In summer I almost invariably use equal parts of arugula (rocket) and basil leaves, sprinkling on nasturtium flowers or leaves or tossing in some radicchio leaves for color when company is coming. In springtime I love to toss wild dandelion leaves with freshly grilled oily fish such as sardines or mackerel. In winter I use endive (both the pale white/yellow variety and the dark purple kind), lamb's lettuce (mâche), radicchio, curly chicory, or tiny leaves of Bibb lettuce. At any time of year I may include raw vegetables such as very thinly sliced fennel or onions or tomato wedges and cooked vegetables such as artichoke hearts, beans (green and others), corn, grilled peppers, and mushrooms. I sometimes toss in capers or pitted imported olives for accent and little croutons, rubbed with garlic and sprinkled with olive oil, for texture.

Many cooks are intimidated by salad dressings, but I almost invariably rely on the easiest of all: extra-virgin olive oil, good wine vinegar (sherry vinegar is my favorite), salt, and pepper. Cookbooks often recommend whisking the vinegar and seasonings and then slowly pouring in the olive oil (four parts oil to one part vinegar). Not only is this a nuisance, but for some mysterious reason whisking extra-virgin olive oil turns it bitter. I just pour a few tablespoons of oil over the salad, sprinkle with vinegar, salt, and pepper, and toss. If I'm in doubt about the proportions, I toss the salad, taste a leaf, and add more oil or vinegar accordingly.

More elaborate salad sauces can be made by incorporating various flavorings such as herbs, shellfish roe or cooking liquid, or aromatic vegetables such as garlic, shallots, or ginger into a vinaigrette or light mayonnaise (essentially a vinaigrette containing egg yolk and whisked into an emulsion). Some of these recipes are given here, but remember when improvising to keep the flavors simple and direct—don't combine too many ingredients. At times you may wish to toss only certain components with a full-flavored complex sauce while tossing the salad greens with a simple vinaigrette so that the flavors of the central component stand out.

❧

Tossed Lobster and Green Salad

I like to serve this salad in summer, when lobster is relatively cheap and plentiful and I can find beautiful tomatoes and an array of flower blossoms—this salad also looks great when served outside in the sunlight. Arrange it in the kitchen and then present it and toss it in front of the guests. The lobster pieces—coated with their own sauce—are then arranged on the individual salads.

This version calls for a sauce, which means you must prepare the lobster the same day since coral is very perishable, but you can simplify matters by leaving out the sauce. You can also prepare the salad with cooked shrimp or crab.

MAKES **4** MAIN-COURSE SERVINGS

four 1¼-pound female lobsters

1 teaspoon wine vinegar

1 teaspoon cognac

½ cup water

¼ cup heavy cream

3 tablespoons sherry vinegar or more to taste

1 tablespoon finely chopped herbs such as parsley, chives, or chervil

mixed greens such as basil, arugula, radicchio, Bibb, and chicory

pesticide-free flower blossoms such as nasturtiums, daylilies, or hyssop flowers

2 tomatoes, peeled, each cut into 6 wedges, seeds removed

½ pound green beans, preferably *haricots verts*, ends broken off, blanched in boiling salted water for 4 to 6 minutes, until still slightly crunchy, rinsed in cold water, and drained

2 hard-boiled eggs, each cut into 4 wedges

1 bunch of chervil (optional), large stems removed

⅓ cup extra-virgin olive oil

2 tablespoons white wine vinegar

salt and pepper

Rinse the lobsters, cut them up, and work the coral and tomalley into a bowl containing the wine vinegar and cognac (see directions in lobster chapter and color page 23). Refrigerate until needed.

Slide a wooden skewer along the length of each lobster just under the bottom to prevent the tails from curling. Steam the cut-up lobsters with the water in a covered pot until all the parts turn red, about 8 minutes. Let the lobsters cool and take the meat out of the shells. Slice the lobster tails into 5 slices each. Strain the steaming liquid into a clean saucepan and boil it down until ¼ cup remains. Pour in the cream and continue cooking until the mixture thickens slightly. Remove from the heat, let cool for about 5 minutes, and whisk in the sherry vinegar, the strained coral/tomalley mixture, and the chopped herbs. Put the pan back over medium heat and whisk the sauce constantly until it turns a deep orange. (The coral turns from dark green to deep orange as it cooks.) Immediately remove from the heat and whisk for 1 minute more to cool the sauce quickly. The sauce must not boil, or the coral will curdle. Refrigerate until needed.

Arrange the greens, flowers, tomatoes, green beans, eggs, and chervil leaves in a deep salad bowl. Coat the lobster pieces with the chilled coral sauce and arrange the lobster in a small bowl. Bring the salad and lobster to the table. Pour the oil and white wine vinegar over the salad and sprinkle with salt and pepper. Toss thoroughly and arrange on wide plates. Arrange 5 slices of lobster tail and 2 claws on top of the greens in the center of each plate and serve.

TOSSING GRILLED FISH WITH GREENS

Although most fish can be incorporated into a salad of fresh greens, it's best to use relatively firm fish that won't fall apart and end up strewn, unrecognizable, throughout. If you're using more fragile fish, toss the salad without the fish, arrange it on plates, and then place a piece of fish on top of each salad. Tuna, swordfish, skate, shark, and other firm-fleshed fish can be arranged on top of the bowl of greens and tossed at the table without falling apart.

While almost any cooking technique can be used to cook fish destined for a salad, I prefer those that bring out the fish's fullest flavor—grilling and hot smoking are my favorites, followed by sautéing, broiling, and frying. Depending on the texture of the fish, I slice it (for very firm fish such as undercooked tuna) or cut it into chunks (for more fragile fish).

❧

Grilled Tuna Salad

(color page 13)

Not too long ago tuna was available only in cans. Times have changed, and we're accustomed not only to fresh tuna but even raw. The secret to this salad is, in fact, to grill the tuna over very high heat so it chars lightly on the outside but stays raw in the center—much like a rare steak. Don't yield to any temptation to overcook it—it will end up dry and will fall apart when you try to toss it.

Adjust this salad according to the season—bitter greens such as wild dandelion or chicory in winter and spring, aromatic herbs, especially basil and arugula, in summer. In winter you may want to replace the tomatoes with sautéed mushrooms or other available vegetables.

This salad is quite rich and wonderfully satisfying, so I serve it as a main course. The tuna is best grilled at the last minute, but you can prepare all the greens earlier the same day and keep them in the refrigerator. I usually figure on about 6 ounces of tuna per serving, but for big eaters, serve 8 ounces.

MAKES 4 MAIN-COURSE SERVINGS

4 medium waxy potatoes such as yellow Finn, Yukon gold, or Bintje

1½ pounds fresh tuna cut into steaks at least 1 inch thick

2 red or yellow bell peppers or 1 of each, roasted and peeled (page 133)

½ cup extra-virgin olive oil or more as needed

salt and pepper

3 shallots, finely chopped

¼ cup sherry vinegar or white wine vinegar or more as needed

2 tablespoons finely chopped parsley

4 large handfuls of mixed greens such as basil, arugula, radicchio, Bibb, chicory, dandelion, and endive (white or purple)

2 tomatoes, peeled, each cut into 6 wedges, seeds removed

Cover the potatoes with cold water in a 4-quart pot and simmer gently for about 25 minutes, until they soften—don't overcook them.

Meanwhile, trim the skin and any dark purple flesh off the tuna steaks and reserve in the refrigerator.

Cut the peeled bell peppers into lengthwise strips about ¼ inch wide and toss them in a bowl with 1 tablespoon of the olive oil. Season with salt and pepper and reserve.

Drain the potatoes and peel them while they're still hot—the skin should pull off easily in strips. Slice the still-warm potatoes into ¼-inch-thick slices and arrange a layer of potatoes in a pie plate or casserole. Sprinkle with shallots, sherry vinegar, olive oil, parsley, salt, and pepper. Continue layering the potatoes, seasoning each layer in the same way until the potatoes are all used.

Lightly rub the tuna steaks with olive oil, season with salt and pepper, and grill them about 2 inches above a very hot bed of coals or sauté them for about 2 minutes on each side. (This will leave the tuna almost raw in the center; if you want the tuna to be pink, cook for 3 to 4 minutes on each side.)

Place the greens in a large salad bowl and arrange the peppers, tomatoes, and potatoes on top. Slice the tuna into ¼-inch-thick strips and arrange on top of the salad.

In front of the guests, pour the remaining vinegar and olive oil over the salad—you may have to use more than is called for if you've used a bit too much on the potatoes. Sprinkle the whole thing with salt and pepper, toss, and serve at the table on wide plates.

Substitutes Firm-fleshed steaks or fillets such as king mackerel, salmon, shark, sturgeon, swordfish. Remember when using fish other than tuna that the fish should be cooked all the way through.

SEAFOOD SALADS WITH NONLEAFY VEGETABLES

These salads are made by tossing cooked or occasionally raw seafood with raw or lightly cooked vegetables in a vinaigrette or light mayonnaise. French classic cookbook writers called these salads *salades américaines*, which is a bit mysterious since they don't seem especially popular in the United States.

The joy of these so-called American salads is that they can be made in almost limitless combinations and can be spectacularly flavorful and colorful. A simple version might be cooked shrimp or scallops tossed with a little chopped celery or fennel in a vinaigrette or lightened homemade mayonnaise. More complicated (and expensive) versions might include crayfish tails, lobster, truffles, and wild mushrooms. Fortunately there are a lot of possibilities between these two extremes.

SALAD SAUCES

The best sauce for a salad of seafood and tossed greens is almost always a splash of extra-virgin olive oil and a sprinkling of vinegar, but for a richer salad with nonleafy vegetables and a higher proportion of seafood I often prepare a more complex sauce. Usually these sauces are based on a simple vinaigrette or mayonnaise flavored with chopped herbs, nut oils such as walnut or hazelnut, vegetable purees, reduced broth, shellfish-cooking liquid, spices, mushroom-cooking liquid, or truffle juice. Whichever flavors you decide to use, be sure they don't overwhelm the seafood.

USING EXTRA-VIRGIN OLIVE OIL

Extra-virgin olive oil is one of the most delicious oils you can use for making vinaigrettes and salad sauces, but there are a few things to watch out for when using it.

Don't beat extra-virgin olive oil in a metal bowl with a metal whisk—for some mysterious reason, metal and rapid beating turn the oil bitter. If you need to beat a vinaigrette or mayonnaise, start out using a flavorless oil—such as canola, safflower oil, or "pure" olive oil—and then stir in extra-virgin oil by hand.

Mustard, which is used in most vinaigrettes, doesn't complement the flavor of olive oil, so you're better off leaving it out.

FLAVORING OILS AND VINEGARS

The easiest way to make flavored oils and vinegars is just to shove herbs or spices into the mouth of the bottle and let the oil or vinegar sit until it takes on the right amount of flavor—usually about a week. If you're in a hurry, the herbs or spices can be chopped or ground and heated gently in the oil or vinegar.

Olive oil is best flavored with Provençal herbs such as thyme, rosemary, marjoram, oregano, basil, and lavender; inert oils such as canola or safflower are good when flavored with spices such as ginger or curry; and vinegar is delicious when flavored with tarragon, lemon or orange zest, or berries such as raspberries or blueberries.

VINAIGRETTE

The simplest vinaigrette is made by whisking oil into vinegar seasoned with salt and pepper and mustard; see the basic vinaigrette on page 337. The mustard not only seasons the dressing but also helps emulsify the oil and vinegar so they don't separate. The secret to a successful vinaigrette is to use the best oil and vinegar you can find.

In less traditional vinaigrette recipes the mustard is replaced with a vegetable puree, which flavors the vinaigrette and also acts as an emulsifier. Two of my favorites are garlic and tomato. Herbs and spices can also be added to the vinegar just before the oil is stirred in, or you can make flavored oils and vinegars in advance and use them as needed.

I always make vinaigrettes just before serving instead of keeping them in the refrigerator, where they separate and end up tasting a little stale.

Seafood Salad with Garlic, Tomato, and Basil Vinaigrette

*H*ere's a rich and extravagant salad for a special occasion. The combination of seafood is so delicious and the vinaigrette so tangy and fresh that it's worth the indulgence.

Any firm-fleshed cooked seafood can be used, and with the flavorful vinaigrette not much else is needed. The cubes of celery are added to give a little bit of crunch.

MAKES 6 FIRST-COURSE SERVINGS

6 jumbo shrimp, lightly sautéed in the shell

two 1¼-pound boiled lobsters

one 6-ounce tuna steak

1 tablespoon extra-virgin olive oil

salt and pepper

½ celery stalk, cut into ¼-inch cubes

1 recipe garlic, tomato, and basil vinaigrette (recipe follows)

Peel and devein the shrimp and reserve in the refrigerator.

Take the lobster meat out of the shell (see color page 22) and slice each tail into 6 medallions. Cut 2 of the largest lobster claws in half crosswise so they keep their shape.

Rub the tuna steak with olive oil, season it with salt and pepper, and sauté it or grill it over high heat for 2 minutes on each side, until very rare in the center. Let cool in the refrigerator for 30 minutes and cut into 6 even long slices. Season each slice with salt and pepper.

Lightly coat the shrimp, lobster, tuna, and celery cubes with the vinaigrette and arrange together on plates in small mounds.

Garlic, Tomato, and Basil Vinaigrette

*T*his vinaigrette is a delicious cold sauce for seafood. You can use the recipe as a model for different vinaigrettes by substituting other purees such as potato, mushroom, or asparagus for the garlic and tomato—and other herbs for the basil.

The garlic and tomato purees can be made in advance and frozen indefinitely or covered with a thin layer of olive oil and kept in the refrigerator for up to a week.

MAKES ²/₃ CUP

1 head of garlic

1 tomato, seeded and chopped

6 to 8 tablespoons extra-virgin olive oil

10 fresh basil leaves

2 tablespoons good-quality wine vinegar

salt and pepper

Preheat the oven to 400°F.

Break the garlic into cloves—don't bother peeling them—and wrap the cloves in aluminum foil. Bake for 30 minutes. You can also simmer the unpeeled cloves in water for 30 minutes, until they've softened completely. Push the cooked cloves through a strainer with a ladle or the back of a spoon to get rid of the skins and extract the pulp. Reserve the pulp.

Cook the tomato in a tablespoon of olive oil in a saucepan over medium heat until it dries into a stiff paste, about 15 minutes. Push it through a strainer with a small ladle to eliminate the skin and any remaining seeds. Reserve the puree.

Rub the basil leaves with a few drops of olive oil so each leaf is coated with a light film. Chop the leaves finely and combine them with the garlic and tomato purees and the vinegar. Season with salt and pepper and slowly stir in the remaining olive oil with a wooden spoon.

Mussel, Tomato, and Parsley Salad

*F*requently steaming mussels in white wine to use the cooking liquid in sauces leaves me with lots of leftover cooked mussels—great tossed with chopped fresh herbs and olive oil. This is the tamer Italian cousin of the mussels in salsa given in the mussels chapter.

You can prepare the tomatoes and mussels earlier the same day, but chop the parsley at the last minute. If you're being formal, you may want to cut the tomatoes carefully into ¼-inch cubes. This salad can also be made with cream vinaigrette (page 256).

MAKES 4 FIRST-COURSE SERVINGS

2 pounds small cultivated mussels or 1½ cups leftover shelled mussels

1 shallot, finely chopped

½ cup dry white wine or water

4 tomatoes, peeled, seeded, and coarsely chopped

1 tablespoon salt, preferably coarse sea salt

¼ cup chopped parsley, preferably flat-leaf

2 tablespoons fresh lemon juice

¼ cup extra-virgin olive oil

pepper

If you're using mussels in the shell, bring the shallot and wine to a simmer in a pot and add the mussels. Cover the pot and turn the heat up to high. When the mussels have opened, about 5 minutes, remove the lid, discard any unopened mussels, let the mussels cool, and take them out of the shells. Discard the shells. (Freeze the cooking liquid for another recipe.)

Toss the tomatoes with the salt and let drain in a colander for 30 minutes.

Just before serving, toss everything together and serve in mounds on small plates.

Italian-Style Octopus Salad

Cold octopus has a meaty texture that makes it especially satisfying in salads. The Italians have a genius for converting octopus into first-course salads, perfect for an outdoor summer meal.

Most octopuses have already been cleaned, but if you find one that hasn't, follow the cleaning directions on page 229.

MAKES 6 FIRST-COURSE SERVINGS OR 8 ON A MIXED ANTIPASTO

salt

one 3- to 3½-pound octopus, cleaned

½ cup extra-virgin olive oil

2 garlic cloves, finely chopped

¼ cup finely chopped parsley

3 tablespoons fresh lemon juice

pepper

Bring to a simmer enough water to cover the octopus generously. Salt the water, simmer the octopus for 1 hour and 15 minutes, drain in a colander, and let cool. At this point you may notice that some of the skin of the octopus has grown slimy or come loose. You can peel this off with your fingers and discard.

Cut the tentacles into 1-inch sections and cut the part where the tentacles join into pieces about the same size. Toss the octopus pieces with the remaining ingredients and serve cool.

Salad of Leftover Grilled Fish

It's always a good idea to grill a little extra fish just to make sure you have some for this salad. Firm-fleshed fish such as tuna or swordfish is best because it won't fall apart when tossed. This is a somewhat bare-bones version to which you can add basil (chopped or whole leaves), cooked beans, cooked rice, mushrooms, tomatoes (peeled, cut into wedges, seeded), olives (pitted), capers, orange wedges, fennel (bulb sliced almost paper-thin with a slicer), pine nuts, raisins, or croutons.

MAKES 6 FIRST-COURSE OR 4 MAIN-COURSE SERVINGS

four 6- to 8-ounce servings of grilled tuna or swordfish steaks or other grilled fish or shellfish

1 large red onion, thinly sliced

1 tablespoon coarse salt

1½ cups cooked rice, pasta, or beans

1 cup cooked green vegetables such as green beans, asparagus, or broccoli in ½-inch pieces

½ cup extra-virgin olive oil

¼ cup fresh lemon juice

¼ cup finely chopped parsley

1 red bell pepper, roasted (page 133), peeled, and cut into julienne strips

salt and pepper

Cut the grilled fish into 1-inch cubes and reserve in the refrigerator.

In a small mixing bowl, toss the onion with the coarse salt. Rub the salt into the onion until the salt dissolves and you don't see any adhering to your fingers. Put the onion in a colander set over a bowl to drain for about 30 minutes. Squeeze the onion—a

small handful at a time—to eliminate moisture and salt.

Toss the fish with the onion, rice, green vegetable, oil, lemon juice, parsley, and red pepper. Season with salt and pepper to taste. (You may not need any more salt since the onions are already salty.)

Cream Vinaigrette

A cream vinaigrette simply replaces the oil in a basic vinaigrette with heavy cream. When I make a cream vinaigrette for seafood salads, I like to add some of the reduced cooking liquid from the seafood.

MAKES ½ CUP

2 tablespoons good-quality wine vinegar

6 tablespoons heavy cream

6 tablespoons seafood-cooking liquid, boiled down to 2 tablespoons

salt and pepper

Whisk together the vinegar, cream, and reduced cooking liquid. Season with salt and pepper to taste. (The sauce may not need any salt because of the salty cooking liquid.)

Scallop and Crayfish Salad with Mushrooms and Chervil

This is another salad that can be used as a model for almost limitless variations. The scallops or crayfish tails can be replaced with cooked shrimp, lobster, or crabmeat or lightly cooked pieces of firm fish such as tuna or salmon. In this version a cream vinaigrette is flavored with the cooking liquid from the scallops, crayfish shells, and mushrooms and then used to coat the ingredients in the salad just before serving. If you're replacing the crayfish with crayfish tails or shrimp, use a simple vinaigrette that doesn't require shellfish-cooking liquid.

Most of the work for this salad can be done earlier in the day—only the final assembly must be done at the last minute.

MAKES 6 FIRST-COURSE SERVINGS

6 large (1 ounce or more) sea scallops, small muscle removed

30 live crayfish or crayfish tails (use tails if you're not making the shellfish vinaigrette)

2 tablespoons pure olive oil

1 shallot, finely chopped

2 tomatoes, seeded and coarsely chopped

½ cup dry white wine

18 small mushrooms, quartered

¼ cup good-quality white wine vinegar or sherry vinegar

¼ cup heavy cream

1 medium bunch of fresh chervil or parsley

salt and pepper

Pull off and discard the small muscle that runs up the sides of the scallops. Cut the scallops in half crosswise and reserve in the refrigerator.

Rinse the crayfish and sort through them to make sure there are no dead ones. Heat the olive oil in a pot large enough to hold the crayfish over medium heat for about 5 minutes. Toss in the crayfish, cover the pot, and turn the heat up to high. Cook the crayfish, stirring every 2 minutes. Sprinkle on the chopped shallots after about 4 minutes and continue cooking for 2 to 4 minutes more, until the crayfish have all turned red. Let cool.

Twist off the crayfish tails, devein them by tugging on the tiny tail flap—both flap and vein should pull out—and take out and reserve the meat by either pinching on the tails to crack them or cutting along one side of the underside of the tail with scissors. Break off the crayfish claws (they damage the food processor blade) and crack them with a rolling pin. Puree the heads and remaining shells in a food processor for about 1 minute.

Combine the pureed shells, claws, tomatoes, and wine in a 4-quart pot and simmer gently, covered, for 30 minutes. Strain the mixture through a fine-mesh strainer into a small pot—discard what doesn't go through the strainer.

Bring the crayfish liquid to a simmer and stir in the scallops. Poach the scallops for 1 to 2 minutes, depending on their size. Take the scallops out with a slotted spoon and let cool in the refrigerator. Stir the mushrooms into the cooking liquid and simmer gently for 5 minutes. Remove with a slotted spoon and let cool, covered with plastic wrap, in the refrigerator.

FLAVORING SALAD SAUCES WITH SHELLFISH-COOKING LIQUIDS AND OILS

Vinaigrette and mayonnaise for seafood salad can be flavored with the liquid released by the seafood while it is being cooked. The shells from crustaceans such as shrimp, lobster, or crayfish can be cooked in liquid and the liquid then reduced and incorporated into a mayonnaise or vinaigrette. Crustacean oil (page 337) can also be whisked into a mayonnaise or vinaigrette along with other, less assertive oil.

Boil down the cooking liquid until ¼ cup remains. Stir in the vinegar and reduce again until only ¼ cup is left. Stir in the cream and bring quickly to a simmer to sterilize the cream. Remove from the heat and while the sauce is cooling, chop half the chervil and stir it into the sauce. When the sauce is cool, season it with salt and pepper to taste. You may also have to adjust its acidity by adding a tablespoon or two more of vinegar or cream.

Just before serving, stir the scallops, crayfish tails, and mushrooms into the sauce. Arrange each of the ingredients in small mounds on plates. Decorate each serving with a small cluster of chervil leaves.

Lobster and Scallop Chat

(color page 2)

*I*ndian cooks make delicious spicy salads that make perfect openers to more elaborate dinners or can be served by themselves as light meals. Many Indian salads also contain fairly substantial ingredients such as potatoes, chicken, or seafood.

One of my favorite Indian dishes is a cold potato and chicken salad called *murgh chat.* It's a delicious dish, cool and tangy with just the right amount of spice. I've adapted it here for use with lobster and scallops. This is also a great salad for the diet-conscious because it contains very little oil.

MAKES 6 FIRST-COURSE SERVINGS

two 1¼-pound lobsters, boiled and shelled (see color page 22)

¾ pound sea scallops, lightly steamed or sautéed and cooled

6 small red potatoes, boiled and peeled while still warm

1 small red onion, thinly sliced

1 teaspoon ground cumin

2 teaspoons ground coriander

1 tablespoon pure olive or vegetable oil

¼ teaspoon cayenne pepper

¼ teaspoon freshly ground white pepper

½ cup water

2 tablespoons fresh lemon juice

2 tablespoons finely chopped cilantro

2 tablespoons finely chopped fresh mint

salt

Slice each of the shelled lobster tails into 6 medallions. Slice the largest 2 lobster claws in half crosswise so each slice retains the shape of the claw. If the scallops are large, cut them into disks about ⅓ inch thick. Reserve the lobster

and scallops on a plate, covered with plastic wrap, in the refrigerator.

Cut the potatoes into ⅓-inch-thick slices and reserve in a mixing bowl with the sliced onion.

In a small skillet or saucepan, stir the cumin, coriander, and oil over low heat until you can smell the fragrance of the spices. Stir in the cayenne, pepper, and water. Bring the mixture to a quick simmer and let cool to room temperature. Stir in the lemon juice, cilantro, and mint. Season to taste with salt, but remember that the spice mixture should taste *too* salty because it's the only seasoning for the vegetables and seafood.

Pour three quarters of the spice mixture over the potatoes and onions and toss. Let sit for about an hour in a cool place. (You can refrigerate the salad for 30 minutes and then let it sit at room temperature for 30 minutes.)

Gently toss the lobster and scallops with the remaining spice mixture. Arrange the potatoes, lobster, and scallops on cool plates. Drizzle on any remaining spice mixture left in the bowl.

Yogurt Sauces for Salads

Yogurt makes an excellent salad sauce for chunks of cold fish or shellfish. It can be somewhat bland, but stirring in chopped herbs such as cilantro, mint, or basil or finely chopped hot chilies and curry mixtures spikes it deliciously. To eliminate excess water, use thick labneh (page 36) or drain regular plain yogurt in cheesecloth for a couple of hours before incorporating it into the salad.

Indian Salmon and Yogurt Salad

I don't know if Indian cooks really make this salad, but the flavors and basic techniques are typical of Indian cooking. Essentially a kind of raita—a traditional yogurt salad—this salad is made more substantial with chunks of seafood.

I usually serve this salad as a main course outdoors on warm summer evenings, but if I'm showing off, I'll serve it as an elaborate first course.

Most of the work for this salad can be done earlier the same day—just squeeze the water out of the vegetables and toss the salad shortly before serving.

MAKES 8 FIRST-COURSE SERVINGS

1½ pounds center-cut salmon fillet, skin and pin bones removed

salt and pepper

2 tablespoons pure olive oil

1 long hothouse or 2 regular cucumbers, peeled

2½ tablespoons coarse sea salt or kosher salt

3 tomatoes, peeled and each cut into 8 wedges

1 red onion, thinly sliced

2 teaspoons ground cumin

1 tablespoon ground coriander

½ teaspoon cayenne pepper

2 tablespoons finely chopped fresh cilantro

2 tablespoons finely chopped fresh mint

1 cup labneh (page 36) or 2 cups regular plain yogurt, drained for 3 hours in a cheesecloth-lined strainer

Season the salmon with salt and pepper and sauté it in 1 tablespoon of the olive oil in a nonstick pan over high heat for 4 minutes on each side

(8 minutes total per inch of thickness). The salmon fillet can also be rubbed with olive oil and grilled. Let the salmon cool and cut it into 1-inch cubes. Reserve the cubes on a plate, covered with plastic wrap, in the refrigerator.

Cut the cucumbers in half lengthwise and scoop out the seeds with a spoon. Slice each half into 1/8- to 1/4-inch-thick crescents. Toss the crescents with a tablespoon of the coarse salt—keep tossing until all the salt has dissolved—and let the cucumbers drain in a colander for 30 minutes.

Scoop the seeds out of the tomato wedges with your fingers and toss the tomatoes in a tablespoon of coarse salt until all the salt has dissolved. Let drain in a colander for 30 minutes.

Rub the onion slices in the remaining coarse salt and let drain for 30 minutes in a colander.

Cook the cumin and coriander in the remaining oil in a saucepan or small skillet over low heat for about 3 minutes, until you can smell their aroma. Remove the pan from the heat and let cool.

Combine the cayenne, cilantro, mint, cooked spice mixture, and yogurt in a mixing bowl. Squeeze the water out of the cucumbers and onions a small handful at a time and combine them with the yogurt/spice mixture. Stir in the tomatoes.

Refrigerate the salad for 30 minutes—just enough to cool it slightly—and gently stir in the cubes of cooked salmon. Serve in mounds on cool plates.

Substitutes Any firm-fleshed delicately flavored fillet or steak that won't fall apart when tossed with the other ingredients. Dover sole, king mackerel, mahimahi, shark, sturgeon, swordfish, tilefish, and tuna are a few possibilities.

USING HOMEMADE MAYONNAISE AS A SAUCE FOR SALADS

(see the flavored mayonnaises on pages 334 and 335)

A light homemade mayonnaise can be the perfect accompaniment to a seafood salad. A basic mayonnaise is made in much the same way as a vinaigrette except that an egg yolk is included in the mixture before the oil is added.

Many cooks make the mistake of using a mayonnaise that is too thick so that too much ends up coating the seafood—making the dish overly rich and gloppy. The easiest way to avoid this is to make a basic mayonnaise and then thin it with flavorful liquids such as wine vinegar, reduced mushroom-cooking liquid, seafood-cooking liquid, heavy cream, or truffle juice. If you're improvising a flavored mayonnaise, make sure it's tangy with plenty of vinegar or lemon juice and be sure to season it with enough salt and pepper—in fact, a mayonnaise for a seafood salad should be *over*seasoned because it's the only seasoning in the dish. Mayonnaise can also be flavored with pureed vegetables, spices such as curry or saffron, almost any chopped herb, aromatic vegetables such as garlic, shallots, or ginger, and chopped olives or capers.

❧

Fresh Bay Scallops with Truffle Mayonnaise

This is one of those luxurious dishes that I serve during the holidays, when I can justify being even more extravagant than usual. You can, if you like, leave out the truffles and use just the truffle juice or oil—a little of either goes a long way.

You can serve other shellfish in the same way as this salad, but bay scallops, fresh out of the shell, are almost magically delicious. The sauce can be made earlier the same day.

MAKES 4 FIRST-COURSE SERVINGS

4 dozen bay scallops, preferably still in the shell (3/4 pound shelled)

salt and white pepper

1 tablespoon extra-virgin olive oil

1/4 cup flavorless oil such as canola or safflower

1 egg yolk

1 tablespoon bottled black truffle oil or canned-truffle juice or more to taste

1 tablespoon finely chopped fresh chives

three 1/8-inch-thick black truffle slices, cut into 1/8-inch julienne (optional)

1 tablespoon white wine vinegar

4 small fresh chervil sprigs

Shuck the scallops if they're still in the shell (see color page 17 or have the fishmonger do it). Remove the small muscle and any membrane surrounding the scallops. Season the scallops with salt and pepper and gently toss them in olive oil in a sauté pan over medium heat for about 2 minutes, until they just start to lose their sheen and release liquid. Transfer the cooked scallops to a bowl with a slotted spoon and let cool. Boil down any liquid in the sauté pan until only about a teaspoon is left.

Make a mayonnaise by slowly beating the flavorless oil into the egg yolk. Stir the reduced scallop-cooking liquid, the truffle oil or juice, the chives, half the julienned truffles, and the vinegar into the mayonnaise. Season with salt and pepper to taste—you may also want to add more vinegar or truffle liquid. (Brands of truffle oil and juice differ in strength.)

Just before serving, toss the scallops in the sauce and arrange on plates. Decorate with the remaining truffle julienne and the chervil.

TRUFFLE JUICE AND TRUFFLE OIL

Most of us can afford the subtle and pervasive flavor of truffles only on those rare occasions when we forget about budgets and common sense.

Fortunately, truffle juice—actually the cooking liquid left over from canned truffles—and truffle oil, made by soaking truffles in olive oil, are relatively inexpensive (although never cheap). The juice can be used in vinaigrettes, mayonnaise, and hollandaise sauces, and truffle oil can be added to any sauce containing oil, butter, or cream.

JAPANESE SALAD DRESSINGS

Japanese salad dressings are often very different from Western versions and only distantly related to mayonnaise and vinaigrette. While some Japanese dressings are indeed thickened with egg yolks and may contain vinegar, because they rarely contain oil they are good low-fat alternatives to Western salad sauces. Japanese dressings also have a special affinity for the flavors of fish and shellfish.

Once you've made one or two of these dressings, you'll probably come up with dozens of ideas for using them. Most of the time I toss them with lightly cooked pieces of firm-fleshed fish (such as lightly grilled tuna) or shellfish such as shrimp, lobster, clams, and mussels. It's always a good idea to include something crunchy—usually a vegetable—to provide contrast and make the dish less rich.

Many Japanese salad dressings contain mirin, sake, dashi, and miso. Some also contain pureed tofu, ground sesame seeds, soy sauce, egg yolks, vinegar, sugar, pickled plums, and starch such as *kuzu* starch or cornstarch. Once you get used to playing around with these ingredients, you'll be able to improvise your own Japanese-style salad dressing. (See glossary for more about the ingredients.)

❧

Basic Japanese Vinaigrette

*J*apanese cooks actually use 3 versions of this basic vinaigrette, but they differ only in amount of sugar. I usually start out making this vinaigrette with no sugar at all and then gradually stir in sugar—tasting with a piece of vegetable or fish as I go along—until the vinaigrette tastes right. Variations on this vinaigrette almost always work for Japanese-style seafood salads.

MAKES ⅔ CUP

¼ **cup rice wine vinegar**

1 **tablespoon Japanese dark soy sauce**

⅓ **cup dashi (page 343)**

1 **tablespoon sugar or more or less to taste**

Stir together all the ingredients. Stir in the sugar a teaspoon at a time, tasting as you go, until the sauce has just the right amount of sweetness.

❧

Japanese-Style Shrimp and Cucumber Salad

*T*his salad makes a refreshing first course, especially when you're serving other Japanese foods. You can substitute other vegetables such as celery (cut into small cubes) or shredded carrots or daikon for the cucumber, but the cucumber provides a crunchy and refreshing contrast to the cooked shrimp.

MAKES 6 FIRST-COURSE SERVINGS

18 **headless extra-large or jumbo shrimp, peeled**

1 **recipe basic Japanese vinaigrette (preceding recipe)**

1 **regular cucumber, peeled**

½ **tablespoon coarse sea salt**

In a sauté pan over high heat, stir or toss the shrimp in 2 tablespoons of the vinaigrette until the shrimp turn red, about 2 minutes. Drain the shrimp—discard the vinaigrette that runs off—and chill in the refrigerator. Once cool, devein the shrimp. (The shrimp shouldn't be deveined before cooking, or the cuts along the back will curl and look ugly in the salad.)

Cut the cucumbers in half lengthwise and scoop out the seeds with a spoon. Slice the cucumber halves into ⅛-inch-thick crescents and toss with coarse salt. Toss the cucumber slices with the salt so each slice is well coated and let drain for 30 minutes in a colander set over a bowl in the refrigerator.

Squeeze the cucumbers to eliminate more liquid and salt and toss them in half the remaining vinaigrette. Arrange the cucumbers in small Japanese-style pottery or lacquer bowls. Toss the shrimp in the remaining vinaigrette and arrange them in the bowls, next to the cucumbers.

Fresh Tuna Salad with Sea Urchin Roe Vinaigrette

I first read about sea urchin vinaigrette in Shizuo Tsuji's wonderful book *Japanese Cooking: A Simple Art.* I love the idea of imparting a subtle sealike flavor to a salad dressing, and being a fan of sea urchins, I came up with my own version of sea urchin vinaigrette. Although this vinaigrette would be delicious in practically any seafood salad, it's irresistible with very slightly cooked tuna. This dish must be prepared the same day it is served.

MAKES 6 FIRST-COURSE SERVINGS

For the Vinaigrette:

3 fresh sea urchins or 3 tablespoons fresh sea urchin roe

2 teaspoons mirin

2 teaspoons sake

1 teaspoon rice wine vinegar

1 teaspoon soy sauce

For the Tuna:

one 12-ounce 1-inch-thick tuna steak

salt and pepper

1 tablespoon safflower, canola, or vegetable oil

1 small daikon or 2 medium carrots

If you're using fresh sea urchins, cut them open and take out the roe (see color page 18). Push the roe through a fine-mesh strainer with the back of a wooden spoon and combine it with the other vinaigrette ingredients. Keep the vinaigrette in the refrigerator, covered with plastic wrap, until needed.

Trim any skin or dark red sections off the tuna steak. Season it with salt and pepper. Heat the oil in a sauté pan until it starts to smoke and brown the tuna for 2 minutes on each side. (You can also grill it.) Pat off any oil adhering to the tuna with paper towels and let the tuna cool in the refrigerator for 30 minutes.

Peel the daikon or carrots and either finely grate them or cut them into very fine julienne with a benriner cutter (a Japanese slicer) or by hand.

Within an hour of serving, slice the tuna steak into 12 strips and then cut each of these strips in half so you end up with 24 rectangles—the tuna should be raw in the center. Just before serving, dip each of the rectangles in the sea urchin vinaigrette and arrange 4 rectangles in a small fanned-out mound in each of 6 small Japanese pottery bowls. Spoon 2 teaspoons of the remaining vinaigrette over each serving of tuna. Arrange a small mound of daikon or carrot next to the tuna. Serve immediately.

SOUTHEAST ASIAN SALADS

Unlike their Western cousins, Southeast Asian salads aren't usually tossed with vinaigrette or mayonnaise but may contain coconut milk, sugar, miso, Thai fish sauce, peanuts, and other ingredients exotic by Western standards. I've given a few of my favorite combinations here.

Thai Shrimp, Cucumber, and Carrot Salad

I've always been intrigued by the slightly sweet first courses that are served in Thai and Indian restaurants. Instead of spoiling my appetite, they perk it up and leave me hungrier than when I started.

This salad with its juxtaposition of sweet, sour, and hot flavors is especially satisfying. The sauce and shrimp can be prepared completely in advance and just tossed together before serving. You can also substitute other seafood such as squid, crabmeat, or pieces of grilled fish such as tuna or swordfish.

MAKES 6 FIRST-COURSE SERVINGS

1½ pounds headless extra-large or jumbo shrimp (5 shrimp per serving), peeled and deveined if desired

2 teaspoons safflower oil

2 regular cucumbers or 1 long European cucumber, peeled

1 tablespoon coarse salt

2 large carrots, cut into 3-inch lengths

2 Thai or jalapeño chilies, seeded and finely chopped

2 large garlic cloves, finely chopped and crushed

½ cup unsweetened coconut milk

3 teaspoons sugar

2 tablespoons crunchy peanut butter without additives

3 tablespoons chopped fresh cilantro

3 tablespoons fresh lime juice (from about 1½ limes)

3 tablespoons rice wine vinegar or white wine vinegar

2 tablespoons Thai fish sauce (nam pla)

6 fresh cilantro sprigs

continued

Sauté the shrimp in safflower oil in a sauté pan over high heat for about 3 minutes and let cool.

Cut the cucumbers in half lengthwise and scoop out the seeds with a spoon. Slice the cucumber halves into ⅛-inch-thick crescents and toss with coarse salt until all the slices are well coated. Let drain in a colander set over a bowl in the refrigerator for 30 minutes.

Finely grate the carrots lengthwise down to the woody core. Discard the cores and reserve the grated carrots in a small mixing bowl.

In a separate bowl, whisk together the rest of the ingredients except the cilantro sprigs to make a smooth sauce.

Squeeze the cucumber slices, a handful at a time, to eliminate as much liquid as you can and place them in a small mixing bowl.

Toss the cucumbers, shrimp, and carrots with the sauce in separate bowls. Arrange the cucumbers in the middle of chilled plates, place a small mound of carrots in the center, and top each plate with shrimp and a cilantro sprig.

❧

Thai Hot-and-Sour Squid Salad

Chilled squid rings tossed with Thai spices make a delicious and refreshing summer salad. Most Thai restaurants serve this salad on a bed of shredded lettuce, but I like to serve it in a stemmed glass as for a shrimp cocktail. See the glossary for information on Asian ingredients.

MAKES 4 FIRST-COURSE SERVINGS

1½ **pounds squid, cleaned and hoods cut into rings (see color page 19)**

2 **tablespoons fresh lemon juice**

1-inch **piece of lemongrass, finely sliced**

1 **kaffir lime leaf, finely chopped**

1 **teaspoon sugar**

1 **Thai chili, seeded and finely chopped**

2 **shallots, finely chopped**

1 **garlic clove, finely chopped**

2 **teaspoons safflower oil**

1 **tablespoon Thai fish sauce**

2 **tablespoons chopped fresh cilantro**

6 **fresh cilantro sprigs**

Toss the squid in lemon juice and marinate for 30 minutes in the refrigerator.

Gently sauté the lemongrass, lime leaf, sugar, chili, shallots, and garlic in safflower oil in a nonstick pan for about 3 minutes. Don't let any of the ingredients brown. Pour in the squid along with the lemon juice and stir over high heat for about 1 minute, until the squid turns from translucent to a matte white. Stir in the fish sauce and chopped cilantro and stir for 30 seconds more over high heat. Pour the contents of the sauté pan into a mixing bowl and let cool. Refrigerate and serve in chilled glasses, topped with a cilantro sprig.

SEAFOOD SALADS MADE WITH STARCHY INGREDIENTS

It's easy to convert a small amount of seafood into a substantial salad course by combining the fish or shellfish with starchy ingredients such as rice, pasta, beans, bread, or even couscous. Although many traditional salads are made this way, I usually make these salads by haphazardly combining leftovers and then adding a few fresh ingredients for color and crunch.

SEAFOOD AND BEAN SALADS

When I first heard of combining beans with shellfish, I thought it sounded awfully improbable, but now that I've sampled a few versions I often make these salads at home.

Dried beans have to be soaked and then simmered for over an hour, but you can use canned beans in a pinch, and once you have the cooked beans

---

HOW TO COOK A BEAN

Although canned beans can be used for salads, they always seem slippery and, like so many canned things, somehow suspect. In any case, you'll get much better flavor by cooking fresh or dried beans with aromatic vegetables and herbs (preferably fresh).

Dried beans should be soaked for at least 2 hours and up to 12 hours (any longer and they may start to sprout). I always know they're ready when all the skins have crinkled and they've doubled in volume. The beans should then be drained and simmered in about three times as much water as the presoaked beans (3 cups water to 1 cup beans) in a covered nonaluminum pot. (If the pot isn't covered, you keep having to add more water. An aluminum pot may turn the beans gray.) I always include some onion, garlic, and celery in the water to flavor the beans. Leave the vegetables whole and remove them when the beans are done or chop the vegetables and just serve them with the beans. I also simmer a few herbs such as parsley, thyme, bay leaf, sage, rosemary, oregano, or marjoram—tied up with string or wrapped in cheesecloth—with the beans. Salt should be added only 30 minutes into the cooking, or it may toughen the skins. Don't, however, wait until the beans are completely cooked or the salt won't penetrate the beans—they'll end up tasting flat. When presoaked, most beans cook in about an hour to an hour and a half.

you just stir in pieces of cooked fish or shellfish, some good extra-virgin olive oil, and a bit of vinegar or lemon juice.

❧

Grilled Shrimp and Bean Salad

This salad makes a great start to an Italian meal. I serve it either by itself as a first course or along with olives, slices of salami, and other salads as part of an antipasto. If you don't want to bother with grilling, just sauté the shrimp in a little olive oil. In either case, the shrimp should be peeled *after* cooking so it doesn't curl up. You can be as generous as you like with the shrimp—here I suggest 3 extra-large or jumbo shrimp per serving. I usually make this salad with cooked dried beans, but if you can find them by all means use fresh. Just substitute 3 cups fresh beans—boiled until done with a sprig of fresh sage or other herb—for the dried beans.

MAKES 6 FIRST-COURSE SERVINGS

1½ cups dried beans such as borlotti or cannellini, rinsed and soaked in 1 quart cold water for 2 to 12 hours

1 medium onion, peeled, cut in half

½ celery stalk

3 garlic cloves

stems from 1 large bunch of parsley, preferably flat-leaf

2 fresh sage leaves

salt

1 cup dry white wine

18 extra-large or jumbo shrimp

pepper

½ cup extra-virgin olive oil

¼ cup fresh lemon juice

2 tablespoons finely chopped parsley

Drain the beans in a colander and combine them with the onion, celery, and garlic in a heavy pot. Tie the parsley stems and sage leaves into a small bundle with string and nestle them into the beans. Add enough water to cover the beans by about 1 inch. Bring to a slow simmer, cover the pot, and simmer gently for 30 minutes. Gently stir in 2 teaspoons salt and white wine and continue simmering, covered, until the beans soften and have no hint of mealiness—usually an hour more. You may have to add a little water from time to time so the beans don't run dry. (Or, if all the liquid isn't absorbed when the beans are finished cooking, pour the liquid into another pan, reduce it to ¼ cup, and pour it back over the beans.)

Meanwhile, sprinkle the shrimp with salt and pepper to taste and grill it for about 2 to 3 minutes on each side. Let cool, peel, and devein.

As soon as the beans are done—all the water should have evaporated—gently stir in the olive oil, lemon juice, and parsley and adjust the seasoning with salt and pepper.

Serve the beans at room temperature in small mounds topped with 3 shrimp per serving.

Using Shellfish-Cooking Liquids to Cook Beans: Most bean and shellfish salads contain separately cooked beans and shellfish that are combined shortly before serving so that both retain their individual flavors. This method works best when the beans are cooked with aromatic vegetables and herbs so the flavor of the beans stands out in contrast to the seafood.

Another approach is to cook the beans in the cooking liquid from the shellfish—the contrast is lost, but the flavor of the shellfish will pervade the entire dish. In the following salad the lobster shells are simmered in water with herbs and aromatic vegetables and the liquid is then used to cook dried beans. This is also a great method for making bean salads with crab, crayfish, and shrimp with heads.

❧

Lobster and Bean Salad

This salad looks so simple and unassuming that you're unlikely to hear any *oohs* and *aahs* when you set it down in front of guests or family. But once they take a bite . . . The beans in this salad end up tasting as much like lobster as lobster itself, and their melting texture is a perfect contrast to the slight crunch of the lobster chunks. Every step of this recipe can be done earlier the same day. (You have to use dried beans for this recipe—fresh and canned beans won't absorb enough liquid.)

MAKES 8 FIRST-COURSE OR SIDE-DISH SERVINGS

For the Lobsters:

two 1¼- to 1½-pound lobsters

2 shallots, finely chopped

1 garlic clove, finely chopped

3 tablespoons olive oil

1 cup dry white wine

½ cup cognac or good brandy

3 tomatoes, peeled, seeded, and chopped

1 cup chicken broth (page 344), fish broth (page 343), or water or more as needed

For the Beans:

2 cups dried beans such as borlotti, cannellini, or navy, rinsed and soaked in 1 quart cold water for 2 to 12 hours

1 teaspoon salt

½ cup extra-virgin olive oil

4 shallots, finely chopped

¼ cup chopped parsley

¼ cup fresh lemon juice

Rinse the lobsters and cut them in half through the head to kill them (see color page 23). Twist off the tail in one piece and take the grain sac out of each side of the head. Snap off the claws (see color page 23).

In a pot large enough to hold the lobsters, cook the shallots and garlic in olive oil over medium heat until they sizzle, about 5 minutes. Add the lobster, wine, cognac, tomatoes, and broth and cover the pot. Simmer over medium heat for about 8 minutes, until the lobster shells have turned completely red.

Take the lobster out of the pot, let the lobsters cool, remove the meat from the shells, and reserve. Put the shells back in the pot with the vegetables and liquids and break up the shells with the end of a handleless rolling pin or a cleaver held up on end. Simmer the shells gently in the covered pot, crushing now and then with the rolling pin or cleaver, for about 20 minutes. Strain the shell liquid and reserve.

Drain the beans and put them in a 4-quart pot with the lobster-shell liquid. If there isn't enough to cover the beans by at least an inch, add a little broth or water. Cook the beans, covered, until they soften, for about 1½ hours. Add the salt ½ hour into the cooking. If, when the beans are done, there is a lot of leftover liquid, drain them in a colander set over a pot, reduce the liquid that runs out to about ¼ cup, and pour it over the beans in a bowl. If there is no extra liquid, just transfer the beans to a mixing bowl. Gently stir in the olive oil, shallots, parsley, and lemon juice. Cover with plastic wrap and let cool at room temperature for at least an hour.

Cut the cooked lobster into cubes or slices and toss with the beans. Serve cool or at room temperature but not cold.

SEAFOOD AND RICE SALADS

Cooked rice is great when tossed with pieces of cooked fish or shellfish. Using cooked rice is also an easy way to stretch a few leftovers into a tasty first course or side dish. Almost any shellfish, left whole, can be stirred into a rice salad, as can most kinds of cooked fish—provided they aren't so fragile that they'll fall apart when stirred with the rice, as would flounder fillets for example.

❧

Improvised Seafood and Rice Salad

Although most of my own seafood and rice salads are last-minute improvisations, tossed together after rummaging around in the refrigerator, a few general principles and all-purpose ingredients make a seafood rice salad a sure success. I always stir in some extra-virgin olive oil to add flavor and to keep the rice from getting sticky. I also like to stir in pieces of raw or lightly cooked vegetables to provide contrasting texture and a fresh flavor. Acidic ingredients such as vinegar, lemon, or lime juice are also essential to keep the salad from tasting flat. To give the salad a fresher and brighter flavor and color, I stir in chopped fresh herbs, especially parsley. Other, more exotic ingredients such as dried fruits (especially raisins or dried currants), walnuts, pine nuts, and cubes of fresh fruit (pineapple is especially good) also make it into my salads if they're on hand.

MAKES 6 FIRST-COURSE OR SIDE-DISH SERVINGS

2 cups cooked long-grain rice, preferably basmati, Texmati, or jasmine

1 cup or more cooked fish and shellfish in ½-inch cubes or left whole

1 cup mixed vegetables such as cooked green beans, carrots, turnips (all cut into ¼-inch cubes), cooked or raw mushrooms (whole or sliced), cooked asparagus tips, peas, tomatoes (peeled, seeded, and cut into ½-inch cubes), celery (cut into ¼-inch cubes), and fennel (coarsely chopped)

½ cup walnut halves or whole pecans or pine nuts; raisins, dried currants, or dried apricots (soaked in barely enough cold water to cover for 30 minutes) (optional)

¼ cup chopped fresh herbs such as parsley, chervil, cilantro, or chives or 2 tablespoons chopped fresh tarragon or 1 tablespoon chopped stronger fresh herbs such as marjoram, thyme, or oregano

½ cup extra-virgin olive oil

¼ cup good-quality wine vinegar or fresh lemon or lime juice

salt and pepper

Gently toss everything together in a large mixing bowl. Taste and adjust the oil, vinegar, salt, and pepper if necessary. Serve at room temperature.

SEAFOOD AND PASTA SALADS

Cooked pasta salads reach new heights when combined with cooked fish and shellfish. Most of my own pasta salads are made with leftovers from the night before and tossed with a few vegetables and herbs. You can also make shellfish sauces, which you can then serve tossed with the cold pasta.

It's best to use pasta that will trap a lot of flavorful sauce—macaroni, penne, conchiglie, and fusilli.

Improvised Seafood and Pasta Salad

MAKES 6 FIRST-COURSE OR 4 LIGHT
MAIN-COURSE SERVINGS

3 cups cooked pasta (2 cups uncooked dried), tossed with 2 tablespoons olive oil to prevent sticking

2 cups cooked fish or shellfish such as shrimp (left whole or cubed), lobster (sliced or cubed), mussels, clams, baby octopus, squid (tentacles left whole, hoods cut into rings), tuna (sliced or cubed), or salmon (cut into ½-inch cubes)

1 cup mixed vegetables such as cooked green beans, carrots, turnips (all cut into ¼-inch cubes), cooked or raw mushrooms (whole or sliced), cooked asparagus tips, peas, tomatoes (cut into ¼-inch cubes), and celery (cut into ¼-inch cubes)

¼ cup chopped fresh herbs such as parsley, chervil, cilantro, or chives or 2 tablespoons chopped fresh tarragon or 1 tablespoon chopped stronger fresh herbs such as marjoram, thyme, or oregano

½ cup extra-virgin olive oil

6 tablespoons good-quality wine vinegar or fresh lemon or lime juice

salt and pepper

Combine all the ingredients. Season with salt and pepper to taste and add more vinegar or olive oil if the salad needs to be tangier or seems dry. Serve at room temperature or slightly chilled.

Mussel, Walnut, and Penne Salad

One easy way to make a salad out of pasta and leftover mussels is to toss both together with olive oil, herbs, and lemon. This recipe goes a step further and uses the cooking liquid from the mussels to make a full-flavored sauce. You can do all the work the day before and just toss things together before serving. Feel free to add different shellfish (clams and cockles are great) or other ingredients.

MAKES 4 FIRST-COURSE SERVINGS

1 shallot, finely chopped

1 small garlic clove, finely chopped

½ cup dry white wine or water

2 pounds small cultivated mussels, scrubbed and sorted

2 tomatoes, peeled, seeded, and coarsely chopped

½ cup heavy cream

¼ cup chopped parsley, preferably flat-leaf

½ cup coarsely chopped walnuts

2 tablespoons extra-virgin olive oil

2 tablespoons fresh lemon juice or more to taste

salt and pepper

2 cups cooked penne (1½ cups uncooked dried)

Bring the shallot, garlic, and wine to a simmer in a pot and add the mussels. Cover the pot and turn the heat up to high. When the mussels have opened, in about 5 minutes, remove the lid, discard any unopened ones, let the mussels cool, and take them out of the shells. Discard the shells.

If the mussel-cooking liquid seems gritty, slowly pour it into a clean pot, leaving behind any sand or grit. Stir the tomatoes into the mussel-cooking liquid and simmer until most of the moisture released by the tomatoes evaporates, about 15 minutes. Stir in the cream and simmer until the mixture barely begins to thicken, about 5 minutes. Stir in the parsley and let cool.

Stir the walnuts and olive oil into the sauce and season to taste with lemon juice, salt, and pepper.

Toss the cooked pasta with the cooked mussels and walnut sauce. Serve slightly chilled.

Soups

Lean and smoky broths from Japan, creamy chowders from New England, pungent lemony soups from Southeast Asia, brightly colored Mediterranean soups redolent of garlic and tomatoes—few dishes are more satisfying or versatile than a good bowl of fish soup. The method is simple too. Almost every fish soup is a variation on the basic approach of tossing cleaned and scaled whole fish into a pot of boiling salted water and then serving the fish surrounded by a ladleful of the hot liquid.

If you prefer to spare your guests the frustration of dealing with a tangle of bones and broth, however, you're better off using filleted fish and making the broth with the fish heads and bones.

Most of the soups here are based on finfish, but some do include shellfish.

FISH SOUPS

ADDING VEGETABLES

Almost all fish soups contain vegetables to accent or round out the basic flavors of the fish, and the types used are often the only thing that distinguishes one fish soup from another. Mediterranean cooks often include fennel, tomatoes, garlic, and orange peel; Japanese cooks will likely add daikon, shiitake mushrooms, or bamboo shoots; and Thai cooks use shallots, galangal, and lemongrass.

Vegetables are added at different stages in the soup preparation. They can be simmered along with the fish heads and bones to make the basic broth and then be strained out and discarded, or they can be simmered in the fish broth after it is strained so they remain in the soup. In the most formal approach the vegetables are cooked separately and then arranged carefully with the seafood in the soup bowls when serving.

Although most recipes describe when and where to add vegetables to a fish soup, I usually take a rough-and-tumble approach and use less presentable vegetables for making the broth and nicer-looking vegetables as part of the final presentation. When using fennel, for example, I throw the woody stalks into the fish broth (saving a few of the leafy fronds to chop and add to the soup at the last minute) and then carefully cut the bulb into wedges. I then either simmer the wedges in the strained broth along with other vegetables and eventually the fish or, if I'm being fancy, braise them separately in a little of the fish broth so that I can carefully arrange them in the bowls along with the fish. The same approach is applicable to other vegetables. For an informal soup I just slice and simmer carrots in the strained fish broth, but when I want the carrots' flavor but don't want them interfering with a dramatic presentation of a formal soup, I simmer them along with the fish heads and bones and strain them out.

WHAT LIQUID TO USE

Water is the usual medium—either for making a fish broth or for cooking the whole fish. In Europe wine is often added to give the broth a little tang and fruitiness. But when you want to make soup out of fillets or fish that doesn't come with heads and bones, you'll need to use another savory liquid. (You could ask the fishmonger for heads and bones from other fish to make a broth, but I'm distrustful of this because it's hard to determine freshness.) One choice is a hearty vegetable broth, such as one based on tomatoes or garlic. Generally you'll do well with a soup that's good in itself but at the same time won't overpower the flavor of the fish.

Japanese fish soups rarely require fish broth because Japanese cooks rely on dashi (page 343), a broth made from seaweed and dried smoked bonito.

Another alternative to fish broth is to make a Southeast Asian soup based on herbs, vegetables, and fish sauce. Thai or Vietnamese aromatic vegetables such as lemongrass and herbs such as cilantro and kaffir lime leaves are a perfect backdrop for fish, and the fish sauce gives the soup a full-bodied flavor. The hot, sour, and spicy taste of these soups is irresistible.

THICKENERS FOR FISH SOUPS

Most thickeners provide little flavor and if not used carefully can make an otherwise delightful soup pasty and unpleasant—just remember your last bowl of clam chowder in a cheap restaurant. Some soups, especially those containing cream or butter, are better when only lightly thickened.

Flour is the most common thickener for European and American soups. The best and easiest way to thicken a soup with flour is to whisk a hot fish broth made with the heads and bones into a roux made by gently cooking flour in butter. Some cooks use as much as 2 tablespoons of flour per quart of fish broth, but I never use more than 1 tablespoon—just enough to give the soup a little texture.

Rice and bread crumbs are also used as thickeners, most often in shellfish bisques. Broken-up crackers are used as a thickener for a traditional chowder, but I sometimes use cooked potatoes.

One of the best methods for thickening a fish soup is to puree some or all of the cooked fish and vegetables and stir the puree back into the soup. This is the method used for a traditional fish soup from Nice.

Cornstarch or arrowroot—first thinned in a little water is sometimes used to thicken Chinese soups and consommé.

FLAVORFUL FINISHES AND ENRICHENERS

Because the flavor of many foods cooks off if simmered for too long, certain ingredients such as delicate herbs are best added to fish soup shortly before serving. Other ingredients such as cream, coconut milk, or mixtures containing eggs may separate if cooked for too long and should be added during the last few minutes of cooking. Flavorful vegetable purees such as those made from garlic, corn, or tomatoes can also be stirred into a soup just before serving.

FISH CONSOMMÉ

Consommé is made by preparing a fish broth with fish bones and heads and sometimes additional whole fish or fish fillets and then clarifying the broth with egg whites, vegetables, and sometimes more fish. The resulting consommé, which should be perfectly clear and golden, is then garnished with carefully cut pieces of vegetable and pieces of fish or shellfish.

SERVING AND PRESENTING FISH SOUPS

One of the most common problems with fish soups is that the fish sits in the broth and ends up overcooked. The best way to avoid this is to completely prepare the soup without the fish and then simmer the fish in the soup just a few minutes before serving.

Another problem with fish soups is that the fish often sinks down into the broth so that it can't be seen. This is a pity, especially if you have pretty pieces of fillet from brightly colored fish such as red snapper. A good trick is to toast a piece of bread—not white bread, but crusty French or Italian bread—and set it in the middle of a wide soup or pasta bowl. Then, instead of throwing all the filleted fish

into the soup at once, poach the fish in just enough soup to cover (so you don't have to dig around in the pot to find the cooked fish). Then carefully prop the pieces of fish on the toasted bread and ladle on the broth so the fish stays at least partially out of the broth where it can be seen. Cooked leafy vegetables such as spinach, broccoli rabe, and sorrel can also be used instead of or in addition to toasted bread as decorative and tasty supports for the cooked fish.

MEDITERRANEAN-STYLE FISH SOUPS

Fish soups are made along the Mediterranean coast from Portugal all the way around to Morocco. Although each region uses different herbs, spices, and vegetables to give its soups a distinctive character, most of these soups are prepared in a similar way.

In most cases you start by cooking a flavor base of aromatic vegetables and sometimes herbs and spices in fat for 10 to 30 minutes, until the vegetables turn translucent or are browned. Usually the fat is olive oil, but occasionally it's pork fat such as rendered pancetta or ham, or butter or even *smen*, the Moroccan version of *ghee*. Then you add the liquid, usually water but sometimes white or even red wine, chopped tomatoes, vegetable broth, fish broth, crustacean-shell broth, mussel- or clam-steaming liquid, or chicken broth. Once the liquid is simmering, fish fillets or shellfish can be added and simmered gently for just long enough to cook through. This rarely takes more than a few minutes, and then the soup is ladled out immediately. Often, however, slower-cooking vegetables (such as fennel, green beans, mushrooms, squash), herbs (such as thyme or marjoram tied into a bouquet garni), or spices such as saffron are added along with the liquid and before any seafood so the ingredients have time to cook through and release their flavor into the broth.

One wonderful Mediterranean trick is to make flavorful purees of herbs, aromatic vegetables (especially garlic), nuts, sometimes spices (especially saffron), and extra-virgin olive oil and whisk them into the soup or stew a minute or two before serving. These pastes and sauces burst with flavor when added to a soup. Pesto is probably the best known, but the French also give us pistou (another pestolike mixture), aïoli (garlic mayonnaise), and rouille (the traditional sauce for bouillabaisse), the Catalans romesco and picada, and the Moroccans charmoula (a paste of cilantro, parsley, and spices). Because the liquid is simmered for only a minute or two after the pastes are added, their pungent flavor doesn't have any time to cook off. Using one of these pastes, you can transform a relatively lightly flavored broth or cooking liquid into a full-flavored soup in just a few seconds.

⤳

Bouillabaisse

(color page 4)

A bouillabaisse is one of those luxurious dishes that I make only for small groups of carefully selected friends who love to eat and drink, even to slight excess.

Purists insist that it's impossible to make an authentic bouillabaisse unless you live within a kilometer or two of the Mediterranean. Whether this is true or not, there is nothing to stop a determined cook from using the same techniques and flavorings to make a delicious soup with other fish.

An authentic bouillabaisse calls for seven kinds of Mediterranean fish, but even in Marseilles it's unusual to find all seven at the same time at least at the same fish market. Most fish soups do seem to be best made with a variety of fish, however. In the United States I use various combinations of rockfish, red snapper, sea bass, striped bass, monkfish, porgy, and conger eel.

A traditional bouillabaisse includes whole fish, but in this version the fish is filleted, a broth is made from the fish heads and bones, and the fillets are simmered in the broth at the last minute. Although bouillabaisse is somewhat complicated, the fish, the basic broth, and the rouille can all be prepared earlier the same day.

MAKES 6 MAIN-COURSE SERVINGS

8 pounds assorted whole fish, scaled and gutted, filleted, heads and bones reserved

6 tablespoons olive oil

6 garlic cloves, chopped

1 small fennel bulb (optional), coarsely chopped

1 medium onion, coarsely chopped

1 bouquet garni: 3 fresh thyme sprigs or ¼ teaspoon dried, a small bunch of parsley, and a bay leaf tied up with string (or in cheesecloth for dried thyme)

a 2-inch strip of orange zest

2 medium leeks, white parts only, halved lengthwise, rinsed, and finely chopped

8 ripe medium tomatoes, peeled, seeded, and chopped

½ teaspoon saffron threads, soaked in 1 tablespoon water for 30 minutes

¼ cup Pernod or Ricard

1 baguette, cut into ¼-inch slices and toasted under the broiler

For the Rouille (makes 2 cups):

2 red bell peppers, grilled or roasted, skin charred and removed (page 133)

2 jalapeño chilies, seeded and finely chopped

3 garlic cloves, chopped

1 teaspoon coarse salt

three 1-inch slices of baguette or 2 slices of regular white bread, crusts removed (¼ pound with crust)

½ cup extra-virgin olive oil

Make 2 rows of diagonal slashes in the skin to prevent the fillets from curling or remove the skin entirely. Pull out any bones with needlenose pliers or cut the fillets into pieces on either side of the bones. Cut the fillets so that each guest gets the same amount of each.

Soak the fish heads and bones in cold water for at least 30 minutes, then drain. Heat half of the olive oil in a 6-quart pot and add the fish heads and bones, garlic, fennel, onion, bouquet garni, and orange zest. Cook over medium heat, stirring occasionally with a wooden spoon, for about 10 minutes, until the fish bones begin to break apart. Add just enough water to cover—about 5 cups—and leave the broth at a slow simmer for 20 minutes more. Strain and discard the bones and vegetables. Reserve the fish broth.

Gently cook the leeks in the remaining olive oil in a 4-quart pot until they soften and turn slightly translucent, about 10 minutes. Add the tomatoes, the saffron with its soaking liquid, Pernod, and fish broth. Simmer for about 10 minutes, until the tomatoes have softened. This soup can be reserved in the refrigerator until just before serving.

continued

Preparing the Rouille: Cut the red peppers in half, remove the stem and seeds, and chop coarsely. Puree the red pepper, chilies, garlic, and salt in a blender or food processor for about 1 minute, until you have a smooth paste. You may have to scrape the sides of the food processor once or twice with a rubber spatula.

Soak the bread slices for a minute in some warm water to soften. Squeeze the excess liquid out of the bread and add the bread to the mixture in the blender. Puree the mixture for 30 seconds more and transfer it to a mixing bowl. Slowly stir in the extra-virgin olive oil with a wooden spoon.

Finishing the Bouillabaisse (last minute): Bring the fish broth to a simmer. Arrange the fillets skin side up in a pan large enough to hold them in a single layer. Pour over the simmering broth and simmer gently until the fillets are done.

Place 2 toasted bread slices in each of 6 wide soup bowls—make sure the bowls have been heated in the oven—and use a slotted spoon to arrange the cooked fish on top of and around the bread.

Put half of the rouille in a large mixing bowl and whisk in the hot liquid used to poach the fish. Ladle this mixture over the fillets and serve immediately. Pass the rest of the rouille and the crusty bread slices in a basket at the table.

A FEW TRADITIONAL MEDITERRANEAN SOUPS AND STEWS

AÏGO SAU: This simple Provençal fish soup is prepared by simmering cut-up pieces of whole fish in water with onion, garlic, tomato, a strip of orange peel, a little fennel, a bouquet garni, and sometimes potatoes. Like bouillabaisse, aïgo sau is thickened at the end with rouille, but aïgo sau is much simpler than bouillabaisse and is made with only one or two kinds of fish.

BOUILLABAISSE: This is the Mediterranean soup/stew par excellence. While the basic techniques for making bouillabaisse are similar to those for many Mediterranean fish soups and stews, ingredients such as saffron (simmered in the fish broth), fennel, pastis (a fennel-flavored aperitif), and most of all rouille, give bouillabaisse its special character.

BRODETTO: Probably the best known of Italian soups, brodetto is a favorite along most of the Adriatic coast. Each region has its own variations, but the basic technique is simple—a basic broth made with aromatic vegetables and fish heads is strained and used to cook chunks of the whole fish. Some versions (from Ravenna and sometimes Venice) contain squid, cuttlefish, or baby octopus, which must be simmered in the strained broth for 30 minutes before the rest of the fish is added. Other ingredients vary from region to region. Venetian versions may not always contain tomatoes (almost universal elsewhere), the brodetto from Emilia-Romagna often contains vinegar (a delicious touch) and perhaps a little lemon zest, a favorite version from Ravenna contains vinegar and dried oregano, a *brodetto marchigiano* (from the Marches) contains saffron, and a version from Abruzzi has hot peppers.

BOURRIDE: A bourride is prepared by poaching one or more kinds of fish in a broth made from their bones and heads and then thickening the broth at the last minute with garlic mayonnaise, aïoli. A bourride can be presented as a soup or stew by using more or less broth.

BURIDDA: This hearty seafood stew from Genoa is filled with fish and shellfish, and while it's prepared in much the same way as cacciucco or many a *zuppa di pesce*, it has a special character of its own because it contains dried or fresh porcini mushrooms and sometimes stoccafisso—air-dried but not salted cod. Don't confuse *buridda* with *burrida*.

BURRIDA: Really more a sauced fish than a stew, burrida is a traditional Sardinian dish made with Mediterranean dogfish, a kind of shark. The sauce is made by grinding walnuts to a paste with garlic and then working in olive oil, vinegar, and parsley.

CALDEIRADA: This is the Portuguese equivalent of the French bouillabaisse except that a caldeirada tends to be more stewlike (less liquid) and is finished with a few leaves of chopped basil instead of rouille. Baby squid is a favorite ingredient.

CALDERATA: A Spanish soup made with both shellfish and finfish. Recipes vary from region to region, but sherry is usually included, as is nutmeg sometimes, giving the soup its own special character. Don't confuse *calderata with caldeirada*, a Portuguese fish stew.

CACCIUCCO: Originally a cheap fisherman's stew, cacciucco is now a favorite along Italy's Mediterranean shores, especially around Livorno. More a stew than a soup, it is usually served as a main course instead of a first course like brodetto or *zuppa di pesce*. Cacciucco always contains chili peppers (little red peperoncini in Italy, but jalapeño chilies will work in the United States), tomatoes, white or red wine, and bay leaves. While traditionalists insist that cacciucco contain five types of fish or shellfish (one for each c in *cacciucco*), many recipes call for even more. Squid, cuttlefish, an assortment of round fish, and shellfish such as clams, mussels, shrimp, or even spiny lobster are often included in more extravagant versions. One of my favorite versions has cuttlefish ink stirred in at the end so it ends up jet-black.

CIUPPIN: This famous soup from Genoa resembles some of the most famous fish soups of southern France (*soupe de poisson niçoise* and *soupe de poisson de roche*) in that the fish is cooked in a flavorful broth (containing tomatoes, garlic, and olive oil) and then pureed so the finished soup is intensely flavorful but contains no solid ingredients.

ROMESCO: Like so many Mediterranean soups, romesco has many variations. It originated in Tarragona, a city in Catalonia, where, depending on where you eat it, it can be served as a soup, a rather thick stew, or chunks of fish with a thick sauce. Whichever version you end up sampling or making, each will include romesco sauce. To complicate matters further there are many variations of romesco sauce, but all contain dried peppers along with almonds, hazelnuts, garlic, and bread crumbs. Romesco sauce is similar to the better-known picada.

SOUPE DE POISSON: A *soupe de poisson* is either a simple fish broth made from whole fish that is then strained (*soupe de roche* and *soupe de poisson de Marseilles* are two versions made from little fish that swim around the rocks along the shore) or a pureed fish soup made by working the cooked fish through a food mill and then whisking the resulting puree into the fish broth (*soupe de poisson provençale* or *soupe de poisson niçoise*). Don't confuse *soupe de poisson* with *soupe aux poissons*, which describes any soup containing whole chunks of fish. Ciuppin is an Italian version of a pureed *soupe de poissons*.

SUQUET: A simple Catalan fisherman's fish soup/stew made with potatoes and Mediterranean fish. A traditional suquet contains the almost-universal Mediterranean ingredients garlic, onion, and tomatoes. What gives suquet its own identity is the pungent bread and almond sauce, picada, stirred into the soup just before serving.

TAGINE: A general word for any kind of Moroccan stew, fish tagines almost always contain charmoula, an aromatic paste of cilantro, parsley, cumin, garlic, paprika, and sometimes saffron, ginger, cayenne, and other ingredients. In addition to charmoula, tagines also contain typically Mediterranean ingredients such as tomatoes, olives, and peppers.

ZARZUELA (Catalan: *sarsuela*): According to Colman Andrews in his wonderful book *Catalan Cuisine*, zarzuela is the object of a certain amount of ridicule—"because it seems too much of a good thing and because, in unscrupulous hands, it can provide an easy way to use up bad fish." But certainly the same caveat could apply to any Mediterranean seafood soup or stew. It would be hard for even the most accomplished connoisseur to distinguish a zarzuela from dozens of other seafood soups because the ingredients are so similar. Colman Andrews's recipe contains rum (most others contain Spanish brandy instead), cinnamon, allspice, and *vi ranci*, a kind of oxidized wine similar to sherry. Penelope Casas, in her book *The Foods and Wines of Spain*, includes saffron, as does Maite Manjon in *The Gastronomy of Spain and Portugal*, who also includes the bread-and-almond sauce picada.

ZUPPA DI PESCE: Of all Italy's fish soups, *zuppa di pesce*, literally "fish soup," is the most loosely defined. In the same way as cacciucco or brodetto, each region or even town has its own variation, based on the local catch. One of the most interesting variations is the Sicilian *zuppa di neonata*, which contains baby anchovies and sardines. A *zuppa di pesce* can be a simple broth made from two or three fish or an elaborate affair containing assorted shellfish and several types of finfish.

Southern French–Style Fish Soup with Garlic Mayonnaise

BOURRIDE

A bourride is one of the most delicious of all Mediterranean fish soups and is certainly one of the easiest to make. An authentic bourride is made with the same fish as a bouillabaisse, but you can get by with just 1 or 2 varieties. Monkfish fillets are especially good because they're easy to slice into attractive medallions, but they don't supply bones and heads for broth. You may want to try a combination of monkfish with sea bass, striped bass, red snapper, or rockfish for the necessary heads and bones. Or if you have access to small inexpensive fish you may want to use a couple of pounds for making the broth.

The real secret to a bourride is the aïoli (garlic mayonnaise), which is whisked into the simmering soup just before serving and then passed at the table for guests to smear on toast.

The fish broth for the bourride can be made earlier the same day.

MAKES 6 LIGHT MAIN-COURSE SERVINGS

1½ pounds monkfish fillets

1½ pounds whole round fish such as black sea bass, striped bass, red snapper, or rockfish, filleted, fillets skinned, heads and bones reserved

2 pounds small whole fish, gutted, gills removed (optional)

1 large onion, chopped

3 garlic cloves, crushed

1 large bouquet garni: 5 fresh thyme sprigs or ¾ teaspoon dried, a medium bunch of parsley, and a large bay leaf tied up with string (or in cheesecloth for dried thyme)

1 cup dry white wine

2½ cups water

4 tomatoes, peeled, seeded, and chopped

pinch of saffron threads

12 slices of large French loaf or 24 slices of baguette

2 cups aïoli (page 334)

2 egg yolks

salt and pepper

Preparing the Fish: Trim any membrane and dark purple flesh off the monkfish fillets (see color page 25) and slice into ½-inch-thick medallions—try to end up with a total of 6 or 12 medallions—and reserve in the refrigerator. Cut each round fish fillet into large chunks—you should get 2 or 3 per fillet (you'll need at least 6). Reserve in the refrigerator.

Preparing the Fish Broth: Thoroughly rinse the fish heads and bones and the small whole fish if you're using them and put them in a pot with the onion, garlic, bouquet garni, white wine, and water. Simmer gently for 30 minutes, skimming off any scum that floats to the surface, and strain into a clean pot.

Finishing and Serving: Bring the strained broth to a gentle simmer and stir in the tomatoes and saffron. Cover the pot and simmer for 10 minutes. Slide in the pieces of fish and simmer for about 5 minutes (8 minutes per inch of thickness).

Lightly toast the bread on both sides and place 1 large slice or 2 small slices in each hot soup plate.

Put half of the aïoli in a mixing bowl and whisk in the egg yolks—the extra yolks give the soup a richer, silkier texture—and about a third of the simmering broth. Remove the remaining broth from the heat and whisk the aïoli mixture into the broth. Return the pot to medium heat for a few seconds, whisking, but don't let

---

AMERICAN SUBSTITUTES FOR MEDITERRANEAN FISH

Those of us who have traveled around the Mediterranean know the frustration of returning home and not being able to find fish for our favorite Mediterranean dishes. The trick to making Mediterranean fish soups or stews is to use as many different fish as possible—a traditional bouillabaisse calls for seven. Unless the soup is to be pureed, the fish should be firm enough not to fall apart in the soup (avoid flatfish except halibut), and none of the fish should be strong or oily, such as salmon, mackerel, or sardines. My favorite fish are chunks of blackfish, black sea bass, cod, grouper, halibut, mahimahi, red snapper, rockfish, sea trout, striped bass, tilefish, and wolffish. Pieces of very firm-fleshed fish such as blowfish, catfish, John Dory, and swordfish can also be added.

When you're making a pureed fish soup, texture is unimportant. Soft-textured fish such as sole and flounder, sea trout, whiting, and rockfish in addition to the fish just mentioned can all be used.

When it comes to flatfish, Americans are at a disadvantage because American flatfish species are very soft-textured and will often fall apart when cooked. Unless you have access to—and can afford—authentic Dover sole, you're better off substituting firm-fleshed round fish fillets such as blackfish, John Dory, or pompano in Mediterranean recipes calling for sole or flounder.

the soup approach the boil or the aïoli will curdle. Season with salt and pepper to taste and ladle into each bowl. Pass the rest of the aïoli and the extra toasts at the table.

Catalan Shrimp Soup with Almonds, Chilies, and Garlic

ROMESCO

I've already written about romesco in my book *Splendid Soups* but can't resist including a somewhat modified version here. The real secret to this soup is the pungent sauce made from nuts, garlic, and chilies, which is stirred in at the end in much the same way as an aïoli is stirred into a bourride or a rouille into a bouillabaisse.

Colman Andrews, author of *Catalan Cuisine,* recommends including an assortment of ocean fish and shellfish in his authentic recipe. But in my own fooling around in the kitchen I've found that the absolute best American version starts out with a broth made from shrimp heads. If you usually can't find shrimp with their heads, it would be worth ordering a few pounds a day or two in advance so you can make this soup.

The time-consuming parts—the shrimp-head broth and the sauce—can be made earlier the same day.

MAKES 8 FIRST-COURSE SERVINGS

3 pounds large shrimp with heads, peeled and deveined, shells and heads reserved

3 tablespoons olive oil

1 medium onion, chopped

2 garlic cloves, crushed

4 tomatoes, chopped

2 cups dry sherry or white wine

3 cups water

For the Romesco Sauce:

1 large slice of French bread (about ¼ pound), crust removed, softened in cold water, and squeezed dry

1 poblano chili, charred, peeled, and seeded (page 133)

2 jalapeño chilies, seeded and chopped

3 garlic cloves, peeled

1 cup blanched almonds, toasted in a 350°F oven until pale brown, about 15 minutes

1 teaspoon salt

½ cup extra-virgin olive oil

12 slices of large French loaf or 24 slices of baguette, lightly toasted on both sides

Making the Shrimp-Head Broth: Combine the shrimp heads and shells in a large pot with the olive oil, onion, and garlic. Stir over medium heat until the shrimp heads turn completely red and the onions turn translucent, after about 10 minutes. Stir in the tomatoes and cook over medium heat for about 10 minutes more. Puree this mixture for about 1 minute in a food processor—you may need to add some of the sherry to get the mixture to turn around—and return the mixture to the pot. Add the rest of the sherry and the water. Cover the pot and simmer gently for 20 minutes. Strain through a food mill or use a ladle to force the mixture through a strainer. Strain a second time through a fine-mesh strainer. Reserve.

Making the Romesco Sauce: Puree all the ingredients except the olive oil in a food processor for 5 minutes. Scrape along the insides of the food processor 2 or 3 times with a rubber spatula to get the mixture to move around. Transfer the sauce to a mixing bowl and stir in the olive oil with a wooden spoon.

Finishing and Serving: Take half of the romesco sauce out of the mixing bowl to serve at the table. Bring the shrimp-head broth to a simmer, whisk half of it into the romesco sauce, and stir the sauce/broth mixture back into the pot with the rest of the broth. Poach the shrimp in the broth for about 4 minutes, being careful not to let the broth boil.

Place 1 or 2 pieces of toast in each of the wide hot soup plates and ladle on the soup. Pass the rest of the toasts and the romesco sauce at the table.

Tuscan Fish and Shellfish Soup with Cuttlefish

ZUPPA DI PESCE

I first encountered this version of *zuppa di pesce* in an unpretentious little restaurant on the Mediterranean coast of Tuscany. It arrived at the table jet-black with cuttlefish ink, a small mound of pasta surrounded by various unrecognizable sea creatures.

Cuttlefish with the ink sac still intact can be hard to find in the United States. Cuttlefish that is perfectly white has probably been frozen and won't contain any ink; fresh cuttlefish is almost always black from leaking ink. You can always use squid instead; the broth just won't be the same startling black.

Most of the work for this dish can be done earlier in the day, but the clams and mussels must be steamed and the pasta cooked at the last minute.

continued

MAKES 6 MAIN-COURSE SERVINGS

1 medium onion, finely chopped

3 garlic cloves, finely chopped

$\frac{1}{2}$ teaspoon chopped fresh marjoram or thyme or $\frac{1}{4}$ teaspoon dried

3 tablespoons olive oil

4 tomatoes, peeled, seeded, and chopped

1$\frac{1}{2}$ cups dry white wine

1 pound cuttlefish or squid

18 littleneck clams

1 pound small cultivated mussels

1 pound fillets of firm-fleshed fish such as halibut or sea bass, cut into $\frac{1}{2}$-inch cubes

$\frac{1}{2}$ pound dried spaghetti or linguine

salt and pepper

Cook the onion, garlic, and chopped herbs in 2 tablespoons of the olive oil in a wide 6-quart pot over medium heat until the onion turns translucent, about 10 minutes. Add the tomatoes and wine, cover the pot, and simmer gently for 10 minutes more.

Clean the cuttlefish or squid. If you're using cuttlefish, cut it into strips and remove the ink sac. Squeeze the ink out of the sac and keep it on a small plate in the refrigerator. If you're using squid, cut it into rings. Put the cuttlefish or squid in the pot with the tomato-and-wine mixture and simmer gently, covered, for 30 minutes.

Bring a large pot of water with the remaining tablespoon of olive oil to a boil for the pasta.

About 15 minutes before serving, put the clams in the pot with the cuttlefish, cover the pot, and simmer until they all open, about 10 minutes. Put the pasta in the boiling water. Add the mussels and fish to the clams and simmer, covered, for 5 minutes more—until all the mussels open and the fish is cooked through.

Drain and arrange the pasta in the center of hot soup plates. With a slot-ted spoon, arrange the fish and shell-fish over the pasta. Whisk the reserved cuttlefish ink into the cook-ing liquid, season with salt and pep-per to taste, and ladle onto each plate. Serve immediately.

❧

Fish Stew with Dried Porcini

BURIDDA

*E*ven though this fish stew is pre-pared in much the same way as other Mediterranean versions, it gets its very special luxurious flavor from the dried porcini mushrooms added to the fish broth. The cubes of pro-sciutto are my own addition and can be left out. If you do decide to include it, try to buy the end piece, which usu-ally sells for about half the price of prime slices.

MAKES 6 LIGHT MAIN-COURSE SERVINGS

1$\frac{1}{2}$ pounds monkfish fillets

1$\frac{1}{2}$ pounds whole round fish such as sea bass, striped bass, red snapper, or rock-fish, filleted, fillets skinned, heads and bones reserved

2 pounds small whole fish, gutted and gills removed

2 medium onions, finely chopped

1 large bouquet garni: 5 fresh thyme sprigs or $\frac{3}{4}$ teaspoon dried, a medium bunch of parsley, and a large bay leaf tied up with string (or in cheesecloth for dried thyme)

1 cup dry white wine

3 garlic cloves, chopped

1 $\frac{1}{4}$-inch-thick slice of prosciutto ($\frac{1}{4}$ pound), cut into $\frac{1}{4}$-inch cubes (optional)

3 tablespoons extra-virgin olive oil

1 ounce dried porcini, quickly rinsed under cold water and soaked in $\frac{1}{2}$ cup warm water for 30 minutes

4 tomatoes, peeled, seeded, and chopped

12 slices of large French loaf or 24 slices of baguette, lightly toasted

salt and pepper

Preparing the Fish: Trim any mem-brane and dark purple flesh off the monkfish fillets (see color page 25) and slice them into $\frac{1}{2}$-inch-thick medallions—try to end up with 6 or 12 medallions—and reserve in the refrigerator. Cut each of the round fish fillets into large chunks—you should get 2 or 3 per fillet. Reserve in the refrigerator.

Preparing the Fish Broth: Thor-oughly rinse the fish heads and bones and the small whole fish if you're using them and put them in a 6- or 8- quart pot with half the chopped onions, the bouquet garni, wine, and just enough water to cover. Simmer gently for 30 minutes, skimming off any scum that floats to the surface. Strain into a clean con-tainer, pushing down on the bones and small fish in the strainer to extract as much liquid as possible. Discard the small fish and bones.

Gently stir the garlic, remaining onion, and prosciutto in the olive oil in a clean 4-quart pot over medium heat until the prosciutto and onions caramelize slightly and leave a brown film on the inside of the pot, about 20 minutes. Squeeze the liquid out of the mushrooms—be sure to save it—and coarsely chop the mushrooms. Stir the chopped mushrooms into the pro-sciutto mixture. Continue stirring over medium heat for about 10 minutes, until the mushrooms caramelize slightly. Carefully pour the mushroom-soaking liquid into the prosciutto/mushroom mixture, leaving any sand or grit behind. Add 2 cups of the strained fish broth and the chopped tomatoes to the mushroom mixture and bring to a gentle simmer. Transfer the mushroom broth to a pan just large enough to hold the fish in a single layer.

Finishing and Serving: Bring the mushroom broth to a gentle simmer and slide in the pieces of fish. Simmer for about 5 minutes. Place 1 large slice or 2 small slices of the toasted bread in the bottom of each hot soup plate. Distribute the fish equally among the soup plates, mounding it on top of the bread slices. Season the hot broth with salt and pepper to taste and ladle it over the fish in each plate. Serve immediately.

CHOWDERS

No one seems to agree on a what a chowder really is. Some insist it must have potatoes (what about corn chowder?), others agree it must be made with bacon fat (I've had perfectly good versions made with butter), and others say the fish must be cooked in milk (I use fish broth). I've finally settled for a looser definition—a fish or shellfish soup containing milk or cream, almost always containing onions, and usually containing some kind of starchy vegetable such as potatoes or corn.

Most chowders we see in restaurants are thickened—usually too much—with flour or cracker crumbs. It is true that some people like their soups thick, but I prefer a light-textured soup that bursts with flavor. Most chowders are also made with milk, which can be a problem because unless you use a fair amount of flour to stabilize the milk, it will curdle. I've had better luck cooking everything in a fish broth with the heads and bones and then adding a relatively small amount of heavy cream at the last minute.

∾

Fish Chowder

*T*his is a slightly modernized version (there's no flour) of a traditional New England fish chowder. Traditional versions are usually made with cod, but since cod is usually sold in steaks, you'll have to ask the fishmonger to give (or sell) you the cod head. If the fishmonger doesn't have the cod head (cod is sometimes shipped to retailers without the head), you may have to ask for fish heads and bones from other fish. This is tricky business since such bones are sometimes not fresh—give them a good sniff before using them in the soup.

I sometimes make more elaborate versions of this soup and add glazed pearl onions, little mushroom caps, or even peas.

The basic chowder—up to the point where the fish is added—can be made earlier in the day.

MAKES 8 FIRST-COURSE SERVINGS

4 pounds whole firm-fleshed fish such as grouper or snapper, filleted, skin and gills removed, bones and head reserved, or 2 pounds cod, haddock, or pollack steaks or fillets, skin removed, plus 2 pounds fish heads and bones for broth

4 medium onions, halved and thinly sliced

1 large bouquet garni: 5 fresh thyme sprigs or ¾ teaspoon dried, a medium bunch of parsley, and a large bay leaf tied up with string (or in cheesecloth for dried thyme)

two ¼-inch-thick slices (or 4 slices if pre-sliced) bacon, cut crosswise into 1-inch strips

3 medium or 2 large potatoes, peeled and cut into ½-inch cubes

1 cup heavy cream or crème fraîche

salt and pepper

1 tablespoon chopped fresh chives

Soak the bones and/or heads in cold water for 30 minutes. Drain them and combine them with one of the onions, the bouquet garni, and enough water to cover (about 5 cups) in a 4-quart pot. Bring the broth to a slow simmer and simmer for 30 minutes, skimming off any froth that floats to the top. Strain the broth through a medium-mesh strainer. Reserve.

Remove any remaining bones from the fillets or steaks with tweezers or needlenose pliers and cut the flesh into 24 equal pieces (3 per serving). Refrigerate until just before serving.

Cook the bacon in a 6-quart pot over medium heat until it renders fat and *barely* begins to turn crispy. Remove the bacon with a slotted spoon, reserve it, and cook the remaining onions and the potatoes in the fat over low to medium heat for about 15 minutes. Don't let the onions brown.

Add the fish broth and the reserved bacon to the onions and bring the soup to a slow simmer. Simmer the soup for 5 to 10 minutes to finish cooking the potatoes. Skim off any fat that floats to the top and check to see if the potatoes are done by pushing one of the cubes against the inside of the pot with a spoon—it should crush easily. If you want a thicker soup, whisk it vigorously to break up some of the potatoes. Add the cream and simmer for 1 minute.

Just before serving the chowder, bring it to a simmer and add the cut-up fish. Simmer the soup with the fish for 5 to 10 minutes, depending on the size of the chunks. Season with salt and pepper to taste.

Ladle the chowder into hot bowls and decorate each one with a pinch of chopped chives.

Indian-Style Sweet-and-Hot Seafood Chowder with Coconut Milk

It may be a stretch to call this soup a chowder, but because it contains onions and potatoes I figure I can get away with it. What sets this soup apart from more traditional chowders is the subtle use of Indian spices.

For the seafood, use what's freshest and looks best. I make this soup with shrimp, lean white fish such as halibut, scallops, steamed mussels, or a combination. In any case the soup is almost completely finished before any seafood is added, so you don't have to worry about overcooking anything. You can make the base up to 3 days in advance and reheat it just before adding the seafood.

MAKES 8 FIRST-COURSE SERVINGS

2 pounds cleaned and trimmed firm-fleshed seafood, cut into approximately 1-inch squares

2 medium onions, finely chopped

1 tablespoon grated fresh ginger

2 garlic cloves, finely chopped

2 Thai chilies, seeded and finely chopped

2 tablespoons peanut oil or vegetable oil

1 teaspoon ground turmeric

1 teaspoon ground cinnamon

½ teaspoon ground cloves

1 teaspoon ground cardamom

2 teaspoons ground cumin

2 teaspoons ground coriander

15 fresh, frozen, or dried curry leaves, coarsely chopped (optional)

1 large russet potato (about 1 pound), peeled and chopped into roughly ¼-inch cubes

1 quart water or chicken broth (page 344) or fish broth (page 343)

2 cups (or one 14-ounce can) unsweetened coconut milk

¼ cup fresh lime juice (from about 2 limes)

2 tablespoons finely chopped fresh cilantro

salt and pepper

Carefully pick over the fish or shellfish and remove any pieces of skin, shell, or pin bones. Refrigerate on a plate, covered, until needed.

Cook the onions, ginger, garlic, and chilies in peanut oil in a 4-quart pot over medium heat for about 10 minutes, stirring occasionally, until the onions turn translucent. Add the ground spices and curry leaves to the hot onion mixture and stir over medium heat for about 2 minutes, until you can smell the fragrance of the spices. Add the potatoes to the pot with the spices and add just enough of the water to cover. Cover the pot and simmer gently for about 15 minutes, until it's easy to crush a potato cube against the inside of the pot with a spoon.

Let the soup cool for 15 minutes, puree until smooth in a blender, and return to the pot. Add the rest of the water, the coconut milk, and the lime juice to the pureed soup. Strain the soup through a food mill or work it through a large strainer with the back of a ladle into a clean pot. Bring to a gentle simmer, stir in the chopped cilantro, and season with salt and pepper to taste. Just before you're ready to serve, stir in the seafood and simmer gently for 5 minutes.

Substitutes Skinless chunks of fish such as blackfish, black sea bass, cod, grouper, halibut, mahimahi, red snapper, rockfish, sea trout, striped bass, tilefish, or wolffish

SOUTHEAST ASIAN–STYLE FISH SOUPS

Until recently few Americans had ever tasted authentic Thai or Vietnamese cooking. Today of course there are Thai and Vietnamese restaurants in practically every American city and most Americans have sampled Southeast Asian cooking at least once. I've yet to meet someone who doesn't like it.

Southeast Asian cooks each seem to have their own recipes with no strict rules—even for the most traditional dishes. This free-and-easy approach in the kitchen is one that I borrow once I've followed a few recipes to get a feel for the ingredients.

One big advantage to Southeast Asian soups is that they usually don't need stock. Fish sauce and the aromatic herbs and vegetables used in Southeast Asian cooking are so flavorful that you can thin the soup with water and it will still be bursting with flavor.

The soul of most Southeast Asian dishes is fish sauce. Fish sauce is made by salting and fermenting fish and capturing the liquid that runs off. This sounds scary to most Westerners, but the flavor of fish sauce is surprisingly subtle and stays in the background, lending support without taking over.

In addition to fish sauce you'll need chilies—the little Thai chilies are best, but you can substitute serrano chilies or hot red pepper flakes. I almost always include a little chopped garlic and shallot (or onion), which I cook in peanut oil with the chopped chilies before I add any liquid. Most Thai and Vietnamese soups have a distinct citrus flavor, which usually comes from lemongrass and kaffir lime leaves. Don't worry if you can't find both of these, but you'll need at least one if you want the soup to taste at all authentic. (I have in a pinch used just strips of lime zest.) All Southeast Asian soups need an acidic tang. Authentic recipes usually call for tamarind paste, but I often use lime juice instead. Most Southeast Asian soups include herbs, usually added at the end, which give the soups an irresistible fragrance. Cilantro is the most common, but basil (preferably holy basil) and mint are also popular and delicious—I sometimes combine all three. Other herbs such as rice-paddy herb and sawtooth herb can also be used, but they're hard to find, so I never count on them, but just grab them in the market when I see them.

One very easy way to make a Thai-style soup is to simmer chilies, shallots, and garlic in water with a little fish sauce and then whisk in a few tablespoons of red or green Thai curry paste (see recipes, page 340). Fish or shellfish—shrimp is especially good and very easy—can then be simmered in the finished soup just a few minutes before serving.

Shrimp paste is often called for in Southeast Asian soups, but recipes written for Americans often leave it out because of its strong odor. Even more than fish sauce, shrimp paste is an acquired taste. While most authentic Southeast Asian soup recipes suggest cooking a chunk of it in hot oil before adding liquid, this could very well drive you out of the house—the odor is strong and pervasive. I prefer to dilute a teaspoon or two in water and then stir it into the soup; it gives the soup an intriguing aroma that reminds me of authentic Southeast Asian foods and not the tamer versions found in restaurants in the United States.

Coconut milk—I usually use canned—is a great way to finish a soup and make it richer and more delicate. I'm always sneaking it in when I have it in the cupboard. Because coconut is rich and contains fat, I sometimes leave it out for dieting guests, who are always surprised and delighted to encounter something at my house that is completely fat-free. (Southeast Asian soups rarely contain much fat.)

Pineapple is another favorite ingredient in Southeast Asian soups. Pineapple not only lightens the soup, making it a perfect addition for summer, but also helps create a delicious sweet-and-sour effect.

One easy way to make a soup more substantial—so you can serve it as a main course—is to add a starch such as rice or noodles. Southeast Asian cooks are fond of cellophane noodles (also called *mung bean noodles* and *bean thread noodles*), which can be soaked for 30 minutes and added to a soup for the last 3 minutes of cooking. Rice—preferably basmati or jasmine—can also be simmered in the soup for 15 minutes or cooked separately in water, drained, and added to the soup just before serving.

While many Southeast Asian soup recipes are very specific about what kinds of seafood to add, I prefer to play it by ear and use what looks good at the fish store. Shellfish such as shrimp or scallops are the easiest to use because they can be tossed into the soup a few minutes before serving with no risk of falling apart. Shellfish such as lobster or crab has to be lightly precooked so you can get the meat out of the shell and cubed, sliced, or shredded (crabmeat). This lightly precooked shellfish should then be added to the soup only long enough to heat it through. Fish fillets or steaks, both cut into bite-size cubes, can also be added shortly before serving the soup, but fish can overcook and fall apart espe-

cially if it sits too long in a soup tureen waiting to be served. When I'm adding fish, I like to add firm-fleshed fish such as swordfish, shark, monkfish, wolffish, or tuna.

Thai-Style Fish Soup

You can use almost any lean nonoily fish for this soup, but I avoid flounder fillets, which fall apart and cloud the soup as soon as they cook through.

This soup can be made almost entirely in advance. See the glossary for information on Asian ingredients.

MAKES 6 FIRST-COURSE SERVINGS

1½ pounds assorted fish fillets or 2 pounds steaks from firm white fish such as haddock, grouper, or black sea bass, skin and bones removed (peeled shrimp and trimmed scallops will also work)

3 shallots, finely chopped

3 garlic cloves, finely chopped and crushed to a paste

4 Thai chilies or 6 jalapeño chilies, seeded and finely chopped

six ⅛-inch-thick slices of peeled galangal (optional)

2 tablespoons safflower oil

5 cups water, chicken broth (page 344), or fish broth (page 343)

5 kaffir lime leaves or two 2-inch strips of lemon zest

3-inch piece of lemongrass, finely sliced

¼ cup fresh lime juice (from about 2 limes)

¼ cup Thai fish sauce (nam pla), or more to taste

3 tablespoons finely chopped fresh cilantro

continued

Diagonally cut the fish fillets or steaks into strips about 1½ inches long and ½ inch wide. Refrigerate until just before serving.

Heat the shallots, garlic, chilies, and galangal in the safflower oil in a 4-quart pot over medium heat for about 2 minutes. Add the water, lime leaves, and lemongrass and simmer gently for 5 minutes.

Add the lime juice and fish sauce and, just before you're ready to serve, the strips of fish and chopped cilantro. Depending on the thickness of the fish, simmer for 2 to 4 minutes. Serve in hot bowls.

Substitutes Fillets such as blackfish, catfish, John Dory, lingcod, monkfish, rockfish, sablefish, shark, swordfish, walleye

❧

Vietnamese Shrimp, Scallop, and Pineapple Soup with Cellophane Noodles

This soup combines all my favorite Southeast Asian flavors—hot, sweet, sour—with an ineffable scent of the sea. I love making this soup fiery-hot and serving it outside on a hot summer evening with lots of ice-cold beer. If I'm unsure of my guests, I tone it down a little and use the minimum number of chilies suggested.

This soup can be made in advance up to the point of adding the herbs.

MAKES 6 MAIN-COURSE SERVINGS

1 pound sea scallops, small side muscle removed, cut into ⅓-inch-thick disks

1½ pounds headless medium shrimp, peeled, deveined if desired

½ pineapple, peeled, cored, and cut into wedges, or one 20-ounce can pineapple wedges, drained

1 tablespoon sugar

¼ cup fresh lime juice (from about 2 limes)

2 tablespoons peanut or vegetable oil

3 shallots, thinly sliced

4 garlic cloves, finely chopped

3 to 5 Thai chilies, seeded and finely chopped

5 cups water or chicken broth (page 344)

6 tablespoons Vietnamese or Thai fish sauce

3 tomatoes, peeled, cut into thin wedges, and seeded

2 tablespoons coarsely chopped fresh mint leaves

2 tablespoons coarsely chopped fresh basil leaves

2 tablespoons coarsely chopped fresh cilantro leaves

two 1.7-ounce packets cellophane noodles or the equivalent, soaked for 30 minutes in cold water, drained

Refrigerate the scallops and shrimp on plates, covered with plastic wrap. Toss the pineapple wedges in a bowl with the sugar and lime juice.

In a 4-quart pot over medium heat, heat the peanut oil and gently cook the shallots, garlic, and chilies until they brown lightly, about 5 minutes. Add the water, fish sauce, and tomatoes. Bring to a simmer, add the pineapple/sugar/lime juice mixture, and bring back to a simmer.

Add the chopped herbs and seafood and simmer the soup for about 3 minutes. Add the noodles and simmer for 1 minute more. Serve in heated deep bowls.

❧

Laotian Catfish Soup with Peanuts and Coconut Milk

I got the idea for this soup from a dish that caught my eye in Alan Davidson's book, unfortunately now out of print, *Fish and Fish Dishes of Laos.* While the flavors in this soup—in its original version actually more a stew—are similar to the basic flavors of Thai and Vietnamese cooking, I was intrigued by the peanuts (glorious combined with coconut milk), the amazing amount of garlic, and the use of catfish.

Catfish takes on great importance in Southeast Asian cooking with Davidson listing 15 species, each with nuances of flavor and texture. The most prized catfish, the giant (up to 10 feet long) Mekong catfish (*Pangasianodon gigas*), is now at the point of extinction because the rituals once followed by fishermen—which made the fish almost impossible to catch—have largely been abandoned.

This soup is perfectly good with American catfish, but in all honesty there's no magical affinity between the flavors that makes catfish better for this dish than other firm-fleshed fish that won't fall apart in the simmering broth. See the glossary for information on Asian ingredients.

MAKES 6 FIRST-COURSE SERVINGS

1½ pounds catfish, monkfish, or blowfish fillets, skin and pin bones removed

3 Thai chilies, seeded and finely chopped

12 garlic cloves, finely chopped

3 kaffir lime leaves, finely chopped

4-inch piece of lemongrass, thinly sliced

2 shallots, finely chopped

2 tablespoons peanut or vegetable oil

1 quart water or chicken broth (page 344)

2 tablespoons fresh lime juice (from about 1 lime)

two ¼-inch-thick slices of fresh or frozen galangal (optional)

¼ cup creamy peanut butter without additives

one 14-ounce can unsweetened coconut milk

6 tablespoons Thai or Vietnamese fish sauce

2 tablespoons finely chopped fresh basil leaves

2 tablespoons finely chopped fresh cilantro

Cut the fillets into strips (blowfish fillets are already the right size) about 1 by ½ inch and reserve in the refrigerator on a plate, covered with plastic wrap.

Cook the chilies, garlic, lime leaves, lemongrass, and shallots in peanut oil in a sauté pan over medium heat for about 5 minutes . Pour in the water, lime juice, and galangal if you're using it and bring to a slow simmer. Thin the peanut butter with 2 tablespoons of the coconut milk and whisk this mixture into the simmering soup. Stir in the fish and the rest of the coconut milk and simmer gently for about 2 minutes. Stir in the fish sauce and the herbs and simmer for 2 minutes more.

Serve immediately in hot bowls.

JAPANESE-STYLE FISH SOUPS

Japanese-style fish soups are easy to make because the basic broth, dashi, is made out of ingredients you keep on the shelf or in the refrigerator; there's rarely any need to make a fish broth out of fish bones and heads. Pieces of fish or shellfish are simmered in the broth at the last minute.

❧

Japanese-Style Salmon, Spinach, and Soba Noodle Soup

(color page 16)

This dish is really a cross between a soup and dish of noodles—it's up to you which of the two you want to emphasize. If you want it soupier, use more broth. If you want it more substantial, use more noodles.

The best and prettiest noodles for this are called *cha-soba*, which are buckwheat noodles made with green tea. The tea not only flavors them but gives them a lovely green hue.

Be sure to serve this dish in small deep bowls, preferably Japanese lacquer. The noodles, salmon, and spinach look beautiful nestled together under the golden broth.

MAKES 4 FIRST-COURSE OR LIGHT MAIN-COURSE SERVINGS

For the Spinach:

1 bunch of spinach, stems removed

½ teaspoon dark sesame oil, preferably Japanese

2 teaspoons Japanese dark soy sauce

For the Glazed Salmon:

1 teaspoon vegetable oil

8-ounce salmon fillet, scaled and skin left on

1 tablespoon dark soy sauce

1 tablespoon mirin

For the Broth and Noodles:

1 quart dashi (page 343)

2 tablespoons mirin

2 tablespoons Japanese dark soy sauce

a 1-inch-thick bundle of *cha-soba* or regular soba noodles

2 scallions, including green, finely chopped

Japanese seven-spice mixture (shichimi)

Blanch the spinach in a pot of boiling water for 30 seconds, drain in a colander, and rinse immediately under cold running water. Gently squeeze the water out of the spinach and toss the spinach in a bowl with the sesame oil and soy sauce. Reserve in the refrigerator.

Heat the vegetable oil in a nonstick sauté pan over high heat. When the oil barely begins to smoke, place the salmon, skin side down, in the hot oil. Hold the salmon down with the back of a fork for about a minute to prevent it from curling. Continue cooking the salmon over high heat for 2 minutes. Take the salmon out of the pan and place it, skin side down, on a paper towel to soak up the oil. Wipe out the sauté pan with a paper towel and pour in a tablespoon of soy sauce and a tablespoon of mirin. Put the salmon back in the pan skin side down and cook over medium to high heat for about a minute, until the mirin mixture almost completely evaporates and glazes the salmon skin. Be careful at this point, however, not to go too far and burn the mirin mixture—keep sniffing so you'll detect any burning. Transfer the salmon to a plate, let it cool slightly, and carefully slice it across the fillet into 4 even long strips with the skin attached. Don't worry if the salmon is raw on one side—it will finish cooking as it sits on top of the hot broth.

Bring the dashi to a slow simmer with the mirin and soy sauce.

Cook the soba noodles in about 3 quarts of boiling water for about 8 minutes—bite into a noodle every few minutes to determine when they are done. Drain the noodles in a colander and divide them among 4 warmed deep porcelain or lacquer bowls. (Porcelain bowls can be warmed in the oven; lacquer bowls are best warmed by filling them with boiling water a minute before serving.)

Push the noodles to one side in each of the bowls and arrange a small mound of spinach next to the noodles. Add the scallions to the simmering dashi, wait about 15 seconds, and ladle the dashi into each of the bowls. Lay a strip of salmon, skin side up, across the middle of each bowl. Serve immediately. Pass the seven-spice mixture at the table for guests to sprinkle into the soup.

PUREE-STYLE FISH SOUPS

Some fish soups are made by simmering whole fish in water or broth—almost invariably flavored with aromatic vegetables or spices such as saffron or curry—and then pureeing the whole soup so that the fish flesh itself ends up in the broth and gives it body and texture. The best known of these soups is *soupe de roche,* one of the contenders—along with bouillabaisse—for the tastiest of all Mediterranean fish soups.

Traditionally, puree-style soups are made by boiling whole fish and vegetables until everything starts to fall apart and then working the whole thing through a food mill. This may be the easiest method if you're given a bucket of fresh whole fish, but working the mixture through a food mill is tedious at best. I find it much easier to have the fishmonger fillet the fish and save me the heads and bones. I then prepare a fish broth with the heads and bones, strain it, and simmer the fillets in the broth until they fall apart. Finally I puree the whole thing in the food processor before straining a last time.

Marseilles-Style Fish Soup

SOUPE DE ROCHE

Unassuming to look at, *soupe de roche* is one of those glories of southern French cooking that I could eat every day of my life. The flavors of this soup are so powerful that the first spoonful almost knocks your head back, but I've never known anyone not to fall immediately in love with it and ask for more.

MAKES 8 FIRST-COURSE SERVINGS

4 pounds assorted lean whole fish such as sea bass, snapper, or flatfish, filleted, skin removed, heads and bones reserved

1 cup dry white wine

1 large bouquet garni: 5 fresh thyme sprigs or ¾ teaspoon dried, a medium bunch of parsley, and a large bay leaf tied up with string (or in cheesecloth for dried thyme)

1 small fennel bulb, stalk removed and chopped

¼ cup olive oil

2 onions, chopped

8 garlic cloves, peeled

6 tomatoes, seeded and coarsely chopped

1 medium russet potato, peeled and cut into approximately ½-inch cubes

pinch of saffron threads, soaked in 1 tablespoon water for 30 minutes

1 recipe rouille (page 269)

salt and pepper

French bread, sliced and lightly toasted

Preparing the Fish Broth: Soak the fish heads and bones in cold water for at least 30 minutes, changing the water at least twice. Drain the bones and heads and make a fish broth by combining the bones and heads with the white wine, bouquet garni, chopped fennel stalk, and enough

water to cover (about 5 cups) in a 4-quart pot. Simmer the broth gently for 30 minutes, skimming off any froth that floats to the top. Strain the broth through a medium-mesh strainer.

Preparing the Flavor Base: Finely chop the rest of the fennel bulb and put it in a 4-quart pot with the olive oil, onions, and garlic cloves. Put the pot over medium heat and stew the vegetables, stirring every few minutes with a wooden spoon, until they are tender but not browned, about 15 minutes.

Finishing the Soup: Add the fish broth, tomatoes, potato, and fish fillets to the vegetable mixture. Simmer the mixture until the fish is ready to fall apart and the potato cubes have softened, about 30 minutes.

Strain the broth into a bowl and puree the solid ingredients in a food processor or blender for about 2 minutes. If the mixture gets too stiff and won't turn around, thin it with some of the broth. After pureeing the fish mixture, work it through a food mill or push it through a strainer with the back of a ladle. If your food mill has various disks, work the mixture through twice, once with the coarse attachment and again with the fine while adding broth from time to time to lubricate the mixture. Most of the fish flesh won't go through, but all the savory juices will.

Combine the pureed fish mixture with the remaining broth and add the saffron threads and their soaking liquid. Whisk half of the rouille into the soup. Bring the soup to a simmer, season it with salt and pepper to taste, and serve it immediately in hot bowls. Pass the remaining rouille and the bread at the table.

USING A VEGETABLE SOUP BASE FOR FISH SOUPS

In these soups the fish can simply be added shortly before serving to make a vegetable soup more substantial or to give it a particular character. In other words, you might come up with a perfectly satisfying cream of tomato soup or a simple corn chowder and one day decide to simmer some pieces of fish or shellfish directly in the soup just a few minutes before serving. This is a simple and great technique because you can use almost any broth or vegetable soup—and you don't need whole fish; fillets work perfectly well.

❧

Fish or Shellfish Corn and Poblano Chili Soup

I came up with this soup one afternoon when I was fiddling around with some recipes out of Rick Bayless's book, *Authentic Mexican.* The magical combination of corn and poblano chilies makes it easy to put together a flavorful soup—adding the fish or shellfish, almost as an afterthought, makes the soup more substantial and even more deeply flavored.

MAKES 6 FIRST-COURSE SERVINGS

4 large ears of sweet corn or two 10-ounce packages frozen white corn

1 large onion, finely chopped

3 garlic cloves, finely chopped

2 jalapeño chilies, finely chopped

3 poblano chilies, seeded and coarsely chopped

½ teaspoon dried oregano, preferably Mexican

2 tablespoons unsalted butter

4 tomatoes, peeled, seeded, and finely chopped

3 cups chicken broth (page 344), fish broth (page 343), or shrimp-head broth (page 201)

1 cup heavy cream

1½ pounds flatfish, tilefish, striped bass, tuna, swordfish, or salmon fillets, cut into ½-inch cubes, or shrimp, scallops (cut into ½-inch-thick disks), or crabmeat

2 tablespoons finely chopped fresh cilantro

¼ cup fresh lime juice (from about 2 limes)

salt and pepper

1 cup sour cream or crème fraîche

Preparing the Corn: Husk the corn and remove any threads clinging to the kernels. Hold the corn vertically in a large bowl and slice off the kernels with a sharp paring knife. If you're using frozen corn, just let it defrost.

Preparing the Flavor Base: Cook the onion, garlic, chilies, and oregano in butter in a 4-quart pot over medium heat for about 10 minutes, until the onions turn translucent. Don't let any of the vegetables brown.

Add the corn, tomatoes, broth, and cream to the vegetables and bring the mixture to a slow simmer. Simmer gently for 10 minutes and let cool. Puree the soup in a blender or food processor for about 1 minute and strain it into a clean pot. If the soup seems too thick, thin it with a little water or broth. (You can also skip the pureeing and straining and leave the soup crunchy.)

Cooking the Seafood and Serving the Soup: Just before serving, bring the soup to a slow simmer and add the seafood, cilantro, and lime juice. Simmer gently for 2 to 3 minutes, ,

season with salt and pepper to taste, and ladle into hot bowls. Decorate each bowl with a dollop of sour cream and serve immediately. Serve the remaining sour cream at the table.

FISH CONSOMMÉ

A fish consommé is clarified by gently simmering the fish broth with egg whites, herbs, vegetables, and sometimes extra filleted fish. Because fish consommé is perfectly clear, it makes an elegant backdrop for delicately shaped pieces of fish, shellfish, vegetables, and herbs.

I always think consommé looks a little austere when served in a wide soup bowl. Try serving consommé in espresso cups—the double size—or in Japanese lacquer bowls with lids.

❧

Basic Fish Consommé

*T*o avoid the expense of buying whole fish for the broth and extra fish to deepen the consommé's flavor, use the heads and bones of your fish for the broth and the fillets to clarify it. Use less expensive lean fish such as small flatfish or round fish including grouper, pollack, porgy, rockfish, sea bass, tilefish, and whiting.

continued

MAKES 6 FIRST-COURSE SERVINGS
(6 CUPS)

For the Basic Broth:

6 pounds whole fish, cleaned and filleted, heads and bones reserved, fillets skinned and cut into 1-inch chunks

1 onion, chopped

1 bouquet garni: 3 fresh thyme sprigs or ¼ teaspoon dried, a small bunch of parsley, and a bay leaf tied up with string (or in cheesecloth for dried thyme)

2 cups dry white wine

For Clarifying the Fish Broth:

fish chunks, from above

1 onion, coarsely chopped

1 carrot, coarsely chopped

1 celery stalk, coarsely chopped

4 tomatoes, chopped

2 teaspoons Tabasco

1 bunch of parsley, coarsely chopped

5 egg whites

Soak the fish bones and heads or whole fish in cold water for 30 minutes, changing the water every 10 minutes, to eliminate blood.

Drain the fish heads and bones and pack them into a 4-quart pot with the onion and bouquet garni. Add the wine and enough water to cover—about 6 cups. Simmer gently for 30 minutes, skimming any froth off the top of the pot with a ladle. Strain the fish broth through a fine-mesh sieve.

Combine the fish chunks with the remaining clarifying ingredients in a food processor. Grind for about 1 minute, until everything is finely chopped. If you don't have a food processor, just chop everything by hand and work the egg whites into the mixture. Put the mixture in a 6-quart pot.

Whisk the warm (but not hot) fish broth into the pot, whisking thoroughly to break up the mixture. Make sure the egg white and vegetables are

well distributed. Bring the broth to a slow simmer over medium heat. Turn down the heat slightly and move the pot to one side of the burner so that it boils gently on one edge. After about 5 minutes, take a long wooden spoon and gently scrape along the bottom of the pot to make sure the solids don't stick to the bottom and burn. Leave the broth at a gentle simmer for 40 minutes more, positioning the pot differently over the burner every 10 minutes so the broth boils in a different place.

By this time a thick layer of coagulated froth should be floating on top. Poke a hole in the froth with a wooden spoon so that the soup simmers up through the hole. Simmer for 10 minutes more or until the broth is completely clear except for little specks of egg white and vegetable.

Line a wide strainer with a triple layer of cheesecloth or a cloth napkin. Be sure to rinse the cloth thoroughly to get rid of any residual soap or bleach. Place the strainer over a pot and ladle in the consommé. To do this you have to break through the layer of coagulated egg, but be careful not to break up the vegetable/egg white mixture too much, or you will cloud the consommé. To strain the last bit of consommé, you'll have to tilt the pot over the strainer. If after a few minutes the consommé starts to drain very slowly through the cloth—the weave of the cloth may become clogged—gently pull on one side of the cheesecloth or napkin so the liquid can drain through an unused section.

GARNISHES FOR FISH CONSOMMÉ

Garnishing a fish consommé with lobster or other fish or shellfish can be approached in one of two ways. The first and simplest is to cook the lobster separately, take the meat out of the

shell, and present the lobster meat—carefully sliced in medallions—in the bowls with the hot consommé. The second method, somewhat more complicated, is designed so that the flavor of the lobster actually makes it into the broth. To do this the lobster must be cooked in the strained fish broth, the meat taken out of the shells, and then the broken-up shells—I just smash them with a handleless rolling pin—combined with the egg whites and filleted fish to be used for the clarification. This technique works with small crabs, crayfish, and shrimp as well.

FISH FOR CLARIFYING

Fish for clarifying should be lean, delicately flavored, and inexpensive; texture isn't an issue. I often use scrod or the least-expensive flatfish fillets, but depending on price you can also use ocean perch, pollack, porgy, rockfish, sea trout, tilefish, or weakfish.

SERVING CONSOMMÉ COLD

Cold consommés are among the most subtle and delicate of all soups and contain not even a speck of fat. They also make the perfect backdrop for fine white wines and Champagnes whose flavor would be lost next to more assertive foods. Cold consommé makes an especially light and delicious summer first course.

When making cold consommé, be sure it isn't too stiff, or it will feel rubbery in the mouth. If you've made your consommé by following the preceding recipe, it should barely set once it chills in the refrigerator. The best way to serve it is just to spoon it out into chilled bowls or, as a nice touch, into Champagne coupes.

Although cold seafood consommé has a lovely delicacy, it can look a little lonely without little cubes of cooked shrimp or lobster and a sprinkling of freshly chopped parsley, chervil, or chives. One last trick is to serve cold consommé with a chilled light sauce. One of my favorites is made with tomatoes and cream (below).

❧

Cold Fish Consommé with Tomato Cream Sauce

A simple fish consommé is itself a delight, but the light tomato cream sauce in this recipe gives the consommé an exciting tangy accent and color that make it irresistible to look at and to taste.

MAKES **12** VERY LIGHT FIRST-COURSE SERVINGS

3 ripe tomatoes, peeled, seeded, and finely chopped

1½ teaspoons coarse salt

3 tablespoons heavy cream

3 teaspoons sherry vinegar

1½ teaspoons chopped fresh tarragon, chives, or parsley

pepper

6 cups basic fish consommé (preceding recipe)

12 tiny tarragon sprigs, parsley sprigs, or chives

Toss the chopped tomatoes with salt and place them in a strainer set over a mixing bowl. Let them drain for 30 minutes.

In a small bowl, combine the tomatoes, cream, vinegar, and chopped herbs and season lightly with freshly ground pepper. Chill the sauce for at least 15 minutes.

Spoon the consommé into 12 chilled small soup bowls, double espresso cups, or Champagne coupes. Carefully spoon the tomato sauce over and around the consommé. Garnish with the herbs.

Stews

The most basic fish stews are made by simmering whole fish in a flavorful liquid and, as soon as the fish is done, stirring in a thickener such as flour or cornstarch. The problem with this approach is that most people have trouble grappling with whole pieces of cooked fish. Another problem with a quickly thrown together fish stew is that the liquid—often wine—doesn't have enough time to cook, so its flavors remain raw and the flavors of the seafood stay weak and diluted.

A better approach to making a fish stew is to prepare a flavorful cooking liquid with the fish heads and bones and then cook only the fillets in the flavorful liquid at the last minute. In this way most of the work can be done ahead of time and there's plenty of time for cook-

ing and perhaps reducing the flavorful liquid without keeping the fish—or the guests—waiting. A liquid base for a fish stew is made in the same way as a basic fish broth except a liquid other than water may be used for simmering the bones and heads, the bones and heads may be caramelized in butter or oil before liquid is added, and the finished liquid may be reduced to concentrate its flavor before it is used for cooking the fish in the stew.

Once you've prepared a flavorful liquid base, the filleted fish is simmered in the liquid shortly before serving, the liquid is usually thickened, other flavorful ingredients may be added (such as herbs or brandy), and a separately prepared garnish of vegetables is stirred in or arranged on the plates just before serving.

FISH TO USE FOR STEWS

Many traditional fish stews are made only from freshwater fish or only from ocean fish, but because it can be difficult to find an assortment of either type, I often include both in the same stew. The most important thing to look for is, of course, freshness. Also look for firm-fleshed fish that won't fall apart when simmered in liquid and keep in mind the kind of stew you're making. Avoid flatfish such as flounder or sand dabs, which have very fragile fillets. Full-flavored red wine stews can incorporate stronger-tasting fish such as salmon, squid, or mackerel, while more delicate stews—those made with white wine or hard cider—need less assertively flavored fish.

Keep in mind the way the stew is going to look and if possible select fish that can be cut into different shapes such as small fillets, strips, or cubes (salmon or swordfish, for example) and fish such as red snapper with attractive skin that can be left on. Try to find whole fish so you can make a full-flavored broth out of the heads and bones. If you can find only filleted fish, consider making a Japanese-style fish stew with dashi.

Shellfish can also be incorporated. Already shucked shellfish such as scallops or peeled shrimp can be added directly to the stew and simmered for a minute or two, while whole or live shellfish such as lobster or crayfish must first be cooked lightly, taken out of their shells (the shells can be simmered with the stewing liquid before straining), and gently reheated in the stew just before serving.

SOUPS, STEWS, AND SAUCES

The difference among soup, stew, and sauced fish is often a matter of how concentrated the surrounding liquid is and how much of it there is. Pieces of fish in a soup are surrounded by relatively large amounts of light-flavored liquid, while stews are surrounded by less liquid but the liquid is richer, thicker, and more intensely flavored. A fish stew is likely to be made with all wine or another flavorful liquid, while a fish soup may contain a little wine but more than likely mostly water. A sauce may be richer still and be the result of long simmering to concentrate its flavors.

LIQUIDS USED FOR MAKING FISH STEWS

WATER

Water can be used for making fish stews in the same way it is used for making soups—as the liquid used to make a fish broth from the fish bones and heads. Because a fish stew requires a more intensely flavored liquid than a soup, a fish broth made from water will usually need to be reduced to concentrate its flavor. The filleted fish can then be simmered in the concentrated fish broth shortly before serving.

WINE

Both red and white wine can be used to make delicious fish stews. The best way to use wine is to use it as the liquid (instead of water) in a fish broth made out of the fish heads and bones.

The techniques for using red and white wine are slightly different because of the tannin contained in red wine. White wine can be used in much the same way as water for making a basic broth, while red wine should be cooked for at least an hour to soften its acidity and eliminate its tannin. It is also helpful when making a red wine–based fish stew to brown the fish bones and heads with aromatic vegetables before adding the wine. Another trick that heightens the wine's flavor is to add it in increments and let it caramelize with the vegetables before the bulk of the wine is added.

Select a white wine with a tart, clean fruitiness. Muscadet is one of my favorites because it's tart and not too expensive. French or California sauvignon blanc also works well.

Select a red wine that is full-bodied with a deep color and preferably a little bottle age. Don't use expensive wine—any delicacy or finesse will be lost in cooking—but don't use a wine you wouldn't drink. Avoid light fruity wines such as Beaujolais or wines with a lot of acidity. My favorites for cooking are Spanish Rioja, California Zinfandel, and French Côtes-du-Rhône.

CIDER

Cooks in Normandy sometimes use cider in fish stews. The easiest way to include cider is to use it to make a basic fish broth and then cook the filleted fish in the broth.

When French cooks talk about cider, they mean hard cider, which has

been fermented so that most of the sugar contained in the apple juice has turned to alcohol. Hard cider is best for cooking because the alcohol evaporates and there isn't a lot of sugar left in the stew. Apple juice or what is sold in the United States as apple cider (virtually the same thing as apple juice) contains considerable sugar. If you can't find hard cider, substitute half apple juice and half water and then add a few tablespoons of cider vinegar to the stew near the end. The effect is different—a kind of sweet-and-sour taste—but still delicious.

DASHI

Japanese cooks usually make fish stews—*nimono*—by simmering pieces of fish or small whole fish in a dashi flavored with mirin, soy sauce, and sake. This is an especially good method for cooking filleted fish when you don't have access to the heads and bones for making a fish broth.

SHELLFISH-COOKING LIQUID

The cooking liquid from steamed mussels or clams and the savory broths made from the shells of lobster and crayfish can be used to make a fish stew. The shellfish itself can then be reheated gently in the stew along with the other fish just before serving. This is a great technique if you're stuck with only fish fillets or steaks and you don't have the bones and heads to make a fish broth. It's also quick, easy, and delicious to quickly steam some clams or mussels and then use the cooking liquid for cooking fish fillets or steaks.

VEGETABLE BROTH (COURT BOUILLON)

Vegetable broth can be used as the base for a fish stew in the same way as fish broth. Although the flavor won't be as pronounced as if a fish broth were made from the fish's head and bones, a vegetable broth makes an excellent base for a stew made with delicately flavored fish or where subtle flavors are being incorporated. A vegetable broth is also an excellent alternative when preparing a fish stew with steaks or fillets when you don't have heads and bones to make a fish broth.

FLAVORING FISH STEWS WITH AROMATIC VEGETABLES

Almost all fish stews contain vegetables added at the end to provide extra flavor, color, and texture. Aromatic vegetables such as onions, carrots, garlic, celery, and shallots are either simmered in the fish broth and strained out and discarded or incorporated into the finished stew and served along with the fish. French cooks call vegetables added to the stew at the end the *garniture*. One of the most common combinations is a mixture of pearl onions, mushrooms, and little strips of bacon (*lardons*)—a combination used to accompany *coq au vin, boeuf bourguignon,* and red wine fish *matelote*. Although many recipes are rigid about what vegetables should comprise the garniture, I usually select vegetables according to what I find at the market. While the most direct approach is to cook these vegetables in the strained stewing liquid (before the fish is added), I usually cook them separately (using the most appropriate technique for each one) and add them to the fish stew only a minute or two before serving. Try braised fennel wedges; coarsely chopped, peeled, and seeded tomatoes; peeled and glazed baby carrots and turnips; blanched and lightly creamed spinach; blanched French string beans; fresh beans; and others.

USING HERBS

Herbs can be added to a fish stew during different stages of cooking in much the same way as vegetables. The herbs most often used for making a fish stew are parsley, bay leaves, and thyme—the traditional components of a bouquet garni—but other herbs can be added to give the stew a special flavor.

The question that confuses most cooks is when different herbs should be added. Although there is no hard-and-fast rule, herbs such as thyme, marjoram, savory, oregano, and lavender—the so-called herbes de Provence—are more aggressive and should be added earlier in the cooking, perhaps included in a bouquet garni used to make a fish broth with the heads and bones. Thyme in particular has a different character when added to a simmering stew just before serving than it does when given 30 minutes to an hour in the liquid; after long cooking its flavor melds with that of the other ingredients and is much more subtle and appealing.

Delicate herbs such as parsley, chervil, chives, tarragon, and basil release their flavor quickly into a surrounding liquid, so it's better to add these herbs—finely chopped—within a minute or two of serving the stew.

THICKENERS FOR FISH STEWS

Once pieces of fish—or shellfish—have been simmered in an aromatic liquid, traditional recipes usually call for thickening the liquid so it will coat the fish. More contemporary recipes often omit the thickener and suggest serving the fish in soup plates surrounded by the concentrated cooking liquid. I often compromise and use only a small amount of thickener.

One of the most common thickeners is flour, which can be used in two ways. The first method is to make a roux by gently cooking the flour in butter for about 3 minutes and then quickly whisking in the hot liquid to be thickened. A second method, usually used for red-wine stews, is to knead equal parts of flour and butter together with a fork to obtain a smooth paste (*beurre manié,* or "worked butter" in French") and then whisk this paste into the simmering liquid just before serving.

FISH STEWS: COMBINING TECHNIQUES

Many stews—especially those using meat—are prepared by sautéing in hot fat before any liquid is added. This is an excellent technique for cooking meat because the browning helps caramelize the meat juices and enhance its flavor. If, however, you're cooking small pieces of fish—or fish that is fragile once cooked—using more than one technique can result in overcooking. Most fish stews are best made by simmering the fish directly in liquid with no preliminary browning.

There are times, however, when the flavor of fish is enhanced by browning. In these situations the fish should be browned, set aside while a sauce is being prepared, and then heated in the sauce at the very last minute. In this way the savory brown crust on the fish's surface stays intact.

Japanese cooks are also fond of precooking fish and then combining it with a concentrated liquid just before serving.

Cornstarch and arrowroot can also be used, combined with an equal volume of water and then whisked into the simmering cooking liquid a minute or so before serving. Their advantage is that they don't require any fat, but be careful not to use too much, or the cooking liquid will take on an artificial-looking sheen.

Butter can also be used as a thickener, but because it is much less efficient than flour, the cooking liquid must be reduced before the butter is added. Because of the extra reduction and flavor of butter, fish stews that have been thickened with butter alone are richer and more deeply flavored than those thickened with flour. You'll end up with less liquid, but it will have more flavor. Fish stews can also be finished with herb butters, crustacean butters, or coral butter.

Cream is an excellent thickener for fish stews made with clear or pale liquids, but don't use it to thicken red-wine fish stews, or they'll come out looking like milk of magnesia. Cream should be added to the cooking liquid shortly before serving and the mixture reduced slightly until it thickens slightly. Many classic French fish stews are thickened with both cream and egg yolks. Egg yolks give the stew a luxurious silky texture. Combine them with the cooking liquid shortly before serving by whisking the cooking liquid into the egg yolks, not the yolks into the hot liquid, or the yolks may curdle. Then gently reheat the liquid, stirring, but don't let it boil, or the yolks will curdle.

Some fish stews can be thickened with vegetable purees. Traditional Italian fish stew recipes include tomatoes for color, flavor, and thickening, but you can also experiment with roast-garlic puree, pureed potato or onion, and pureed green vegetables such as sorrel, spinach, or watercress.

Many of the thickeners used to finish fish soups, such as rouille, aïoli, picada, and Thai curries, can also be used for stews.

❧

Burgundy-Style Red Wine Fisherman's Stew

MATELOTE À LA BOUR-GUIGNONNE

This red wine *matelote* is traditionally made only with freshwater fish. Since in some areas finding an assortment of fish is almost impossible, I make it with what I can find—ocean fish included.

Although any fish stew should be made the same day the fish is bought, the red wine cooking liquid, the vegetable garnish, and the flour thickener (*beurre manié*) can all be prepared earlier in the day. Only the fish needs to be cooked at the last minute.

MAKES 6 MAIN-COURSE SERVINGS

6 pounds whole firm-fleshed fish (preferably at least 3 kinds), filleted, skinned (optional, depending on the fish), heads and bones reserved, gills removed from heads

For the Aromatic Vegetable Base:

1 large onion, chopped

4 garlic cloves, unpeeled, cut in half

1 medium carrot, sliced

2 tablespoons unsalted butter

For the Liquid:

6 cups full-bodied red wine

For the Herbs:

1 bouquet garni: 3 fresh thyme sprigs or ¼ teaspoon dried, a small bunch of parsley, and a bay leaf tied up with string (or in cheesecloth for dried thyme)

For the Beurre Manié:

3 tablespoons unsalted butter, softened

3 tablespoons all-purpose flour

For the Garnish:

1 cup pearl onions, peeled (about 5 per serving)

3 tablespoons unsalted butter

salt and pepper

2 tablespoons finely chopped parsley

½ pound mushrooms, quartered

For the Final Flavorings:

1 tablespoon cognac, Armagnac, or marc (grappa)

1 tablespoon good-quality red wine vinegar or sherry vinegar

2 tablespoons finely chopped parsley

Preparing the Red Wine Fish Broth: If you've decided to leave the skin on the fillets (I usually leave it on bass and red snapper), make shallow incisions diagonally across the skin—about ¾ inch apart—to keep the fillets from curling. Cut the fillets as decoratively as possible, keeping in mind the number of fish and guests and how the finished stew is going to look in the bowl. The stew will look most attractive if each serving has an odd number of pieces of fish, such as 3 or 5. I sometimes cut the fillets in half lengthwise so the 2 pieces look like fillets from smaller fish. Try to keep all the pieces the same size. Keep the fillets covered in the refrigerator.

Preparing the Aromatic Vegetable Base: Soak the fish bones and heads in cold water for 30 minutes, changing the water at least twice during the soaking. Drain in a colander.

Cook the vegetables and fish heads and bones in butter in a 4-quart pot over medium heat for about 20 minutes—stirring every few minutes with a wooden spoon—until the bones fall apart and a brown crust forms on the bottom and sides of the pot. Don't let the pot burn. Add 1 cup of the wine to the browned bones and vegetables and continue stirring, scraping the bottom and sides of the pot with the wooden spoon to dissolve the caramelized juices into the wine.

Turn the heat up to high and simmer the wine until it completely evaporates and a brown glaze forms for a second time on the sides and bottom of the pot. Add the rest of the wine and the bouquet garni. Bring the wine to a simmer and adjust the heat to maintain a slow simmer. Simmer, partially covered, for 45 minutes.

Strain the cooked red wine through a fine-mesh strainer into a sauté pan (preferably one with straight sides) just large enough to hold the fillets in a single layer. Discard the bones and vegetables. There should be about 3 cups of red wine broth. Set this pan aside while you prepare the thickener and garnish.

Preparing the Beurre Manié: On a small plate, work the butter and flour together into a paste with the back of a fork. Reserve until needed.

Preparing the Garnish: Glaze the pearl onions by arranging them in a sauté pan or pot just large enough to hold them in a single layer. Put in a tablespoon of butter and enough water to come halfway up their sides. Partially cover the pan and cook gently for about 15 minutes until all the liquid evaporates and leaves the onions with a shiny glaze. Season with salt and pepper and sprinkle with some chopped parsley. Sauté the mushrooms in another pan in the remaining butter, season with salt and pepper, and sprinkle with the remaining parsley. Reserve the onions and mushrooms, covered, in the refrigerator until needed.

Cooking the Fish (last minute): Bring the red wine mixture to a simmer in the sauté pan and quickly arrange the fish in the simmering liquid—skin side up if the skin is on the fish; otherwise skin side down—sprinkle with salt and pepper, and place a flat pan lid or plate over the fillets to keep them flat. Simmer gently for about 5 minutes (8 minutes per inch of thickness). If the fish fillets have different thicknesses, add them in stages—thickest first, thinnest last.

When the fish is done, quickly arrange it in hot wide soup plates or bowls. Keep warm in a 200°F oven.

Whisk the *beurre manié* into the red wine liquid left in the pan and bring the broth back to the simmer to thicken it.

Add the cognac, vinegar, parsley, mushrooms, and pearl onions to the red wine mixture and simmer for about 30 seconds to evaporate the alcohol and heat the vegetables. Season with salt and pepper to taste. Arrange the mushrooms and onions around the fish and ladle on the sauce.

The Best Fish for Stews Atlantic cod, blackfish, grouper, John Dory, lingcod, Pacific cod, red snapper, rockfish, sablefish, salmon, sea bass, stripe bass, walleye, wolffish

❧

Alsatian-Style White Wine Fish Stew

MATELOTE ALSACIENNE

I don't know of many dishes that are more satisfying than this creamy white wine fish stew. I always make sure I have plenty of bread on hand for mopping up the winy broth.

An Alsatian fish stew is approached in much the same way as the preceding red wine version from Burgundy, but there is no need to caramelize the vegetables with the fish bones before adding the wine. This stew is thickened at the end not only with roux but also with cream and egg yolks.

Although you can get by using an inexpensive dry white wine for making this dish, you can come up with interesting flavor nuances by experimenting with wines with a distinct character. Cooks in Alsace use a local sylvaner, pinot blanc, or even the more expensive Riesling, but I've had good luck using California chardonnay or sauvignon blanc.

Traditionally this stew would be made with small freshwater fish such as eels, small carp, or pike, but I use whatever nonoily firm-fleshed freshwater or ocean fish I can find.

Most of this dish can be prepared in advance—only the final poaching of the fish and the thickening of the poaching liquid should be done at the last minute.

MAKES 6 MAIN-COURSE SERVINGS

6 pounds whole firm-fleshed fish (preferably at least 3 kinds), filleted, skinned, heads and bones reserved, gills removed from heads

For the Aromatic Vegetable Base:

1 large onion, chopped

1 leek, halved lengthwise, rinsed, and chopped

1 medium carrot, sliced

For the Liquid:

2 cups dry white wine

For the Herbs:

1 bouquet garni: 3 fresh thyme sprigs or ¼ teaspoon dried, a small bunch of parsley, and a bay leaf tied up with string (or in cheesecloth for dried thyme)

continued

FISH SOUPS AND STEWS

	Origin	Flavor Base	Moistening Liquid(s)	Types of Fish	Finish	Garnish
Anguille au Vert	Belgium Flanders	Onions Bouquet garni	Fish broth made with trimmings White wine	Eels and other freshwater fish	Egg yolks Cream Herbs	Croutons
Bourride	Provence	Onions Fennel Thyme Bay leaf Orange zest	Fish stock made with trimmings	Mediterranean (firm-fleshed fish can be substituted)	Aïoli	Aïoli
Bourride Sétoise	Languedoc	Leeks Onions Swiss chard Bouquet garni	Fish stock White wine	Monkfish	Aïoli	Aïoli
Caldeirada	Portugal	Onions Green bell peppers Garlic Tomatoes Thyme	Fish broth made with trimmings and white wine	Saltwater fish: Sea bass, cod, monkfish, etc. Squid Bay scallops	None	Basil cut in strips
Calderata	Spain	Olive oil	Sherry	Cod, sea bass	None	None
Asturiana	Spain	Onions Red bell peppers Nutmeg	Water	monkfish, etc.		
Caudière	Flanders	Onions Cloves Bouquet garni Garlic	Fish stock made with trimmings and water White wine Mussel-cooking liquid	Small Atlantic fish: baby sole, flounder, conger eel	Cream	Mussels
Chaudrée	Charente	Bouquet garni Bell peppers	White wine Water	Squid or cuttle-fish, baby skate, eel, mullet	Butter	Buttered croutons
Chirinabe	Japan		Konbu-flavored water	Firm-fleshed whitefish		Chinese cabbage Spinach *Enokitake* mushrooms Wheat gluten *(fu)* White radish Bean curd
Chowder	North America	Onions Salt pork Bacon Potatoes	Milk Fish broth	Cod, white firm-fleshed ocean fish	Cream	Crackers
Chowder	Mexico	Roasted chilies Jalapeño chilies	Fish broth made with trimmings	Firm-fleshed round fish	Cream	Tortilla chips Sour cream
Cotriade	Cornwall (England)	Onions Sorrel Potatoes	Water Vinegar	Conger eel, mackerel, cod	Butter	Stale bread
Indian-Style Coconut Curry	India	Ginger Onions Fish trimmings Hot chilies	Fish broth made with milk Tomatoes	Firm-fleshed fish	Coconut Cilantro	Rice

	ORIGIN	FLAVOR BASE	MOISTENING LIQUID(S)	TYPES OF FISH	FINISH	GARNISH
MATELOTE ALSACIENNE	Alsace	Leeks Carrots Onions Bouquet garni	Fish broth made with vegetables and fish trimmings Riesling	Freshwater fish: carp, eel, perch, etc.	Cream Egg yolks *Beurre manié*	Buttered croutons
MATELOTE À LA BOURGUIGNONNE	Burgundy	Onions Garlic Bouquet garni	Red wine Marc de Bourgogne	Freshwater fish: trout, eel, perch, etc.	*Beurre manié* Butter	Garlic-rubbed croutons
MATELOTE À LA CANOTIÈRE	Alsace	Leeks Carrots Onions Bouquet garni	Fish stock made with vegetables and fish trimmings Riesling or Sylvaner	Carp and eel only	Butter	Mushrooms Crayfish
MATELOTE NORMANDE	Normandy	Onions Garlic Bouquet garni	Hard cider Calvados	Saltwater fish: sole, flounder, conger eel	*Beurre manié* Cream	Croutons Mussels
POCHOUSE	Burgundy	Onion Garlic cloves Bouquet garni	White wine (Bourgogne Aligote)	Freshwater fish: trout, perch, eel, pike, etc.	*Beurre manié*, Cream	Pearl onions Bacon Mushrooms, Croutons
ROMESCO	Spain	Onions Leeks	Fish broth made with trimmings Sherry	Mediterranean (firm-fleshed fish can be substituted)	Romesco (picada)	None
SOUPE DE POISSON NIÇOISE	Nice (France)	Olive oil Onions Garlic Saffron Tomatoes	Fish broth made with trimmings	Mediterranean (firm-fleshed fish can be substituted)	Rouille	French bread
TTORRO	Basque Country	Olive oil Onions Garlic Red bell peppers Hot peppers Saffron Bouquet garni	Stock made with fish trimmings and vegetables	Saltwater fish and shellfish: mussels, langoustines, monkfish, conger eel, shrimp, lobster, etc.	None	Croutons cooked with olive oil Chopped parsley
VATAPA	Brazil	Onions Hot peppers Tomatoes Ginger	Coconut milk Water	Small ocean fish Shrimp	Coconut puree Peanut puree	Chopped cilantro
WATERZOOÏ	Belgium	Butter Onions Bouquet garni Sage	Stock made with fish trimmings and vegetables	Freshwater fish: trout, eel, perch, pike, etc.	Butter Heavy cream	Chopped parsley Croutons
ZARZUELA	Catalan	Onions Red bell peppers Green bell peppers Garlic Ham Tomatoes Saffron Bouquet garni	White wine	Lobster Large shrimp Mussels Bay scallops Sea scallops	None	Almonds Chopped parsley

For the Garnish:

6 square slices of white bread, crusts removed

½ cup (¼ pound) unsalted butter, clarified (page 336)

1 tablespoon finely chopped parsley

For the Thickeners:

2 tablespoons unsalted butter

2 tablespoons all-purpose flour

1 cup heavy cream

5 egg yolks

For the Final Flavorings:

1 tablespoon finely chopped parsley

2 tablespoons fresh lemon juice

salt and white pepper

Preparing the Fish: Cut the fish fillets so you have 3 pieces per serving. Fillets can be cut in two lengthwise so the pieces have the same shape. Cover the fish with plastic wrap and store it in the refrigerator.

Preparing the Fish Broth: Soak the fish bones and heads for 30 minutes in cold water and drain. Combine the fish bones and heads, chopped vegetables, white wine, bouquet garni, and enough cold water to cover in a sauté pan just large enough to hold the fish in a single layer. Bring the reduced fish broth to a slow simmer in the sauté pan.

Preparing the Garnish: Cut the bread slices in half diagonally. Round off one pointed end and the side of each triangle to make elongated heart shapes. Gently brown these on both sides in clarified butter. Dip the tip of each crouton in chopped parsley.

Poaching the Fish and Thickening the Poaching Liquid (last minute): Heat the croutons and 6 soup plates in a 200°F oven.

Prepare a roux by cooking the butter and flour in a 2-quart saucepan over medium heat for about 5 minutes, stirring with a wooden spoon. Don't let the flour brown. Set aside.

Whisk together the cream and egg yolks in a 2-quart mixing bowl.

Pour the broth through a fine-mesh strainer into a clean pot. Bring the broth to a simmer and reduce it to 2 cups, about 30 minutes, skimming off froth with a ladle. Arrange the pieces of fish in a single layer in the simmering broth and place a flat lid or plate directly on the fish to keep them at least partly submerged in the stewing liquid and to prevent them from curling.

When the fish is done, about 5 minutes, arrange it in the hot soup plates and keep the plates in the oven with the door cracked while you prepare the sauce.

Finishing and Serving: Whisk the hot poaching liquid into the roux. Bring to a simmer and whisk half of this roux-thickened poaching liquid into the egg yolk/cream mixture. Return this mixture to the saucepan with the roux mixture and stir constantly over medium heat until it thickens slightly and takes on a silky texture. Don't let the sauce boil, or the egg yolks will curdle. Remove from the heat, stir in the parsley and lemon juice, and season with salt and pepper to taste. Ladle the sauce over the fish in the bowls. Arrange 2 croutons— parsley-coated tip pointed in—on the rim of each bowl.

Thai-Style Fish Sauté with Yellow Curry

Thai curries have the almost miraculous ability to make the simplest dishes taste exotic. Yellow curry is virtually the same as green curry with some turmeric added, so use some of your own green curry or buy it canned.

For a sauté, the pieces of fish or meat are sautéed in hot fat, a sauce is made in the sauté pan, and just before serving the pieces of fish or meat are reheated in the sauce. Don't try this dish with fragile fish, or they may fall apart by the time they are browned and reheated.

This dish can be made in a few minutes. I like to serve a bowl of jasmine or basmati rice alongside.

MAKES 6 MAIN-COURSE SERVINGS

2½ pounds swordfish, marlin, or shark steaks, skin and bones removed, cut into strips about 1½ inches long and ½ inch wide

salt and pepper

2 tablespoons vegetable oil

3 tablespoons green curry paste (page 340)

2 teaspoons ground turmeric

2 tomatoes, peeled, seeded, and chopped

one 14-ounce can unsweetened coconut milk

2 tablespoons Thai fish sauce (nam pla) or more to taste

1 tablespoon lemon juice

2 tablespoons finely chopped fresh cilantro

Dry the strips of fish with paper towels and season them with salt and pepper. In a sauté pan just large enough to hold the fish in a single layer, heat the oil until it begins to smoke. Sauté the pieces of fish for about 1 minute on each side and place them on a plate covered with paper towels. Pat the oil off the fish.

Let the sauté pan cool slightly and wipe it out with a paper towel. Whisk in the green curry and turmeric and place the pan over medium heat. Spread the mixture around the bottom of the pan with a whisk for about 1 minute so the heat brings out its flavor. Add the tomatoes and cook over high heat for about 5 minutes, until the mixture thickens. Stir in the coconut milk, the fish sauce, and the lemon juice and simmer for 5 minutes more. Stir in the cilantro. Add the fish, simmer for 1 minute, and serve on hot soup plates.

❧

Moroccan Swordfish Tagine with Olives and Saffron

I've never been fortunate enough to sample Moroccan cooking in its native environment, but I have sampled it in Paris and New York and have Paula Wolfert's *Couscous and Other Good Food from Morocco* in my kitchen library.

This tagine is flavored with a potpourri of my favorite Moroccan flavors—saffron, olives, preserved lemon, and of course charmoula. Traditional tagine recipes always seem to me to overcook the fish—in this version the cooking times are more restrained.

My favorite fish for this recipe is swordfish because I can cut it into meaty chunks and brown it without overcooking it. If you don't have

access to swordfish, other firm-fleshed fish such as shark, salmon, or halibut also work well.

Don't be distressed if you don't have preserved lemons. You can use sliced fresh lemons instead, but I highly recommend putting up a small batch of preserved lemons for next time (see box).

This tagine is best served with couscous, but basmati rice is also delicious.

MAKES 4 MAIN-COURSE SERVINGS

two 1-pound 1-inch-thick swordfish steaks, bones and skin removed

1 recipe charmoula (see recipe, page 294)

salt and pepper

3 tablespoons olive oil

3 tomatoes, peeled, seeded, and chopped

2 teaspoons sugar

pinch of saffron (about 10 threads), soaked in 1 tablespoon water for 30 minutes

½ pound large green Greek or Italian olives, pitted and very coarsely chopped

½ preserved lemon, salt rinsed off and cut into ¼-inch cubes, or 2 fresh lemons, skin cut off with a knife and pulp sliced into ¼-inch-thick rounds

1 cup slivered almonds, toasted in a 300°F oven until light brown, about 15 minutes

Cut the swordfish into 18 equal chunks about an inch on each side. Toss the chunks in the charmoula and refrigerate for 1 hour.

Wipe the charmoula off the fish and save it for use later. Season the fish with salt and pepper and brown the chunks in olive oil in a sauté pan just large enough to hold them in a single layer over high heat for about 3 minutes. Take the swordfish out of the pan and pour out the olive oil in the pan. Put the swordfish back in the pan and stir in the tomatoes, sugar, and saffron. Bring the mixture to a gentle simmer and simmer covered for about 1 minute. Stir in the olives, lemon, charmoula, and almonds and season with salt and pepper to taste. Serve immediately on hot plates.

PRESERVED LEMONS

Preserved lemons are an essential ingredient in Moroccan cooking, but once you get used to their flavor you may find yourself using them in all sorts of highly flavored dishes. They're great with chicken and fish.

You may be able to find preserved lemons in fancy-food shops, but it's easy to make your own provided you're willing to wait a month. Once ready, preserved lemons will last for at least a year in a cool place.

To fill a pint mason jar you'll need about 9 lemons—5 for preserving and 4 more to provide extra juice—and about 5 tablespoons coarse salt. Scrub 5 of the lemons thoroughly with hot water and quarter them vertically. Stack them, a layer at a time, in the mason jar, distributing the salt equally over each layer. Press the lemon wedges tightly into the jar, squeeze the remaining lemons, and pour the juice into the jar—the lemons should be completely covered in juice. Screw on the lid and keep in a cool place or the refrigerator for a month before using. During the first 2 weeks, leave the jar upside down for several hours every couple of days to redistribute the salt and juice.

Moroccan Herb and Spice Mixture

CHARMOULA

This mixture is not only good when whisked into traditional Moroccan tagines but is also a delicious finish to almost any seafood soup or stew, Moroccan or otherwise.

MAKES ⅔ CUP

1 teaspoon ground cumin

2 teaspoons paprika

1 tablespoon grated fresh ginger

2 tablespoons extra-virgin olive oil

leaves from 1 large bunch of cilantro

leaves from 1 large bunch of parsley

4 garlic cloves, peeled

½ teaspoon cayenne pepper or more to taste

¼ cup fresh lemon juice

¼ cup sherry vinegar or good-quality red wine vinegar

Gently cook the cumin, paprika, and ginger in olive oil in a small saucepan over medium heat until you can smell their fragrance, about 2 minutes. Puree this spice mixture with the rest of the solid ingredients in a food processor for about 2 minutes. Slowly add the lemon juice and vinegar through the top of the food processor to get the mixture to move around.

Indonesian Fish Curry

KARÉ IKAN

I first read a recipe for this dish in Sri Owen's wonderful book *Indonesian Food and Cookery*. I've been deliberately evasive about what kind of fish to use, but it should be firm enough so that it won't fall apart in the sauce. Usually I don't recommend stronger-tasting fish in saucy dishes like this one, but the flavors here are so assertive that salmon, Spanish mackerel, or king mackerel would be fine. I also like to use monkfish or wolffish because they won't fall apart if I happen to overcook them a tad. See the glossary for information on Asian ingredients.

You can make the liquid mixture for this dish a day or two in advance and put the fish in just before serving. Serve with plenty of plain rice.

MAKES 4 MAIN-COURSE SERVINGS

2 pounds fish fillets or steaks such as king mackerel, Spanish mackerel, monkfish, swordfish, or salmon, skin and pin bones removed

1 long European cucumber or 2 regular cucumbers, peeled

1 tablespoon coarse salt

3 shallots, chopped

2 garlic cloves, finely chopped

1 tablespoon freshly grated ginger

2 teaspoons finely chopped fresh turmeric or ½ teaspoon ground

2 to 3 Thai chilies, halved, seeded, and finely chopped

1 kaffir lime leaf, finely chopped

3-inch piece of lemongrass, finely sliced, then finely chopped

1 tablespoon ground coriander

2 tablespoons peanut or vegetable oil

1 salam leaf (optional)

juice of 2 limes

2 teaspoons shrimp paste, worked to a thin paste with 1 tablespoon water (optional)

leaves from 1 bunch of mint, coarsely chopped within an hour of serving

1 cup unsweetened coconut milk

salt and pepper

Cut the fish into pieces about 1 inch square and refrigerate, covered with plastic wrap, until needed.

Slice the cucumbers lengthwise and scoop out the seeds with a spoon. Slice the halves into ¼-inch-thick crescents. Rub the slices thoroughly with coarse salt for a couple of minutes until you can't feel the salt grains and let drain in a colander for about 20 minutes. Squeeze the cucumbers in small bunches in your palm to eliminate excess water. Reserve in a bowl in the refrigerator.

Prepare a *bumbu* by combining the shallots, garlic, ginger, turmeric, chilies, lime leaf, lemongrass, coriander, and peanut oil in the bowl of a (preferably miniature) food processor and pureeing for about 3 minutes, until you get a fairly smooth paste.

Cook the *bumbu* in a 4-quart pot over medium heat, stirring, for about 5 minutes, until its aroma fills the room. Stir in the rest of the ingredients, adding salt and pepper to taste.

Bring the liquid to a gentle simmer and slide in the fish. Simmer for 3 to 8 minutes (8 minutes per inch of thickness).

Fricassee of Blowfish Fillets with Cockles, Clams, or Mussels

*S*eafood dishes using the cooking liquids from bivalves, especially cockles, clams, and mussels, are special favorites of mine. The juices make a wonderful sauce, and the bivalves themselves look elegant scattered over or around pieces of more substantial fish or miniature fillets.

A fricassee is a kind of miniature stew made by sautéing pieces of fish or meat in hot fat, discarding the fat, and then simmering the lightly browned fish or meat in a liquid such as water, wine, or broth. Thickeners and flavorings are then added to the cooking liquid.

Although blowfish fillets are called for in this dish because they hold together and take well to two-stage cooking—preliminary cooking in fat, simmering in liquid—pieces of firm-fleshed fish such as salmon, swordfish, marlin, tuna, and shark all work well. This recipe is also well suited to fish steaks or fillets because the shellfish provides the broth—there's no need to make a fish broth out of the fish bones and heads.

The cooking liquid from this dish is thickened with butter, so if you're concerned about its richness, cut the butter in half or eliminate it altogether.

The most time-consuming part of this recipe—steaming open the mussels and taking them out of their shells—can be done earlier in the day.

MAKES 6 FIRST-COURSE OR 4 MAIN-COURSE SERVINGS

2½ pounds blowfish without heads or skin, trimmed and filleted, or 2½ pounds other firm-fleshed fish fillets, bones and skin removed, cut into 2- by ½- by ½-inch strips

1 small garlic clove, finely chopped

1 shallot, finely chopped

½ teaspoon finely chopped fresh thyme

1 cup dry white wine

2 pounds small cultivated mussels, cockles, or clams, scrubbed and drained

salt and pepper

½ cup all-purpose flour

2 tablespoons pure olive oil

1 tomato, peeled, seeded, and chopped

¼ teaspoon saffron threads, soaked in 1 tablespoon water for 30 minutes

½ cup (¼ pound) cold unsalted butter, cut into 4 chunks

2 tablespoons finely chopped parsley

Preparing the Fish and Mussels: Reserve the trimmed fish, covered, in the refrigerator.

Combine the garlic, shallot, thyme, and wine in a pot large enough to hold the mussels. Cover the pot and simmer gently for 5 minutes to infuse the flavors in the wine. Add the mussels, cover the pot, and place over medium heat for 5 minutes, until all the mussels open. If they haven't opened after 5 minutes, steam them for 2 minutes more. Discard any unopened ones at that point.

Take the mussels out of the shells and reserve. Discard the shells. Check the mussel-cooking liquid—if it's sandy, pour it carefully into a clean container, leaving the sand behind in the pot.

Cooking the Fish and Serving: Season the fish with salt and pepper and dredge it in flour. Carefully pat off any excess flour. (Flour the fish just before cooking, or the pieces will stick to each other.)

Brown the fish in olive oil in a sauté pan over high heat. When the fish feels firm to the touch—after about 5 minutes—drain it on a plate covered with paper towels and keep it warm in a 200°F oven.

Throw the cooked fat out of the sauté pan and pour in the mussel-cooking liquid. Add the tomato and saffron with its soaking liquid and boil the mixture until about 1 cup remains. Whisk the butter and parsley into the sauce and season with salt and pepper to taste.

Gently reheat the pieces of fish in the sauce—don't let the sauce boil—and serve in heated wide soup plates.

Substitutes Dover sole, frogs' legs, John Dory, sea scallops, shark, swordfish

INDIAN FISH AND SEAFOOD CURRIES

Most Westerners think of an Indian curry as a stew or sauce to which a few teaspoons of commercial curry powder have been added. Indian cooks never use already combined curry powder—unless they've made it themselves—but rely on subtle mixtures of spices that differ for almost every dish.

Because fish and seafood curries are essentially stews, most fish and shellfish are best added to an already-prepared sauce mixture just minutes before serving so the seafood doesn't overcook.

Even though cooking a traditional curry may seem mysterious, there is a certain order and logic to adding the ingredients. Typically, aromatic vegetables—especially onions, garlic, ginger, and chilies—are cooked lightly in vegetable oil, ghee, or mustard oil. Once the vegetables have softened or, for some recipes, browned, ground spices are added and the mixture is cooked for a few seconds to release the flavor of the spices. This cooking of the spices is important, especially if the spices haven't been roasted before they've been ground.

Once the spices have released their flavor—they'll start to smell good—liquid is added to the spice/aromatic vegetable mixture. Water or broth is sometimes added at this point. Although Indian recipes don't usually suggest it, I sometimes make a flavorful broth out of the main stew ingredients—such as fish stock from fish heads and bones or shrimp or lobster broth from heads and shells. Acidic liquids, especially tamarind extract or lemon juice, are also sometimes added at this point. Once the liquid has been simmered with the spices and aromatic vegetables for 5 to 10 minutes, an enrichener is usually stirred into the curry to give it a silky texture and soften its flavor. In northern India the enrichener is likely to be a dairy product such as heavy cream, yogurt, or a combination of the two, while in southern India coconut milk is likely to be used. While Indian curries are often quite thin, Indian cooks often use cooked vegetables or vegetable purees made from spinach, tomatoes, potatoes, or legumes such as lentils or dried beans to give curries more body.

The last ingredients to go into an Indian seafood curry are the seafood itself and chopped green herbs such as cilantro or mint. The seafood is gently cooked through, the seasonings adjusted with salt and often cayenne pepper. Most of the time the curry is served with rice or traditional Indian breads.

Shrimp Curry

I never encountered a dish exactly like this one in India, nor have I ever seen a recipe exactly like it. This is a result of my own tinkering following the suggestions of my two favorite Indian cookbook writers, Julie Sahni and Madhur Jaffrey, and using some of my own favorite methods for getting the flavor out of shrimp.

I suggest making a shrimp-head broth, but don't despair if you can't find shrimp with their heads—just use water or chicken broth instead. I also suggest coconut milk as a possible substitute for the heavy cream and yogurt—probably heretical but delicious nonetheless.

The time-consuming part of making this dish, the sauce, can be made ahead of time and the shrimp just reheated in the sauce at the last minute. I like to serve this dish with plenty of basmati rice.

MAKES **6** MAIN-COURSE SERVINGS

3 pounds medium to large shrimp with heads or 2 pounds headless

2½ cups chicken broth (page 344) or water

2 tablespoons ghee or clarified butter (page 336), butter, or vegetable oil

2 medium onions, finely chopped

4 garlic cloves, finely chopped

1 tablespoon grated fresh ginger

2 to 5 Thai or serrano chilies, halved, seeded, and finely chopped

½ teaspoon ground turmeric

1 teaspoon ground cumin

1 tablespoon ground coriander seeds

2 teaspoons paprika

1 teaspoon ground fenugreek

1 tablespoon fresh lemon juice

½ cup plain yogurt combined with ½ cup heavy cream or 1 cup unsweetened coconut milk

salt and cayenne pepper

2 tablespoons chopped fresh cilantro

Peel and devein the shrimp. If you have shrimp with the heads, reserve the heads and shells and puree them for about 1 minute in a food processor with just enough of the broth or water to get the mixture to move around. Combine the head/shell mixture with the rest of the broth or water in a saucepan and simmer gently for 30 minutes. Strain through a fine-mesh strainer and reserve.

Heat the ghee in a 4-quart pot over medium heat and stir in the onions, garlic, ginger, and chilies. Continue to stir every few minutes for about 15 minutes, until the onions turn translucent and begin to brown slightly.

Stir the turmeric, cumin, coriander, paprika, and fenugreek into the onion mixture. Continue stirring over medium heat for about 1 minute and then pour in the reserved shrimp broth. Bring to a gentle simmer and whisk in the lemon juice and yogurt/cream or coconut milk. Season with salt and cayenne to taste.

Five minutes before you're ready to serve, add the cilantro and the shrimp and simmer gently for 3 to 5 minutes. Serve immediately.

Swordfish Vindaloo

*B*ecause I love vindaloo dishes, usually made with meat or poultry—I always order them in Indian restaurants—I set out to adapt the technique for cooking seafood. After a bit of research I discovered that the secret (and essential) ingredient is mustard oil, which has a peculiar smell and flavor that must be softened by first heating it in the pan until it smokes slightly and then letting it cool.

I've never encountered swordfish in Indian cooking, but I like to use it in saucy dishes because I know it won't fall apart. Other firm-fleshed fish fillets or steaks such as Dover sole, John Dory, pompano, or tuna can be cut into cubes or strips and used in this dish. Shellfish such as scallops or shrimp are also delicious.

I like to serve this dish with plenty of rice.

MAKES 6 MAIN-COURSE SERVINGS

2½ pounds skinless and boneless swordfish (3 pounds if swordfish is in steak form) or other firm-fleshed fish

salt

3 tablespoons vegetable oil

5 tablespoons mustard oil

2 medium onions, finely chopped

3 garlic cloves, finely chopped

2 tablespoons ground coriander seeds

2 teaspoons turmeric

2 teaspoons ground cumin

2 teaspoons black mustard seeds

1 teaspoon ground cinnamon

¼ teaspoon ground cloves

2 teaspoons paprika

2 teaspoons cayenne pepper

1 tablespoon grated fresh ginger

4 tomatoes, peeled, seeded, and chopped

½ cup fish broth (page 343) or water

2 tablespoons sherry vinegar or red wine vinegar

2 walnut-size chunks tamarind paste or 2 tablespoons fresh lemon juice

2 tablespoons chopped fresh cilantro

Browning the Fish: Cut the swordfish into 1-inch cubes and sprinkle with salt. Brown the cubes in vegetable oil in a skillet over high heat. Be careful not to let the fish overcook—the browning shouldn't take longer than 2 minutes. Set the cubes on a plate covered with paper towels to drain. Refrigerate while you're preparing the vindaloo sauce. Wipe out the skillet with a paper towel.

Preparing the Vindaloo Sauce: Heat the mustard oil over high heat until it barely begins to smoke in the skillet used for browning the fish. Turn off the heat, wait 5 minutes, and then turn the heat back to medium.

Cook the onions and garlic in the mustard oil over medium heat until the onions begin to brown slightly, about 15 minutes. Stir in the spices, up to and including the ginger, and cook over medium heat, stirring constantly, for 2 minutes more. Add the tomatoes, broth, and vinegar and simmer gently for about 15 minutes.

While the sauce is simmering, pour ½ cup boiling water over the tamarind in a small mixing bowl. Let sit for 5 minutes and work to a paste with the back of a fork. Strain into the simmering vindaloo sauce. Stir in the chopped cilantro. Season the sauce, if necessary, with salt or more cayenne.

Finishing and Serving: Stir the cubes of swordfish into the simmering sauce about 2 minutes before serving. Serve immediately on hot plates.

Pasta and Rice Dishes

A simple rice or pasta dish can be converted into a flavorful meal by combining it with seafood. One of the most popular of these dishes is linguine with clam sauce, but the principle of tossing cooked seafood with pasta just before serving can be used with almost any shellfish. Asian cooks are fond of stirring chunks of seafood into cooked rice, and Europeans are likely to incorporate shellfish into rice dishes such as risotto and pilaf.

PASTA

Almost any seafood soup, stew, braised dish, or sauce can be converted to a pasta dish by tossing the finished dish with cooked pasta. Cooked seafood can also easily be turned into a stuffing for filled pasta such as ravioli, agnolotti, or tortellini. Seafood pasta dishes can be presented in several ways. One of the easiest and most obvious is simply to make some kind of seafood stew and then toss the mixture over the cooked noodles. A seafood soup can also be served over noodles so that the broth comes halfway up the sides of the noodles and the solid pieces of fish or shellfish remain on top. A third method, more popular in Italy than in the United States, is to prepare a seafood stew and then finely chop the fish or shellfish so that it becomes an integral part of the sauce.

❧

Linguine with Lobster Basil Sauce

This is an example of how a simple seafood dish can be converted into a delicious pasta sauce. If you haven't cooked lobster before, you'll probably want to read some of the basic information in the lobster chapter. In this pasta dish the lobster is

steamed, a simple sauce is made from the steaming liquid, and the lobster meat is cut into small chunks used in the sauce.

While this recipe is kept simple by design, you can make an even fuller-flavored version by crushing the cooked lobster shells and simmering them with just enough liquid to cover. This lobster-shell broth can then be reduced and incorporated into the pasta sauce. The same method can be used for shrimp or crabs.

MAKES 8 FIRST-COURSE OR 4 MAIN-COURSE SERVINGS

three 1¼-pound lobsters
1 cup dry white wine
1 cup chicken broth (page 344) or water
2 garlic cloves, finely chopped
½ cup heavy cream
6 tablespoons extra-virgin olive oil
salt and pepper
about 20 fresh basil leaves
2 pounds fresh linguine or 1 pound dried

Rinse the lobsters under cold running water. Bring the wine, broth, and garlic to a simmer in a pot large enough to hold the lobsters over medium heat. Put the lobsters in the pot, turn the heat up to high, and cover the pot tightly—you may have to hold down the lid during the first couple of minutes of cooking. Check the lobsters after 6 minutes. If they are bright red all over, take the pot off the heat, let cool for a minute or two, and take out the lobsters. If the lobsters still have dark patches, steam them for 2 minutes more.

Cut the lobsters in half, take the grain sacs out of the head, and take the meat out of the tail and claws. Cut the meat into 1/4-inch cubes. Be sure to scoop out any tomalley or coral and include it by chopping it up with the meat. You can also freeze the lobster shells for lobster butter, seafood broth, or another recipe.

Add the cream to the liquid in the pot and boil it down for about 5 minutes, until it thickens slightly. Whisk in 1/4 cup of olive oil and season with salt and pepper to taste. Sprinkle the basil leaves with a tablespoon of olive oil—this keeps them from turning dark—and finely chop them. Whisk the chopped basil into the reserved sauce.

Just before you're ready to serve, gently heat the cubes of lobster in the sauce.

Bring a big pot of water to the boil, add a tablespoon of olive oil to the water, and cook the linguine. Drain the linguine in a colander and distribute it evenly among hot soup plates. Ladle the sauce over each serving and serve immediately.

❧

Homemade Cuttlefish-Ink Linguine or Fettuccine

I'll never forget my first encounter with black pasta, years ago in a restaurant in Florence—I thought I had reached the height of culinary sophistication. I now see strands of black pasta, both dried and fresh, at fancy food stores displayed nonchalantly with pasta of every conceivable shape and color. The disappointing thing about the store-bought variety is that it doesn't seem to have any of the wonderful sealike flavor I remember in my first tasting. This homemade version, while subtle, captures the flavor of the sea.

I haven't given directions here for rolling pasta out by hand, assuming there's a pasta machine available. Be sure to wear an apron when working with the cuttlefish ink.

MAKES ABOUT 1½ POUNDS, ENOUGH FOR 6 FIRST-COURSE OR 4 MAIN-COURSE SERVINGS

5 large eggs

2 tablespoons extra-virgin olive oil

ink from 2 cuttlefish (clean and freeze the cuttlefish for recipe at right)

1 teaspoon salt

½ teaspoon freshly ground pepper

3 cups all-purpose flour or a little more

1 cup semolina flour or cornmeal

Whisk together the eggs, oil, cuttlefish ink, salt, and pepper in a large mixing bowl. Strain the mixture through a regular strainer, scraping against the inside of the strainer to get all the ink to go through. Add the flour and work the mixture into a ball either by hand, in a food processor, or in an electric mixer with the paddle blade or dough hook. The dough should feel moist but not at all sticky—pasta dough feels to me like a new suede coat—but you may need to add a little water or flour to the dough to get it to feel right. Knead the dough in the pasta machine, roll it as thinly as you can, and cut it into linguini or fettuccine. Gently toss each batch of pasta with semolina flour or cornmeal to prevent it from sticking to itself and gently coil it on a baking sheet covered with flour. The pasta can be cooked right away or stored in a dry place for up to 24 hours.

❧

Cuttlefish Linguine with Tomato Basil Sauce

The obvious way to serve black pasta is to make some kind of sauce out of the cuttlefish since you will have had to track one down to get the ink. The disadvantage is that the flavor of the sauce completely dominates the subtle sealike flavor of the pasta—hence my preference for this simple tomato and basil sauce. One of my favorite tomato sauce tricks is to partially cook the tomatoes until they release liquid but then, instead of cooking the sauce until the liquid evaporates and the sauce thickens, strain the tomatoes and boil down the liquid that comes through the strainer. In this way the tomatoes themselves are only very lightly cooked and retain their fresh flavor.

MAKES 6 FIRST-COURSE OR 4 LIGHT MAIN-COURSE SERVINGS

2 garlic cloves, finely chopped

1 medium onion, finely chopped

¼ cup extra-virgin olive oil

8 ripe tomatoes, peeled, seeded, and coarsely chopped

about 30 fresh basil leaves

salt and pepper

1 recipe cuttlefish-ink pasta (preceding recipe)

Cook the garlic and onion in 2 tablespoons of the olive oil in a 6-quart or larger pot over medium heat until the onion turns translucent but doesn't brown, about 10 minutes. Add the tomatoes and bring the mixture to a simmer over medium heat. Simmer gently for 10 minutes—the tomato should release its liquid and make the sauce very runny.

Strain the tomato sauce into a saucepan and return the tomatoes to the first pan. Boil down the liquid that runs through the strainer until only about ½ cup of syrupy liquid remains. Stir this liquid into the tomato mixture.

Bring a pot of water—for cooking the pasta—to the boil with the last tablespoon of olive oil.

Sprinkle the basil leaves with a tablespoon of olive oil (to keep them from turning dark) and finely chop them. Stir the chopped basil into the tomato sauce and season with salt and pepper to taste. Bring the sauce to a gentle simmer.

Cook the pasta in the boiling water for about 2 minutes—bite into a piece to make sure it's done—and coil the pasta in the center of hot soup plates. Ladle on the hot tomato sauce.

STUFFED PASTA
ravioli, tortellini, agnolotti

The big question when making stuffed seafood pasta is whether to put the seafood into the stuffing, the surrounding broth or sauce, or even the pasta itself (as in cuttlefish-ink pasta). The key to success is that the flavors of the stuffing contrast with those of the sauce or broth surrounding the cooked pasta. So if ravioli is stuffed with shrimp and basil, you shouldn't serve the ravioli in a basil shrimp sauce.

One of my favorite approaches is to make an intensely flavored stuffing and then serve the pasta surrounded with a very delicately flavored—even slightly insipid—broth so that the flavor of the stuffing bursts in the mouth all at once. One of the best ways to accomplish this is to include a fair amount of butter in the stuffing so the stuffing liquefies inside the pasta and

rushes out with a burst of flavor as soon as you take a bite.

Another approach is to make a delicate stuffing—a mixture of ricotta and fresh sage is one of my favorites—and then surround it with a flavorful seafood sauce or broth. In this way the stuffed pasta acts as a backup or foil for the flavor of the seafood.

❧

Shrimp and Fresh Marjoram Ravioli with Light Chicken Broth

This is one of those dishes that can be as simple or as complicated as you like. The simplest—but nonetheless delicious—stuffing calls for just chopping the shrimp in the food processor, stirring in some chopped fresh marjoram or other fresh herb, and then seasoning with salt and pepper. I usually opt for this simple approach, but I do occasionally spend obsessive afternoons in the kitchen using any complicated alchemy to get the most flavor out of the shrimp and into the ravioli. On such days I buy shrimp with the heads and use the heads and shells to make a shrimp butter, which I then incorporate into the stuffing.

MAKES APPROXIMATELY 64 RAVIOLI, ENOUGH FOR 10 FIRST-COURSE OR 6 MAIN-COURSE SERVINGS

1 pound headless shrimp, peeled and deveined

2 tablespoons finely chopped fresh marjoram

¾ cup (6 ounces) unsalted butter

1½ teaspoons salt

1 teaspoon freshly ground pepper

2 recipes cuttlefish-ink pasta (page 300) or plain pasta (just leave the ink out of the cuttlefish recipe)

½ cup semolina flour or cornmeal

1 tablespoon olive oil

1 quart chicken broth (page 344)

1 tablespoon finely chopped parsley

Making the Stuffing: Puree the shrimp, marjoram, butter, salt, and pepper in a food processor for about a minute, scraping down the sides of the processor once or twice, until the mixture is smooth. Reserve this mixture, covered with plastic wrap, in the refrigerator.

Making the Ravioli: Meanwhile, roll out the pasta dough with a pasta machine, stopping at the second-to-last setting. If you're not using the dough right away, cover it with plastic wrap so it doesn't dry out. Cut the strips lengthwise into 2 strips, making one strip about ¼ inch wider than the other. Brush the narrower of the 2 strips with cold water and place teaspoons of stuffing about 2 inches apart along the center of the strip. Drape the wider strip over the mounds of stuffing and press all around the mounds to seal in the stuffing. Cut the ravioli apart with a knife or fluted pastry cutter. If you're using a ravioli mold, arrange the wider strips of pasta over the mold, fill with stuffing, moisten the top with water, and seal on another strip of pasta. Reserve the ravioli on a plate or baking sheet covered with a thin layer of semolina flour or cornmeal to prevent sticking. Refrigerate the ravioli until needed.

Cooking and Serving the Ravioli: Bring about 4 quarts of water to a boil in a large pot with the olive oil. Bring the broth to a simmer and season with salt and pepper to taste. Toss the ravioli into the boiling water—the water will immediately stop boiling—and leave the water on high heat until the water comes to a very slow simmer. Turn down the heat and simmer the ravioli gently for 5 minutes after the water comes back to the boil. Don't allow the water to boil, or the ravioli may burst open.

Gently transfer the ravioli to hot soup plates with a slotted spoon or a skimmer. Toss the parsley into the simmering chicken broth and ladle the broth over the ravioli. Serve immediately.

❧

Ricotta and Sage Agnolotti in Tomato Shrimp Broth

I love the simple and delicate flavor of ricotta with fresh sage. These agnolotti are satisfying enough to serve very simply—tossed with a little butter or olive oil is great—and also make a fabulous backdrop for the flavor of seafood. I've suggested using shrimp in this recipe because they're relatively inexpensive and easy to find (although you will need shrimp with the heads unless you have some heads on hand in the freezer). You can also use crayfish, lobster, or crab to make the broth—anything with a shell from which you can extract flavor. This is also a good method if you find yourself stuck with a single lobster or a pound of shrimp with 8 people coming to dinner.

The agnolotti are fun and easy to make once you've rolled out the

sheets of fresh pasta. I once encountered agnolotti in an Italian restaurant that were made with both plain and cuttlefish-ink pasta. If you're feeling especially ambitious, you can make two-toned sheets of pasta by rolling out sheets of cuttlefish-ink pasta and plain pasta, cutting them in half lengthwise down the middle, and then rolling them together through the pasta machine to seal them into a single sheet. The squares for the agnolotti can then be cut from the black-and-white sheets.

MAKES ABOUT 32 AGNOLOTTI, ENOUGH FOR 8 FIRST-COURSE OR 4 MAIN-COURSE SERVINGS

For the Agnolotti:

one 8-ounce container ricotta

1 large egg, beaten

1 tablespoon finely chopped fresh sage

salt and pepper

1 recipe plain pasta (page 300, omitting the ink) or ½ recipe plain pasta and ½ recipe cuttlefish-ink pasta

½ cup semolina flour

1 tablespoon olive oil (for the pasta water)

For the Shrimp Broth:

1 pound small or medium shrimp with heads

1 garlic clove, chopped

1 small onion, chopped

6 medium tomatoes, quartered

1 teaspoon finely chopped fresh or dried rosemary

salt and pepper

Making the Agnolotti: Stir together the ricotta, beaten egg, and sage. Season with salt and pepper to taste.

Roll the pasta into sheets with a pasta machine and cut the sheets in half lengthwise. Cut each half into 2-inch squares. Brush each square with cold water and place about a teaspoon of filling in the center of each. Fold

one corner of the square over to the other corner—you'll end up with a triangle—and pinch all around the stuffing to make a seal. Wet the outside of the triangle, wrap one of the ends around to the other end, and pinch it to form a ring. Spread the agnolotti on a baking sheet or plate covered with a thin layer of semolina flour to prevent the agnolotti from sticking.

Preparing the Shrimp and Shrimp Broth: Twist the heads off the shrimp and peel and devein the shrimp. Reserve the shrimp in the refrigerator and puree the heads and shells in a food processor with the garlic, onion, tomatoes, and rosemary for about 1 minute. Transfer the mixture to a small pot, bring to a slow simmer over medium heat, and simmer for 30 minutes. Strain the broth through a regular strainer and then through a fine-mesh strainer. Season the broth with salt and pepper to taste and reserve.

Finishing and Serving: Bring a large pot of water with the olive oil to a boil. Bring the shrimp broth to a simmer in a small pot. Simmer—don't boil—the agnolotti for about 5 minutes. Plunge the shrimp into the shrimp broth about 3 minutes before the agnolotti are ready. Drain the agnolotti in a colander and distribute them among hot soup plates. Ladle the shrimp broth with the shrimp over the agnolotti and serve.

BAKED PASTA

pasticci and timballi

A pasticcio is a dish of baked pasta made by spreading cooked pasta in a casserole or gratin dish and then baking it with enough liquid to keep it moist. A timballo is similar except that the pasta is then baked in a relatively deep and narrow mold and in fancier versions the mold is lined with pastry—to me a needlessly complicated and redundant addition. The French have their own versions, one of my absolute favorites being leftover linguine dolloped with disgraceful amounts of crème fraîche and baked until crusty. Americans also have their own baked pasta variations—macaroni and cheese (delicious) and tuna noodle casserole (not so delicious).

Baked pasta dishes are excellent for using leftover seafood—true, the fish or shellfish ends up overcooked, but this is less important when it's nestled in moist and crispy pasta.

Leftover Pasta and Seafood Pasticcio

MAKES 4 FIRST-COURSE OR LIGHT MAIN-COURSE LUNCH SERVINGS

2 tablespoons unsalted butter

**1 to 2 cups leftover seafood in
1/2- to 1-inch cubes**

**3 to 4 cups leftover cooked pasta such as
linguine, spaghetti, or macaroni**

2 tablespoons extra-virgin olive oil

2 cups heavy cream, milk, or half-and-half

salt and pepper

Preheat the oven to 400°F. Butter an oval or square baking dish. Toss the seafood with the pasta and olive oil

and spread the mixture in the baking dish—ideally the pasta mixture should be about 1 inch thick in the dish. Pour in the cream or milk—which should barely come up to the surface of the pasta but not com-pletely cover it—and season the whole thing with salt and pepper. Bake until the surface of the pasta turns crusty and brown and there's no excess liquid in the baking dish, 30 to 40 minutes. Push down on the pasta every 10 minutes during baking to moisten the top crispy layer with cream. Serve at the table on hot plates.

RICE DISHES

Mediterranean cooks have long been fond of rice. Italy has its risotto, Spain its paëlla, and Portugal its *arroz de sustância*. Rice pilaf, of Middle Eastern origin, shows up throughout the Mediterranean. While each of these dishes is distinct and is made using entirely different techniques, there are certain methods for cooking rice with seafood that will yield especially marvelous results. Most important, each variety of seafood should be cooked so that it produces a flavorful cooking liquid that can in turn be used for cooking the rice: steam mussels and clams in white wine to yield a briny broth; lightly precook lobsters and simmer the shells with water, wine, and tomatoes into a flavorful broth; use fish heads and bones for making fish broth; slowly simmer squid in wine. . . .

At least as important as getting the most flavor out of the seafood is using the right kind of rice. Ordinary long-grain Carolina rice not only doesn't have any flavor but will turn mushy and sticky as soon as it's cooked. Basmati, Texmati (a cross of basmati and American long-grain rice grown in the United States), and jasmine rice from

Southeast Asia are all excellent for making rice pilaf. Risotto must be made with short-grain rice, preferably Vialone Nano, Arborio, or Carnaroli from Italy. Paella must also be made with short-grain rice, preferably authentic Spanish rice from near Valencia, but Italian short-grain varieties will do. Whatever you do, don't use long-grain rice in paella.

Mediterranean-Style Shrimp and Tomato Pilaf

The trick to this dish is to buy whole shrimp with their heads and make a flavorful broth with the shrimp heads, shells, and tomatoes. Then use the broth to cook the pilaf and grill or sauté the shrimp at the last minute and serve over the rice. This method can also be used for lobster by lightly cooking a cut-up live lobster in olive oil, using the same olive oil to precook the rice, making a broth with the lobster shells, and then using it to cook the rice. Bivalves such as mussels and clams can also be steamed open in white wine and their liquid used for cooking the rice.

MAKES 4 MAIN-COURSE SERVINGS

**2 pounds medium to large shrimp with
heads, heads and shells removed and
reserved, deveined if desired**

4 tomatoes, chopped

1 cup dry white wine

2 cups water

salt and pepper

6 tablespoons extra-virgin olive oil

1 medium onion, finely chopped

2 garlic cloves, finely chopped

**1/2 teaspoon chopped fresh thyme or
marjoram or 1/4 teaspoon dried**

**1 1/2 cups long-grain rice, preferably
basmati or jasmine**

continued

Preparing the Shrimp Broth: Combine the shrimp heads and shells with the tomatoes in a food processor and puree for about 30 seconds. Add some of the wine to the mixture if necessary to get the shrimp to move around.

Add the water and the wine to the shrimp/tomato mixture in a saucepan and gently simmer the mixture for 30 minutes. Strain through a fine-mesh strainer into a measuring cup. If you end up with more than 3 cups, boil the mixture down; if you end up with less, just add enough water to make 3 cups. Season to taste with salt and pepper.

Cooking the Rice: Preheat the oven to 350°F. Heat ¼ cup of the olive oil in a heavy ovenproof pot over medium heat. Stir in the onion, garlic, and thyme and continue stirring over medium heat until the onion turns translucent, about 10 minutes. Pour in the rice and stir for about 5 minutes more, until the rice starts to turn milky white.

Pour the shrimp broth over the rice, bring to a simmer over high heat, and stir quickly, scraping along the bottom of the pot to dislodge any rice that may be sticking. Place a sheet of buttered aluminum foil loosely over the rice and slide the pan into the oven and bake for 20 minutes, or until there is no liquid left.

Cooking the Shrimp and Serving the Pilaf: When the rice is ready, sauté the shrimp in the remaining olive oil or toss the shrimp with the olive oil and grill it. Season with salt and pepper.

Mound the pilaf in an oval gratin dish and arrange the cooked shrimp over the rice. Serve at the table.

RISOTTO

The best risotto has a texture in between a rice pilaf and a cream soup if such a thing can be imagined. Each grain should retain its integrity without in any way tasting raw. See clam risotto (page 145) and lobster risotto (page 186).

Seafood Paella

PAELLA MARINERA

For an authentic paella, the short-grain rice should be Spanish Bahia, although Italian risotto rice will do, the seafood must be perfectly fresh, and you must use real saffron. For strict authenticity the paella should be cooked outdoors on a wood fire, but you can sneak by and make a delicious paella in your kitchen. At the risk of being inauthentic, the rice in this recipe is cooked with a broth made from shrimp heads while traditional recipes call for water. You don't need to follow this recipe exactly—skip the shrimp broth if you wish and use any seafood you want.

I usually make paella for at least 6 people, and while most of the cooking has to be done at the last minute, the flavorful broth can be made earlier the same day. Paella looks best served in an authentic paella pan—a wide flat pan with handles on both sides—but a large skillet works equally well.

MAKES 8 MAIN-COURSE SERVINGS

2½ pounds extra-large or jumbo shrimp with heads or 1¾ pounds headless, peeled, deveined if necessary, heads and shells reserved

4 tomatoes, chopped

1 small bunch of parsley

5 fresh thyme sprigs

1 bay leaf

1 pound squid, cleaned and hoods cut into rings (color page 19)

2 pounds small cultivated mussels, clams, or cockles, scrubbed and drained

1 pound firm-fleshed white fish fillets such as tilefish, halibut, or swordfish, skin and bones removed, cut into 8 equal pieces

½ teaspoon saffron threads, soaked in 1 tablespoon water for at least 30 minutes

¼ cup extra-virgin olive oil

1 medium onion, finely chopped

3 garlic cloves, finely chopped

3 cups short-grain Spanish or Italian rice

lemon wedges

Chop the shrimp shells and heads in a food processor for about 30 seconds and put them in a pot with the tomatoes, herbs, and just enough water to cover. Simmer gently for about 30 minutes. Strain this shrimp broth into a clean pot and discard the shells. Bring the broth to a gentle simmer and slide in the squid. Simmer gently, partially covered, for 30 minutes. Scoop the squid out of the broth with a slotted spoon and reserve. Add the mussels to the simmering broth, cover the pot, and simmer gently until the shellfish open, about 5 minutes (10 minutes for clams). Scoop out the shellfish and reserve on a plate.

Submerge the fish in the simmering broth for 5 minutes, depending on thickness—it should be left undercooked—scoop out with a slotted spoon, and reserve on a plate. Stir the saffron and its soaking liquid into the broth and remove the broth from the heat.

Heat the olive oil in a large iron skillet, sauté pan, or paella pan over medium heat. Stir in the onion and garlic and cook gently for about 5 minutes. Add the rice and stir for a minute or two until it's coated with oil. Preheat the oven to 300°F.

Pour the broth into a measuring pitcher and if necessary add enough water to make 6 cups. Pour into the rice and bring to a simmer on top of the stove. Simmer very gently—without stirring—for about 2 minutes. Nestle the seafood into the rice, loosely cover the pan with a sheet of aluminum foil, slide the pan of rice into the oven, and bake for 15 minutes or until the seafood and rice are completely cooked. Remove the paella from the oven and, without removing the aluminum foil, let rest for 10 minutes. Place the whole pan on a trivet in front of the guests and serve on hot plates at the table. Pass a plate of lemon wedges.

SEAFOOD PILAF

A pilaf differs from risotto or paella in that long-grain rice is used and the rice is never stirred once liquid has been added. Usually the rice is cooked in oil or butter before any liquid is added.

There are a number of ways to incorporate the flavor of seafood into a rice pilaf. The most obvious is to use fish broth or the cooking liquid from shellfish to cook the rice. Depending on the type of seafood being used, it can be cut into small pieces and cooked with the rice throughout the cooking or cooked separately and folded gently into the rice before serving. Another method, great for crustaceans, is to cook the rice in lobster, shrimp, or crayfish butter (page 330) before adding liquid.

Usually rice pilaf is served as a starchy accompaniment to other foods, but seafood pilaf is substantial enough to serve as a main course. One of my favorite methods is to make a pilaf with broth made from fish or shellfish trimmings and then serve the pilaf garnished with the whole fish or shellfish.

Mousses, Soufflés, and Other French Classics

When I was first studying cooking in the early 1970s, the food processor, then called a robot coupe, had just appeared on the market. The magic of the food processor was not that it could chop vegetables or puree soup (other machines could already do this) but that it could puree raw meat and fish into a smooth paste. The result was that a whole collection of elaborate dishes—quenelles, fish and poultry mousses—until then inaccessible to home cooks, could now be made in minutes. For the next decade it seemed as if every fish ended up pureed and served as a fish terrine or mousseline. While it's fortunate that the puree fad is on the wane, there are still times when a carefully made quenelle or fish mousse is the perfect way to start an elegant meal.

MOUSSES AND MOUSSELINES

The difference between a mousse and a mousseline is that a mousse is made with cooked fish and a mousseline from raw. A mousseline is a mixture of raw fish and cream that is then cooked gently in a mold such as a *dariole* mold, a small individual mold which looks a little like an oversize cocktail jigger. Mousseline can also be baked in a terrine or poached, unmolded, in the form of quenelles.

PREPARING A BASIC MOUSSELINE

To make a fish or shellfish mousseline you must have very fresh fish or shellfish that has never been frozen. Avoid fish that is watery—especially flounder, fluke, or sand dab—or fish that has a strong flavor or high oil content such as bluefish or most jacks. The best fish and shellfish for making mousseline are rich and dense-fleshed such as scallops (preferably just-shucked) and salmon.

The first step is to puree the fish or shellfish in a food processor (this is the part that used to be done by hand in giant mortars) and then chill the pureed seafood in a bowl set over another bowl of ice. When the puree is well chilled, you gradually work heavy cream into the mixture with a wooden spoon until the raw mousseline has the consistency of fluffy mashed potatoes. Although most recipes give exact proportions, it's hard to predict exactly how much cream should be added for the mousseline to have the right consistency. The general rule is to combine equal parts by volume of puree and cream, but the only way to know if you've added the right amount of cream is to poach a dollop of the mixture in a pot of simmering water for about 5 minutes. If the dollop dissolves in the water, you've added too much cream and you will need to work some raw egg whites into the mixture to get it to hold together. If, on the other hand, the cooked mousseline seems hard or has a dry, chalky texture, you'll need to add more cream. Another thing to consider when tasting the cooked mousseline is of course taste. You'll probably need to add salt and pepper (use white pepper so you won't see it), and you may want to jazz up the mixture by adding chopped fresh herbs (tarragon is especially good) or by pureeing in something savory and extravagant such as smoked salmon or even foie gras.

Another thing to consider when making a mousseline mixture is whether you're going to be cooking it in a mold or shaping it into quenelles

A FEW DEFINITIONS

aspic: In American usage a consommélike clear jelly used for coating cold foods or served in its own mold. In French usage *aspic* refers to the whole dish, not just the clear jelly, which the French call gelée.

chaud-froid: A fish or meat aspic (gelée) containing heavy cream.

cold soufflé: A fish mousse allowed to set in a mold with a paper collar so that it appears like a hot soufflé. Not a true soufflé.

gelée: The French word for clarified broth, usually called "aspic" in English. What would be described as "in aspic" in English is called *en gelée* in French.

mousse: Any molded dish made from cooked and pureed fish or shellfish. Mousses can be served hot or cold.

mousseline: Mixture of pureed raw fish or shellfish, heavy cream, and usually egg whites that is then cooked either in a mold or as quenelles.

quenelle: Mousseline mixture shaped into the form of an egg or small sausage and then poached.

seafood sausage: Made by rolling fish mousseline into a sausage shape and poaching. Served in round slices, cold or hot.

soufflé: A light and puffy form of fish mousse served hot. Made by combining mousseline or concentrated fish velouté (fish broth thickened with flour) with egg whites and baking in a mold.

terrine: Mousseline mixture baked in a terrine (pâté mold) and served sliced.

and poaching directly in contact with liquid. If you're cooking the mixture in a mold, the consistency of the raw mixture can be as loose as you like because the mold will hold its shape. You do, however, need to make sure the mixture will set once it's hot. The best way to make sure of this is to place a tablespoon or so of the mixture in a small ramekin or mold and simmer it gently for 10 minutes in a shallow layer of water in the bottom of a pot. If the mixture refuses to set, stir a couple of egg whites into the mixture and try again. Keep repeating until the mixture sets. If you're using your mousseline mixture to make quenelles, then of course the raw mixture must be stiff enough to shape into the quenelles such that you may not be able to keep adding egg whites to get it to hold without making the raw mixture too runny. If you've added too much cream to a quenelle mixture, the only solution is to puree more fish and work it into the mixture.

~

Individual Mousselines with Crayfish or Lobster Sauce

This is one of those French dishes—actually it's from Lyons—that has come to represent French cooking at its most snobbish and refined. While today's cooks have moved on to lighter and perhaps more inventive cooking, even the most modern interpretations are based on the same techniques.

A mousseline should be light—almost like a soufflé—and have a rich and subtle flavor. A well-made mousseline is delicious in itself as well as the perfect backdrop for elaborate and deeply flavored sauces.

If you're in an extravagant mood, you can also fold diced black truffles into the mousseline, which will give it a deep and mysterious flavor as well as contrast nicely with its color and texture.

The mousseline mixture can be made earlier in the day or even the night before, but it must be baked just before serving. If you're not up to making a lobster or crayfish sauce, try serving the mousselines with a light tomato cream sauce.

MAKES 8 FIRST-COURSE SERVINGS

For the Mousseline Mixture:

1¼ pounds sea scallops, small white muscle removed, or salmon fillet, skin and pin bones removed

2 egg whites

2 to 3 teaspoons salt, to taste

1 teaspoon freshly ground white pepper

2 cups heavy cream or more as needed

1 or 2 medium black truffles, peeled, cut
  into ¼-inch cubes, and peels chopped
  (optional)

4 tablespoons unsalted butter, softened

For the Sauce and Garnish:

1 recipe lobster *à l'Américaine* (page 177)
  using 1¼-pound lobsters or ½ crayfish
  and sauce from fillet of grouper with
  crayfish sauce (page 217) or tomato
  cream sauce (page 283), heated

6 tiny fresh chervil or dill sprigs

Preparing the Mousseline: Cut the
fish into 1-inch chunks and combine
with the egg whites, 2 teaspoons of
the salt, and pepper in the bowl of a
food processor and puree for about 1
minute. Scrape down the sides of the
food processor twice while pureeing
the fish.

Transfer the puree to a mixing bowl
and place the bowl over a bowl of ice.
Cover the puree with plastic wrap and
refrigerate the bowls for 1 hour.

Work half the cream, a bit at a time,
into the fish mixture with a wooden
spoon. Beat the remaining heavy
cream to medium peaks—don't overdo it—and fold it, along with the truffle cubes and chopped peels if you're
using them, into the mousseline mixture with a spatula. Chill the mousseline mixture for 30 minutes more.

Test the flavor and consistency of
the mousseline mixture by poaching a
dollop in simmering water and if
necessary by adding more cream
or egg whites and adjusting the salt
and pepper.

Coat the inside of 8 dariole molds or
½-cup porcelain ramekins with a generous layer of butter with a small
brush or your finger. Bring about 2
quarts of water to a boil for a bain-
marie (see box). Preheat the oven to
300°F.

Fill the molds with the mousseline
mixture and give each of them a hard

tap on the work surface to knock out
any air bubbles. Cover each mold
loosely with a small piece of buttered
aluminum foil to prevent a crust from
forming on the mousselines during
baking. Place the mousselines in a
pan—a large cake pan is perfect—just
large enough to hold them.

Pour enough boiling water into the
pan to come halfway up the sides of
the molds and slide the whole thing
into the oven. Bake for about 40 minutes—a knife or skewer slid into one
of the mousselines should come out
clean. When the mousselines are done,
turn off the oven, but leave them in
their molds in the bain-marie to keep
warm until just before serving.

Just before serving, unmold the
mousselines onto a large plate or baking sheet—don't unmold them directly on the serving plates, because
they release liquid—and then set them
in the center of warmed plates. Spoon
lobster, crayfish, or tomato sauce over
and around the mousselines and surround with lobster medallions or crayfish tails. Decorate with chervil or dill.

Substitutes Mild-flavored whitefish such as cod, flatfish (flounder,
sole, or halibut), monkfish, Northern
pike, rockfish, scrod, tilefish, walleye

USING A BAIN-MARIE

A bain-marie is a pan of hot water in which soufflés, custards, and mousselines are baked to prevent them from being exposed to the direct heat of the oven and to help them bake evenly. If a
mixture containing eggs or other proteins (such as fish or shellfish) gets too hot—over 175°F—
the protein breaks apart and causes liquid held in an emulsion to separate out, leaving a runny,
curdled mess.

When using a bain-marie, make sure the bain-marie water is boiling before you pour it into the
baking pan—or you may wait all day for your mousselines or custards to bake. Check the bain-
marie water every 10 or 15 minutes during baking—at no point must it boil. If you see even one
bubble appear, turn down the oven.

QUENELLES

A quenelle is a mousseline formed into
egg shapes with spoons and then
poached in simmering water. Occasionally quenelles are piped out into
sausage shapes with a pastry bag, but
they are still poached in salted water.

Before anyone heard of nouvelle
cuisine, the quenelle represented the
very apex of luxurious dining and
sophistication. Today, the pale
quenelle stands opposed to our lean
and simply prepared food with its
bright colors, direct flavors, and forthright textures. But as for so many
things that have been out of fashion
long enough, there is a certain novelty
in bringing them back. I like the look of
confusion on my guests' faces when I
announce the first course, and I give a
nod to current preferences by serving
quenelles in lighter-textured almost
brothlike sauces instead of the rich and
complicated sauces favored at the turn
of the century. I also like to serve
quenelles alongside other fish or
shellfish so there is something firm to
contrast with the airy texture of the
quenelles. In the following dish,
quenelles are served around a simple
square of sautéed fish.

Sautéed Striped Bass Fillet with Oysters and Quenelles

You can make this dish as simple or as complicated as you like. Here the method for making the tomato broth is somewhat elaborate because a fish stock is first made from the fish bones and heads. This fish broth is then combined with the tomatoes and cooking juices from the oysters. If you want to simplify things, use a simple tomato puree diluted with a little broth or water instead of making a fish broth. (Make the tomato broth tangy with vinegar so that it contrasts with the richness of the quenelles.) Or add vegetables or different kinds of seafood instead of the oysters.

The quenelles can be prepared the day before serving and the tomato broth earlier the same day.

MAKES 4 MAIN-COURSE SERVINGS

For the Quenelles:

6 ounces sea scallops, small white muscle removed, or skinless salmon fillet, pin bones removed, or firm-fleshed mild-flavored whitefish

1 egg white

1 teaspoon salt

½ teaspoon freshly ground white pepper

1 cup heavy cream or more as needed

1 tablespoon unsalted butter, softened

For the Rest of the Dish:

one 1½- to 2-pound whole firm-fleshed nonoily fish such as striped bass, black bass, rockfish, tilapia, or red snapper, scaled, filleted, skin left on, head and bones reserved

1 large onion, sliced

SHAPING AND REHEATING QUENELLES

Shaping a mousseline mixture into classic egg-shaped quenelles may take a little practice. The easiest method is to take two spoons of the same size and dip them in a glass of cold water before scooping into the mousseline mixture. To shape the mousseline mixture, mound it on one spoon by holding the other spoon in the opposite direction and using it to smooth over the mound. Once you've shaped the quenelle, the trick is to gently nudge it off the spoon and slide it onto a buttered pan.

An easier method but with less attractive results is to use a pastry bag with a ¾-inch-diameter tip and pipe out quenelles in sausage shapes.

While some recipes suggest shaping the quenelles and placing them immediately in simmering water as you go along, it's easier to arrange them on a buttered pan and then pour in enough boiling water to cover them. This way you can cook them at the last minute, all at the same time.

Quenelles are too time-consuming to shape and cook at the last minute, so they are best made the day before or earlier the same day and then reheated gently, covered with a damp towel, in a 250°F oven for 20 minutes.

1 bouquet garni: 3 fresh thyme sprigs or ¼ teaspoon dried, a small bunch of parsley, and a bay leaf tied up with string (or in cheesecloth for dried thyme)

1 cup dry white wine

12 oysters, shucked

4 ripe tomatoes, seeded and chopped

1 tablespoon sherry vinegar or white wine vinegar

salt and pepper

1 tablespoon olive oil

2 tablespoons mixed chopped fresh chervil, chives, and parsley

4 fresh chervil, parsley, dill, or fennel green sprigs

Making the Quenelles: Prepare a mousseline mixture by pureeing the scallops with the egg white and seasoning in a food processor for about 2 minutes, chilling the mixture in a mixing bowl set over ice in the refrigerator, and then slowly working in ¾ cup of the cream with a wooden spoon. Test the quenelle mixture by poaching a dollop in a saucepan of simmering salted water and adjust the cream and

seasoning, adding more egg white if the mixture is too loose and more cream if it seems too stiff. Be sure to chill the finished quenelle mixture in the refrigerator over ice for at least 2 hours so it's stiff enough to shape into quenelles.

Bring about 2 quarts of water to a boil and with the softened butter brush or rub the bottom of a pan, roasting pan, or casserole large enough to hold a dozen quenelles.

Shape 8 quenelles the size and shape of small eggs using 2 oval soup spoons (see box) and arrange them in even rows in the buttered pan. Gently pour boiling water down one side of the pan until the quenelles begin to float. Place the pan on the stove over medium heat to keep the water at a slow simmer. After about 3 minutes, gently turn the quenelles over with a slotted spoon and poach for 3 minutes more. Transfer the finished quenelles to a baking sheet covered with a wet towel. (Don't use paper towels, or they'll rip and stick to the quenelles.) Cover the baking sheet with aluminum foil and reserve in the refrigerator.

Preparing the Oysters and Tomato Broth: Carefully scrape any remaining scales off the fish fillets, remove any pin bones, and cut each fillet in half crosswise so you end up with 4 attractive pieces of fish. Make 3 diagonal slits in the skin side of each piece. Refrigerate until needed.

Place the fish bones and heads, onion, bouquet garni, wine, and barely enough water to cover in a 4-quart pot. Simmer gently for 30 minutes, skimming any froth off the surface, then strain the fish broth and reserve.

Heat the oysters in a small saucepan until the edges curl slightly. Don't let their liquid boil. Transfer the barely cooked oysters to a clean towel. Strain the oyster liquid through a fine-mesh sieve into a clean saucepan. Add the tomatoes and 1 cup of the fish broth (freeze the rest for another recipe). Simmer the mixture gently for about 20 minutes to cook the tomatoes. Strain the mixture, stir in the vinegar, and season with salt and pepper to taste. Reserve.

Cooking the Fish and Serving: Place the pan containing the quenelles in a 300°F oven for 15 minutes. Leave covered. Bring the tomato broth to a slow simmer. Season the fish and sauté, skin side down first, in the olive oil for about 3 minutes on each side (8 minutes per inch of total thickness). Pat off any oil clinging to the fish with paper towels.

Arrange the fish in the center of 4 soup plates. Arrange 3 quenelles around each piece of fish. Using a slotted spoon, submerge the oysters in the hot tomato broth for about 15 seconds and arrange them over and around the fish. Stir the chopped chervil into the

hot tomato broth and carefully ladle the broth around the fish, quenelles, and oysters. Decorate with a chervil sprig and serve immediately.

SEAFOOD TERRINES

A seafood terrine is simply a mousseline mixture that has been baked in a pâté mold. It is then served sliced, usually cold, with a sauce such as a light mayonnaise, a strained tomato puree (coulis), or a light cream-based sauce. Some recipes suggest folding pieces of lightly cooked shellfish into the mousseline mixture before filling the mold; other recipes divide the mousseline into three batches and color each one differently; some recipes line the mold with strips of vegetables such as leeks or eggplant. I like to serve a small salad of green vegetables such as green beans, asparagus, or artichokes so there is something a little crunchy to contrast with the terrine.

Whichever approach you use, the important thing is to keep the mousseline as light as possible—this may require several tests (poaching in simmering liquid) and adjustments (adding more cream or egg whites). Otherwise the terrine, when served cold, may not be set or may have an unpleasant rubbery texture.

A seafood terrine is best made the day before serving so it will have time to chill.

Three-Color Seafood Terrine

To make this terrine you simply make 3 mousselines and layer them in the terrine mold. The easiest approach is to puree one batch of seafood in the food processor, divide it into thirds, and then color one third with blanched and pureed watercress leaves, another third with saffron, and leave the last third alone. But this approach always seems a little bit phony, so I make each layer with different fish so each has a subtle flavor.

MAKES 12 FIRST-COURSE SERVINGS

6 ounces skinless salmon fillet, pin bones removed

6 ounces sea scallops, small muscle removed

3 egg whites

6 ounces firm-fleshed fillets of whitefish such as cod, flatfish, tilefish, rockfish, red snapper, sea bass, or striped bass

leaves from 1 bunch of watercress, blanched for 1 minute in boiling water, rinsed in a colander, and excess water squeezed out

1½ teaspoons salt

1½ teaspoons white pepper

3 cups heavy cream

3 tablespoons unsalted butter, softened

Puree the salmon and scallops separately, each with one egg white, in a food processor for about 2 minutes each. Puree the fish fillets with the watercress and the remaining egg white in the food processor, also for 2 minutes. Reserve the purees in separate bowls, each covered with plastic wrap, in the refrigerator for 2 to 4 hours. Season each puree with ½ teaspoon salt and ½ teaspoon pepper.

Beat half the cream in a bowl set over ice until the cream begins to stiffen but is less stiff than whipped cream.

continued

Reserve in the refrigerator and work ½ cup of the remaining cream into each puree. Fold the whipped cream into the purees. Poach a dollop of each of the mousselines in a pot of simmering salted water for about 5 minutes and taste. If necessary, season the mixtures with more salt and pepper. If the samples seem too stiff, add more cream to the mixtures; if the samples fall apart in the simmering water, work an additional egg white into each. You may have to perform 2 or 3 tests to get the consistency and flavor just right.

Bring about 2 quarts of water to a boil and preheat the oven to 300°F. Thickly butter the inside of a 6-cup terrine or loaf pan (a 9- by 5-inch loaf pan holds 6 cups) and spread a layer of salmon mousseline in the bottom with a rubber spatula. The salmon mousseline should come one third of the way up the sides of the terrine. Fill up the next third of the terrine with the white mousseline and then fill the terrine with the green watercress mousseline.

Place a double sheet of buttered aluminum foil over the top of the terrine, sealing it tightly around the outside. Place the terrine in a pan or casserole and pour in enough boiling water to come at least a third of the way up the sides of the terrine. Place in a 325°F oven and bake until the inside of the terrine reaches 140°F. Start checking with an instant-read thermometer after 45 minutes. The terrine usually takes between 45 minutes and an hour to bake.

The terrine can be unmolded at this point and served hot, or you can chill it overnight in the refrigerator and serve it cold. To serve the terrine, run a knife around the inside of the mold and carefully turn the finished terrine out onto a cutting board or platter. Slice the terrine into ¼-inch slices with a very sharp knife, using long cutting motions but applying very little pressure.

❧

Seafood Sausages

A seafood sausage is simply a mousseline mixture that has been wrapped up and cooked in a cylindrical shape. Unless I'm including the slices in another dish, I rarely bother making seafood sausages with mousseline alone because there's something monotonous about the texture and look of the slices. My favorite mixture for seafood sausage is chunks of colorful seafood such as lobster and just enough mousseline to hold the whole thing together. Because of its firm texture, shellfish works better than finfish, but I do sometimes include cubes of salmon. I usually make seafood sausages when I have a little bit of raw mousseline left over from another recipe. Seafood sausages are best served hot with a tasty sauce such as a beurre blanc, a lobster or crayfish sauce, or a light tomato sauce. To serve them cold—they make a perfect first course—I avoid rich sauces and serve them with a seafood aspic (page 316) or a light vinaigrette flavored with chopped fresh tarragon.

Seafood sausage can be made a day ahead and simmered just before serving. If you're serving it cold, it will last a day longer.

MAKES FOUR 5- TO 6-INCH SAUSAGES, ENOUGH FOR 8 FIRST-COURSE SERVINGS

For the Mousseline:

10 ounces sea scallops, small white muscle removed, or salmon fillet, pin bones and skin removed, or firm-fleshed mild-flavored whitefish

1 egg white

1 teaspoon salt

½ teaspoon freshly ground white pepper

1 cup heavy cream or more as needed

or

2 cups raw mousseline mixture left over from another recipe

For Incorporating into the Sausages:

1 pound cooked shelled shellfish such as lobster, shrimp, scallops, crabmeat, or crayfish tails cut into ⅓-inch cubes or finfish such as salmon, cut into ½-inch cubes

salt and pepper

2 tablespoons chopped fresh chives, parsley, chervil, or tarragon

3 quarts water

1 tablespoon unsalted butter, softened

Puree the scallops, egg whites, and salt and pepper for 1 minute in a food processor. Chill in a bowl over a bowl of ice for an hour. Work half of the cream into the puree, then beat the rest to soft peaks and fold in. Test the mousseline mixture by poaching a dollop in simmering salted water. Add more salt and pepper if necessary; if the mixture seems too stiff, work in additional cream; if too runny, work in another egg white.

Sprinkle the cubed seafood with salt and pepper and herbs and fold into the mousseline mixture.

Bring the water to a simmer in a pot at least 10 inches in diameter. Cut out four 10-inch squares of aluminum foil and brush them with the softened butter. Place a 10-inch square of plastic wrap (Saran Wrap works best) over each square of foil.

Shape the sausage mixture into a roughly cylindrical shape along one side of each square, running about 3 inches from the edge. Leave about 2 inches of the square uncovered on each side of the sausage for twisting the ends.

Roll the squares, leaving the sausage sealed inside. Twist the ends of each square in opposing directions until the sausage forms a tight cylinder.

Place the sausages in the pot with the simmering water and partially cover the pot. Adjust the heat from time to time to keep the water at a bare simmer. Roll the sausages over every 5 minutes to make sure they're cooking evenly.

Check the inside temperature of the sausages with an instant-read thermometer. They are done when the temperature reads 140°F, after about 15 minutes.

Carefully take the sausages out of the water and let cool for about 5 minutes, even if you're serving them hot. (Otherwise they may fall apart when you cut into them.) If you're serving them cold, refrigerate for at least 2 hours.

Unwrap the sausages and slice each sausage into 6 slices and place 3 slices on each plate. If you're serving a sauce, spoon 2 to 3 tablespoons of it over each serving.

SLICING SAUSAGES AND TERRINES

Especially when there are chunks of shellfish surrounded by a relatively soft mixture such as mousseline, a delicate seafood sausage or terrine can break apart and crumble during slicing. Use a long very thin sharp slicing knife and slice back and forth using long strokes but hardly any force. Pushing down into the sausage or terrine will cause it to break. Hold your other hand against the end of the sausage or terrine to support the slice as it comes away.

SEAFOOD SOUFFLÉS

A soufflé is simply a thick and flavorful sauce or mixture lightened with beaten egg whites and then baked. There are two basic approaches to making seafood soufflés. One method is to make a seafood mousseline, fold in beaten egg whites, and bake it. The other is to use a flavorful liquid such as fish broth or shellfish-cooking liquid, thicken it with butter and flour (roux), and then fold this mixture with beaten egg whites. Both methods give similar soufflés—mousseline soufflés are slightly denser and creamier, while roux-thickened soufflés are airier and less substantial. I usually use the mousseline method for making fish soufflés because fish is easy to work with raw. I use the roux method for shellfish because I can use the shells and juices to make a very tasty cooking liquid for the base. Sometimes I fold in chunks of shellfish so the soufflé has some texture.

I usually bake soufflés in 10-ounce individual soufflé dishes, but some cooks like to serve soufflés in empty lobster, crab, or scallop shells—pretty but hard to cook evenly because of the irregular shape of the shells.

Sea Urchin Soufflés

When I first returned to the United States after living in France, I was amazed to discover that some of the foods I could never afford in France were sold here for almost nothing. One of these was sea urchins. For a few dollars I bought a giant case and set out cooking dishes that would have raised the eyebrows of many a

parsimonious French cook.

To make these soufflés the sea urchins must be impeccably fresh—taste a few to make sure there is none of that peculiar iodine taste that sea urchins take on after a few days out of the water.

If you don't have sea urchins, you can still make this soufflé without them, but make sure you add something to the fish mousseline base to give it extra flavor, such as chopped fresh tarragon, reduced and strained tomato puree, chopped truffles, lobster or crab roe, or smoked salmon.

You must beat the egg whites at the last minute, but you can make the mousseline mixture earlier in the day or the day before.

MAKES SIX INDIVIDUAL SOUFFLÉS, 6 FIRST-COURSE SERVINGS

For the Mousseline:

3 tablespoons unsalted butter, softened

½ pound sea scallops or skinned fillets of firm-fleshed white fish such as black sea bass, flatfish, red snapper, rockfish, or striped bass, cut into 1-inch cubes

½ cup sea urchin roe (If you're taking it out of the sea urchins, you'll need 8)

3 egg yolks

½ teaspoon salt

¼ teaspoon white pepper

1½ cups heavy cream

3 quarts water

6 egg whites

pinch cream of tartar

Thickly butter six 8- to 10-ounce individual soufflé molds and keep them in the refrigerator until needed.

Puree the fish fillets, sea urchin roe, egg yolks, salt, and pepper to a smooth paste in a food processor, about 1 minute. With the food processor on, pour the cream through the top and puree until smooth, about 30 seconds. Reserve in the refrigerator.

continued

Preheat the oven to 375°F and bring the water to a boil. Beat the egg whites to stiff peaks. (Add the cream of tartar if you're not using a copper bowl.) Beat a quarter of the beaten egg whites into the mousseline mixture to lighten it and then carefully fold in the rest all at once with a rubber spatula.

Fill the buttered molds with the soufflé mixture and smooth the tops with the back of a knife or metal spatula. Wipe off any mixture that drips over the sides. Hold the thumb of your right hand about ½ inch into the soufflés along the edge and rotate the molds with your left hand so a moat forms along the edge of the soufflé—this helps in the formation of a cap.

Put the soufflés in a roasting pan or casserole and pour the boiling water around them—it should come between a third and halfway up the sides of the molds. Bake until the soufflés rise about 1½ inches above the rim of the molds, about 25 minutes. (If you're uncertain whether the soufflés are done, quickly poke into one with a knife. If the mixture looks raw, bake for another 5 minutes and check again.) Serve immediately when cooked through.

Blue Crab Soufflés

I'm so inept at getting the delicious meat out of whole blue crabs that I always want someone else to do the work for me. This soufflé captures all the flavor of blue crabs, but no one has to fuss.

The trick to making a crab soufflé is to make a flavorful base with the crab shells as if you were making a crab soup or sauce, also a good

method for making soufflés out of lobster, shrimp, or crayfish. I usually add extra crabmeat to give the soufflé some texture. Most of the preparation—making the crab-shell base and separating the eggs—can be done earlier in the day.

MAKES 6 INDIVIDUAL SOUFFLÉS, 6 FIRST-COURSE SERVINGS

1 small onion, chopped

1 small carrot, chopped

½ celery stalk, chopped

2 tablespoons olive oil

6 live blue crabs, cleaned (see color page 20)

3 medium tomatoes, cut in half crosswise and seeds squeezed out, or 1½ cups drained and seeded canned tomatoes

2 cups fish broth (page 343), chicken broth (page 344), or water

½ teaspoon cayenne pepper

4 tablespoons all-purpose flour

4 tablespoons unsalted butter

3 quarts water

2 tablespoons unsalted butter, softened

¼ cup freshly grated Parmesan cheese or flour

5 egg yolks

½ teaspoon salt

¼ teaspoon white pepper

2 teaspoons finely chopped fresh tarragon (optional)

10 egg whites

10 ounces lump crabmeat (about 2 loosely packed cups)

Cook the vegetables in olive oil in a 4-quart pot over medium heat until soft, about 10 minutes.

Meanwhile, crack the crab legs and bodies with a rolling pin and add them to the softened vegetables. Stir over medium heat until the crab parts have turned red, about 5 minutes. Add the tomatoes and broth, cover the pot, and simmer for 30 minutes, stirring and pounding on the shells

every few minutes with a large wooden spoon or the end of a cleaver.

Strain the mixture through a heavy-duty strainer (the crab shells will poke holes in anything too delicate), pushing hard to extract as much liquid as you can, and then strain again through a fine-mesh strainer into a clean pot. Boil this crab-cooking liquid down to 2 cups. Add the cayenne and set aside.

Prepare a roux by cooking together the flour and 4 tablespoons butter in a 2-quart saucepan over medium heat for about 5 minutes, until the mixture is smooth and has a pleasant toasty smell. Whisk in the crab-cooking liquid and bring the mixture to a boil while whisking—it should turn into a thick paste. If you're making this mixture in advance, cover it with plastic wrap and refrigerate until needed.

About 30 minutes before serving, preheat the oven to 400°F and bring the water to a boil. Butter six 8- to 10-ounce soufflé molds and coat them lightly with cheese or flour. Refrigerate the molds until needed. Beat the egg yolks, salt, pepper, and tarragon into the flour/crab mixture. Beat the egg whites to stiff peaks and whisk about a quarter of the beaten egg whites into the flour/crab mixture. Fold in the crabmeat and the rest of the whites with a rubber spatula.

Fill the prepared molds with the soufflé mixture and smooth the tops with the back of a knife or metal spatula. Wipe off any mixture that drips over the sides. Dip your thumb about ½ inch into one side of each soufflé and rotate the soufflé until you've formed a moat around the entire edge. This helps in the formation of a cap.

Put the soufflés in a small roasting pan or casserole and pour the boiling water around them—it should come between a third and halfway up the sides of the molds. Bake until the soufflés rise about 1½ inches above the rim of the molds, about 15 to 20 minutes. (If you're uncertain whether the soufflés are done, quickly poke into one with a knife and see if the mixture is raw. If so, cook for another 5 minutes and check again.) Serve immediately.

❧

Rolled Seafood Soufflé

The first time I saw a recipe similar to this one, I had to teach it to a group of 20 students at Peter Kump's Cooking School in New York. Fortunately the recipe didn't let me down, and I've ended up teaching it at the school for many years.

This soufflé never fails to get *oohs* and *aahs* because it's presented as a large roll—almost like a rolled chocolate cake—and then sliced at the table. The soufflé itself is actually a cheese soufflé with seafood—at the school we use crab, but you can use any kind of fish or shellfish—rolled up inside. You can use a béchamel sauce or even some of the more elaborate crustacean sauces such as the one for lobster à l'Américaine sauce on page 177 instead of the tomato sauce in the filling.

The tomato sauce can be made up to 2 days in advance or even longer if you freeze it. You can make the soufflé itself up to an hour ahead and keep it warm in the oven. Before setting out to make this soufflé, make sure you have a 12- by 17-inch baking sheet (a standard size) with 1-inch-high sides.

MAKES 8 FIRST-COURSE OR LIGHT MAIN-COURSE SERVINGS

For the Tomato Sauce:

1 onion, finely chopped

2 garlic cloves, finely chopped

2 tablespoons olive oil

8 tomatoes, peeled, seeded, and chopped, or 4 cups drained, seeded, and chopped canned tomatoes

5 fresh thyme sprigs or ½ teaspoon dried

salt and pepper

For the Soufflé:

4 tablespoons unsalted butter

6 tablespoons all-purpose flour

2 cups milk

tiny pinch of nutmeg

pinch of cayenne pepper

½ teaspoon salt

¼ teaspoon pepper

4 egg yolks

2 tablespoons unsalted butter, softened

8 egg whites

½ cup grated Gruyère cheese

½ cup grated Parmesan cheese

2 cups cooked shellfish meat such as crab, shrimp, lobster, or crayfish, cut into about ½-inch cubes

Making the Tomato Sauce: Cook the onion and garlic in the olive oil in a wide pot (the wider the pot, the more quickly the tomatoes will cook down) over medium heat until the onion turns translucent, about 10 minutes. Add the tomatoes and thyme and bring the mixture to a simmer over high heat—the tomatoes will release a lot of liquid—and then turn down the heat to maintain at a simmer. Stir every few minutes to prevent sticking. When the sauce has thickened, after about 30 minutes, season it with salt and pepper to taste and reserve in a covered container in the refrigerator. You should end up with about 2 cups.

Preparing the Soufflé Base: Prepare a roux by stirring together the 4 tablespoons butter and 4 tablespoons flour in a 2-quart saucepan over medium heat until the mixture is smooth and takes on a pleasant, toasty aroma, about 5 minutes. Whisk in the milk and seasonings and bring to a boil, whisking. Boil for about 1 minute, until the mixture is quite thick. Let cool for 2 minutes and stir in the egg yolks, combining thoroughly. Set aside.

Finishing and Baking the Soufflé: Preheat the oven to 400°F. Line a 12- by 17-inch baking sheet with aluminum foil, being sure to cover the sides of the pan. Coat the foil with softened butter, then with the remaining flour. Beat the egg whites to stiff peaks and beat a quarter of the beaten whites into the soufflé base. Fold in the rest of the egg whites with a rubber spatula while sprinkling in the cheese. Spread this mixture evenly over the foil. Bake until the mixture browns on top and doubles in height, about 10 minutes.

Meanwhile, place a kitchen towel, at least as large as the pan, on a counter and cover it with a sheet of plastic wrap. Bring the tomato sauce to a simmer. When the soufflé comes out of the oven, align the baking sheet next to the towel and quickly flip the pan down on top of the towel. Pull off the pan and carefully peel off the foil.

Spread the soufflé with half the tomato sauce and sprinkle on the cubes of shellfish. Carefully lift the towel on one of the long sides of the soufflé and gently roll the soufflé over itself. If you're not serving the soufflé immediately, leave it wrapped in the towel in a 200°F oven for up to an hour.

Serving the Soufflé: Cut the soufflé into three-inch-thick slices and spoon 2 tablespoons of tomato sauce over each serving.

ASPICS

Aspics can be the most delicate, delicious, and elegant of all seafood dishes, and they're completely fat-free. Unfortunately, either our only experience with aspic has been with Jell-O or the aspic-coated dishes we've tasted have been prepared so badly they're like eating rubber.

Originally aspics were simply leftover dishes—usually meat stews—that were served cold, surrounded by their natural juices, which had set into a natural jelly. French chefs, especially in the 19th century, were quick to invent complicated dishes coated in aspic, often set in special decorative molds. The problem with many of these dishes was that for the aspic to hold its shape a large amount of gelatin had to be added. The results may have been visually pleasing, but the rubbery texture was not.

The best aspics are light and delicate and contain only the natural gelatin released by fish or shellfish. They are served, almost melting, next to or combined with cold fish and shellfish.

PREPARING A BASIC FISH ASPIC

The easiest and least expensive way to make fish aspic is to make a fish broth with fish heads and bones and then clarify the broth with some chopped vegetables and egg whites in the same way as for consommé. The clear broth should then be boiled down to concentrate its gelatin. A *small* amount of commercial gelatin is then added to get the aspic to set. The aspic can then be flavored with chopped herbs, flavorful wines, or vegetables cut into tiny cubes and used to coat chilled fish or shellfish.

ABOUT GELATIN

Gelatin is a clear protein that dissolves in warm water. When fish or meat is heated in liquid, certain proteins break down and release gelatin. When a liquid containing a sufficient amount of gelatin is cooled, the gelatin causes the mixture to set.

Commercial gelatin is made from different sources—including pig skin and fish bones—and is sold in either powder form, most popular in the United States, or transparent sheets, popular in Europe. Both forms of gelatin work equally well and can be dissolved in warm liquid (gelatin won't dissolve in cold liquid) to make the liquid set once chilled. Sheet gelatin should be soaked for 5 minutes before it is used and powdered gelatin should be soaked for 30 minutes.

You can concentrate the natural gelatin contained in an aspic by cooking the aspic down on the stove. In this way you'll end up with less aspic, but its natural gelatin will be more concentrated and the aspic will be more likely to set. You can also add commercial gelatin to the warm aspic to get it to set. I usually start out by adding ½ teaspoon powdered unflavored gelatin per cup of aspic. These amounts are half as much as suggested on the package.

Canned broth, while good for some things, won't work for aspics, chaud-froid, or mousses, because it has no (or very little) gelatin—notice how canned broth never sets, even when left in the refrigerator.

∽

Seafood Aspic with Green Herbs

This recipe makes a quart of aspic, which is probably more than you'll need for most recipes, but it's hard to make less, and you can freeze what you don't use. If you can't find all the herbs, just substitute more of one of the others.

MAKES 1 QUART

1 recipe basic fish consommé (page 281)

1 fresh tarragon sprig

1 tablespoon finely chopped fresh chives

1 tablespoon finely chopped fresh chervil

2 tablespoons finely chopped parsley

salt

one ¼-ounce envelope unflavored gelatin, soaked for 30 minutes in 2 tablespoons cold water

Once the consommé has been clarified, add the tarragon and simmer over medium heat until reduced to 1 quart. If specks of egg white appear during this stage, strain the broth a second time through cheesecloth.

Discard the tarragon sprig and stir the other herbs into the simmering broth. Season with salt to taste. (When aspic chills, it tends to taste less salty, so it should taste slightly too salty when hot.) Take the broth off the stove, place a lid on the pot (to keep in the aroma of the herbs), and let cool for about 30 minutes. Stir the gelatin and its soaking liquid into the still-warm aspic until the gelatin dissolves. Pour the aspic into containers. Refrigerate.

USING ASPIC TO COAT WHOLE FISH, FISH FILLETS, AND SHELLFISH

There are two basic methods for coating fish and shellfish with aspic. The most common is to spoon chilled aspic—right on the verge of setting—over chilled whole fish, fillets, or shellfish. You'll need to apply at least two or three coats to end up with a ¼-inch-thick layer of aspic. The second method is to line a mold or small individual molds with aspic, arrange fish or shellfish inside the molds, and top them off with more aspic.

❧

Crayfish, Artichoke, and Wild Mushroom Aspic

*T*his brightly colored aspic is not only delicious, but the textures of the crayfish, mushrooms, and artichokes make it irresistible. While the overall effect may be simple, be prepared to spend money and time in the kitchen making crayfish aspic, cooking and peeling crayfish tails, and trimming and cooking artichokes. My favorite way to serve this aspic is to allow it to set in a decorative mold—I often use a soufflé dish—and then spoon it out into glasses at the table. I like to serve this aspic with a delicate tomato salad, which the guests can spoon over the aspic. And since I'm going all out anyway, I usually serve this dish with a vintage Champagne.

MAKES 6 FIRST-COURSE SERVINGS

For the Crayfish Aspic:

60 live crayfish (about 3 pounds)

2 tablespoons olive oil

1 leek, both white and green parts, chopped

1 carrot, coarsely chopped

2 tomatoes, chopped

1 bunch of parsley, coarsely chopped

1½ quarts fish broth (page 343)

5 egg whites and eggshells

For the Artichokes and Mushrooms:

4 large artichokes

1 lemon

8 medium shiitake mushrooms, stems removed and caps cut into ¼-inch cubes

2 tablespoons finely chopped parsley, chives, or chervil

one or two ¼-ounce envelopes unflavored gelatin if needed

For the Tomato Salad:

4 tomatoes, peeled

1 tablespoon coarse salt

2 teaspoons white wine vinegar

2 tablespoons extra-virgin olive oil

10 fresh basil leaves

Making the Crayfish Broth: Rinse the crayfish with cold water in a colander and sauté them for 5 to 8 minutes—until they turn at least partly red—in olive oil in a large covered pot over high heat. Stir the crayfish every couple of minutes to redistribute them.

Remove the crayfish and twist off the tails and claws, reserving everything. Pull the vein out of the crayfish tails by pinching the piece of shell at the end and giving a gentle pull. Peel the tails, reserving the shells.

Combine the crayfish heads, claws, and shells with the leek, carrot, tomatoes, and parsley in a large pot. Crush the shells with the end of a handleless rolling pin or with the end of a cleaver—this should take about 10 minutes. Pour in the fish broth and simmer the mixture, covered, for 30 minutes, stirring every 10 minutes.

Strain the crayfish broth through a strainer into a clean pot and let cool for 15 minutes. Break up the eggshells with your hands—make sure your hands are clean—and add them to the strained broth. Pour in the egg whites and whisk the mixture vigorously to distribute the whites and shells throughout the broth. Bring the mixture to a slow simmer, simmer for 40 minutes, gently scraping the bottom of the pot once or twice with a wooden spoon to prevent the mixture from sticking, and strain through a triple layer of wet cheesecloth. Simmer the broth to reduce it to 3 cups. Strain the broth a second time through cheesecloth if any specks appear and place in the refrigerator to cool.

Preparing the Artichokes: Trim the artichokes into bottoms (page 144) and rub each bottom with ½ lemon. Place the artichokes in a nonaluminum pot and the juice of ½ lemon (don't throw the whole lemon half in with the artichokes, or it will take over their flavor) and simmer them, partially covered, until they soften yet still feel firm when poked with a knife, about 20 minutes. Drain in a colander, sprinkle with the juice from the other lemon half, and let cool. Carefully pull out and discard the chokes with a spoon and cut the bottoms into approximately ¼-inch cubes. Cover with plastic wrap and refrigerate until needed.

Cooking the Mushrooms and Finishing the Aspic: Rinse the mushroom cubes and simmer them in just enough of the crayfish broth to cover for 10 minutes or until they soften. Sprinkle with parsley during the last 2 minutes of simmering. Place in the refrigerator to cool.

continued

Check the broth in the refrigerator to see if it has set. If not, reheat it slightly and stir in an envelope of gelatin until the gelatin is well dissolved. Chill once again, and if the broth still doesn't set, reheat and stir in the second envelope of gelatin. Chill a 1½-quart soufflé dish or other decorative dish in the refrigerator.

Fill the mold with alternating layers of artichoke cubes, crayfish tails, and mushrooms. Spoon in just enough cool but unset broth to fill the mold, tap it against a hard surface to release any trapped air, and put it back in the refrigerator to set for at least 2 hours.

Making the Tomato Salad: Cut the tomatoes vertically into 6 wedges each. Take the seeds out of each wedge and cut out and discard the inner pulp. Cut the flat outer sections of the tomatoes into small cubes. Toss the cubed tomatoes with coarse salt and drain the tomatoes in a strainer for an hour.

Toss the drained tomatoes with the vinegar, olive oil, and basil leaves, cut into thin shreds at the last minute.

Serving the Aspic: Bring the set aspic to the table in its dish. Spoon the aspic into chilled glasses (small old-fashioned or large balloon wineglasses look great). Pass the tomato salad at the table for guests to spoon over the aspic. Serve immediately.

❧

Cold Trout Fillets with Green Herb Aspic

These glittering trout fillets are best served outside for lunch so the sun catches the light of the herb-specked aspic. This dish can be completely finished the day before. If you're making the green herb aspic at the same time you're cooking the trout, poach the trout in the fish broth you're using for the aspic before you clarify it.

MAKES 6 FIRST-COURSE OR LIGHT MAIN-COURSE SERVINGS

three 1-pound trout

2 quarts fish broth (page 343), vegetable broth (page 66), or water

1 quart seafood aspic with green herbs (page 316) or fish broth from poaching trout to prepare aspic

Arrange the trout in a square casserole or pan just large enough to hold them in a single layer. Bring the fish broth to a simmer and pour it over the trout. Place the pan of trout over medium heat and keep at a slow simmer for about 10 minutes. Check for doneness by sticking a paring knife into a trout along the dorsal fin and gently pulling the fillet away from the spine. If the fillet adheres or appears translucent inside, simmer for 2 minutes more and check again.

When the trout are done, place them on a cutting board and peel off and discard the skin. (You can freeze and reuse the poaching liquid.) Be sure to peel the skin off the trout while they are still hot, or it will stick. Let the trout cool for about 10 minutes and carefully remove the fillets by sliding a small knife along the back and pulling

off the top fillet. Remove the second fillet by just lifting up the trout skeleton with its head. Pull the pin bones out of the fillets with tweezers.

Arrange the fillets, skin side up, on a cake rack set over a clean baking sheet and place the whole rack in the refrigerator for about an hour, until the trout fillets are well chilled.

If the herb aspic is set, put it in a saucepan and heat it while stirring just enough so it melts—it should still feel cool to the touch. Quickly spoon a small amount of the aspic over the trout fillets and put them back in the refrigerator. Coat them again after about 10 minutes and again 10 minutes later. Keep coating the fillets until they are coated with about ¼ inch of aspic.

When the trout fillets are coated, scoop up any remaining aspic—including what has fallen down on the baking sheet—and chop it up on a cutting board. Spread the chopped aspic on a chilled serving platter and arrange the trout fillets on top. Don't take the platter out of the refrigerator until just before serving. Serve each trout fillet on a chilled plate with a small mound of chilled aspic.

USING BEEF OR CHICKEN BROTH FOR SEAFOOD ASPICS

Beef or chicken broth sometimes provides a more subtle backdrop for certain seafood flavors than fish broth. It's also easier to make a quick chicken broth if you can't get perfectly fresh fish heads and bones. The best beef or chicken broth for aspics is made by browning bones and/or meat in the oven before simmering in water.

Salmon and Truffle Aspic

This sublimely delicious and elegant dish looks like a sparkling black sapphire; only when you cut into it do you see the bright orange salmon and the golden aspic. If you don't want to spring for the truffle, finely chopped green herbs and cubes of cooked vegetables such as mushroom or artichoke can also be used between the layers.

MAKES 4 FIRST-COURSE SERVINGS

1 recipe clear chicken broth (page 344)

¾ pound salmon fillet with skin, pin bones removed

2 tablespoons extra-virgin olive oil

salt and pepper

one 1- to 1½-ounce fresh or frozen black truffle

½ teaspoon powdered unflavored gelatin soaked in 1 tablespoon cold water for 30 minutes, until dissolved, if needed

Gently simmer the chicken broth for about 45 minutes until only 1½ cups remains. Skim off and discard any fat or froth that floats to the broth's surface, strain through a fine-mesh strainer, and reserve in the refrigerator.

Using a long thin knife, slice the salmon into 5-inch squares ⅛ inch thick. This is the same method used for slicing smoked salmon and may take a little practice. If you're having a hard time, put the salmon in the freezer for about 20 minutes—just long enough to give it a firmer texture, not long enough to freeze it. Preheat the oven to 300°F.

Place each slice on a small square of aluminum foil brushed very lightly with olive oil. Sprinkle the slices with salt and pepper. Place the sheets of aluminum foil with the salmon slices on a baking sheet and bake for approximately 2 minutes or until the surface of the salmon just begins to turn pink and slightly opaque. Do not allow the slices to cook all the way through. Remove the slices from the oven and let cool in the refrigerator.

Peel the truffle, chop the peelings, and slice the truffle as thinly as you can, with a benriner cutter (a Japanese slicer) if available. A large truffle should provide approximately 60 very thin slices.

Cover each salmon slice with the chopped peelings and the sliced truffles, saving half the slices for lining the mold. Gently stack the truffle-covered slices of salmon, leaving the slices on the aluminum foil. Place the stack on a plate, cover with plastic wrap, and refrigerate for 2 to 3 hours so the aroma of the truffle permeates the salmon.

Check the chilled concentrated chicken broth, which should have the consistency of firm jelly. If it remains runny or seems too loose to hold together, warm it on the stove and stir in the dissolved gelatin. If the chilled broth has the right consistency, simply warm it in a saucepan. Remove the broth from the heat and add the chopped truffle peelings and the remaining truffle slices. Cover the saucepan and let it cool for 20 minutes to flavor the broth with the truffles.

Strain the truffle-flavored broth into a mixing bowl and place the bowl over a bowl of ice. Stir the broth until it is cold but not set.

Place a 1 quart round-bottomed bowl in a bowl of ice. Pour about ¼ cup of the chilled broth into the bowl and keep spinning the bowl so the broth goes up along the sides and sets. Repeat this with more jelly until there is a ¼-inch-thick layer of jelly around the inside of the bowl.

Line the inside of the bowl with the simmered truffle slices (in the strainer) so that none of the bowl is visible from the inside.

Fill the bowl with alternating layers of the truffled salmon slices and the almost-set truffle-flavored broth. Continue until the bowl is full and all the ingredients have been used. Cover the bowl with plastic wrap and refrigerate for 2 hours or overnight.

To serve the salmon, place the bowl in another bowl of hot water for 10 to 15 seconds. Place a silver tray upside down over the bowl and flip the whole thing over, carefully holding the bowl against the tray. Lift off the bowl. If you've found that any of the truffles have stuck to the inside of the bowl, just peel them off and use them to cover up any exposed pieces of salmon. Spoon the aspic onto chilled plates at the table.

CHAUD-FROID

Chaud-froid (pronounced "show fwah") is almost the same as aspic except that cream is added so the aspic becomes white or pale brown and completely opaque. Cream has a way of amplifying subtle flavors, so I sometimes make a chaud-froid to take advantage of truffles, mushrooms, tomatoes, and certain herbs. Chaud-froid is also easier to make than aspic because you don't have to worry if the aspic is perfectly clear—the cream clouds it anyway. And if you're serving cold fish fillets, you can mask any imperfections in your filleting technique with chaud-froid.

I like to add ingredients such as pureed tomatoes, saffron, finely chopped herbs, and chopped mushrooms to chaud-froid to vary its color and texture.

～

Striped Bass Fillets with Tomato Chaud-Froid and Parsley Vinaigrette

*T*hese lightly coated fillets make a delicious main course for an outdoor luncheon. Any lean white fish fillets can be used, but I often use striped bass because it is easy to find fresh and I can then use the heads and bones for making the basic broth. One way to prepare a seafood chaud-froid is to make a fish broth with the striped bass heads and bones and then reduce it by half to concentrate its gelatin, but the chaud-froid sometimes ends up too fishy. A better method is to make fish broth with the heads and bones but use a gelatinous chicken broth instead of water. The easiest method, given here, is to add a small amount of powdered gelatin to the fish broth instead of reducing it.

MAKES 8 LIGHT MAIN-COURSE SERVINGS

For the Chaud-Froid:

four 1-pound striped bass, filleted, skin removed, heads and bones reserved

1 medium onion, sliced

4 tomatoes, seeded and coarsely chopped

3 fresh tarragon sprigs or 1 bouquet garni: 3 fresh thyme sprigs or ¼ teaspoon dried, a small bunch of parsley, and a bay leaf tied up with string (or in cheesecloth for dried thyme)

1 cup dry white wine

one ¼-ounce envelope powdered unflavored gelatin, soaked for 30 minutes in 2 tablespoons water

2 tablespoons finely chopped fresh chives or chervil

1 cup heavy cream

2 tablespoons white wine vinegar or sherry vinegar

salt and white pepper

For the Parsley Vinaigrette:

leaves from 1 bunch of flat-leaf parsley

¼ cup white wine vinegar

2 teaspoons Dijon mustard

½ cup extra-virgin olive oil

salt and pepper

Making the Chaud-Froid: Pull the pin bones out of the bass fillets with tweezers and refrigerate the fillets. Take the gills out of the bass heads and soak the bones and heads in cold water for 30 minutes. Combine the heads and bones, onion, tomatoes, tarragon, and wine in a 4-quart pot and add barely enough cold water— about a quart—to cover. Bring to a slow simmer and simmer gently for 30 minutes. Strain first through a regular strainer, pushing hard to force through the tomato pulp, and a second time through a fine-mesh strainer.

Pour the fish broth into a pan just large enough to hold the fish fillets in a single layer. Bring the broth to a simmer and gently poach the fillets for about 6 minutes (8 minutes per inch of thickness). You may have to poach in 2 stages if your pan isn't large enough. Transfer the fillets, in a single layer, to a plate and refrigerate until chilled thoroughly.

Stir the gelatin with its soaking liquid into the fish broth used for poaching the fish. Stir the chopped herbs into the broth and chill the broth in the refrigerator or, if you're in a hurry, over a bowl of ice. When the broth is cool but not set, stir in the cream and vinegar and season with salt and pepper to taste.

Arrange the chilled fillets, skin side up, on a cake rack set over a clean baking sheet and spoon on the chaud-froid. Chill the fish for 10 minutes in the refrigerator or freezer and repeat until the fillets are covered with about a ¼-inch-thick layer of the chaud-froid. If the chaud-froid in the bowl starts to set, warm it on the stove while stirring to loosen it up, but be careful not to overheat it or it will melt the layers of chaud-froid already on the fish.

Making the Parsley Vinaigrette: Don't prepare the parsley vinaigrette more than 15 minutes before serving, or the flavor of the parsley will turn stale.

Combine the parsley leaves, vinegar, and mustard in a blender and blend at high speed until the parsley is very finely chopped. You'll probably need to push the parsley down several times with a wooden spoon to get it to move around. Strain the mixture through a fine-mesh strainer into a small mixing bowl. Gently whisk the olive oil into the strained parsley mixture and season with salt and pepper to taste.

Serving: Spoon 2 tablespoons of the parsley vinaigrette onto each of 8 chilled plates. Carefully place a chaud-froid-coated fillet on top of the sauce.

Substitutes Fillets of blackfish, black sea bass, flatfish, grouper, red snapper, rockfish, tilefish

MOUSSES

Fish and shellfish mousses are one of those great classics of French cooking that had a momentary craze after the invention of the food processor. Seafood mousses then died a rather sudden death, in part because they contain velouté (roux-thickened broth) and lightly whipped cream—undesirable ingredients when fat became taboo. Admittedly, seafood mousse is not everyday fare, but I do occasionally like to start a fancy dinner with something rich and luxurious.

A fish or shellfish mousse has almost the same texture as a mousseline except that a mousse is always served cold while a mousseline is often served hot, and a mousse is made from cooked seafood while a mousseline is made from raw. The classic approach to making a seafood mousse is to combine cooked and pureed fish or shellfish with the velouté, aspic, and cream and allow the mousse to set in a metal mold, usually lined with aspic. I use a similar method but leave the flour out of the broth and just reduce it to intensify its flavor and its natural gelatin. Because I don't bother lining the mold with aspic, I can get by using a simple broth instead of a clarified aspic. I like to mold mousses in either individual molds such as dariole molds (3- to 4-ounce metal molds that look like large cocktail jiggers) or ½-cup ramekins.

~

Individual Shrimp Mousses

These rich little mousses will startle your guests because for all their creamy delicacy they are intensely flavorful. If you can't find shrimp with their heads—essential for deep flavor—you can make these mousses with crayfish, lobster, or smaller crabs such as blue crabs. Although these mousses are complicated, you can make them a day ahead.

MAKES 8 FIRST-COURSE SERVINGS

2 pounds large or extra-large shrimp with heads (you should have about 60 shrimp)

2 tablespoons olive oil

1 medium carrot, coarsely chopped

1 medium onion, coarsely chopped

1 garlic clove, crushed

½ celery stalk, coarsely chopped

4 tomatoes, chopped

3 fresh tarragon sprigs or 1 bouquet garni: 3 fresh thyme sprigs or ¼ teaspoon dried, a large bunch of parsley, and a bay leaf tied up with string (or in cheesecloth for dried thyme)

6 cups chicken broth (page 344)

½ envelope powdered gelatin soaked in 1 tablespoon cold water for 30 minutes if needed

1 cup heavy cream

salt and pepper

1 ounce sevruga or osetra caviar or 1 tomato, peeled, seeded, and cubed, and 8 fresh chervil sprigs

Sauté the shrimp in the olive oil in a sauté pan over high heat for about 5 minutes, until the shrimp turn completely red. Let the shrimp cool, twist off the heads, and peel the tails, reserving the heads and shells.

Combine the shrimp shells and heads and chopped vegetables in a food processor—you may have to do this in 2 or 3 batches—and puree for

about 1 minute. Combine the pureed shrimp/vegetable mixture with the tomatoes, tarragon, and broth in a 4-quart pot and simmer gently for about 40 minutes. Strain through a fine-mesh strainer. Boil to reduce the broth to 2 cups. Reserve the broth in the refrigerator—over a bowl of ice if you're in a hurry. When the broth is well chilled, check its consistency. If it's not that of a firm jelly, gently warm 1 cup of the shrimp broth in a saucepan and stir in the gelatin with its soaking liquid until it melts.

Devein the shrimp if necessary and reserve 16 shrimp. Puree the rest of the shrimp in a food processor and chill the puree in the refrigerator in a covered bowl.

Chill eight 4-ounce ramekins or dariole molds.

Cut 8 of the reserved shrimp into ¼-inch cubes and combine them with the pureed shrimp. Whip the cream over ice or in a chilled bowl to medium stiffness. Stir 1 cup of barely melted shrimp broth (the cup with the gelatin if the gelatin was needed) into the puree and then gently fold in the cream. Season with salt and pepper to taste and gently fill the molds with the mousse mixture. Tap each mold firmly on the counter to drive up any air bubbles.

Chill the mousses for at least 2 hours. Unmold the mousses by dipping each mold in a bowl of hot water for about 10 seconds, quickly running a knife around the insides, and then inverting a chilled plate over each mold and turning the whole thing over. You may need to tap on the molds to get the mousses out.

Depending on its consistency, the remaining chilled shrimp broth can be spooned out next to each mousse as a sauce or a lightly set aspic. Place one of the reserved shrimp on each plate and decorate each mousse with a tiny spoonful of caviar or chopped tomato and chervil sprig. Serve immediately.

USING PUFF PASTRY

bouchées, vol-au-vents, and feuilletées

Each of these pastries is made with *pâte feuilletée* better known as puff pastry. You don't have to make your own, because very good quality puff pastry is available frozen in sheets in gourmet stores and even some supermarkets. When buying puff pastry, check the ingredients to make sure it's made with butter and doesn't contain any margarine (which usually appears euphemistically on the label as hydrogenated something-or-other). Puff pastry made with margarine may rise adequately, but it doesn't taste good.

A FEW PUFF PASTRY DEFINITIONS

bouchée: This is a little puff pastry cup sometimes used for holding miniature shellfish ragouts. In more modern French cooking bouchées have been replaced largely by the lighter feuilletées.

feuilletée: This term can refer to the pastry itself or a square or rectangle of baked puff pastry used to present fish or shellfish. Feuilletées represent a more contemporary alternative to bouchées and vol-au-vents.

fleuron: This is a miniature crescent or fish-shaped piece of puff pastry used as a decoration on plates of fish or shellfish.

mille-feuille: This is the French word for the American napoleon—a rectangular stack of puff pastry layers containing pastry cream. Placing pieces of fish between delicate cooked layers of puff pastry is popular in French restaurants.

vol-au-vent: This is a large dome-shaped version of a bouchée and is (or was) used for holding and serving various ragouts for more than one person.

~

Bay Scallop Bouchées

This is just one of many examples of how you can use puff pastry bouchées to turn a simple dish of sautéed seafood into an elegant first course or light main course with very little effort. Bouchées can be used for any combination of sautéed seafood and vegetables.

Bouchées are best baked just before serving so you can serve them straight out of the oven, but the raw bouchées can be completely assembled several days in advance, left on the baking sheet, and frozen. You can then take them straight out of the freezer, brush them with a little egg, and put them in the oven.

MAKES 8 FIRST-COURSE OR LIGHT MAIN-COURSE SERVINGS

2 pounds puff pastry

all-purpose flour

1 egg

1 teaspoon salt

1½ pounds bay scallops

2 tablespoons extra-virgin olive oil

2 shallots, finely chopped

¼ cup finely chopped parsley

2 garlic cloves, finely chopped and crushed to a paste

salt and pepper

1 tablespoon fresh lemon juice

Preparing the Bouchées: Roll the puff pastry into a ³⁄₁₆-inch-thick sheet (about the thickness of 2 dimes) on a floured surface. Cut 16 rounds out of the pastry with a 3-inch fluted cookie cutter (or cut around an inverted glass or cup with a sharp knife). Place 8 of the rounds upside down on a baking sheet sprinkled lightly with cold water. Brush the rounds with

cold water. Cut 2-inch rounds out of the center of the 8 remaining rounds with a 2-inch cookie cutter and place them next to the larger rounds on the pan. Place the outer rings left from the small cutouts on top of the wet rounds on the pan. Press gently to attach the rings.

Place the pan in the refrigerator or freezer for at least 10 minutes but up to a week if needed. If you're freezing the bouchées for more than a day, cover the pan with aluminum foil. Immediately before baking, combine the egg and salt in a small bowl and beat for about 2 minutes with a whisk, until the egg turns dark and becomes very runny. Carefully brush this egg wash on the top rims of the bouchées, being careful not to let any drip down the sides (which could keep the pastry from rising).

Baking the Bouchées: Preheat the oven to 400°F and slide in the tray of chilled or frozen bouchées. Check the bouchées after about 12 minutes to see how they're browning. Continue checking every 5 minutes until the bouchées are golden brown and then turn the oven down to 250°F. Continue baking for 20 minutes more to make sure the pastry cooks all the way through. Sometimes when the bouchées are done you'll find that the inside center has risen almost as much as the sides so there's no room to put the scallops. If this happens, cut carefully around the inside of the outer rim with a sharp knife, lift out the top crispy part of the center ring, and peel out any excess dough. Replace the crispy ring.

Sautéing the Scallops and Serving the Bouchées: Rinse the scallops, dry thoroughly, and pull off the small muscle running up the sides. Heat the olive oil in a sauté pan over high heat until the oil barely begins to smoke and toss in the scallops and shallots. Toss over high heat for about 2 minutes, sprinkle with the parsley, garlic, salt, and pepper, and continue tossing or stirring over high heat for 1 minute. Sprinkle with lemon juice and spoon immediately into the hot bouchées. Place a lid atop each bouchée and serve immediately.

Note: The purpose of sautéing over very high heat is to brown the scallops and seal in the juices, but the scallops sometimes release juices so quickly that it is impossible to get them to brown. If this happens, transfer the scallops to a bowl with a slotted spoon after they've been sautéed for about 2 minutes and boil down the juices in the sauté pan until only about 2 teaspoons remain. Stir the parsley, garlic, and seasonings into the juices—if you haven't already sprinkled them over the scallops—and toss the scallops in their reduced juices over high heat for 1 minute more. Serve in the hot bouchées.

❦

Sautéed Boneless Cod Steaks with Oyster Sauce in Feuilletées

When perfectly fresh, whole cod provides delicious delicately flavored steaks. If you can't find it, use one of the substitutes listed below.

Because larger pieces of fish won't fit into a bouchée, they're better served loosely enclosed in a rectangular feuilletée. This is also true of dishes with sauce, where the sauce would end up absorbed by the bouchée instead of staying on the plate or on the fish. In this dish both the shape and texture of the rectangular feuilletée contrast with the round cod steak.

This dish is at its best when everything is synchronized so each component is ready at the same time, but to avoid going crazy you can cook the leeks and the feuilletées and shuck the oysters (or have them shucked) earlier in the day. The oyster sauce can be prepared up to an hour in advance.

MAKES 6 MAIN-COURSE SERVINGS

six 6- to 8-ounce cod steaks, center bone removed, shaped into rounds, and tied with string (see color page 25)

all-purpose flour

1 pound puff pastry

1 egg

1 teaspoon salt

3 leeks, including 1 inch of green, cut into fine julienne

6 tablespoons unsalted butter

1 cup dry white wine

1 shallot, finely chopped

18 oysters

1 tablespoon fresh lemon juice

1 tablespoon finely chopped fresh chives or parsley

salt and pepper

2 tablespoons olive oil

Remove any pin bones that stick out the sides of the cod steaks and reserve the steaks on a plate in the refrigerator.

Preparing and Baking the Feuilletées: If you're baking the puff pastry right away, preheat the oven to 400°F. On a floured surface, roll the puff pastry into a $3/16$-inch-thick (the thickness of 2 dimes) rectangle measuring $9^1/2$ by $5^1/2$ inches. Quickly cut away a $1/4$-inch-wide strip all around the pastry rectangle with a sharp knife to get rid of the crimped edges that may prevent the pastry from rising. Cut six $1^1/2$- by 5-inch rectangles out of the puff pastry rectangle with a sharp chef's knife (cut quickly to

avoid crimping the edges of the pastry) and quickly place the rectangles upside down on a baking sheet sprinkled with cold water. Put the baking sheet in the refrigerator or freezer for at least 15 minutes. (You can leave the pastry on the pan in the freezer for up to a week if you cover it with aluminum foil.)

Immediately before baking, combine the egg and salt in a small bowl and beat for about 2 minutes with a whisk, until the egg turns dark and becomes very runny. Carefully brush a thin layer of this egg wash onto the tops of the rectangles, being careful not to let any drip down the sides. Gently cut a series of about 10 diagonal lines, about $1/16$ inch deep, across the top of the rectangles and slide the pan into the oven. Check the feuilletée rectangles after about 12 minutes to see how they're browning. Continue checking every 5 minutes until the rectangles are golden brown and then turn the oven down to 250°F. Continue baking for 20 minutes to make sure the pastry cooks all the way through.

When the feuilletées are done, cut through them horizontally and carefully pull out any raw or undercooked dough in the center. If you're making the feuilletées in advance, you'll need to reheat them gently before serving.

Cooking the Leeks: Cook the leeks in 1 tablespoon butter in a heavy pot over low to medium heat for about 20 minutes, until they're soft to the bite but not mushy. Refrigerate until needed.

Making the Oyster Sauce: Combine the wine and shallot in a saucepan and gently reduce to $1/4$ cup. Shuck the oysters into another saucepan and heat gently until the oysters curl slightly, about 3 minutes. Don't let the liquid boil. Transfer the oysters to a clean kitchen towel or cloth napkin with a slotted spoon and pour the poaching liquid through a fine-mesh strainer into the reduced shallot mixture. Reduce the shallot mixture again to ¼ cup and whisk in the lemon juice, remaining butter, and chopped herbs. Season with salt and pepper to taste and put the oysters back in the sauce. Remove from the heat.

Cooking the Cod Steaks and Assembling the Finished Dish: Season the cod steaks with salt and pepper and coat them with 2 tablespoons flour, being sure to pat off any excess.

Sauté the steaks in the olive oil over high heat for about 4 minutes on each side (8 minutes total per inch of thickness) and transfer to a paper towel–covered plate to soak up any cooked oil. Remove the string and peel off the skin.

Gently reheat the oysters in their sauce. Place a bottom feuilletée on each plate, spread on a layer of leeks, place a steak on top, and spoon a tablespoon of sauce and 3 oysters over each steak, letting the sauce drip down the sides onto the plate. Place the feuilletée lid on top and serve immediately.

Substitutes Firm-fleshed fish steaks such as Atlantic pollack, haddock, king mackerel, salmon, shark, swordfish, tuna, wolffish

Salmon and Smoked Salmon Mousse Napoleons

A napoleon is a sweet pastry made traditionally by spreading thin layers of baked puff pastry with pastry cream. In this version smoked salmon mousse and lightly cooked fresh salmon replace the pastry cream, and the salmon napoleon is served as an elegant little first course.

The smoked salmon mousse gets its consistency entirely from crème fraîche and butter—a great technique for making a silky smooth mousse. The trick to making these napoleons light and delicate is to bake the puff pastry in thin layers and then slice the layers horizontally in half so they end up containing half as much pastry as a classic napoleon.

The napoleons should be put together within a couple of hours of serving so the pastry won't get soggy. The mousse, however, can be made a day or two in advance and the fresh salmon cooked earlier in the day.

MAKES 8 FIRST-COURSE SERVINGS

For the Smoked Salmon Mousse:

6 ounces smoked salmon

¼ pound unsalted butter

½ cup crème fraîche

salt and pepper

For the Pastry:

½ pound puff pastry

all-purpose flour

1 tablespoon unsalted butter, softened

For the Salmon and Final Assembly:

1½ pounds center-cut or tail-end salmon fillet with skin

1 tablespoon olive oil

salt and pepper

3 tablespoons very finely chopped parsley or ¼ pound sevruga or osetra caviar

Making the Smoked Salmon Mousse: Puree the smoked salmon and butter in a miniature food processor until the mixture is smooth, about 2 minutes. (You can use a standard food processor, but you'll need to scrape the mixture off the insides of the food processor continually to get it to turn around.)

Transfer the mixture to a small mixing bowl and work in the crème fraîche with a small whisk. Don't overwork the mixture, or the crème fraîche may separate. Season to taste with salt—it will need very little because of the saltiness of the smoked salmon—and pepper and keep covered in the refrigerator until needed.

Preparing and Baking the Puff Pastry: Roll the puff pastry into an ⅛-inch-thick square slightly larger than 8 inches on each side on a floured surface. Because you are rolling the pastry so thin, you may have to do the rolling in 2 stages. Whatever you do, don't force the pastry—if it becomes elastic or hard to roll, put it on a baking sheet and refrigerate for at least 30 minutes before rolling some more. Trim the edges of the pastry with a sharp chef's knife to make a perfect square.

Preheat the oven to 375°F. Cut the square in half so you end up with 2 rectangles, each 4 by 8 inches. Place the pastry rectangles on a baking sheet sprinkled with cold water. Brush the bottom of a second baking sheet—the same size as the first—with butter and place it on top of the pastry. (This prevents the pastry from rising, keeping it in a thin crispy layer.) Bake for 30 minutes. Check the pastry—lift up the top baking sheet—after 15 minutes to make sure the pastry rectangles aren't getting too dark; if they are, turn the oven down to 325°F.

Gently transfer the pastry rectangles to a cutting board and slice through them horizontally with a long bread knife so you end up with 4 very thin rectangles (you'll use only 3). Set these aside. Don't panic if you cut through one of the rectangles with the bread knife—you can use any broken pieces for the bottom or middle layers.

Slicing and Cooking the Fresh Salmon: Preheat the oven to 350°F.

Slice the fresh salmon lengthwise into sheets between 1/8 and 1/4 inch thick. Arrange the salmon slices on a baking sheet brushed with olive oil and bake until the edges of the salmon just begin to turn pink and opaque, about 2 minutes. Lightly season the salmon with salt and pepper and refrigerate the whole pan for 20 minutes.

Assembling and Serving the Napoleons: Dollop a small spoonful of the smoked salmon mousse on a small baking sheet to hold the pastry in place while you're constructing the napoleons. Place one of the rectangles on the baking sheet—save the best-looking rectangle for the top—and arrange the salmon slices in an even layer on the rectangle. Using a thin metal spatula (preferably an offset spatula), spread a quarter of the smoked salmon mousse in an even layer on top of the salmon. Place a second pastry rectangle over the salmon and spread on half of the remaining mousse. Set the third pastry rectangle on top of this whole assembly, being sure that the smooth bottom of the last pastry rectangle becomes the top of the napoleons. (The bottom is smoother and more even.)

With a small spatula, carefully spread a very thin layer of mousse over the top. Spread the remaining mousse around the sides of this layered rectangle in much the same way as icing a cake, filling up any spaces as you go. With a sharp bread knife, slice the rectangle crosswise into 8 small rectangles, each an individual napoleon. Rinse the knife off between slices.

Minutes before serving, sprinkle each napoleon with chopped parsley or very gently spread the caviar in an even layer on top. Place each napoleon on a cool plate and serve immediately.

❧

Tomato, Cucumber, and Fresh Crab Napoleon

I first encountered this dish in Joël Robuchon's legendary Paris restaurant, Jamin. As so often seems to happen in the greatest restaurants, the presentation of the dish took me by surprise. I expected to find pieces of crab and cucumber between thin layers of puff pastry, in typical napoleon fashion. What arrived instead was a completely flourless construction where the outer pulp of ripe tomatoes replaced the puff pastry. The result was light, delicate, and bursting with flavor.

Even though I've tried to simplify the dish somewhat in re-creating it here, this is a painstaking dish that will probably take most of the afternoon. The first time you make it, don't try it for more than 4 people.

MAKES 4 FIRST-COURSE SERVINGS

6 large bright-red ripe tomatoes, all the same size, peeled

coarse salt

1/2 cup heavy cream

leaves from 2 fresh tarragon sprigs, finely chopped

1 cup fresh crabmeat

salt and pepper

1 regular cucumber, peeled

1 tablespoon finely chopped fresh chives

Carefully cut a slice off the top and bottom of the tomatoes so the tomatoes each end up 1 1/2 inches high. Reserve the slices. Make sure you cut the same amount off the top and bottom so the amount of exposed pulp on each side of the tomato is the same. Cut around the inside of the tomato with a sharp paring knife through both the top and bottom openings to detach most of the pulp from the sides of the tomatoes. Push the pulp out through the openings and reserve with the tomato tops and bottoms for the sauce. Cut vertically through one side of each of the tomatoes and carefully spread open the tomatoes into strips. Cut away, spoon out, and reserve any remaining pulp from each tomato. Sprinkle the 6 tomato strips on both sides with coarse salt and place them on a cake rack over a baking sheet in the refrigerator to drain for about an hour.

Gently simmer the tops, bottoms, and inside pulp from the tomatoes in a saucepan for about 10 minutes. Add half of the cream to the tomato mixture and simmer for 5 minutes more. Strain into a clean saucepan and simmer for 5 to 10 minutes more, until the mixture becomes very stiff. Let this sauce cool. Stir in the tarragon and crabmeat and season with salt and pepper to taste. Cover with plastic wrap in a small bowl and refrigerate.

Slice the cucumber into strips about 1/8 inch thick with a mandoline or vegetable slicer and slice each strip into fine julienne. The easiest way to slice a cucumber into strips is to cut off one end so the cucumber can be stood up on end and then slice 1 or 2 slices off each of the 4 sides, down to the seedy center section. Slice across the julienne strips so you end up with ⅛-inch cubes. Sprinkle the cubes generously with salt and place them in a fine-mesh strainer over a bowl in the refrigerator to drain for at least 30 minutes.

Boil the remaining cream in a small saucepan until reduced by about half and very thick. Stir in the chives and let cool. Just before you're ready to assemble the napoleons, put the cucumber cubes in a kitchen towel and squeeze tightly to eliminate excess water. Stir the cucumbers into the cream/chive mixture. Season with pepper to taste.

Assembling the Napoleons: Cut the strips of tomato in half so you end up with 12 strips each measuring about 4 by 1½ inches. Place 4 of these tomato strips on a clean flat surface and carefully spread all the cucumber mixture in a thin even layer over each one. Place a second tomato strip on top of the cucumber mixture and spread on a layer of the crab mixture. Place a third tomato strip on top. Carefully transfer the napoleons to chilled plates and serve.

QUICHE

After the quiche's couple of decades in the limelight, I'm afraid that the craze is finally on the wane. I for one got a little tired of being offered the same combinations of insipid, undercooked vegetables in soggy crust anytime I went to an inexpensive restaurant for lunch.

Seafood—especially shellfish—makes a great quiche because it's full of flavor and retains its texture when baked. Making a quiche is also a great way to turn very little seafood into something substantial enough for a light meal.

I never follow a recipe for quiche but instead reach into the refrigerator and pull out whatever I think might go with whatever seafood I've chosen. This almost always includes onion and garlic, often tomatoes, and usually some thyme or marjoram I have growing up on the roof. A quiche should always contain at least some milk or cream and of course eggs to hold the whole thing together. I just figure out how much liquid my quiche pan will hold and then calculate based on 1 egg per ¾ cup of liquid—usually I use 2 or 3 eggs. The custard mixture for the quiche usually consists mostly of milk and eggs flavored with some lightly cooked onion, garlic, and herbs, but if you want to take the time and make the quiche more flavorful, you can make a flavor base with shrimp or crayfish heads or lobster or crab shells—as though you were making a sauce or soup—and reduce the flavor base before combining it with an equal amount of milk. Seafood used for making quiche should be precooked lightly, or it will release liquid into the custard during baking and each piece of seafood will be surrounded by a little puddle.

If you don't want to make your own pie dough, you can use store-bought dough, but check the ingredients carefully to make sure the dough is made only with butter and that it contains nothing suspect (hydrogenated this-or-that, preservatives, etc.).

LINING AND PREBAKING A QUICHE SHELL

One of the mistakes often made by beginning cooks is undercooking—or not cooking at all—the pastry in a quiche pan before adding the custard filling. Once you pour in the custard mixture, the pie dough won't cook anymore, so it must be *completely* cooked in advance.

To precook a quiche shell, line it with pie dough, cover with a sheet of aluminum foil, and fill it with dried beans. Bake the shell in an oven preheated to 400°F until the outer rim of the shell turns pale brown, about 15 minutes. Take out the beans (save them) and foil and continue baking the shell until it turns pale brown in the center, about 10 minutes more. Let cool for at least 5 minutes before pouring in the custard mixture.

PIE DOUGH FOR QUICHE

1¼ cups all-purpose flour

10 tablespoons unsalted butter, cut into
    ½-inch cubes and frozen

1 egg yolk

1½ tablespoons heavy cream

½ teaspoon salt

MAKES ¾ POUND, ENOUGH FOR ONE 10-INCH QUICHE

Combine all the ingredients in a food processor and pulse for about 30 seconds. Keep the processor on until the dough starts to come together but doesn't quite yet form a ball. Turn the dough out onto the work surface and knead it very quickly, just long enough to get it to hold together.

❧

Scallop Quiche

I especially like this version of scallop quiche because it contains garlic and tomatoes and has such a bright and savory flavor. While scallops are especially simple to use in a quiche, this method can also be used for shrimp.

MAKES ONE 10-INCH QUICHE, ENOUGH FOR 8 FIRST-COURSE OR 6 LIGHT MAIN-COURSE SERVINGS

1 recipe pie dough (see box)

¾ pound scallops, small white muscle removed, rinsed, and dried

2 tablespoons olive oil

1 garlic clove, finely chopped

1 shallot, finely chopped

salt and pepper

2 tablespoons finely chopped parsley

1 tomato, peeled, seeded, and chopped

½ cup dry white wine

½ cup milk

3 eggs, beaten

Line a 10-inch quiche pan with pie dough, making sure the dough comes well up the sides of the pan. Prebake the pastry (see box on page 326).

If the scallops are large, cut them into ⅓-inch-thick disks. Sauté the scallops in the olive oil in a sauté pan over high heat for about 1 minute. Sprinkle the scallops with the garlic, shallot, salt, and pepper and sauté for 1 minute more. Sprinkle with parsley and sauté for another 30 seconds. Slide the scallops into a mixing bowl to let cool. Add the tomato and wine to the still-hot sauté pan and simmer for about 5 minutes to cook the alcohol out of the wine. Let cool in the pan. Preheat the oven to 275°F.

Arrange the scallops on the prebaked quiche shell, leaving any juices in the mixing bowl. Combine the cooked tomato mixture and the milk in the mixing bowl containing the scallop juices. Season with salt and pepper to taste and stir in the beaten eggs. Pour the mixture over the scallops.

Bake the quiche on a baking sheet (so you don't mess up your oven if it overflows) until it sets, for 45 minutes to 1 hour. (Gently move the pan back and forth, watching the center of the quiche—when it's set, it won't swish back and forth.) Serve immediately.

Crayfish and Sorrel Quiche

(color page 7)

This quiche is somewhat elaborate, but with the intense wonderful flavor of crayfish I think it elevates the quiche to new heights. The sorrel gives the quiche a zesty tang, but don't worry if you can't find it—you can leave it out or use spinach instead. You can use this recipe for shrimp, provided they still have their heads (for flavoring the custard).

MAKES ONE 10-INCH QUICHE, ENOUGH FOR 6 FIRST-COURSE OR LIGHT MAIN-COURSE SERVINGS

1 recipe pie dough (see box)

3 pounds live crayfish

2 tablespoons olive oil

1 garlic clove, finely chopped

2 shallots, finely chopped

½ teaspoon fresh thyme or marjoram leaves, finely chopped, or ¼ teaspoon dried

2 tomatoes, peeled, seeded, and chopped

1 cup dry white wine

2 tightly packed cups sorrel leaves (about ½ pound)

salt and pepper

½ cup heavy cream

3 eggs, beaten

Line a 10-inch quiche pan with pie dough and prebake it (see box on page 326).

Preparing the Crayfish: Rinse the crayfish with cold water in a colander and sauté them in olive oil in a large covered pot over high heat for 5 to 8 minutes—until they turn at least partly red. Stir the crayfish every few minutes so they're redistributed and cook evenly. Take the cooked crayfish out of the pot and sauté the garlic, shallots, and thyme leaves in the remaining hot oil for about 2 minutes. Add the tomatoes and wine and simmer gently for 10 minutes. Let cool.

Twist the tails and claws off the crayfish, reserving the claws and heads in separate bowls. (The claws are cracked by hand because their hard shells can damage the food processor blade.) Pull the vein out of the crayfish tails by pinching the piece of shell at the end and giving a gentle pull. Peel the tails, putting the shells with the reserved heads.

Combine the crayfish heads and shells (but not the claws) with the tomato/white wine mixture in a food processor and puree the mixture for about 1 minute.

Crack the reserved crayfish claws with a rolling pin and combine them with the crayfish/tomato mixture in a 2-quart pot. Bring the mixture to a slow simmer and simmer gently for 20 minutes. Strain through a regular strainer—pushing with a wooden spoon to extract as much liquid as possible—and then again through a fine-mesh strainer into a small saucepan. Boil the crayfish liquid down until only ¾ cup remains.

Preparing the Sorrel: Stir the sorrel leaves in a 4-quart pot over medium heat until they melt and turn gray, about 4 minutes. Simmer gently, uncovered, for about 10 minutes, until the liquid released by the sorrel evaporates. Stir every minute or two to prevent sticking. Season with salt and pepper to taste and spread evenly over the prebaked quiche shell.

Assembling and Baking the Quiche: Preheat the oven to 275°F. Spread the crayfish tails over the sorrel. Whisk together the reduced crayfish liquid and the cream and season with salt and pepper to taste. Whisk in the beaten eggs and pour the mixture into the quiche shell. Bake on a baking sheet (to catch drips) until the quiche sets, 45 minutes to an hour. Serve immediately.

Sauces and Salsas, Condiments and Broths

FLAVORED BUTTERS

A slice or dollop of flavored butter is a great way to transform a simple piece of grilled, poached, or broiled fish into a delightfully savory dish—and very little butter will do the trick. The easiest way to serve a flavored butter is to dollop a teaspoon or two on top of a piece of hot fish. You can also roll the butter into a cylinder, chill it for 20 minutes, and slice it into disks. A slightly more sophisticated method is to whip the butter for 3 minutes in an electric mixer and serve it in a sauceboat at the table.

Flavored butters can also be used as flavorings for more elaborate sauces such as beurre blanc or in sauces made by incorporating butter into hot poaching or braising liquid.

Flavored butters are easiest to make in a food processor. It's best to start out with cold butter, but you may have to push it down away from the sides of the food processor to get it to turn around.

One of the advantages of flavored butters is that they keep almost indefinitely, tightly wrapped in the freezer. Most of the recipes that follow are for slightly more than ¼ pound. Depending on how generous you are, ¼ pound of flavored butter is enough for 8 to 12 servings.

Almond Butter

MAKES ABOUT ½ POUND

Lightly toast ½ cup blanched almonds in a 350°F oven for about 10 minutes, until they turn very pale brown and smell toasty. Grind the almonds in a food processor for 5 minutes, scraping the sides from time to time with a rubber spatula until the mixture has the consistency of peanut butter. Add ¼ pound of cold butter and a pinch of salt and process until smooth.

Anchovy Butter

A tiny dollop of anchovy butter gives a savory and salty zing to a simple piece of sautéed or grilled fish.

MAKES ABOUT ¼ POUND

Soak 15 anchovy fillets (preferably the kind packed in salt or in extra-virgin olive oil) in cold water for 10 minutes. Dry the anchovies on paper towels and puree them in a food processor with ¼ pound of butter. If you want to get rid of the tiny bones—I usually don't bother—work the butter through a fine-mesh strainer with the back of a ladle.

Basil Butter

It's amazing how a sliver of this delicious butter gives a fragrant freshness to a piece of grilled, broiled, or sautéed fish.

Once fresh basil leaves are taken off the plant, they quickly wilt and lose their flavor. If you chop the basil and combine it with butter, it will retain its flavor and won't turn dark the way it does if simply chopped. Basil butter can also be tightly wrapped and frozen almost indefinitely.

MAKES ABOUT 6 OUNCES

Combine 1 tightly packed cup of basil leaves with ¼ pound of butter in a food processor. Puree the mixture for 2 or 3 minutes. Scrape the sides of the food processor every 30 seconds with a rubber spatula.

❧

Bercy Butter

The gently winy tang of Bercy butter makes a great accent to delicately flavored fish and shellfish.

MAKES ABOUT ¼ POUND

Gently simmer ½ cup of dry white wine with 2 finely chopped shallots until only 2 tablespoons remain. Meanwhile, cream a stick of butter in a food processor, electric mixer, or by hand. Work the wine mixture and a tablespoon of finely chopped parsley into the butter. Season with a pinch of salt and a few grinds of white pepper.

❧

Coral Butters

I know of no better method for capturing the flavor of the sea than making a butter out of the coral of certain fish and shellfish.

The coral (roe) from sea urchins, lobster, and some sea scallops as well as salmon roe can each be combined in a food processor with butter— usually an equal amount butter to coral—and the mixture then dolloped on grilled fish or shellfish or whisked into poaching or braising liquids to convert them into sauces. When a hot sauce is finished with coral butter, don't allow the sauce to come to a boil or the coral will curdle (remember, coral consists of eggs).

❧

Garlic Butter

Because of its full flavor, garlic butter is best with grilled rather than poached fish. Small amounts of garlic butter can also be combined with other flavored butters and beurre blanc–like sauces.

MAKES ¼ POUND

Peel and finely chop 2 garlic cloves. Crush the chopped garlic to a paste with the side of a chef's knife or in a mortar and pestle. Combine the garlic paste with ¼ pound of butter in an electric mixer with the paddle blade or in a food processor.

❧

Crustacean Butter (Lobster, Crayfish, Shrimp, Crab)

Unlike most flavored butters, crustacean butters are not very good served by themselves on top of hot fish but are best combined with other ingredients as components in more complex sauces or as a finish to soups such as bisques. Crustacean butters have a bright orange color that looks great in fish sauces, and because of their strong flavor a little goes a long way. Crustacean butters are prepared by stewing crustacean shells in butter. Crustacean butters can be prepared in batches and refrigerated or frozen until needed.

Crustacean shells can be pureed with butter in several ways. The easiest is just to put the shells in a food processor with the butter. This is the best method for pureeing shrimp heads or the softer tail shells of lobster and crayfish, but harder shells such as crab shells or the claw shells of crayfish and lobster will damage the food processor blade and are best worked with butter in an electric mixer using the paddle blade.

MAKES ABOUT 1 CUP

Combine a pound of cooked crustacean shells with ¾ pound butter cut into large chunks in the bowl of an electric mixer or food processor. If you're using the electric mixer, use the paddle blade and attach the guard to the mixer to prevent the shells from flying out. Work the shells with the butter at slow speed until the mixture starts to hold together in a single mass—usually after about 5 minutes. Turn the mixer up to medium speed and work the mixture for 10 minutes more. If you're pureeing softer shells such as shrimp heads or lobster tail shells, combine them with the butter in a food processor and puree for about 1 minute. Don't use the food processor for grinding very hard shells, especially the claws of lobsters, crayfish, and larger crabs.

Transfer the butter into a heavy pot and cook it gently for 20 minutes over medium heat, stirring every couple of minutes, until the butter turns oily and bright orange. Add enough warm water to cover the shells by about 2 inches, remove the pot from the heat, and let sit for 5 minutes. Skim off and reserve the butter that floats to the top or chill the pot overnight in the refrigerator and remove the butter once it has congealed. Discard the crustacean shells and the liquid. Heat the crustacean butter in a small saucepan and strain it through a fine-mesh sieve to remove fragments of shell and other particles.

Maître d'Hôtel Butter

MAKES ¼ POUND

This is France's most popular flavored butter. It's usually served with grilled steaks, but I like it even more with fish. Combine ¼ pound of butter with 2 tablespoons finely chopped parsley, a teaspoon of lemon juice, and a pinch of salt in a food processor, in an electric mixer with the paddle blade, or by hand.

Montpelier Butter

This butter is elaborate and complicated to make, but it's so good dolloped on hot or cold fish that it always seems worth it. Olive oil gives Montpelier butter its special luxurious creamy texture. If wrapped carefully, Montpelier butter will keep in the freezer for months, so it may be worth doubling or tripling the recipe to have extra on hand.

MAKES ABOUT 12 OUNCES

Blanch in boiling water for 30 seconds the leaves from ½ bunch each of parsley, watercress, chervil, chives (chopped before blanching), a large fresh tarragon sprig, a small handful of spinach leaves, and 2 peeled and chopped shallots. Rinse the blanched greens and shallots in cold water, dry them off in a towel, and grind them in a food processor for about 1 minute. Add 4 cornichons (gherkins), a heaped tablespoon of capers, a peeled garlic clove, and 4 anchovy fillets (soaked in cold water for 5 minutes to remove salt and oil). Puree the mixture for about 2 minutes more until it is smooth. Add to the mixture 2 raw egg yolks (if you're worried about eating raw eggs, leave these out) and 3 cooked egg yolks and work again until smooth. Add ¼ pound of butter and continue working the butter until it is smooth. (Working the butter through a drum sieve will give it a perfectly smooth texture—a pleasant but unnecessary refinement.) Stir ½ cup of extra-virgin olive oil into the butter with a wooden spoon. Season the butter with salt, pepper, cayenne, and 2 tablespoons lemon juice or good wine vinegar.

Morel Butter

Although this butter can be made with any kind of mushroom, it is most dramatic with morels. Dried and fresh mushrooms work equally well.

MAKES ABOUT 6 OUNCES

If you're using dried mushrooms, soak a small handful—about 12 mushrooms—in just enough water to cover until the mushrooms soften. (This takes about 20 minutes for morels and somewhat longer for porcini.) Squeeze the excess water out of the soaked mushrooms.

Sauté the reconstituted dried mushrooms or ¼ pound of fresh mushrooms (sliced if large) in a tablespoon of olive oil, butter, or duck fat. Season with salt and pepper and continue sautéing until there is no moisture left in the pan, about 5 minutes.

Let the mushrooms cool and combine them with ¼ pound of butter in a food processor. Puree until the butter is smooth.

Mustard Butter

This simple butter is great on poached or grilled fish when you want the flavor of mustard but straight mustard would be too strong.

Mustard butter can be prepared with smooth Dijon-style mustard or with whole-grain Meaux-style mustard.

MAKES ¼ POUND

Combine 2 tablespoons mustard with a stick of butter in a food processor and work until smooth.

Parsley and Garlic Butter

SNAIL BUTTER

With the pungency of garlic combined with the fresh flavor of parsley, snail butter is easy to make and intensely aromatic when dolloped on grilled fish and shellfish.

This butter is a lot easier to make than Montpelier butter, and although not as suave it's just as good in its own, more assertive way.

MAKES ABOUT 6 OUNCES

Peel and finely chop 3 garlic cloves. Crush them on a cutting board with the side of a chef's knife until you obtain a paste. Finely chop the leaves from 1 bunch of flat-leaf Italian parsley. Soak 3 anchovy fillets in cold water for 5 minutes and drain on paper towels. Blend the garlic, parsley, and anchovies with ¼ pound butter in a food processor until smooth, about 3 minutes. Transfer to a mixing bowl and work in ¼ cup extra-virgin olive oil with a wooden spoon. Season with salt and pepper to taste.

Red Pepper and Chili Butters

Chilies and bell peppers are delicious when combined with butter and served with hot fish. You'll need to vary the amounts depending on what kind of chili you're using. Chilies are best grilled or charred over a gas flame to remove their skin and cook them.

MAKES ¼ POUND

For mild chilies such as poblanos or for bell peppers, puree 1 pepper with ¼ pound butter in a food processor. Season with salt to taste. Dried chilies can also be soaked and used in butters as can canned chilies such as chipotle.

Red Wine Butter

My guests are always struck by this dark purple butter and its tangy winy flavor. This butter is excellent on hot grilled or poached fish.

MAKES ABOUT ¼ POUND

Simmer 1½ cups of full-bodied red wine with 2 finely chopped shallots until only about 2 tablespoons of wine remain. Work the mixture with ¼ pound of butter, ½ teaspoon of salt, and 1 tablespoon of finely chopped parsley in a food processor or electric mixer with a paddle blade.

Smoked Salmon Butter

This butter is delicious on hot grilled or poached fish.

MAKES ABOUT 6 OUNCES

Combine 2 ounces of good-quality smoked salmon in a food processor with ¼ pound of butter for about 1 minute. If you want the butter to be perfectly smooth, work it through a drum sieve or through a fine-mesh strainer with the back of a ladle.

Tarragon Butter

I never tire of the heady anise flavor of fresh tarragon. This butter is great dolloped on a piece of hot fish or shellfish, but it can also be used to finish more elaborate sauces such as beurre blanc or hollandaise (see recipes later in this chapter).

MAKES ABOUT ¼ POUND

Blanch the leaves from 12 tarragon sprigs for about 15 seconds in boiling water. Rinse the leaves with cold water in a strainer and pat them dry on paper towels. Combine the leaves with ¼ pound of butter in a food processor. Puree the mixture for about 2 minutes, until the leaves are finely chopped and well incorporated.

Tomato Butter

When tomatoes are cooked down to a thick sauce and combined with butter, they make a bright colored and savory condiment that's great on pieces of hot fish or shellfish.

MAKES ABOUT 6 OUNCES

Cut 2 ripe tomatoes in half crosswise and squeeze out the seeds. Chop the halves and cook them over medium heat in a small saucepan until all their moisture has evaporated and the tomato pulp is stiff and dry. Work this mixture through a fine-mesh strainer with the back of a ladle.

Combine this homemade tomato paste and 2 teaspoons of good-quality white wine vinegar or sherry vinegar with ¼ pound of butter in a food processor with the paddle blade, electric mixer, or by hand. A tablespoon of chopped fresh marjoram added to the butter at the end makes it even more delicious.

Truffle Butter

Most people are so horrified by the price of truffles that they'll skip over any recipe that calls for them. But making truffle butter is one way of getting the most out of a truffle or two. There are 2 ways of making truffle butter. The most subtle and least expensive method is to store butter with a couple of black truffles overnight in a tightly sealed jar in the refrigerator. The next day the butter will be saturated with the aroma of truffles, and the truffles themselves can be used for something else. More traditionally, a whole black truffle can be pureed in a food processor with a stick of butter. Even butter prepared in this way can be used in small amounts and is much more economical than working with a whole truffle at a time.

❧

Beurre Blanc

A traditional beurre blanc is made by simmering chopped shallots with white wine and white wine vinegar and then whisking in butter until the sauce takes on a creamy consistency. Once you've learned this technique—not as hard as it sounds—it's easy to make beurre blanc variations with chopped herbs, garlic, tomatoes, crustacean butter, truffles, or different-flavored butters or by using different wines (a beurre blanc made with red wine becomes a beurre rouge) and wine vinegars such as balsamic or sherry.

Beurre blanc can be made an hour or two before it is served, provided it doesn't get too hot or too cold. Leave it in a covered saucepan in an oven set to warm or on the back of the stove while you're cooking. You can also set the saucepan in a pan of hot (not boiling) water.

MAKES 1¼ CUPS, ENOUGH FOR 8 SERVINGS OF SEAFOOD

3 medium shallots, finely chopped
½ cup dry white wine
½ cup good-quality white wine vinegar
2 tablespoons heavy cream
1 cup (½ pound) unsalted butter
salt and white pepper

Combine the shallots with the wine and vinegar in a heavy saucepan. Gently simmer the mixture until only about ¼ cup of liquid is left, about 15 minutes.

Add the cream to the reduced shallot mixture and bring the mixture back to a simmer. Cut the butter into 1-inch cubes and whisk them, all at once, into the shallot mixture. Whisk the sauce over medium heat until all the butter has been incorporated.

Season with salt and pepper. If the sauce seems flat, add wine vinegar a few drops at a time to perk it up. If the sauce tastes harsh or overly acidic, whisk in more butter. Strain the sauce.

MAYONNAISE

Fresh homemade mayonnaise is a revelation for those of us who grew up eating mayonnaise out of a jar. A basic mayonnaise is easy to make and is easy to flavor in different ways by adding capers, saffron, garlic, curry, or fresh herbs.

Traditional mayonnaise is made by whisking oil drop by drop into one or more egg yolks seasoned with salt, lemon juice, and most of the time a little mustard. As the mayonnaise starts to thicken, you can add the oil more quickly. With a little practice, making a cup of mayonnaise by hand shouldn't take more than 10 minutes. Another foolproof method is to pour oil in a steady stream into the seasoned egg yolks in a food processor or blender. The only time I don't recommend this last method is when making mayonnaise that contains extra-virgin olive oil, which turns bitter when beaten.

Mayonnaise can be served with poached, grilled, broiled, or fried fish in one of two ways. The first and most obvious is just to serve the mayonnaise with hot or cold fish for guests to dol-

lop on as much as they want. The other method, best for braised or poached fish, is to whisk the hot poaching or braising liquid into a small amount of mayonnaise and serve the hot broth-like mixture around the fish in a wide soup plate.

Count on 2 tablespoons per serving with cold or hot fish.

Basic Mayonnaise

MAKES ABOUT 1 CUP

1 egg yolk
½ teaspoon salt
pinch of finely ground white pepper
1 to 2 tablespoons wine vinegar or lemon juice, to taste
1 tablespoon Dijon mustard (optional)
1 cup safflower, canola, or other flavorless vegetable oil

Combine the egg yolk, salt, pepper, a tablespoon of vinegar or lemon juice, and the mustard in a small mixing bowl or in the food processor.

If you're making the mayonnaise by hand, carefully pour a tablespoon of the oil down the side of the bowl. Whisk the egg yolk mixture on the side of the bowl opposite the oil. Work the oil into the egg yolk mixture a bit at a time. This should take about 1 minute. Add more oil and repeat in the same way until the mixture starts to thicken. Once the mixture thickens you can pour in the oil in a thin steady stream.

To make mayonnaise in the food processor, turn the food processor on and add the oil in a thin steady stream through the top.

If the mayonnaise becomes too thick, add about a tablespoon more wine vinegar, lemon juice, or water until it has the consistency you want.

FLAVORED MAYONNAISES

Aïoli

GARLIC MAYONNAISE

Aïoli is a specialty of Provence, where it is served in big bowls—or in a mortar and pestle—with hot poached fish and vegetables. Be forewarned: It is highly addictive.

MAKES 1 CUP

Crush 2 peeled garlic cloves into a paste in a mortar and pestle or chop the garlic and then crush it into a paste with the side of a chef's knife on a cutting board. Combine the paste with 2 egg yolks, salt and pepper, and a teaspoon of lemon juice in the mortar or in a small mixing bowl. Gently work ³⁄₄ cup of extra-virgin olive oil into the mixture gradually with the pestle or with a wooden spoon. If the mayonnaise starts to get too thick, stir in a teaspoon or two of water or lemon juice.

Saffron Aïoli

Soak a pinch of saffron threads in a tablespoon of water for 30 minutes. Stir the saffron and soaking liquid into a cup of aïoli.

Gribiche Sauce

Gribiche sauce is a mayonnaise that traditionally contains extra egg yolks (some raw, some hard-boiled), herbs, capers, and the little French gherkins called *cornichons*. In this version the extra egg yolks are left out and more of the other ingredients are added.

MAKES 1½ CUPS

Combine 1 cup of basic mayonnaise with 1 tablespoon Dijon mustard. With a wooden spoon, slowly work in ¼ cup extra-virgin olive oil. Stir in 2 heaped tablespoons coarsely chopped capers, 6 chopped cornichons, 2 tablespoons finely chopped parsley, 1 tablespoon finely chopped chives, 1 tablespoon finely chopped fresh tarragon, and salt and pepper to taste.

TIPS FOR MAKING MAYONNAISE

1. Add the oil slowly at the beginning. Rather than adding the oil drop by drop, I usually add about a tablespoon of oil to one side of the bowl and incorporate it bit by bit into the egg yolks with a whisk. This keeps one arm from getting tired holding the bottle of oil over the bowl.

2. Don't beat extra-virgin olive oil with a whisk or in a food processor—the violent action causes it to turn bitter. It's better to work extra-virgin olive oil slowly into the yolks with a wooden spoon or start out using half vegetable or pure olive oil, which can be beaten, and then finish by working in the extra-virgin olive oil with a wooden spoon by hand.

3. If you're worried about salmonella, cook the egg yolks, with a little water in the same way as starting a hollandaise (see page 335) before adding the oil. If the mayonnaise is being used in a hot sauce, you needn't bother because the egg yolks are being cooked anyway.

4. If the mayonnaise breaks—you'll see it thin all of a sudden, or it never thickens—beat it slowly into a new yolk or into 2 tablespoons of heavy cream.

5. Mayonnaise can be kept covered in the refrigerator for up to 3 days, but it may separate. You can bring back broken mayonnaise by working it for a few seconds in a food processor or by working it by hand into cream or a new yolk.

Mustard-Flavored Mayonnaise

You can use any kind of mustard to flavor a basic mayonnaise. My favorites are Dijon mustard and whole-grain mustard from Meaux. Because mustards differ in strength, you'll need to add the mustard a bit at a time and taste as you go, but figure on 2 to 3 tablespoons per cup of basic unflavored mayonnaise.

Rémoulade Sauce

*A*lthough rémoulade sauce is traditionally served with fried fish, it is also great on poached or grilled fish.

MAKES 1 CUP

Combine 1 cup basic mayonnaise with 2 tablespoons mustard, ¼ cup drained and chopped capers, and 2 tablespoons mixed finely chopped parsley, fresh chervil leaves, and fresh tarragon leaves. If you don't have all 3 herbs, just use more of the others.

Tartar Sauce

*T*artar sauce is easy to make and is classic with fried fish. There are lots of variations, but this version is tasty and easy.

MAKES 1 CUP

Combine 1 cup of basic mayonnaise with 2 finely chopped shallots, 2 tablespoons finely chopped chives, and a tablespoon of Dijon mustard. Season with salt and pepper to taste.

Mayonnaise Lightened with Whipped Cream

Mayonnaise that has been lightened with whipped cream has a delicate, melting texture that makes it delicious with cold or hot fish. Any flavored mayonnaise can be lightened by folding it with half as much cream, whipped—½ cup heavy cream whipped to medium stiffness, folded with 1 cup mayonnaise.

Don't combine whipped cream with mayonnaise until the last minute, or the mixture will break down and lose its airiness.

Cilantro and Hot Chili Mayonnaise

*T*his mayonnaise is excellent with grilled or deep-fried fish.

MAKES 1¼ CUPS

Seed and chop a tomato and stew it gently in a small saucepan over medium heat until it forms a thick sauce, about 15 minutes. Work the tomato through a strainer—to eliminate the peel—into a cup of mayonnaise. Stir in 3 tablespoons finely chopped cilantro, a clove of garlic crushed to a paste in a mortar or with the side of a chef's knife on a cutting board, and 2 seeded and finely chopped jalapeño chilies. Add 1 to 2 tablespoons of wine vinegar to taste. Season with salt.

Hollandaise Sauce

*D*espite somewhat of a fall into disrepute, a hollandaise flavored with a touch of lemon is one of the best and easiest sauces for poached, baked, or broiled fish. The trick to a good hollandaise is to beat water into the egg yolks before adding any butter. Melted butter that has not been clarified can then be whisked into the egg yolks, but the sauce will remain somewhat thin because of the water contained in the butter. If you want a looser hollandaise, don't clarify the butter. Because hollandaise is rich, you don't need a lot. I usually count on 2 to 3 tablespoons per serving (5 to 8 servings per cup of hollandaise).

MAKES 1½ CUPS

4 egg yolks

¼ cup cold water

1 cup (½ pound) unsalted butter, clarified (see box on page 336)

1 teaspoon fresh lemon juice or to taste

salt and white pepper

Combine the egg yolks with the cold water in a saucepan (preferably one with sloping sides) and whisk the mixture for about 30 seconds, until it becomes light and frothy. Place the saucepan over medium heat and whisk rapidly until the mixture triples in volume and suddenly thickens—you will start to see the bottom of the saucepan while whisking. Immediately remove the egg mixture from the heat and whisk for about 20 seconds so that it cools.

Ladle the clarified butter into the egg mixture while gently stirring with the whisk. Add the lemon juice and season with salt and pepper.

CLARIFIED BUTTER

Clarified butter is butter that has been cooked to eliminate moisture (most butters contain at least 25 percent water) and milk solids. Clarified butter, which burns at a higher temperature than whole butter, is used for sautéing when high heat is required and for making hollandaise sauce.

To make 1 cup, gently cook 1½ cups (¾ pound) of butter in a heavy saucepan over medium heat for about 15 minutes. When the foam that floats to the top of the butter begins to subside and form golden-brown specks, strain the butter through a fine-mesh strainer, coffee filter, or paper towel. Clarified butter keeps for up to a year, tightly covered in the refrigerator. Clarified butter made in this way—cooked until the milk solids turn into golden-brown specks—is also called *beurre noisette* by French cooks and *ghee* by Indian cooks.

Béarnaise Sauce

This delicious sauce is made in the same way as hollandaise sauce except that a tangy mixture of fresh tarragon, wine vinegar, dry white wine, shallots, and cracked peppercorns is used instead of lemon juice. Because very little of the tarragon mixture is needed at a time, it is convenient to make a batch—it keeps in the refrigerator indefinitely—and use it as needed.

MAKES ½ CUP FLAVOR MIXTURE FOR BÉARNAISE

4 sprigs fresh tarragon
1 shallot, finely chopped
1 teaspoon cracked black peppercorns
¾ cup dry white wine
¾ cup good-quality white wine vinegar

Combine the ingredients in a small saucepan and simmer gently—for about 20 minutes—until approximately ½ cup remains. Strain through a fine-mesh strainer and reserve in the refrigerator. Prepare béarnaise by substituting a tablespoon of this mixture for the lemon juice in the hollandaise sauce recipe.

VEGETABLE PUREES

Artichoke Puree

MAKES ½ CUP

Cut off and discard the top two thirds of three medium artichokes and trim the tough outer leaves off the sides of the bottom. Rub the artichoke bottoms with half a lemon, put the artichokes in a 4-quart nonaluminum pot, and add enough water to cover by 2 inches. Add 2 tablespoons of olive oil to the pot to keep the artichokes from darkening. Put a plate or lid directly over the artichokes so they stay submerged during cooking. Simmer for 20 to 30 minutes, until the artichokes are easily penetrated with a knife.

Drain the artichokes, let them cool for 10 minutes, and scoop out and discard the chokes with a spoon. Puree the artichoke bottoms for 1 minute in a food processor. Strain the puree through a food mill fitted with the finest disk or work it through a strainer.

Asparagus Puree

MAKES ⅔ CUP

Cut off and discard the woody 2 or 3 inches at the base of 1 pound of asparagus spears. Blanch the asparagus in 2 quarts of salted boiling water until they soften, about 7 minutes. Take the asparagus out of the boiling water with a slotted spoon or skimmer and rinse with cold water. Cut off and save the asparagus tips for garnish. Squeeze excess water out of the asparagus stems with your hands. Puree the asparagus stems in a food processor for about 1 minute, until you have a smooth paste. Work the puree through a food mill with the finest attachment, through a drum sieve, or through a strainer.

Garlic Puree

MAKES ½ CUP

Break three large heads of garlic into cloves. Simmer the unpeeled cloves for 20 to 30 minutes in a pot of water until they are completely soft—you'll be able to crush one against the side of the saucepan with a spoon.

Drain the garlic, puree it in a food processor, and work it through a drum sieve or a fine-mesh strainer. Garlic puree keeps in the refrigerator for up to a week and for several months in the freezer if tightly covered.

Mushroom Puree

MAKES ½ CUP

Slice ½ pound of very fresh mushrooms (if they're not perfectly fresh, the puree will be dark) and toss them in the juice of a lemon. Puree the slices for 1 minute in a food processor. Transfer the puree to a 2-quart non-aluminum pot and cook it on the stove over medium heat until it is completely dry and stiff, about 20 minutes.

If you want a very fine puree, work the puree through a drum sieve or fine-mesh strainer. Mushroom puree is best used right away—it turns dark in a few hours—or it can be frozen for several months in a tightly sealed container.

Tomato Puree

MAKES ½ CUP STIFF PUREE

Cut four medium tomatoes in half crosswise and squeeze the seeds out of each half. Chop the tomato halves and stew them over medium heat in a 2-quart pot until the liquid they release evaporates and the mixture thickens, about 20 minutes. Stir every few minutes to make sure the mixture doesn't stick and burn. Work into a clean saucepan through a food mill or a strainer with the back of a ladle to eliminate any seeds and pieces of peel. Cook the puree over medium heat for about 15 minutes more, until it becomes stiff.

VINAIGRETTES

Vinaigrette can be a simple mixture of oil and vinegar seasoned with salt and pepper or an elaborate mixture containing so many chopped herbs or other flavorings that it becomes stiff enough to be dolloped on hot or cold fish.

One of the simplest ways to serve a vinaigrette is to follow the traditional Mediterranean habit of putting a small pitcher of extra-virgin olive oil and a pitcher of good wine vinegar on the table for guests to sprinkle over grilled fish. You can vary this simple method by steeping herbs for a week or so in the oil or vinegar.

Basic Vinaigrette

MAKES ⅔ CUP

2 tablespoons good-quality wine vinegar
salt and pepper
2 teaspoons Dijon mustard
6 to 8 tablespoons olive oil

Season the vinegar with salt and pepper in a small mixing bowl. Whisk in the mustard until the mixture is smooth and then whisk in the oil in a slow stream so that the sauce thickens. If you're using extra-virgin olive oil, use a nonmetal mixing bowl and stir the oil into the sauce with a wooden spoon.

Balsamic Vinegar and Herb Vinaigrette

This tasty hot vinaigrette looks and tastes great lightly spooned over poached, baked, or grilled fish fillets. Balsamic vinaigrette can also be made in advance and reheated just before serving.

MAKES ½ CUP, ENOUGH FOR ABOUT 4 SERVINGS

2 tablespoons finely chopped fresh basil or chives
1 teaspoon fresh thyme or marjoram leaves, finely chopped, or ½ teaspoon dried
½ cup balsamic vinegar
½ cup extra-virgin olive oil
½ teaspoon salt
pepper

Combine the herbs and vinegar in a small saucepan and cook gently over low heat until the vinegar is reduced by half, about 5 minutes. Stir in the olive oil, salt, and pepper and whisk the mixture over very low heat for about 5 minutes more. Stir again just before serving because this vinaigrette separates and the vinegar sinks to the bottom.

Crustacean Oil

MAKES ABOUT 1 CUP

Crustacean oil (lobster, crayfish, shrimp, crab) can be prepared in much the same way as crustacean butter by substituting olive oil for the butter. Crustacean oil is best in cold sauces such as vinaigrettes or mayonnaise in which crustacean butter would congeal. Unlike crustacean butter, crustacean oil cannot be prepared in an electric mixer, but must be prepared by breaking up the shells in a food processor.

Combine 1 pound of cooked crustacean shells with 1¼ cups olive oil in the food processor. Don't put lobster claws or crayfish claws or hard-shell crabs in the food processor or you may damage the blade. Puree the mixture for about 1 minute. Transfer the mixture to a heavy-bottomed pot and cook gently for 20 minutes over medium heat, stirring every couple of minutes, until the oil turns bright orange. Add enough warm water to cover the shells by about 2 inches, remove the pot from the heat and let sit for 5 minutes. Skim off, strain, and reserve the oil that floats to the top.

Sicilian Olive Oil, Lemon, and Garlic Sauce

SALMORIGLIO

This simplest of all sauces is just a mixture of extra-virgin olive oil, lemon juice, and crushed garlic. It is best made in a mortar and pestle, but as long as you crush the garlic to a very fine paste you can get by making it in a mixing bowl. Whatever you do, don't make it in a blender or food processor, which will turn the olive oil bitter.

MAKES ABOUT ¾ CUP, ENOUGH FOR 4 SERVINGS

¼ cup fresh lemon juice

4 garlic cloves, chopped and crushed to a fine paste

1 tablespoon finely chopped dried oregano leaves

½ cup extra-virgin olive oil

salt

Whisk together the lemon juice, garlic, and oregano. Let sit for 15 minutes, whisk in the rest of the olive oil, and season with salt to taste. This sauce needs to be shaken or well stirred before it is served, or all the lemon juice will have sunk to the bottom.

Green Sauce

A green sauce, whether it be a classic French ravigote sauce, an Italian salsa verde, or a traditional English version, is essentially a vinaigrette containing so many chopped herbs, bread crumbs, and/or pickled things (such as cornichons or capers) that it has a stiff texture. Because of their tangy flavor and bright color, green sauces make wonderful accompaniments to grilled or poached fish.

Salsa Verde

This classic Italian sauce is traditionally used for *bollito misto* (simmered meats served with their own broth), but it also has a delicate tang that makes it great with fried and grilled fish and shellfish. Adjust the flavors as you like—some people like it a bit tangier and add extra vinegar. Salsa verde will keep for up to a week in the refrigerator.

MAKES 2 CUPS

2 garlic cloves, finely chopped

½ cup tightly packed fresh basil leaves

½ cup tightly packed flat-leaf parsley leaves

3 slices of white bread, such as Pepperidge Farm, crust removed

¼ cup white wine vinegar or sherry vinegar

1 tablespoon Dijon mustard

3 tablespoons drained capers

6 cornichons

½ cup extra-virgin olive oil

salt and pepper

Combine the garlic with the basil and parsley leaves, the bread slices, and the vinegar in the bowl of a food processor. Puree the herb/bread mixture for about 1 minute, scraping down the sides of the food processor with a rubber spatula every 10 or 15 seconds. Add the mustard, capers, and cornichons and chop for about a minute more, until the mixture is granular but smooth. Put the mixture in a bowl, work in the olive oil with a wooden spoon, and stir in the salt and pepper to taste.

Pestos and Salsas

Mint and Cilantro Yogurt Pesto

This is one of the most refreshing sauces I know. Although this minty pesto is perfectly good year-round, I usually make it when the summer heat is at its worst. Depending on the kind of yogurt you use, you might want to give it a little extra zip with the juice of a lemon. This pesto is best with grilled or fried fish.

MAKES 1½ CUPS

½ cup plain yogurt

1 small onion, coarsely chopped

1 or 2 jalapeño chilies, to taste, seeded and coarsely chopped

½ cup tightly packed mint leaves, from 1 good-size bunch

½ cup tightly packed fresh cilantro leaves

salt and pepper

Combine all the ingredients except the salt and pepper in a food processor and process for about 1 minute, scraping down the sides every 15 seconds, until the ingredients are finely chopped and the mixture is smooth. Season with salt and pepper to taste.

Tapenade

While usually not thought of as a pesto, tapenade is made in much the same way as traditional Italian pesto, except that olives replace the basil. This wonderful salty paste is delicious on just about anything but is especially good on grilled fish or shellfish such as shrimp. All tapenade recipes include capers and olives, but few include dried currants as does this one, given to me by my food writer friend Sally Schneider. The gentle sweetness of the currants relieves some of the tapenade's saltiness. Most versions of tapenade found in restaurants tend to be too smoothly pureed, and the original texture of the olives is lost. Tapenade is best when coarse and almost chunky.

MAKES ABOUT 2 CUPS, ENOUGH FOR ABOUT 8 SERVINGS

6 tablespoons dried currants

1 pound imported large black olives, preferably Moroccan, French, or Italian

12 salt- or oil-cured anchovy fillets, soaked in cold water for 5 minutes, drained, and patted dry

3 tablespoons small nonpareil capers

1 garlic clove, finely chopped and crushed to a paste

¼ cup extra-virgin olive oil

pepper

Soak the currants for 1 hour in just enough warm water to cover. Pit the olives by squeezing them on each end so the pit just slips out. Chop the anchovies into a coarse paste with a chef's knife.

Combine all the ingredients except the salt and pepper in a food processor and pulse for about 5 seconds. Scrape down the sides with a rubber spatula and pulse again. Repeat as long as necessary until you come up with a chunky mixture with the texture of hamburger relish—don't overdo it; it's better to err on the side of chunkiness.

Tropical Fruit Salsa

This salsa is really a hot and spicy salad but with each ingredient chopped finely so that it becomes a savory sauce instead. The hot and sweet and cool flavors of this salsa make it perfect for grilled seafood, and the festive colors look great at an outdoor barbecue.

Because this salsa takes so much fruit, I usually make it when I'm having dinner for at least 6 so it will all get eaten. You can also make half a recipe and use the leftover fruit in a tropical fruit salad. Tropical fruit salsa will keep for up to 3 days in the refrigerator. This salsa is best with grilled fish.

MAKES 4 CUPS

¼ small pineapple, peeled, cored, and cut into wedges

1 Hawaiian papaya, peeled, seeded, and cut into chunks

2 kiwi fruit, peeled and sliced

1 mango, halved, pit removed, and fruit spooned away from the skin

1 medium red onion, finely chopped

1 red bell pepper, grilled (page 133), peeled, seeded, and finely chopped

3 jalapeño chilies, seeded and finely chopped

juice of 2 limes

leaves from 1 small bunch of cilantro, finely chopped

salt

MEDITERRANEAN SAUCES FOR GRILLED FISH

Mediterranean cooks have a long tradition of grilling seafood outdoors. Except for minor variations—Moroccan cooks may coat fish with spices; Provençal cooks are likely to grill over fennel twigs—basic grilling techniques are the same all along Mediterranean shores. While a well-grilled fish has little need for an elaborate sauce—a dribble of olive oil will usually suffice—Mediterranean cooks are experts at making pungent, rough-hewn sauces, usually with a lot of garlic and olive oil. A good way to make a summer barbecue a little special is to grill a few different fish—or one big one—and serve a couple of different sauces at the table for people to pass around and dollop. See aïoli, tapenade, and *salmoriglio* in this chapter as well as rouille (page 269) and *romesco* (page 273).

Combine the fruits in a food processor and pulse them to a chunky semi-liquid consistency, but don't overdo it and turn the salsa into soup. Combine the chopped fruit mixture with the other ingredients in a mixing bowl. Cover with plastic wrap and chill in the refrigerator for 2 hours.

❧

Tomato and Avocado Salsa

*T*his cool and spicy salsa is similar to guacamole except the vegetables are chopped instead of crushed. You can make it in a food processor, but you'll get a much nicer effect if you chop the ingredients by hand. I like this salsa best with grilled fish.

MAKES ABOUT 4 CUPS

6 plum tomatoes, peeled, seeded, and chopped

1 garlic clove, finely chopped

1 red bell pepper, finely chopped

1 jalapeño chili, seeded and finely chopped

1 poblano chili, seeded and finely chopped

1 medium red onion, finely chopped

1 avocado, pitted, peeled, and chopped

½ cup tightly packed cilantro leaves (from about 1 bunch)

juice of 2 limes

salt to taste

Combine all the ingredients and let the mixture sit for an hour or two in the refrigerator.

ASIAN SAUCES AND CONDIMENTS

THAI CURRIES

Unlike Indian curries, Thai curries are pastes made from fresh herbs and aromatic vegetables—they're hot, pungent, intensely flavorful, and can be whisked into a simple broth or sauce, instantly transforming it into something delicious and authentically Thai.

While very good Thai curries are available in cans—use a few spoonfuls at a time and freeze the rest in a plastic container—you'll get better results and have a lot more fun making your own. Making your own Thai curries will also get you used to working with Thai ingredients and familiarize you with their flavors. The best Thai curries are ground to a very smooth paste in a large mortar and pestle, a process that can require more than an hour to make a few tablespoons. Most of us don't have large mortars and pestles—and those little porcelain ones are too small—so your best bet is to grind all the ingredients in a food processor (a miniature food processor for small batches). You won't get a perfectly smooth paste, but for most recipes the effect will be close enough. If you're fortunate to have a big mortar and pestle, grind the mixture first in a food processor and then in the mortar.

Thai curries come in assorted colors—red, green, and yellow—and while most curries contain similar ingredients, the proportions are different so they all have different effects. One distinctly different curry is Mussaman curry used mostly by Thai Muslims.

Be careful when making and tasting curry pastes—they're fiery-hot and can burn your fingers, so you may want to wear gloves. If some of these ingredients are unfamiliar, check the glossary.

Green Curry Paste

*T*his is justifiably the most popular of the Thai curries. Green curry is pungent, hot, and easy to make. See the glossary for information on Asian ingredients.

MAKES 1¼ CUPS

⅓ cup tightly packed cilantro leaves

1 tablespoon ground coriander seeds

3 tablespoons chopped peeled galangal

3 kaffir lime leaves, coarsely chopped, or a 1-inch strip of lime zest, coarsely chopped

2 teaspoons shrimp paste (optional)

2 teaspoons salt

4 garlic cloves, chopped coarsely

¼ cup chopped lemongrass

3 shallots, chopped

12 green Thai chilies, seeded and chopped

¼ cup peanut oil

Combine the ingredients in a food processor or in a large mortar and work the mixture to a paste (for about 5 minutes in a food processor, an hour in a mortar and pestle). Store the green curry in a jar in the refrigerator for up to a week or in the freezer for up to a year.

❧

Red Curry Paste

*R*ed curry paste is very similar to the green version. One obvious difference is that red chilies are used instead of green. Another, more subtle difference is that red curry always contains ground coriander seeds. See the glossary for information on Asian ingredients.

MAKES 1¼ CUPS

⅓ cup tightly packed cilantro leaves

1 tablespoon ground coriander seeds

3 tablespoons chopped peeled galangal

3 kaffir lime leaves, coarsely chopped, or a
1-inch strip of lime zest, coarsely
chopped

2 teaspoons shrimp paste (optional)

2 teaspoons salt

4 garlic cloves, coarsely chopped

¼ cup chopped lemongrass

3 shallots, chopped

12 red Thai chilies or 3 red serrano chilies,
seeded and chopped

1 teaspoon freshly ground black pepper

¼ cup peanut oil

Follow the directions for green
curry paste (preceding recipe).

Mussaman Curry Paste

Mussaman curry is almost a cross
between an Indian curry powder and a Thai curry paste. See the
glossary for information on Asian
ingredients.

MAKES ½ CUP

¼ teaspoon ground cloves

4 teaspoons ground coriander

1 teaspoon ground cinnamon

1 teaspoon freshly ground white pepper

1 teaspoon ground cumin

½ star anise, crushed

½ teaspoon ground cardamom

7 Thai chilies, seeds and stems removed

4 shallots, chopped

4 garlic cloves, chopped

3 kaffir lime leaves, chopped

3-inch piece of lemongrass, chopped

½-inch piece of galangal, peeled and
chopped

2 teaspoons shrimp paste (optional)

¼ cup peanut oil

Combine everything in a food
processor or mortar and pestle and
work the mixture to a paste. If you're
using a food processor, you may have
to add 2 or 3 tablespoons of water to
get the mixture to move around.
(Count on about 5 minutes in a food
processor, an hour in a mortar and
pestle.) Mussaman curry will keep in
a jar in the refrigerator for up to a
month or indefinitely in the freezer.

INDONESIAN SAMBALS

These saladlike Indonesian relishes
are especially delicious with baked or
grilled fish.

Sambal Kelapa

COLD COCONUT SAUCE

I first read a version of this in Sri
Owen's book *Indonesian Food and
Cookery*. This sauce is best on grilled
fish or shellfish.

MAKES ENOUGH FOR 10 SERVINGS

1 fresh coconut

4 garlic cloves, finely chopped

4 shallots, finely chopped

5 Thai or jalapeño chilies, halved, seeded
and finely chopped

½ cup Thai fish sauce (nam pla)

½ cup unsweetened coconut milk

2 tablespoons granulated or palm sugar

juice of 4 limes

salt

**Preparing the Grated Fresh
Coconut:** When buying a fresh
coconut, give it a shake to make sure
you can hear liquid sloshing around
inside—otherwise it may be stale or
dried out.

When you get your coconut home,
hammer a screwdriver into 2 of the
eyes—the brown circles—near the end
and drain out the liquid (which I usually drink on the spot). Bake the
coconut for about 15 minutes in a
350°F oven and let cool for 5 minutes
before wrapping it in a kitchen towel
and hitting it with a hammer to break
it up and get the white pulp to pull
away from the shell. Peel the brown
membrane off the outside of the pulp
with a vegetable peeler. Grate the
coconut with a hand grater or in a
food processor with the grater attachment.

Finishing the Sambal: Combine the
reserved grated coconut with the rest
of the ingredients and refrigerate,
covered, for 2 hours.

Cucumber Sambal

This lemony mixture of spices,
cucumber, coconut milk, and
peanut butter is a delicious condiment
for grilled fish.

MAKES ENOUGH FOR 6 SERVINGS

2 long European cucumbers or 4 regular
cucumbers, peeled

1½ tablespoons coarse salt

2 Thai chilies, seeded and finely chopped

1 shallot, finely chopped

3-inch piece of lemongrass, finely sliced,
then finely chopped

continued

2 teaspoons grated fresh ginger

2 tablespoons Thai fish sauce (nam pla)

1 tablespoon creamy natural peanut butter

1 cup unsweetened coconut milk

2 teaspoons granulated or palm sugar

juice of 2 limes

Cut the cucumbers in half length-wise and scoop out the seeds with a spoon. Cut the cucumbers into strips and then into ⅓-inch cubes. Rub the cubes with coarse salt—rub for a couple of minutes until all the salt has dissolved—and place in a colander to drain for 30 minutes. Squeeze the cucumber cubes in small handfuls to eliminate more water. Reserve in a covered bowl in the refrigerator.

Combine the rest of the ingredients in a small bowl and stir into the cucumbers. Serve cold.

INDIAN CHUTNEYS

In Indian cooking the word *chutney* refers to almost any sauce or condiment served at the table with hot foods. A chutney can be as simple as a little chopped onion flavored with a little lemon juice or as complicated as fruits or vegetables flavored with an array of spices. Chutneys are sometimes sweetened with sugar or honey and given an acidic tang with vinegar or lemon juice so they end up with a characteristic sweet-and-sour flavor.

Mint, Cilantro, Cucumber, and Yogurt Chutney

*I*t's sometimes hard to tell if this cool refreshing sauce is a condiment or a salad. I love to serve this chutney at a summer barbecue with grilled fish. Chutneys made with cucumber will keep covered in the refrigerator for several days but may get a little runny.

MAKES 2 CUPS, ENOUGH FOR ABOUT 8 SERVINGS

1 long European cucumber or 2 regular cucumbers, peeled

1 tablespoon coarse sea salt or kosher salt

1 small red onion, finely chopped

½ teaspoon cayenne pepper

1 teaspoon grated fresh ginger

2 tablespoons finely chopped fresh mint

2 tablespoons finely chopped fresh cilantro

1 tablespoon fresh lemon juice

½ cup labneh (page 36) or 1 cup regular plain yogurt, drained for 2 hours in a cheesecloth-lined strainer

freshly ground white pepper (to taste)

Cut the cucumbers in half length-wise and scoop out the seeds with a spoon. Cut each half into strips and then into ¼-inch cubes. (You can also do this in a food processor with the pulse mechanism—just be sure not to overdo it.) Toss the cucumber cubes with a tablespoon of the coarse salt—keep tossing until all the salt has dissolved—and let drain in a colander for 30 minutes.

Squeeze the water out of the cucumbers a small handful at a time. Toss the cucumbers with the remaining ingredients and refrigerate for at least 30 minutes.

Tomato Chutney

*T*his simple chutney is prepared like most tomato sauces (by gently stewing the tomatoes until they lose their liquid) except that it contains spices and is made sweet and sour with sugar and vinegar. Tomato chutney can be served cold or hot, but I usually serve it cold with grilled foods. Tomato chutney will keep for 2 days in the refrigerator.

MAKES 1½ CUPS, ENOUGH FOR ABOUT 8 SERVINGS

1 medium onion, finely chopped

2 garlic cloves, finely chopped

2 Thai or serrano chilies, seeded and finely chopped

2 tablespoons olive oil or vegetable oil

1 tablespoon grated fresh ginger

1 teaspoon ground cumin

2 teaspoons ground coriander

1 teaspoon ground fenugreek

¼ teaspoon ground cloves

½ teaspoon ground cinnamon

6 tomatoes, peeled, seeded, and coarsely chopped

3 tablespoons sugar

⅓ cup sherry vinegar or good-quality wine vinegar

salt

Cook the onion, garlic, and chilies in the oil in a heavy pot over medium heat for about 10 minutes, until the onion turns translucent but has not browned. Add the ginger and spices and stir over medium heat until you can smell the fragrance of the spices, about 2 minutes. Add the tomatoes, sugar, and vinegar and simmer gently for about 40 minutes, until the sauce thickens and takes on a jamlike consistency. Season with salt to taste and let cool.

Mango Chutney

*O*ne of the great things about making this chutney is that you can use unripe mangoes—in fact they're essential—so it's easy to make almost any time of year.

Traditionally this chutney is served with cooked meat dishes, but I like it equally well with grilled fish. Mango chutney will keep for several weeks, tightly sealed in a jar in the refrigerator. This recipe is adapted from a microwave version in Julie Sahni's book *Moghul Microwave: Cooking Indian Food the Modern Way.*

MAKES 2 CUPS, ENOUGH FOR ABOUT 8 SERVINGS

2 unripe mangoes

1 cup sugar

½ cup good-quality wine vinegar

1 tablespoon grated fresh ginger

2 Thai or serrano chilies, seeded and finely chopped

2 teaspoons dry mustard

¼ cup slivered almonds, lightly toasted

¼ cup raisins

Peel the mangoes with a vegetable peeler and slice the pulp away from the pit. Cut the pulp into ½-inch cubes.

Simmer the sugar and vinegar in a 4-quart pot until the sugar dissolves. Add the mango cubes, simmer gently for 10 minutes, and remove the mango with a slotted spoon. Add the ginger, chilies, and mustard to the vinegar/sugar mixture and simmer gently until it looks syrupy, about 15 minutes.

Stir the almonds, raisins, and mango cubes into the syrup and simmer for 1 minute. Let cool.

BROTHS

Fish broth can be kept in the refrigerator for 3 days and in the freezer for up to 6 months. Dashi can be kept in the refrigerator for a week and in the freezer

for up to 6 months. Chicken broth and clear broth sauce can be kept in the refrigerator for 3 days and in the freezer for up to 6 months.

Fish Broth

To make the best fish broth, use the freshest fish (don't buy stale-smelling heads and bones), soak the heads and bones for at least 30 minutes, don't let the broth boil (it should simmer gently), and don't cook the broth for more than 30 minutes, which will give it a stale fishy taste.

MAKES 2½ QUARTS

4 pounds fish bones and heads (from about 6 pounds of whole fish)

2 medium onions, sliced

1 bouquet garni: 5 fresh thyme sprigs or 1 teaspoon dried, 1 bunch of parsley, and a bay leaf tied with string (or in cheesecloth for dried thyme)

1½ cups dry white wine

Preparing the Fish Bones and Heads: Fish bones and heads need to be rinsed thoroughly before being used to make broth, or traces of blood adhering to the bones will cloud the broth and make it gray.

If the fishmonger has not removed the gills from the base of the head, you'll have to take them out yourself. The easiest way to do this is to reach under the base of the head with a pair of scissors, cut the gills on each end and along the sides, and just pull them out with your fingers.

Break the bones into several pieces with a cleaver or an old knife. Put them in a large bowl and cover them with cold water. Let them soak for about 30 minutes, change the water

every 10 minutes, rinse them thoroughly one last time, and drain.

Combine the onions, bouquet garni, fish bones and heads, and wine in a 4-quart pot. Add enough cold water to barely cover the bones and bring the water to a slow simmer. Skim off any froth that floats to the top with a ladle. After the broth has simmered slowly for about 30 minutes, strain it and throw out the bones.

To make a clarified broth, follow the directions under basic fish consommé (page 282).

Dashi

Dashi is a basic broth made from kelp and specially dried and smoked fish, usually bonito. It's hard to imagine Japanese cooking without dashi; it's as fundamental to Japanese cuisine as stocks and broths are to European and American cooking. Dashi is easy to make and amazingly delicious and satisfying.

There are three ways to make dashi. The easiest method is to dissolve instant dashi granules (called *hon dashi* or *dashi-no-moto*) in hot water or to steep dashi teabags—also called *dashi-no-moto*—in hot water. These are modern-day shortcuts for authentic dashi, but unlike so many convenience foods they're of very good quality.

The second method, itself a shortcut, consists of making a kind of kelp tea with a Japanese seaweed called *konbu.* Shaved dried bonito flakes (*hana-katsuo*) are then soaked in this tea for a minute or two, and the mixture is strained. The used bonito flakes can be used to make a coarser-tasting *dashi* called *secondary dashi* (*niban dashi*).

To make *dashi* following the original and most traditional method, you'll need to obtain a solid chunk of dried bonito called *katsuo-bushi*. *Katsuo-bushi* looks something like an overripe banana but feels like a chunk of hardwood. To find it you'll need to go to a Japanese specialty shop, and to complicate matters further you'll need a special gadget—a kind of wooden shoe box with a blade attached—for shaving the *katsuo-bushi*. Aficionados of Japanese cooking say that freshly shaved bonito flakes have a more delicate forthright flavor than preshaved flakes, but I've found that because of the inconsistent quality of *katsuo-bushi* this isn't always true.

MAKES 1 QUART

one 18-inch piece of giant seaweed (konbu) (about 1 ounce)

5 cups water

1 ounce shaved bonito (*hana-katsuo*) (1 cup tightly packed, 4 cups unpacked)

Wipe the konbu with a damp towel, but don't get carried away and wipe the delicate white minerals off its surface. Fold it over itself and place it in a saucepan with a quart of cold water. Put the saucepan over low heat. When the water comes to a simmer, after about 15 minutes, remove the konbu. (You can save it for secondary dashi.) Turn the heat to high. As soon as the broth comes to a full boil, stir in the bonito flakes and immediately take the saucepan off the heat. Let the bonito flakes sit in the broth for 1 minute and immediately strain the soup through a fine-mesh sieve or through an ordinary sieve lined with a double layer of cheesecloth.

∾

Chicken Broth

Many of us make the mistake of adding too much water to too few chicken parts or bones so that the broth ends up too weak. When making chicken broth, add only enough water to barely cover the bones or parts and don't let the broth boil—keep it at a gentle simmer—or it will turn cloudy and greasy.

MAKES 3½ QUARTS

6 pounds chicken backs, necks, and/or bones

1 medium onion, coarsely chopped

1 medium carrot, coarsely chopped

1 celery stalk, chopped

1 bouquet garni: 3 fresh thyme sprigs or ¼ teaspoon dried, a small bunch of parsley, and a bay leaf tied with string (or in cheesecloth for dried thyme)

4 ½ quarts cold water or enough to cover

Trim excess fat off the chicken parts. Put the chopped vegetables and the bouquet garni in the bottom of a 10- or 12-quart pot (these are added first so they don't float to the top and interfere with skimming), add the chicken parts, and pour over enough water to barely cover.

Put the pot on the stove over medium to high heat until the water comes to a simmer. Turn the heat down low enough to keep the broth at a slow simmer. Cook the broth for about 3 hours. For the first 30 minutes, skim off any fat or froth that comes to the surface. Add small amounts of cold water as needed to keep the chicken parts submerged.

When the broth is done, strain it into a clean pot or heat-resistant plastic container. Let it cool, uncovered, for an hour before putting it in the refrigera-

tor. The next day, when the broth is cold, spoon off and discard any fat that has congealed on its surface.

∾

Clear Chicken Broth

To prepare the clear chicken broth called for in the salmon and truffle aspic recipe on page 319, you must start out with good homemade chicken broth (see preceding recipe).

MAKES APPROXIMATELY 1 QUART

2 quarts homemade chicken broth

1 pound boneless chicken breasts

1 celery stalk

1 small onion

1 bunch of parsley

3 fresh tarragon sprigs (optional)

5 egg whites

Skim off and discard any fat that has floated to the top of the chicken broth. Combine the rest of the ingredients in a food processor and chop together for about 1 minute. Put the chopped mixture into a 6-quart pot and pour in the chicken broth. The chicken broth can be warm or cold but must not be hot enough to cook the egg whites.

Place the pot on the stove over medium to high heat and bring to a gentle simmer. Five minutes after the broth comes to a simmer, scrape against the bottom of the pot with a wooden spoon to prevent any of the mixture from adhering and burning. Simmer gently for about 30 minutes, moving the pot to a different position over the burner about every 10 minutes.

Carefully strain through a strainer lined with a triple layer of cheesecloth.

Finfish Dictionary

SALTWATER FISH

ANCHOVIES (various species of the Engraulidae family)

Even when we're lucky enough to encounter fresh anchovies—most end up in cans or packed in salt—they are often confused with sardines. This isn't a serious problem since cooking methods for one work for the other. Imported sardines are larger than anchovies, but American "sardines" are actually herring and are about the same size as anchovies. One sure way to tell the difference between anchovies and sardines: The lower jaw of sardines protrudes farther than the top part—a characteristic they share with other members of the herring family. Anchovies have the reverse characteristic—the top jaw protrudes farther than the lower.

Like sardines, anchovies are delicious grilled, but they may be too small and fragile to grill on a barbecue. Sprinkling with herbs and oil and then broiling is an easier, if not quite as tasty, approach. Anchovies are also delicious lightly panfried and marinated—in escabeche.

BEST METHODS: broiling, grilling, baking, in escabeche, panfrying

AVOID: including in soups and stews

YIELD: 45 percent skin-on fillets from ungutted fish

APPEARANCE WHEN COOKED: off-white flesh

TEXTURE WHEN COOKED: soft

FAT CONTENT: low

FLAVOR: pronounced

BARRACUDA (Atlantic: *Sphyraena barracuda*; Pacific: *Sphyraena argentea*)

The Pacific barracuda, *Sphyraena argentea*, is all we're really concerned with here because for all practical purposes its Atlantic cousin, the great barracuda—*Sphyraena barracuda*—is inedible due to its tendency to carry ciguatera toxins. While Bahamian and Caribbean locals insist that barracuda under 5 pounds are free from ciguatera poisoning, why take a chance when there are, as they say, other fish in the water?

The Pacific barracuda found off the Pacific coast from Alaska to southern California is considered entirely safe, and while I've never tasted it, it's reported to have a good flavor and moderately firm flesh that makes it well suited to grilling.

BEST METHODS: grilling, broiling

AVOID: eating Atlantic species

YIELD: 35 percent skinless fillets from ungutted fish

APPEARANCE WHEN COOKED: off-white

TEXTURE WHEN COOKED: moderately firm

FAT CONTENT: moderate

FLAVOR: moderately pronounced

BASS (SALTWATER)

Bass is a vague term applied haphazardly to a wide variety of completely unrelated fish. In a stricter scientific sense those fish that are indisputably bass are members of the family Percichthyidae or Serranidae (actually the grouper family, included within the bass family) and include the European bass as well as the American striped bass and American black sea bass. The confusion starts when the word *bass* is attached to the name of an unrelated fish as a marketing tactic. Several members of the drum and other families are labeled *bass*, which of course adds to the confusion. And then of course there are the freshwater bass.

The true saltwater basses are delicious fish with lean white flesh and not too many bones. Most are large enough to provide thick fillets but also make exciting presentations when cooked whole.

BEST METHODS: baking whole, grilling (either whole, fillets, or steaks of Chilean sea bass, which are oily enough so they won't stick), panfrying (whole smaller fish and fillets), braising (whole and fillets), deep-frying (boneless and skinless fillets, not Chilean sea bass)

AVOID: deep-frying Chilean sea bass (too oily)

YIELD: 40 percent to 45 percent skinless fillets from ungutted fish for most species

APPEARANCE WHEN COOKED: very white, tight small flakes

TEXTURE WHEN COOKED: moderately firm

FAT CONTENT: very low except Chilean sea bass, which is moderately fatty

FLAVOR: Delicate, crustaceanlike; Chilean sea bass has a fuller flavor

Black Sea Bass (*Centropristis striata*)

This is one of the most popular fish along the Eastern Seaboard and is surprisingly inexpensive considering its quality. I've heard about black sea bass weighing up to 5 pounds, but most weigh between 1 and 2 pounds. Almost completely black, at least until it is scaled, when it reveals a certain amount of white coloration underneath, black sea bass lives up to its name. Black sea bass flesh is perfectly white and has a delicate flavor and a moderately firm texture.

Chilean Sea Bass (*Dissostichus yanezei*)

This scary-looking fish is not really a bass but a member of an unusual family of fish found only in the Southern Hemisphere. Biologists insist the Chilean sea bass's name should be the Patagonian toothfish, which seems reasonable considering that this fish has very visible and very pointed teeth. Toothfish or bass, this fish has large winglike pectoral fins, glassy sunken eyes, and typically weighs about 20 pounds. But it's unlikely that you'll encounter a whole Chilean sea bass because most are gutted and have their heads removed before they are shipped to the United States, usually frozen. Often they are available only as steaks or fillets. Chilean sea bass is a moderately oily fish with a firm texture and a delicious full flavor. It is particularly good grilled.

European Bass (*Dicentrarchus labrax*)

This is one of the most prized of all European fish and is the only bass called for with any regularity in European recipes. Found in both the eastern Atlantic and the Mediterranean, it has always been so expensive in Europe that it would have been impractical to import it into the United States. Now, though, European sea bass is farmed in Norway, so it may become more available in years to come. European sea bass typically weighs between 1½ and 3 pounds and has a silvery skin, much like striped bass without the stripes. The French call Mediterranean European bass *loup de mer* (meaning "sea wolf"), but it should not be confused with wolffish.

Giant Sea Bass (also called black sea bass and grouper) (*Stereolepis gigas*)

This enormous gray fish can weigh up to 500 pounds and was once popular along the coast of California and Mexico, but it is now quite rare. The giant sea bass is similar to the jewfish, a kind of grouper, with which it is sometimes confused.

Striped Bass, Wild (also called rockfish) (*Morone saxatilis*)

This is one of America's favorite fish, especially on the East Coast, where it is fished both commercially and by sportfishermen. Striped bass has shiny silvery scales with dark stripes running horizontally along its sides and can be found from northern Florida to the Saint Lawrence River. In the last decade, because of overfishing and dangerous levels of PCBs found in some bass, many states have declared a moratorium on commercial striped bass fishing, so much of the striped bass on the market is of the smaller farmed variety. Before the moratorium most of the striped bass for sale in retail fish markets weighed about 3 pounds, but 10-pound specimens weren't hard to come by. Apparently 100-pound specimens were not uncommon before the turn of the century. Striped bass has a delicate flavor that varies depending on where and when the fish is caught. The numbers of striped bass are apparently increasing in some areas, so we may see a loosening of the moratorium where PCBs are not a problem.

Striped Bass, Farmed (also called California bass and sunshine bass) (hybrid cross of wild striped bass/*Morone saxatilis* and white bass/*Morone chrysops*)

Farm-raised striped bass has come about largely as a response to the dearth of wild striped bass, but it has the advantage of arriving at the market extremely fresh. The farmed variety is a cross between wild striped bass and a freshwater species called *white bass* and usually weighs between 1 and 2 pounds. Farmed striped bass has a milder flavor than wild striped bass and a slightly higher fat content.

White Sea Bass (*Atractoscion nobilis*)

Despite its name, this fish is neither a bass nor white but bluish-gray and a member of the drum family. It is also called *sea trout* in California.

BLACK COD: See Sablefish.

BLACKFISH (*Tautoga onitis*)

This underrated fish is also called by its Indian name, *tautog*. Blackfish is dark gray to black and has a characteristic short plump body with a flat little head. It has sharp front teeth and a set of molars in the back of its mouth that it uses for grinding up the mollusks it so enjoys eating. Blackfish grow up to 25 pounds, but the largest I've ever seen was 5 pounds. Three pounds is more typical.

Blackfish are caught along the Atlantic coast from North Carolina to Cape Cod. Because they enjoy eating shellfish attached to rocks near the shores, out of reach of the large nets of the large commercial fishing boats, they are popular with sportfishermen. They are most often available in East Coast markets during the summer. In some ethnic markets blackfish are even sold alive.

Blackfish belong to the wrasse family (Labridae) of which there are hundreds of members, most of which are caught in tropical waters. Those members that do make it to American shores include the cunner, a smaller, more slender version of the blackfish, which I've seen only at the Fulton fish market in New York, never in a retail store. Apparently cunners were popular in the late 19th century. Other wrasse are the hogfish (*Lachnolaimus maximus*), a colorful tropical fish sometimes found as far north as North Carolina, and the California sheephead (*Semicossyphus pulcher*), a large Pacific version caught (or speared) mostly by sportfishermen but occasionally appearing in retail markets. I've never tasted one, but they're supposed to be delicious.

Blackfish have firm, lean, and perfectly white flesh with a delicate flavor. The skin sometimes has a bitter taste, so I remove it. Don't confuse blackfish with a bony freshwater fish by the same name harvested and raised by aquaculture in California (*Orodan macrolepododus*) and often found live in Chinese markets.

BEST METHODS: panfrying (skinless fillets), braising (skinless fillets), deep-frying (skinless fillets), soups and stews (skinless fillets), poaching (whole), baking (whole)

AVOID: smoking (the flesh is too lean)

YIELD: 40 percent skinless fillets from ungutted fish

APPEARANCE WHEN COOKED: very white, tight small flakes

TEXTURE WHEN COOKED: firm, finely flaked

FAT CONTENT: very low

FLAVOR: very delicate, crustaceanlike

BLOWFISH (*Sphoeroides maculatus*)

Blowfish are members of the puffer family, Tetraodontidae, of which there are at least 100 members. The only puffer I would ever recommend eating is the blowfish—sometimes called *sea squab*—fished off the Atlantic coast, because most of the other species are poisonous. In Japan about 20 Tetraodontidae members are known as fugu and may be dissected only by specially licensed experts who manage to prevent any of the toxic innards from coming in contact with the flesh before it is eaten raw. Despite this precaution, several people die each year from eating fugu.

East Coast blowfish are another story and may be eaten safely, especially if you buy them at the fish store, where everything conceivably dangerous about the fish—the skin and innards—has been removed. Blowfish "fillets" look like miniature chicken drumsticks and have a single bone running between two tasty little morsels of chicken-like flesh. They're easy to pick up with your fingers and gnaw, but if you want to be more refined it's also easy to slice the pieces of flesh off each side of the backbone before cooking. While good in themselves, blowfish are also a great substitute in recipes for sautéed shellfish such as scallops or shrimp, or for frogs' legs.

BEST METHODS: sautéing, deep-frying, soups and stews (remove bones from the "fillets")

AVOID: baking (blowfish are so small they must be cooked with rapid searing heat)

YIELD: 60 percent boneless flesh from "fillets"

ROUND FISH

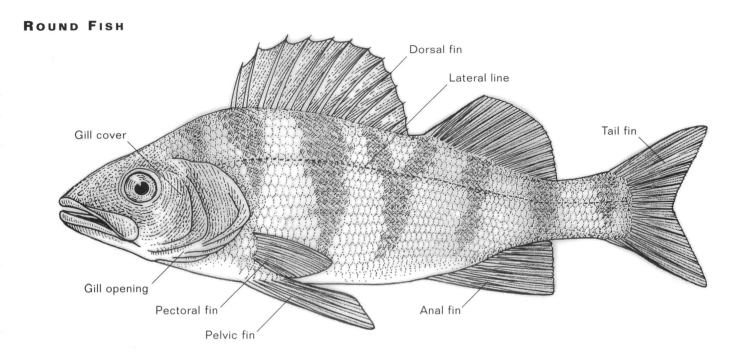

Dorsal fin

Lateral line

Gill cover

Tail fin

Gill opening

Pectoral fin

Anal fin

Pelvic fin

FLATFISH

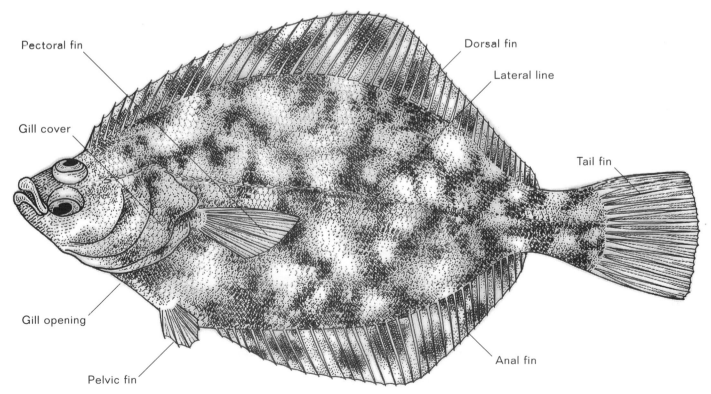

Pectoral fin

Dorsal fin

Lateral line

Gill cover

Tail fin

Gill opening

Anal fin

Pelvic fin

APPEARANCE WHEN COOKED: white (like chicken), meaty rather than flaky

TEXTURE WHEN COOKED: firm, meatlike or shellfishlike

FAT CONTENT: very low

FLAVOR: delicate, not at all fishy

BLUEFISH (*Pomatomus saltatrix*)

These fish are extremely popular along the Atlantic coast, especially during the summer, when they're also very plentiful. They're a favorite among sportfishermen because they swim near the surface and make a beautiful and tasty catch.

Bluefish grow to 20 pounds but are usually sold in sizes ranging from about a pound—these small ones are sometimes called *blue snappers*—up to about 10 pounds. They're an especially beautiful fish—thick, silvery, and streamlined—and especially during the summer can be found very fresh. Bluefish are usually sold whole but also occasionally as skin-on fillets.

Because of its strong flavor, bluefish is an acquired taste. The flavor will be much milder if the bluefish is bled properly (by making an incision above the tail or behind the gills) and gutted as soon as it is caught. Bluefish is especially good on the grill, sprinkled with chopped herbs such as thyme, marjoram, or rosemary or marinated. You can also improve the flavor and texture of bluefish by first soaking it in brine (see box). Be careful when turning the fish during cooking because the flesh is soft and easily torn. Fish between 1 and 2 pounds as well as fillets are also excellent panfried. When not iced properly, bluefish can cause scombroid poisoning.

BEST METHODS: grilling (whole fish up to 5 pounds, fillets with skin), panfrying

AVOID: deep-frying

YIELD: 45 percent skin-on fillets from gutted fish (bluefish should always be bought gutted)

APPEARANCE WHEN COOKED: brownish gray with darker sections, medium flake

TEXTURE WHEN COOKED: soft

FAT CONTENT: moderate

FLAVOR: strong, fishy (less so when brined)

BUTTERFISH (also called harvestfish, star butterfish, and Pacific pompano) Atlantic: *Peprilus triacanthus; Peprilus alepidotus* (also called harvestfish or star butterfish); Pacific: *Peprilus simillimus* (also called Pacific pompano)

BRINING BLUEFISH

One way to improve the texture of bluefish and at the same time give it a milder taste is to soak the fillets in a salt-and-herb solution. To marinate 2 pounds of bluefish fillets, combine 1 cup of kosher salt and 2 cups of water with 2 bay leaves and about 10 fresh thyme or marjoram sprigs in a small saucepan. Bring to a simmer and simmer gently for about 5 minutes, until the salt dissolves. Remove from the heat and let cool at room temperature for 15 minutes. Stir a quart of cold water into the salt mixture along with a dozen ice cubes. After 10 minutes, pour this mixture over the bluefish fillets in a nonreactive container (glass, stainless steel, or porcelain) and refrigerate for 1 hour. Drain and dry the fillets before cooking.

These delicious silvery little fish are a great bargain, but at least on the East Coast you'll need to go to a Caribbean or Chinese market to find them. Once you have tracked them down, they're so ridiculously cheap that you may wonder if they can possibly be any good.

Butterfish—don't confuse them with so-called butterfish fillets, which are actually sablefish—look vaguely like miniature pompano. They are small—rarely longer than 8 inches—with thin, tightly compressed bodies, a sharply forked tail, and bright silvery bodies with scales that just rub off. They're too small to bother filleting, but they're easy to eat when cooked whole because they don't contain many bones.

My favorite way to cook butterfish is to panfry them whole, but they are also quite good when grilled over very high heat—they're so thin that they cook in just a few minutes.

BEST METHODS: panfrying (whole), grilling (whole)

AVOID: adding to soups and stews

YIELD: 35 percent fillets with skin from gutted fish

APPEARANCE WHEN COOKED: white, fine flake

TEXTURE WHEN COOKED: soft, buttery

FAT CONTENT: moderate

FLAVOR: mild but tasty

THE COD FAMILY

At least until recently, the cod and its close relatives were among the most important food fish in the world. This is still largely true except that certain species—particularly the Atlantic cod for which the entire family is named—have been so overfished that there aren't many left.

The cod family, Gadidae, includes not only the so-called true cods—the Pacific and Atlantic cods—but also haddock, whiting, hake, pollack, scrod (a name for baby cod), grenadier, and cusk. Even though all of these groups of fish are related, the quality of the flesh varies, with some species having a firmer texture and a sweeter flavor.

Depending on species, members of the cod family are sold whole, with the head off, or as skinless or skin-on fillets. Larger specimens are also sometimes sold as steaks. Much cod and the closely related pollack are also processed and frozen into packaged foods such as fish sticks.

Because most members of the cod family have lean and delicate flesh, they are adaptable to most cooking techniques and recipes using delicately flavored ingredients. Don't confuse authentic members of the cod family with black cod—really a sablefish—or with rock cod, which is a member of the unrelated rockfish family, or with lingcod, which is actually a greenling.

BEST METHODS: panfrying, braising, poaching, in chunks in soups and stews, deep-frying

AVOID: serving whole fish with the skin still attached or with the skin on; raw (because of parasites)

YIELD: 30 percent to 40 percent fillet from ungutted fish

APPEARANCE WHEN COOKED: white, flaky

TEXTURE WHEN COOKED: moderately firm; soft to slightly firm (hakes and whitings)

FAT CONTENT: very low

FLAVOR: delicate, sweet

ATLANTIC VARIETIES

Atlantic Cod (*Gadus morhua*)

This best-known member of the cod family has long been one of the world's staples, but overfishing has caused its numbers to decline dramatically in recent years. Perhaps because of its abundance, until recently cod was thought of as an ordinary fish. But cod's sweet lean flavor and relative scarcity have now made it a favorite in some of the best seafood restaurants.

Fresh whole cod is easy to recognize because it has a single whisker (barbel) jutting out of its chin and a clear white lateral line that curves gently up the side of the fish as it approaches the head. Cod are usually brown or greenish gray with darker brown mottling and weigh between 3 and 25 pounds with the most common weight being about 10 pounds. Cod is fished from North Carolina up to Greenland and is available year-round.

Cod are sold fresh with the head on or off but more often as fillets with the skin removed. Cod fillets, especially when small, are sold as scrod, but the word *scrod* really means just "small" and is used with many fish in the cod family. So you might be getting pollack or cusk, which aren't as tasty, when you buy scrod. Strictly speaking, the fish should be marketed as scrod cod, scrod haddock, etc. Cod freezes well, so unless you see perfectly fresh-looking whole cod at the market, you may be better off buying frozen fillets. Cod is also sold dried as stockfish and salt cod.

Atlantic Pollack (also called blue cod, Boston bluefish in the Northeast, and, in Great Britain, saithe or coalfish) (*Pollachius virens*)

While pollack isn't quite as delicate-tasting as cod, it's surprisingly sweet and satisfying for such an inexpensive fish. It's especially wonderful coated in a light batter and deep-fried (the British serve it up in fish and chips). Unfortunately most pollack is sold already filleted as scrod, so it's hard to be sure of what you're getting. As cod stocks decrease, occasionally fresh whole pollack does show up at market, often under a different name (I've even seen it sold as blue snapper). Whole pollack are usually sliced into steaks.

Pollack has much the same shape as Atlantic cod but is easy to distinguish because it doesn't have a whisker (barbel) sticking out of its chin. Also, pollack has an almost straight lateral line and evenly colored gray skin, except on the belly, which is white. Whole pollack usually weigh between 4 and 8 pounds. Pollack fillets are darker than cod fillets and have a duller, almost gray appearance.

Cusk (also called torsk or tusk) (*Brosme brosme*)

It's unlikely you'll ever run into whole cusk at the fish market because it's usually sold already filleted as scrod. It is, however, easy to recognize a whole specimen because, unlike most other members of the cod family, cusk has a single dorsal fin that runs all along the back of the fish to the tail, giving this fish a vaguely eellike appearance. Cusk weigh up to 20 pounds but are usually much smaller. Cusk has excellent firm white flesh that can be cooked in the same way as that of other members of the cod family.

Haddock (*Melanogrammus aeglefinus*)

Because of its delicate flavor and relatively firm flesh, haddock is perhaps the most prized member of the cod family. Haddock usually weigh between 2 and 5 pounds and, like cod, are sometimes sold filleted as scrod or with the skin on so you can verify that you're really getting haddock. Haddock have a dark lateral line and a dark spot above the pectoral fin (which sticks out along the side behind the gills). They are caught on both sides of the Atlantic and on the American side from Newfoundland all the way down to New Jersey. In recent years haddock has become relatively scarce and expensive because of overfishing.

Haddock is sometimes split and smoked to make finnan haddie, originally a Scottish preparation but now made in Canada, Denmark, and to a small extent New England. As haddock stocks diminish, so does the supply of finnan haddie. Authentic finnan haddie is made from the split haddock and has the backbone still attached.

Hake/Whiting

Even though there are subtle biological differences between hake and whiting, both belong to the cod family, and are marketed interchangeably. Most varieties of hake and whiting have a reputation for mushiness, but this is largely due to lack of freshness or proper handling (though they do have a softer texture than cod, haddock, or pollack).

Atlantic Whiting (also called silver hake) (*Merluccius bilinearis*)

In most fish markets Atlantic whiting is sold simply as whiting. Whiting are often sold whole with their heads and usually weigh just slightly less than a pound. Larger whiting are also sold filleted. Whiting are best in February and March, just before they spawn. Whiting, called *merluzza*, is the fish consumed most widely in Spain. French cooks are fond of deep-frying whole whiting, curled around with their tails in their mouths, called *merlan frit en colère*—translated as "angry whitings." Who would blame them?

Red Hake (also called squirrel hake; ling in parts of the Northeast) (*Urophycis chuss*)

Red hake once was little seen in American fish markets, but with supplies of cod and haddock dwindling it's becoming more popular and very well might be what you're buying as "scrod." Most red hake caught weigh about a pound—although they grow much larger—and have reddish brown coloring with a dorsal fin that runs along the back of almost the entire fish. Red hake has a long antennalike ray on the front of the dorsal fin. It can be cooked in the same way as other members of the cod family.

White Hake (also called Boston ling or steakfish) (*Urophycis tenuis*)

These large hake can weigh up to 30 pounds but are usually only 1 or 2 pounds and are often sold in steak form, especially around Philadelphia and Baltimore, where they are most popular. White hake has lean delicate flesh and can be cooked the same way as cod.

NORTH PACIFIC VARIETIES

Alaskan Pollack (also called walleye pollock and bigeye cod) (*Theragra chalcogramma*)

Alaskan pollack is only distantly related to Atlantic pollack and is considerably smaller, typically weighing between $\frac{1}{2}$ and 2 pounds. In terms of quantity, Alaskan pollack is the most important fish in U.S. waters and by weight comprises almost 10 percent of all the fish caught in the world. So, it's peculiar that more of us haven't heard of it or seen it (at least knowingly). The reason is that almost all Alaskan pollack is frozen—some of it is frozen twice and of inferior quality—and sold already filleted, in Japan converted to surimi, which is used to make fake crab sticks or in commercially prepared foods such as fish sticks.

Pacific Cod (also called true cod or gray cod) (*Gadus macrocephalus*)

These cod are close relatives of the Atlantic cod and, except for being slightly smaller—5 to 10 pounds—and having pale gray coloring, are almost identical to their eastern cousins. Most Pacific cod ends up filleted and frozen, but occasionally fresh cod shows up in better fish markets. Pacific cod is caught from Oregon up to the Bering Sea.

OTHER VARIETIES

Hake/Whiting

Several species of hake and whiting are imported from South America and New Zealand to make up for the dwindling supply of cod-related fish in the Northern Hemisphere.

Antarctic Queen (also called New Zealand hake) (*Merluccius australis*)

Antarctic queen is a marketing name for what is actually a hake. Antarctic queen usually weigh between 7 and 9 pounds and are sold as fresh or frozen fillets, although occasionally you'll see them whole at the fish store with their heads and guts removed. Antarctic queen are among the more desirable hakes because they have slightly firmer flesh and a mild flavor.

Argentine Hake (also called Uruguayan whiting or Patagonian whiting) (*Merluccius hubbsi*)

This is another fish you're unlikely ever to see whole since it's usually sold as frozen fillets.

Chilean Hake (also called hake, Peruvian whiting, or Peruvian hake) (*Merluccius gayi*)

Similar to Argentine hake but because it has softer flesh, not as desirable.

Hoki (also called blue hake or blue grenadier) (*Macruronus novaezelandiae*)

Most hoki is consumed in New Zealand where it is caught, but some is exported in the form of frozen fillets. Hoki is marketed as a substitute for Atlantic cod, but it has a somewhat higher fat content and slightly pink coloring.

CONGER EEL (American conger: *Conger oceanicus*)

You'll probably run into conger eel only if you shop at an ethnic market or special-order it. Conger eel has never been popular in the United States but is a favorite in Europe, where it enters into soups and stews, the most famous being bouillabaisse. Conger eels are scary-looking with pointed heads and sharp teeth, but you'll usually be able to buy a section without the head. To use conger eel in soups and stews, remove the skin and bone and just cut the flesh into chunks before simmering it directly in the soup or stew.

CUSK: See Cod.

CUTLASS FISH (also called ribbonfish, silver scabbardfish) (Atlantic: *Lepidopus caudatus*)

This horrifying-looking fish is actually quite good to eat if you can get beyond its serpentine shape and vicious-looking teeth. Most ribbonfish are bright silver and about 3 feet long. Only the front half is fleshy enough to be worth filleting. The only place I ever see ribbonfish is in Chinese markets. I have had luck panfrying ribbonfish without the skin and grilling it with the skin.

DORY

The most famous species of this weird-looking fish is the John Dory (*Zeus faber*), which is found mostly on the eastern side of the Atlantic. In most languages the John Dory is called St. Peter's fish (Saint Pierre, San Pietro, etc.) because of the black spot on both of its sides, which is supposed to represent St. Peter's thumbprint. John Dory fish are extremely expensive in Europe, and because a whole fish yields a relatively small amount of fillet, the flesh itself is exorbitant. Fortunately there is an American dory (*Zenopsis ocellata*) that swims in the western Atlantic and is just as delicious as its European counterpart. You can't count on finding American dory at the fish store—it's not fished commercially and shows up only now and then—so it's best to grab it when you see it. Dories are easy to recognize. They are flat with a large protruding lower jaw; most have the characteristic "thumbprint" and large fins that run all the way back to the tail. Most dories weigh about 2 pounds.

In addition to the American dory, two closely related fish, the black oreo dory (*Allocyttus niger*, sometimes called *deepsea dory*) and the smooth oreo dory (*Pseudocyttus maculatus*), are being imported into the United States from New Zealand, usually as frozen fillets. While technically oreos, not dories, these fish look similar and have the same lean and firm white flesh that makes dories such a treat. Black oreo dory fillets tend to be small, however, and not as desirable as those of the smooth oreo dory. Because these two New Zealand varieties are marketed as frozen fillets, they won't be as exciting as a fresh European or American dory.

If you luck upon a whole dory, remember that the yield of flesh is small. On the other hand, you'll have a lot of bones and head to make a delicious fish broth. Dory should always be cooked filleted.

BEST METHODS: panfrying (skinless fillets), steaming, poaching, soups and stews

AVOID: baking whole (there's too little usable flesh) and smoking (flesh is too lean)

YIELD: 25 percent fillets from ungutted fish

APPEARANCE WHEN COOKED: pure white except for black oreo dory, which is slightly off-white

TEXTURE WHEN COOKED: firm

FAT CONTENT: very low

FLAVOR: mild, delicate

DRUMS, CROAKERS, AND SEA TROUT

This large family of mostly saltwater fish is divided—at least in the vernacular—by whether the fish produces a drumming or a croaking sound when it sticks its head out of the water. Drums and croakers comprise a large collection of fish, many of which are quite delicious. But sorting through the collection of drums and croakers is especially confusing since some members of this family have names like *sea trout* and *white bass* but have no relation to either trout or bass.

There is so much variation in quality that it's almost impossible to give general tips on how to cook drums and croakers. A word of warning, however, does apply to most species: Don't eat drums or croakers raw. They often contain parasites, which are rendered harmless once the fish is cooked.

BEST METHODS: panfrying, braising, poaching, in chunks in soups and stews, deep-frying

AVOID: raw

YIELD: 40 percent fillet from ungutted fish

APPEARANCE WHEN COOKED: white to off-white, fine flake

TEXTURE WHEN COOKED: slightly firm to very firm depending on species

FAT CONTENT: very low

FLAVOR: delicate, sweet

ATLANTIC AND GULF VARIETIES

Atlantic Croaker (also called golden croaker) (*Micropogonias undulatus*)

These small golden silvery fish are caught and eaten along the Atlantic coast from New York to southern Florida. They are inexpensive and tasty, lean with moderately firm flesh. Because of their small size—up to 3 pounds but usually under a pound—they are almost always sold whole, especially in ethnic markets, though sometimes they appear dressed, with the head cut off. They are best served whole as individual servings, either panfried or broiled.

Black Drum (*Pogonias cromis*)

This is one of the larger drums, typically weighing between 5 and 10 pounds but growing as large as 100 pounds. Black drums have black silvery skin and small barbels (whiskers) on the lower jaw. The flesh of black drum has a very firm, almost meaty, texture, so it will hold up under almost any cooking method. I especially like it in fish stews and soup because it won't disintegrate.

Kingfish (northern: *Menticirrhus saxatilis*; southern: *Menticirrhus americanus*; Gulf: *Menticirrhus littoralis*)

Unfortunately these delicious fish are hard to find in fish markets, although apparently a large number is caught by anglers. Kingfish—not to be confused with king mackerel—are rarely over a foot long.

Red Drum (also called redfish or channel bass) (*Sciaenops ocellata*)

Most of us had never heard of these fish until about 10 years ago, when Paul Prudhomme's blackened redfish became all the rage. The dish in fact became so popular that red drums almost ended up being fished out and a moratorium was placed on fishing for red drum in the Gulf. Red drums, raised by aquaculture in Texas and Ecuador, have helped meet some of the demand. Fortunately, blackened redfish is just as good when made with any firm-fleshed fish.

Red drums can be found infrequently as far north as Massachusetts all the way down to the Gulf of Mexico, where they are (or were at least until recently) most abundant. Red drums grow to be quite large—up to 30 pounds—but are usually sold in 1- to 2-pound sizes, which connoisseurs say is the best size anyway. They are easy to recognize because of their coppery sheen and pronounced scales. They also have a black spot on both sides of their tails and don't have whiskers (barbels) on their chins as do black drums. Redfish often contain parasites—in the same way as pork—and should be cooked thoroughly.

Spot (also called goody, Lafayette, and Norfolk spot) (*Leiostomus xanthurus*)

These are the smallest members of the croaker family that are sold with any regularity. Most specimens weigh only about ¼ pound. Spots are easy to recognize by their spot right behind the gill opening. Spots are best panfried whole.

Spotted or Speckled Sea Trout (*Cynoscion nebulosus*)

This member of the croaker family is absolutely no relation to a trout (except that it's a fish) but looks vaguely like a trout because of its silvery skin and black spots. The sea trout's closest relative is in fact the weakfish, which tends to swim in more northern waters. To add to the confusion, the names *sea trout* and *weakfish* are sometimes used interchangeably. This is no tragedy since both fish are very good.

Sea trout are caught along the southern Atlantic, especially Florida, and in the Gulf of Mexico.

Weakfish (also called gray trout or sea trout) (*Cynoscion regalis*)

This delicious fish is especially pleasant to eat because it doesn't have any pin bones. I used to be puzzled by the name—the flesh is moderately firm, so there seemed to be nothing weak about it—but fishermen now tell me that the name comes from the fish's weak mouth, which easily tears and lets go of the hook.

This fish grows quite large—up to 40 pounds—but most of the weakfish I see for sale in New York weigh about 2 pounds. Weakfish is found all along the Atlantic coast from Florida to Massachusetts (in the summer only), but it is hard to describe because its markings vary from fish to fish. In general weakfish are silver-gray with more or less densely packed clusters of spots sometimes forming subtle stripes. Weakfish is delicious when panfried whole—especially since there are so few bones to contend with.

PACIFIC VARIETIES

Unless you fish, you're unlikely to encounter the many varieties of Pacific drums and croakers, because commercial fishing of these species has been outlawed. Among the favorites are the California corbina (*Menticirrhus undulatus*), the spotfin croaker (*Roncador stearnsi*), and the yellowfin croaker (*Umbrina roncador*).

Totuava (*Cynoscion macdonaldi*)

A. J. McClane tells a sad story in his book *The Encyclopedia of Fish Cookery* of how this wonderful fish was driven almost to extinction during the 1920s and 1930s when it was caught and massacred for its swim bladder, which was sent to China for use in soups. It seems that this once-abundant fish has never quite recovered and only occasionally shows up in fish markets. Totuava apparently (I've never seen or tasted one) grow up to 80 pounds and according to McClane are best broiled or barbecued.

White Sea Bass (*Atractoscion nobilis*)

Not really a bass but a drum, white sea bass is one of California's most prized fish. Unfortunately it's hard to find on the open market, and most of it is sold to fancy restaurants in southern California during the late summer and fall. Regionally it is known as *corbina*, *California white sea bass*, and *king croaker*, but the FDA-approved market name is *sea trout*. White sea bass grows quite large—over 75 pounds—but most of the time is sold in the 15-pound range. Grab it when you can.

FLATFISH: SOLE, FLOUNDER, AND HALIBUT

Flatfish are well named: they spend much of their time resting flat, half buried in sand, on the ocean floor. The skin on the top of a flatfish is usually gray or almost black but may be slightly mottled or have a brownish hue—it's designed to match the surrounding sand—so the fish can hide from predators and disguise itself so as not to scare off unsuspecting prey. The underside of most flatfish is white.

Flatfish begin their lives with eyes on both sides of their heads and swim upright in the same way as round fish. But as the fish matures, one of the eyes actually migrates to the other side. During the same period the fish begins to swim on its side—flat—so the side with the two eyes is now the top, dark side. In this way the fish can use both eyes while resting flat in the sand. Some flatfish appear to have eyes on the left side, others on the right. Flatfish such as winter flounder and gray sole seem to swim from left to right (so-called *right-eyed flatfish*), while others such as Dover sole and summer flounder (fluke) seem to swim from right to left (so-called *left-eyed flatfish*). It's easy to tell the difference between the two: just arrange (or imagine) the fish in front of you—going sideways, the backside away from you and the belly toward you—and see what direction the fish is facing. None of this has much importance for the cook except that it may sometimes be useful for identifying an unknown species.

Almost all the flatfish available in the United States are flounders, but many flounder species are commonly called *sole*. The only species of the true sole family (Soleidae) sold commercially in the United States is imported Dover sole from Europe. While many of the flounders available in the United States under such names as *lemon sole, gray sole,* and *petrale sole* are similar in texture and flavor (freshness is more important than species), authentic Dover sole has an unmistakable firm meaty texture that distinguishes it from flounder. While four species of halibut are marketed in the United States, halibut is easy to distinguish from other flatfish just because of its size. Halibut have been known to reach 700 pounds, but nowadays it's unusual to find them so large. Most halibut ranges from 4 pounds (for the smallest species, California halibut) to 40-pound samples of other species. But even the smallest halibut are larger than any sole or flounder you're likely to encounter.

BUYING SOLE, FLOUNDER, AND HALIBUT

Most flounder is sold filleted. There are two types of fillets: so-called quarters, which are narrow strips (four fillets per fish, two per side), and halves, which consist of two fillet strips connected at the middle by a thin gristly strip (two fillets per fish, one per side). When using halves it's best to separate the two strips by cutting along each side of the center strip, at the same time eliminating any trace of gristle. Buying filleted flounder not only makes it difficult to figure out what kind of fish you're getting but also makes it hard to determine freshness. If you want filleted flounder, buy a whole flounder and have the fishmonger fillet it or take it home and fillet it yourself. In this way you can also use the heads and bones for making fish broth.

When buying whole flounder it's important to inspect it carefully since all flatfish, because they are so thin, are very perishable. Very fresh flounder should be stiff and have red gills that smell like the ocean and not like fish. Beware of flounder that is coated with white slime. Transparent slime is a sign of freshness, but when it turns white the fish is growing stale.

Halibut is usually sold in the form of steaks but is also sometimes available filleted. If you look closely at a halibut steak, you can see that it is a cross section of the fish and has four sections separated from each other by either membrane or bone. Halibut steaks are fine for most cooking methods, but if the steaks are very large or you prefer serving the halibut in smaller pieces, it's easy to separate the four sections by carefully cutting along each side of the membrane or bone with a sharp knife (see color page 28). Halibut is often sold frozen, usually in steaks. Frozen halibut tends to be opaque and very white, while fresh halibut is more ivory-colored.

PREPARING AND COOKING

Fillets

The obvious advantage of cooking fillets is convenience—fish fillets, except for cutting out the center gristly strip, are ready to cook. The major drawback of cooking flounder fillets is that the flesh becomes very fragile once cooked. The flesh not only takes on a mushy texture in the mouth but also becomes very difficult to handle and transfer from pan to plate. This problem applies less to halibut

and larger flounder fillets, which are less fragile partly just because they are much thicker. Authentic Dover sole fillets have a firm texture and have none of the disadvantages of flounder fillets. Be aware that the fillets from the bottom white side of flatfish are thinner than those on the top dark side.

Whole fish

Cooking the whole fish is the tastiest and most appealing way to prepare sole or flounder. Fish cooked whole retains its shape—fragility isn't a problem—and flavor. The only disadvantage is that large specimens must be carved at the table—reintroducing the fragility problem—and smaller specimens must be served whole to each guest. Many people don't know what to do when confronted with a whole flatfish and need a quick demonstration at the table (see color page 29).

Flatfish destined to be served whole must be cleaned and dressed. The top gray skin of sole and certain flounders is tough and scaly and must be peeled off, while on some kinds of flounder it need only be scaled. The bottom white skin of most flounder can be left attached and need only be scaled. If you buy a flatfish and are unsure about what to do with the top or bottom skin, have the fishmonger scale both sides. When you get the fish home, inspect both the white and dark skins and scrape off any stray scales left by the fishmonger. If the top skin seems thick or you can't get the scales off, peel it off.

Steaks

The only flatfish steaks you're likely to encounter with any regularity are halibut steaks. They require no preparation unless you want to cut the four boneless sections out of each steak (see color page 28).

BEST METHODS: panfrying, braising, poaching, grilling (whole fish only), soups and stews (large chunks taken from halibut steaks or Dover sole only)

AVOID: grilling fillets (which will stick and tear), using in stews or soups (fillets fall apart; large chunks of halibut are all right)

YIELD: 28 percent to 35 percent skinless fillets from whole ungutted fish

APPEARANCE WHEN COOKED: very white, flaky

TEXTURE WHEN COOKED: very fragile, soft, except halibut, which is firm, and Dover sole, which is very firm

FAT CONTENT: very low

FLAVOR: delicate, sometimes iodinelike

ATLANTIC SPECIES

Gray Sole (also called witch flounder) (*Glyptocephalus cynoglossus*)

This East Coast favorite has perfectly white and relatively firm flesh. Gray sole—actually a flounder—gets its name because the top skin is pale gray rather than dark or tinted with brown. Whole gray sole are easy to recognize because the fillets can be seen as relatively narrow strips running along the center of the fish. The bottom or "white side" of a gray sole is also pale gray. Gray sole fillets are long and narrow and perfectly white. Because gray sole has a very small yield, the fillets are quite expensive. The best way to eat gray sole is cooked whole with both the white and black skin scaled and left attached but the fins removed with heavy scissors. Gray sole grow quite large—occasionally about 2 feet long and up to 5 pounds—but are relatively elongated rather than round. (Yield: 28 percent.)

Halibut

Four species of fish are marketed as halibut, two from the Atlantic and two from the Pacific.

Atlantic Halibut (*Hippoglossus hippoglossus*) Atlantic halibut is generally considered the best of the four halibut species because of its firm texture and delicate flavor. Atlantic halibut is usually sold fresh or frozen in steaks. I like best to buy it in fish stores where I can see them slice the steaks off a section of the whole fish.

Greenland Turbot (*Reinhardtius hippoglossoides*)

Even though Greenland turbot is often marketed as halibut or black halibut, it's not a true halibut. Greenland turbot doesn't swim just off the coast of Greenland but is found in the northernmost areas of both the Atlantic and Pacific although at times it is found in the Atlantic as far south as Cape Cod. Greenland turbot is much fattier than Atlantic halibut, has a softer texture, and is generally less desirable. It's unlikely that you'll encounter a whole section of Greenland turbot, but if you do, notice that the underside is quite dark, unlike Atlantic halibut, which has a pure white underside. In some parts of the country Greenland turbot is sold simply as turbot even though it sells for about a tenth of the price of authentic European turbot.

Sand Dab (also called dab) (*Hippoglossoides platessoides*)

Sand dab, sometimes called *American plaice* or *Canadian plaice,* has a gray to reddish brown top skin. It grows quite large—up to about 2 feet long and about 5 pounds—and is marketed as flounder or, when filleted, as fillets of sole even though the FDA considers that label unacceptable. Sand dab fillets have reddish lines running lengthwise along the middle of the filets. Don't confuse this fish with a smaller species, *Scophthalmus aquosus,* also called *sand dab* or *windowpane.* Windowpane is very thin and doesn't yield much flesh.

Southern Flounder (*Paralichthys lethostigma*)

Fished off the coast of North Carolina all the way around to Texas, this small flounder reaches a maximum weight of about 3 pounds but is usually marketed between 1 and 1½ pounds. Southern flounder has a plain and somewhat drab dark side with a greenish hue and is often caught "accidentally" by shrimp fishermen. (Yield: 40 percent.)

Summer Flounder (also called fluke) (*Paralichthys dentatus*)

This flounder is usually sold under the name *fluke.* Well known by recreational anglers, it is a left-eyed flounder caught inshore in summer. The top skin of a fluke is usually slightly orange or brown rather than black or gray and has black spots; it has a larger mouth than other flounders. Like most flounder, fluke is fragile once cooked, but because fluke is relatively large (up to 2 feet long and 2 to 5 pounds), the fillets are thick and substantial. (Yield: 40 percent.)

Winter Flounder (*Pseudopleuronectes americanus*)

This relatively large oval flounder has a dark top skin and is also called *lemon sole* when it weighs more than 3½ pounds and *blackback* flounder when it weighs less. Winter flounder is usually marketed only in the winter and spring since it lives offshore during the summer. Winter flounder is one of the tastiest flounder available in the United States but has the disadvantage of being very fragile once cooked. Large fillets are sold as lemon sole or simply fillet of sole. Lemon sole fillets often have dark gray coloration on the skin side. (Yield: 40 percent.)

Yellowtail Flounder (*Limanda ferruginea*)

This common East Coast flounder weighs an average of only 1 or 2 pounds but for its small size is one of the most important commercial Atlantic species. It is sometimes called *rusty dab* or *yellowtail dab.* Recently, however, its numbers have been diminishing and it's harder to find. (Yield: 40 percent.)

PACIFIC SPECIES

"Dover" Sole (*Microstomus pacificus*)

Unfortunately this insipid-tasting fish is never marketed with the quotation marks, which may lead the unwary to confuse it with authentic Dover sole from Europe. The two have nothing in common. This fish, also called *Pacific flounder,* is considerably larger (2 to 10 pounds) than authentic Dover sole and has a mushy texture when cooked; authentic Dover sole has a very firm texture.

English Sole (*Pleuronectes vetulus*)

Almost always sold in fillets, English sole, a flounder, is sometimes called *lemon sole* but is much smaller than East Coast lemon sole. English sole is not found in English waters.

Halibut

Two species of halibut are found along the Pacific coast of the United States.

California Halibut (*Paralichthys californicus*) This fish is actually a flounder and is much smaller than either Atlantic or Pacific halibut (a California halibut typically weighs between 4 and 12 pounds). Its flesh is less firm than either Pacific or Atlantic halibut and because of its size is usually sold in fillet form rather than in steaks.

Pacific Halibut (*Hippoglossus stenolepis*) This is by far the most common halibut on the West Coast. The season for Pacific halibut is run on a strict quota system and usually lasts only a day or two, so except for a short period each year, all Pacific halibut available at fish markets has been frozen. Unlike Atlantic halibut, which is usually sold in steaks, Pacific halibut is often sold filleted and sliced. Pacific halibut is a delicious fish but slightly less flavorful than Atlantic halibut.

Petrale Sole (*Eopsetta jordani*)

Petrale sole—again, really a flounder—is one of the best flatfish found on the Pacific coast. It can be found as large as 5 pounds but more commonly weighs about a pound. While much of the catch ends up filleted, the fish tastes a million times better when cooked whole—dressed and scaled with both white and dark skin attached (sometimes called *rexing*). Removal of the heads is optional.

Rex Sole (*Glyptocephalus zachirus*)

This delicious little fish—actually a flounder—was once common in Pacific waters but is becoming harder to find. Rex sole can weigh up to a pound but more typically weighs about ½ pound. It is too small to fillet but tastes better cooked whole anyway. Rex sole need only be scaled before cooking—both the dark and white skin can be left attached. My favorite way to eat rex sole is *à la meunière*, but it is also great grilled. (Yield: 35 percent.)

Rock Sole (*Lepidopsetta bilineata*)

This is one of the best soles for filleting because it has a relatively firm texture and won't fall apart. It has a sweet delicate flavor and is one of the most desirable Pacific flatfish. Whole rock sole weigh up to 5 pounds.

Sand Dab (*Citharichthys sordidus*)

These little fish—they weigh up to a pound but are sold as small as 4 ounces—are a West Coast favorite and always sold and cooked whole; the fillets would be microscopic. Sand dabs appear to swim to the right. They are best cooked *à la meunière* or grilled over a very hot fire.

Starry Flounder (*Platichthys stellatus*)

Starry flounder are easy to recognize because of the distinctive orange stripes on their fins. They weigh 1 to 5 pounds and have very delicate flesh, which unfortunately falls apart easily when cooked.

EUROPEAN SPECIES

It's unusual for European fish to be imported into the United States because the best fish, already so expensive in Europe, would become prohibitively so once they get here. But occasionally European fish do show up in American markets, and aquaculturists are starting to experiment with growing European varieties in other parts of the world, so we may start seeing some of the more famous species in several years.

Dover Sole (*Solea solea* and *Solea vulgaris*)

This is the only true sole available in the United States, although it has to be imported from the European side of the Atlantic. It has firm flesh (unlike flounder) and a delicate flavor. It's delicious when cooked whole and in fillets. Dover sole has a very elongated elliptical shape with a tough dark top skin that must be peeled off before cooking. Dover sole is expensive. Most Dover sole weighs from 14 to 16 ounces. Don't confuse Dover sole with Pacific flounder (*Microstomus pacificus*), which sometimes is sold under the name *Dover sole*. (Yield: 40 percent.)

Brill (*Scopthalmus rhombus*)

Sometimes used as a substitute for turbot, brill is somewhat smaller and not as thick as turbot, so the fillets are not quite as meaty and thick. It's easy to tell the difference between brill and turbot: brill is oval, turbot diamond-shaped. While brill doesn't reach the culinary heights of turbot, it is still an excellent fish, better than most American flatfish. Pick it up when you can.

Plaice (*Pleuronectes platessa*)

This common and inexpensive European fish is occasionally sold in the United States, usually already filleted. Plaice doesn't have the firm meaty texture of turbot or brill, but when compared in price to American fillets of sole it's worth the money.

Turbot (*Rhombus maxima* or *Psetta maxima*)

This large (up to 30 pounds but usually sold around 10 pounds) diamond-shaped fish, with the possible exception of Dover sole, is the most prized of all European flatfish. It has four thick perfectly white fillets that keep their firm texture and delicate flavor when cooked. Turbot has a very rough and very black top skin with little barnaclelike growths on its surface. Other species such as Pacific arrowtooth flounder and Greenland turbot are sometimes sold as turbot, but these soft and thin fillets have nothing in common with the real thing. In fact you can be sure that any fillet sold as turbot in the United States is not the real thing. Unless aquaculturists manage to bring down the price of authentic turbot, your only encounter with genuine turbot is likely to be in a fine (and expensive) French restaurant.

Greenling: See Lingcod.

GROUPER

Groupers are hard to describe because each species is so different. Some are brightly colored, some drab; some weigh a pound or two, others up to 1,000 pounds. But most have thick bodies and firm excellent-tasting flesh. Because groupers are members of a subgroup within the sea bass family, Serranidae, they are occasionally marketed as bass.

There are hundreds of species of grouper, but only a couple dozen or so are regularly sold in fish stores in the United States—and most of these are sold in Florida. Most of the groupers sold in the United States come from along the coast of Florida, the Gulf of Mexico, and the Caribbean, but there are also Pacific varieties caught off the coast of southern California, Mexico, and Central America.

In ethnic markets grouper is sold whole, but grouper fillets often show up in other places and can be quite large, with cherry-red coloring on the skin side of each fillet. The coloring turns a chocolate hue as the fish loses freshness, so buy fillets accordingly. In any case, the skin of most groupers is too thick to be eaten and should be removed either before or after cooking.

Grouper is most plentiful in the summer.

BEST METHODS: panfrying, braising, poaching, grilling, in chunks in soups and stews

AVOID: serving whole fish with the skin still attached; raw; large groupers of uncertain origin (they may contain ciguatera toxins)

YIELD: 30 percent to 40 percent skinless fillets from ungutted fish

APPEARANCE WHEN COOKED: white, flaky

TEXTURE WHEN COOKED: moderately firm

FAT CONTENT: very low

FLAVOR: delicate, mildly pronounced flavor

ATLANTIC AND GULF SPECIES

Black Grouper (*Mycteroperca bonaci*)

Caught mostly off the coast of Florida and in the Caribbean, black grouper can weigh as much as 100 pounds but more typically weighs 10 to 15 pounds. It has dark brown or gray blotchy skin with black spots and squiggly pale horizontal lines. It is often confused with the gag, another popular grouper of similar quality. Because of its size and thick skin, black grouper is often sold filleted.

Gag (*Mycteroperca microlepsis*)

This fish is similar to and more common than the black grouper, so what is sold as black grouper is often gag. This isn't a serious problem because gag is just as tasty, possibly even more so.

Jewfish (*Epinephelus itajara*)

The jewfish is the largest of all the groupers, weighing up to 700 pounds, although most specimens weigh about 200. Because of overfishing, there is a moratorium on jewfish and it no longer appears in the markets. It's a tasty fish and before the moratorium was very popular with Chinese cooks. Sometimes confused with Nassau grouper, jewfish is caught all along the western Atlantic coast from southern Florida to Brazil.

Nassau Grouper (*Epinephelus striatus*)

Because of its size, abundance, and tasty flesh, Nassau grouper is one of the most popular groupers along the Eastern Seaboard—especially off the coast of Florida—and around the Bahamas. Nassau groupers grow to be quite large—up to more than 50 pounds—but most that I see at the market weigh between 5 and 10 pounds. A Nassau grouper is easy to recognize by the distinctive dark spot on its back between its dorsal fin and tail. It also has brownish gray coloration and wavy or barlike lines running down its sides.

Red Grouper (*Epinephelus morio*)

This is one of the most common and one of the best groupers. Red grouper is easy to recognize because of its even brownish red coloring and faint white spots. As with most groupers sold in the United States, it is most common around southern Florida and in the Gulf of Mexico, but it often shows up in New York markets, especially in summer. Red groupers grow up to 50 pounds, but most weigh around 5 to 10 pounds.

Red Hind (*Epinephelus guttatus*)

I always snatch up this tasty little fish when I see it at the market. Red hind—sometimes called *strawberry grouper*—usually weighs between 1½ and 2 pounds and has greenish yellow coloring and brownish red spots along its back. The spots closer to the belly are bright red.

Warsaw Grouper (*Epinephelus nigritus*)

This is another large grouper, weighing up to 300 pounds (although specimens 100 pounds or smaller are more common), and is sometimes sold as jewfish. Warsaw grouper is colored an even gray and has small white blotches. It has delicious firm flesh.

Yellowfin Grouper (*Mycteroperca venenosa*)

The name of this fish is confusing because only a tiny strip along the pectoral fin—the little fin next to the gills—is yellow. The rest of the fish is colored with red, black, and silver-gray and is covered with little red spots. This tasty little fish usually weighs between 1½ and 2 pounds.

Yellowmouth Grouper (*Mycteroperca interstitialis*)

This is one of the most common grouper species sold along the Eastern Seaboard. Most yellowmouth groupers weigh about 2 pounds and have brown spots with yellow coloration around the jaws.

PACIFIC SPECIES

Broomtail Grouper (*Mycteroperca xenarcha*)

This large grouper—it weighs up to 100 pounds—is rarely seen in California fish markets but is more likely to be encountered in Mexico. I've never tasted broomtail grouper but hear that its flavor is not as delicate as that of most Atlantic species.

Cabrilla (*Epinephelus* spp.)

There are several cabrilla species, the most famous of which is the spotted cabrilla, *Epinephelus analogus*. Much like the broomtail grouper, these large and delicious groupers are more likely to be found in fish markets in Mexico, where they are much appreciated, than in California markets. Cabrilla are comparable in quality to the best Atlantic groupers.

Hapu'upu'u (also called grouper or sea bass) (*Epinephelus quernus*)

The color of the hapu'upu'u varies from dark brown to dark gray with scattered white spots. It weighs from 5 to 30 pounds and is popular in Hawaii, especially in ethnic restaurants, where small fish are often served steamed and whole.

Grunt (white grunt: *Haemulon plumieri*; porkfish: *Anisotremus virginicus*)

You're not too likely to encounter grunts unless you live along the southern part of the Eastern Seaboard, especially in the Carolinas or Florida. I have seen grunts for sale at New York's Fulton fish market but never in a New York retail store, so I'm not sure where they end up.

Grunts get their name from the grunting sound they make when taken out of the water. There are dozens of varieties of grunts that are either caught by sportfishermen or sold commercially, but the two most common are the white grunt and the porkfish (not to be confused with the hogfish or the pigfish, another grunt). While these grunts can grow up to 2 pounds, neither often makes it to much more than a pound. White grunts are easy to recognize because of their pale metallic blue and gold stripes, which span the length of their bodies, including their heads.

Grunts have lean white rather soft flesh. They are usually deep-fried or panfried.

Herring (Atlantic: *Clupea harengus harengus*; Pacific: *Clupea harengus pallasi*)

Even though herring is (or was until recently) one of the most abundant foods in the sea, it's unusual to see herring for sale fresh. Until I found where to buy it fresh—from fishermen at Sheepshead Bay in Brooklyn—I had seen it only smoked or in its many preserved forms in jars. A fresh herring is beautiful to look at, with bright silvery scales that slide off easily and beautiful deep green coloring along its back. Most fresh herring are about 10 inches long; herring 3 and 4 inches long are also abundant but are usually sold as sardines.

Because herring have a high fat content, they are especially delicious when grilled or broiled. Herring roe is considered a delicacy by the Japanese, who marinate it in mirin, rice wine vinegar, broth, and soy sauce, which gives it a golden color, and then serve it as part of their traditional New Year's celebration.

Most of us have encountered herring only in one of its many preserved forms. So many methods are used for preserving herring, especially in Scandinavia, that it's almost impossible to keep track of them. But here are a few examples:

BISMARK HERRING: Vinegar-cured skin-on herring fillets, usually containing sugar and sliced onions

BLOATER: Whole salted and smoked herring

HERRING IN SOUR CREAM SAUCE: Also common in New York, in supermarkets, this is salted herring marinated in vinegar and finished with sour cream and usually sliced onions.

KIPPER: Made by splitting the whole herring, leaving the two sides attached, and cold-smoking. The best kippers have a silver red color from long smoking, although some manufacturers also use red dye.

PICKLED HERRING: This is the herring often found in delicatessens, especially in New York—herring fillets marinated in vinegar and spices. Elsewhere herring is pickled in brine.

ROLLMOPS: These are pickled herring fillets—bismarks—that are rolled up and held together with a toothpick.

BEST METHODS: grilling, panfrying, smoking (both hot and cold), broiling

AVOID: using in soups and stews

YIELD: 45 percent skinless fillets from ungutted fish

APPEARANCE WHEN COOKED: off-white

TEXTURE WHEN COOKED: soft

FAT CONTENT: moderate to high

FLAVOR: mildly pronounced

THE JACK FAMILY

Most members of the jack family (Carangidae) are easy to recognize because of their distinctive forked tails and smooth, often shiny skin. There are more differences in quality among species of jacks than within almost any other group of fish. Some members have too strong a flavor, while others, such as pompano, are among the best of all saltwater fish.

One way to eliminate some of the strong flavor of certain jacks is to fillet them, remove the skin, and cut away any strips of red muscle that run along the fillets, usually under the skin, along the lateral line and around the belly flaps.

Most jacks have firm flesh and a full flavor that makes them particularly well suited for grilling or hot smoking. Because of their firm flesh, less strong-tasting jack fillets can also

be simmered in full-flavored fish soups or stews without falling apart. While some jacks are too strongly flavored for some cooking techniques and delicate-flavored ingredients, others such as pompano are excellent regardless of method.

Most commercially sold jack fish come from the Atlantic. Pacific waters, along the coasts of Mexico and California, have their own jack species, but fishing restrictions allow only sportfishermen to take these fish.

BEST METHODS: grilling (whole, fillets), smoking (cold or hot), panfrying (smaller fish, fillets, steaks), raw (yellowtail only)

AVOID: deep-frying (except pompano); large amberjacks, which may have ciguatera toxins

YIELD: usually 40 percent skinless fillets from ungutted fish, but sometimes much less

APPEARANCE WHEN COOKED: white or off-white depending on species, dense very fine flake

TEXTURE WHEN COOKED: usually firm

FAT CONTENT: moderate to high

FLAVOR: full or even strong for most members of the jack family; delicate for pompano and permits

Amberjack (*Seriola dumerili*)

This beautiful silver and amber fish is one of the most important of the jack species. Amberjack is found on both sides of the Atlantic from Cape Cod to South America and from the Mediterranean to Southern Africa. It grows to well over 100 pounds, but since larger specimens develop a stronger flavor and often contain parasites, most jacks sold in fish markets weigh under 15 pounds and often as little as 2 pounds.

Even small jacks have a full, somewhat strong flavor. The easiest and tastiest way to cook a whole small jack is to grill it, but if you want a milder flavor, buy a whole small one, fillet it, and cut off any strips of dark flesh. The dark flesh can also be cut off steaks or fillets taken from larger specimens. Once filleted and trimmed, the amberjack fillets can be grilled, panfried, or hot-smoked.

Crevalle Jack (*Caranx hippos*)

Crevalle jack is one of the most common jacks fished off the coast of Florida but also appears as far up the East Coast as Massachusetts. While some specimens reach 30 pounds or more, smaller specimens of about 2 pounds are best. Crevalle jacks are best prepared in the same way as amberjacks.

Pacific Gafftopsail Pompano (*Trachinotus rhodopus*)

This fish, found off the coast of southern California and Mexico, is virtually identical to the palometa (see below).

Palometa (*Trachinotus goodei*)

This fish is found along the coast of Florida and South America. A palometa looks somewhat like a Florida pompano except that the palometa has two very long fins that reach almost all the way to the end of the tail and dark vertical bars that come halfway down the body. The tail itself is forked and the body less plump than a pompano's so that palometa isn't nearly as desirable as pompano.

Permit (also sometimes sold as pompano) (*Trachinotus falcatus*)

Because permit swim in the same water as pompano—off the coast of Florida and the Carolinas—and look almost identical, they are often sold along with pompano for the same price. This is of little consequence when buying smaller fish, but any fish larger than 3 pounds is almost certainly a permit (pompano don't grow any larger) and should be less expensive. A permit larger than 4 or 5 pounds won't have as delicate a flavor as a pompano or a smaller permit, but provided you're not paying pompano prices, a larger permit is certainly worthwhile on the grill or cut up and simmered in a fish soup or stew.

Pompano (*Trachinotus carolinus*)

Its firm white flesh and smooth silvery skin make pompano the star of the jack family. Most pompano is fished off the coast of Florida and the Carolinas and in the Gulf of Mexico. Pompano is available year-round but is more abundant and usually less expensive in the spring and late fall. Most pompano weigh between 1 and 1½ pounds but occasionally can be found in the markets as large as 3 pounds. Be suspicious of any fish much larger, which will probably be the very similar-looking permit.

My favorite way to cook a pompano is to grill it whole over very hot coals so the skin gets crispy and the flesh stays juicy. Pompano are also delicious when panfried whole or filleted (especially *à la meunière*) or when baked.

Yellowtail (*Seriola dorsalis, Seriola lalandei, Seriola lalandei dorsalis, Seriola quinqueradiata*)

The yellowtail is one of the world's most delicious jacks. Unless you sport-fish and have been lucky enough to catch a yellowtail jack somewhere off the coast of southern California or in the western Pacific, you're most likely to have encountered yellowtail in a sushi bar under its Japanese name, *hamachi*. All the *hamachi* eaten in the United States comes from a subspecies of yellowtail—*S. quinqueradiata*—which is farm-raised in Japan and harvested when it reaches optimum size, about 15 pounds. The harvested yellowtail is then carefully frozen and made available year-round. The yellowtail caught wild off the coast of California is delicious but a little lean for Japanese tastes. It can be prepared in the same way as amberjack. The best way to eat Japanese yellowtail is raw, being sure to take the usual precautions.

JOHN DORY: See Dory.

KINGKLIP (also called cusk eel and ling) (golden: *Genypterus blacodes*; red: *Genypterus chilensis*; black: *Genypterus maculatus*)

While you wouldn't mind biting into a piece of one of these delicate firm-fleshed fish, you probably wouldn't want to encounter a whole one. Kingklips look like fish in the front and eels in the back and can measure up to 6 feet long. Most weigh a more manageable 10 pounds.

Even though most kingklips are caught far away from the United States—off the coast of South America and New Zealand—they are starting to appear more regularly, in fillet form, in American fish markets. The quality of red and golden kingklip is considered much better than that of black kingklip.

BEST METHODS: panfrying, poaching, braising, soups and stews

AVOID: strong sauces because flavor is very mild

YIELD: 40 percent skinless fillets from ungutted fish

APPEARANCE WHEN COOKED: pure white with large flakes

TEXTURE WHEN COOKED: firm

FAT CONTENT: very low

FLAVOR: mild, delicate

LINGCOD (*Ophiodon elongatus*)

This is another fish that has *cod* tagged onto its name even though it has no relation to the cod family. Lingcod is in fact a member of the greenling family, which no doubt got its name from the fact that freshly filleted members of this family have pale green flesh. This color is offputting to some, but in any case lingcod turns pure white once it is cooked.

Lingcod is caught off the coast of California during the summer and off the coast of Alaska during the winter. Lingcod typically weigh about 12 pounds but can grow to 50 pounds. When whole, lingcod do in fact look vaguely like cod but are more elongated, don't have a whisker on their chins, usually have darker, more pronounced mottling, and have tiny flaps over their eyes.

Because of its firm texture, lingcod is excellent for grilling and, because it won't fall apart when cooked, in soups and stews.

BEST METHODS: grilling (steaks), panfrying (steaks and fillets), steaming, poaching, braising, soups and stews

AVOID: strong sauces because flavor is very mild

YIELD: 40 percent skinless fillets from ungutted fish

APPEARANCE WHEN COOKED: pure white with large flakes

TEXTURE WHEN COOKED: firm

FAT CONTENT: very low

FLAVOR: mild, delicate

THE MACKEREL FAMILY

While I might not serve mackerel as the star attraction at an important dinner party, the mackerel is a most unjustly maligned little fish. Part of the problem is that most of us have been exposed to canned mackerel or fresh mackerel that has been handled improperly. Mackerel must be iced carefully as soon as it is caught, or it will develop a strong fishy flavor. Perfectly fresh mackerel is surprisingly delicate.

Tuna and bonito are also members of the mackerel family, Scombridae, but because of their size they are prepared and cooked in entirely different ways. Members of the mackerel family have sleek, efficiently designed bodies with distinctive forked tails. Some of the members, especially the best known of the bunch, the Atlantic mackerel, have beautiful coloration.

Most members of the mackerel family have a fairly high fat (oil) content—and hence a full flavor—but the intensity and subtlety of their flavor varies considerably. Because of their high fat content, mackerel are especially delicious when grilled or smoked, but they are also good panfried or simply baked. Mackerel or Spanish mackerel fillets panfried with their skin left on so it becomes slightly crispy are a particularly tasty treat. These fillets are also good prepared in escabeche or served raw as sashimi with the usual precautions.

BEST METHODS: grilling (whole, fillets, steaks), smoking (cold or hot), panfrying (smaller fish, fillets, steaks), baking, in escabeche, raw

AVOID: braising, deep-frying, fish that have been stored or handled improperly because they are susceptible to scombroid poisoning

YIELD: 45 percent to 50 percent skinless fillets from ungutted fish for most species

APPEARANCE WHEN COOKED: gray or pale brown, medium flake

TEXTURE WHEN COOKED: depends on species; Atlantic mackerel has a soft texture; Spanish and king mackerel are slightly firm

FAT CONTENT: varies according to species; Atlantic mackerel and king mackerel are moderate to high; wahoo has a low fat content

FLAVOR: full (Atlantic, king, Spanish) to moderate (cero and wahoo)

Atlantic Mackerel (also called mackerel or Boston mackerel) (*Scomber scombrus*)

This is the best known of the mackerel species and one of the more oily and strongly flavored. Atlantic mackerel is also one of the most beautiful fish in the sea. I rarely see Atlantic mackerel in upscale fish markets, but in the ethnic markets where I usually shop it makes a beautiful and tempting sight. When very fresh, mackerel has greenish blue coloring on its back and distinct squiggly blue-gray lines along its back. When fresh, Atlantic mackerel should be stiff—it shouldn't sag too much when you hold it sideways by its head—and it should be perfectly shiny. Its eyes should be clear and protruding, and there should be no fishy smell.

Most Atlantic mackerel weigh between 1 and 2 pounds and measure between 12 and 15 inches long. Even though mackerel are caught year-round in the North Atlantic, mackerel is at its best in the fall and early winter, when it's had all year to fatten up.

Cero Mackerel (also called painted mackerel) (*Scomberomorus regalis*)

Cero mackerel looks similar to Spanish mackerel, except cero mackerel is usually somewhat larger—typically 5 to 8 pounds—and has horizontal golden stripes in addition to gold spots. Cero is most popular in Florida, where most of it is caught, but I grab it whenever I see it for sale in New York. It has leaner flesh and a more delicate flavor than king mackerel, but larger specimens are usually sold in the same way, as steaks.

King Mackerel (also called kingfish) (*Scomberomorus cavalla*)

King mackerel look somewhat like giant elongated Spanish mackerel, typically 5 to 15 pounds and about 3 feet long. While young they have golden spots like Spanish mackerel, but the spots fade as they get older. I never see them for sale in upscale fish markets, but they are very popular in ethnic markets, especially in Caribbean neighborhoods. King mackerel is usually sold in steaks that are cut off the whole fish to order. The flesh has a peculiar gray color that turns off-white when the fish is cooked. King mackerel steaks are delicious, especially when barbecued.

Pacific Mackerel (also called chub mackerel or blue mackerel) (*Scomber japonicus*)

Pacific mackerel is the closest West Coast equivalent to the Atlantic mackerel. It has a lower fat content than Atlantic mackerel but a strong flavor, and most of it is canned.

Spanish Mackerel (*Scomberomorus maculatus*)

It's easy to recognize a Spanish mackerel because of its sleek tuna-shaped body with its forked tail, shiny silver skin, and golden spots. It also has a set of small triangular fins running along the rear half of its back to its tail. Because Spanish mackerel has a much more delicate flavor than Atlantic mackerel, it is a much appreciated fish along the Atlantic coast. It runs in warmer water than Atlantic mackerel—all the way from the Gulf of Mexico to Cape Cod—and is better and easier to find during the winter.

Spanish mackerel are usually about 2 feet long and typically weigh about 3 pounds. They are sold both whole and as skin-on fillets.

Wahoo (in Hawaii, also called ono) (*Acanthocybium solandri*)

This sleek elegant-looking fish is the most delicately flavored in the mackerel family. Whole wahoo typically weigh between 8 and 30 pounds and look much like a mature king mackerel. The best way to recognize a wahoo is by its gray-silver skin and the faint dark vertical bars along its body. Unlike other mackerel, wahoo flesh is pale pink and slightly translucent—like very pale tuna—that turns white when cooked. Wahoo are fished in the Caribbean, off the coast of Central America, and near Hawaii. They are most often available in summer.

Mahimahi (also called dolphinfish and dorado) (*Coryphaena hippurus*)

Don't confuse this colorful fish with the mammalian dolphin—they are unrelated. When mahimahi are just pulled out of the water, they are colorful creatures with blue-green backs and yellow along their bellies, but once they die their color fades quickly so that after a few days they are completely gray. Mahimahi have a distinctive shape that makes them easy to recognize. They have square heads with high foreheads—their profiles are strangely primatelike—and a body that tapers toward a very angular V-shaped tail.

Despite their Hawaiian name, mahimahi are fished along the Atlantic Coast—mainly in Florida—and along the Pacific coast all the way down to South America as well as in Hawaiian waters. They are most abundant in late spring and during the summer. Mahimahi grow as large as 50 pounds, but most specimens I see in stores in New York range between 5 and 10 pounds. Mahimahi is also sold filleted, both skinless and skin on.

When cooked, mahimahi has a delicate mildly pronounced flavor and medium texture. It turns off-white when cooked. The flesh of mahimahi usually has strips of brown running down the center of the fillets. This discoloration is perfectly harmless, but some people feel it makes the cooked fillets less attractive and trim it off. Mahimahi can also cause scombroid poisoning when mishandled.

BEST METHODS: grilling (small whole fish, fillets with skin), panfrying, soups and stews, braising, baking (fillets)

AVOID: deep-frying, fish that have been stored or handled improperly, as they are susceptible to scombroid poisoning

YIELD: 35 percent skin-on fillets from gutted fish

APPEARANCE WHEN COOKED: off-white with small light brown sections, fine flake

TEXTURE WHEN COOKED: moderately firm

FAT CONTENT: very low

FLAVOR: mildly pronounced

Marlin (in Hawaii, also called a'u) (blue marlin: *Makaira nigricans*; striped marlin: *Tetrapturus audax*; shortbill spearfish: *Tetrapturus angustirostris*; white marlin: *Tetrapturus albidus*; black marlin: *Makaira indica*)

Unless you're a fisherman, you're unlikely to encounter these beautiful giants in a fish store. In many states it's even illegal to sell marlin, and catching large fish is limited to sportfishermen. Commercial marlin fishing does take place in Hawaii, where the fish is highly prized as sashimi. A large amount is also sent to Japan. Because of their bills, marlins look vaguely like swordfish from the outside, but their flesh is leaner and more tunalike. They can be eaten raw or cooked in the same way as tuna—following the same precautions.

Monkfish (also called anglerfish or bellyfish) (*Lophius americanus, Lophius piscatorius*)

When I was cooking in France in the mid-1970s, monkfish—in France, called *lotte*—was as expensive as Dover sole. When I returned to work in a restaurant in the United States and ordered bellyfish from the confused fish wholesaler (I was the first ever to have ordered it), it sold for less than a dollar a pound. Today monkfish has become culinarily chic, and while it never reaches European prices, it is never cheap.

A whole monkfish is a rather horrifying sight. The head is about twice as wide as the tail and has a huge wide mouth (which seems to be smiling maliciously) filled with dozens of sharp pointed teeth. In most places monkfish is sold with the head already cut off, and in fact at one time in France it was illegal to bring monkfish into port with their heads for fear of frightening passersby.

American monkfish (*Lophius americanus*) is found all along the Atlantic coast as far south as Brazil and as far north as the Grand Banks off the coast of Newfoundland. It is available during most of the year with a peak from September through April. Monkfish usually measure from 1 to 4 feet long and weigh from 1 to 50 pounds; the tails measure and weigh about half as much.

Monkfish are usually sold as whole tails with the black outer skin removed, but the tails are also sometimes sold already filleted. If you're buying monkfish tail with the skin still attached, have the fishmonger remove the outer black skin or do it yourself once you get the tail home—it peels off fairly easily with the help of a paring knife. Below the black skin is a thin membrane with tiny black spots, which should also be peeled off with the help of a paring or boning knife. For most dishes the fillets should be removed from the central backbone—the only bone—by just slicing next to the bone on each side. Monkfish flesh has purple colorations that, while perfectly harmless, turn dark brown once cooked, so you may want to trim these off.

Monkfish has very lean delicate-flavored white flesh with the texture of shellfish and no visible flaking. Despite claims that monkfish is the "poor man's lobster," it tastes nothing like lobster; only its texture is somewhat reminiscent. Whichever method you use for cooking monkfish, be careful not to overcook it, or it will dry out. When cooking filleted monkfish tail, slice the fillets before serving to make them more presentable and easier to eat.

BEST METHODS: panfrying (fillets), baking (whole trimmed tail and fillets), steaming (fillets), soups and stews, braising (whole tail or fillets)

AVOID: grilling (masks the flavor, and monkfish tends to stick to the grill) smoking (too lean)

YIELD: 35 percent skinless fillets from ungutted fish, 60 percent fillets from skinless tail

APPEARANCE WHEN COOKED: white with brown discoloration on untrimmed pieces, no flake, even shellfishlike structure

TEXTURE WHEN COOKED: moderately firm

FAT CONTENT: very low

FLAVOR: mild

Moonfish (called opah in Hawaii) (Atlantic: *Lampris guttatus*; Pacific: *Lampris regius*)

Unless you live in Hawaii, you're unlikely to encounter this fish very often, and even in Hawaii opah are not caught regularly because they are solitary and don't swim in schools. Along the Atlantic coast encountering a moonfish is rare indeed. When you do, you'll need to adjust your shopping plans to accommodate this delicious fish.

Moonfish are well named because they are almost completely round and have silvery skin flecked with white spots. They have brilliant red fins and pink to red flesh that looks somewhat like tuna. Hawaiian opah are caught as large as 200 pounds, and the Atlantic species grows even larger, although those moonfish I've encountered in New York markets are much smaller, weighing about 15 pounds. If the moonfish is small, you may have to buy the whole thing. Even if you do buy the whole thing, moonfish yields about 35 percent skin-on fillets, so even a whole fish will leave you with a manageable amount of flesh.

If you're buying opah already filleted, try to get a piece of the long piece of loin rather than the triangular stomach section, which can be stringy. Moonfish can be cooked and served the same way as tuna.

Mullet (also called lisa) (striped mullet: *Mugil cephalus*; silver mullet/also called white mullet: *Mugil curema*)

Mullet is another one of those underrated fish that's a revelation once you taste it. There are many species of mullet, but the one that pops up most often in American fish markets is the striped mullet, followed by the smaller silver mullet. Striped mullet have blue-gray coloration along their backs, and silver mullet are almost all silver with some gray coloring along their backs. Most mullet weigh between 1½ and 4 pounds.

Perhaps the mullet's less-than-stellar reputation is due partly to the fact that it doesn't travel well from where it's caught—usually along the southern Atlantic coast and along the Gulf Coast of Florida. I often see it in markets in New York, but it's rarely fresh enough, so I don't often buy it. Most striped mullet is harvested from November through March and silver mullet from April to July.

If you manage to find mullet sparklingly fresh—not a problem if you live where it's caught—be sure to try it. Because of its moderately high fat content, mullet takes well to grilling and hot smoking. Mullet sometimes contain parasites, so it should not be cold-smoked or eaten raw. Most mullet has a delicate flavor but sometimes, because mullet bottom-feeds on vegetation in brackish water, the flesh may have an earthy taste. To stave off this possibility, trim off the strong-tasting dark strip that runs down the center of the fillets—or the fishmonger may have already done this.

Mullet roe is a delicacy much prized by the Japanese, who eat it salted and dried, and to a lesser degree by Americans, who fry it up and eat it for breakfast with scrambled eggs.

Don't confuse mullet with red mullet, which is really a goatfish and completely unrelated.

BEST METHODS: grilling (fillets), baking (whole), hot smoking (butterflied or filleted), panfrying (skin-on fillets), deep-frying (skinless fillets)

AVOID: eating raw

YIELD: 45 percent skin-on fillets from ungutted fish

APPEARANCE WHEN COOKED: white

TEXTURE WHEN COOKED: moderately firm

FAT CONTENT: low to moderate

FLAVOR: moderately pronounced to pronounced

OCEAN PERCH: See Rockfish. Ocean Pout (also called eel pout) (*Macrozoarces americanus*)

This is one of those fish that's starting to show up in fish markets because other better-known (and better-looking) fish are becoming more scarce. An ocean pout looks somewhat like an eel (never an American favorite) and has rather long winglike pectoral fins and yellow or brownish green skin. It's usually 1½ to 2 feet long. In Chinese markets I've seen ocean pout sold live from tanks. Ocean pout has firm and very lean white flesh with a delicate flavor. The fillets should be skinned and are good panfried, but because of its firm texture I especially like to put it in soups, where it won't fall apart. Avoid dry heat and overcooking.

Orange Roughy (*Hoplostethus atlanticus*)

Orange roughy, a beautiful fish with bright red coloring turning into silver and gold near the fish's head, is a 1980s success story. It is a deep-water fish found off the coasts of New Zealand and Australia. Unfortunately you're unlikely ever to see one whole because virtually all orange roughy available in the United States is sold as skinless fillets. Because orange roughy grows slowly—the average fish is between 30 and 50 years old—the New Zealand government has imposed fishing restrictions; consequently it is not as abundant as during the 1980s. Usually the fish is frozen on board ship, thawed again on shore, where it is filleted, and then frozen again. None of this does much for its quality, and in fact I find orange roughy somewhat insipid-tasting, although it is surprisingly firm—more so than flounder or American varieties of so-called sole. But because of its firm texture and perfectly white flesh, it's an excellent substitute for the ubiquitous fillet of sole.

Most orange roughy fillets weigh between 6 and 8 ounces. Smaller oreo dory fillets—which usually have a slight yellow coloration—are sometimes sold as orange roughy but should be less expensive.

BEST METHODS: panfrying, braising, soups and stews

AVOID: grilling (the fillets tends to stick to the grill); smoking (too lean)

YIELD: always sold as skinless fillets

APPEARANCE WHEN COOKED: pure white

TEXTURE WHEN COOKED: moderately firm

FAT CONTENT: very low

FLAVOR: mild

OREO DORY: See Dory.

PARROTFISH (*Sparisoma virida* and *Scarus coelestinus*)

This rather plump foot-long fish is neither commercially important nor terribly great eating. But when it shows up now and then in ethnic fish markets, its bright blue color with orange on the fins attracts a lot of attention. Disappointingly, it loses much of its color once scaled. Parrotfish is best filleted, the beautiful skin removed, and panfried in butter or used in soups since it has a moderately firm texture. The flavor is mild.

PERMIT: See Jack Family.

POLLACK: See Cod Family.

POMPANO: See Jack Family.

PORGIES

Porgies are members of the Sparidae family, which includes hundreds of species. In Europe and other parts of the world porgies are called *sea bream*. In Mediterranean countries bream are especially prized and usually cooked simply, by grilling or panfrying.

Almost all the porgies eaten in the United States are caught off the Atlantic coast or in the Caribbean. There are some delicious Pacific species, but most come from the Indo-Pacific and are seen only rarely in fish markets in the western United States.

While porgies have delicious lean and flaky flesh, some species contain a lot of bones, which makes for difficult eating. It's always a good idea to buy the largest porgies you can find so the bones aren't so difficult to remove. Because even large porgies come in manageable sizes, I prefer to cook and eat porgies whole rather than in the small, less flavorful fillets. Most porgies have tough skin that is difficult to scale, so if you're cooking whole fish, leave the scales attached and remove skin and all after cooking. If you're cooking fillets, don't bother scaling; just skin the fillets before cooking.

BEST METHODS: panfrying (whole), grilling (whole with scales left on), baking (whole, plain, or in salt crust), braising (skinless fillets), deep-frying (skinless fillets)

AVOID: smoking, soups and stews (porgy fillets tend to fall apart)

YIELD: 35 percent to 40 percent skinless fillets from ungutted fish

APPEARANCE WHEN COOKED: very white, small flakes

TEXTURE WHEN COOKED: slightly firm, flaky

FAT CONTENT: low

FLAVOR: very delicate

ATLANTIC AND CARIBBEAN VARIETIES

Jolthead Porgy (*Calamus bajonado*)

This porgy is not only delicious but beautiful to look at. It has golden silver coloring and pale blue markings next to its gills, and because it's plumper than most porgies, it's easier and more satisfying to eat. Jolthead porgies also grow quite large, up to 8 pounds but commonly to 2 pounds. Jolthead porgies are most popular along the coast of North Carolina, in Bermuda, and in the Bahamas.

Red Porgy (also called pink porgy, pink or silver snapper) (*Pagrus sedecim*)

This fish is in fact so close to a species of Mediterranean sea bream (*Pagrus pagrus*) that icthyologists now think the eggs actually ride a current all the way across the Atlantic and hatch along the southeastern coast of the United States.

Red porgy is one of the most appealing of the porgies because of its pink hue, its slightly firmer flesh, and its tendency to be a bit bigger than other species, typically about 1½ pounds but occasionally much larger.

Scup (also called porgy) (*Stenotomus chrysops*)

This is the most common, popular, and inexpensive porgy found in the waters (and markets) of the Eastern Seaboard. Scup are silvery gray with rounded backs and fairly flat. They grow up to 5 pounds, but those that show up in the market usually weigh only a pound or less.

Sheepshead (*Archosargus probatocephalus*)

This porgy is easy to spot because of its distinctive vertical black stripes and arching back. At one time many sheepsheads were caught in Sheepshead Bay in Brooklyn, but now most are caught off the coast of the Carolinas and Virginia. Sheepsheads are tasty—if somewhat undistinguished—and have the advantage of being slightly larger than scups. They have distinctive black stripes, for which they're sometimes called *convictfish*. Most sheepsheads weigh between 1½ and 2 pounds. Don't confuse sheepsheads with California sheepheads.

Whitebone Porgy (*Calamus leucosteus*)

This is one of the most popular porgies along the southeast coast of the United States. It tastes and looks similar to a jolthead porgy except that is usually somewhat smaller and lacks the jolthead's golden hues.

RED MULLET (*Mullus surmuletus*)

It wasn't until recently that this Mediterranean fish started showing up—much to my delight—in New York fish markets. Red mullet brings a high price in Europe, where it is one of the Mediterranean's most prized fish—the famous *rouget de roche* and *triglia di scoglio* of French and Italian cooking. It's easy to understand why: Red mullet has firm tasty flesh, and its bright red or orange color is irresistible. Perhaps because Americans have not yet caught on, red mullet is cheaper in ethnic fish markets in New York than in the south of France and in Italy, where it is caught.

Red mullet isn't really mullet at all but a member of the goatfish family, Mullidae. Red mullet looks somewhat like red snapper but smaller, brighter red, more elongated, and with chin whiskers (barbels).

Red mullet is delicious grilled whole, baked, panfried, broiled, or panfried and then marinated in escabeche. Red mullet livers are also prized. French cooks like to chop up the liver, work it with a little butter, and then stuff this liver butter into the fish before they are baked. One popular method in the south of France is to grill red mullet ungutted, scales and all. The scale-encrusted skin then just peels off at the table. But for most guests it's probably better to scale and gut the red mullet before grilling.

America also has its own species of goatfish, most important the spotted goatfish (*Pseudupeneus maculatus*) with pink to orange coloring. Spotted goatfish swim off the coast of Florida and can grow up to a foot long. Buy them when you can.

BEST METHODS: grilling (whole, with or without scales), panfrying (whole or filleted), deep-frying (whole), broiling (whole or filleted), baking (whole or filleted), in escabeche (whole or filleted), soup (whole, especially in bouillabaisse)

AVOID: eating raw

YIELD: 45 percent skin-on fillets from ungutted fish

APPEARANCE WHEN COOKED: white

TEXTURE WHEN COOKED: moderately firm

FAT CONTENT: low

FLAVOR: mildly pronounced

RIBBONFISH: See Cutlass Fish.

ROCKFISH

Except for the Atlantic ocean perch (not really a perch at all but a rockfish), the only commercially important rockfish are caught along the Pacific Coast as far south as Baja California and as far north as the Bering Sea. The whole matter becomes especially confusing when most of the Pacific species—and there are well over 50—are marketed under misleading names such as red snapper, rockcod, and Pacific snapper. All rockfish are from the genus Sebastes and are completely unrelated to snappers and cod.

It's surprising that rockfish don't show up more often in upscale fish markets on the Pacific Coast, especially considering that they are caught locally and can be had very fresh. The trick is to shop in an ethnic market—San Francisco's Chinatown is especially wonderful—and buy the freshest and, I hate to say it, the most expensive you see. There are so many species of rockfish that it's almost impossible to figure out which you're getting, and the chances of successfully setting out to find a particular species in perfect condition are practically nil. I follow the advice given in

Isaac Cronin's book *The California Seafood Cookbook* and buy those rockfish with thicker bodies—which usually have firmer flesh—and again I also look for the most expensive, which in any case is never very high.

Rockfish are among the most colorful and beautiful of all fish and are easy to recognize because of their long spiny dorsal fins, usually bright colors, big eyes, and generally jagged appearance. Rockfish are deep-water fish and usually weigh between ½ pound and 20 pounds.

Most rockfish are excellent cooked both whole and filleted. If you're serving whole rockfish or filleting the rockfish yourself, be certain to trim off the very sharp spiny fins before cooking or cutting into the fish.

BEST METHODS: steaming (whole), deep-frying (whole), baking (whole), braising (fillets), poaching (fillets), in chunks in soups and stews

AVOID: grilling (rockfish tends to stick)

YIELD: 30 percent to 40 percent fillets from ungutted fish

APPEARANCE WHEN COOKED: white, fine flake

TEXTURE WHEN COOKED: soft to moderately firm

FAT CONTENT: very low

FLAVOR: delicate, mildly pronounced

ATLANTIC VARIETIES

Atlantic Ocean Perch (sometimes called redfish) (*Sebastes marinus, Sebastes mentella*)

Most ocean perch are sold already filleted with their pink skin left on so that the fillets look somewhat like red snapper. Because ocean perch fillets sell for considerably less than red snapper fillets, you should learn to tell the difference. Red snapper fillets, which are usually larger, have a more deeply colored skin, and the flesh side has a line of cherry-red running lengthwise down the middle; the flesh side of ocean perch is evenly white or pale pink. During the spring ocean perch are often available whole.

Ocean perch is fished off the coast of Labrador to as far south as southern Maine. Atlantic ocean perch weigh up to 3 pounds but more typically weigh only a pound. The fillets usually weigh about ¼ pound each. Ocean perch has delicately flavored moderately firm flesh.

PACIFIC VARIETIES

Bank Rockfish (also called rockcod, redwidow rockfish, snapper, Pacific red snapper) (*Sebastes rufus*)

This moderate-size (usually 12- to 15-inch) rockfish is light brown on the back, light red on the body, and often but not always has black spots on its body and dorsal fin.

Blue Rockfish (also called rockcod, black rockfish, priestfish, blue bass, snapper, Pacific snapper, and reef perch) (*Sebastes mystinus*)

Despite its name, this rockfish isn't always blue but may be colored olive brown, grayish black, or dark blue on its back with lighter coloring on its body. Blue rockfish grow to about 20 inches long but are more typically about 10 inches long.

Bocaccio (also called salmon grouper, grouper, mini-grouper, snapper, Pacific snapper, Pacific red snapper, jack, and meru) (*Sebastes paucispinis*)

This rockfish grows quite large—up to more than 15 pounds—but is sold mostly in smaller sizes. It has pink-brown coloring and is considered less desirable than other rockfish species because of its soft flesh.

Bolina (also called brown rockfish) (*Sebastes auriculatus*)

Because of its relatively firm flesh, this is one of the best of the Pacific rockfish. Bolina is brown with orange markings and usually weighs about 2 pounds, although it can grow as large as 5 pounds.

Canary Rockfish (also called orange rockfish, red rock, Pacific red snapper, fantail, canary, and rockcod) (*Sebastes pinniger*)

This rockfish is easy to spot because of its yellow-orange coloring along its back and fins. Canary rockfish also have gray mottling and pale gray on their sides. While canary rockfish grow to about 30 inches, most of those in the markets are half as long.

Chilipepper (also called chili, rockcod, snapper, Pacific snapper, and Pacific red snapper) (*Sebastes goodei*)

These tasty and bright-colored little fish are usually pink and white (white especially near the belly) with a bright red line (lateral line) on their sides. Most chilipeppers in the fish market are about 12 inches long.

Olive rockfish (also called rockcod, johnny bass, kelp bass, johnathans, snapper, Pacific snapper, Pacific red snapper) *(Sebastes serranoides)*

As their name implies, these fish have olive brown coloring along their backs and a light green hue on the sides. Olive rockfish have yellow fins and are typically about 14 inches long.

Pacific Ocean Perch *(Sebastes alutus)*

Pacific ocean perch is fished from southern California up to the Bering Sea and is one of the most important of the Pacific rockfish. It's very similar to Atlantic ocean perch except that it grows to be slightly larger, up to 8 pounds (although 2 pounds is typical), and has black markings along with its red coloring. Pacific ocean perch is usually sold as skin-on fillets weighing about $1/2$ pound.

Vermilion Rockfish (also called rockcod, red rock, red rockcod, scarletino, rasciera, rasher, snapper, Pacific snapper, and Pacific red snapper) *(Sebastes miniatus)*

This rockfish is easy to spot because of its beautiful bright red coloring and big black eyes. It has a delicate flavor and moderately firm flesh. I've never tried it, but most people I talk to insist that, unlike other rockfish species, vermilion rockfish can't be frozen. Most vermilion rockfish I've spotted in the markets weigh about 2 pounds.

Other Varieties

A few of the most important rockfish are goldeneye rockfish *(Sebastes ruberrimus)*, yellowtail rockfish *(Sebastes flavidus)*, black and yellow rockfish *(Sebastes chrysomelas)*, starry rockfish *(Sebastes constellatus)*, and black rockfish *(Sebastes melanops)*.

Sablefish (also called blackcod) *(Anoplopoma fimbria)*

The sablefish gets its name because of its furry black skin. Although it is sometimes called *blackcod*, sablefish is not related to cod but is a member of the obscure skilfish family.

Sablefish typically weigh between 3 and 10 pounds—they can grow as large as 40 pounds—and are caught off the coast of Alaska all the way south to California from January through September. During these months they are available fresh, but sablefish is often frozen and sold year-round, usually in the form of fillets or steaks. Sablefish is often sold as *butterfish*—probably because of its rich texture—but it has no relation to authentic butterfish.

Because of its high fat content, sablefish has a rich, buttery texture that makes it perfect for grilling and smoking. Sablefish is in fact smoked commercially and sold simply as *sable*.

BEST METHODS: grilling (fillets and steaks), hot smoking (fillets), broiling (fillets), panfrying (fillets and steaks)

AVOID: cooking whole, soups and stews (tends to fall apart)

YIELD: 40 percent skin-off fillets from ungutted fish

APPEARANCE WHEN COOKED: white with large flakes

TEXTURE WHEN COOKED: slightly firm

FAT CONTENT: high

FLAVOR: mild to slightly pronounced

SAND EEL: See Whitebait.

SARDINES (European: *Sardina pilchardus*; Atlantic: *Clupea harengus harengus*; Pacific: *Sardinops sagax* and *Clupea harengus pallasi*)

Although I think of the big fat sardines from Portugal as true sardines and the others as more or less adequate substitutes, obviously several species are available. All sardines are members of the herring family (Clupeidae)—a large group of fish that includes shad, anchovies, and herring. Members of this family are easy to recognize because they have no lateral line, they have shiny, easily detached scales, and they have a single soft dorsal fin.

The best and plumpest sardines come from the European side of the Atlantic and are easier than ever to find in East Coast fish stores. Atlantic sardines—most of which are caught off the coast of Maine and end up in cans—are actually herring. Atlantic sardines look similar to their European cousins but aren't as plump or meaty. Pacific sardines were abundant along the California coast during the 1930s and during that time were the main source of canned sardines in the United States. They were so overfished that they are now virtually extinct. Any sardine found along the Pacific coast is nowadays more likely to be a herring (*Clupea harengus pallasi*).

Sardines have very thin light scales that you can rub off while you're washing the sardines under cold running water. Sardines must be gutted before they are cooked, but whether or not you leave the head attached is up to you. The easiest way to gut a sardine is to pinch the gills on both sides at the base of the head and pull them out. Sometimes the innards will pull out with the gills, but if they don't, slide your finger along the belly cavity and pull out all the innards. Rinse the sardines in cold water while rubbing—to get rid of the scales—and wipe them with a towel. Any remaining scales will come off as the sardines are being wiped dry. If you're removing the heads, gutting is even easier: simply snap back the head and pull it off; the guts should remain attached and come with it. Sardines can also be gutted and boned through the back, a particularly good method for stuffing and baking.

My favorite way to cook sardines is to toss them in a little olive oil, sprinkle them with salt, and grill them over wood coals. The best way to eat them is to pick them up with the fingers and nibble off the flesh on each side. (I was once almost laughed out of a Portuguese street-side restaurant when I delicately attempted to fillet my sardines with knife and fork.)

Sardines are also delicious filled with a savory stuffing and baked or panfried and served in escabeche.

BEST METHODS: grilling, baking, in escabeche, hot smoking, broiling, panfrying

AVOID: including in soups and stews (the flavor is too strong and the flesh will fall apart)

YIELD: 45 percent to 50 percent skin-on fillets from ungutted fish

APPEARANCE WHEN COOKED: off-white flesh

TEXTURE WHEN COOKED: soft

FAT CONTENT: moderate

FLAVOR: pronounced

SCABBARDFISH: See Cutlass fish.

SCULPINS AND SCORPIONFISH

These fish are actually members of two entirely different families, but since the names *scorpionfish* and *sculpin* are often used interchangeably, it seems worthwhile to sort out the confusion. Scorpionfish are members of the family Scorpaenidae, a large family that also includes all the rockfish. Scorpionfish are also members of their own genus,

Scorpaena. (Rockfish and ocean perch are members of the genus *Sebastes.*) Scorpionfish get their name from the fact that many have venomous spines that can inflict a painful sting or even be fatal. They also sometimes look like rocks (which furthers the confusion because sometimes they are called *rockfish*) so they can hide in the background. The most famous scorpionfish is the Mediterranean *rascasse rouge,* which is one of the fish essential to a bouillabaisse, but unfortunately this fish isn't found on the American side of the Atlantic. The most common scorpionfish found on the western side of the Atlantic is the blue-mouth (*Helicolenus dactylopterus*), also called *black bellied rosefish,* which I've seen sold under the name *scorpina* in ethnic markets. The blue-mouth is closely related to the Mediterranean rascasse rouge (*Scorpaena scrofa*) and can be used in recipes such as bouillabaisse that call for rascasse. Unfortunately blue-mouth doesn't appear on the market very often. The most common Pacific scorpionfish is the California scorpionfish (*Scorpaena guttata*), which shows up for sale from time to time in West Coast fish markets. The California scorpionfish has venomous spines, so if you encounter one, handle with care.

Sculpins belong to the Cottidae family—whose members look somewhat like scorpionfish—and here is where the confusion begins. The sculpin (*Myoxocephalus scorpius*) is found on both the northern Pacific and Atlantic coasts and is sometimes called a *scorpionfish.* The West Coast also has the great sculpin (*Myoxocephalus polyacanthocephalus*) and the best known of all, the cabezon (*Scopaenichthys marmoratus*). All of these sculpins have mild-flavored but firm flesh that makes them good in soups. Cabezons are the largest of the lot and can weigh up to 10 pounds. If you catch your own, remember that cabezon roe is poisonous.

SEA ROBIN (*Prionotus carolinus*)

The first time I saw anything resembling a sea robin was in France, where the red gurnard—a close relative of the sea robin—is a popular, inexpensive fish best known as an ingredient in bouillabaisse but also baked whole for simple family dinners. It wasn't until years later that I realized that its American relation, the sea robin, was plentiful along the Atlantic coast and long disregarded—and discarded—by fisherman. The reason for the sea robin's lack of popularity is probably its somewhat frightening long winglike pectoral fins and its bizarre vaguely triangular body. In fact its flesh is delicately flavored and quite firm. Unlike the French version, which can be cooked whole, the sea robin has tough skin that must be removed. The easiest way to remove the skin is to fillet the fish—by sliding a knife down along each side of the sea robin's backbone—and then take the skin off each fillet as with any other fish.

If your sea robin is small, cut off the head, clean the tail, and skin it in the same way as monkfish (see color page 25). Cook the whole tail and then let guests take the meat off their own at the table.

BEST METHODS: panfrying (fillets), soups and stews (fillets), baking (fillets)

AVOID: grilling (fillets will stick to the grill), baking whole (skin is too tough)

YIELD: 35 percent skinless fillets from ungutted fish

APPEARANCE WHEN COOKED: off-white

TEXTURE WHEN COOKED: moderately firm

FAT CONTENT: low

FLAVOR: mild

SHARKS

Sharks come in and out of fashion. Until recently shark was likely to be the cheapest fish at the market, but lately the price of mako shark steaks has been approaching—although never reaching—that of swordfish and tuna. While a good shark steak is certainly comparable to the more expensive swordfish, the shark's dubious status probably has more to do with its own eating habits than with its quality as a food fish. Actually it's fortunate that shark has never been wildly popular—sharks grow and reproduce slowly, so a diminished population takes a long time to replenish itself.

There are hundreds of species of sharks, but only seven or so are marketed and eaten with any regularity in the United States. Europe has its own favorite species, most of which never make it to American shores. Most species of shark that you're likely to find for sale make delicious eating. The flesh is firm and sweet and holds up with fairly direct treatment, the only danger being that some kinds of shark meat dry out easily when overcooked.

It's sometimes easy to confuse shark steaks with swordfish. Shark has thicker sandpaper-like skin; swordfish skin is usually smooth. Swordfish steaks usually have a smooth surface with the meat forming four symmetrical swirls. The grain of shark meat tends to be more amorphous and doesn't seem to go in any particular direction. Most shark meat is white—darker-colored meat should be avoided because of its strong taste—with a fairly coarse structure. A cooked shark steak usually has a sort of rippled surface—the grain seems to protrude—which makes it easy to distinguish from swordfish. While most shark bought from a fishmonger will have been treated properly, it is occasionally possible to run into a shark that hasn't been bled properly. Because sharks don't have a separate urinary system, urealike substances are secreted through the skin. If the shark is not bled soon after it's been caught—by cutting a notch just above its tail—then the urea accumulates in the tissues and turns into ammonia. If you get a steak that smells strongly of ammonia, take it back. If there's just a hint of ammonia, it's easy to get rid of by rubbing the steaks with a little lemon juice about 30 minutes before cooking.

Preparing and Cooking

Most larger sharks such as mako, thresher, and blacktip are sold as steaks. Remove any dark sections of meat from the steaks since these sections can sometimes taste bitter. It's best to leave the skin attached if you're grilling or panfrying the steaks whole—it helps seal in moisture—but you might have to take it off while you're removing the sections of red meat. Smaller sharks, such as dogfish (cape shark is the name accepted by the FDA) or sand shark, are sometimes sold as large skinless sections called *loins.*

Shark is best grilled. You can leave the steaks whole, but shark is firm enough to be cut into cubes and grilled on skewers. Shark is also excellent panfried and in soups and stews because it keeps its shape and doesn't fall apart. The most important precaution is to avoid overcooking shark, or it will dry out.

BEST METHODS: grilling (in steaks or kebabs), panfrying, stewing, deep-frying, soups

AVOID: You can cook shark using any method. Avoid overcooking and rich sauces for fattier species such as dogfish.

YIELD: 75 percent skinless steaks from steaks with cartilage and skin

APPEARANCE WHEN COOKED: white, with a distinct swirling grain

TEXTURE WHEN COOKED: moderately firm to very firm

FAT CONTENT: low to moderate

FLAVOR: delicate, clean, sealike

Blacktip Shark (*Carcharhinus limbatus*)

This is another large and excellent-flavored shark that is usually sold in steaks. It's easy to recognize blacktip shark steaks because they are circled by a ring of ruby-colored flesh just under the skin. This should be cut off, along with the skin, before cooking. The rest of the blacktip meat should be pale pink and contain no gristle. Blacktip shark, which got its name because the fin tips of younger specimens are black, are found in warm water off the coast of Florida and in the Caribbean.

Mako (*Isurus paucus* and *Isurus oxyrinchus*)

This is the best-known shark in the United States and is usually sold in steaks. Mako shark meat is pale pink with two little blotches of red on each side of the steak. The meat is moist and flavorful without being strong. It is quite lean but slightly fattier than swordfish. Shortfin mako (*I. oxyrinchus*) is caught mostly in the Atlantic and Caribbean, while longfin mako (*I. paucus*), the larger of the two, comes mostly from Pacific waters and is sometimes called *bonito* not because of any relation to the true bonito but because bonito is an important part of this shark's diet.

Smooth Dogfish (also called sand shark or cape shark) (*Mustelus canis*)

Smooth dogfish are similar in size and flavor to spiny dogfish and can be prepared in the same way. Various sand shark species are found throughout the world's oceans and are particularly well thought of in Japan.

Spiny Dogfish (also called cape shark or sand shark) (*Squalus acanthias*)

These small sharks—rarely weighing more than 12 pounds—are found in both the Atlantic and Pacific oceans and in both the Northern and Southern hemispheres. In the United States they are hard to find in the market because fishermen who have traditionally thought of them as nuisance fish throw them back to sea. I do occasionally see them whole at wholesale fish markets and skinned at the fishmonger. Dogfish is amazingly cheap and likely to become more widely available soon, and since it's a favorite of mine I snatch it up when I find it.

Because dogfish is somewhat fatty—more so than mako shark or swordfish—it stays moist even if you happen to overcook it a little. On the other hand, because of its richness, I don't serve it with rich cream or butter sauces. Dogfish is very popular in Europe—the Germans smoke the belly flaps to make a preparation called *schillerlocken*, and the British use it in fish and chips.

Thresher Shark (*Alopias vulpinus*)

Even though this shark swims all over the world, it's little appreciated except on the West Coast of the United States, where it appears regularly in fish stores. Thresher shark is usually sold as steaks and has pink flesh similar to mako.

SHEEPSHEAD

I've never figured out why so many fish remind people of sheep, but there are three fish that go by this name. The most common (*Archosargus probato cephalus*) is a member of the porgy family, but there is also the California sheephead, which is related to the Atlantic blackfish, and then there is a freshwater drum called a sheepshead. See Porgies, Drums in the freshwater chapter, and Blackfish.

SILVERSIDE: See Whitebait.

SKATE (Atlantic: *Raja radiata, Raja ocellata*; Pacific: *Raja binoculata, Raja inornata*)

Skate is one of those underrated fish, long popular in Europe, that is beginning to be appreciated in America. It's having been ignored probably has more to do with its bizarre looks than with the flavor of its flesh, which is delicious.

Fortunately, skate is almost always sold in the form of wings rather than as the whole creature, which would be a scary sight indeed. Now that skate is beginning to appear in fancy fish stores, the wings are frequently available completely boneless with their skin removed. Skate wings with their skin still attached are slippery and fan-shaped with hard little nodules on their surface. The skin on top is typically dark brown or gray with spots, while the skin on the bottom is white in the same way as flatfish. When shopping for skate, make sure the wings are shiny and have no odor of ammonia.

Some cooks like to remove the skin from skate wings by poaching the wings in salted water for about 2 minutes and then peeling off the skin, but I prefer to fillet the wings and then strip the skin off the flesh in the same way as for any fish fillet (see color page 24).

Filleted and skinned skate wings are easy to recognize because of their fan shape and distinct ribbed texture. If the skate fillets have any smell of ammonia, rub them with lemon juice or a little wine vinegar about 30 minutes before cooking.

Because of its high gelatin content, skate should always be served piping hot, or it may feel sticky in the mouth.

Skate is sometimes confused with ray, which is very similar. Rays are more likely to be members of genera *Myliobatus* or *Rhinoptera*.

BEST METHODS: panfrying, deep-frying (cut lengthwise along the ribbing to separate the flesh into strips)

AVOID: grilling (fillets will stick to the grill) serving cold (because of gelatinousness)

YIELD: 50 percent boneless skinless meat without cartilage from wings with skin

APPEARANCE WHEN COOKED: off-white

TEXTURE WHEN COOKED: firm

FAT CONTENT: very low

FLAVOR: mildly pronounced

SNAPPER

Few varieties of fish cause as much confusion as snapper. Because red snappers are beautiful to look at (most but not all have varying amounts of pink or red markings) and delicious to eat, the name red snapper has been foisted off on practically any fish that happens to be red. And the confusion is compounded by the fact that there are several hundred species of snapper, all with their own variations in color and size. In the midst of all this, purists (and the FDA) insist that only one of these hundreds of fish, *Lutjanus campechanus*, can be called an authentic red snapper.

Snappers are found throughout the world's tropical and semitropical waters, but most of the snapper eaten in the United States comes from the Caribbean and from off the coast of Virginia down to Florida. There's also an abundance of closely related fish in the Pacific, but except for Hawaiian varieties most of these don't make it to market. While authentic snapper is found off the coast of southern California and Mexico all the way down to South America, most of the fish sold on the Pacific coast as snapper is usually from the gulf of Mexico or is actually rockfish, an unrelated species. Rockfish can be excellent fish, but they have a completely different flavor and texture from red snapper and other tropical snapper species.

While most snappers have a moderately firm texture and a delicate flavor, snapper is somewhat overrated (probably because of its color), especially considering how many delicious fish are completely ignored. My favorite way to cook it is to serve it whole in some way. Larger specimens—1½ pounds or more—are good baked and dramatic when presented and served at the table. Smaller fish can be grilled—leave the scales on, or the fish will stick—or panfried whole (remove the scales). Snapper fillets are also good panfried with the skin left on, scales of course removed. The skin turns crispy but retains its color. I don't like using snapper in soups or stews, because it tends to fall apart.

I always recommend buying whole snapper and either cooking it whole or having the fishmonger fillet it for you, but if you must buy filleted fish, make sure the fillets still have the skin so you can be sure of what you're getting.

BEST METHODS: Baking whole (large fish), grilling or panfrying (smaller fish), panfrying (fillets), deep-frying (small whole), steaming (whole)

AVOID: Soups (unless pureed), stews

YIELD: 45 percent skinless fillets from ungutted fish, but most red snapper is sold already gutted; 55 percent skinless fillets from gutted fish

APPEARANCE WHEN COOKED: very white with strip of brown, visible flaking

TEXTURE WHEN COOKED: soft to moderately firm

FAT CONTENT: very low

FLAVOR: delicate, crustaceanlike, shrimplike

ATLANTIC AND CARIBBEAN VARIETIES

Lane Snapper (*Lutjanus synagris*)

This easy-to-recognize snapper is small—usually about 1½ pounds—with pale pink coloration and, most characteristically, bright yellow stripes running along its sides all the way along its head. Because of its size, it's best cooked and eaten whole.

Mangrove Snapper (also called gray snapper) (*Lutjanus griseus*)

This snapper is well named, being almost completely gray with very little of the usual pink coloration, although it does have red markings. Gray snappers typically weigh about a pound. (Don't confuse mangrove snappers with Hawaiian gray snappers.)

Mutton Snapper (*Lutjanus analis*)

This is one of my favorite snappers because it has a firmer texture than most other species. It has the same rounded profile as red snapper but is usually sold in larger sizes—4 to 5 pounds or more—and has a grayish hue rather than the pure pink of red snapper. I like to serve this fish baked whole because of its size, color, and texture.

Red Snapper (*Lutjanus campechanus*)

This is the best-known red snapper in the United States and the only one the FDA allows to use the name. I've never understood this because there are other similar species that are just as tasty if not better. Red snappers grow to be quite large—around 40 pounds—but most specimens I see for sale in New York weigh only about 2½ pounds. Authentic red snapper is easy to tell from other species because its profile is more rounded and less streamlined. It also has consistently pink coloration unlike the bright red or gray and brown tints of other species.

Vermilion Snapper (also called b-liner) (*Rhomboplites aurorubens*)

This tasty little fish is smaller than red snapper—usually weighing 1½ to 2 pounds after gutting—and is easy to recognize because of its bright red color and its streamlined shape. Its yellow stripes are broken where lane snapper's are solid. Vermilion snapper is usually less expensive than red snapper and to my mind every bit as good. It is the most common snapper caught in American waters.

Yellowtail Snapper (*Ocyurus chrysurus*)

This grayish snapper is easy to recognize because of the single yellow stripe that runs along its entire length, even along the head (lane snapper has several stripes). Yellowtail snapper is considered one of the best-flavored snappers and is more often sold in Florida than in northern states. This may be due partly to the fact that it is very perishable.

EASTERN PACIFIC VARIETIES

Pacific Red Snapper (*Lutjanus peru*)

This is one of several important species of snapper found in the eastern Pacific off the coast of Mexico and Baja California. Pacific red snapper looks very similar to the familiar red snapper of the Gulf of Mexico except that Pacific red snapper is slightly more elongated.

HAWAIIAN VARIETIES

There are several species of snapper that reach American soil only in Hawaii, although some of these fish are so good that they're beginning to be air-freighted to the mainland. Some of these snappers are closely related to the Caribbean variety—members of the genus *Lutjanus*—but others belong to a different group of very similar fish, often called *jobfish*. None of this is terribly important for the cook except to help put a little order into the jumble of names.

Hawaiian Red Snapper (also called ruby or longtail snapper; called by its Japanese name, onaga, in Hawaii (*Etelis coruscans*)

This beautiful bright red snapper looks a little like a vermilion snapper except that it has an especially long tail. One-pound specimens are common in markets in Hawaii, but Hawaiian red snapper is occasionally caught up to 18 pounds. Hawaiian red snapper is at its best in winter—peak season is December—and is popular among the Japanese as sashimi.

Jobfish (also called green jobfish, gray snapper or, in Hawaii, uku) (*Aprion virescens*)

Perhaps because a jobfish isn't technically a snapper, it has none of the snapper's pink or red coloring but is instead gray all over, sometimes with a greenish hue. Jobfish is highly prized in Hawaii, where it is cooked or eaten raw. It is best and most available in the summer.

Pink Snapper (also called crimson or rosy jobfish or, in Hawaii, opakapaka (*Pristipomoides filamentosus*)

This gray and pink snapper has rather somber coloring compared to most snappers but is highly prized in Hawaii, where it is often served raw as sashimi. Pink snapper usually weigh from 3 to 5 pounds but can grow to as large as 18 pounds. Connoisseurs consider pink snapper to be at its best in winter, when its fat content increases.

Surfperches (also called seaperch) (*Amphistichus* spp., *Cymatogaster aggregata*)

About 20 species of surfperches are caught along the Pacific coast from Alaska to Baja California. While most surfperches are caught and eaten by sportfishermen, some are also sold in local fish markets. Surfperches are members of the family Embiotocidae and range in size from 5 to 25 inches. They have compressed bodies and are usually silvery with stripes or bars, although some are brightly colored. The most popular species are the redtail surfperch (*Amphistichus rhodoterus*), which while basically silver has subtle red coloring on its fins and tail; the barred surfperch (*Amphistichus argenteus*), which is silver with golden vertical bars running down its sides; and the shiner surfperch (*Cymatogaster aggregata*), which has large golden silver scales. Other surfperch species are considered inferior eating fish, but these species are considered quite good. Surfperch have lean flesh and are best panfried or steamed.

Swordfish (*Xiphias gladius*)

Unfortunately few of us ever get to see whole swordfish because they are so large that few fish stores want to deal with them. A whole swordfish is indeed an impressive sight. The sword itself can comprise as much as a third of the swordfish's maximum 15-foot length. Swordfish weigh up to 1,000 pounds but average between 50 and 100 pounds. Whole swordfish is mostly white but colored with bands of blue or deep purple. Fish stores buy sections of swordfish called wheels, the thickness of which are measured in knuckles, each knuckle corresponding to one of the fish's vertebrae. Depending on the size of the original fish, the wheel is then either sliced into whole steaks or quartered lengthwise into loins, which can then be sliced into more manageable pieces. Smaller swordfish are also sometimes sold to retailers as logs, which are whole headless and gutted fish.

Swordfish are found throughout the world and are available year-round but are usually somewhat more abundant and less expensive in the summer. In the United States swordfish

are caught off the coast of California, occasionally in Alaskan waters, and off the coast of New England in the summer and fall and in the Gulf of Mexico and off the Florida coast in the winter.

The color of swordfish steaks varies from ivory white to slightly pink, but the color doesn't seem to affect their flavor much. You do, however, want to avoid swordfish steaks that show signs of browning. This is referred to in the trade as *burning* and may indicate that the fish struggled when it was caught and overheated, changing the color and flavor of its flesh. Swordfish steaks also have dark red areas in the same way as tuna steaks. These should be dark cherry red rather than brown. Don't be misled into buying shark steaks for swordfish prices. Swordfish steaks have four symmetrical whorls and smooth skin; shark steaks have a distinct grain but without the symmetry of swordfish steaks. Sharks have rough sandpaperlike skin.

Swordfish steaks can be cooked in the same way as tuna steaks—panfrying and grilling are the best methods—but while tuna is delicious when undercooked or raw, swordfish should be cooked all the way through. But be careful not to overcook it, or it may dry out.

BEST METHODS: grilling, panfrying, baking, broiling

AVOID: overcooking regardless of method, deep-frying, eating raw

YIELD: 80 percent meat from steaks

APPEARANCE WHEN COOKED: off-white with some brown sections, compact dense grain

TEXTURE WHEN COOKED: firm

FAT CONTENT: low

FLAVOR: delicate yet flavorful

Tilefish (*Lopholatilus chamaeleonticeps*)

It's hard to imagine that this popular and inexpensive East Coast fish wasn't even discovered until 1879, when fishermen found it in deep offshore waters. Since then, tilefish has been fished all along the Atlantic coast and in the Gulf of Mexico, but tilefish is most abundant off the coast of New Jersey and Long Island. Tilefish is beautiful to look at with its various shades of gray and yellow spots and its big head with big eyes. It's available year-round along the Eastern Seaboard and—at least in ethnic markets—is quite inexpensive.

Tilefish are usually about 2½ to 3 feet long and typically weigh from 5 to 10 pounds, although they can weigh as much as 60 pounds. Tilefish have perfectly white, very delicately flavored lean flesh. They are always cooked in fillets or in steaks, never whole.

BEST METHODS: steaming, poaching, braising, baking, frying, soups and stews

AVOID: aggressive flavorings and sauces that will mask the flavor of the fish

YIELD: 40 percent skinless fillets from ungutted fish

APPEARANCE WHEN COOKED: white

TEXTURE WHEN COOKED: slightly firm

FAT CONTENT: low to very low

FLAVOR: delicate

TRIGGERFISH (*Balistes* spp., such as queen triggerfish) (*Balistes vetula*)

If you're lucky enough to spot one of these at the market—and you'll run into one only if you live along the Eastern Seaboard or in the Caribbean—snatch it up right away. Triggerfish have delicious firm flesh that takes well to almost any cooking method. They are peculiar-looking with long hairlike rays sticking out of the tail and the rear dorsal fin. The name *triggerfish* refers to an unusual interlocking dorsal fin that has to be "unlocked" by releasing a trigger-shaped spine. Most triggerfish are slightly longer than a foot and weigh about 2 pounds. They have very strong scales and tough skin, so I usually just fillet them and remove the skin from the fillets. The flesh is very firm and lean and can be used in soups and stews, panfried, or braised.

TUNA

Before I lived in France in the 1970s, the only tuna I had ever tasted came out of a can. The fresh tuna I first tasted in the south of France was an unexpected pleasure; the raw tuna I tasted in Japan a few years later was a revelation.

Nowadays excellent-quality fresh tuna is available throughout the United States, although much of the very best is sent to Japan. While there are several species of tuna, with some clearly more prized than others, the price of an individual tuna is often determined by appearance and taste. The best tuna is usually translucent, ranges in color from pink to bright red, and has a high fat content.

Buying, Preparing, and Cooking

While smaller tuna is sometimes sold in steaks made by simply slicing the whole fish, most tuna is sold in loins—actually thick fillets—that are then cut into smaller, easier-to-manage steaks. I always prefer having the fishmonger slice tuna steaks off the loin instead of buying already-sliced tuna steaks so that the surface of the tuna steaks is not exposed to air, which causes the tuna to discolor and spoil more quickly. Look for tuna that's moist and shiny and pink or red and avoid tuna that has any hint of browning or with a multicolored rainbowlike pattern on its surface. While some oily tuna may have a rainbow pattern, this may also indicate deterioration and is best avoided. I usually avoid buying the last piece in the case and ask the fishmonger if there are any fresh loins in the back. Another trick, if you're cooking for six or more people, is to buy a whole section of loin and cut it yourself.

When you get the tuna home, keep it tightly wrapped in plastic wrap and well iced until you're ready to serve—hopefully the same day. You'll probably also want to remove the strip of dark meat that runs through each steak or along the side of the loin. While this dark meat is perfectly harmless, it has a stronger taste and its appearance might put people off. (Chopped up, it's a thrill for the cat.)

The best tuna such as bluefin, yellowfin, bigeye, or albacore should never be marinated. Its flavor is too delicate and would be masked by a marinade, and a marinade cooks the tuna and turns it white. If you're grilling tuna, a marinade can cause the tuna to stick. If, however, you're cooking a stronger-flavored variety such as skipjack, little tunny, or bonito, a marinade can help balance the tuna's stronger taste.

If you're cooking your tuna—not serving tuna raw in the form of sushi or sashimi—always remember to undercook it. (Don't worry about squeamish guests; after one bite they'll be convinced—completely cooked tuna will be thoroughly dry and uninteresting.) Do keep in mind, though, that to be perfectly safe tuna to be eaten raw should be bought from a reliable, preferably Japanese fish market, where they know you're planning to eat it raw. If you have any doubts about the tuna, freeze it (page 90).

Tuna is best grilled, panfried, or broiled very quickly so that a savory outer crust forms (just like a rare steak) but the inside stays anywhere from completely raw to pink and no longer translucent. To achieve this effect the tuna steaks should be at least $\frac{1}{2}$ inch thick—but preferably closer to an inch thick—and then cooked over the most intense heat for about 2 to 4 minutes on each side. If this seems like too much food, remember that tuna steaks are best served in slices—so one steak may be enough for two or more people. Lightly cooked and sliced tuna is also excellent tossed in salads.

BEST METHODS: panfrying, grilling, eating raw as sashimi, very lightly cooked in salads

AVOID: overcooking, deep-frying

YIELD: 85 percent from steaks after removing skin and dark sections

APPEARANCE WHEN COOKED: deep pink to dark red when raw and lightly cooked; pink but opaque like medium-rare meat when moderately cooked; brown or white, completely opaque when overcooked

TEXTURE WHEN COOKED: firm

FAT CONTENT: very low (yellowfin and bigeye) to low (skipjack) to moderate (bluefin)

FLAVOR: when raw, very delicate with fresh clean, sealike aroma and flavor; when moderately cooked, gentle meat and fish flavors

Albacore (longfin tuna also called tombo in Hawaii) (*Thunnus alalunga*)

Albacore tuna has the palest flesh of all tuna species and is often canned as so-called white tuna. It's a relatively small species—typically about 40 pounds—and while it's popular as sashimi, it's not as desirable as yellowfin, bluefin, or bigeye because of its softer flesh. Albacore tuna is found in both the Pacific and Atlantic oceans and is in season in the summer.

Bigeye (called ahi in Hawaii) (*Thunnus obesus*)

Unlike most tuna species, which are at their best during the summer, bigeye tuna is best and easiest to catch in the winter (though it is also caught in the summer). It is a large species and typically weighs 200 pounds and occasionally more than 400 pounds. Lately, however, small specimens of about 20 pounds are being sold, but they have a lower fat content and so are of lower quality. Because bigeye tuna has a higher fat content than yellowfin, it is more prized for sashimi and so of course more expensive. It ranks with bluefin in price and quality. Much bigeye tuna has never been frozen, so if you're lucky enough to find some, it will most likely be fresh. Bigeye flesh is bright translucent red with an almost orange cast.

Blackfin (*Thunnus atlanticus*)

This tuna is found only in the western Atlantic from Cape Cod to Brazil. Most of the U.S. catch is off the coast of Florida. Although it grows up to 50 pounds, specimens weighing about 10 pounds are much more typical. Blackfin has pale flesh and a delicate flavor but strangely is rarely found for sale.

Bluefin (*Thunnus thynnus*)

Bluefins are the largest and usually the most prized of all tuna. A large bluefin tuna can weigh up to 1,500 pounds, although most tuna caught nowadays typically weigh only about 150 pounds. A large specimen may sell—to a Japanese wholesale buyer—for up to $20,000 or even more. The best bluefin meat is medium red to deep red. Bluefin tuna migrate up the Atlantic coast from South America and reach New England in the middle of the summer, when they also have the highest fat content and are at their best. While much of the best bluefin is sent to Japan, it is possible to find excellent-quality fresh bluefin on the East Coast during the summer.

Bonito (Atlantic bonito: *Sarda sarda*; Pacific bonito: *Sarda chiliensis*)

This underrated fish often shows up for sale during the summer at bargain prices. Most bonito weigh about 5 pounds and have dark stripes running horizontally along their silvery bodies. While not technically tuna, bonito are sometimes confused with skipjack tuna because of their similar size and shape. But bonito have their stripes on the back, while skipjack tuna have their stripes on the stomach. The flesh of the bonito is also pale pink, while that of the skipjack tuna is dark red. Atlantic bonito is also sometimes confused with little tunny (*Euthynnus alletteratus*), which is about the same size, about 5 pounds. But little tunny has spots near the base of their pectoral fins and, like the skipjack, darker flesh and a stronger flavor.

Skipjack (*Katsuwonus pelamis*)

This is the world's most abundant tuna and is mostly converted into canned tuna. Fresh skipjack swim in both the Pacific and Atlantic but are far more common in the Pacific. In fresh form skipjack is popular in Japan and in Hawaii, where it is the main ingredient in the traditional Hawaiian dish, poke. Because of its small size—typically 6 to 8 pounds—skipjack is one of the few tuna you're likely to encounter whole at the retail fish market. It's easy to recognize by its bluish back and silver stomach with long gray stripes running along its stomach. Skipjack has a stronger flavor than yellowfin, bluefin, and bigeye, so it is not to everyone's taste. The quality of skipjack tuna is greatly improved by bleeding the fish—making a cut a few inches above the tail—immediately after it has been caught. In this way much of the strong-tasting blood is eliminated. A. J. McClane in *The Encyclopedia of Fish Cookery* recommends soaking tuna steaks in 2 tablespoons of salt dissolved in 1 quart of water for about 1 hour to extract some of the strong flavor. This, however, will change its color, leaving it much paler.

Yellowfin *(Thunnus albacares)*

Named after its bright yellow fins and markings, yellowfin tuna is the second-most-abundant tuna (only skipjack is more so) and is the one you're most likely to encounter at the fish store. Yellowfin tuna are also smaller than bluefin and typically weigh in at a relatively small 20 to 100 pounds although they can grow as large as 375 pounds. Yellowfin flesh is dark pink to medium red but in general is lighter than bluefin and darker than albacore. Yellowfin swim worldwide, but most are caught in the Pacific. It's also abundant on the Atlantic coast in the summer. Much yellowfin is caught far out to sea and is quickly frozen. The best-quality frozen yellowfin is so-called clipper grade yellowfin, which is immediately flash-frozen at sea.

WEAKFISH: See Drums, Croakers, and Sea Trout.

WHITEBAIT

There's no such thing as a whitebait fish. *Whitebait* is just a word for almost any silvery or transparent fish (usually an immature specimen of something that grows much larger) no more than 2 inches long. The English, who have eaten whitebait for centuries, simply roll the little fish in flour, plunge them into hot oil, and sprinkle them with a little lemon juice and cayenne. The French love to

serve them as a little crunchy introduction to a fine dinner and usually sip on a dry white wine at the same time.

We Americans have access to our own whitebait varieties on both coasts—usually sand eel (*Ammodytes americanus*) and silversides (*Menidia menidia*) on the Atlantic coast and various herrings, silversides, or anchovies on the Pacific coast. While whitebait are cheap and easy to prepare—just dust them whole and ungutted, in flour and deep-fry—you may have to special-order them or look for them in ethnic markets.

WOLFFISH (striped wolffish: *Anarhichas lupus*; spotted wolffish: *Anarhichas minor*; Pacific wolffish, (sometimes called wolf-eel): (*Anarhichas ocellatus*)

These fish are well named because they have large heads and mouths filled with vicious caninelike teeth. They in fact can inflict a serious wound if not handled carefully after they've been caught.

Wolffish usually measure about 3 feet and have no scales. Even when they're fresh, their leathery skin wrinkles up in a very unfishlike way when they're moved from side to side. The difference among the three species of wolffish is relatively minor. The striped and spotted wolffish are found in the Atlantic from Cape Cod north and around all the way to Greenland, Iceland, and the Barents sea. The Pacific wolffish (or wolf-eel) is found along the Pacific coast from southern California to Japan.

Wolffish is wonderful to eat because its flesh is lean, relatively firm, and very delicately flavored. Wolffish is always cooked filleted or in steaks, never whole.

BEST METHODS: poaching, braising, panfrying, steaming, deep-frying

AVOID: grilling or at least take care—wolffish tend to stick

YIELD: 40 percent fillets from ungutted fish

APPEARANCE WHEN COOKED: white, large flake

TEXTURE WHEN COOKED: moderately firm

FAT CONTENT: low

FLAVOR: delicate yet flavorful

YELLOWTAIL: See Jack Family.

FRESHWATER FISH

ARCTIC CHAR (also called char, blueback trout, or Quebec red trout) (*Salvelinus alpinus*)

I first encountered this delicious fish at an inn on the shores of Lake Annecy in the French Alps, but it wasn't until years later that I realized that what I had eaten—an *omble chevalier*—was Arctic char, available in fancy fish stores in the United States.

Arctic char is closely related to trout and to salmon, and in fact the three can sometimes be difficult to tell apart. Arctic char *usually* has large pink spots running along its sides, especially below the lateral line, but so may Dolly Varden trout, the char's closest relative. The flesh of an Arctic char can be as dark red as that of salmon or as pale as that of trout; the color depends on what the char has been eating. The only foolproof way to identify a char is by analyzing something about its mouth that I've never been able to figure out. None of this makes a great deal of difference, because chances are you'll be buying a clearly labeled farm-raised Arctic char, pink spots and all. In the wild, Arctic char swims in the cold lakes of Canada and northern New England, and like certain trout and salmon much Arctic char is anadromous—making its way between salt water and fresh, where it spawns.

While wild Arctic char can grow to 25 pounds, most farm-raised specimens weigh about 4 pounds. Arctic char has a higher fat content than most trout and less fat than most salmon. It can be cooked in the same way as trout and salmon.

BEST METHODS: panfrying (fillets and steaks), poaching (whole), grilling (steaks, fillets), broiling (steaks, fillets), hot or cold smoking, baking (whole)

AVOID: eating raw

YIELD: 55 percent skin-on fillets from ungutted fish

APPEARANCE WHEN COOKED: pink, pale yellow, or off-white

TEXTURE WHEN COOKED: moderately firm

FAT CONTENT: moderate

FLAVOR: moderately pronounced (similar to salmon and trout)

FRESHWATER BASS AND SUNFISH

The reason that these two completely unrelated families are listed together is that most so-called freshwater bass are actually members of the sunfish family, Centrarchidae. The only two authentic bass mentioned here are the white bass and the yellow bass, both of which are close relatives of the ocean-going striped bass. In fact, wild white bass is crossed with striped bass to produce farmed striped bass.

BEST METHODS: panfrying (whole or split), deep-frying (whole, split, or filleted)

AVOID: serving larger black bass with the skin on

YIELD: 25 percent to 40 percent skinless fillets from ungutted fish

APPEARANCE WHEN COOKED: white, small flakes

TEXTURE WHEN COOKED: soft

FAT CONTENT: very low

FLAVOR: usually delicate but sometimes muddy flavor (especially larger bass); removing the skin helps

Black Bass *(Micropterus* spp.)

The many species of black bass in the lakes and ponds of the United States (bass prefer still water) are the object of much enthusiastic sportfishing. The most important species are the largemouth bass (*Micropterus salmoides*) and the smallmouth bass (*Micropterus dolomieui*). Largemouth bass are dark green, almost black, and can grow up to 15 pounds but are usually caught much smaller. Small-mouth bass usually have brown coloring and typically weigh about 2 pounds. Like many freshwater fish, black bass sometimes have a mossy or muddy taste, which can usually be eliminated by filleting the fish and removing the skin.

Sunfish *(Lepomis* spp.; *Ambloplites* spp.; *Pomoxis* spp.)

Sunfish swim in amazing variety in American lakes, streams, and ponds. Unless you're a fisherman or are friends with one, you're unlikely ever to have an opportunity to eat sunfish since they rarely appear in fish stores. I have seen sunfish for sale at New York's Fulton fish market and in Chinatown. Most sunfish are quite small—under a pound—so they are best cooked whole by panfrying or deep-frying rather than cooked in fillets. A. J. McClane, in *The Encyclopedia of Fish Cookery*, lists nine species including the well-known bluegill, crappie, pumpkinseed, and redear. Sunfish often have a mossy taste, which is attenuated by not eating the skin.

White Bass *(Morone chrysops)*

This close relative of the striped bass is a popular game fish. Unlike its cousin the yellow bass, white bass grows to be quite large—up to 2 pounds—and can be cooked either whole or in fillets.

White Perch *(Morone americana)*

A small pan fish taken mostly by sportfishermen in lakes and estuaries of the eastern United States and Canada, white perch is not really a perch but is more closely related to striped bass.

Yellow Bass *(Morone mississippiensis)*

This freshwater bass is closely related to striped bass and even looks similar, having dark stripes and yellow sides. Although it a small fish—a 1-pounder is large—it is much prized by anglers.

BUFFALOFISH (Largemouth: *Ictiobus cyprinellus*; Smallmouth: *Ictiobus bubalus*)

Buffalofish are members of the sucker family, Catostomidae, so named because suckers have odd-looking mouths that they use as suction cups for eating their favorite foods, small insects and crustaceans. Because of their large brown scales, buffalofish look somewhat like carp and in fact are sometimes sold live along with the carp in Chinese markets. Like carp, buffalofish have small bones that run along their backs and that are almost impossible to fillet out. Buffalofish should always be cooked with the skin off.

While some buffalofish, especially the big-mouth variety, grow up to 50 pounds, most buffalofish that show up in the market weigh between 3 and 5 pounds.

BEST METHODS: (all for skin-off fillets): baking, braising, deep-frying, steaming, sautéing

AVOID: cooking whole, leaving the skin on

YIELD: 25 percent skin-off fillets from ungutted fish

APPEARANCE WHEN COOKED: white to off-white; flaky

TEXTURE WHEN COOKED: soft

FAT CONTENT: high

FLAVOR: usually somewhat bland but sometimes with muddy or mossy flavor

BURBOT (also called ling or lawyer) *(Lota lota)*

The burbot is the only member of the cod family that is found in fresh water. Although burbot are found in the lakes and rivers of most of North America, you're unlikely to run into burbot at the fish market since most are caught by game fishermen. While burbot can grow quite large, most are little more than a foot long and weigh less than a pound. The burbot has a distinctive shape that looks like a fish on the head end and an eel on the tail end. It's usually dark brown mottled with yellow markings. Like pike, burbot is covered with a slime layer that is best removed by pouring boiling water over the gutted fish. Don't leave the fish in contact with hot water for more than 5 seconds, and unless you're cooking it immediately, quickly dip it in ice water before putting it on ice or in the refrigerator.

The flavor and texture of burbot are similar to those of cod, but what has brought this fish more notice than it probably deserves is its large fatty liver, which is highly prized by European chefs. (Authors sometimes confuse burbot with monkfish because they are often spelled the same—*lote* or *lotte*—in French. Monkfish livers are also much appreciated.) Burbot roe, however, is poisonous, and the liver should no longer be eaten because of its tendency to accumulate environmental pollutants.

ANADROMOUS AND CATADROMOUS FISH

While most fish live in either fresh water or salt water, a number of species spend time in both. Many oceangoing fish—so-called anadromous varieties such as shad and certain varieties of trout and salmon—swim up rivers to spawn. Whether they're caught at sea or in fresh water influences the flavor and texture of their flesh.

Far less common are catadromous creatures such as eels, which spend most of their adult lives in fresh water but then go to sea to spawn.

CARP (*Cyprinus carpio*)

I always enjoy watching the tourists in Chinatown who gaze fascinated and horrified at the tubs of live carp. Indeed carp can be a bit scary to look at with their large scales and usually impressive size of 10 pounds or more.

Despite my attempts to appreciate carp, I've always found them difficult to eat because of their bones, arranged in such a way that it's almost impossible to extricate them from the flesh when raw.

If you don't mind the bones, carp is surprisingly good eating. The flesh is very mild—although occasionally I encounter a carp with a muddy flavor—and has a firm texture. Carp can be cooked by several methods, including deep-frying, braising, pan frying, and grilling, but whatever method you use the carp should be completely skinned. Because carp has large scales embedded in its skin, it can't be scaled in the same way as other fish—you must remove the skin and scales together. The easiest way to do this is to use a very sharp, preferably somewhat flexible knife and cut the skin off in long strips while working from the tail to the head. Once the skin and scales have been removed, carp can be cooked whole or filleted in the same way as other fish.

BEST METHODS (all for skinless fillets): braising, panfrying, deep-frying, gefilte fish

AVOID: cooking whole, leaving the skin on

YIELD: 25 percent skinless fillets from ungutted fish

APPEARANCE WHEN COOKED: white to off-white

TEXTURE WHEN COOKED: firm

FAT CONTENT: moderate

FLAVOR: usually delicate but sometimes muddy flavor

CATFISH (from the Ictaluridae family)

Of the more than 2,000 species of catfish, the channel catfish (*Ictalurus punctatus*) is the one most eaten by Americans. Until the 1970s, most of the channel catfish eaten in the United States were caught in the rivers of the southern United States, but now most are farmed. Unlike many fish that taste best when caught in the wild, farmed catfish have none of the muddy taste often found in their wild cousins.

Because catfish farming and distribution have grown into such a huge industry, it's possible to find catfish in almost any form—

from live in ethnic markets to frozen fillets in supermarkets.

Catfish range in size from 1½ to 5 pounds and are easy to recognize by their barbels, which look a little like cats' whiskers. If you buy a whole catfish—unusual except at ethnic markets—fillet it and remove the skin from the fillets. Catfish weighing 4 pounds or more can be cut into steaks.

Catfish is somewhat bland in taste but has a firm texture that makes it useful as a relatively inexpensive substitute for more firmfleshed fish fillets such as pompano, Dover sole, or dory.

BEST METHODS: (fillets or steaks only): grilling, deep-frying, panfrying, baking, braising

AVOID: cooking whole

YIELD: 40 percent skinless fillets from ungutted fish

APPEARANCE WHEN COOKED: white, fine flake

TEXTURE WHEN COOKED: firm

FAT CONTENT: low to moderate

FLAVOR: mild

DRUM, FRESHWATER (*Aplodinotus grunniens*)

Most drums are saltwater fish, but there is one freshwater drum, called simply *freshwater drum* or *sheepshead*. (Don't confuse this fish with the California sheephead, a fish related to the blackfish, or with the member of the porgy family.) I've never tasted freshwater drum, but A. J. McClane, in *The Encyclopedia of Fish Cookery*, describes it as "only fair." Freshwater drums typically weigh between 2 and 5 pounds.

EEL (American Atlantic: *Anguilla rostrata*; European: *Anguilla anguilla*)

Few creatures inspire more revulsion in the squeamish diner than the eel. And unless you have a cooperative fishmonger who will skin and gut the eel for you, you will have to wrestle with the living beast to prepare it for cooking (see box on page 371). All of this is unfortunate because most of us end up going through life never tasting eel, much less treating it with the reverence bestowed on it by Europeans and the Japanese.

Eels are catadromous, which means they spawn in the ocean and then return to live their adult lives in fresh water. Most eels are caught during the freshwater phase of their existence, although some babies, called *elvers*

(*angulas* in Spanish), are caught on their way upstream. In Spain elvers are sautéed whole, usually with garlic and olive oil, and sold at an exorbitant price.

Eel must be bought alive, or the flesh will be mushy.

Shopping for eel—a bit of an adventure in itself—can be tricky because eels caught in stagnant water or held for long periods in tanks can have an unpleasant muddy taste. If you're an eel aficionado who's caught the bug in Europe or Japan, it might be worthwhile to shop around if you live in a big city with plenty of ethnic markets or to talk to local fishermen if you live in the country, so you can try eel from different sources.

Eel is delicious grilled, sautéed, hot-smoked, or simmered in a stew. The usual way to deal with a gutted and skinned eel is to cut it into 1- to 1½-inch sections, but eel can also be filleted—by cutting alongside the backbone in the same way as with round fish—or butterflied by cutting out the backbone from the underside and leaving the fillets attached down the middle. The butterfly technique works best for grilling and smoking. If you're gutting your own eel, be aware that the viscera tend to adhere to the inside of the eel. I've found it helpful to use a spoon to scrape it out (see color page 32).

While Europeans are fond of eel in many guises, it is the Japanese—or at least those who can afford it—who make eating eel a national pastime. In fact the easiest way to sample eel in the United States is to order *unagi* in a Japanese restaurant. *Unagi* is never eaten raw but is made from eel fillets that have been grilled while being basted with a mixture of mirin and soy sauce. *Unagi* never has the muddy flavor sometimes encountered in American eel because it comes from Japan, where eel is farm-raised carefully to develop the best flavor. In the average Japanese restaurant, *unagi* is served atop a bowl of rice.

BEST METHODS: grilling (butterflied, large fillets, or chunks), hot smoking (butterflied or large fillets), panfrying (butterflied, fillets, or sections), stewing (sections)

AVOID: rich sauces—eel is already rich enough; eating raw

YIELD: 60 percent skinless fillets from whole eel

APPEARANCE WHEN COOKED: white to off-white

TEXTURE WHEN COOKED: moderately firm

FAT CONTENT: high

FLAVOR: rich and usually delicate but sometimes with a muddy flavor

NILE PERCH (also called Lake Victoria perch) (*Lates niloticus*)

This rather impressive-looking fish is not really a perch but a member of the snook family, Centropomidae. Originally swimming only in the Nile River, Nile perch was transplanted in the early 1960s to Lake Victoria—bordering Tanzania, Uganda, and Kenya—to help stimulate the fishing industry. The Nile perch completely took over the lake (the size of South Carolina) such that close to 400,000 tons of Nile perch are now harvested each year. Unfortunately the voracious Nile perch has annihilated most of the lake's indigenous species and wreaked havoc on the lake's ecosystem.

Nile perch is rarely seen in the United States—most is sold to Israel, Europe, and South America—but commercial fish importers are excited by the amount of fish being caught and are already licking their chops over future sales. When you do spot Nile perch, it will probably be in the form of skinless and boneless fillets that have been frozen. Nile perch can grow to 300 pounds, but most are harvested at between 5 and 15 pounds. Because the yield is 35 percent, most fillets weigh between 14 ounces and 2½ pounds. Nile perch fillets are moderately lean and pale pink when raw but white when cooked. Some people find that Nile perch has too strong a taste, but in my experience it's very mild.

THE PERCH FAMILY

This is a confusing group of fish because so many unrelated species, from both fresh and salt water, are marketed as perch. Ocean perch is really a rockfish, white perch is either a freshwater bass or a freshwater drum, the surfperches have a family of their own, and Victoria perch (also called *Nile perch*) is a member of still another unrelated family, Centropomidae.

Of the authentic perch that swim in American waters only two, the walleye and yellow perch, are large and tasty enough to have commercial importance.

Sauger (also called pickerel) (*Stizostedion canadense*)

More commonly called *pickerel* than by its correct name, *sauger*, this fish is very similar in taste and texture to the walleye. Sauger are usually smaller than walleye, and the fillets

SKINNING AN EEL

If you buy your eel as I do, from a Chinese fish stall, chances are the quality of service will correspond to the low prices and you'll have to skin your live eel at home. Don't plan on doing a lot of shopping once you've bought your eel, because people will notice that your plastic bag is moving . . .

The easiest way to kill the eel is to grip it at the base of the neck with a towel and whack its head as hard as you can on the kitchen counter. You may also want to hit it over the head with a hammer to assure yourself that the creature is really dead—because the eel itself, dead or alive, will still wrap around your arm as you grip its neck. If at this point you're still standing, make a shallow cut into the skin around the base of the head and use a pair of pliers to fold back a tiny bit of the skin all around the neck. Grip the folded-back skin with a kitchen towel and pull firmly; the skin should roll off like a glove. Pull the skin completely off. Gut the eel by making a shallow incision on its underside near the base of the head all the way down to the anus.

The skinless eel will still be wiggling around—I usually pour myself a glass of wine at this point—and is ready to be sectioned, filleted, or butterflied (see color page 32).

have a very thin row of tiny needlelike bones that need to be pulled or cut out.

Walleye (also called yellow pike, doré, or pike perch) (*Stizostedion vitreum*)

I first encountered a close relative of the walleye's, called a *sandre,* when working in a restaurant in Paris. Only one small fish arrived, carefully wrapped in a box of its own, reserved for a special customer. The reverence with which the creature was handled—and the price that was charged—intrigued me, but it wasn't until years later that I could afford to sample a *sandre* of my own. Needless to say the fish was delicious (and of course dear), so I was thrilled when I discovered that a very similar fish could be bought in a Chinese fish stall in New York for one-tenth the price.

The walleye is one fish whose freshness cannot be judged by the clarity of its eyes—the eyes of even the freshest specimens are cloudy. Even though walleye are sometimes called *yellow pike,* they don't look anything like pike and are completely unrelated. Walleye have long elegantly tapering bodies with brown or yellow coloration on a silvery background. Like all perch, they have hard spiny dorsal fins. There are stories of 25-pound walleyes, but most of the walleyes I've seen for sale in New York and the Midwest weigh between 1 and 2 pounds.

Unlike pike, walleye doesn't have a lot of bones, and the pure white flesh has a very delicate flavor. Walleye can be scaled and baked whole, or filleted, scaled, and cooked as either skinless or skin-on fillets.

BEST METHODS: baking (whole, scaled), poaching (whole), panfrying (skin-on or skinless fillets), braising

AVOID: smoking or overcooking (flesh is too lean)

YIELD: 45 percent skinless fillets from ungutted fish

APPEARANCE WHEN COOKED: pure white; very fine flake

TEXTURE WHEN COOKED: slightly firm

FAT CONTENT: very low

FLAVOR: sweet, delicate

Yellow Perch (also called just perch) (*Perca flavescens*)

Yellow perch is abundant in most of the eastern half of the United States and Canada and is a popular sportfish. I rarely see yellow perch in East Coast fish markets, but it does often show up for sale in the Midwest, especially anywhere near the Great Lakes, where it is caught commercially.

Most yellow perch weigh between ½ and 1 pound and are easy to recognize because of their yellow-brown coloration and by the black vertical bars running up their sides.

When I first encountered a perch, I tried to panfry it but discovered it was impossible to scale. So I ended up filleting it and removing the skin. (I read somewhere that you can scale a perch immediately after it comes out of the water, but I've never verified this.)

BEST METHODS: (all for skinless fillets only): pan-frying, deep-frying, braising

AVOID: overcooking (flesh becomes tough)

YIELD: 40 percent skinless fillets from ungutted fish

APPEARANCE WHEN COOKED: white; moderately fine flake

TEXTURE WHEN COOKED: moderately firm

FAT CONTENT: very low

FLAVOR: sweet, delicate

THE PIKE FAMILY

When I learned to cook in France, buying pike was simple because there was one kind. In North America there are three species of pike—the northern pike, which is very similar to the pike I first encountered in Europe, a smaller version called the *chain pickerel*, and a giant that I've never seen since they aren't sold, called *muskellunge*. To add to the confusion, walleye is sometimes incorrectly called *yellow pike* or *blue pike*.

All members of the pike family are very lean and have a large number of bones, which makes larger specimens more desirable because the bones are bigger and easier to pick out. I have seen elaborate instructions for filleting pike to minimize the bones, but I've never figured out how to end up with truly boneless fillets. I fillet pike in the same way as any round fish and then pick out as many bones as I can with needlenose pliers. French cooks get around the bone problem by pureeing pike for fish mousses, terrines, and quenelles. And of course there is gefilte fish of which pike is a traditional ingredient. Pike caught from ponds sometimes has a muddy taste that can be attenuated by removing the skin. Try also to select pike with bright silvery scales rather than with brown coloration. Brown pike may have spent too much time in stagnant water and may have a muddy taste.

Scaling pike can be a problem because pike are often covered with a thick layer of slime, which makes the job messy. One way to get around this is to poach the pike whole, scales and all, and then remove the skin and scales as soon as you take the pike out of the

poaching liquid. Another approach, if you want to use another cooking method, is to pour boiling water over the gutted pike, which helps coagulate the slime and make the scales easier to remove.

BEST METHODS: poaching (whole), steaming (steaks), baking (whole, scaled), panfrying (steaks), pureeing for quenelles, fish mousses, etc.

AVOID: small fish whose bones are hard to remove or negotiate; overcooking will make pike very dry

YIELD: 30 percent skinless fillets from ungutted fish

APPEARANCE WHEN COOKED: white, flaky

TEXTURE WHEN COOKED: slightly to moderately firm

FAT CONTENT: very low

FLAVOR: usually delicate but sometimes muddy flavor

Chain Pickerel (*Esox niger*)

Don't confuse this authentic member of the pike family with a walleye, which is sometimes incorrectly called a *pickerel*. I've never seen chain pickerel—a small version of the northern pike—for sale in fish stores. Chain pickerel are rarely caught weighing more than 2 pounds and so, because of their small bones, can be difficult to eat.

Muskellunge (also called muskie) (*Esox masquinongy*)

This giant pike, a popular sportfish, grows up to 60 pounds. It looks much like a northern pike but is often preferred because its large size facilitates removing bones and eating the fish.

Northern Pike (also called pike) (*Esox lucius*)

This is the most distinctive-looking fish of the pike family and is the most closely related to the European pike. Northern pike has a straight, almost cylindrical body with a long pointed mouth that I've heard best described as looking like a duck's bill. But if you look closely, this duck's bill is filled with scary little teeth. Northern pike are usually dark brown or gray with pale yellow elongated spots.

Even though pike are caught in the United States by game fishermen, the only pike sold commercially comes from Canada, where there are commercial freshwater fisheries.

Northern pike can grow up to 20 pounds, but I've never seen one larger than 4 or 5 pounds in New York fish markets.

SALMON

Deservedly one of the most popular fish in the United States, salmon is one of the few foods that has actually dropped in price over the last decade. Not only is salmon almost always available at reasonable prices, but it's almost always fresh and of excellent quality.

Most of the salmon consumed in the United States is farmed rather than caught wild. The Norwegians were among the first to farm salmon in cagelike contraptions in the open sea—a method that gives the salmon a natural "wild" flavor—but now salmon farming has caught on throughout the world so that prices have dropped dramatically.

Salmon is a versatile fish that is delicious when cooked using almost any method except, perhaps, deep-frying. It is sold whole, in fillets, and in steaks. Whole salmon fillets have a row of pin bones running along the front third, but these are easy to remove with a pair of pliers or tweezers. Salmon steaks, if they've been cut from the front third of the fish, will also have pin bones, but these are easily pulled out of the sides of the steaks.

BEST METHODS (STEAKS AND FILLETS): panfrying, steaming, grilling (leave skin on), hot or cold smoking (especially Atlantic salmon), poaching, braising, curing (gravlax), microwave

BEST METHODS (WHOLE): baking, poaching; **(FILLETS):** panfrying, grilling, braising; **(STEAKS):** grilling

AVOID: deep-frying

YIELD: 60 percent to 65 percent skinless fillets for 8-pound or larger gutted fish (salmon are usually already gutted)

APPEARANCE WHEN COOKED: pale pink to red

TEXTURE WHEN COOKED: moderately firm

FAT CONTENT: low (chum and pink), moderate (coho, Atlantic, sockeye), high (king)

FLAVOR: delicate, sealike, rich

All of the salmon available in the United States is either Atlantic salmon (*Salmo salar*) or Pacific salmon, of which there are five species. The situation gets even more confusing because Atlantic salmon is sometimes farmed in Pacific waters. (Chile provides much Atlantic salmon to the United States.) Atlantic salmon is the salmon most commonly eaten in the United States, and most of it is of consistently excellent quality. Most Pacific salmon is caught in the wild instead of being farmed, and it has more flavor variation than Atlantic salmon, which, while excellent, ends up all tasting the same—especially if you eat a lot of it.

ATLANTIC VARIETY

Atlantic Salmon (*Salmo salar*)

Most Atlantic salmon is farmed and is shipped quickly (often by air freight) so that it arrives in pristine condition at the fish market. The best Atlantic salmon has a delicate pink hue and a rich sealike flavor. Atlantic salmon has a fairly high fat content, which is partly responsible for its melting texture and rich flavor. The richest (and fattiest) part of the salmon are the belly flaps—they're excellent cut into strips and grilled—and the leanest part is the tail. Many people wrongly assume that redder salmon has a higher fat content than pale salmon, whereas the opposite is sometimes true. Salmon's red color is caused by astaxanthin, a nonfatty compound that accumulates in salmon that eat crustaceans and certain insects. Atlantic salmon is usually sold gutted with the head on and weighs from 8 to 12 pounds.

PACIFIC VARIETIES

All five species of Pacific salmon are members of the genus *Oncorhynchus*, which means "hooked nose." Unfortunately this isn't much help when it comes to distinguishing Pacific salmon from Atlantic—Atlantic salmon, depending on its age and stage of development, often has a hooked nose too. Unlike Atlantic salmon, which is available year-round, each species of Pacific salmon is traditionally available only at certain times of year, although some farming is beginning, so this may not be true for long.

Chinook (also called king salmon) (*Oncorhynchus tshawytscha*)

This is the largest of all salmon and typically weighs from 15 to 40 pounds, although specimens of over 100 pounds are sometimes caught. It can be difficult to tell this salmon from other, less expensive varieties, especially if you can't see the whole fish with the head on. Typically chinook salmon is the fattiest, and it has the largest scales of any salmon. The most distinguishing characteristic of a

chinook salmon is that it has black gums. Chinook salmon also have black spots covering their tail and black spots on the back of the fish above the lateral line. The color of chinook flesh can range from pale, almost white, to deep red. Chinook salmon that is overly mature—with a hooked nose and rough-edged tail—will not have as good a flavor as younger specimens.

Most chinook salmon is available in the summer, although Columbia River chinook is available in the fall and a small amount of farmed chinook is now available in the winter.

Chum (also called dog or keta salmon) (*Oncorhynchus keta*)

Chum salmon is one of the least expensive salmon and is often frozen to be sold in supermarkets. Chum salmon usually weigh from 8 to 10 pounds—and have distinctive V-shaped tails. Chum's flavor and texture deteriorate as the salmon approaches spawning, so if you happen to be buying from a whole fish—where you can see the skin color—choose one with bright silvery skin and avoid dark salmon or salmon with mottled and blotched skin. In the trade, chum salmon are referred to as *silverbrites*, *semi-brites*, and *darks*, with silverbrites being the most desirable.

Coho (also called silver or jack salmon) (*Oncorhynchus kisutch*)

Because coho salmon contain less fat than Atlantic, chinook, and sockeye salmon, they tend to be less flavorful and more flaky when cooked. Coho salmon typically weigh from 5 to 12 pounds but can grow as large as 25 pounds. Coho salmon have silver-blue coloring along their backs. They are only sparsely spotted—on their backs and on the top part of their tails. It's hard to tell the difference between a coho salmon and the less expensive chum salmon, but chum salmon have distinctive V-shaped tails. Coho salmon flesh is usually somewhat paler than chinook or sockeye flesh. Farmed coho is available year-round, but wild coho is in season from July until early October with the peak in August. Baby coho salmon (about ½ to 1 pound), which look somewhat like trout except for their orange flesh, are now being farmed and marketed year-round. Usually they are boned but with the heads still on. The flesh has a delicate flavor, but it isn't as tasty or pronounced as that of adult salmon or trout.

Pink (also called humpback salmon) (*Oncorhynchus gorbuscha*)

Most of these inexpensive salmon end up in cans, but some show up in ethnic fish markets, where there is a demand for inexpensive fish. In fact these small salmon—usually between 3 and 5 pounds—are often good bargains. I like to have them scaled and gutted and bake them whole. Pink salmon is easiest to recognize by the characteristic hump in its back.

Sockeye (also called red or blueback salmon) (*Oncorhynchus nerka*)

In Japan, sockeye is the most prized of all salmon; in the United States it runs a close second to chinook. Sockeye salmon are generally somewhat small—6 pounds is typical—but sometimes grow up to about 15 pounds. It's hard to tell what you're getting unless you can see the whole fish, but in general sockeye salmon has consistently dark red flesh while other species are often paler. Sockeye salmon has bright silver skin—sometimes with a bluish cast—and much less spotting than chinook salmon.

Most sockeye salmon are available in the summer with peak availability occurring the first two weeks in July. Most sockeye salmon comes from Alaska and Canada.

SHAD (*Alosa sapidissima*)

Because shad are anadromous—they spawn in rivers but spend most of their lives at sea—most are caught as they make their way up the rivers and streams of both the Atlantic and Pacific coasts to lay their eggs. The result is that the height of shad season ends up lasting only a month or two in the spring. (Ocean-run shad is occasionally available at other times of the year.) Shad on the Atlantic coast start their expedition in Florida and make it to New York in March and April but don't get to the Saint Lawrence River— another one of their favorite spawning grounds—until May. On the Pacific coast, shad work their way up the Columbia River from May to July.

Shad are members of the herring family (Clupeidae) and have the same soft single dorsal fin and large silvery scales. Most shad have a black spot on their sides just behind the gills and weigh from 3 to 5 pounds.

My guess is that we're much less enthusiastic about shad fish than we are about shad roe (see entry below) because shad flesh is full of little bones. And despite theories that baking the fish for 6 hours or simmering it with sorrel will dissolve the bones, nothing seems to get rid of them. I have cookbooks that give elaborate descriptions for boning shad, which I've never been able to follow, and "boned" shad fillets still seem to have bones most of the time. But shad is such delicious fish that I remain undaunted and just pick out the bones as well as I can while I'm eating.

The filleted and "boned" shad is usually sold in upscale markets, while at ethnic places you may be able to find shad whole. Even if you do find whole shad, they will be gutted so the roe can be sold at a premium.

BEST METHODS: panfrying (fillets), baking whole (if you can live with the bones), broiling (fillets), hot smoking, grilling (skin-on fillets)

AVOID: serving to small children (because of the bones), eating raw

YIELD: 55 percent skin-on fillets from gutted fish

APPEARANCE WHEN COOKED: off-white

TEXTURE WHEN COOKED: soft

FAT CONTENT: high

FLAVOR: mildly pronounced

Shad Roe

Americans have a long history of eating shad roe—and in fact pay quite dearly for it—but have shown much less interest in eating the fish. (In Europe the opposite is true; shad roe is rarely mentioned, but the fish is considered a delicacy.) Shad roe is best when panfried in butter or bacon fat. It has a firm but delicate texture.

BEST METHOD: panfrying in butter or bacon fat

AVOID: eating more than once a week (roe accumulates environmental contaminants)

YIELD: 100 percent

APPEARANCE WHEN COOKED: brown

FAT CONTENT: high

FLAVOR: pronounced

SMELTS (depending on species, also called candlefish, whitebait, jacksmelt, grunion, capelin, surf smelt, eulachon) (Atlantic: rainbow smelt: *Osmerus mordax*; Pacific: eulachon: *Thaleichthys pacificus*; surf smelt: *Hypomesus pretiosus*)

Smelts are small silvery fish with olive-green coloring on their backs and white on their bellies. Smelts grow up to 14 inches, but most of the smelt you're likely to encounter in the market are only about 6 inches long. I actually prefer small smelts to large ones because the bones are smaller and I can eat practically the whole thing. Many writers say that smelts taste of cucumbers or violets; I've never noticed this, but in any case they have very delicate sweet and satisfying flesh.

The best known of all American smelts is the rainbow smelt, which is found not only in the Atlantic and Pacific oceans but also in freshwater lakes and streams. An oilier Pacific species, the eulachon—sometimes marketed as Columbia River smelt—is also popular along the Pacific coast, especially during the late winter and spring. Occasionally the leaner surf smelt is also harvested in the same locations as the eulachon.

While most smelts are harvested in the spring, they are also fished during the off-season in (sometimes frozen) lakes and streams. They also freeze well, so in one way or another it's possible to buy them year-round.

Smelts are often sold already headed and gutted, but if you encounter them whole you can remove the guts by snapping back and pulling off the head and pulling out the entrails with it or, if you want to leave the head on, by pinching the gills and pulling gills and guts out together.

My favorite way to eat smelts is to behead them and gut them, coat them in a very light batter, deep-fry them, and serve them with lemon. If they're small enough, you can eat them bones and all, but even large smelts are easy to eat by just nibbling the flesh off the backbone.

BEST METHODS: frying (whole, beheaded and gutted), broiling (whole), baking (whole), panfrying (whole), grilling (use skewers to hold them together)

AVOID: eating raw, using in soups and stews

YIELD: 45 percent skin-on fillets from ungutted fish

APPEARANCE WHEN COOKED: white flesh

TEXTURE WHEN COOKED: soft

FAT CONTENT: rainbow smelts: low; eulachons: high

FLAVOR: rainbow smelts: mild; eulachons: mildly pronounced

STEELHEAD: See Rainbow Trout.

STURGEON (Atlantic: *Acipenser oxyrhynchus*; Atlantic shortnose: *Acipenser brevirostrum*; lake: *Acipenser fulvescens*; Pacific white: *Acipenser transmontanus*; Pacific green: *Acipenser medirostris*)

Many of us have tasted smoked sturgeon or have been lucky enough to sample its delicious eggs, but few of us have tasted fresh sturgeon. Unfortunately very little sturgeon makes it to market because most of the wild varieties have been fished out or their habitats have been destroyed by pollution. California has a small sturgeon-farming industry, but it still isn't large enough to make sturgeon regularly available.

Before the turn of the century sturgeon was so common that it practically clogged the Hudson River. Sturgeon was not only abundant, but some specimens grew to 30 feet long and weighed 4,000 pounds. Nowadays a 30-pound wild sturgeon is considered rather large, and farmed sturgeon are rarely sold larger than 20 pounds. While farmed sturgeon will hopefully become more abundant so that it's available year-round, most wild sturgeon is caught in the spring and fall, especially in September, which is the best time to look for it.

Sturgeon isn't covered with scales or the usual kind of fish skin but instead has a series of thick steellike plates. When I used to buy whole sturgeon to cook at my restaurant, I hacked at the underside of the fish with a cleaver to cut through the skin, cut all the way through the flesh to the armor plating on the back of the fish, and then again attacked with a cleaver. Fortunately, at the fish store sturgeon is usually sold in skinless steaks or fillets.

Sturgeon flesh is light pink with strips of yellow-orange fat that is easy to remove with a sharp knife. Beware of sturgeon whose flesh is orange-colored since this may be the less expensive and not as tasty as green sturgeon, indigenous to the western United States. Sturgeon is very firm—it has almost the texture of meat—and has a delicate flavor. (Although I have heard it sometimes has a muddy flavor, I've never encountered this.) Sturgeon is adaptable to almost any cooking method; my favorites are grilling and smoking.

BEST METHODS: grilling (skinless fillets or steaks), hot or cold smoking (fillets), broiling (skinless fillets or steaks), braising (skinless fillets or steaks)

AVOID: cooking whole; leaving the skin on; eating raw

YIELD: 50 percent skinless steaks from gutted fish, 45 percent skinless fillets from gutted fish, 62 percent skinless fillets from headless and gutted fish (bullet)

APPEARANCE WHEN COOKED: white to off-white

TEXTURE WHEN COOKED: firm

FAT CONTENT: moderate

FLAVOR: usually delicate but may on occasion have a muddy smell and flavor, sniff before buying

TILAPIA (also called St. Peter's fish—not to be confused with Dory) (*Tilapia* spp.)

Virtually all tilapia is raised on fish farms. Most of the fresh tilapia we see in the United States comes from farms in California, while a considerable amount of frozen tilapia comes from Taiwan.

There are so many species of tilapia—some are even a different genus—that it's almost impossible to give an accurate description that will fit all. Tilapia can be black, red, or golden. Tilapia grow quickly and can be raised up to 3 pounds, but most fish are sold when they weigh about 1½ pounds.

I find the taste of tilapia to be somewhat insipid, but an efficient distribution system means that sometimes tilapia is the freshest fish I see at the fish market. In Chinese markets it is sometimes kept alive in tanks. I don't recommend buying tilapia that has already been filleted because the fillets have probably been frozen, which further depletes tilapia's delicate flavor.

Smaller fish can be scaled and panfried whole. Tilapia fillets are best with the skin on, lightly panfried.

BEST METHODS: panfrying (skin-on fillets or whole fish), braising (skinless fillets)

AVOID: strong sauces that will completely mask its flavor, raw

YIELD: 35 percent skin-on steaks from ungutted fish

APPEARANCE WHEN COOKED: white to off-white

TEXTURE WHEN COOKED: slightly firm

FAT CONTENT: low

FLAVOR: usually delicate, almost insipid; wild tilapia from Florida may have a muddy flavor

CAVIAR

A few other foods may be more expensive by weight (saffron and truffles), but I know of no other food that is more expensive per serving. Most of us haven't even tasted authentic sturgeon caviar, much less ever had enough of it not to leave us craving more. A 1-ounce portion is considered standard, but for some of us anything less than 2 ounces is a tease.

The best caviar is malossol, meaning lightly salted, which must be kept tightly sealed and well refrigerated. Caviar comes in large round tins with large lids held in place by thick rubber bands. Smaller quantities may be repacked in jars and sold refrigerated. Avoid pasteurized caviar, which is usually sold unrefrigerated in vacuum-packed jars.

Most caviar comes from the Caspian Sea, bordered by Russia and Iran, but a small amount of so-called Imperial caviar is imported from China. There is also a small amount of very high-quality caviar produced in the United States, mainly in Louisiana and Oregon.

There are four kinds of Caspian sturgeon caviar, each coming from a different sturgeon species. Beluga, the most expensive, has the largest grains and comes from the largest sturgeon, the beluga; osetra—from the osetra sturgeon—consists of slightly smaller eggs but is considered by some experts to be as good if not better; sevruga consists of the smallest eggs and is usually less expensive, which makes it a good value (if any caviar can be a good value). The fourth variety of caviar is the pale sterlet caviar from the almost-extinct sterlet sturgeon.

In America the eggs of other fish may not be called simply caviar; the fish name must precede the word *caviar* (e.g., salmon caviar, whitefish caviar, and lumpfish caviar). While these other eggs can be delicious, none of them compares with authentic sturgeon caviar. Good-quality unpasteurized salmon and trout eggs and whitefish caviar are much less expensive than sturgeon caviar and can be substituted in some situations calling for caviar. Least expensive of all are lumpfish eggs, which come pasteurized in small jars. While perhaps amusing in small amounts, they are salty and strong-tasting and lack the melting texture of unpasteurized eggs.

Cookbooks abound with elaborate suggestions for serving caviar, but any accompaniment such as lemon juice or chopped onion only interferes with caviar's delicate flavor. Nor should caviar be served on crackers—their brittleness interferes with the caviar's delicate texture. Lightly toasted white bread is suitable, but my own favorite way is to serve caviar with blinis and plenty of melted butter.

TROUT

Anyone who has camped alongside a rushing stream and caught trout for dinner knows that trout can be one of the most delicious things there is. Those of us who hardly ever escape the city, much less go fishing, must settle for farmed trout. And while farmed trout never reaches the celestial heights of its wild cousins, such a trout can certainly make a tasty meal.

While there are several varieties of trout, a trout's flavor, texture, and color (which ranges from almost pure white to a rich salmon color) have far more to do with diet and habitat than with species. A well-managed trout farm can sometimes produce trout with a good wild flavor and a firm texture, while lesser places produce trout with an unpleasant earthy flavor and a mushy texture. So if you cook trout with any regularity and have access to trout from more than one farm, it pays to compare.

While most trout live in either lakes or streams, some varieties—so-called anadromous species—migrate between fresh and salt water. An example of this is the steelhead—a West Coast rainbow trout that goes to sea. Europe also has its own anadromous version, called sea trout (not to be confused with the member of the drum family similar to weakfish).

When you're buying trout it's impossible to judge which have the best flavor, but it is at least possible to determine freshness. The freshest trout is covered with a slippery layer of perfectly transparent slime. In fact a perfectly fresh trout should be so slippery that it's almost impossible to hold. Trout is one of the longest-lasting small fish and will keep in the refrigerator for several days without losing flavor. (Blue-style trout is the only dish that requires a trout caught the same day it is cooked.)

Trout scales are so minute that there's no need for scaling, and most trout is sold already gutted and ready to cook. If you catch your own trout, they must of course be gutted. Trout is sometimes sold already boned but, like anything, has more flavor when cooked with its bones.

The very delicate flavor of trout shouldn't be masked with strong-tasting ingredients or with aggressive cooking techniques (such as blackening). The most delicate treatment and the one least likely to alter a trout's flavor is blue-style trout, but because the trout needs to have been killed just hours before it is cooked I usually opt for trout meunière. Trout is also good grilled, but be sure to use a grilling basket, or the skin may stick and tear.

BEST METHODS: poaching (especially blue-style), meunière, grilling (with grilling basket), steaming, smoking (especially lake trout)

AVOID: deep-frying

YIELD: 50 percent to 55 percent fillets with skin on from larger gutted whole trout

APPEARANCE WHEN COOKED: white to pale pink with gray coloration along the lateral line, distinct angular flakes

TEXTURE WHEN COOKED: soft to moderately firm

FAT CONTENT: low to moderate; high (lake trout)

FLAVOR: wild trout and the best farmed trout have a delicate herbaceous, grasslike flavor; inferior farmed trout sometimes have a muddy flavor

Brook Trout (*Salvelinus fontinalis*)

Brook trout is indigenous to the eastern United States and Canada. Much like the rainbow trout, its indigenous western cousin, the brook trout has been transplanted throughout the United States and is also farmed. Fishermen tell me that wild brook trout is the most delicious of all trout. Brook trout grow up to 6 pounds in the wild but typically weigh about a pound. Brook trout is usually dark olive in color with red-orange spots on its sides.

Brown Trout (*Salmo trutta*)

This is the original trout of Europe that was transplanted to the United States in the 19th century. Like native American species, brown trout can live in lakes and streams or migrate to the sea. Brown trout that swim to the sea are sometimes called *sea trout* or *salmon trout*. Salmon trout is a popular delicacy in Europe and looks somewhat like coho salmon. But the closest American equivalent to salmon trout is steelhead. Brown trout can grow up to 40 pounds, but most brown trout caught in rivers or streams weigh between 1 and 2 pounds. Salmon trout typically weigh 4 to 5 pounds.

Lake Trout (*Salvelinus namaycush*)

These wild trout are netted in the cold-water lakes of the northern United States and Canada. Lake trout have the highest fat content of almost any fish and for this reason aren't to everyone's taste. The biggest problem with lake trout is that their fat content varies so that some are quite delicious while others are just too oily. Hot smoking is the most reliable method for preparing lake trout. Lake trout grow to be very large—up to 100 pounds—but most I see for sale weigh about 10 pounds.

Rainbow trout (*Oncorhynchus mykiss*)

Rainbow trout is the most common species of farmed trout and the variety most often used to replenish rivers and streams in the American West, where it originated. It gets its name from the pinkish hue that runs along its lateral line. Steelhead is rainbow trout that runs to sea and can grow up to 12 pounds. Wild steelhead is even more delicious than inland rainbow trout. Most farm-raised rainbow trout weigh 12 to 16 ounces.

WALLEYE: See Perch.

WHITEFISH

There are actually several varieties of whitefish, but the most common, at least when sold fresh, is the lake whitefish, *Coregonus clupeaformis*. Whitefish is beautiful to look at because it has bright fine silvery scales and a beautiful shape, almost like that of a salmon, to which it is related. Most whitefish comes from Canada, where it is harvested commercially, but much whitefish is also caught by sportfishermen in New England and around the Great Lakes. Whitefish grow up to 20 pounds, but most that I've encountered in the markets weigh between 3 and 5 pounds. Whitefish is best in the spring and fall.

Because whitefish are moderately fatty, they should be cooked accordingly. They are especially good when smoked; in fact their smaller cousins, ciscos, are smoked and sold as chubs. Whitefish is one of the traditional ingredients in gefilte fish. Whitefish roe is also a popular and inexpensive substitute for caviar.

BEST METHODS: baking (whole), broiling (steaks and fillets), grilling (steaks and fillets), hot smoking

AVOID: deep-frying (whitefish is already fatty enough)

YIELD: 55 percent skinless fillets from ungutted fish

APPEARANCE WHEN COOKED: white; fine flake

TEXTURE WHEN COOKED: moderately firm

FAT CONTENT: moderate to high

FLAVOR: mild

Glossary of Foreign Ingredients

ASIAN INGREDIENTS

Bonito

Dried bonito is the main ingredient in dashi, the soul of Japanese broths and sauces. Japanese cooks use the dried bonito in one of three ways: The most traditional and best method is to shave the bonito shortly before it is cooked on a shoe box–like gadget with a blade on top. A second and much easier method is to buy the bonito already flaked in cellophane bags. Bonito flakes, called *hana-katsuo*, look like wood shavings. The easiest method is to use instant dashi—called *dashi-no-moto*—which comes either in instant granules or in teabags.

Bumbu

Bumbu, a word often encountered in Indonesian recipes, is a mixture of spices and aromatic vegetables such as chilies and garlic that is usually cooked in oil before other liquid ingredients are added. A *bumbu* is much like a Thai curry except that the ingredients differ somewhat, and a Thai curry is usually stirred into a preparation at the end while a *bumbu* is cooked at the beginning.

Chilies (Thai)

Southeast Asian cooks use these chilies—also called *bird chilies*—in almost all their seafood soups, stews, and sauces. Thai chilies are about 1 inch long and are usually green, although occasionally red ones show up in a batch (their heat is the same). Thai chilies' small size is deceiving—they are very hot.

The easiest way to use Thai chilies is to slit them lengthwise down the middle, scrape out the seeds, and chop them finely. (Wear gloves and don't touch your eyes after chopping chilies.) Thai chilies can also be ground, with other ingredients, in a food processor or in a large mortar and pestle.

LATIN: *Capsicum frutescens*

THAI: *prik e noo*

VIETNAMESE: *ot*

STORING AND PRESERVING: Thread the chilies with a string and hang them in a warm dry place until they dry out. Once dried, they will keep for months. Whole chilies can be also be kept in plastic bags in the refrigerator for at least a week or in the freezer, tightly wrapped, for up to a year.

SUBSTITUTES: Serrano chilies are best. Although individual chilies vary enormously in heat, I usually substitute 1 red or green serrano chili for 2 Thai chilies. Jalapeños can also be used in larger amounts.

Chinese Mushrooms

So-called Chinese mushrooms are actually dried shiitake mushrooms and are used throughout Asia. There are many different grades ranging from fairly inexpensive to very pricy indeed. The least expensive have relatively smooth deep brown caps that are less than an inch in diameter. The most expensive are over 2 inches in diameter and have brown caps covered with weblike white fissures. The fissure type are much more flavorful, but I've found that size doesn't affect the flavor much, so I usually opt for the small fissure type, which are half the price of the largest fissure type.

Chinese mushrooms should be soaked in water until soft—about 30 minutes in hot water, 5 hours in cold. Their flavorful soaking liquid is worth saving for soups and sauces.

LATIN: *Lentinus edodes*

JAPANESE: *shiitake*

THAI: *hed hom*

ENGLISH: black oak, black forest, black mushroom

STORING AND PRESERVING: Dried mushrooms will keep indefinitely when tightly sealed in jars and kept in a dry place.

SUBSTITUTES: Fresh shiitake mushrooms (which need no soaking), regular cultivated mushrooms (in a pinch), dried porcini

Coconut Milk

Coconut milk is not the liquid contained in a fresh coconut but is extracted by soaking the grated coconut pulp in hot water.

While you can make your own coconut milk, canned coconut milk is so inexpensive and of such good quality that I rarely bother. There are several brands on the market. The best brands always seem to come from Thailand, but I've heard there are some acceptable Spanish brands. Avoid sweetened coconut milk (or cream) containing sugar or stabilizers, which is meant for piña coladas.

To make your own coconut milk, buy a coconut that has liquid (shake it to make sure you hear the liquid sloshing around inside). Use a hammer and a screwdriver to puncture holes in two of the coconut "eyes"—the dark oval spots near the top. Drain out the liquid—I usually just drink it as a little reward for going through all this work—and bake the coconut in a 375°F oven for 20 minutes to get the pulp to separate from the shell. Wrap the coconut in a towel and hit it with a hammer to crack it open. Pull out the pulp. Peel the thin dark peel off the sections of pulp with a vegetable peeler. Grind the pulp in a food processor for about 1 minute or grate it with a hand grater.

Put the grated pulp in a mixing bowl and pour on 1 cup of boiling water. Let the mixture sit for 10 minutes and then strain the mixture through a medium-mesh strainer over another bowl, reserving the liquid. Wrap the drained pulp in a kitchen towel and wring out any remaining liquid over the bowl. Put the pulp in the original mixing bowl and pour on another cup of boiling water. Repeat the straining process.

One fresh coconut should give you 2 cups coconut milk. If you're left with extra coconut milk (either canned or fresh) after making a recipe, freeze the coconut milk in a plastic container—it keeps for months.

THAI: *Nam katee*

VIETNAMESE: *nuoc cot dua*

INDONESIAN: *santen*

STORING AND PRESERVING: While canned coconut milk will keep for several months if stored in a cool place, it doesn't last forever—I have had cans turn rancid that I've stored for six months. Fresh coconut milk or coconut milk out of the can will last for a week in the refrigerator or indefinitely when frozen in tightly sealed containers.

SUBSTITUTES: There is really no substitute, but I have used heavy cream in Thai soups with OK results.

Fish Sauce

This is *the* universal Southeast Asian sauce and condiment. Fish sauce is made by salting anchovies and sometimes squid or shrimp in barrels and capturing the liquid that runs out over several months. Fish sauce is surprisingly delicate when combined with other ingredients. Because its strength differs among brands, you may have to adjust the quantities given in a particular recipe. The best way to do this is to add a little bit at a time, tasting as you go along. I usually think of fish sauce as a substitute for salt, and when the saltiness of the dish is right, I've added enough fish sauce.

Tiparos brand, Flying Lion brand "Phu Quoc," and Ruang Tong brand are particularly good and available in most parts of the country.

THAI: *nam pla*

VIETNAMESE: *nuoc mam*

LAOTIAN: *nam pa*

CAMBODIAN: *tuk trey*

TAGALOG (Philippines): *patis*

BURMESE: *ngan-pya-ye*

STORING AND PRESERVING: In the bottle in the refrigerator for up to 1 year

SUBSTITUTES: There are no substitutes. I have made Thai seafood soups and sauces and left the fish sauce out. While these dishes were good, they lacked soul.

Galangal

Galangal looks like a root but is actually an underground stem called a *rhizome*. It looks somewhat like ginger but has a completely different taste—a pleasant pine resin flavor. Southeast Asian cooks use galangal in many of their dishes—the Thais and Vietnamese slice it and simmer it in soups and sauces or grind it into their curries, while Indonesian cooks are more likely to use it in powdered form in a *bumbu*—the cooked flavor base for many of their dishes.

If you live near an Asian market, you should be able to find frozen whole galangal or fresh galangal, which you can store indefinitely in your freezer at home. Galangal is also sold in powder form under the Indonesian name *laos*.

LATIN: *Alpinia galanga*

THAI: *kha or ka*

VIETNAMESE: *rieng*

INDONESIAN: *laos*

ENGLISH: Sometimes galanga or galanga root

STORING AND PRESERVING: Fresh galangal can be wrapped tightly in plastic wrap and frozen for a year. Ground galangal will keep in a cool place for 1 year.

SUBSTITUTES: Although many recipes suggest ginger, it has a completely different flavor. While there is really no substitute, I sometimes substitute a bay leaf (one per ¼-inch slice galangal).

Holy Basil

Sometimes called *Thai basil* or *Asian basil*, holy basil has smaller leaves and a more pungent licoricelike flavor than our large-leaf Italian basil. Fortunately, Italian basil is similar enough to holy basil that it can be substituted.

LATIN: *Ocimum sanctum linn*

THAI: *bai horapa*

VIETNAMESE: *rau que or rau húng*

STORING AND PRESERVING: Up to 1 week by putting roots in a glass of water, covering the whole plant with a plastic bag held around the glass with a rubber band. Up to several months by packing the leaves into mason jars and filling the jars with olive or vegetable oil and refrigerating. Up to 1 year by pureeing the leaves with a little olive oil in a blender and freezing the mixture.

SUBSTITUTES: Italian basil. Mint, parsley, and cilantro can also be used even though their flavors are much different. (Don't substitute dried basil.)

Kaffir Lime Leaves

Kaffir lime trees are closely related to our common lime, but the flavor of kaffir lime is more pungent and aromatic. Kaffir lime leaves are used throughout Southeast Asia and are added whole or shredded to soups and sauces or finely ground as an ingredient in Thai curry pastes. The zest (the green outer part of the rind) of the kaffir lime can also be grated and used as a flavoring.

LATIN: *Citrus hystrix*

THAI: *makrut*

VIETNAMESE: *la chanh*

LAOTIAN: *mak khi hout*

INDONESIAN: *jeruk purut*

PRESERVING AND STORING: Leaves and fruit will keep in the refrigerator for up to two weeks if wrapped tightly in a plastic sandwich bag or for several months in the freezer.

SUBSTITUTES: Two 1- by ¼-inch strips of common lime zest—blanched for 1 minute to remove bitterness—can be substituted for each kaffir lime leaf.

Kemiri Nuts

These nuts, popular in Indonesian cooking, have a dark smooth and very hard shell and vaguely resemble chestnuts. Because the shell is so hard—I remember using them to make neckerchief clasps in Cub Scouts—the nut itself ends up in little pieces by the time you get it out. Kemiri nuts are sold in little cellophane bags by Asian grocers. When raw, kemiri nuts are known to be mildly toxic.

LATIN: *Aleurites moluccana*

INDONESIAN: *kemiri or buah keras*

ENGLISH: candlenut

STORING AND PRESERVING: Like all nuts, kemiri nuts are best kept in the freezer—they'll keep for up to a year—to prevent rancidity.

SUBSTITUTES: Macadamia nuts

Kinome (*Zenothoxylum piperitum*)

Because these bright green leaves of the prickly ash tree are one of the most popular garnishes used by Japanese cooks, they are relatively easy to find in the United States. Kinome leaves have a pungent cinnamonlike flavor that makes them delicious with grilled or simmered Japanese seafood dishes. The same tree produces little red berries that are ground into a Japanese pepper called *sansho*.

Lemongrass

Lemongrass grows in stalks about 18 inches long that look a bit like miniature ears of corn but more elongated. Lemongrass has a subtle lemon aroma and taste and is very popular in Southeast Asian cooking—either thinly sliced in soups or ground to a paste in a food processor or with a mortar and pestle for use in curries and the Indonesian flavor base, *bumbu*. To use lemongrass, pull away the fibrous outer sheath and slice or grind only the bottom half.

LATIN: *Cymbopogon citratus*

THAI: *takrai*

VIETNAMESE: *xa*

INDONESIAN: *sereh*

STORING AND PRESERVING: Keeps up to a month in the refrigerator, but the outer sheath will become dry and woody and should be removed before slicing or grinding. Will keep for up to 1 year wrapped tightly in the freezer.

SUBSTITUTES: A 2- by ½-inch strip of lemon zest, blanched for 1 minute to remove bitterness, can be substituted for a 1-inch piece of lemongrass.

Mint

Southeast Asian cooks use mint, chopped or torn into small pieces and often combined with basil or cilantro, as a finish for seafood soups and stews. Several varieties of mint can be found at different times of the year, and while any kind of mint can be used in Southeast Asian cooking, the most typical are the more pungent small- and dark-leaved varieties of peppermint and spearmint.

LATIN: *Mentha* spp.

VIETNAMESE: *bac-ha*

STORING AND PRESERVING: Fresh mint will keep for up to 2 weeks if the roots are submerged in a glass half full of water and the whole thing is then covered with a plastic bag attached tightly to the glass with a rubber band. Mint leaves, left whole or finely chopped, can be packed into jars, covered with peanut oil, and frozen for up to 1 year.

SUBSTITUTES: None. More of other herbs such as cilantro or parsley can be used if no mint is available. Don't use dried mint.

Mirin

A sweet sake used in Japanese cooking, mirin is never drunk but is used as a sweetener in Japanese broth, glazes (for grilling), and dipping sauces. Mirin is inexpensive and keeps for months on the shelf.

Miso (Japanese fermented soybean paste)

Miso is a stiff paste that comes in various colors, each corresponding to a different strength and saltiness. The lightest miso, called *shiro-miso*, is pale yellow bordering on white and is considered the sweetest and mildest. Darker misos, called *inaka-miso* or *hatcho-miso*, come in various shades of brown and red and are saltier and stronger-flavored. Many Japanese cooks combine different kinds of misos to come up with different nuances of flavor. Miso is most often used in miso soup—a perfect backdrop to small pieces of fish or shellfish—and is sometimes combined with other ingredients such as soy sauce or mirin as a marinade for grilled fish.

The best miso is usually sold in plastic bags, which make a mess as soon as you open them (I put the opened bag in a sandwich bag), but occasionaly you'll be able to find miso in small and convenient plastic tubs. Miso, when wrapped tightly, keeps in the refrigerator for at least a year and probably indefinitely.

Palm Sugar

Many Southeast Asian and Indonesian recipes call for palm sugar, made from the sap of various palm trees, including the coconut palm. It's sold in several forms—in plastic containers or sometimes logs—under the name *coconut sugar, Java sugar,* and of course *palm sugar.* The Indians have a version of cane sugar called *jaggery,* which makes a suitable substitute if you can't find the Southeast Asian or Indonesian version. While granulated sugar has none of the flavor of palm sugar, I sometimes use it as a substitute—at least it provides the necessary sweetness.

Sake

Also known as *Japanese rice wine,* sake is sold in most liquor stores in the United States, and while some sake is very expensive, an inexpensive brand will work for cooking. Sake is often used along with soy sauce, dashi, and mirin to make the basic broths, sauces, marinades, and glazes essential to Japanese cooking. It is especially useful in seafood cooking because, when used as a marinade, it eliminates salt and any traces of "fishiness."

Salam Leaves

Popular in Indonesian cooking, salam leaves are used in the same way as bay leaves in Western cooking or curry leaves in Indian cooking.

LATIN: *Eugeneia polyanza*

Seaweed

Two kinds of seaweed are called for in this book. The best known is *nori,* the dried black or very dark green paperlike seaweed used for wrapping sushi. Nori comes in large rectangular sheets that are then usually cut into strips. Some nori needs to be toasted slightly (by holding it over a gas flame for a few seconds) before it is used, but most nori sold in Japanese grocers has already been toasted. *Konbu* is a relatively large type of seaweed that is sold in long dried strips that are simmered gently as the first step in making dashi.

Sesame Oil

The extract of toasted sesame seeds, sesame oil is a potent flavoring used in Chinese and Japanese soups and sauces. Sesame oil is especially delicious when combined with soy sauce, ginger, and garlic. Be sure to buy *dark* sesame oil, which is made from toasted seeds. Kodaya brand from Japan is especially good.

Seven-Spice Mixture (*Shichimi*)

This popular Japanese spice mixture contains red pepper flakes, sansho pepper pods, dried mandarin orange peel, white poppy seeds, white sesame seeds, mulberry, and ground nori seaweed. The Japanese sprinkle this spice mixture on foods in much the way Westerners use pepper. I place a small container of the mixture on the table whenever I'm serving Japanese seafood soups.

Shrimp Paste

While this is a popular condiment in Southeast Asia, it's not often used in restaurants in the United States because of its taste and pungent aroma. In the same way as fish sauce, shrimp paste—made by fermenting shrimp in the sun—gives such a depth of flavor to seafood stews and soups that once you're used to it you'll begin to miss if it's not there.

If used in the way most recipes recommend—cooking in oil before liquid is added—shrimp paste will smell up the house for days. It's better to stir small amounts of paste into a dish near the end. My favorite brand is Trachang brand from Thailand.

THAI: *kapee*

VIETNAMESE: *mam tom* or *mam ruoc*

INDONESIAN: *trassi* (*terasi*)

MALAYSIAN: *balachan*

BURMESE: *ngapee*

STORING AND PRESERVING: In the refrigerator for up to a year; in the freezer indefinitely.

SUBSTITUTES: While there's no perfect substitute, powdered dried shrimp will contribute some of the same effect.

Soy Sauce

Made by fermenting roasted soybeans, soy sauce comes in so many strengths and colors that hunting down a good brand can sometimes be confusing. Buy only authentic soy sauce that has been brewed naturally—it should say so on the label—and avoid synthetic soy sauces such as the La Choy brand found in supermarkets. Kikkoman from Japan is a reliable brand and is usually easy to find.

To add to the confusion, Japanese and Chinese soy sauces have different flavors. While it's almost impossible to describe the nuances, Chinese soy sauce is usually saltier and should be used more sparingly than Japanese. The recipes in this book are made with Kikkoman, so if you're substituting another brand, taste as you go along to control the salt. Many of the recipes call for dark versus light soy sauce. Dark soy has a deeper flavor and is usually less salty.

Tamarind (*tamarindo*)

This is a sour fruit that looks somewhat like fava beans except that the husk of the tamarind is brown and shriveled instead of green. The sticky pulp that surrounds the beanlike fruit is used in Asian cooking to give a pleasant sour tang to soups and sauces.

Because taking the pulp out of fresh tamarind pods can be a nuisance and fresh tamarind isn't always available, I usually rely on blocks of tamarind paste, easily found in ethnic markets. Tamarind paste contains pieces of pulp; strain it through a fine-mesh strainer after dissolving a walnut-size chunk by working it around with a wooden spoon in 1/2 cup of boiling water.

LATIN: *Tamarindus indica*

THAI: *mak kam*

VIETNAMESE: *me chua*

INDONESIAN: *asam*, also known as *asam jawa*

STORING AND PRESERVING: Tamarind pods will keep for several weeks in the refrigerator or indefinitely in the freezer. Blocks of tamarind paste, wrapped tightly in plastic wrap, will keep indefinitely in the refrigerator and freezer.

SUBSTITUTES: Lime or lemon juice. In general, a walnut-size piece of tamarind paste or pulp will provide about the same amount of sourness as 2 tablespoons lime juice.

Turmeric

Most of the turmeric I encounter comes powdered in jars and has practically no aroma or flavor. I use powdered turmeric mainly as a coloring to brighten up murky-looking curries. Fresh turmeric, however, has a special pungent flavor all its own and looks somewhat like ginger and galangal. If you're lucky enough to find fresh turmeric—it shows up from time to time in Asian markets—chop it very finely (in the same way as garlic, chilies, or galangal) and cook in a little oil before liquids are added.

LATIN: *Curcuma domestica*

INDONESIAN: *kunyit*

THAI: *kamin*

VIETNAMESE: *nghe*

Wasabi

In Japan the root of this hot variety of horseradish is freshly grated and served with sushi and sashimi. I've never found fresh wasabi root in the United States, but I keep a constant eye when in Japanese markets in the hopes that it will show up. In the United States we must make do with powdered *wasabi*—worked to a paste with water—or *wasabi* in tubes. Common horseradish cannot be substituted.

Yuzu

Yuzu is a small yellow fruit that looks like a small lemon but has a bitter rind that tastes like kumquats. Japanese cooks use slivered *yuzu* rind (but rarely the juice) to flavor and decorate soups, light stews, and pickles. Substitute lemon, lime, or kumquat zest.

INDIAN SPICES

Fortunately most Indian spices can be found on the spice rack of a decent supermarket. A few exotic ingredients such as curry leaves or black mustard seeds may mean a trip to an Indian grocer (usually not a problem in a large city) or waiting for a mail order.

Spices are most aromatic when they're ground shortly before use. I use a coffee grinder, but I don't grind my spices each time I make an Indian dish. Instead I grind a small batch of a particular spice—enough for a month or two—and then keep the spices in tightly sealed jars in the freezer. I also keep whole spices in the freezer, where they keep for up to a year without losing their aroma.

Indian cooks insist that most spices be roasted before they are added to a dish. The traditional Indian method consists of spreading the whole spice over the surface of a wok-like pan or skillet and then toasting the spices on the stove until they brown slightly and release their aroma. Because each spice takes a different amount of time to roast—anywhere from 4 to 10 minutes—you have to roast one spice at a time. Roasting whole spices is worth the effort if you're making batches of premixed spice mixtures (curry powders) to keep on hand, but I usually cook the ground spices in the butter or oil that will be used to cook aromatic vegetables in oil at the beginning of a soup or sauce instead.

Cardamom

These aromatic little black seeds come in pods that look a little like pistachio nuts. Most cardamom is the so-called green cardamom, but if you have access to an Indian market you may want to try the more subtle-tasting black cardamom. Cardamom has a very pronounced flavor that can easily take over the flavor of a dish—use it carefully.

Cinnamon/Cassia

Most of the "cinnamon" sold in the United States is actually cassia, which has a harder, more woodlike texture and a stronger flavor than authentic cinnamon, which has a flakier, more brittle texture and a more subtle flavor. Real cinnamon is hard to find—I'd never even seen it until I took a trip to Mexico—but fortunately Indian cooks usually use cassia anyway.

Because of its hard texture, cassia is one of the few spices that can't be ground in a coffee grinder. (Authentic cinnamon with its softer texture works fine.) The best way to grind cassia is to break it up into pieces with a cleaver and then grind it for several minutes in a food processor. You'll need to grind a couple of handfuls at once, or it won't move around in the processor. Keep your freshly ground cassia in the freezer—it will be much more aromatic than what you buy already ground in a jar.

Cloves

Ground cloves are an essential Indian spice. If you're improvising your own spice mixtures, use cloves very sparingly—1/4 teaspoon too much and it'll take over the flavor of the whole dish.

Coriander

These are the seeds of the coriander plant, usually called *cilantro*. Even though there is a slight resemblance between the aroma of leaf and seed, the seeds have a far more delicate and elusive flavor. Coriander seeds look very similar to white peppercorns. The ground seeds are used frequently in Indian spice mixtures. Coriander root is also sometimes used in Thai cooking, especially for making Thai curries. Most Asian markets sell cilantro with the small root still attached.

Cumin

One of the most often used spices in Indian cooking, cumin seeds look a little like caraway seeds but have a completely different flavor. I use cumin in practically all my curry mixtures, usually in conjunction with coriander.

Curry Leaves

Don't confuse curry leaves with curry powder. Curry leaves look somewhat like bay leaves but have a distinct spicy quality that gives a subtle and intriguing flavor to soups and sauces. Available frozen, fresh, or dried at Indian groceries, they can also be ordered by mail (see "Sources").

Fennel Seeds

Ground fennel is often included in commercial curry powders, but I see it only occasionally in Indian recipes.

Fenugreek

Even though fenugreek leaves are available in some Indian groceries, the most common form of fenugreek is the seeds. Fenugreek seeds are brown and rectangular and are actually a kind of pungently flavored mung bean. Fenugreek seeds can be bought both powdered and whole. I usually buy them whole and grind them for a minute in a coffee grinder. Fenugreek has a rich aroma and flavor of maple—fenugreek is in fact used for flavoring artificial maple syrup.

Mustard

Indian cooks are fond of mustard and use not only the whole and ground seeds but the oil as well. While I sometimes substitute ordinary yellow mustard powder for the mustard called for in Indian recipes, Indian cooks use black mustard seeds, which look somewhat like poppy seeds. Black mustard seeds are available at Indian groceries and should be toasted, Indian style, in a heavy iron skillet for about 2 minutes before they are ground, or they can be ground raw and cooked in a little oil before they are used. Mustard oil is sometimes used for cooking but should be heated until it smokes to eliminate some of its strong flavor.

Paprika

Unless you have access to authentic Hungarian paprika, which has a subtle flavor of its own, ordinary store-bought paprika is used mostly for its color. I sometimes add a tablespoon or two of paprika to stews, soups, or sauces that have a dull or muddy color. The recipes that call for paprika assume you're using a mild supermarket version. If you're using one of the hotter Hungarian varieties, taste as you add it, to avoid making the dish too hot.

MEDITERRANEAN INGREDIENTS

Capers

These tangy little berries are usually sold packed in brine but occasionally are sold packed in salt. They come in two sizes. While both types have a similar flavor, I prefer the smaller variety, called *nonpareil,* which has a brighter taste and is less likely to take over a dish's flavor. Capers are best added as briny accents to sauces shortly before serving. They're especially good tossed into a tomato sauce in combination with coarsely chopped olives.

Fennel

The flavor of fennel seems to go naturally with seafood. Fennel is in season in the United States during the winter months, but at other times imported fennel is sold, albeit at a premium. If you can't get your hands on fresh fennel, a little splash of Pernod can be used to give seafood soups and stews a distinct fennel flavor.

Herbs

Most Mediterranean herbs are indigenous to the area and have a high oil content, which helps keep them from drying out in the hot sun. Thyme, rosemary, oregano, marjoram, sage, lavender, basil, mint (basil and mint are the only ones with *low* oil contents), and both winter and summer savory are all used in Mediterranean cooking.

Because of their high oil content, most Mediterranean herbs dry well, although they always retain a better flavor when dried on the branch rather than when packed into little jars. Basil and mint can be used only fresh.

Olive Oil

Olive oil is the cooking fat of the Mediterranean and shapes the flavor of Mediterranean dishes more than any other ingredient.

Extra-virgin olive oil—made by crushing whole olives under relatively low pressure and without heat—is by far the most delicious and expensive but need be used only when the dish isn't being exposed to high heat, which would destroy its delicate flavor. Pure olive oil is made using heat and chemicals, and while it doesn't have the delicate flavor of extra-virgin olive oil, it's perfectly acceptable for sautéing, panfrying, and deep-frying.

Olives

Pitted and chopped olives are great stirred into a Mediterranean-style sauce such as a tomato sauce just before serving but shouldn't be cooked for more than a few seconds, or they will turn bitter. Avoid pitted olives—unless you're careful to taste them first—and never buy olives out of a can, which have no flavor. Pitting olives is easier than it looks. Just pinch the olive on both ends between your thumbs and forefingers, and the pit will pop right out.

Pernod

The southern French are fond of drinking this delicious aperitif, well mixed with water as an accompaniment to almost anything, including their favorite sport, *petangue.* Pernod is actually only one of the better-known brands of this drink, which is known more generically, in France, as *pastis.* Other brands are Ricard and Pastis. A few drops of any brand can be sprinkled into a fish soup or stew to give it a delightful fennel flavor.

Pine Nuts

These are the most commonly used Mediterranean nuts and are wonderful for giving crunch and an exotic flavor to seafood dishes. Pine nuts are best lightly toasted, either tossed in a sauté pan over medium heat for 5 to 8 minutes or baked on a sheet pan in a 375°F oven for 15 to 20 minutes.

Saffron

In spite of its expense, saffron is one of the most commonly used spices in Mediterranean cooking and ends up in all sorts of soups, stewed dishes, and sauces. It has an almost magical affinity for garlic, fennel, and tomatoes.

Saffron is sold in powdered form and in threads—the actual stamen of the crocus flower. Unless certain of your source, you're better off buying saffron in threads, because they're harder to adulterate than the powder. Saffron threads should all be dark red—saffron that contains pale or bright orange threads doesn't have as much flavor. Saffron threads should be soaked for 30 minutes in a tablespoon of water before they are added to a dish to help release their flavor. The soaking water should be added to the dish along with the saffron.

Tomatoes

Tomatoes are made up almost entirely of water, so unless they're going into a soup or a very liquid sauce, they must be cooked to eliminate or reduce their moisture. Tomatoes used in soups and sauces are usually peeled (dip in boiling water for 20 seconds, rinse under cold water, and pull away the skin), seeded (cut in half crosswise and squeeze the seeds out of each half), and chopped. In soups or sauces that are going to be strained there is no need to peel or even seed the tomatoes because the cooked peels and seeds will be strained out anyway.

Canned tomatoes can be substituted when fresh tomatoes are out of season. To get rid of the seeds, I dig my thumb into each tomato and squeeze over a bowl before chopping the pulp. Don't bother saving the juice because it has little flavor and sometimes a slightly metallic taste.

Sources

1. American Spoon Foods
   PO Box 566
   Petoskey, MI 49770
   800-222-5886
   Fax 616-347-2512

2. Anzen Oriental Foods and Imports
   736 N.E. MLK Jr. Blvd.
   Portland, OR 97232
   503-233-5111
   Fax 503-233-7208

3. Arrowhead Mills
   PO Box 866
   Hereford, TX 79045
   806-364-0730

4. Atlantic Seafood Direct
   21 Merrill Dr.
   Rockland, ME 04841
   800-227-1116

5. Aux Délices Des Bois
   4 Leonard St.
   New York, NY 10013
   212-334-1230
   Fax 212-334-1231

6. Bayou-to-Go Seafood Inc.
   PO Box 20104
   New Orleans, LA 70141
   800-541-6610

7. Blue Crab Bay Co.
   108 Market St.
   PO Box 180
   Onancock, VA 23417
   800-221-2722
   Fax 804-787-3430

8. Bridge Kitchenware
   214 E. 52nd St.
   New York, NY 10022
   212-688-4220

9. Broadway Panhandler
   520 Broadway
   New York, NY 10012
   212-966-3434

10. Brumwell Flour Mill
    Highway 6
    South Amana, IA 52334
    319-622-3455

11. C.M. International
    PO Box 60220
    Colorado Springs, CO 80960
    719-390-0505

12. Caviarteria
    29 E. 60th St.
    New York, NY 10022
    800-221-1020

13. Charcoal Companion Inc.
    7955 Edgewater Dr.
    Oakland, CA 94621
    800-521-0505
    Fax 510-632-1986

14. The Chef's Catalog
    3215 Commercial Ave.
    Northbrook, IL 60062
    800-338-3232

15. Cinnabar Specialty Foods
    1134 W. Haining St.
    Prescott, AZ 86301
    602-778-3687
    800-824-4563

16. The CMC Co.
    PO Box 322
    Avalon, NY 08202
    800-CMC-2780
    Fax 609-861-0043

17. Don Alfonso Foods
    PO Box 201988
    Austin, TX 78720-1988
    800-456-6100
    Fax 800-765-7373

18. Ducktrap River Fish Farm
    Lincolnville, ME 04849
    800-828-3825
    Fax 207-763-4235

19. El Paso Chile Co.
    909 Texas Ave.
    El Paso, TX 79901
    800-274-7468
    Fax 915-544-7552

20. Estius Gourmet
    1555 Park Ave. Unita
    Emeryville, CA 94608
    510-653-0496
    Fax 510-530-7428

21. Frieda's Rare and Exotic Foods
    PO Box 58488
    Los Angeles, CA 90058
    800-241-1771
    Fax 213-741-9443

22. Hasty-Bake
    PO Box 471285
    Tulsa, OK 74147
    918-665-8220
    800-4AN-OVEN

23. Hot Stuff
    227 Sullivan St.
    New York, NY 10012
    800-466-8206
    Fax 212-254-6120

24. Kalustyan's
    123 Lexington Ave.
    New York, NY 10016
    212-685-3888
    Fax 212-683-8458

25. Kam Man Chinese Supermarket
    200 Canal St.
    New York, NY 10013
    212-571-0330

26. Katagiri
    224 E. 59th St.
    New York, NY 10022
    212-752-4197

27. King Arthur Flour
    PO Box 876
    Norwich, VT 05055
    800-827-6836
    Fax 802-649-5359

28. Charles LaMalle
36 W. 25th St., 6th Floor
New York, NY 10036
212-242-0750

29. Lazzari Fuel Co., Inc.
PO Box 34051
San Francisco, CA 94134
415-467-2970
Fax 415-468-2298

30. Legal Seafoods Market
5 Cambridge Center
Cambridge, MA 02139
800-343-5804
Fax 617-254-5809

31. Little India Store
128 E. 28th St.
New York, NY 10016
212-683-1691

32. Luhr-Jensen and Sons Inc.
Customer Service Dept.
PO Box 297
Hood River, OR 97031
503-386-3811

33. Lunber and Family Farms
5370 Church St.
PO Box 369
Richvale, CA 95974-0369
916-882-4551

34. Mo Hotta—Mo Betta
PO Box 4136
San Luis Obispo, CA 93403
800-462-3220
805-545-8389

35. Nancy's Specialty Market
PO Box 1302
Stamford, CT 06904
800-462-6291
Fax 410-364-5215

36. Northwest Mushroom Co.
PO Box 2997
2506 Adams Ave.
La Grande, OR 97850
503-963-6999
Fax 503-963-5533

37. Oriental Food Market and Cooking
School Inc.
2801 W. Howard St.
Chicago, IL 60645
312-274-2826

38. Penzey's Spice House
PO Box 1448
Waukesha, WI 53187
414-574-0277

39. Phipps Ranch
PO Box 349
Pescadero, CA 94060
415-879-0787

40. Russ and Daughters
179 E. Houston St.
New York, NY 10002
212-475-4880
Fax 212-475-0345

41. Santa Cruz Chili and Spice Co.
Box 177
Tumacacori, AZ 85640
602-398-2591

42. The Sausage Maker
26 Military Rd.
Buffalo, NY 14207-2875
716-876-5521
Fax 716-875-0302

43. Spiceland Inc.
3206 N. Major
Chicago, IL 60634
312-736-1000

44. Spice Merchant
PO Box 524
Jackson Hole, WY 83001
800-551-5999

45. Spice and Sweet Majal
135 Lexington Ave.
New York, NY 10016
212-683-0900

46. Stonewall Chili Pepper Co.
PO Box 241
Highway 290 East
Stonewall, TX 78671

47. Sur la Table
84 Pine St.
Pike Place Farmers' Market
Seattle, WA 98101
800-243-0852

48. Urbani Truffles and Caviar
29-24 40th Ave.
Long Island City, NY 11101
718-392-5050
800-587-2264

49. Uwajimaya
519 Sixth Ave. S.
Seattle, WA 98104
206-624-6248

50. Walnut Acres
Penns Creek, PA 17862
800-433-3998

51. Weber-Stephen Products Co.
250 So. Hicks Rd.
Palatine, IL 60067-6241
800-446-1071
Fax 708-705-7971

52. Williams-Sonoma
PO Box 7456
San Francisco, CA 94120
800-541-2233
Fax 415-421-5153

53. The Wooden Spoon
PO Box 931
Clinton, CT 06413
800-431-2207

54. Yaohan
333 S. Alameda Rd.
Los Angeles, CA 90013
213-687-0501
Fax 213-687-0573

55. Yaohan
595 River Rd.
Edgewater, NJ 07020
201-941-9113

56. Zabar's
2245 Broadway
New York, NY 10024
212-496-1234
Fax 212-580-4477

KITCHENWARE

Benriner cutter: 26
Chimney charcoal starter: 9, 52
Chinese bamboo steamer: 16, 9
Copper fish pans: 8, 28, 47, 56
Copper sauté pans: 8, 28, 47, 56
Fish poacher: 8, 28, 47, 56
Grilling equipment: 13, 22, 51
Food mill: 9, 47, 52, 56
Hardwood charcoal: 13, 29
Kitchen tools: 9, 14, 47, 52, 53, 56
Nonstick pans: 9, 14, 47, 52, 53, 56
Pasta machine: 9, 14, 47, 52, 56
Outdoor smoker: 32, 42
Stovetop smoker: 11, 56
Sudare: 26, 49, 54, 55
Wood chunks and sawdust for
    smokers: 13, 22, 29, 32, 42, 56

MISCELLANEOUS INGREDIENTS

Beans, dried: 35, 39, 50
Buckwheat flour: 3, 10, 27, 50
Chilies, fresh (in season only): 46
Chinese ingredients: 2, 16, 23, 25,
    37, 44
Herbs, fresh: 5
Herbs, dried: 35, 38, 39, 43
Indian ingredients: 15, 16, 23, 24,
    31, 35, 45
Japanese ingredients: 12, 15, 16,
    26, 35, 49, 54, 55
Mexican ingredients: 16, 17, 19,
    23, 34, 35, 41, 46
Mushrooms, dried: 1, 5, 16, 35, 36
Mushrooms, fresh or frozen, wild:
    5, 48
Rice: 16, 20, 33, 35
Southeast Asian ingredients: 12,
    15, 16, 23, 35
Spices: 35, 38, 39, 43
Truffles: 5, 48
Vegetables, exotic: 21

SEAFOOD

Caviar: 4, 12, 40, 48
Clams: 7, 30
Crabs/crabmeat: 6, 7, 30
Fish (in season): 4, 30
Lobster: 4, 30
Oysters: 6, 30
Smoked seafood: 4, 12, 18, 40

Index

Page numbers in **bold type** refer to recipes. Recipe variations appear on pages indicated by *bold italics.*

Abalone, 235–236
    medallions with parsley sauce, **236**
agnolotti in tomato shrimp broth, ricotta and
    sage, **302**
aïgo sau, 270
aigrelette, salmon with hazelnut, **62–63,**
    color page 16
aïoli, **334**
    as garnish, 73
    shrimp and red snapper fillets *en bourride,*
      72–73
aïoli, saffron, **334**
    grilled tuna steaks with tomato broth and,
      56–57, color page 13
    shrimp with tomato sauce, pesto and, **194**
Alaskan crabs, 205–206
Alaskan pollack, 349–350
albacore tuna, 367
almejas al horno (Spanish-style baked clams),
    143
almond(s), 79
    butter, **329**
    Catalan shrimp soup with chilies, garlic
      and (romesco), 271, **273**
    coating, 82
    curry, and herb crust, halibut fillets with,
      20
Alsatian-style white wine fish stew,
    289–290
aluminum foil, as wrapping, 53
amandine, 79
amberjack, 356
anadromous fish, 369
ancho chili sauce, oysters with, **152–153,**
    color page 6
anchovy(ies), 345
    butter, **329**
    escabeche, *93–94*
    grilled, 52, 53, *55–56*
    tapenade, **339**
anglaise, à l', 80
    fillets of sole, with watercress sauce, 81
Antarctic crabs, 205–206
Antarctic queen, 350

aoyagi (red clams), 117
appetizers:
    cold mussels in herb and caper sauce, **133**
    cold mussels with herb mayonnaise, **129**
    oysters with ancho chili sauce, **152–153,**
      color page 6
    sautéed Thai fish cakes with dipping
      sauce, **86–87**
    scallop yakitori, **164–165**
    Venetian creamed salt cod or stockfish,
      104–105
Arctic char, 368
    baked in salt, **22–23**
    with fennel and tomatoes in a roasting bag,
      whole, *21*
    grilled whole, *54–55*
    in puff pastry, *24*
Argentine hake, 350
aromatics, 28, 29
    for fish stew, 287
    for marinades, 90
    for shrimp soups and stews, 198
aromatic Thai shrimp soup, **196**
artichoke(s), 144
    clam stew with beans, wild mushrooms
      and, **144,** color page 8
    crayfish, and wild mushroom aspic, **318**
    as garnish, 73, 241
    individual lobster aspics with chervil and,
      183–184
    puree, **336**
    red wine octopus and clam stew, **244–245,**
      color page 16
    sardines escabeche, **93–94**
    tomato squid stew with pearl onions,
      garlic and, **224–225**
Asian sauces and condiments:
    Indian chutneys, **342–343**
    Indonesian sambals, **341**
    Thai curries, **340–341**
asparagus:
    puree, 37, **336**
    salad of leftover grilled fish, **256**
aspic(s), 308, 316
    beef or chicken broth for, **318**
    chaud-froid, 308, 319
    cold trout fillets with green herb,
      317
    crayfish, color page 7

    crayfish, artichoke, and wild mushroom,
      318
    individual lobster, with artichokes and
      chervil, **183–184**
    salmon and truffle, **319**
    seafood, with green herbs, **316**
    striped bass fillets with tomato chaud-froid
      and parsley vinaigrette and, **320**
assorted:
    cold-smoked fish with blinis and crème
      fraîche, **103**
    fish and shellfish with butter-enriched
      poaching liquid, **71–72,**
      color page 4
    steamed fish and shellfish in Thai-spice-
      scented broth, **108–109**
Atlantic croaker, 351
    fillets simmered in sake-flavored dashi,
      73–74
    meunière, *78*
    see also croaker(s)
Atlantic mackerel, 357–358
    fillets with white wine, butter, and parsley,
      113–114
    see also mackerel
Atlantic pollack, 349
    steaks with white wine, butter, and
      parsley, *113–114*
    see also pollack
Australian crayfish, 214
Australian rock lobsters, 168
avocado(s):
    mackerel seviche, *90–91*
    in marinades, 90
    mixed shellfish seviche, **91,**
      color page 5
    and tomato salsa, **340**

Baby octopus, 229
    and pasta salad, improvised, *265*
bacalao en samfaina (salt cod with peppers,
    tomatoes, and eggplant), **106**
bacalhau à lisbonense (Lisbon-style salt cod or
    stockfish), 104, **105**
baccalà mantecato (Venetian creamed salt cod
    or stockfish), **104–105**
bacon, in New England clam chowder,
    139

About the Author

James Peterson grew up in northern California. After majoring in chemistry with a minor in philosophy at the University of California at Berkeley, Jim took a year off to travel around the world. Near the end of his trip, he ended up in the south of France picking grapes for a family of wine makers. Impressed by their love of good food and drink and by the good things to eat in Paris and throughout the French countryside, Jim decided that he wanted to study cooking professionally.

After returning to the United States, where he worked for two years in restaurants to save money to pay for a prolonged return to France and for cooking school, Jim packed up his things and moved to Paris, where he stayed for two years. He spent six months at the Cordon Bleu, and funds ran low but Jim was fortunate to obtain a job at the then three-star Le Vivarois. It was here that he worked with some of France's most talented chefs. The next year Jim moved to Vonnas, near Macon, where he worked at the renowned three-star restaurant Chez La Mére Blanc (now Georges Blanc).

In 1979 Jim begrudgingly moved back to the United States where a French friend had opened Le Petit Robert in Greenwich Village. Jim and his friend became partners—eventually Jim took over the restaurant with another partner—and cooked innovative yet rustic and traditional French food. During this period the restaurant was reviewed by major magazines throughout the United States and abroad.

In 1984 Jim Peterson began teaching at The French Culinary Institute in Manhattan, where he wrote the advanced curriculum, and later at Peter Kump's New York Cooking School, also in Manhattan.

In addition to his teaching career, Jim has translated six French books on pastry and baking, has published a comprehensive book on sauce making titled *Sauces: Classical and Contemporary Sauce Making*, which won the 1991 James Beard Cookbook of the Year Award, and has written an acclaimed book on soups called *Splendid Soups*, which was nominated for a James Beard Award in 1994.

Jim has spent the last three years working on *Fish & Shellfish*, his most ambitious project to date. Experts in the field consider *Fish & Shellfish* to be an essential classic on the subject. Jim is currently working on a book about vegetables due to appear in early fall 1997.